MW00964026

Applied Ethics
Reflective Moral Reasoning

SUSAN DIMOCK

York University

CHRISTOPHER TUCKER

York University

THOMSON

NELSON

Australia   Canada   Mexico   Singapore   Spain   United Kingdom   United States

THOMSON

NELSON

Applied Ethics:
Reflective Moral Reasoning
by Susan Dimock and Christopher Tucker

Editorial Director and Publisher:
Evelyn Veitch

Executive Editor:
Chris Carson

Marketing Manager:
Lenore Taylor

Senior Developmental Editor:
Rebecca Rea

Production Editor:
Carrie McGregor

**Copy Editor and
Proofreader:**
Erin Moore

Production Coordinator:
Helen Jager Locsin

Creative Director:
Angela Cluer

Interior Design:
Liz Harasymczuk

Cover Design:
Liz Harasymczuk

Cover Image:
Wieland, Joyce, Canadian
   1930–1998
Time Machine Series 1961
Oil on canvas
203.2 x 269.9 cm
© National Gallery of Canada
Gift of the Estate of Joyce
   Wieland

Compositor:
Starlight Design

Printer:
Transcontinental Printing Inc.

**National Library of Canada
Cataloguing in Publication Data**

Main entry under title:

Applied ethics: reflective moral
reasoning / edited by Susan
Dimock and Christopher Tucker.

Includes bibliographical
references.
ISBN 0-17-622444-0

1. Ethics, Modern—20th century.
2. Reasoning. I. Dimock, Susan,
1963- II. Tucker, Christopher

BJ319.A67 2004   170
C2003-905889-1

TABLE OF CONTENTS

PREFACE

The principal objective of this book is to teach students how to think critically about moral matters. This goal drives the organization of the work. The book is divided into six chapters. The first provides an overview of the subject, explaining what morality is and how philosophy can improve our thinking about moral issues. The remaining chapters each present a moral theory that has been central in the Western philosophical tradition: Utilitarianism, Kantian Deontology, Libertarianism, Modern Liberalism, and Feminism. After a brief characterization of the moral theory, each chapter then contains a set of readings on some specific moral issues or problems. The issues have been selected because they highlight something important about the moral theory being considered: a problem for it, a relative strength of it, an ambiguity or inconsistency within it, its under-determination of some case, or some difficulty of interpretation or application. Thus our organization reflects our belief that "applied ethics" really should be treated as applying something, namely moral theories, to a range of concrete moral problems.

The organization of the book differs from others on applied ethics or moral issues. The standard approach in texts on this subject is to select a few moral issues for discussion, and then to present all of the possible positions one might take with respect to those issues. Thus you get a chapter on abortion that includes a hard-line anti-abortionist paper, a staunch defence of abortion on demand, some middle-of-the-road pieces that would gradually restrict access to abortion as a pregnancy continues, etc. The problem, as we see it, with such books is that they fail to teach students how to think critically about moral issues, because they fail to teach students how to think philosophically. Rather, the result of such organization is that students are able to simply find the paper representing their pre-theoretical position on the issue in question and use it to defend their view. They often do not advance beyond the level of intuition with which they began. They have not learned much about either good moral reasoning or philosophy through such an exercise.

Rather than simply providing students with an opportunity to defend their pre-theoretical views in this way, our book challenges them to think through the implications of their intuitions and about how moral judgements might be justified or critically examined. Indeed, we push back where intuitions seem most strong. Our desire to encourage students to think critically about their own moral positions has in large part dictated our choice of topics, for we wanted some topics about which students might be thought to have very strong views. Among those we selected are abortion, organ sales from live donors, human cloning, cruelty to animals, same sex marriage, female circumcision, and pornography. But we also want to provide students with an opportunity to think about the difficulty of applying basic moral principles and moral theories to some issues, to think about the consistency of their overall moral position, and to think through the implications of a given theory for subjects about which they may not yet have developed strong opinions. Thus we also examine nuclear deterrence, world hunger, aboriginal rights, welfare rights, war, in vitro fertilization and surrogate motherhood. Many of the topics are taken up only once, while others reoccur twice or even three times. In no case have we tried to present an even minimally comprehensive view of the range of positions one could take with respect to the issues we discuss. Instead, we have tried to provide a theoretical framework within which the issues can be critically examined. The cumulative effect, we hope, will be a greater insight into the moral theories and principles that undergird the specific judgements that students want to make about the issues themselves.

Each reading is preceded by a brief introduction and followed by any definition or explanation of terms that is necessary to understand it. Each paper is also accompanied by detailed study questions. The questions include not only queries designed to ensure that students understand the central positions taken in the paper and the arguments given for those positions, but also questions designed to provoke further thought about other implications a position has, as well as the various kinds of arguments that get used in moral thinking and their strengths and limitations. The assumption is that the book will be studied more or less in order. The questions get harder, more thought provoking, and more critical as the book proceeds, and later questions sometimes refer back to earlier material.

The book includes both seminal works in applied ethics—Judith Jarvis Thomson on abortion, James Rachels on euthanasia, Peter Singer on animals, and Susan Sherwin on in vitro fertilization—and less well known readings on numerous other topics. We thank all of the publishers and authors who have given us permission to reproduce their work here.

CHAPTER ONE

Critical Moral
Reasoning

MORALITY

We begin our exploration of ethical thinking with a seemingly uncontroversial thought: that there is moral disagreement in the world. Thoughtful people seem to disagree, for example, over the moral status of abortion, capital punishment (the death penalty), euthanasia (mercy killing), and the justice of war. And it is not just over issues involving death that we see moral disagreement manifest itself. Is there a duty to provide assistance to the poor? Is it wrong to use animals for food or various kinds of research? Should we clone animals, including humans? Do people who belong to groups that have suffered adverse discrimination in the past have a right to be compensated now through affirmative action programs? These are just a few of the many issues and questions about which people have different moral views.

To understand why these are *moral* questions we need to step back from the specific issues about which people disagree to consider what morality is and what makes some issue a moral one. Morality is a system of norms that sets standards of right and proper conduct. Those standards then play two roles within moral thinking. First, they *govern our judgements* about the rightness or wrongness of actions, the goodness or badness of certain states of affairs, the virtue or viciousness of people, the justice or injustice of social practices and institutions. Second, having set those standards of right and proper conduct, they *direct us to act* in conformity with those standards. In this way morality concerns what we ought to do. As such, it is a **normative** system. Behaviour that conforms to the standards set by morality is **prescribed** as what a person ought to do, while actions that violate the standards are **proscribed** as wrong or bad, and ought not to be done. Thus morality governs a particular range of judgements (concerning what is right, good, virtuous or just, and their contraries), as well as issues prescriptions concerning what people ought to do (we ought not to lie, we ought to keep promises, we ought to avoid acting cruelly, and we ought not to kill).

To specify more precisely the content of morality is complicated by two important considerations. First, morality is only one among a number of normative systems within human societies. Other normative systems that are commonplace in human communities are law, religion, and etiquette. These are normative systems because they set standards of right and proper conduct and prescribe actions that conform to those standards. As we shall see later, there are good reasons to treat these various normative systems as independent of one another, and very good reason to be concerned with morality in its own right. Unfortunately, it is sometimes unclear which normative system a person is using when condemning or praising certain actions. Do we condemn spitting on people for moral reasons or the sake of politeness? Is forgiving someone's transgressions against you required by morality, or by religious edict? These are difficult questions, to be sure, but important if we wish to engage in deliberation concerning morality exclusively.

The second complication we face in specifying the content of morality, and determining what makes something a moral issue rather than some other normative issue, is that people disagree over how to answer this question. Some people think that morality includes standards of human excellence and of what kind of person one should be. Others think that morality is centrally about our actions and especially our actions as they affect other people.

We allow that both personal ideals and actions may fall within the scope of morality. They may even in some cases be related, with people disagreeing about which action is best because they adopt different ideals of human excellence. But we shall be concerned here primarily with the morality of actions. That is because we want to discuss moral disagreement, particularly disagreements about what we ought to do when our actions affect the world at large. These disagreements may be over individual actions, social policies, or the design of our social and political institutions and the like. Moral disagreement, as we will usually understand it, arises when two or more people disagree about what we should do. Disagreement about actions that affect more than just the person so acting are particularly pressing, in a way that conflicts about models of perfection or excellence may not be. People who hold different ideals of human excellence or disagree about what the best kind of life is for people, may be able to "agree to disagree," as the common expression has it. That is, people who hold differing ideals of what kind of person to be or what kind of life is best need not settle their differences before living peacefully together. But when we have conflicting moral claims about what we ought to do, when the consequences are not purely private, or which social policy we ought to adopt, or how we should organize our central political institutions, we cannot simply agree to disagree. We must choose, and act. And this gives us a reason to want to settle our moral disputes when they involve competing claims about what we ought to do. The potential for serious conflict is here too significant to ignore.

We adopt the view that moral issues are issues that affect the significant interests of people (and perhaps other kinds of creatures that have interests, such as animals). Morality sets the standards of proper conduct toward creatures that have significant interests. Its central content takes the form of norms governing how we ought to act toward creatures with interests, and especially toward other people. Its most central requirements will be universal in scope, covering all creatures with significant interests. And it receives its authority from the protection it gives to those interests. Only those norms that in fact serve important interests are truly moral norms. And given that the interests of everyone matter, only those norms that serve our interests in an impartial way will be endorsed by a rationally defensible morality.

We concentrate on interests because we think that moral disagreement often arises out of competing or conflicting interests. What people disagree about in moral disputes is which of the competing interests that are at stake should be protected or served, and which interests can be subordinated. So, for example, if we are disagreeing about whether we ought to use animals in medical experiments or not, it is helpful to think about what interests are in conflict in the case. On the one hand, the animals surely have an interest in not being subjected to painful treatment, not to be intentionally infected with a fatal disease, and not to be caged in a laboratory. On the other hand, human beings surely have an interest in collecting scientific data about the causes and treatment of diseases, the safety of new drug therapies, and the like. People who disagree about the moral status of such research can usually be seen to give different weight to these competing interests. So a moral issue is one involving significant interests, moral disputes are disagreements about competing interests, and moral norms are standards governing how we ought to act toward creatures with interests and settle disputes when interests conflict.

Moral Relativism

Philosophers and other theorists who think about the nature of morality disagree about the answer to one important question: is morality a single set of universal norms, or are there many moral systems, each tied to a particular cultural tradition and history. The view that there are many moral systems, tied to different cultures, is known as moral relativism. (It is sometimes also called social or cultural relativism.)

Moral relativists begin with the obvious fact that different societies, with different cultural histories and traditions, often endorse different moral norms. That there is diversity in the moral codes that different societies endorse seems too well supported by historical, anthropological, and sociological study to dispute. But moral relativists conclude from this fact of moral diversity that all there is to morality is whatever a society or cultural group accepts. Thus they hold that moral judgements simply express the attitudes of approval or disapproval of the culture in which they are made. On this view, to say that some action is right is just to say that it is approved of in our society. Thus moral statements will be true only relative to a particular social group. Moral statements will be true or false for a particular society. Thus we can say that the moral statements, "Slavery is wrong" and "Everyone has a right to freedom of religion" are true for contemporary Canadian society. Relative to that social group, these statements are true. But of course we can also say that, relative to the cultural group in ancient Athens, "Slavery is right, or morally permitted" and "Discrimination against women is just."

Moral relativists deny that the two claims, "Slavery is right" and "Slavery is wrong" are inconsistent or logically incompatible. Once you say which group and time they are relative to, you can see this. "Slavery is wrong" means "Slavery is disapproved of by society A at time T." "Slavery is right" means "Slavery is approved of by society B at time T." Both of these claims could be true, and so we see that what looked to be a moral disagreement over the moral status of slavery really was no dispute at all. This same way of relativizing moral claims can also be used to show that there is no conflict in describing the moral views of the same society when they change over time.

Moral relativism then makes sense of moral diversity in the world, but it does so at the cost of eliminating genuine moral disagreement between cultural groups. On this view, two different cultural groups cannot have a genuine moral disagreement, since all they are saying is that one approves of one norm and the other approves of a different norm. It is like saying that one person likes chocolate ice cream and the other likes vanilla. There is simply no problem. However, this does not capture what most people think they are doing when they engage in moral debate or when they morally criticize other cultures.

The fact that moral relativism cannot make sense of cross-cultural moral disagreement and does not allow genuine moral praise or criticism of other cultures makes this view problematic as a general account of morality. It does not square with our moral practices when we engage in moral debate or criticism. But there are further difficulties with this view as well.

First, if moral relativism is right then a person cannot coherently dissent, on moral grounds, from the morality that is endorsed within his or her society. For it makes no sense to say, from within a culture, that the moral norms of that culture are wrong. After all, the moral norms just are those of which are approved. The only kind of criticism that is possible within a group is a charge of inconsistency: that the group is not actually acting consistently with its own approved standards. But moral reformers and critics want to say that the norms that are approved of within their societies are wrong and ought to be changed. Such a claim makes no sense on a moral relativist view.

For the same reason, minority moral positions, moral views held by a minority of people in a society that differ from those of the majority, must always be wrong. For the minority says, in effect, "Even though the majority in my society thinks slavery is morally permissible, we think it is wrong." But to say that slavery is wrong is just to say that the majority disapproves of it, which is not the case (the majority approves of it).

Likewise, it is impossible to speak of moral progress on such a view. We can say that the moral norms endorsed by a society have changed, but not that they have changed for the better or worse. For there is no independent standard by which the change can be evaluated as better or worse.

Finally, there is a practical difficulty of deciding what a society's moral position is. Is morality set by what is approved of by everyone, almost everyone, a bare majority, the political leaders, the judges, or the clergy? Whose approval represents the view of the society? And how do we determine what a cultural group or a society is for these purposes? Is a cultural group just a group of people that share a common set of moral judgements? If so, then there are many cultures, and so many moralities, within any pluralist or multicultural state, such as Canada.

Many people have been drawn to moral relativism because they think it is truer to the fact of moral diversity in the world than a universal conception of morality. However, many others have clung to this view, despite the problems with it that we have just outlined, for a different reason. Some people think that we should be moral relativists because it supports an attitude of toleration and respect for other cultures. This idea comes out of the unfortunate history of moral imperialism that accompanied colonialization of many parts of Africa, the Middle East, and the Americas by the great Western powers (especially England, Spain, Portugal, and France). The Western powers not only wanted to bring other peoples under their political control, but wanted also to "reform" their normative practices and beliefs (their religions, their laws, and their moralities). As part of spreading civilization, the colonializing powers sought to impose their moral beliefs upon others. The result was often devastating, with whole cultures being disrupted or even lost.

The legacy of this history lingers with us still. Consider the problem we face in deciding what do with respect to cultures that deny basic human rights to some of their members, cultures that stone women to death or subject them to genital mutilation, for example. *We* may think these practices are morally wrong, but should *we* impose our views on others who have a different moral tradition? Many people, who think we should not—that we should respect or at least tolerate such cultural differences—think moral relativism supports that view. But in fact it does not. The relativist says that *if* we value toleration and mutual respect, *then* such a policy is right for us. We should not impose our moral views on others. But other cultures (or even our culture) may not value toleration, or not value it as much as the basic rights of women, and may therefore not believe that they have any duty to respect the moral traditions of others. For them, imposing their views on others is right. Thus relativism does not support toleration or mutual respect within cultures that do not already share a commitment to these values. This is so because relativism cannot support any universal values, values that transcend cultures, including the value of tolerance between cultures.

Can we do better than moral relativism? Can we develop a way of thinking about morality that allows for the diversity in moral opinion that we actually see in the world, but which makes it possible for us to engage in real moral debate and evaluate the moralities of cultures against a set of universal norms? We think so.

CRITICAL AND CONVENTIONAL MORALITY

We begin by adopting a distinction well known in philosophical discussions of morality, namely, the distinction between conventional and critical morality.

Conventional morality refers to the set of moral beliefs, norms, rules, and practices that are endorsed within a given community. Thus we can speak of the conventional morality of Canadians, and contrast that with the conventional moralities of some other communities. Thus we could say that Canadian morality supports extensive individual freedoms, including freedom of speech and religion. We might contrast this with the morality of some Islamic countries, say, in which freedom of speech and religion are not respected as moral rights or treated as having moral value. Similarly, we can speak, in this conventional sense, of the moralities of a culture changing over time. Thus we could say that the moralities of the West once upheld the rightness of practices that denied the equal worth of women and non-white men. But these moral views have undergone significant revision in the past century, and Western morality now accepts that men and women, whites and non-whites have equal moral worth and that certain forms of discrimination against women and non-whites is morally unacceptable. The conventional morality of any group of people is, then, just the set of norms that those people endorse as defining the rights, duties, and ideals of individuals and the moral status of various actions, institutions, and practices. There may be significant differences between the conventional moralities of different cultures and peoples, as well as within the morality of a single culture over time. The study of such cultural differences is the subject matter of many social sciences, such as history, anthropology, sociology, and political science. At the conventional level we acknowledge moral diversity as a social fact.

We contrast conventional morality with critical morality, however. Critical morality is ideal morality. It may be that no actual cultural groups or people have ever fully endorsed the norms of critical morality, actual societies always falling short of the ideal to a greater or lesser extent. The study of critical morality is the subject matter of moral philosophy, or ethics. It consists of the set of moral beliefs, norms, ideals, institutions, and practices that would be endorsed as those which are rationally most defensible.

Critical morality is a corrective to conventional morality. For conventional morality, the actual moral beliefs and practices of some group, may be rationally defective and indefensible in important ways. The moral beliefs of a people might be based on ignorance of relevant facts, superstition, or prejudice. In a conventional sense we can speak of the morality of the Nazi regime in Germany, the morality of South Africa under apartheid, or the morality of the Afghanistan people under the Taliban. The first was committed to the position that exterminating millions of Jews was morally right; the second to the moral legitimacy of a form of social organization that denied basic human rights and opportunities to the majority of its black citizens and the privilege of the white minority who exercised virtually total political and economic control; the last was committed to the establishment of what it took to be an ideal Islamic state in which women are treated as chattel, the property of men. Although we can refer, in the conventional sense, to the morality that was or is endorsed by these social groups, we can also question the legitimacy of these views. When we do so, we are engaged in critical moral thinking, and we are asking whether the moral positions adopted in these social groups is justifiable. Are these moral positions rationally defensible?

Different moral theories, such as we shall examine in the following chapters of this book, attempt to identify the content of critical morality, the set of moral beliefs and practices that are most rationally defensible. They also typically provide guidance as to the right method for thinking critically about moral issues, including the issue of whether any particular conventional moral belief is defensible and so deserving of rational support.

MORAL JUDGEMENTS AND MORAL PRINCIPLES

When thinking about critical morality, we must distinguish between two different things: between moral judgements and moral principles. Moral judgements are specific judgements we make when we call some person or action or practice good or bad, right or wrong, just or unjust, virtuous or vicious. So, for example, if you were to turn a street corner and see a group of young people beating an elderly person, you might be expected to make the moral judgement that what they were doing is morally wrong. Likewise, if a business acquaintance tells you that she has been interviewing candidates for a job, and that she has decided to hire a candidate from a First Nations community even though he is not strictly the best qualified for the job, you might applaud this decision as an instance of justice. And if you read in the newspaper that cosmetics companies have been using animals to test their products in ways that cause considerable pain to the animals, you might think the researchers involved to be vicious and their activities to be bad. These are examples of specific moral judgements that a person might be expected to make; other people may make different judgements, of course, and so we have moral disagreement at the level of moral judgements.

Critical moral thinking begins with the judgements that we make, but it does not stop there. We also formulate moral principles. Moral principles are general in a way that specific judgements are not. Principles identify types of actions as morally right or wrong, good or bad, and the like. And these principles are then used as the foundations of competing ethical theories, which attempt to explain what it is that makes particular actions or practices or people right or good or just or virtuous. Such principles, and the theories that are built upon them, attempt to systematize and explain the particular moral judgements that we make, to identify what properties make right actions right and wrong actions wrong, and to guide our thinking about new or difficult moral issues. Examples of moral principles are the following: All persons deserve equal concern and respect; That action is right which produces the greatest happiness for the greatest number of people affected by it; Every person ought to enjoy the most extensive liberty compatible with everyone else enjoying the same liberty. These are general moral principles, which are used both to explain the specific judgements we make and to justify those judgements that conform to them. We shall return later to the ways in which moral judgements and principles interact in critical moral thinking.

Critical Moral Thinking

What role can philosophy and philosophical inquiry play in resolving moral disputes? And how do we proceed in developing a critical morality, a morality that is rationally defensible and genuinely worthy of support? We think philosophy can guide critical thinking about moral issues in a number of ways.

Scope

One of the contributions which philosophical reflection on moral issues and moral disagreements can offer is making explicit certain scope limits on moral principles and moral judgements. Take the following claim that someone might make in a dispute about, say, abortion: "Killing is wrong." As stated, the claim is certainly false and, moreover, no one actually means it. No one thinks that killing vegetables or cancer cells is morally wrong. So the person who says, "Killing is wrong," is implicitly restricting the scope of his claim in ways that must be made explicit. What kinds of killings are wrong? Once we have an answer to that question we can move closer to figuring out why such killings are wrong. Because if the person replies, for example, that of course he only meant "Killing people is wrong," we can then press further and ask if he thinks that *all* instances of killing people are wrong. Will he accept further limits on the scope of this claim? Suppose he says, "Yes, all acts of killing people are wrong." Then we might press his judgements on a number of fronts: what about killing in a defensive war, or in self-defence, or as legal retribution for particularly heinous crimes, or as an act of mercy of a terminally ill person who wants to die but cannot kill herself? It may be that he wants to allow that these too constitute exceptions to his general claim that "Killing people is wrong," and so he will have to further refine his principle about the morality of killing. It may be that he decides that what he really means is something like "Killing all innocent people is wrong" or "Killing people who do not want to die is wrong." It may be that once the scope restrictions on moral principles are made fully explicit we not only improve our ability to think about what might ultimately justify or ground such a principle, but also that people who thought they were disagreeing with one another find that they actually can agree on the more refined moral principle.

Questions of scope arise in many contexts of moral thinking. Consider, as a different example, the claim that "Discrimination is wrong." Such a claim, like the one we considered above, is clearly false as stated. Even allowing that what it means is that discrimination between people is wrong (though not among possible sofas or television shows or vacation destinations), it is still false. We discriminate between people in a wide variety of contexts, without committing any moral wrong in doing so. We discriminate between people in the choice of friends and a mate. We discriminate between students in the assignment of grades and between applicants for entrance to universities or employment. We discriminate between authors in the giving of literary awards and between researchers in the assignment of research grants. We discriminate between politicians in selecting who will represent us in our elected political offices. In each of these cases, and numerous others that could be mentioned, we might commit no moral wrong in so discriminating.

Indeed, not to discriminate might itself be wrong. To see this, consider the case of assigning grades to students. If we discriminate according to performance as determined against a publicly announced set of standards of academic merit then we do no wrong in giving different grades to different students. Indeed, to ignore these standards and assign grades on any other basis would itself be wrong. Discrimination is only wrongful if it is unjust, if it denies benefits or rewards to some people who deserve them on arbitrary grounds. Thus someone who holds that discrimination is wrong will come to refine his or her moral view in specifying when it is wrong, and what criteria are used in determining what people deserve and what criteria of assessment are legitimate compared with those that are arbitrary.

Question-Begging Language

Those engaged in moral disputes often fall prey to using not merely inflammatory but also question-begging language. Examples of this are readily seen in disputes involving the right to kill people under certain circumstances. Those arguing against a right to abortion, against the permissibility of mercy killing, against capital punishment and the like are often heard to say, "Abortion/euthanasia/capital punishment is murder!" This is an abuse of language, and entirely question-begging in any discussion of the moral status of the acts being assessed. The reason is that the term "murder" is a morally loaded one. "Murder" means "wrongful killing." Thus to say that abortion is murder is to say that it is wrongful, which is precisely what is at issue in a disagreement on the moral status of abortion. People who use such language have already begged the moral question about which they are disputing, and they have done so through an abuse of language. The question at the heart of the dispute is whether abortion is wrongful; to call it murder begs that question and cannot help the disputants to reach a resolution to their problem or even to identify why the anti-abortionist thinks abortion is wrongful. But critical moral thinking asks the question *why* we hold the moral opinions that we do.

Conceptual, Factual, and Normative Claims

The above example of question-begging language leads to a more general error into which people can fall when engaging in moral disputes. We might distinguish between three general types of claims that people make: conceptual, factual, and normative.

Conceptual claims are claims that are true in virtue of the way we use language and concepts; they are often true by definition. Thus, for example, "Murder is wrongful killing" is true by definition; it is part of our concept of murder that it is wrongful and that it is killing. A person who says, "Bill murdered Ted, but it was morally right that he did so" is as conceptually confused as a person who says, "Bill murdered Ted but Ted didn't die." Likewise, to say, "Bill was hired under an affirmative action plan even though he is a male and not a member of any group that has been discriminated against in the past" is conceptually confused, because affirmative action plans are plans that give an advantage to those who do belong to groups that have been discriminated against in the past. The important point to this is that conceptual truths tell us something about how we use language and carve up the world (how we divide the world into concepts), but by themselves they cannot tell us anything about the morality or immorality of anything. The fact that when we use the word "murder" we mean "wrongful killing" cannot tell us which are examples of wrongful killing and which are not. It cannot tell us whether abortion or mercy killing or capital punishment or killing in wars are cases of murder or not; to decide that we have to decide if they are, in fact, wrongful, and how we use language cannot answer that moral question.

Factual claims are claims about the world, and their truth or falsity is determined in principle by some test in the world. Most of the claims that we make in ordinary life are of this type, and they include historical claims such as "Brutus killed Caesar," psychological claims like "Everyone cares only about himself," scientific claims such as "Black holes exist," sociological claims such as "The majority of Canadians support the death penalty for some crimes," etc. Factual claims purport to tell us something about the way the world is, was, or will be, and there is, in principle at least, some test that we could perform in the world to determine if they are true or false.

Now there are many important things to say about factual claims in the context of moral thinking, though we will highlight only one here. (Others will be treated as topics in their own right in what follows.) The important point here is that from the mere fact that something *is* the case it does not follow that it *ought to be* the case. That is, we cannot derive any normative claim from a factual claim. This is easily illustrated. From the (unfortunately true) factual claim that "There are tens of thousands of children living in poverty in Canada" it does not follow that "There ought to be tens of thousands of children living in poverty in Canada." The attempt to derive moral claims directly from factual ones is a mistake, and a mistake so common that it has a name: it is the **"is-ought fallacy."** Like all **fallacies**, it is poor reasoning and must be avoided.

But now, you might say, surely no one would commit such a fallacy. The example illustrates so clearly that we cannot infer what ought to be the case from what is the case that no one would do so. But other examples show the force of the fallacy more readily. Many people, for example, reason from the fact that something is illegal to the further claim that it is also morally wrong. Thus the mere fact that the use of certain narcotics is illegal is taken by many people to be evidence that drug use is also morally bad. This is an instance of the is-ought fallacy, since the report that something is illegal is just a report of fact about the particular legal code in force in a particular jurisdiction, and by itself cannot tell us anything about the moral status of the actions that are legally forbidden. After all, we know that sometimes we forbid in law activities that are not immoral, and some immoral behaviour is not also forbidden by law. It is a moral question whether the particular laws we have are morally justified, and it can only be answered by examining whether the law serves the interests of the people in an impartial way. Many laws in Western democracies will pass that test, but their moral status is independent of their legal status and the one cannot be inferred directly from the other.

The same thing can be said, more briefly, of appeals to "what everyone thinks." It is not uncommon to hear people, when engaged in moral disputes, to appeal to the shared moral judgements held by members of their community, to current consensus, or to tradition and history. But even if it is true (as a sociological or historical report) that our country has historically considered some practice (say, homosexuality) to be morally wrong, and even if most people in Canada still hold that belief, those facts alone do not license the conclusion that homosexuality is wrong. We need to assess those judgements to determine if they are supported by justified moral principles.

Normative claims differ from both factual and conceptual claims. Normative claims concern what ought to be the case or what people ought to do. "People ought to keep their promises," "Slavery is wrong/ought not to be practised," "We should not pollute the environment," and "You ought to honour God" are examples of normative claims. They are true, we say, just in case they are supported by the normative system in which they are made. And that in turn depends upon the basic principles that define the normative system. The ultimate justification of normative claims depends, then, on the principles that define the system, and how well or ill these claims serve the goals of the normative system in question. In the case of morality, we assess proposed principles in light of the point of morality, which is to help us all live better together and achieve our important interests as rational and social creatures.

Basic and Derived Principles

We have distinguished between moral judgements and moral principles, but we must now look more closely at the role principles play in moral reasoning. When we look at moral reasoning we see that some principles are more basic than others are. Consider the following piece of moral reasoning.

> Premise 1: The action is right (morally required) that will bring about the greatest amount of happiness possible for those affected by it. (Basic moral principle)
>
> Premise 2: Happiness will be maximized if we set up a mandatory system for redistributing wealth in society, in the form of a social welfare system. (Non-moral factual claim)
>
> Conclusion: It is right (morally required) that we set up a social welfare system. (Derived moral principle)

In this very simple example, Premise 1 is a basic moral principle. As we shall see, it is the most basic principle in one version of the moral theory known as Utilitarianism. Premise 2 is a factual claim about what will produce the most happiness in society. We may suppose that the alternatives that were considered and rejected included a proposal for non-mandatory or voluntary relief for the poor through charitable donations, and a proposal to simply let people care for themselves, with no relief being given by the rich to the poor. Premise 2 claims that of all the proposals considered, a mandatory social welfare system is the one that will produce the most happiness for everyone affected (rich and poor alike). The conclusion is the moral claim that we are morally required to establish such a system. This conclusion has the status of a derived moral principle within the normative system that we are considering. We might state the derived principle as "It is right that the rich give to the poor" or "The rich have a duty to give to the poor."

If more complex moral reasoning has this same basic structure, then we can say a number of important and general things about moral reasoning and moral disagreement. The first is that many disagreements that seem to be *moral* disagreements may not in fact be that at all. That is, it may be that people accept different derived moral principles and claims about what we ought to do, only because they disagree about the *non-moral* premises that they rely on in their reasoning.

Consider, for example, two people who disagree about the morality of a mandatory welfare system. One of the disputants thinks we ought to have such a system where the rich have a duty to give to the poor, while the other thinks there is no such duty and that to force the rich to give to the poor is itself morally wrong. This alone does not establish that they are having a genuine moral dispute. We have to ask *why* they hold the positions that they do. It may be that they agree at the level of basic moral principles; they might both, for example, accept that we ought to do whatever produces the most happiness for everyone affected. Yet they might disagree about whether or not this entails that it is right to establish a mandatory welfare system. They could disagree about this derived moral principle because they disagree about the facts with respect to what will actually make people most happy. Thus the person who is opposed to such a welfare system may base her opposition on a belief that such a welfare system leads to cycles of dependency and deprives the welfare recipients of the dignity and self-respect that are necessary to happiness. She would then be opposed to mandatory welfare schemes even though she agrees with her opponent that the most basic moral consideration is that happiness should be maximized.

Many disputes have this structure. The parties to the dispute share a commitment to the same basic moral principles, but disagree over derived principles because they hold different factual beliefs that are crucial in their reasoning from the basic principles to the derived. Philosophers are not in a unique position to resolve such factual disputes; often social sciences such as economics, sociology, anthropology, history, psychology, or political science are the proper source to look to for resolving them. But philosophers are uniquely qualified to explain the structures of moral reasoning, and so to make transparent the source of such disagreements, which is the first step to their resolution.

Not all moral disagreements hinge on factual disagreement, however. Sometimes people disagree about basic moral principles themselves. Using our welfare case again for illustrative purposes, it may be that two disputants who disagree over the moral status of a welfare system do so because they disagree at the level of basic principles. This would be the case, for example, if the defender of a mandatory welfare system bases his arguments on considerations of overall happiness (the utilitarian principle we considered in our example) while his opponent based her opposition to such systems on a competing basic principle. Candidates for such principles may be based in a theory of virtue, for example, which holds that only those actions that are undertaken *voluntarily* can have moral worth, and so a *mandatory* system of charity cannot serve moral goodness. Alternatively, a person might take as his most basic principle a commitment to individual *liberty*. Since mandatory welfare systems require that people be *forced* to give, thus violating their liberty, such systems may be deemed unjustified. In cases such as these, there is genuine moral disagreement, and a person must evaluate the competing basic principles themselves. We shall propose a method of evaluation for this purpose shortly.

We can also use the distinction between basic and derived principles to illustrate another important feature of moral reasoning. This involves the use of hypothetical counter-examples. Moral philosophers are notorious, as the readings in this text will amply demonstrate, for creating sometimes quite outrageous counter-examples to proposed moral principles. The method is simple. Take any proposed moral principle and see what can be derived from it, in terms of further derived principles or specific recommendations as to what a person should do in a given case. If those derived principles or specific recommendations are contrary to our judgements about such cases then we have a counter-example to the principle.

An example will illustrate the point. Consider again the utilitarian principle that we ought to do what maximizes happiness overall. A frequently cited counter-example to this principle is found in the following hypothetical case. Suppose you are a surgeon, with five critically ill patients, all of whom need organ transplants to survive (two need kidneys, one a lung, another a heart, and the last a liver). Each of these five patients is a model citizen, loved by many and all are significant contributors to the happiness of their communities. The loss of any of them would create significant misery for many other people. Imagine, too, that you have another patient, who just happens to come to you for the treatment of some minor ailment. This patient, you know, is loved by no one, is a parasite on his community, is cruel and selfish, and relishes causing misery for all those with whom he comes into contact. But he is very healthy, and has all five organs that your other patients need. Should you not kill this patient and harvest his organs to save the other five? Is this not what the utilitarian principle tells you ought to be done? The reasoning involved in this example can be formalized as follows:

Premise 1: We ought always to do whatever maximizes happiness for all those affected by our actions. (Basic moral principle)

Premise 2: The action that would maximize happiness in the example we are considering is the surgeon killing the healthy patient and using his organs to save the other five patients. (Hypothetical factual claim)

Conclusion: The surgeon ought to kill the healthy patient to save the five others. (Derived moral claim)

If this is in fact what the basic moral principle of utilitarianism recommends (that surgeons ought to kill their healthy patients to save other patients when doing so would maximize happiness) then this is a counter-example to that principle, because our judgement about such a case is that it would be morally wrong for the surgeon to kill the one patient even to save the five others. The argument can be formalized as follows:

Premise 1: No moral principle that endorses sacrificing an innocent person for the benefit of others is an adequate moral principle.

Premise 2: Utilitarianism endorses so sacrificing an innocent person.

Conclusion: Utilitarianism is not an adequate moral principle.

Such a use of hypothetical examples is legitimate against basic moral principles. The reason is because basic moral principles claim to identify the properties that make something good or right universally. If those principles then identify monstrous actions such as surgeons killing their patients for the benefit of others as right or good, this indicates that the principle's identification of the good or the right is inadequate. We must search for another, or refine it in such a way that it does not have these counter-intuitive results.

Using a hypothetical example to test the implications of the basic moral principle of utilitarianism works, though, only because the hypothetical factual assumption (that we could produce more happiness by killing the one patient to save the five) is plausible. It seems reasonable to suppose that this action would in fact maximize happiness overall given that people are made happier by living than dying, and by having beloved fellow citizens rather than public parasites in their communities. This example works, in other words, because the factual assumptions of the case are reasonable given what we know about what makes real people happy.

The general lesson to be learned here is important. Derived principles and specific recommendations as to what we ought to do are derived not only using more basic moral principles but also using factual premises or assumptions. In constructing counter-examples to basic principles, we must be sure not to use completely implausible or unrealistic non-moral assumptions in the derivation. To illustrate the mistake that must be avoided, consider the following objection that someone might make to the utilitarian principle: "It says that maximizing happiness is the right thing to do. But suppose [here is the hypothetical factual assumption] that people liked being tortured, and were made extremely happy that way. Then the utilitarian principle would say that torture is right." Since any principle that implies that torture is right must be considered highly questionable, this might be thought to be a counter-example to the utilitarian principle in the same way that the surgeon example was. Formally the suggested argument is this:

> Premise 1: We ought to do whatever maximizes happiness for all those affected by our actions. Maximizing happiness is the right thing to do in all cases. (Basic moral principle)
>
> Premise 2: People are made very happy by being tortured. (Hypothetical factual claim)
>
> Conclusion: We ought to torture people. Torturing people is the right thing to do. (Derived moral recommendation and derived moral principle)

This would be a *mistake*.

To see why this is an illegitimate use of a hypothetical example, consider the following. It is true (we may assume) that in the real world and given the way people actually are, torture makes people miserable rather than happy. And so the utilitarian principle would condemn torture as morally wrong. If, as the hypothetical example supposes, people were very different and actually liked being tortured, then the principle would support torture as right. But that does not show that torture being right is a derived principle of utilitarianism in the real world, and so it is not a counter-example to the principle. A utilitarian insists that what is right is what makes everyone as happy as possible. If we supposed that people derived happiness from radically different things than what we think makes them happy, then what the principle endorses would be radically different than we think it is. But that would not in any way show that morality is not centrally determined by what makes people happy.

The lesson is simple. The plausibility of derived moral principles and moral recommendations concerning what we ought to do rest on two factors: the justification of the basic moral principle and the plausibility of the factual premises from which they are derived. If you use completely implausible factual premises (like the claim that people are made happy by being tortured) then you make the derived principle equally implausible. But that implausibility does not reflect back to any basic moral principles used in the derivation.

There is another lesson to be learned here as well. Once we have a set of derived principles, we must use considerable care in constructing hypothetical examples to test their acceptability. Because derived principles have been derived from a more basic principle together with one or more non-moral premises, we must be sure not to change those non-moral assumptions in constructing our hypothetical cases. Suppose we reconsider our case for a mandatory welfare system.

We illustrated earlier how someone could reason from the basic utilitarian principle that we ought to maximize happiness, together with the assumption that a welfare system would in fact maximize happiness, to the conclusion that we ought to establish a welfare system. Suppose that the conclusion that we ought to establish a welfare system was then formulated as a derived principle within a utilitarian theory.

Now suppose that someone wanted to test or challenge that derived principle. She could do so in the same way that we test basic principles, namely by trying to construct a counter-example to it. But it is crucial that in doing so she not change the non-moral factual assumption upon which the derived principle is derived. The *mistake* would be to reason as follows.

> Premise 1: Establishing a welfare system is the right thing to do. Perhaps we might express this by saying that the rich have a duty to support the poor. (Derived principle within utilitarianism)
>
> Premise 2: If we force the rich to support the poor then the rich will have no incentive to labour, and everyone will end up poorer and less happy than they were before introducing the welfare system. (Hypothetical factual claim)
>
> Conclusion: We ought not to have a mandatory welfare system. It would be wrong to establish a welfare system. (Derived moral claim)

This reasoning is faulty because Premise 2 changes the factual assumption under which the duty claimed in Premise 1 was derived. In the original derivation of the duty to aid the poor it was assumed that enforcing such a duty would maximize happiness overall. In this new argument it is assumed that enforcing such a duty would not maximize happiness overall. It is no surprise then that the two arguments would lead to different recommendations as to what we should do with respect to welfare.

This simply represents the fact that the people who are disagreeing about the moral status of mandatory welfare are having a factual dispute about the effects of such a system on the happiness of those affected, rather than a meaningful moral debate.

Again, the lesson is simple. We must be very cautious when using counter-examples to test derived principles within a moral theory. And, more specifically, we must ensure that we do not change any of the non-moral assumptions used in the derivation of that derived principle when we test it against possible hypothetical counter-examples.

Conceptual Analysis

We distinguished above between conceptual, factual, and normative claims, and said that conceptual claims alone do not support any particular normative judgement. From the conceptual claim that "Murder is wrongful killing" we cannot determine what is or is not an act of murder. But philosophers often contribute to critical moral thinking by making certain concepts clearer. The process by which this is done is usually called conceptual analysis. The concepts that are analyzed might be moral or non-moral.

Many moral disputes involve confusion about the concepts that are being used. Sometimes people literally don't know what the words they are using really mean, and other times people are using the same term to refer to different concepts and so simply talk past one another. Again, some examples will help make this clearer.

Consider some of the many disputes that arise concerning *rights*. People claim a right to life, a right to an education or a job or welfare, a right to a decent standard of living, a right to dignity, a right to self-determination, etc. But what do they mean when they say they have a right to these things? What is a right? This is a normative concept, and one that is notoriously unclear. Philosophers can help to resolve moral disputes by making such concepts clearer. Thus philosophers point out that people understand the concept of a right in two importantly different ways, as being positive or negative. We will take the right to life as our example in making clear the distinction between the positive and negative concepts of a right.

Suppose we agree that people have a right to life. What follows from that in terms of derived principles and specific recommendations about how we ought to act? The answer will depend upon whether we think the right to life is a negative or a positive right. As a negative right, the right to life is the right not to be killed. As a positive right, the right to life is a right to whatever the right-holder needs to live. Furthermore, rights are held against other people. Others must respect the right-holder's right. Let us suppose that the right to life is universal, both in the sense that everyone has such a right and each person's right is held against every other person. Thus everyone must respect the right to life of everyone else.

If the right to life is a negative right then this means that everyone must refrain from killing everyone else. This seems an easy enough right to satisfy; people could actually respect the rights of everyone else simply by not killing them. But if the right to life is a positive right then everyone must do whatever it takes to keep all people alive. Some people will not need anything from you, we may suppose, to stay alive. But there are many needy people in the world who face the risk of death without the aid of others. If the right to life is a positive right then they have a right against all other people to provide them with what they need to live. Thus a positive construction of the right to life would support extensive systems of aid to the poor, the sick, the displaced, and any others who cannot live without the help of others. Such rights might be very hard to respect.

But consider another possibility. What if what a particular person needs to live is my kidney? Suppose I am the only suitable donor. And suppose I don't want to give up my kidney. It is true that people only need one functioning kidney to live, but I simply don't want to give one up. My reaction would certainly indicate that I am not the nicest of persons, but that is neither here nor there. What is at issue is whether the person who needs my kidney has a right to it. If a positive conception of rights implies that she does have a right to my kidney, and if we find this unacceptable, then we have reason to adopt the negative conception of rights.

We can employ this distinction when thinking about other rights claims, like those mentioned above. Are they claims to negative or positive rights, and what corresponding duties do they put on others by way of respecting those rights? Here conceptual analysis can help us to be clearer about the moral concepts we use.

Non-moral concepts are often equally unclear. Consider, for example, the concept of a *human being*. This concept, while itself non-moral (perhaps), is frequently used in moral disputes. When we say that human beings ought to be treated with respect, or that human beings have a right to life, what do we mean by "human being"?

Perhaps we mean just an entity with a particular DNA code, using "human being" to mean the biological category of *Homo sapiens*. But perhaps we mean something more, reserving the term "human being" for creatures with a particular kind of self-consciousness and experience of themselves as continuing creatures separate from their environments. People use the term in both these ways, and others. Thus the concept is vague. And it matters which conception of a human being is being used in many moral disputes.

Take disputes over abortion or the treatment of brain dead patients. Fetuses and brain dead patients are not human beings in regards to the negative, or second, concept of a right, since they lack self-consciousness and the experience of themselves as continuing creatures separate from their environments. Thus, even if we agree that human beings have a right to life, say, neither abortion nor the killing of brain dead patients would be a violation of that right. Of course if, on the other hand, someone means by human being any creature with human DNA then fetuses and brain dead patients are covered by the right to life. Here, again, we see how the use of vague concepts can confuse moral thinking, and why we need to reach agreement about how we are using our terms when we engage in moral discussion.

In some cases, such as that of "human being," the situation can be even more complicated because people sometimes use this concept in normative rather than merely descriptive ways. Thus many people think the concept of "human being" refers to creatures with inherent dignity, making this normative notion part of their very conception of a human being. In cases like this, conceptual analysis is crucial, not only to prevent people from just talking past each other, because they are literally talking about different things, but also to avoid the use of question-begging language mentioned previously.

Many concepts are vague in the way we have identified here. Some notorious examples, often invoked in moral discourse, are the following: right, duty, good, bad, intrinsic value, dignity, respect, liberty or freedom, happiness, rational, human being, and person. When these concepts are used in the making of moral claims a critical thinker must examine very carefully what they mean in that context, and determine whether parties to a moral dispute are all using these concepts in the same way. We believe that a considerable amount of what looks like moral disagreement can be resolved by eliminating conceptual confusions.

REFLECTIVE MORAL REASONING

There are some genuine moral disagreements, however, which cannot be resolved by the methods just canvassed. In this section we propose a method of critical or reflective moral reasoning that should be employed in thinking about moral issues. This method will yield a critical morality, in the sense discussed above. It will yield the most rationally defensible and coherent system of moral judgements and principles.

Reflective moral reasoning follows a path set out by the American philosopher John Rawls. He called his method "reflective equilibrium." We do not follow Rawls in all the details of his discussion of reflective equilibrium, but our account is certainly inspired by his work. Critical moral reasoning must instruct individuals concerning what they ought to do. It must do so, especially, in hard cases—cases in which there is genuine moral disagreement. Critical moral reasoning must help us decide between the competing claims that make up moral disputes. And it must resolve such disputes in a reasoned and principled way.

We said that moral concerns are those that significantly affect the interests of people and, perhaps, other creatures that have interests. Moral disputes are essentially disputes about conflicting interests. Thus we can think of the dispute about abortion as involving the conflicting interests of pregnant women and the fetuses they carry. We think of issues involving the proper treatment of animals as arising from the conflicting interests of animals not to be harmed in certain ways and the interests that some people have in using them for food or experimental purposes. Critical moral reasoning must help us to decide, in cases of competing interests, which interest is most important or deserving of respect and protection. In this way, critical morality will provide guidance as to what we ought to do in cases of conflicting interests.

This approach takes actions and policies or rules dictating actions to be basic to moral thinking. We want to know what action is required in situations of conflicts between interests or which policy or rule we should follow in adjudicating such conflicts. But there is another stream of moral thinking, which has as its focus how to be a good person, that is, what makes a good moral character. This is the domain of virtue ethics. We do not deny that this is an important moral question, but we insist that action rather than character is the more basic level of moral concern. The reason for this, roughly, is that a good person is one who acts well and a good character is displayed by a person who does what is right for the right reasons. This requires that we already know what acting well and doing the right thing is before we can say that a person is good. But the notion of virtue and good character is richer than the notion of a right action, because it looks not just at what we do but the motives that lead us to act as we do. Thus, although we take critical moral thinking to involve, in the first instance, an attempt to decide the question of what we should do, we allow a partly independent and important role for theories of virtue and good character to be developed within critical moral thinking.

Moral Judging

How do we engage in critical moral thinking about conflicting interests? To begin, we might think of the parallel between deciding moral disputes about interests and the way in which interest-based disputes are resolved in law. In particular, we might use the model of a good legal judge or arbitrator to guide us in our thinking about how we, as evaluators of competing claims, should and should not approach the dispute. Some obvious points can be made.

First, a good judge does not decide a case when she is drunk, under serious emotional distress, very tired, or distracted. These and other influences we commonly recognize can impair the judgement of a person and a good judge would postpone making decisions if she was influenced by such factors.

Likewise, a good judge never decides a case in which his own interests are personally involved. The fact that the judge's own interests would be affected by the outcome of a case disqualifies the judge. The worry, of course, is that in such cases the judge would not be impartial, and would be biased toward a solution that favoured his own interests, regardless of the relative merits of the competing positions. At the most extreme, judges must never be allowed to judge cases in which they themselves are a party to the dispute.

A more positive way of putting this general requirement is that a judge should be impartial among the disputants. This also requires that judges not bring to their task any of the biases that afflict human beings. If the judge has strong feelings of affection or hatred, is prejudiced positively or negatively toward any of the disputants, then this reduces the likelihood that he or she will make the most reasonable choice between them.

A judge must also be sensitive in considering who has interests that are at stake in any dispute. For only if all the competing interests are considered will a reasoned resolution of their conflict be possible. One common reason why people find themselves in difficult conflict situations is that they fail to give due weight to the interests of those whose interests conflict with their own, dismissing the other party's concerns as irrelevant or unimportant. A judge must never dismiss the interests of any of the disputants in this way.

Finally, a judge must do the best he or she can to ascertain any facts that are relevant in the dispute. This is often a difficult task. But if it becomes clear that any of the conflict rests on disputes about the facts (such as whether animals really feel pain), the judge must use all the methods of respectable investigation appropriate to the domain to decide which set of facts is most fully supported by the evidence.

These are requirements of good judging because, when they are satisfied, we can be as sure as possible that the judge has considered all the relevant moral and non-moral facts of a case, taken full and unbiased account of all the interests that are in conflict in the situation, and impartially weighed the competing claims of the disputants. When such a judge renders a verdict in favour of one of the disputants against the other, or settles on a compromise between their competing claims, we can be as sure as we can be that that is the most reasonable judgement that could be made. We can also assume that any other similarly good judge would agree with the judgement, or at least see it as fully justified.

We propose that a similar model should be imposed upon moral judging. For judging between competing interests is equally involved in this case. And judges of moral disputes are susceptible to all of the kinds of weaknesses, biases, and lack of information that legal judges are. Thus when we engage in critical moral reasoning we must try to emulate as fully as possible the ideal of a good moral judge. We must take into account all of the competing interests, we must be impartial between the different moral positions being put forward, we must be as fully informed of any relevant facts as is possible, we must be impartial between the disputants, and we must be free of influences that distort our judgement. When we make moral judgements under such ideal conditions we can be as confident as possible that those judgements are as reasonable as could be made, and that other similarly good moral judges would agree with our judgement, or at least see it as justified.

Moral Reasoning

Having characterized the ideal moral judge, we must now say something about the method of moral reasoning that he or she employs. We call this method "reflective moral reasoning." Often we talk of critical moral reasoning as a mere stylistic variation.[1] We said above that good moral reasoning begins with the specific moral judgements we make but it does not end there. We now explain that remark, relying on the distinction between moral judgements and moral principles.

Moral questions arise when we are confronted by clashing interests and must decide what we ought to do. Often our decisions about what to do will be driven by our judgement that one of the possible actions available to us is clearly the right one, or that one action or policy we could adopt would clearly produce more good than the other options we face. Consider some everyday cases that a person might face. You see a person or group of people acting cruelly toward another, and you judge that their behaviour is wrong. A friend lies to her parents for personal gain, and you judge that your friend's action is wrong. Another friend is considering having an extra-marital affair, and you condemn the proposal. You read in the newspaper about a terrorist attack on innocent people in some distant part of the world, and you judge their action to be unjust. You read an historical account about the actions of armies raping the female civilians of the enemy population in order to demoralize them, and you judge such a tactic to be unjustifiable. You read about societies that systematically exploit segments of their populations for the good of the rulers, about slave societies, or societies in which women or particular racial groups are denied basic rights and you deem such societies unjust. You find out that your employer refuses to hire members of visible minorities and you judge such actions to be immoral. You see a person who relishes in the misery of others and you judge such a person to be vicious. You see a group of young people light a cat on fire and you judge what they are doing to be bad. These are just a few examples of the moral judgements a person might make in assessing the situations he confronts in the world as we know it.

These examples all fit the model of conflicting interests. We suppose that burning cats, denying people jobs because of racial prejudice, slavery, adultery, rape, cruelty, and the like are wrong and ought not to be engaged in because the interests involved are too important to be sacrificed, at least in favour of the interests that such actions serve in the cases as we have imagined them. Parents have an interest in not being lied to by their children in the kind of case we imagined, women have an interest in not being raped, people have an interest in being free, etc., and these interests are so important that we judge actions that violate them to be wrong.

Now we are supposing that everyone, in reaching normal moral maturity, has formed a set of judgements of this kind. These judgements are pre-theoretical, and are made prior to or independently of any systematic study of moral philosophy. They are not guided by a theoretical commitment to any particular moral theory or general moral principles.

The moral judgements with which we begin our critical moral thinking are of this type. We assume that those judgements have been made under something like the conditions needed for ideal moral judging. Thus we assume that when you make the judgements you make that you are not impaired in some way, that your interests are not directly affected by actions being assessed, etc. Of course, often we do form our judgements in contexts that directly involve our interests. Consider the difference between the case we mentioned (you learn that a friend has lied to her parents), and the case in which your friend has lied to you. In the latter case you might be expected to judge your friend's actions very harshly, since it is your interests that are in conflict with hers. Even here, too, we need certain factual information, including information about why your friend lied. Did she lie to spare your feelings, to save another friend from even greater harm, or for self-serving reasons? History is a great tool of moral education because through history we have the actions of others laid bare, the relevant facts explained, and our interests are not affected. Thus the judgements we make about the actions and policies of individuals and societies distant from us in history are often such that they satisfy the conditions for ideal judging. And we see, as we should expect given the account of ideal judging given above, that there is much more agreement among individuals about the moral quality of the actions described in history than there was by the participants in those events, whose information was perhaps more limited, whose biases were directly involved, and whose competing interests were at stake.

Of the moral judgements we make, some we feel very certain about while others we make much more tentatively. We are very sure, in other words, that some of our judgements are correct or fully justified and others we are less sure of. We are most sure of those that we cannot imagine changing our minds about without radically transforming our entire moral outlook. Our conviction that slavery is wrong is such a judgement. We do not believe that any further information could be found that would make us change our minds about the injustice of slavery. And we could not revise our judgement about the immorality of slavery without changing our entire moral outlook, about the value of persons, the rights that people have, and the point of morality itself. For us, the moral status of slavery is an easy case; we have no difficulty reaching a firm conclusion about its immorality.

Consider, by way of contrast, our attitudes toward cloning or genetic engineering. Here our moral judgements concerning whether we ought to engage in these activities might be much more tentative. This will often be the case when assessing new technologies. It is so in part because we recognize that we probably don't have all the relevant facts, such as the long-term health effects of these technologies on people or the environment, we don't know the uses to which such technologies might be put in the future if they are allowed, etc. We don't even have a clear sense of what interests are involved in using or banning such technologies, and so it is very difficult to reach a firm conclusion as to the moral status of them. The expectation of agreement upon the morality of such issues is much less reasonable in these cases. These are hard moral cases.

It is not, of course, solely new situations in which hard moral cases arise. The moral status of affirmative action policies is often only weakly agreed upon. The same person may recognize that there are good moral reasons for hiring policies that favour members of historically disadvantaged groups (correcting past injustices, for example) and also recognize that there are good moral reasons for rejecting the implementation of such policies (it will lead to hiring people for reasons other than their qualifications—the very thing that led to the need for corrective measures). If a single person is unclear regarding which course of action is correct, it is difficult to be optimistic regarding the possibility of agreement between different people.

Reflective moral thinking begins with those judgements about which we have the greatest certitude, about which we feel confident that we know the relevant facts, the interests that are at stake, and the consequences of deciding between those interests one way rather than another. We begin our critical thinking with our firmest moral judgements.

The methodology of reflective moral thinking then requires that we move from the level of specific moral judgements to the formulation of general moral principles. In formulating principles, we are trying to find a principle or set of principles, which explains the particular moral judgements we make, which explains why the easy moral cases are easy, and systematizes those judgements into a coherent moral point of view.

Suppose that my set of firm moral judgements includes the following: "Slavery is wrong." "The use of torture, rape, and brutality against human beings is never permissible." "We ought not to lie." "We ought to keep our promises." "It is wrong to engage in terrorist attacks." "The intentional killing of people is wrong." And so on. Critical morality requires that I think about *why* I think all these things are wrong. Do they have something in common that makes them all wrong, and which explains why I think them wrong? In answering this question I am trying to formulate a general principle under which all the specific judgements form a coherent moral point of view.

What doing lying, promise breaking, killing, rape, torture, slavery, terrorism, and brutality have in common? What common interest do they offend? There are a few possibilities that come readily to mind. Perhaps they are wrong because they all involve the infliction of pain upon the victim of the wrongful action. And so the principle I might think systematizes and explains my specific moral judgements would be "It is wrong to inflict pain upon people."

Now there are two stages to testing this proposed principle. First, does it explain all the specific judgements it is meant to explain and systematize? And, second, what implications does it have in terms of further specific judgements it supports?

In applying these tests we note that actions may have one of three moral statuses. An action may be morally required, forbidden, or permitted. In each stage of testing, a proposed principle must require only those actions that are right or good, forbid only those actions that are wrong or bad, and permit those actions that are neither right nor wrong. It must, furthermore, forbid all wrong actions, require all right actions, and permit all permissible actions.

Consider the first test. Does the principle "It is wrong to inflict pain upon people" explain all the moral judgements it was meant to explain? No. It does not adequately explain what is wrong with breaking our promises and lying, since both of these actions can be done without the victim knowing and, therefore, without the victim experiencing any pain as a result. This principle does not forbid some actions that are clearly wrong: promise breaking and lying. Thus it is inadequate according to our first test.

An alternative principle that might explain all the specific judgements that need to be explained is "You must always respect other persons." This principle is better than the first attempt because it covers all the cases; every wrong that I was trying to explain can be seen as covered by this principle, since cruelty, promise breaking, and the rest fail to respect the person who is wronged.

The principle of respect for persons is not the only principle that could explain the judgements in question, however. I might instead think that the judgements are best explained by the principle that "We ought to follow moral rules that produce the most happiness for every being whose interests are concerned." Rules which forbid torture, killing, lying, promise breaking, and the like are likely to produce more happiness for the people whose interests are concerned than rules that allow or require such actions, and so this principle explains the cases equally well.

When we have more than one principle that systematizes and explains the specific judgements that we make, how do we decide between them? One thing we can do is expand the range of judgements to see if both principles can accommodate the expanded set. So suppose we add the judgement that when kids light cats on fire what they are doing is wrong. The principle that "You must always respect other persons" cannot explain this judgement, since cats are not persons and so they are not covered by this principle. It cannot explain why we think burning cats is wrong. By contrast, a principle that requires that "We ought to follow moral rules that produce the most happiness for every being whose interests are concerned" can explain the judgement we make about cat burning being wrong. If cats are made very unhappy by being burned alive, and their pain outweighs the happiness that people might get from burning them, then this principle would support a rule against burning cats and, presumably, other acts of wanton cruelty toward animals just for kicks. Thus this principle explains the broader range of judgements and so would be deemed superior.

But now we come to the second way in which we test our principles. We must ask what further judgements are implied by our principles. Whereas in the first stage of critical moral thinking we moved from our firm moral judgements to the level of general principles, in this stage we move from the general principles to the specific judgements they require in further cases. Take, for example, the principle that "Killing human beings is always wrong." And suppose we stipulate that "human being" means "entity with the DNA of a *Homo sapien*." If you accept this principle then you must accept, as an implication of this principle, that killing even in a defensive war is wrong, that killing in self-defence is wrong, that abortion is wrong, that suicide is wrong, etc. If you are not willing to accept all of these implications, then you must refine your principle.

Reflective moral thinking requires that we move back and forth between the levels of specific moral judgements and general moral principles. What we are trying to do is construct a moral point of view that is coherent, within which all of our firm moral judgements are explained by our general principles, and the implications of our principles in deciding further specific cases are acceptable. The resulting point of view should allow us to say why easy moral cases are easy, being directly explained by the basic principle or principles in the view, and why hard cases are hard. It must also provide us with guidance in deciding hard or novel cases, and its direction in such cases must be such that we can accept it as ideal moral judges.

Reflective moral thinking requires that we move back and forth between the levels of moral judgements and moral principles, in order to test both. We must be willing to refine and revise our principles when we find that they are too narrow to explain all the firm moral judgements that we make or when we find that they have implications for specific cases that would be unreasonable to an ideal moral judge. But we must also be willing to revise our specific moral judgements when they cannot be supported by the best set of principles we have been able to formulate. Revision works in both directions. This is why Rawls called his method reflective equilibrium: we are trying to bring our moral judgements and our moral principles into equilibrium, into a coherent balance in which they are mutually supportive and explanatory. Our principles are supported by their ability to explain our firmest moral judgements and our further judgements are supported by the principles from which they can de derived. There is a balance and mutual support between the levels, producing a moral point of view that is in equilibrium. It is reflective because it has been produced by a method that begins but does not end with a person's uncritical moral judgements. Both the principles and specific moral judgements that come to make up a coherent point of view have been subjected to scrutiny, they have been tested for fit with one another, and in terms of their implications for deciding further moral questions. When the person engaged in critical moral thinking reasons from the perspective of an ideal moral judge, the moral point of view that results from this process is reflective, and has been selected as the most coherent and rationally defensible moral position available. This is the goal of critical moral thinking. Its output is what we call critical morality.

LAW AND RELIGION

Morality is only one of many normative systems typically found within human communities. Other important normative systems are those of law and religion. All three are normative systems, in that they set standards of right and proper conduct, and prescribe actions that conform to those standards of what people ought to do. We have already pointed out that the norms of a legal system and that of critical morality may differ. We know, for example, that some legal systems have explicitly supported the institution of slavery and denied basic rights to women. Critical morality, we assume, would condemn such laws as morally unjustified. Thus there may be a significant gap between the legal code of a given society and the ideal moral code identified by critical morality.

It would be unreasonable to expect the legal code and conventional moral code of a society to be entirely unrelated, however. Human beings often use law to reinforce their moral systems. Moreover, law serves many of the same purposes as morality does. It should provide rules governing human behaviour that allow for peaceful and cooperative interaction in society, and mechanisms for resolving disputes when the interests of some come into conflict with the interests of others. But just as the conventional moral system of a society may be defective, influenced by ignorance, prejudice and the like, so can a legal system be defective. In both cases our standard of deficiency is set by critical morality. Critical morality provides an independent standard against which we can test both the moral opinions of our fellows and the laws of our society. Ideally, both will be reformed to bring them into closer harmony with the dictates of critical morality over time.

Religion is, of course, also an important normative system within many cultures. It often influences both the legal code of a society and the moral beliefs of individuals. But it is an independent normative system. It has a different purpose than that of either law or morality, namely, to render us pleasing to the deity. If the deity requires that we treat each other well (because He loves us, say), then there will be some overlap again between the dictates of religion with those of law and morality. All three, for example, will typically forbid the killing of other people in most circumstances. Killing is a sin, a crime, and a moral wrong, because it is forbidden under all three normative systems.

Despite the fact that religion and morality are often bound up together in the moral outlook of those who believe, religion can play no role in critical morality, and moral opinions that are based on religious authority alone must be given no weight in reflective moral reasoning. This is so for the following reason.

Religious authority faces a challenge that all appeals to authority in moral disputes face. Advertising crucially rests on appeals to authority to sell products in the market, but consider how baseless many such appeals are. A famous athlete endorses a medical drug or a car, and we are supposed to accept him as an authority on the goodness of medications or cars. To do so is unreasonable, because there is no reason to think that an athlete has any special expertise on what makes one drug or car superior to another. By contrast, an athlete might have some special insight into what makes a good basketball shoe or tennis racket.

This is meant to illustrate a general point. Appeals to authority depend for their strength upon the likelihood that the authority in question has any particular experience, insight, or expertise that makes him or her better than most people to decide some question or to offer direction as to what we should do. We rely upon the advice of many professionals, such as doctors and lawyers, in deciding what we should do because they have the relevant expertise that we lack. But notice that their expertise, and so the reasonableness of accepting them as authorities, extends only to those areas over which they do have superior relevant knowledge or experience. It would not be reasonable for me to take my doctor's advice as authoritative on matters of gardening or auto repair.

Let us return now to the place of religion in reflective moral thinking. Why should we take the dictates of any particular religion, or the judgements of any particular group of clerics, as authorities in moral matters? This is an especially troubling question, given that there are differences of religious opinion in the world. They all claim the same source for their authority, namely divine revelation, yet they offer conflicting prescriptions concerning what we ought to do. But the problem is deeper than that. Even if we knew which was the one true religion, and what the will of its deity was, we would still face the question of why we should accept that deity as a moral authority and not just as a religious authority.

The answer given to that question usually relies on three properties that the deity is supposed to have: perfect goodness or benevolence, complete power, and perfect knowledge. For ease of exposition we shall simply refer to the deity as God, though that is not meant to imply any judgement about what is the one true religion. Someone claiming that God is the proper moral authority could first argue that, as God is all knowing, He therefore knows what the good is, and so all we have to do is listen to what God tells us to know what morality requires. But someone else could respond that perhaps God is not inclined to tell us what morality requires, or is being prevented by some other powerful entity (perhaps the devil) from telling us what morality requires. To this response, the person arguing for appealing to God's authority would have a ready response: God is all-powerful and perfectly good. If He is all-powerful, none could restrain Him, and His being perfectly good ensures that He would be inclined to tell us what morality requires. But this is the crux of the matter. How do we know that God is perfectly good? If we answer "because God said so" we are question-begging. Only if God is truly good would we have a reason to take His word for the fact that He is good, and this is the point that is at issue. On the other hand, to identify God as good ourselves, we would have to already know what goodness is. It is only by recognizing that everything that God has ever done was good that we could even attempt to argue that God is, in fact, perfectly good. But in this case we must already know what it is to be good. And so, in critical morality, appeals to God's word are either question-begging or redundant.

No doubt those who have strong religious convictions will be dissatisfied with this conclusion. But note that we are not denying that religion often plays a significant role in the lives of individuals, that it makes those lives more meaningful, connects people to a broader community, and often is a strong support to morally good action and the building of virtuous and happy characters. We are not saying that religion itself is arbitrary or irrelevant. We are only saying that critical morality is independent of religion, that it can be studied in its own right, and that appeals to religious authority alone cannot be an acceptable method of resolving moral conflicts.

WHY CRITICAL MORALITY MATTERS

Why should we go to all the trouble of engaging in critical moral thinking? There are two reasons. First, we must decide moral disputes, both as individuals and as societies. Individually we must act, often in contexts where people make competing moral demands on us. Reflective moral reasoning is the best method we have for deciding what to do in a responsible way. A person who acts according to the dictates of critical morality can justify his actions to others as rationally defensible. He can invite others to share his moral point of view. And he can hope for success if his fellows are trying to reach a reasoned resolution to the dispute.

The alternatives to critical morality, furthermore, are simply unacceptable: blind adherence to tradition or authority, decisions based on unreflective and disputed moral opinions, disagreements that never go anywhere because the people simply talk past one another, and the interests of some being discounted by those making decisions. At best these methods can result in an agreement to disagree—something that is unlikely given that significant interests are at stake. At worst, they result in moral disagreements being solved by might rather than right, by power rather than reason. We think we can and should do better.

And even if individuals can simply live with disagreement, societies often cannot. Laws have to be passed, policies have to be set, funding has to be distributed, and disputes have to be settled. Our choice is stark. We can have governments act on whatever moral feelings the governors have at the moment, or even on the moral feelings of the majority of citizens, no matter how ill-informed, biased, self-serving, incoherent, and unprincipled those feelings might be, or we can insist that governments subject their laws, policies, and the like to critical scrutiny. Only a critical morality guarantees to all that their interests will be taken into account when they conflict with the interests of others, in an impartial and informed way. This is the way to a reasonable resolution of disputes, to an accommodation of conflicting interests in society, and to genuine moral progress in the world. We think that is worth the effort.

What follows in this book is designed to provide its readers with material on which to develop and exercise their skills at critical moral reasoning. We begin, in each of the subsequent chapters, with an introduction to a moral theory that has been widely influential in the Western philosophical tradition. The theories we present are Utilitarianism, Kantian Deontology, Libertarianism, Liberalism, and Feminism. These are competing theories, each of which is organized around a set of moral principles and factual beliefs, which it is claimed, provide the most defensible basis for critical moral thinking. Our assessment of these theories will depend upon how well they explain and systematize our most firmly held moral judgements, and the acceptability of their advice in deciding controversial or novel moral issues. To provide material against which students may test the theories, each chapter contains a number of readings that concern a particular moral issue (such as abortion, nuclear deterrence, cloning, organ sales, duties to the poor, etc.). By examining how well a theory can explain why some practices are wrong and others right, and by assessing the kind of guidance each theory gives in hard cases, we will be able to apply the skills of critical moral reasoning and judging so as to do two things. We will be able to assess the theories themselves, according to how well they explain and systematize our most firmly held moral judgements, and the acceptability of their advice in deciding controversial or novel moral issues. And we will reach reasoned judgements on a wide range of specific moral issues or problems. The result, we hope, will be a more defensible and coherent moral outlook than we started with, and a greater understanding of why we make the moral judgements and evaluations that we do. We cannot guarantee that critical morality will allow us to resolve all moral disputes, or that all good moral judges will reach agreement on which are the correct moral principles. But our hope is that many moral disputes may be found to be resolvable, once they have been clarified by critical moral reasoning.

DEFINITIONS AND EXPLANATIONS

Is-ought fallacy: A pattern of faulty reasoning that must be avoided. The mistake involved is reasoning from what is the case (from some set of facts) to what ought to be the case (to some normative claim). The mistake is in trying to infer the truth of a normative claim from the truth of some factual claim(s). The term **fallacy** refers to any such mistaken patterns of inference, bad reasoning, or logical mistake. The is-ought fallacy is only one of a number of fallacies. Students wishing to learn more about fallacies should consider studying logic or critical thinking.

Normative: Setting a norm or standard of conduct; normative statements typically take the form of "ought" judgements, as in "I ought to tell the truth."

Prescribe: To recommend or require; to set down a rule of action; a prescription is an order, command, or recommendation that one should act in a particular way, as required by a norm or rule.

Proscribe: To denounce, forbid or condemn; a proscription is an order, command, or recommendation that one should not act, should refrain from acting, in a particular way because such action is forbidden by a norm or rule.

CHAPTER TWO

UTILITARIANISM

———

Introduction

We begin with a moral theory that will be familiar, at least in broad outline, to most readers: utilitarianism. Roughly, utilitarians believe that that morally right thing to do is whatever will produce the best consequences for all those affected by your action. Foremost among those who developed this way of approaching moral questions were Jeremy Bentham, John Stuart Mill, and Henry Sidgwick.

Consequentialism

Utilitarianism is a **consequentialist** theory. It evaluates the morality of actions, rules, decisions, laws, and institutions in light of their consequences. Utilitarians say that what any individual or government ought to do is whatever will have the best consequences. We shall speak here just of actions and individuals for the sake of simplicity in setting out the view. In saying that individuals ought to do whatever will produce the best consequences, utilitarians are rejecting the competing view that some actions are right or wrong in themselves, that is, right or wrong independently of their results. To understand the difference here, consider the example of lying. Some people say that lying is wrong in and of itself, and in all cases. They say that lying is wrong independently of the consequences of lying. Thus, even if you could avert a serious harm to someone by lying, you ought not to lie. But utilitarians find the notion of actions being right or wrong, independently of their consequences, to be rather mysterious. They deny that we really know what we mean when we say that some action or type of action is wrong *per se*, other than that we don't like it. They ask us to think more deeply. *Why* do we think that lying is wrong? Because, utilitarians say, it almost always has bad consequences for the person being lied to, as well perhaps as to others. That is why lying is wrong: because it usually has bad consequences. And if there are exceptional circumstances in which lying would not have bad results then it may not be wrong to lie. A classic example of such a case is this. Suppose you are living in a state in which a group of innocent people is being persecuted and murdered by your own government. Suppose, further, that you are hiding some of those victims in a secret room in your house. If a member of the state death squad comes to your door and asks, "Are you hiding any members of the group?" it seems that you will do significantly more good than harm if you lie and deny that you are hiding your unfortunate fellow citizens. It seems, in other words, that in such a case you ought to lie and save the lives of the innocent people you are hiding. If this is so, if you can imagine any cases in which the right thing to do is to lie, then lying is not wrong *per se* and the utilitarian explanation of what makes lying wrong when it is wrong seems on strong ground. This is the way in which consequences matter to utilitarians. All actions are evaluated, ultimately, in terms of their good or bad consequences, and moral rules such as "Do not lie" are justified rules only if the behaviour that is forbidden by the rule does generally have very bad consequences.

Suppose we accept for the moment this core commitment of utilitarians, that the rightness or wrongness of actions depends on their consequences. How are we to distinguish good from bad consequences? Obviously we must be able to do this if we are to follow the utilitarian's advice to do what will bring about the best results. How do we decide which are the best results? To answer this question utilitarians must provide a theory of value, which tells us which results are good and which are bad.

Value

Utilitarianism in fact begins with a theory of value, that is, a theory of what is good. Different utilitarians have offered competing conceptions of value, but we will begin by distinguishing various ways in which something can be valued. First, many things are valued only instrumentally, that is, as a means to something else. A prime example of something that is valued only instrumentally is money. Most people do not value money for its own sake, but rather they value it for what it can be exchanged for: fun, food, housing, prestige, etc. Money is a means to getting other things that we value. Thus it has only **instrumental value**. But we cannot value everything only instrumentally. If some things are valued as a means to something else, then there must be some other things that we value for their own sakes. To say that we value something for its own sake is to say that we value it intrinsically. **Intrinsic values** are those things we think are good in and of themselves. While some goods are easily classified into one or the other categories of goods, others may be valued differently by different people. Consider, for example, the value of higher education. For some people, education is valued purely instrumentally. They see getting an education, say a university degree, as merely a means to other ends, such as a higher salary, a more fulfilling career, or making their parents happy. Others, by contrast, value education for its own sake. They find the pursuit of knowledge valuable in and of itself, quite independently of any other rewards that being educated might bring. Thus the same thing may be valued differently by different people. But utilitarians will insist that every person must have some things which he or she values intrinsically. And the theory of value they offer is of intrinsic goods.

Most utilitarians have offered **subjective theories of value**. A subjective theory of the good finds intrinsic value in certain subjective states of the individual, such as pleasure, happiness, or preference satisfaction. Now such a conception of the good is not susceptible of direct proof, but it is clear that people value many things because they are either enjoyable in themselves or contribute to their happiness instrumentally. If you ask them why they value pleasure, or why they think happiness is good, or why they want to have their preferences satisfied, they can give no other answer than that those things are good. On such conceptions it is individuals who are the ultimate judges of value, however, for what is good is just what makes them happy, what gives them pleasure, or what satisfies their individual preferences. The theory of value is thus "subjective" in the common usage of that term.

Other utilitarians have defended **objective theories of value**. An objective theory of value holds that some things are good independently of whether they are valued by anyone at all. Often these theories take the form of objective lists of goods, things that it would be good for people to have or experience whether they want them or not. Common items on such lists would be health, sufficient financial resources to live a decent human life, education, meaningful work, fulfilling relationships, political freedom, etc. Such theories are often couched in the language of basic needs, welfare, or objective interests. Thus it might be said that everyone has an objective interest in health, even if some individuals subjectively prefer to ruin their health by smoking, overeating, or using harmful drugs. In such cases the objective and subjective conceptions of value come apart, and the utilitarian must decide which good matters in assessing the consequences of actions. Furthermore, it is not only human interests that might appear on a list of objective goods. Anything that is such that its existence is a good thing in and of itself, can be an objective good. One test for the intrinsic value of an object or state of affairs is that developed by the objective value utilitarian G. E. Moore. Moore proposed what has come to be called the test of radical isolation as a test of intrinsic value: if you want to know whether something is intrinsically valuable, ask yourself whether it would be valuable even if nothing else existed. On this score, Moore thought we could determine that beauty has intrinsic value, for example, since a world in which beauty existed would be better than one in which it did not, even if nothing else exists (including people to appreciate the beauty). This approach has been adopted by many in the environmental movement, who claim that some states of affairs are valuable quite independently of human beings valuing them and even if they alone existed; examples include wilderness, species diversity, and the like. If such thinkers are also utilitarians, then such goods must be included in the assessment of consequences when deciding what actions are right or wrong.

In what follows we shall concentrate either on subjective theories of value or on objective (welfare based) theories, which include a significant subjective component. Conceptions of welfare often straddle the fence between the two broad categories of value in fact, since they typically combine some objective list of goods as components of welfare along with subjective states of happiness and preference satisfaction. No one could have a very high level of welfare who was subjectively miserable and frustrated all the time, but subjective happiness is not enough to constitute welfare when it is based in delusion or the continuous use of intoxicants. The person who does not know that his girlfriend is cheating on him may be happy, and the wealthy crack addict may be able to satisfy most of her preferences, but being an addict or being cheated on does not contribute to their welfare as most people understand it. This ambiguity in the notion of welfare, involving both subjective and objective components, will resurface as a concern in its own right in the last two chapters of the book. But for now we shall move along.

Whatever conception of the good a utilitarian adopts, it then becomes the standard by which consequences are evaluated. One result is better than another if it produces more good (more intense pleasure, more lasting happiness, a higher level of welfare, etc.) for an individual, or if it produces good for more people rather than less. We refer to the amount of good a state of affairs contains as its **utility**. Utility is, then, just a measure of the overall goodness of a state of affairs. Utilitarianism tells us to produce that state of affairs that has the highest utility score, meaning just that state of affairs with the greatest amount of good in it. Disutility is, correspondingly, a measure of the bad (pain, unhappiness, preference frustration, unmet needs, etc.). Disutility is to be reduced so far as possible and utility is to be produced as far as possible. The alleviation of distress and pain is just as important as the production of pleasure or happiness. As Jeremy Bentham put it, "By utility is meant that property in any object, whereby it tends to produce benefit, advantage, pleasure, good, or happiness (all this in the present case comes to the same thing) or (what comes again to the same thing) to prevent the happening of mischief, pain, evil, or unhappiness to the party whose interest is considered: if that party be the community in general, then the happiness of the community: if a particular individual, then the happiness of that individual."[1]

As this passage makes clear, Bentham (and other utilitarians) sees utility as the proper standard by which actions are to be judged. To do so we must take into account not only the good but also the bad possible consequences of our actions, and do so for everyone whose interests might be negatively or positively affected by what we propose to do.

Such a calculation might be incredibly complex. To see what kinds of considerations might be taken into account in determining which of a number of possible states of affairs will be best, let us take the simplest case in which utility is just a measure of pleasure. This was Bentham's own understanding. It will be incredibly difficult, you might think, to compare different possible outcomes in terms of their overall level of pleasure or absence of pain. But Bentham thought it was possible to compare states of affairs according to their overall level of utility, and he provided what has come to be called the felicific calculus as a guide for decision making.

First, every pleasure or pain will be greater or less according to the following four circumstances:

1. Its intensity.
2. Its duration.
3. Its certainty or uncertainty.
4. Its propinquity or remoteness.[2]

Other things being equal, pleasures that are more intense, more lasting, more certain or more immediate in time are greater than those that are less intense, of briefer duration, less certain, or more distant in time. The opposite is true of pains.

Furthermore, the same action that produces any given pleasure or pain may also have further consequences that must be taken into account in assessing the overall utility of the state of affairs it would produce. Thus we can consider

5. Its *fecundity*, or the chance it has of being followed by sensations of the *same* kind: that is, pleasures, it be a pleasure: pains, if it be a pain.

6. Its *purity,* or the chance it has of *not* being followed by sensations of the *opposite* kind: that is, pains, if it be a pleasure: pleasures, if it be a pain.[3]

Thus an action will produce greater amounts of utility if it produces fecund pleasures and unfecund pains, and pure pleasures and impure pains.

Finally, in the case of actions that produce pains or pleasures for more than a single individual, we must consider

7. Its *extent;* that is, the number of persons to whom it *extends;* or (in other words) who are affected by it.[4]

Having thus provided the elements by which the value of individual pleasures and pains can be assessed, Bentham then explains how they come together in an overall assessment of the utility of any given action. We quote the entire paragraph.

> To take an exact account then of the general tendency of any act, by which the interests of a community are affected, proceed as follows. Begin with any one person of those whose interests seem most immediately to be affected by it: and take an account,
>
> 1. Of the value of each distinguishable *pleasure* which appears to be produced by it in the *first* instance.
> 2. Of the value of each *pain* which appears to be produced by it in the *first* instance.
> 3. Of the value of each pleasure which appears to be produced by it *after* the first. This constitutes *the fecundity* of the first *pleasure* and the *impurity* of the first *pain.*
> 4. Of the value of each *pain* which appears to be produced by it after the first. This constitutes the *fecundity* of the first *pain,* and the *impurity* of the first pleasure.
> 5. Sum up all the values of all the *pleasures* on the one side, and those of all the pains on the other. The balance, if it be on the side of pleasure, will give the *good* tendency of the act upon the whole, with respect to the interests of that *individual* person; on the side of pain, the *bad* tendency of it upon the whole.
> 6. Take an account of the *number* of persons whose interests appear to be concerned; and repeat the above process with respect to each. *Sum up* the numbers expressive of the degrees of *good* tendency, which the act has, with respect to each individual, in regard to whom the tendency of it is *good* upon the whole: do this again with respect to each individual, in regard to whom the tendency of it is *good* upon the whole: do this again with respect to each individual, in regard to whom the tendency of it is *bad* upon the whole. Take the *balance;* which, if on the side of *pleasure,* will give the general *good* tendency of the act, with respect to the total number or community of individuals concerned; if on the side of pain, the general *evil tendency,* with respect to the same community.[5]

This may seem an unduly cumbersome process. Imagine having to undertake a full utility calculation before you could ever decide what you ought to do. Bentham immediately points out, however, that individuals typically do not have to undertake such a calculation before they act, both because most individuals cannot affect the interests of very many people when they act, and they typically know sufficiently well what the tendency of their actions is likely to be in terms of their own happiness and the happiness of those others who might be affected by what they do. By contrast, Bentham does urge legislators and those charged with the good of groups to always keep the basis of the calculation in mind when they decide what to do. John Stuart Mill most forcefully made the point that the basic utilitarian calculation is not unduly difficult in the following famous passage of his essay "Utilitarianism."

> Again, defenders of utility often find themselves called upon to reply to such objections as this–that there is not time, previous to action, for calculating and weighing the effects of any line of conduct on the general happiness. This is exactly as if anyone were to say that it is impossible to guide our conduct by Christianity because there is not time, on every occasion on which anything has to be done, to read through the Old and New Testaments. The answer to the objection is that there has been ample time, namely, the whole past duration of the human species. During all that time mankind have been learning by experience the tendencies of actions; on which experience all the prudence as well as all the morality of life are dependent. People talk as if the commencement of this course of experience had hitherto been put off, and as if, at the moment when some man feels tempted to meddle with the property or life of another, he had to begin considering for the first time whether murder and theft are injurious to human happiness.... It is truly a whimsical supposition that, if mankind were agreed in considering utility to be the test of morality, they would remain without any agreement as to what *is* useful, and would take no measures for having their notions on the subject taught to the young and enforced by law and opinion. There is no difficulty in proving any ethical standard whatever to work ill if we suppose universal idiocy to be conjoined with it; but on any hypothesis short of that, mankind must by this time have acquired positive beliefs as to the effects of some actions on their happiness; and the beliefs which have thus come down are the rules of morality for the multitude, and for the philosopher until he has succeeded in finding better.[6]

Thus utilitarianism requires that we evaluate our actions in terms of their overall effect on the happiness of those who will be affected by them. Following the accumulated wisdom of the species we can know roughly which actions contribute to our own happiness and the happiness of others. At a minimum, we must aim to do more good than harm. Ideally, we should try to produce the greatest amount of pleasure over pain as is possible.

Egalitarian and Impartial

One virtue of utilitarian thinking can be seen implicitly in Bentham's description of the felicific calculus, namely, its **egalitarianism**. This aspect can easily be missed, if you think that utilitarianism simply tells people to do what will promote *their own* happiness. In fact, utilitarianism does tell individuals to act so as to bring about the greatest amount of happiness they can. If an action will have consequences only affecting the agent who acts himself, then utilitarianism tells him to act so as to make himself as happy as possible. In that case, where the only consequences fall upon the individual whose action is in question, utilitarianism counsels prudent self-interest. But, of course, most actions have consequences affecting the happiness of others as well as oneself. In this case, utilitarianism does not tell people to selfishly pursue their own interest at the expense of others. If it did, it would be a poor moral theory. For one of the hallmarks of morality and what distinguishes it from mere prudence, is that it should be for the benefit of all people. Morality requires that we think about others, and the right thing to do will take into account the interests of others and not just yourself. Utilitarianism captures these aspects of morality in its commitments to equality and impartiality.

The commitment to equality and impartiality is commonly captured by saying that, within utilitarianism, "everyone counts for one and none for more than one." More carefully, utilitarians say that the happiness of each person counts and counts equally in the felicific calculus. In other words, utilitarianism treats as equally valuable the good wherever it is found. If pleasure and pain are good and bad, they are so whenever they occur. The pains of the poor are as great an evil as the pains of the rich and powerful. Likewise, animals doubtlessly suffer pain. They cannot suffer all the pains that human beings typically can suffer, such as the pains of embarrassment, shame, and fear, yet insofar as they can suffer their pain is bad and ought to be alleviated if it can be without imposing greater suffering on others. As Mill put it, "the happiness which forms the utilitarian standard of what is right in conduct is not the agent's own happiness but that of all concerned. As between his own happiness and that of others, utilitarianism requires him to be as strictly impartial as a disinterested and benevolent spectator."[7]

While many people will see this commitment to everyone's happiness mattering equally as a virtue of the theory, others may find this aspect of the theory problematic. The worry is that it may be too demanding a moral theory if it requires us to be strictly impartial between the happiness of strangers and the well-being of those closest to us: our parents, our children, our siblings, our lovers, and our friends. After all, we would expect a moral theory to explain why we have extraordinary duties to promote the happiness of those closest to us, and if utilitarians say we don't have such extraordinary duties, but we owe the same consideration to everyone's happiness, it will not be able to capture all of our settled moral judgements (about the responsibility of parents and children to one another, the duties of loyalty and care that are involved in friendship, etc.).

The Principle of Utility

We come now to the normative aspect of utilitarianism. On the basis of his theory of the good, Bentham describes what he calls the principle of utility. "By the principle of utility is meant that principle which approves or disapproves of every action whatsoever, according to the tendency which it appears to have to augment or diminish the happiness of the party whose interest is in question: or, what is the same thing in other words, to promote or oppose that happiness. I say of every action whatsoever; and therefore not only of every action of a private individual, but of every measure of government."[8] This principle allows us to move from a theory of the good to a theory of what is right or obligatory in action. It thus allows us to develop a moral theory with prescriptive force, one that tells individuals what they morally may or must do, what is right and wrong in action, what is our duty to do or refrain from doing. One ought to act conformably with the principle of utility. One ought, in other words, to act so as to augment happiness and diminish pain.

> Of an action that is conformable to the principle of utility one may always say either that it is one that ought to be done, or at least that it is not one that ought not to be done. One may say also, that it is right it should be done; at least that it is not wrong it should be done: that it is a right action; at least that it is not a wrong action. When thus interpreted, the words *ought*, and *right* and *wrong*, and others of that stamp, have a meaning: when otherwise, they have none.[9]

This is, perhaps, the weakest possible interpretation of the principle of utility. It says only that one may (is not wrong to) act in such a way that one's action has a tendency to promote happiness and oppose misery. Such an action is right. But there have been stronger interpretations of the principle of utility, which not only permit individuals to promote happiness but require it. This seems to be Bentham's own understanding of the principle in some of the other passages in the book that we have been considering, as well as in other writings. Elsewhere he referred to the principle as the "greatest happiness principle" and indicated that, at least when applied to the actions of governments rather than individuals, it requires, "as the only *right* and justifiable end of Government, the greatest happiness of the greatest number."[10] Indeed, even when writing of individuals Bentham often indicates that he thinks the principle of utility requires individuals to act so as to produce the greatest amount of happiness possible by their actions, for themselves only if it affects only themselves, and for all those affected when the consequences are more far-ranging. Thus, he says, "Ethics at large may be defined, the art of directing men's actions to the production of the greatest possible quantity of happiness, on the part of those whose interest is in view."[11] Here we come closer to the current understanding of the principle of utility, which requires that individuals act so as to produce the *greatest amount* of happiness possible. In this form, utilitarianism is a maximizing doctrine: everyone must act so as to maximize the total amount of good in the world, insofar as they have it within their power to do so.

Act or Rule Utilitarianism

There has been an important debate internal to utilitarianism that we have simply glossed over in the preceding description of the theory. It concerns what exactly it is that must be evaluated: individual actions or rules, laws, institutional arrangements, etc. Act utilitarianism is typically presented as requiring that we evaluate every possible *action* available to an agent to determine how much good it would produce if taken. The principle of utility then tells us to choose that action which will produce the highest level of utility, i.e., the most good.[12] We have already seen that many people have worried about the computational complexity of such an approach. As a result, very early in the development of utilitarian moral theory, John Stuart Mill explicitly advocated thinking about the utility of *rules* rather than actions. In this way we could apply utilitarian reasoning to questions of which moral rules we should support, as well as what kinds of laws and other political arrangements would be morally justifiable. As typically interpreted today, rule utilitarianism asks which rules it would maximize utility to adopt, on the assumption that everyone followed them. In this way we determine which rules are morally justified according to the measure of utility. Right action, what we ought to do, and moral duty are then defined in terms of rule-following. An action is right when it conforms to a justified rule; an action is obligatory when it is required by a rule.

The distinction between act and rule utilitarianism has been an important source of disagreement among utilitarians, and raises interesting questions that a defender of the view must answer. Our earlier example of the moral status of lying highlights the difference between the two approaches. Suppose you are the person hiding your unfortunate fellow citizens from the state death squad, and you are asked if you are doing so. Should you lie? If you are an act utilitarian, the answer seems relatively easy. You calculate the consequences of the two options that are open to you: lying or telling the truth. You must assess the consequences of the options both for yourself and everyone else involved. If you lie (successfully), you save the lives of the people you are hiding (a result with considerable positive utility). You also thwart the plans of the government and its death squad (a result with negative utility to them, presumably). Of course, there may be additional consequences that you must consider: you may raise suspicions against yourself, thus putting yourself in future danger. You may contribute (to a small degree) to the instability of your political society by disobeying your government. No doubt these and other consequences are difficult to determine. But consider the calculation if you tell the truth. The people you are hiding will surely die a mean death, and you may also be punished for hiding them in the first place. You will have also contributed (however much against your will) to the support of an unjust political regime. When you weigh the benefits of saving people from unjust persecution and certain death, and the negative consequences that might be involved in such a case, you surely ought to lie. Lying will maximize utility. Indeed, it seems as though for any general moral rule (keep your promises, don't steal, tell the truth, even don't kill), an act utilitarian must accept that there may be exceptional circumstances in which the right act is contrary to the rule. In other words, an act utilitarian must be prepared, in principle at least, to grant that there may be occasions when the right thing to do is to break the moral rule, because doing so has overwhelmingly better consequences than would following the rule. This is so, even if we are supposing that the moral rules in question are good rules, that is, rules the following of which generally does produce the best results.

Rule utilitarians, by contrast, object to this way of thinking about moral rules. Moral rules get treated just as "rules of thumb" within act utilitarian thinking: they may be good general guidelines in deciding what to do, but they have no real weight and can be over-ridden anytime breaking the rule would have better consequences than following the rule, that is, not to treat them as rules at all.

Rule utilitarians ask us not to assess every individual action in terms of its consequences, but rather to think about which rules it would be best to adopt on the assumption that everyone will follow them. What we must do then is compare possible sets of rules (rather than individual actions as our options). On this test, rules against lying, promise breaking, stealing, killing, and the like would surely be justified. It would be best if everyone refrained from these kinds of actions. Proscribing such actions would surely have better results than allowing them.

Of course, we may want to refine our rules somewhat, once we consider what will happen if two rules come into conflict with each other (such as a rule not to be knowingly cruel to a friend and the rule to tell the truth might, should your friend ask you if she looks fat in her new polka dot dress). We may also have to refine our rules somewhat once we acknowledge that not everyone will in fact follow them. Thus we might refine our rule against killing to allow killing in self-defence, recognizing that not everyone will follow the rule proscribing personal violence. But modifying our general rules to take into account legitimate exceptions (the killing in self-defence rule) and adopting procedures for deciding what to do in cases of conflicts between rules do not pose any undue difficulty for rule utilitarians. For their utilitarian standard can be applied to ask whether the modified rule against killing is better than the unmodified one, and whether in settling conflicts between rules we should give priority to one concern rather than another.

It might seem, in light of this flexibility, that rule utilitarianism is clearly superior to act utilitarianism. Certainly as a guide for action it seems much simpler. Rather than having to calculate the consequences of every action that is available to us, we simply have to decide (usually as a society or group) which rules it would be best to adopt and then follow those rules. I would not have to calculate the consequences of lying every time I could lie; I simply have to know the rule against lying and follow it. This is not to say that it is always easy to know what is required by a rule, or what action would conform to the rule, but in most cases rule utilitarianism would be easier than act utilitarianism to follow. And such a theory would explain why so much of our moral thinking seems to rely upon general rules.

Yet there are serious problems with rule utilitarianism as a form of utilitarianism. The most important has to do with how rule utilitarians treat exceptions to the rules, such as the one we considered above involving lying to the death squad. Let us accept for the sake of argument that the rule forbidding lying would be adopted on rule utilitarian grounds. Now the rule utilitarian seems to face two options with respect to our case. She can say that the person ought to lie, and treat the situation as an exception to the rule. But if she does, she too is just treating the rule as a rule of thumb. Any time breaking the rule will have better consequences than following it (even taking into account the consequence that your breaking the rule might ultimately contribute to general disrespect for and disregard of the rule itself) then we should break the rule and maximize utility directly. If this is what rule utilitarianism recommends—follow the rules when doing so maximizes utility and otherwise break them—then it simply collapses into act utilitarianism. There is no difference between the two. If, on the other hand, the rule utilitarian says that we ought to follow the moral rules even if we know (with all the certainty we can have about the likely consequences of our actions) that doing so will produce more harm than good, then she no longer seems to be a utilitarian at all. How can a utilitarian of any kind counsel us to act in ways we know will bring about more harm than good, when we have other options available that would produce better consequences? To do so she must give up consequentialism altogether. As one philosopher put it, to adopt such a position that says follow the moral rules even when doing so will have worse consequences than breaking the rule would, is to engage in a kind of "rule worship," which is utterly incompatible with consequentialist reasoning.[13]

It seems, then, that rule utilitarians face a problem. Either they too can only treat moral rules as rules of thumb, or they lack an explanation of the authority of the rules in exceptional cases. Now rule utilitarians are quick to point out, and quite rightly, that the idea of exceptions to moral rules is not unproblematic. If you think about when people are most likely to say that a situation involves an exception to a moral rule you will see that they often involve cases in which a person wants to break the rule because it serves his own interests to do so. Most people will accept that lying, stealing, cheating, promise breaking, and the like are wrong, and will condemn others for actions that violate these moral rules. But when it comes to themselves they seem all too ready to find exceptions everywhere. Cheating on school work is wrong for everyone else, but I can do it because I was too busy working to get my essay finished, because I was too upset to write my essay because my boyfriend broke up with me, because…. Rule utilitarians are particularly aware of the general tendency in human nature to make exceptions to the rules for themselves, for reasons of self-interest, or even just convenience. As a result, rule utilitarians might say that the genuine exceptions to a moral rule are rare. This is no doubt true, and worth remembering if we want to be good moral judges. But whether it solves all the problems with rule utilitarianism we leave for the reader to decide.

DEFINITIONS AND EXPLANATIONS

Act utilitarianism: Moral assessment is primarily of actions rather than rules. The principle of utility is applied to all of the possible actions that an agent could perform, and tells us to act so as to bring about the best consequences possible. Right action and duties are directly defined in terms of whatever acts will maximize utility in the circumstances.

Consequentialism: Consequentialism is a type of moral theory whose proponents hold that what is most basic in moral assessments are consequences. Such consequences are often described as outcomes, results, or states of affairs. In moral theorizing, consequentialists are most often concerned with the consequences of human action (rather than natural causes, say, or acts of God). They insist that we cannot know whether an action is right or wrong until we know what consequences it had, or was likely to have.

Egalitarianism: The root of this term is equality. Egalitarian moral theories insist that every person (or creature) covered by the theory is equal in some morally important sense. Utilitarianism is egalitarian in its insistence that the happiness of everyone capable of happiness matters equally. All of the moral theories we look at have an egalitarian component, though what that is differs in each theory. The term is often used as well to describe a particular conception of distributive justice (a theory about what goods and opportunities people should enjoy), which says that everyone should have an equal share of goods and opportunities. We shall see this understanding of the term come to the fore when we reach the discussion of modern liberalism.

Instrumental value: The distinction between instrumental and intrinsic value can be understood in one of two ways. First, we might think about the way in which something is actually valued by a person. On this understanding, to say that something is instrumentally valued is to say that it is valued (desired, wanted, approved of) as a means to something else. Thus money might be valued as a means to health, or power, or leisure. If you want any of these other things, money is often useful for acquiring them, and so you would value money as a means to these other ends. A person might value any number of things only or to a large extent instrumentally. A person in a menial and unrewarding job might value that job only instrumentally, as a means to a paycheque and the things money provides. Second, we sometimes speak of things having only instrumental value when we want to say that they are not valuable in and of themselves, that they are not worthy as ends in themselves. Here we are not talking about how people value the things they value (the ways in which people value what they do), but rather we are speaking of the kind of value a thing actually has. Thus we might say that a miser, who loves money for its own sake, who takes delight in his riches even though he does not spend them on anything else of value, has a skewed sense of value, because he seems to value money as an end in itself, whereas it is really only of instrumental value. Thus we sometimes talk of the "real" value of things, independently of how they are actually valued. This use is more properly tied to the next distinction we mention, between subjective and objective theories of value.

Intrinsic value: Again we have two ways of using this term. First, we use the term "intrinsic value" to refer to the way in which something is valued. If something is valued intrinsically, it is valued as good in itself, as worthy of having or enjoying just because of what it is rather than as a means to anything else. Such values are often called ultimate, basic, or final ends. They are wanted for their own sake, and everything else is wanted as a means to them. Among the things that people cite as being intrinsically valued are happiness, pleasure, leisure, meaningful work, satisfying personal relationships, and the like. Second, corresponding to the second way of speaking about instrumental values, intrinsic value is often used to describe the actual kind of value that some things have, regardless of how they are actually valued by anyone, indeed, whether they are valued by anyone at all. Environmentalists often claim that some aspects of the environment have intrinsic value in this sense, by which they mean that wilderness or species or ecosystems are valuable for their own sakes, even if human beings do not value them and even if they provide no instrumental benefit to people. This is the sense of intrinsic value that Moore's test of isolation is supposed to identify: would something have value even if no one was there to value it? If so, then it has intrinsic value in this second sense.

Non-consequentialism: There are many forms of non-consequentialist moral theories. Among the most popular are those that hold that some actions are right or wrong *per se*, as such, independently of their consequences. Alternatively, a person might be a non-consequentialist because she thinks that what matters most in moral assessments are motives or intentions rather than outcomes, so that one would be a good person or have done the right thing so long as one's motives were virtuous, even if through bad luck or unforeseen influences one's actions actually produced very bad results. Kant, as we shall see in the next chapter, held both of these non-consequentialist views.

Objective theories of value: Those who hold an objective theory of value usually believe that some things are intrinsically valuable, independently of being valued by any one. This is a theory about what is worth valuing, rather than a theory of what is valued. Thus a person might think that truth, beauty, or the natural world has value, even if it is not valued by any valuing subject.

Rule utilitarianism: Moral assessment is primarily of rules rather than individual actions. The principle of utility is applied to possible rules, and tells us to adopt the rule that would have the best consequences were everyone to follow it. Right action and duties are then defined in terms of following the rules that have been selected as maximizing utility.

Subjective theories of value: The distinction between subjective and objective theories of value is obviously related to the previous distinction between instrumental and intrinsic theories of value, but it is different. Subjective theories of value hold that things have value only to the extent that someone (or some entity) values them. On such a view, there is no value without a valuing subject. And, of course, that subject will presumably value some things intrinsically (for their own sakes) and others instrumentally (as means to others ends that he has). This is, we think, probably the most proper use of the term. But a theory of value is often called subjective in another sense as well, namely when what is considered to be of value is just subjective mental states of a person, such as happiness and pleasure. To be happy or to experience pleasure are both subjective states of a person; whether a person is happy or in pain is determined just by his own physical and psychological states, which are subjective in the sense of being personal and unique to him. Most utilitarians are subjectivist about value in both senses. They think that subjective states of the agent are what has value and that they have value only because the agent values them. Thus it is only because we all value (want, desire, approve of) our own happiness or pleasure that these psychological states are in fact valuable for us.

Utility: Utility is a technical term often used in modern moral philosophy. It is simply a measure of the good. To say that some state of affairs (way the world is) has a certain utility value, or to say that one state of affairs has a higher amount of utility in it than another, is just short hand for saying that it has a certain amount of good in it or that it has more of whatever has been deemed good and of which utility is the measure. To say of any action that it would maximize utility is just to say that, of all the options available to the person acting, this action will produce the most good.

✦ ✦ ✦

Peter Singer, All Animals are Equal

Peter Singer gives us good reason to suppose that the ability to suffer pain or experience physical pleasure is the ultimate basis for being worthy of moral consideration, and explores the implications of this supposition for the issue of animal rights. Identifying rational agency as the popular alternative base for being a moral patient (worthy of moral consideration), Singer suggests that this alternative does not sit well with our considered moral judgements. For example, no infant is capable of purposeful behaviour, nor thought to have preferences and beliefs about the world (two common components in definitions of rational behaviour), and so no infant would be afforded moral consideration; they could be treated any way at all. A defender of rationality as the basis of moral consideration might try to solve this problem by saying that it is in light of their *potential* rationality that infants are afforded moral consideration, but as Singer points out, this would imply that abortion is a moral wrong. The ability to suffer, alternatively, does track our moral judgements: infants are surely able to suffer, and so are worthy of moral consideration, and thus cannot be significantly harmed unless it led to some greater good.

Animals also have the ability to suffer, and so on this version of utilitarianism, are worthy of equal moral consideration. The ability to take seriously wrongs to animals, and explain why wanton cruelty to animals is a moral wrong, is in fact one of the unique strengths of utilitarianism; no other moral theory that we look at can explain why lighting cats on fire just for kicks is a moral wrong done to the cat. Singer suggests that this has two significant and immediate implications: we should not eat animals at all, nor should we experiment on them. Since we eat animals only due to the difference in taste between eating meat and eating the viable alternatives, we inflict a great deal of suffering on animals (due to the current conditions of production) for a trivial gain in our satisfaction. Further, it is inefficient to produce food via animals. We would save money, and reduce suffering (given world hunger), if we did not eat animals, and so we ought not to do so. Singer's argument against animal experimentation depends on a call for consistent behaviour. If we are willing to experiment on animals because they are not rational then we should be willing to experiment on brain-damaged humans who are equally non-rational. If, on the other hand, we don't experiment on brain-damaged humans because they can still feel pain, then we ought not to experiment on animals that are equally capable of suffering. The inconsistency in our treatment of animals and brain-damaged humans reflects what Singer calls "speciesism," a form of prejudice analogous to racism and sexism.

Singer is the very embodiment of the impartiality of utilitarianism: each is to count as much as any other. He also raises a tension in utilitarianism between their commitment to a critical morality, and their (usual) acceptance of a subjective theory of value. Singer points out that, if we think about it, we have no reason to think that animals are worthy of less moral consideration than are people. This is a hallmark of a good critical thinker—we must all strive to uncover blind spots in our thinking. The fact that there is no reason for us to prefer avoiding inflicting suffering on people but preferring to inflict it on animals, however, does not necessarily defeat that preference. Suspiciously absent from Singer's argument that we must not experiment on animals if we would not experiment on brain-damaged humans is the fact that we would greatly prefer not to experiment on brain-damaged humans. If our taste for meat is included as a legitimate, if trivial, taste for a utilitarian calculation, then why exclude our taste for who we would experiment on? A theorist committed to a subject theory of value has no easy reply to make.

✦ ✦ ✦

Peter Singer, "All Animals are Equal." Reprinted by permission of the author. Part of this essay appeared in the *New York Review of Books* (5 Apr. 1973), and is reprinted by permission of the Editor.

All Animals Are Equal

PETER SINGER

In recent years a number of oppressed groups have campaigned vigorously for equality. The classic instance is the Black Liberation movement, which demands an end to the prejudice and discrimination that has made blacks second-class citizens. The immediate appeal of the Black Liberation movement and its initial, if limited, success made it a model for other oppressed groups to follow. We became familiar with liberation movements for Spanish-Americans, gay people, and a variety of other minorities. When a majority group—women—began their campaign, some thought we had come to the end of the road. Discrimination on the basis of sex, it has been said, is the last universally accepted form of discrimination, practiced without secrecy or pretence even in those liberal circles that have long prided themselves on their freedom from prejudice against racial minorities.

One should always be wary of talking of 'the last remaining form of discrimination.' If we have learnt anything from the liberation movements, we should have learnt how difficult it is to be aware of latent prejudice in our attitudes to particular groups until this prejudice is forcefully pointed out.

A liberation movement demands an expansion of our moral horizons and an extension or reinterpretation of the basic moral principle of equality. Practices that were previously regarded as natural and inevitable come to be seen as the result of an unjustifiable prejudice. Who can say with confidence that all his or her attitudes and practices are beyond criticism? If we wish to avoid being numbered amongst the oppressors, we must be prepared to re-think even our most fundamental attitudes. We need to consider them from the point of view of those most disadvantaged by our attitudes, and the practices that follow from these attitudes. If we can make this unaccustomed mental switch we may discover a pattern in our attitudes and practices that consistently operates so as to benefit one group—usually the one to which we ourselves belong—at the expense of another. In this way we may come to see that there is a case for a new liberation movement. My aim is to advocate that we make this mental switch in respect of our attitudes and practices towards a very large group of beings: members of species other than our own—or, as we popularly though misleadingly call them, animals. In other words, I am urging that we extend to other species the basic principle of equality that most of us recognize should be extended to all members of our own species.

All this may sound a little far-fetched, more like a parody of other liberation movements than a serious objective. In fact, in the past the idea of 'The Rights of Animals' really has been used to parody the case for women's rights. When Mary Wollstonecraft, a forerunner of later feminists, published her *Vindication of the Rights of Women* in 1792, her ideas were widely regarded as absurd, and they were satirized in an anonymous publication entitled *A Vindication of the Rights of Brutes*. The author of this satire (actually Thomas Taylor, a distinguished Cambridge philosopher) tried to refute Wollstonecroft's reasonings by showing that they could be carried one stage further. If sound when applied to women, why should the arguments not be applied to dogs, cats, and horses? They seemed to hold equally well for these 'brutes'; yet to hold that brutes had rights was manifestly absurd; therefore the reasoning by which this conclusion had been reached must be unsound, and if unsound when applied to brutes, it must also be unsound when applied to women, since the very same arguments had been used in each case.

One way in which we might reply to this argument is by saying that the case for equality between men and women cannot validly be extended to non-human animals. Women have a right to vote, for instance, because they are just as capable of making rational decisions as men are; dogs, on the other hand, are incapable of understanding the significance of voting, so they cannot have the right to vote. There are many other obvious ways in which men and women resemble each other closely, while humans and other animals differ greatly. So, it might be said, men and women are similar beings, and should have equal rights, while humans and non-humans are different and should not have equal rights.

The thought behind this reply to Taylor's analogy is correct up to a point, but it does not go far enough. There *are* important differences between humans and other animals, and these differences must give rise to *some* differences, in the rights that each have. Recognizing this obvious fact, however, is no barrier to the case for extending the basic principle of equality to non-human animals. The differences that exist between men and women are equally undeniable, and the supporters of Women's Liberation are aware that these differences may give rise to different rights. Many feminists hold that women have the right to an abortion on request. It does not follow that since these same people are campaigning for equality between men and women they must support the right of men to have abortions too. Since a man cannot have an abortion, it is meaningless to talk of his right to have one. Since a pig can't vote, it is meaningless to talk of its right to vote. There is no reason why either Women's Liberation or Animal Liberation should get involved in such nonsense. The extension of the basic principle of equality from one group to another does not imply that we must treat both groups in exactly the same way, or grant exactly the same rights to both groups. Whether we should do so will depend on the nature of the members of the two groups. The basic principle of equality, I shall argue, is equality of consideration; and equal consideration for different beings may lead to different treatment and different rights.

So there is a different way of replying to Taylor's attempt to parody Wollstonecraft's arguments, a way which does not deny the differences between humans and non-humans, but goes more deeply into the question of equality, and concludes by finding nothing absurd in the idea that the basic principle of equality applies to so-called 'brutes.' I believe that we reach this conclusion if we examine the basis on which our opposition to discrimination on grounds of race or sex ultimately rests. We will then see that we would be on shaky ground if we were to demand equality for blacks, women, and other groups of oppressed humans while denying equal consideration to non-humans.

When we say that all human beings, whatever their race, creed, or sex, are equal, what is it that we are asserting? Those who wish to defend a hierarchical, inegalitarian society have often pointed out that by whatever test we choose, it simply is not true that all humans are equal. Like it or not, we must face the fact that humans come in different shapes and sizes; they come with differing moral capacities, differing intellectual abilities, differing amounts of benevolent feeling and sensitivity to the needs of others, differing abilities to communicate effectively, and differing capacities to experience pleasure or pain. In short, if the demand for equality were based on the actual equality of all human beings, we would have to stop demanding equality. It would be an unjustifiable demand.

Still, one might cling to the view that the demand for equality among human beings is based on the actual equality of the different races and sexes. Although humans differ as individuals in various ways, there are no differences between the races and sexes *as such*. From the mere fact that a person is black, or a woman, we cannot infer anything else about that person. This, it may be said, is what is wrong with racism and sexism. The white racist claims that whites are superior to blacks, but this is false—although there are some differences between individuals, some blacks are superior to some whites in all of the capacities and abilities that could conceivably be relevant. The opponent of sexism would say the same: a person's sex is no guide to his or her abilities, and this is why it is unjustifiable to discriminate on the basis of sex.

This is a possible line of objection to racial and sexual discrimination. It is not, however, the way someone really concerned about equality would choose, because taking this line could, in some circumstances, force one to accept a most inegalitarian society. The fact that humans differ as individuals, rather than as races or sexes, is a valid reply to someone who defends a hierarchical society like, say, South Africa, in which all whites are superior in status to all blacks. The existence of individual variations that cut across the lines of race or sex, however, provides us with no defence at all against a more sophisticated opponent of equality, one who proposes that, say, the interests of those with IQ ratings above 100 be preferred to the interests of those with IQs below 100. Would a hierarchical society of this sort really be so much better than one based on race or sex? I think not. But if we tie the moral principle of equality to the factual equality of the different races or sexes, taken as a whole, our opposition to racism and sexism does not provide us with any basis for objecting to this kind of inegalitarianism.

There is a second important reason why we ought not to base our opposition to racism and sexism on any kind of factual equality, even the limited kind which asserts that variations in capacities and abilities are spread evenly between the different races and sexes: we can have no absolute guarantee that these abilities and capacities really are distributed evenly, without regard to race or sex, among human beings. So far as actual abilities are concerned, there do seem to be certain measurable differences between both races and sexes. These differences do not, of course, appear in each case, but only when averages are taken. More important still, we do not yet know how much of these differences is really due to the different genetic endowments of the various races and sexes, and how much is due to environmental differences that are the result of past and continuing discrimination. Perhaps all of the important differences will eventually prove to be environmental rather than genetic. Anyone opposed to racism and sexism will certainly hope that this will be so, for it will make the task of ending discrimination a lot easier; nevertheless it would be dangerous to rest the case against racism and sexism on the belief that all significant differences are environmental in origin. The opponent of, say, racism who takes this line will be unable to avoid conceding that if differences in ability did after all prove to have some genetic connection with race, racism would in some way be defensible.

It would be folly for the opponent of racism to stake his whole case on a dogmatic commitment to one particular outcome of a difficult scientific issue which is still a long way from being settled. While attempts to prove that differences in certain selected abilities between races and sexes are primarily genetic in origin have certainly not been conclusive, the same must be said of attempts to prove that these differences are largely the result of environment. At this stage of the investigation we cannot be certain which view is correct, however much we may hope it is the latter.

Fortunately, there is no need to pin the case for equality to one particular outcome of this scientific investigation. The appropriate response to those who claim to have found evidence of genetically-based differences in ability between the races or sexes is not to stick to the belief that the genetic explanation must be wrong, whatever evidence to the contrary may turn up: instead we should make it quite clear that the claim to equality does not depend on intelligence, moral capacity, physical strength, or similar matters of fact. Equality is a moral ideal, not a simple assertion of fact. There is no logically compelling reason for assuming that a factual difference in ability between two people justifies any difference in the amount of consideration we give to satisfying their needs and interests. The principle of the equality of human beings is not a description of an alleged actual equality among humans: it is a prescription of how we should treat humans.

Jeremy Bentham incorporated the essential basis of moral equality into his utilitarian system of ethics in the formula: 'Each to count for one and none for more than one.' In other words, the interests of every being affected by an action are to be taken into account and given the same weight as the like interests of any other being. A later utilitarian, Henry Sidgwick, put the point in this way: 'The good of any one individual is of no more importance, from the point of view (if I may say so) of the Universe, than the good of any other.'[1] More recently, the leading figures in modern moral philosophy have shown a great deal of agreement in specifying as a fundamental presupposition of their moral theories some similar requirement which operates so as to give everyone's interests equal consideration—although they cannot agree on how this requirement is best formulated.[2]

It is an implication of this principle of equality that our concern for others ought not to depend on what they are like, or what abilities they possess—although precisely what this concern requires us to do may vary according to the characteristics of those affected by what we do. It is on this basis that the case against racism and the case against sexism must both ultimately rest; and it is in accordance with this principle that speciesism is also to be condemned. If possessing a higher degree of intelligence does not entitle one human to use another for his own ends, how can it entitle humans to exploit non-humans?

Many philosophers have proposed the principle of equal consideration of interests, in some form or other, as a basic moral principle; but, as we shall see in more detail shortly, not many of them have recognized that this principle applies to members of other species as well as to our own. Bentham was one of the few who did realize this. In a forward-looking passage, written at a time when black slaves in the British dominions were still being treated much as we now treat non-human animals, Bentham wrote:

> The day *may* come when the rest of the animal creation may acquire those rights which never could have been witholden from them but by the hand of tyranny. The French have already discovered that the blackness of the skin is no reason why a human being should be abandoned without redress to the caprice of a tormentor. It may one day come to be recognized that the number of legs, the villosity of the skin, or the termination of the *os sacrum*, are reasons equally insufficient for abandoning a sensitive being to the same fate. What else is it that should trace the insuperable line? Is it the faculty of reason, or perhaps the faculty of discourse? But a full-grown horse or dog is beyond comparison a more rational, as well as a more conversable animal, than an infant of a day, or a week, or even a month, old. But suppose they were otherwise, what would it avail? The question is not, Can they *reason*? Nor can they *talk*? but, *Can they suffer*?[3]

In this passage Bentham points to the capacity for suffering as the vital characteristic that gives a being the right to equal consideration. The capacity for suffering—or more strictly, for suffering and/or enjoyment or happiness—is not just another characteristic like the capacity for language, or for higher mathematics. Bentham is not saying that those who try to mark 'the insuperable line' that determines whether the interests of a being should be considered happen to have selected the wrong characteristic. The capacity for suffering and enjoying things is a pre-requisite for having interests at all, a condition that must be satisfied before we can speak of interests in any meaningful way. It would be nonsense to say that it was not in the interests of a stone to be kicked along the road by a schoolboy. A stone does not have interests because it cannot suffer. Nothing that we can do to it could possibly make any difference to its welfare. A mouse, on the other hand, does have an interest in not being tormented, because it will suffer if it is.

If a being suffers, there can be no moral justification for refusing to take that suffering into consideration. No matter what the nature of the being, the principle of equality requires that its suffering be counted equally with the like suffering—in so far as rough comparisons can be made—of any other being. If a being is not capable of suffering, or of experiencing enjoyment or happiness, there is nothing to be taken into account. This is why the limit of sentience (using the term as a convenient, if not strictly accurate, shorthand for the capacity to suffer or experience enjoyment or happiness) is the only defensible boundary of concern for the interests of others. To mark this boundary by some characteristic like intelligence or rationality would be to mark it in an arbitrary way. Why not choose some other characteristic, like skin colour?

The racist violates the principle of equality by giving greater weight to the interests of members of his own race, when there is a clash between their interests and the interests of those of another race. Similarly, the speciesist allows the interests of his own species to override the greater interests of members of other species.[4] The pattern is the same in each case. Most human beings are speciesists. I shall now very briefly describe some of the practices that show this.

For the great majority of human beings, especially in urban, industrialized societies, the most direct form of contact with members of other species is at meal-times: we eat them. In doing so we treat them purely as means to our ends. We regard their life and well-being as subordinate to our taste for a particular kind of dish. I say 'taste' deliberately—this is purely a matter of pleasing our palate. There can be no defence of eating flesh in terms of satisfying nutritional needs, since it has been established beyond doubt that we could satisfy our need for protein and other essential nutrients far more efficiently with a diet that replaced animal flesh by soy beans, or products derived from soy beans, and other high-protein vegetable products.[5]

It is not merely the act of killing that indicates what we are ready to do to other species in order to gratify our tastes. The suffering we inflict on the animals while they are alive is perhaps an even clearer indication of our speciesism than the fact that we are prepared to kill them.[6] In order to have meat on the table at a price that people can afford, our society tolerates methods of meat production that confine sentient animals in cramped, unsuitable conditions for the entire durations of their lives. Animals are treated like machines that convert fodder into flesh, and any innovation that results in a higher 'conversion ratio' is liable to be adopted. As one authority on the subject has said, 'cruelty is acknowledged only when profitability ceases.'[7]

Since, as I have said, none of these practices cater for anything more than our pleasures of taste, our practice of rearing and killing other animals in order to eat them is a clear instance of the sacrifice of the most important interests of other beings in order to satisfy trivial interests of our own. To avoid speciesism we must stop this practice, and each of us has a moral obligation to cease supporting the practice. Our custom is all the support that the meat industry needs. The decision to cease giving it that support may be difficult, but it is no more difficult than it would have been for a white Southerner to go against the traditions of his society and free his slaves: if we do not change our dietary habits, how can we censure those slave-holders who would not change their own way of living?

The same form of discrimination may be observed in the widespread practice of experimenting on other species in order to see if certain substances are safe for human beings, or to test some psychological theory about the effect of severe punishment on learning, or to try out various new compounds just in case something turns up . . .

In the past, argument about vivisection has often missed this point, because it has been put in absolutist terms: Would the abolitionist be prepared to let thousands die if they could be saved by experimenting on a single animal? The way to reply to this purely hypothetical question is to pose another: Would the experimenter be prepared to perform his experiment on an orphaned human infant, if that were the only way to save many lives? (I say 'orphan' to avoid the complication of parental feelings, although in doing so I am being over-fair to the experimenter, since the non-human subjects of experiments are not orphans.) If the experimenter is not prepared to use an orphaned human infant, then his readiness to use non-humans is simple discrimination, since adult apes, cats, mice, and other animals are more aware of what is happening to them, more self-directing and, so far as we can tell, at least as sensitive to pain, as any human infant. There seems to be no relevant characteristic that human infants possess that adult mammals do not have to the same or a higher degree. (Someone might try to argue that what makes it wrong to experiment on a human infant is that the infant will, in time and if left alone, develop into more than the non-human, but one would then, to be consistent, have to oppose abortion, since the foetus has the same potential as the infant—indeed, even contraception and abstinence might be wrong on this ground, since the egg and sperm, considered jointly, also have the same potential. In any case, this argument still gives us no reason for selecting a non-human, rather than a human with severe and irreversible brain damage, as the subject for our experiments.)

The experimenter, then, shows a bias in favour of his own species whenever he carries out an experiment on a non-human for a purpose that he would not think justified him in using a human being at an equal or lower level of sentience, awareness, ability to be self-directing, etc. No one familiar with the kind of results yielded by most experiments on animals can have the slightest doubt that if this bias were eliminated the number of experiments performed would be a minute fraction of the number performed today.

Experimenting on animals, and eating their flesh, are perhaps the two major forms of speciesism in our society. By comparison, the third and last form of speciesism is so minor as to be insignificant, but it is perhaps of some special interest to those for whom this article was written. I am referring to speciesism in modern philosophy.

Philosophy ought to question the basic assumptions of the age. Thinking through, critically and carefully, what most people take for granted is, I believe, the chief task of philosophy, and it is this task that makes philosophy a worthwhile activity. Regrettably, philosophy does not always live up to its historic role. Philosophers are human beings and they are subject to all the preconceptions of the society to which they belong. Sometimes they succeed in breaking free of the prevailing ideology: more often they become its most sophisticated defenders. So, in this case, philosophy as practiced in the universities today does not challenge anyone's preconceptions about our relations with other species. By their writings, those philosophers who tackle problems that touch upon the issue reveal that they make the same unquestioned assumptions as most other humans, and what they say tends to confirm the reader in his or her comfortable speciesist habits.

I could illustrate this claim by referring to the writings of philosophers in various fields—for instance, the attempts that have been made by those interested in rights to draw the boundary of the sphere of rights so that it runs parallel to the biological boundaries of the species *Homo sapiens*, including infants and even mental defectives, but excluding those other beings of equal or greater capacity who are so useful to us at meal-times and in our laboratories. I think it would be a more appropriate conclusion to this chapter, however, if I concentrated on the problem with which we have been centrally concerned, the problem of equality.

It is significant that the problem of equality, in moral and political philosophy, is invariably formulated in terms of human equality. The effect of this is that the question of the equality of other animals does not confront the philosopher, or student, as an issue itself—and this is already an indication of the failure of philosophy to challenge accepted beliefs. Still, philosophers have found it difficult to discuss the issue of human equality without raising, in a paragraph or two, the question of the status of other animals. The reason for this, which should be apparent from what I have said already, is that if humans are to be regarded as equal to one another, we need some sense of 'equal' that does not require any actual, descriptive equality of capacities, talents, or other qualities. If equality is to be related to any actual characteristics of humans, these characteristics must be some lowest common denominator, pitched so low that no human lacks them—but then the philosopher comes up against the catch that any such set of characteristics which covers *all* humans will not be possessed *only by humans*. In other words, it turns out that in the only sense in which we can truly say, as an assertion of fact, that all humans are equal, at least some members of other species are also equal—equal, that is, to each other and to humans. If, on the other hand, we regard the statement 'All humans are equal' in some non-factual way, perhaps as a prescription, then, as I have already argued, it is even more difficult to exclude non-humans from the sphere of equality.

This result is not what the egalitarian philosopher originally intended to assert. Instead of accepting the radical outcome to which their own reasonings naturally point, however, most philosophers try to reconcile their beliefs in human equality and animal inequality by arguments that can only be described as devious.

As an example, I take William Frankena's well-known article, 'The Concept of Social Justice.' Frankena opposes the idea of basing justice on merit, because he sees that this could lead to highly inegalitarian results. Instead he proposes the principle that '… all men are to be treated as equals, not because they are equal, in any respect, but simply because they are human. They are human because they have emotions and desires, and are able to think, and hence are capable of enjoying a good life in a sense in which other animals are not.'[8]

But what is this capacity to enjoy the good life which all humans have, but no other animals? Other animals have emotions and desires, and appear to be capable of enjoying a good life. We may doubt that they can think—although the behaviour of some apes, dolphins, and even dogs suggests that some of them can—but what is the relevance of thinking? Frankena goes on to admit that by 'the good life' he means 'not so much the morally good life as the happy or satisfactory life,' so thought would appear to be unnecessary for enjoying the good life; in fact to emphasize the need for thought would make difficulties for the egalitarian since only some people are capable of leading intellectually satisfying lives, or morally good lives. This makes it difficult to see what Frankena's principle of equality has to do with simply being *human*. Surely every sentient being is capable of leading a life that is happier or less miserable than some alternative life, and hence has a claim to be taken into account. In this respect the distinction between humans and non-humans is not a sharp division, but rather a continuum along which we move gradually, and with overlaps between the species, from simple capacities for enjoyment and satisfaction, or pain and suffering, to more complex ones.

Faced with a situation in which they see a need for some basis for the moral gulf that is commonly thought to separate humans and animals, but can find no concrete difference that will do the job without undermining the equality of humans, philosophers tend to waffle They resort to high-sounding phrases like 'the intrinsic dignity of the human individual.'[9] They talk of the 'intrinsic worth of all men' as if men (humans?) had some worth that other beings did not,[10] or they say that humans, and only humans, are 'ends in themselves,' while 'everything other than a person can only have value for a person.'[11]

This idea of a distinctive human dignity and worth has a long history; it can be traced back directly to the Renaissance humanists, for instance to Pico della Mirandola's *Oration on the Dignity of Man*. Pico and other humanists based their estimate of human dignity on the idea that man possessed the central, pivotal position in the 'Great Chain of Being' that led from the lowliest forms of matter to God himself; this view of the universe, in turn, goes back to both classical and Judaeo-Christian doctrines. Modern philosophers have cast off these metaphysical and religious shackles and freely invoke the dignity of mankind without needing to justify the idea at all. Why should be not attribute 'intrinsic dignity' or 'intrinsic worth' to ourselves? Fellow humans are unlikely to reject the accolades we so generously bestow on them, and those to whom we deny the honour are unable to object. Indeed, when one thinks only of humans, it can be very liberal, very progressive, to talk of the dignity of all human beings. In so doing, we implicitly condemn slavery, racism, and other violations of human rights. We admit that we ourselves are in some fundamental sense on a par with the poorest, most ignorant members of our own species. It is only when we think of humans as no more than a small sub-group of all the beings that inhabit our planet that we may realize that in elevating our own species we are at the same time lowering the relative status of all other species.

The truth is that the appeal to the intrinsic dignity of human beings appears to solve the egalitarian's problems only as long as it goes unchallenged. Once we ask *why* it should be that all humans—including infants, mental defectives, psychopaths, Hitler, Stalin, and the rest—have some kind of dignity or worth that no elephant, pig, or chimpanzee can ever achieve, we see that this question is as difficult to answer as our original request for some relevant fact that justifies the inequality of humans and other animals. In fact, these two questions are really one: talk of intrinsic dignity or moral worth only takes the problem back one step, because any satisfactory defence of the claim that all and only humans have intrinsic dignity would need to refer to some relevant capacities or characteristics that all and only humans possess. Philosophers frequently introduce ideas of dignity, respect, and worth at the point at which other reasons appear to be lacking, but this is hardly good enough. Fine phrases are the last resource of those who have run out of arguments.

READING ENDNOTES

1. *The Methods of Ethics* (7th edn.). p. 382.
2. For example, R. M. Hare, *Freedom and Reason* (Oxford, 1963) and J. Rawls, *A Theory of Justice* (Harvard, 1972); for a brief account of the essential agreement on this issue between these and other positions, see R. M. Hare, 'Rules of War and Moral Reasoning', *Philosophy and Public Affairs*, vol. 1, no. 2 (1972).
3. *Introduction to the Principles of Morals and Legislation*, ch. XVII.
4. I owe the term 'speciesism' to Richard Ryder.
5. In order to produce 1 lb. of protein in the form of beef or veal, we must feed 21 lb. of protein to the animal. Other forms of livestock are slightly less inefficient, but the average ratio in the US is still 1:8. It has been estimated that the amount of protein lost to humans in this way is equivalent to 90 per cent of the annual world protein deficit. For a brief account, see Frances Moore Lappé, *Diet for a Small Planet* (Friends of The Earth/Ballantine, New York, 1971), pp. 4–11.
6. Although one might think that killing a being is obviously the ultimate wrong one can do to it, I think that the infliction of suffering is a clearer indication of speciesism because it might be argued that at least part of what is wrong with killing a human is that most humans are conscious of their existence over time, and have desires and purposes that extend into the future—see, for instance, M. Tooley, 'Abortion and Infanticide', *Philosophy and Public Affairs*, vol. 2, no. 1 (1972). Of course, if one took this view one would have to hold—as Tooley does—that killing a human infant or mental defective is not in itself wrong, and is less serious than killing certain higher mammals that probably do have a sense of their own existence over time.
7. Ruth Harrison, *Animal Machines* (London, 1964). For an account of farming conditions, see my *Animal Liberation* (New York, 1975).
8. In R. Brandt (ed.), *Social Justice* (Englewood Cliffs, 1962), p. 19.
9. Frankena, op. cit., p. 23.
10. H. A. Bedau, 'Egalitarianism and the Idea of Equality' in *Nomos IX: Equality,* ed. J. R. Pennock and J. W. Chapman, New York, 1967.
11. G. Vlastos, 'Justice and Equality' in Brandt, *Social Justice*, p. 48.

QUESTIONS

1. Peter Singer is a utilitarian. What does "the basic principle of equality" mean to him as a utilitarian?

2. What does it mean to give "equal consideration" to some group?

3. Singer argues that the same grounds or reasons we give for treating all human beings equally (and so opposing discrimination against some people on the grounds of race or sex) require us also to extend equal consideration to non-human animals. How does such a consistency argument work?

4. Why must we not base the moral requirement that we treat all people equally on any factual assumptions about the equality of people (their equal abilities, characteristics, etc.)? Why are such facts irrelevant to deciding what treatment people deserve? Can you relate this to the is-ought fallacy discussed in Chapter 1?

5. Bentham grounds the right to moral consideration in sentience (the capacity for suffering or enjoyment, the capacity to feel pain or pleasure). But is this not just another fact about some creatures? If so, how can it have the moral significance it needs to ground the moral right to consideration? Why is the capacity to feel pain or pleasure morally significant, when other capacities (for rationality, language, political activity, etc.) are not?

6. Consider the fact that animal food production is inefficient. We must grow much more food, for animal feed, than we get at the other end in the form of meat. In other words, we could produce much more human food by growing protein providing grains and vegetables directly for human consumption than we can by using that food as animal feed and then consuming the animals. But since a deplorably large number of people in the world are hungry (literally do not have sufficient caloric intake to maintain their physical functioning at a normal human level) and even more have to devote such a large part of their resources (time as well as money) to securing food that they do not live full and enjoyable human lives, such an investment in food resources seems not only inefficient but morally wrong. Does this provide a different argument, independent of the one from animal suffering, for thinking that eating animals is morally wrong and that we all have a duty to become vegetarians? What is the argument?

7. Singer raises concerns about experimentation on animals. But many people will insist that such experimentation is justified because of the possible benefits it provides in the form of understanding disease and new drugs and other therapies. Even if many animals have to suffer to make possible a cure for cancer or HIV/AIDS, many people will accept that price. But now consider another set of practices involving animal experimentation: those involving the perfume and cosmetics industries. Can Singer's arguments be extended to provide a conclusion about the morality of the use that these industries make of animals?

8. Would it undercut Singer's arguments against using animals for food and experiments if we could add a "happy pill" to their diets so that they were content (or even ecstatic) with their condition?

9. If we follow Singer's advice and all became vegetarians, wouldn't there be considerably fewer of the animals in question? Is it better that they don't exist at all, compared with existing under current conditions? If we could raise them in decent conditions, would it not be better to have more, minimally happy animals, than for them not to exist at all?

✦ ✦ ✦

Bernard E. Rollin, Keeping Up with the Cloneses—Issues in Human Cloning

Bernard E. Rollin argues persuasively that the possibility of human cloning, like many new technologies, creates a gap in our ethical judgements. Reactions to new technologies may be thus irrational, and bear close scrutiny. Rollin thus scrutinizes various reactions to the issue of cloning, and finds the negative reactions lacking in merit. He divides the reactions into three categories: 1. Cloning is one of the sciences that people were just not meant to know, or is inherently wrong; 2. Cloning is one of the sciences that will bring about harm for society; and 3. Cloning will produce harms/problems for the creature cloned. In fine utilitarian fashion, he dismisses as nonsense the claim that cloning is wrong in and of itself. There is no plausible way to argue (rather than assert) that cloning is wrong (or right) independent of the consequences. The closest one can come to such an argument is to suggest that cloning disrupts the natural order of things, but this requires that one be able to provide a compelling account of the natural order of things, which would require insight far beyond our abilities.

Turning then to the consequences of the science of cloning, Rollin considers the state of affairs where the technique of cloning has been perfected on animals (leaving aside the thorny question of whether animal experimentation is permissible in these circumstances) and is now being used to create humans. Rollin defeats many arguments that suggest that human cloning will bring harm to society, and suggests that some good may be plausibly thought to arise from human cloning, for example, a mother and father may be able to clone their child should he or she die. As to potential harms to the clone, Rollin considers both harm from others, and harm from the procedure of cloning. In considering harm from others (like religious witch-hunts seeking to destroy the "soulless clones") Rollin concludes that the best way to avoid such harm is to keep secret the origin of such clones. Concerning harms due to cloning, Rollin acknowledges that the possibility of physical harm exists and not all of the potential risks to clones are yet known, and so he counsels that we should proceed to expand our knowledge of cloning but with caution.

Rollin too embodies the tension between a critical morality and people's prefer-ences. Rollin appears to be a preference-based utilitarian (note his inclusion of the desires of the tragic parents mentioned above in the moral calculus), but nowhere does his calculation regarding the permissibility of cloning include the large majority's negative reactions to it. On what grounds can a proponent of the subjective theory of value exclude such preferences (even the witch-hunter's)? Rollin also relies on a slightly risk-seeking principle of utility maximization under uncertainty. This is contentious. As we will see in Douglas P. Lackey's "Missiles and Morals," when the potential problems and the probabilities of those problems occurring are unknown, many suggest that a risk-adverse strategy is the rational one to adopt.

✦ ✦ ✦

Bernard E. Rollin, "Keeping Up with the Cloneses—Issues in Human Cloning," *The Journal of Ethics* 3 (1999): 51–71. ©1999 Kluwer Academic Publishers. Reprinted with the permission of Kluwer Academic Publishers.

Keeping Up With the Cloneses—Issues in Human Cloning

BERNARD E. ROLLIN

I

With the advent of Dolly, the first animal cloned from a somatic cell, has come a cacophony of voices inveighing against cloning of both animals and, especially, humans. Citizens ranging from the United States President to the proletariat have trumpeted the "immorality" of cloning, and research funding in the areas of animal and/or human cloning has been truncated or blocked in numerous countries and states. Highly diverse theological and political traditions have been uncommonly univocal in their condemnation of cloning humans, and significant legislation is being promulgated internationally and in many states to prevent cloned humans from becoming a reality.

Amongst all of this furor, one can find remarkably little clear argumentation laying bare what, if anything, is morally problematic about cloning animals or humans. In a recent paper,[1] I argued that, in fact, the cloning of animals raises only two substantive concerns with ethical implications, neither of which is very deep, new, or surprising:

(1) How do we prevent cloning from further accelerating our unfortunate and self-destructive tendency towards monocultural agriculture, and;

(2) Are we certain that the very process of cloning will not harm the cloned animal's well-being later in life?

Question (2), of course, will be answered empirically, as we track cloned animals through lifetime studies (in April, 1998, Dolly had a little lamb by normal means). Question (1) is subordinate to the general question of whether we ought to be backing off from highly productive monocultural agriculture in general, given the risks regarding sustainability and crop devastation it entails. Neither of these questions, of course, licenses the furor attendant to the announcement of Dolly's creation, which includes survey evidence that the majority of the general public found cloning morally unacceptable.[2]

In this paper, I set myself two tasks. In the first place, I wish to expand the discussion of human cloning that I began in the previous paper, to see whether there are any weighty issues which license society's profound unrest at its very possibility. Second, in light of my belief that there are in fact no such issues, I want to explain why the prospect of cloning has led to such a maelstrom. I will begin by engaging the latter question first.

II

Any new technology, of whatever form, will create a lacuna in social ethical thought. To put it simply, powerful new devices and tools, when first introduced, cause us to wonder about the positive and negative effects and implications they will have on our lives. For example, with the introduction of the automobile, people immediately worried (and rightly so) about the possible dangers cars posed to pedestrians and to horses. On the other hand, less obvious concerns probably did not get discussed, for example, the proliferation of respiratory disease or the growth of suburbs or the decline of close families. The more esoteric the technology, the less its nature is understood; and the less experts in the area articulate socio-ethical implications of the technology, the more likely it is that the lacuna in social ethical questions will be replaced by lurid, ill-defined concerns. Thus, for example, when computers were first introduced, experts such as Norbert Wiener saw no downside at all, and predicted only that computers would accelerate, as one of his book titles put it, *The Human Use of Human Beings*. Ordinary people, however, were suspicious, and expressed concern about computers "making people obsolete," or "taking over the world." As a result, serious issues such as privacy, child pornography, the increasing elimination of literacy and the decline in the reading of books by young people were never envisioned until they became acute problems.

The lesson here is simple. In the absence of good, reflective, careful ethical thinking about technology initiated by those who introduce a technology, and who should (in principle) understand it well enough to think through its implications, the social-ethical lacuna created by the technology will be filled by sensationalistic, simplistic, emotionally-based slogans which dominate social thought and whose intuitive appeal make them difficult to dislodge. I have called this phenomenon a "Gresham's

Law for Ethics," for it describes a state of affairs quite analogous to what Thomas Gresham noted in economic life; to wit, that "bad money" (e.g., hugely inflated paper money such as what was found in post-World War I Germany, with low intrinsic value) will drive "good money" (e.g., gold coins with high intrinsic value) out of circulation. Clearly if one owes a million dollars, one is wise to pay it off with money possessing no inherent value, and the gold will be hoarded.

Similarly, this is precisely and manifestly what has taken place in the area of cloning. Virtually no ethical discussion of animal cloning was forthcoming from the scientist who had effected the cloning of Dolly; in fact, he specifically affirmed that, as a scientist, socio-ethical discussion of this achievement was outside of his bailiwick. He did, however, opine that cloning humans was morally unacceptable. Period. Nor did other people in the field leap to fill the ethical lacuna since most scientists have typically been raised in what I have elsewhere called "scientific ideology," a view which affirms that science is value-free, hence ethics-free, and thus it is society's job (if anyone's) to articulate the ethical implications of science and technology.[3] What quickly filled the vacuum turned out to be in large measure classic examples of bad ethical thinking, based on the philosophically problematic, but psychologically powerful, principle that whatever clashes with one's cherished basic assumptions tends to be seen as violating the moral order, and thus as ethically wrong.

In earlier writings on biotechnology (including animal cloning), I used the Frankenstein story to disambiguate the three possible types of issues that emerge from new techniques for manipulating life.[4] The relevance of this story is patent, as it is clearly a myth that pervades Western thinking's attempts to wrestle with breathtaking—yet ever-emerging—new technologies. The Mary Shelley novel, unreadable and dense though it may be, has nonetheless appeared in numerous editions (145 by 1984), and inspired thousands of other novels, stories, poems, films, cartoons, etc., painstakingly enumerated in the extraordinary *Frankenstein Catalogue*, appropriately edited by one Donald Glut.[5]

The Frankenstein story has been used to articulate social concerns about the full range of new scientific discoveries, from nuclear power (*Time* magazine, at the 40th anniversary of the Hiroshima bombing) to human cloning (Willard Gaylin in 1972) and continues to flourish. In part to explain the pervasiveness of this myth, one can dissect out three distinct themes pertaining to ethics in the story:[6]

(1) There are certain things humans were not meant to know or do, a line familiar to aficionados of old (and new) horror movies, and one ideally delivered by Maria Ouspenskaya. This proposition expresses the idea that, in and of themselves, certain scientific activities are inherently wrong, regardless of ensuing consequences. The theme of forbidden knowledge (pure or applied) and human *hubristic* attempts to attain it is an ancient one, and is vividly epitomized through the ages in the stories of the Garden of Eden, the Tower of Babel, Daedalus and Icarus, the three great rabbis who "entered the garden" of forbidden mystical knowledge with only one emerging unscathed, the Golem, the Sorcerer's apprentice, and of course, Dr. Frankenstein who, despite his noble intentions, transgressed against limits on human knowledge and thus against the moral order.

I would venture the claim that it is the above theme that underlies most of the horrified reactions to cloning (and to genetic engineering) and the notions that these are "just wrong" or "inherently wrong." The proliferation of comments affirming that these technologies are "against God" (affirmed by 75% of the American public),[7] or involve "playing God," or "violating natural barriers," or "failing to respect species boundaries" or "trying to be God," are all examples of the first aspect of the Frankenstein story. Yet despite the genuine horror, fear, and rage that they clearly encompass, in my view they do not represent defensible moral claims. In fact, they are quite the opposite: examples of bad ethics seizing center stage when rationally based moral discussion is not forthcoming. For it is difficult to see what would count as making any piece of pure or applied knowledge intrinsically wrong, rather than wrong in virtue of its likely consequences and results. Perhaps the consequences of some knowledge are so likely to be harmful as to be virtually inexorable; but that does not prove the knowledge in itself to be inherently wrong, only its consequences, effects being, as David Hume taught us, logically separable from causes.

Defending the inherent wrongness of cloning, for example, requires an argument showing some *logical* connection between the knowledge and some harm or evil. As soon as one moves to affirming such wrongness on the basis of possible or even probable consequences of possessing such knowledge, one has moved away from an intrinsic wrongness position to a consequentialist one. One can, of course, argue that good consequentialist reasons warrant the claim that humans should not achieve knowledge of cloning—that is a reasonably arguable point. But that is quite different from saying that such knowledge is *inherently* wrong, regardless of what consequences—even good ones—do in fact result. And it is clear that many critics are in fact divorcing the alleged wrongness of cloning from whatever consequences it engenders—even if one could show them a scenario where only good came out of cloning, that would not move them off the position that it is intrinsically wrong.

One possible way to salvage an inherent wrongness of cloning position is to provide a metaphysical argument showing that cloning breaches the moral order even if it engenders no bad effects. Such an argument must in turn appeal to something like Leibniz's theology, viz., that this is the best of all possible worlds, or that the world without cloning is the world that God (or nature) intends. The former is of course indefensible without innumerable *ad hoc* hypotheses. The latter requires that we know God's (or nature's) will or design. Further, even if we did "know" God's will (as if we were all to believe cloning was forbidden explicitly by a sacred text we all shared), it is not obvious why violating it is immoral—at best, as Bertrand Russell pointed out, such disobedience is imprudent, since God is stronger than we are, not a proof of intrinsic immorality, unless we add the ancillary premise that (God's) might makes right, vitiating morality as we know it! In the case of nature rather than God, one obviously must show why cloning is unnatural and caesarian sections are not, and why the unnatural is necessarily immoral.

In sum, our inability to provide a rational interpretation to the claim that cloning is inherently or just wrong makes the first aspect of the Frankenstein story morally meaningless in a secular society, however widely held it may be.

(2) As implied by our foregoing discussion, one can only extract a moral issue in any new technology or area of knowledge from the claim that it is just wrong by modifying that claim to one which affirms that the area in question is wrong because of the likely negative consequences or harms likely or highly likely to emerge from it. To do this, however, is to give up the inherent wrongness claim. As stated above, there is a major conceptual gap separating the claim that cloning will inevitably cause bad results from the claim that cloning is intrinsically wrong, regardless of consequences.

Thus, we encounter a second aspect of the Frankenstein story, namely that some scientific activity is wrong because it will produce bad consequences for nature or society. The Frankenstein story is quite explicit on this. Despite Dr. Frankenstein's noble goals in undertaking his experiments (or those of the Rabbi of Prague who creates the Golem), the creation runs amok. I call this aspect of the story "rampaging monsters," and it is the view that a given piece of science or technology will cause disastrous results in virtue of our imperfect understanding of all of its causal ramifications. Such an argument must rely heavily on past history, and invoke such examples as the Chernobyl catastrophe, Three Mile Island, Killer Bee escapes, Challenger, introduction of new species such as the mongoose into Hawaii or the Australian possum into New Zealand, and so forth. A common argument to this effect affirms that science can never possibly anticipate all glitches, and when we are dealing with powerful technologies, glitches are equivalent to disasters. In the case of cloning, one such argument might emphasize the deleterious effect multiplication of the same genes might have on the human gene pool. We will return to this issue.

(3) A final aspect of the Frankenstein story concerns what I have called "the plight of the creature," and is especially useful in discussing biological technologies such as genetic engineering and cloning. The moral concern here, of course, is the effect on the creature created or manipulated by the technology. In the case of the genetic engineering of animals, a major moral problem arises in this area, as one could increase productivity of farm animals, or create animal models of human genetic disease, at the expense of animals' well-being, so that they experience life-long pain and suffering. This concern is obviously a serious moral question when cloning of animals or humans is being contemplated—does the process of cloning do any long-term damage to the organism cloned?

III

When one examines the social response to the possibility of cloning humans, one can readily find examples of alleged moral concerns falling under each of the above categories. Most prevalent, given public, religious—and consequently political—hysteria about cloning, are the sort of bad ethics claims comprising our first category, namely that cloning of humans is intrinsically wrong, regardless of consequences. A survey of salient examples from this category will make it clear why they have little if any substance.

Within a week of Dolly's cloning, CNN/*Time* had done a poll indicating that 69% of the public was "scared" by the prospect of cloning humans, 89% said that such cloning of humans was "morally unacceptable," and 75% said that cloning is "against God's will."[8] Regrettably, the poll did not indicate the grounds upon which people based their claim of "moral unacceptability" or their basis, theological or otherwise, for claiming that cloning violates God's will.

The first point to stress is that religious or theological pronouncements or beliefs, however ubiquitous, even those extending to 100% of the population, do not necessarily constitute a moral argument. It is, of course, often the case that moral injunctions are couched in religious terms—*vide* at least some of the Ten Commandments, but the moral content must be in principle conceptually separable from the religious for it to constitute a truly moral claim. Similarly, much of our social ethic is doubtless historically derived from religious sources, but we do not validate our ethics by appeal to religion in a secular society. On the other hand, religious traditions have indeed given much thought to how humans ought morally to live, and much of that thinking may be viable even outside of the theological tradition in which it is embedded. For example, the Thomistic moral-psychological point that society should prohibit overt cruelty to animals even though animals lack immortal souls, and thus are not direct objects of moral concern, since people who are allowed to abuse animals are psychologically disposed to abusing people, can be restated independently of the theological assumption about animals lacking soul. So restated, it has received succor from twentieth-century socio-psychological research linking early animal abuse with subsequent abuse of humans.

Merely because a practice violates a religious tradition does not render a practice immoral for those of us outside that tradition, which in terms of social ethics in a secular society, is all of us. For example, many women's styles violate the moral precepts of Orthodox Judaism or Islam, yet we do not consider women so attired as socially immoral. To be sure, religious traditions may work to affect our social morality and may even do so, as in Sunday Blue Laws, but the results must putatively and theoretically stand as moral principles independently of their religious origins. In those cases where they do not, and instead bespeak inordinate political power of a religious tradition, we are rightly suspicious and fear a loss of separation of church and state.

There is nothing wrong with looking to pronouncements from religious leaders as a heuristic device when one is attempting to unpack the moral implications of some new technology such as cloning—many religious leaders may be well-trained in identifications of moral issues. A problem arises only if we assume that anything declared to be a moral issue by such leaders automatically becomes one, in a performative way. As we look to such pronouncements, we must be prepared to recast them in strictly secular moral terms, and, if we cannot, to reject them as not morally significant. The Pope, for example, may be infallible in matters of faith and Catholic morals, but certainly not in secular ethics.

Having said all this, what sorts of religious ethical concerns emerged at the prospect of human cloning? Not surprisingly, religious leaders, even within a given community of faith, did not speak with one voice. Even for strict fundamentalists possessed of ancient sacred texts, there is little likelihood of univocal readings of those texts as applied to current technological innovations. Thus, while some Christians have condemned genetic engineering, others have said that, like other works of man, it is acceptable as continuing human "cocreation" of nature in partnership with God.

Surprisingly, the claims about cloning advanced by religious leaders yielded significantly divergent pronouncements and arguments, some of which can be distilled down into sensible moral claims, while others cannot. In this portion of our discussion, we will focus on those that cannot, *i.e.*, on the claims that cloning is intrinsically or "just" wrong.

A particularly valuable source of religious and cultural perspectives on cloning was a newsletter, *Reflections*, which garnered comments from representatives of almost every major faith tradition in America.[9] One argument, from Stanley Harakas, a Greek Orthodox theologian, affirmed the following:

> Whatever motivations and intentions there might be to take this immoral step, I can think of none that would escape the charge of manufacturing a human being for the purpose of exploiting him or her in a way that depersonalizes the human clone.... Further, in itself, cloning would violate practically every sacramental dimension of marriage, family life, physical and spiritual nurture, and the integrity and dignity of the human person.[10]

Insofar as one can extract an argument from this claim, it appears to be that there is no possible way in which a human derived by cloning could enjoy full humanity by virtue of the fact that the motivation for so creating a person would of necessity be exploitative.

This is clearly question-begging. Later on in our discussion we will cite an example where it would seem perfectly reasonable to clone a child for decent, very human reasons. Further, even if a child is created for exploitative reasons, it is difficult to see why such a child would not enjoy full personhood. Many humans have children for exploitative reasons—e.g., to care for them later in life, to have someone to shape, etc.—yet the child's personhood does not depend upon the parent's intention. The claim clearly commits a version of the genetic fallacy, confusing the origin of a child with its subsequent moral status. A human created by cloning is still a human, even as one can love and respect an adopted child as much as a natural one.

Although I have always found the phrase "human dignity" to be more a matter of moral rhetoric than content, it is difficult to see why one's dignity should depend on one's origin rather than on one's nature. Nonetheless, the claim that clonal derivation deprives humans of dignity is a common reason for rejecting it out of hand as just wrong (See, for example, the comments by Demetri Demopoulos.[11] See also National Bioethics Advisory Commission (NBAC) Report, explaining the Catholic Position).[12] Some notion of the elusiveness of this concept can be garnered from the testimony of Catholic Theologian Albert Moraczewski before the National Bioethics Advisory

Commission. Said Moraczewski: "In the cloning of humans there is an affront to human dignity. . . . Yet in no way is the human dignity of the [cloned] person diminished."[13] One is tempted to invoke the old Logical Positivist category of "nonsense" here.

One perennial theme that emerges in attacks on the intrinsic wrongness of cloning and genetic engineering is the "playing God" claim—that such activities involve humans aspiring to decision-making that ought to be reserved to the Deity: In the NBAC Report, this claim is "unpacked" in the following way:

> This slogan is usually invoked as a moral stop sign to some scientific research or medical practice on the basis of one or more of the following distinctions between human beings and God:
>
> • Human beings should not probe the fundamental secrets or mysteries of life, which belong to God.
> • Human beings lack the authority to make certain decisions about the beginning or ending of life. Such decisions are reserved to divine sovereignty.
> • Human beings are fallible and also tend to evaluate actions according to their narrow, partial, and frequently self-interested perspectives.
> • Human beings do not have the knowledge, especially knowledge of outcomes of actions, attributed to divine omniscience.
> • Human beings do not have the power to control the outcomes of actions or processes that is a mark of divine omnipotence.
>
> The warning against "playing God" serves to remind human beings of their finiteness and fallibility. By not recognizing appropriate limits and constraints on scientific aspirations, human reenact the Promethean assertion of pride or hubris. In the initial theological discussions of cloning humans, Paul Ramsey summarized his objections by asserting: "Men ought not to play God before they learn to be men, and after they have learned to be men, they will not play God."[14]

While such an account presumably makes sense within the theological context or universe of discourse of Judaeo-Christianity but not, notably, of Hinduism or Buddhism, it is difficult to extract secular moral sense from it, save by seeing it as an admonishment against human "arrogance." As the NBAC summary puts it: "If making people in your laboratory isn't playing God, the phrase has no meaning."[15]

There is a serious point to such warnings, but it is first of all not restricted or special to cloning or biotechnology, and secondly, it does not justify the intrinsic wrongness of cloning, but only stresses the possibility of unanticipated risks which may emerge from it. Let us pause briefly to examine these points.

The theme of humans sawing off limbs on which they are seated, painting themselves resolutely into corners, or being left up the creek without a paddle, is an ancient one. The aforementioned chutzpah stories of the Tower of Babel, Daedalus and Icarus, the Golem, Frankenstein, and the Sorcerer's Apprentice, all warn of excessive optimism by humans in deploying new knowledge or *techné*. "Oops" should be the logo for humanity.

A *locus classicus* for the discussion of this phenomenon is David Ehrenfeld's *The Arrogance of Humanism*,[16] wherein Ehrenfeld relates countless examples of humans marching resolutely off cliffs from the unanticipated consequences of building the Aswan Dam to ecological disasters we have perpetrated. After living through sundry Ebola spills, Challenger and Chernobyl disasters, Killer Bee escapes, and iatrongenic diseases, society is far less likely to buy "Trust me, I'm a scientist." And things are no different in the area of biotechnology. In fact, I have argued elsewhere that only when society in general is consulted on biotechnology, through some such vehicle as local review of projects, will they feel a stake in it.[17] And this is as it should be in a democratic society.

Yet there is nothing especially arrogant about human cloning—indeed, the scientific community has itself been relatively circumspect in not pressing it hell for leather forward, as the response to Richard Seed's suggestion that he will clone people as rapidly as possible demonstrates. In my view, the creation of herbicide-resistant crops without public discussion is the more "arrogant," as is basing admission into medical schools on a few hours of "scientific" exams. The key point, in any case, is that the whole concern about arrogance associated with cloning is a *consequentialist* one, based on dangerous unanticipated results, not on inherent wrongness.

Enough has been said, I hope, to lay bare the point that arguments about the intrinsic wrongness of cloning either are:

(1) Meaningless; or,

(2) May have meaning within a given religious tradition, but are not subject to secular translation; or,

(3) *Evolve* into points about the likely and significant dangers that cloning must inevitably engender. (1) and (2) are clearly irrelevant to social decision-making, so we must turn to the second aspect of the Frankenstein story as it applies to human cloning, namely the manifest dangers and risks it will likely occasion.

IV

The way most critics have argued, cloning of humans is fraught with risks, and can have no conceivable benefits. Let us first focus on risks to society and others, leaving until our final discussion possible risks to the organism being cloned. Obviously, our discussion is focused on a scenario where sometime in the future, cloning has been perfected in animals, and the technology proceeds as smoothly as any other assisted reproductive technology such as surrogate motherhood or in-vitro fertilization. To attempt cloning today, via the technology that produced Dolly, would clearly violate established medical-ethical principles, since hundreds of attempts would be required, and risk of late term spontaneous abortion threatening the life of the mother would be significant. Furthermore, we are not yet in a position to judge the potential deleterious consequences to the cloned child, and thus, again, it would be immoral to proceed with cloning in a cavalier fashion. The requisite certitude can be achieved only after years of research—it is for this reason that the scientific and medical communities univocally rejected Seed's plan to clone humans "immediately" (We are also here holding in abeyance the question of whether the requisite animal experimentation is morally acceptable, as it almost certainly will proceed!).

In any event, let us suppose that the technique for cloning humans has been sufficiently refined as to pose no significant risk to the health of mother or cloned infant. Does this reproductive technology pose significant risks to society in general?

The standard response, thanks to *The Boys from Brazil*, is the spectre of cloning dozens, scores, hundreds or thousands of Hitlers, all identically evil, demented, and charismatic, as if cloning were a form of xeroxing all aspects of a human being's physical, mental, personality, and social traits. This is, of course, a highly misleading analogy. First of all, we have the evidence of natural clones—"identical" twins. Not only do identical twins have the same genetic structure, they are often raised in as close to the same environment as humans can be raised. Yet, though they may end up similar in many ways, they also end up dissimilar, in indefinite numbers of other ways. Certainly, they are not the same person, thinking the same thoughts at the same moment.

This is *a fortiori* true of artificial clones relative to the cell donor from whom he or she is cloned. First of all, in *all* clones a host of random and prenatal factors will create differences in gene expression that ramify in significant phenotypic differences. Thus, when George Seidel cloned the first Holstein calves by splitting a developing embryo, people were surprised to find that the pattern of black and white in the twins was significantly different. Second, and even more important, we know through both science and ordinary experience and common sense that a person is shaped by both heredity and environment. What we are is underdetermined both by our genes alone and by our experiences alone. The child of highly athletic parents raised as a bookworm and couch potato is likely to turn out less athletic than the child of klutzes whose body is trained in a variety of athletic pursuits from infanthood through maturity. And most assuredly, an adult who clones himself or herself will inevitably be unable to provide an environment for the clone similar to what he or she grew up in 30 or 40 years earlier, thereby diminishing the likelihood of similarity of the resultant child to oneself.

Let us suppose that I am cloned (something my colleagues have frequently suggested, given my type A personality, my tendency to over-commit, and my cavalier disregard for calendars, which has led me on occasion to promise to be in two places at once). Tired of these embarrassing scenarios, I decide to create a clone of myself and, as tomorrow's vernacular might have it, "do a Dolly." Let us further assume that I have had my genetic material inserted into an egg, and it is developing happily. A variety of forces will influence gene expression, including random factors and the prenatal environment. Thus, which genes express, and to what extent, will vary from clone to clone. In this way, variation will be assured from the earliest stages of development.

So from birth and even before, all clones will be different from each other and different from the parent organism. Differentiation will continue to occur as little Bernie grows in virtue of environmental or natural considerations. For example, whereas I was raised in New York, Bernie Jr. will be raised in Colorado. Whereas I was raised with one parent and a grandmother, Jr. will be raised by two parents, one of whom is me. If my wife hates the idea of a cloned Bernie, that will certainly shape the child's emotional life, as my wife's cooking will shape his physical development. Although my mother discouraged my participation in sports, I will bestow a set of weights on Jr. while he is in his crib, and so on. In fact, my identical twin—if I had one—is far more likely to be similar to me than my artificial clone, since the twin and I experienced more or less the same environment. Yet that situation did not make us the same person.

Obviously, the same logical point holds of the cloned Hitlers. Hitler was a product of an elaborate congeries of historical events. He was raised in anti-Semitic Austria, and worked his evil upon Germany, a country with a long history of seeing the Jew as a pathogen in the body politic. Further, Germany had lost a complex war; anarchists and left-wing revolutionaries ran rife, opposed by disenfranchised, right-wing, ex-soldiers; the Allies imposed Draconian terms on the defeated Germany; inflation reached unprecedented heights; Hitler was rebuffed in his attempts to become an artist; his father was a very strict authority figure; etc., endlessly. A cloned Hitler raised in Wyoming ranch country; upon West Side Manhattan; or even today's Germany would not be in a position to actualize the abilities that made him a dictator, even assuming that these abilities were strictly genetically determined, which they most likely were not. A young Hitler given art lessons and choice opportunities in art might well blossom in that direction; one whose debating skills were nurtured may well have become a lawyer.

Again, the same logic prevails regarding the other favored media example—cloning a basketball team of Michael Jordans. In the first place, the cloned Jordans might not even be authentically interested in basketball, might excel in some other sport, might pursue no sport, and might well rebel against the reason they were created, even as many children rebel against what their parents push them towards. Further, a team of Jordan clones would, even if greatly interested in basketball, probably not get much better than Jordan. If we wished to significantly progress beyond Jordan's genetic abilities, we would probably do better to have him impregnate some world class women basketball players, and pay the mothers to raise the children in an environment focused on basketball, though here too there is no guarantee we would create ball players.

In any event, it is difficult to see what dangers would emerge from cloning individuals, even "bad" individuals, given that how they turn out is a crapshoot, even as how natural children turn out is a crapshoot. Surely the majority of people would not clone themselves. So what harm is there in freezing a small portion of the gene pool? Again, even if large numbers of healthy individuals were cloned, what danger would this pose to the gene pool? Since the bulk of human adaptation is technological, rather than biological, it is difficult to see what harm a large number of clones would cause, assuming they were possessed of normal abilities.

In my view, a far greater threat lies in our current approach to genetic disease. At present, largely out of fear of a religiously based, "there are certain things humans were not meant to do" mind set, the strategy for fixing genetic diseases is to attempt to supply the missing gene product—so-called somatic cell therapy—rather than to repair the defect at the genomic level. The result of such an approach—if successful—is to proliferate defective genes in the human population whose deleterious effects are masked by therapy. In the event of nuclear winter, or other natural disasters, disabling our technological capabilities, vast numbers of people will be unable to survive. I see no comparable danger in a cloned population.

One persistent claim regarding the alleged risks of cloning concerns the negative impact it is likely to have upon the nature and structure of the traditional family. In the words of the National Bioethics Advisory Commission:

> In recent years, there has been a heightened awareness of the immense danger done to a child and to a society when fathers are missing from the home. In Washington, D.C., homicide is the leading cause of death for young men; there are many factors that contribute to the pattern of violence, but fatherlessness is among them. Cloning brings children into the world with not one but two missing parents. Genetically, the parents of a cloned child are the parents of the cell donor; they may have been dead for 30 years. Further, the parents are missing or hard to identify not because of specific tragedies but as a matter of planning.
>
> Further, with a cloned child, the basic human relationships need to be redefined. Is the cell donor your brother or father? Is the cloned child a sister or daughter.[18]

Though piously couched and invoking echoes of "family values," there is little content to this argument. "Missing fathers" is a major pattern of behavior in certain subcultures, where it indeed may be part of the causal conditions for violence, but the same pattern of evidence does not occur in some other subcultures with missing fathers. Furthermore, if a married couple cloned the husband or wife (or someone else) as an answer to childlessness, it is manifest that the children would indeed have two parents! Though cell donors may be deceased, so too may be sperm and egg donors.

Cloning is no more necessarily erosive of family life than are a wide variety of other parenting modalities. Does adoption erode families? How about cross-racial adoption? Does going to a sperm bank or fertilizing a donor egg? If gay or lesbian couples have children using assisted reproduction, is it similarly an attack on the sanctity of the family? Is the child equally confused about who the parents are? Perhaps so, but there has been no comparable bioethical outcry in that area. Indeed, if one did raise the same concerns about same-sex parents, one would be rapidly denounced as homophobic, and we have seen no presidential panel raising these concerns!

What of single parents who adopt or use assisted reproductive technology to have a child? What of the huge percentage of marriages ending in divorce? What of illegitimate children? These surely pose as great a threat, or probably a greater one, to the traditional family as does cloning. But where is the outcry to legislate an end to divorce?

Parenting is a functional role. Certainly parenting is most often associated with permanent, identifiable, biological mates, but it need not be so, as all of the above examples well illustrate. Adoptive parents, or single parents, or gay parents may function better as parents than "normal" married couples. Even animals will "parent," or "adopt," other animals, sometimes animals of a different species. So what? People with cloned offspring may treat them well or badly, be good or bad parents, but that will not be decided by whether or not the child is cloned.

One can similarly dismiss the NBAC "argument" that cloning is an assault on the "dignity of human procreation." As in so many "human dignity" locutions, I have a hard time understanding what that means. As many literary figures have pointed out, there is little "dignity" in the sex act, whether performed by humans or ostriches. If the sex act is so "dignified," why do so few official portraits or statues depict the relevant "dignity" *in flagrante delicto*? If there is "dignity" here at all, it lies in how one shoulders the burden of parenting, not in a particular biological route to having a child. Is there more "dignity" in poor Third World slum dwellers who have a child because they don't understand birth control than in an educated person who chooses to implant an embryo derived from cells of a deceased infant? (We shall return to this case shortly.)

The same sort of objection can also be raised against the NBAC Report's claim that cloning represents "an assault on the dignity of the conjugal union." The report says:

> The existence of children is a persistent sign of the parents' mutual love, and an invitation to ponder the endless mystery of gender differences. The potent and universal sign of hope is blurred or lost when the child's life begins in a laboratory.[19]

Surely, the first claim is false. Children may be a "sign of mutual love," but they can also be a sign of lust, drunkenness, ignorance of conception, apathy, rape, immaturity, etc. And the claim that "hope is lost when life begins in a laboratory" is a classic example of the genetic fallacy. A child is still a child regardless of how it is occasioned, whether in loving bliss, or teenage revelry—or in a laboratory!

It is particularly ironic to me that the tempest about human cloning was roughly contemporaneous with the announcement that a U.S. woman who had been taking fertility drugs gave birth to septuplets. She was not confronted with social outrage— instead she became a cultural hero and was showered with positive publicity, money, and gifts. Yet it is far easier to envision a negative or tragic outcome to her story than to a couple who quietly cloned a child. Without external interference, the latter can set about the task of parenting, whilst the other woman (or couple) are playing against a stacked deck. As any parents of triplets will tell you, parenting three infants simultaneously presses human beings to their limits—how, then, can one manage seven? I would venture a guess that a cloned child not labeled a clone has a better chance of a good childhood than a child who is one of a set of septuplets. In any case, one cannot decide this sort of issue *a priori*, which is precisely what these who reject cloning would do.

A final risk-related argument evolves around the claim that cloning "smacks of eugenics," a claim that is little more than guilt by association. Granted that eugenics has in fact been associated with much evil at the hands of the Nazis and even in the U.S.—forced sterilization, euthanasia of the "unfit," and so on. That does not mean that all genetic improvement is conceptually connected with evil. Who would object if we could, through genetic engineering with no untoward consequences, ablate the gene or genes for cystic fibrosis, Lesch-Nyhan's syndrome, Cruzon's syndrome, and other hideous genetic diseases? That is surely "eugenics," yet seems to be a paradigmatically good sort of thing to do, leading to a better universe. To stop genetic improvement of this sort because Hitler or others did evil things under the same rubric is to succumb to the most simplistic sort of slippery slope argument—"today we ablate cystic fibrosis; tomorrow we make everyone genetically Caucasian." No—we ablate cystic fibrosis, and guard against making everyone Caucasian!

This brings up a related issue. Some minority group members fear cloning as inherently connected with racism. For example, African-American medical ethicist Marian Gray Secundy affirms that:

> Ethnic Americans are extraordinarily suspicious of *any new* scientific technologies. This is particularly true for, but not confined to, the African-American community. . . . The prevailing sentiment is that scientists cannot be trusted, that white scientists particularly are dangerous, that abuses are inevitable and that all manner of evil can and will most likely be visited upon the most vulnerable, e.g. ethnic groups and the poor. A family practice resident commented, "*The White Man has a God complex.*" Others raised concerns about possible abuses, among them that "they" would clone soldiers for war, making "*us*" subservient tools.[20]

On the other hand, other ethics embrace cloning. In the same publication, Reverend Abraham Akaka, a Hawaiian Native American minister argues:

> For aboriginal people of our planet who see themselves as dwindling and endangered species, cloning of the best of their race will be a blessing—a viable avenue for preserving and perpetuating their unique identities and individualities upon lands they revere as father and mother; a way to extend their longevity on earth.[21]

A final argument regarding danger inherent in cloning is extremely widespread, yet almost impossible to take seriously. This is the notion that people will clone themselves in order to create spare parts—hearts, lungs, livers, etc. Despite our encountering this concept in medical thrillers, this is a truly stupid idea. For one thing, one would need to wait until the clone reached adulthood—almost two decades! For another, animals whose organs have been genetically engineered to be compatible with the human immune system—xenotransplantation—are close to realization. (This, of course, raises a separate moral issue of animal exploitation.) Third, such use of a human is clearly covered and forbidden by our current social ethic—it would be premeditated murder. Society would not allow this any more than one is allowed to sell one's children for their organs. Fourth, it would be enormously inefficient to raise people for spare parts. What seems much more likely to me is the development of a technology whereby one can clone "spare organs" from the relevant tissue, rather than growing and discarding the entire person. Such organ cloning seems in principle possible, and research in this area is in fact underway.

Having examined the alleged risks of cloning and finding them to be trivial, or at least no greater than those of other technologies—including reproductive technologies—we already accept, it remains to consider possible benefits of cloning. Let us begin by citing a case that strikes most people one discusses it with as plausible: Imagine a couple who have struggled to have a child naturally. The child is born, and they can never have another. The child, at 1 month of age, is struck by lightning in a freak accident, and is dying and irreversibly comatose. The child has not developed a personality yet, and they wish to replace him. Would they be justified in cloning another child from the dying child's tissue? (It's not as if the new child would always be measured against the idealized and deified dead child—that would create moral problems in terms of unfair demands on the new child.) Basically, they want to have a child of their own. They are not cloning themselves, only the dying baby. Intuitively, few of us would say they are *morally wrong* to create the clone, though we might still feel some squeamishness.

Second, we have already encountered the sort of case raised by Akaka, wherein cloning would be used to save a people whose numbers have been decimated in one way or another. Though the suggestion is staggering, I see no moral issue in cloning victims of genocide, assuming the children would be placed in proper families, etc. The cloning of Jewish Holocaust victims whose genetic material we had, for example, while certainly eerie, would not be morally problematic, but rather a reasonable attempt to replenish the Jewish gene pool so cruelly robbed. (Here, of course, we assume that we can clone effectively from deceased people, or perhaps that the Nazis had saved cell lines.)

Third, as is in fact discussed in the NBAC Report (p. 55), we can imagine parents whose infant requires, say, a bone marrow transplant, cloning that infant *in part* to provide the marrow, assuming, of course, that the parents genuinely want another child. Such situations have already arisen with parents in this sort of situation electing to have another child in part to save the first, ailing one. It is difficult of course to judge parental motivation in having a child, but that is the case for normal reproduction as well.

Fourth, a celibate person may wish to pass on his or her genes. It is hard to see why this is morally unacceptable if gay couples or single people may morally use assisted reproductive technology to reproduce.

Fifth, one can imagine a devastating disease that wipes out large portions of the population, but to which a small percentage of people are naturally resistant. Surely it would be reasonable and acceptable to clone such people so as to assure the further spread of that resistance in the population, assuming that the people were willing to be cloned.

Thus, it seems to me, that there are possible scenarios where cloning might be beneficial to individuals and to society, and free of risk, or at least where it would be a plausible reproductive strategy with only a religious or very weak "intrinsic wrongness" argument against it.

V

The final area of possible moral concern about cloning of humans evolves around possible harm to the clone—what we have called in our Frankenstein typology "the plight of the creature." If, for example, clones inevitably develop some wasting disease with the advent of puberty, cloning would clearly become a morally unacceptable reproductive modality. This is the most powerful reason against anyone undertaking to clone a human at this stage of knowledge, and explains why even strong advocates of cloning research were furious at Seed's irresponsible announcement that he would begin cloning shortly—it is the same concern that greeted the vastly premature attempt to provide a baboon heart to Baby Fae.

Is cloning likely to engender untoward effects in a cloned organism? No one knows. Cloned calves created by splitting embryos were oversized, required birthing by caesarian section, and were behaviorally retarded. By the same token, there are suggestions that any assisted reproduction techniques involve more risks for the resulting organism than normal reproduction does, ranging from problems with infections to possible intellectual impairment. As Te Velde et al. remark in a commentary in the *Lancet*:

> Manipulation of human genetics or embryos and intervening with the natural process of conception may induce subtle, complex, and far-reaching changes in the genetic material of the offspring and perhaps also of the next generation. Before new assisted reproduction techniques are adopted as routine treatment for infertility, they should be assessed extensively in animal and human embryo research, then in clinical trials, during which the children must be monitored long term. Lessons learnt from the unexpected effects on fetal development of drugs that were not adequately assessed before introduction should apply here. Scientists and governments should be discussing how the introduction of assisted reproduction techniques should be regulated.[22]

Though this is good common sense, it has not been done in a systematic, publically discussed way with previous assisted reproductive technologies, which were largely developed and promulgated in an unregulated, entrepreneurial fashion. Though cloning is being intensely discussed, it is largely in the sensationalistic, empty manner we have indicated. In all of these areas, a democratic society should have a public, informed discussion regarding steering a course between *laissez-faire* and unjustified regulatory constraint.

One genuine risk to a cloned human grows out of their possibly being identified and labeled by others as monstrous, or less than human. This, of course, is not a risk of cloning *per se*, but of social reaction to it. If religious leaders lead a witch hunt to "ferret out soulless clones," clearly cloned humans would be at risk, though of course it would equally be a risk to anyone misidentified as a clone. The best way to guard against this risk is to maintain strict confidentiality about who is cloned until such time as cloning is socially accepted or at least widespread.

Given environmental influences, pre- and postnatal, age differences, differences in hair and clothing styles, etc., no one could recognize my clone as a clone, rather than as my normally derived progeny or grandson, were I older when he was cloned.

Assuming no untoward effect of cloning, neither he nor anyone else would ever need to know that he was clonally derived, any more than children need to know they were adopted. To say that cloning is unacceptable because cloned children will be unfairly stigmatized for no good reason begs the question against cloning—the plausible response is to assure that they are not so marginalized.

VI

Biotechnology, still in its infancy, will not go away, nor can it be banned—it will simply go underground or to unregulated venues. In barely two decades, it has presented us with questions for which we are totally unprepared morally, and which we consequently answer very poorly. As biotechnology develops exponentially, such vexatious questions will proliferate and grow more complex. With scientists tending to divest themselves of responsibility for defining ethical issues to the public (or to themselves), the resulting ethical lacuna will inevitably be filled with bad ethics. One way to forestall this would be for the general citizenry to understand the science well enough to reflect ethically upon it, but this too is unlikely. In my view, this bespeaks a significant social role for applied ethics-oriented philosophers. They can assure that the science is properly understood and the ethical issues properly analyzed so that a minimal amount of time and energy is wasted on bad ethics. As one who served a similar role in creating federal legislation protecting the interests of laboratory animals, I can attest to its social utility and to the satisfaction one experiences. An ethical and conceptual framework for assessing new biological technological advances is as necessary today as the new philosophical frameworks created by thinkers like René Descartes, Benedict Spinoza and Gottlob Leibniz were at the time to accommodate and interpret the New Physical Science.

READING ENDNOTES

1. B. E. Rollin, "Send in the Clones … Don't Bother, They're Here," *Journal of Agricultural and Environmental Ethics* 10 (1997), pp. 25–40.
2. CNN/*Time* Poll, "Most Americans Say Cloning is Wrong" (1 March 1997).
3. B. E. Rollin, *The Unheeded Cry: Animal Consciousness, Animal Pain, and Science* (expanded edition, Ames, IA: Iowa State University Press, 1998).
4. B. E. Rollin, *The Frankenstein Syndrome: Ethical and Social Issues in the Genetic Engineering of Animals* (New York: Cambridge University Press, 1995).
5. D. Glut, *The Frankenstein Catalogue* (Jefferson NC: McFarland, 1984).
6. Rollin, *The Frankenstein Syndrome*, Part I.
7. CNN/*Time*, 1997.
8. CNN/*Time*, 1997.
9. J. Woolfrey, and C. Campbell, *Reflections*, Special Edition. "Human Cloning: Fact, Fiction and Faith" (Corvallis, OR: Department of Philosophy, Oregon State University, May 1997).
10. Woolfrey and Campbell, p. 3.

11. Woolfrey and Campbell, p. 4.
12. National Bioethics Advisory Commission, *Cloning Human Beings* (Rockville, MD: June 1997), pp. 42–49.
13. NBAC, p. 50.
14. NBAC, pp. 44–45.
15. NBAC, Summary of Arguments against Cloning (http://www.al.org/clontx01.htm), p. 2.
16. David Ehrenfeld, *The Arrogance of Humanism* (New York: Oxford University Press, 1978).
17. Rollin, *The Frankenstein Syndrome*, Part II.
18. NBAC, Summary of the Arguments Against Cloning, p. 2.
19. NBAC, Summary of the Arguments Against Cloning, p. 1.
20. Woolfrey and Campbell, p. 5.
21. Woolfrey and Campbell, pp. 2–3.
22. Quoted in Cummins, *Embryo Mail News* (26 May 1998), p. 768 (see http://www.thelancet.com/newlancet/reg/isues/vol351n o9115/article1529.htm).

DEFINITIONS AND EXPLANATIONS

Ad hoc: Latin, meaning 1. For this specific purpose only (e.g., An *ad hoc* committee was formed to deal with the emergency); 2. Often used as a derogatory term, when an argument is said to rest on *ad hoc* premises or assumptions, that is, premises brought into the argument only to save the speaker's position; a logical fallacy or faulty form of reasoning.

A fortiori: Latin, meaning from strong reason, even more conclusively. Used in reasoning to indicate that a claim that has already been established is now supported even more strongly by additional reasons.

A priori: Latin, meaning prior to experience. Reasoning from abstract notions or concepts to their consequences (e.g., Sanjay is a bachelor, and therefore he is unmarried) or from propositions or axioms that are assumed to be true prior to experience (e.g., Every thing either exists or does not exist). *A priori* knowledge is not gained through experience; it is of self-evident truths that are not contingent (true in fact but they could have been false if the world was different), but of necessary truths (truths which must be true no matter what the world is like). No factual claim about the way the world was, is or will be can be known *a priori.*

Begs the question, or question-begging: Again this is a charge of bad reasoning. Begging the question is something good reasoners avoid, because it is a fallacious form of reasoning. We discussed the way language is often used in moral debates to beg the question in Chapter 1, under "Critical Moral Thinking." The mistake is to simply reassert the very point that you are trying to argue for. Consider, for example, the use of "unnatural" in moral debates. We often hear that homosexuality is unnatural, or cloning is unnatural, or using animal organs for transplantation in people is unnatural and the like. Such claims are often offered as grounds or reasons for thinking that such practices are bad or wrong. But look at how the reasoning actually goes. The person says that cloning is unnatural and so wrong. But then we ask, what do you mean when you say that something is unnatural, and the person says he means that it is wrong. In other words, the explanation of cloning's badness is that it is unnatural, and the explanation of its unnaturalness is that it is bad. This is just begging the question at issue, which is whether or not cloning is bad. This is perhaps the most common form of bad moral reasoning, and it is often masked by the use of vague and emotionally loaded terms. It happens when people smuggle into an argument premises that are equivalent to the very conclusion they are supposed to be giving independent reasons for.

Eugenics: The science that deals with the improvement of races and breeds, through the control of hereditary factors. It is very problematic when applied to the human race, since it depends upon a notion of "improvement" and hence "perfection," which might be quite controversial, and it has been associated with some of the most brutal practices of human kind (including experiments upon Jews and other prisoners by the Nazis during World War II). Less emotionally laden eugenic practices are used in refining thoroughbred animals like dogs and horses.

Genetic fallacy: Another instance of faulty reasoning, and a very common mistake seen in moral reasoning. It involves erroneously drawing conclusions about the current properties of a thing (such as its moral status) on the basis of its origin. In this case, we must avoid drawing any conclusions about the moral status, potential for happiness, or moral personhood of clones just on the basis of their origin or genesis. To conclude anything about the moral status of a clone, on the basis of her origin, would be exactly the same mistake as saying that a child born as a result of rape is of lower moral status or is not a person, just because of his origins. Another example of the genetic fallacy is seen when people conclude that certain information must be false just on the basis of its origin. Concluding that any claim of fact is false just because it has an immoral or disreputable source is fallacious, whereas concluding that it should be treated suspiciously and double checked need not be a faulty conclusion. If you have reason to distrust a source of information, you should double check the information yourself. But you cannot just conclude that it must be false because you disapprove of its origin or source.

Hubristic: Demonstrating hubris, which is undue arrogance or insolence, excessive pride.

Lacuna: A gap or break. In this case, Rollin is speaking about the gap in our critical moral thinking generated by rapidly developing new technologies, whose moral implications have not been fully studied by moral philosophers and others with relevant expertise.

Slippery slope argument: Again this is a name of a common fallacy. A slippery slope argument takes the following form: if we allow some practice then we will find ourselves on a slippery slope that leads to other practices we find unacceptable. Some examples that we have heard recently include (1) if we allow same sex marriages then we will open the door to polygamy (multiple spouses married to a single individual) and pedophilia (sexual relations between adults and children); (2) if we allow abortion on demand then we will undermine the sanctity of life and ultimately accept the killing of other unwanted human beings like the sick, the disabled, and the elderly; (3) if we allow experimentation on cloning then we will end up in a society where people clone themselves for spare body parts; (4) if we legalize or decriminalize the use of marijuana then everyone will end up smoking it, and taking heroine and cocaine, and our children will all become addicts. All of these arguments have the same structure: if we take the first step on a particular road then we will find ourselves unable to stop (as though we are on a slippery slope). But the strength of any such argument depends upon the likelihood that the dire consequences really will follow inevitably from our taking the first step. Will we really be unable to stop the other consequences from following if we take the action being contemplated? In all of the examples given, there is good reason to think that we can draw a principled line between the proposed first step and the subsequent results that we don't want to adopt. Nothing about taking any of the steps contemplated in our examples would commit us (even for reasons of consistency) to also accept the feared consequences that are mentioned, because there are important differences between them and the original action whose morality we are trying to assess.

Somatic cells: Somatic cells become differentiated so as to make up the tissues, organs and other parts of the body of an organism. Somatic cells are contrasted with **germ cells**, which are cells from which a new organism can develop; in mammals, sperm and eggs are germ cells.

QUESTIONS

1. Why does Rollin think those arguments against cloning on the grounds that it is unnatural or "playing God" cannot be defended in a secular society?

2. What are the goods of human cloning? Can you think of others not given in the text?

3. Why would it be immoral to proceed with cloning in a cavalier fashion?

4. In what way is the thought that a clone will be identical to the donor mistaken? Does this fact undermine other arguments you have heard against cloning?

5. A common argument against human cloning is that it will erode "normal" forms of family. What kind of argument is this? What reasons does Rollin give against such arguments?

6. Does cloning children threaten to undermine the bonds of love and care that ideally shape relations between parents and children, or between spouses?

7. If missing parents is a bad, would Rollin advocate banning divorce?

8. In what way are fears that cloning would be used for eugenic purposes misguided? Why do they often take the form of slippery slope arguments?

9. If we can choose who to clone, will we not be tempted to clone only those whose characteristics are currently valued in our society (the strong, the talented, the highly intelligent, and the rich)? If so, do we not then run the risk that we will not clone members of racial minorities, the disabled, the poor, members of native groups, etc.? Does this worry create a new reason to condemn human cloning?

10. Why should we not worry about people cloning themselves for spare parts, for the creation of organs that the donor can use later? What does this issue imply about parents who have a child by "natural" methods who will donate a kidney or bone marrow to his or her sibling or parent?

11. If we could clone single organs (say a liver or heart), as Rollin indicates scientists are working on, would such a practice be ethically problematic?

12. Should we think of cloning as just one of many existing reproductive technologies (like fertility drugs, in vitro fertilization, adoption, etc.)?

13. What does Rollin say about potential harms to the clone? If such harms were established through future research (if clones were more likely to suffer from debilitating diseases, or have certain disabilities, say), would Rollin accept that such consequences would provide a valid reason not to engage in human cloning?

14. Consider your answer to question 13. Now think through the following situation. We currently allow parents to continue a pregnancy even if pre-natal testing has revealed health risks that allow us to know with certainty that the resulting child will be severely mentally or physically defective, will have a life-threatening and debilitating disease, or will lead a life of unremitting pain and disability. If we allow parents to bring such children into the world by existing methods, do we not have to allow (for reasons of consistency) that they may do so through cloning? Or do our reflections here raise doubts about our current practices?

✦ ✦ ✦

James Rachels, Active and Passive Euthanasia

James Rachels offers utilitarian arguments against the distinction between killing (active euthanasia) and letting die (passive euthanasia) commonly accepted by health care professionals. Passive euthanasia is acceptable, while active euthanasia is forbidden. We are asked to consider two cases. In the first case, if a doctor does nothing (withholds treatment), a patient will eventually die. It is decided (by all concerned) that it would be better if this patient died, as his suffering would only be prolonged should the treatments continue. But, Rachels argues, if we are concerned with minimizing needless suffering in this case, should we not engage in active euthanasia? The patient will die sooner and there will be less suffering involved if we humanely kill him rather than simply let him die. It seems that if mercy suggests letting the patient die, it suggests even more strongly killing the patient. In the second case, Rachels enjoins us to consider babies with extreme examples of Down syndrome. Some of these babies also have operable conditions that would be fatal if not corrected. Doctors sometimes fail to operate on such children, letting them die. But if (as we must assume) these doctors are allowing these children to die because it has been determined that Down syndrome renders their life to be not worth living, why do they not kill the other babies with similarly severe Down syndrome? It seems that, in order to be consistent in their consideration of the alleviation of suffering, doctors who have found two children with the same degree of Down syndrome, one of whom will die if left alone, and one who will not, have only two available options. They must either let one die and kill the other, should their quality of life be found intolerably dismal, or they must save the first child and let the other live. The distinction between killing and letting die seems arbitrary.

We must here caution against undue outrage at Rachel's proposal. Rachels is not proposing that even one baby be killed—just that if a life has been found to be not worth living, that the principle through which that life has been found wanting be applied equally, so as to not have cases distinguished between due to morally irrelevant differences. Critical moral reasoning, as we have previously mentioned, must be dispassionate. Many utilitarian proposals have been met with outrage, but we must meet them instead with argument.

✦ ✦ ✦

James Rachels, "Active and Passive Euthanasia," *The New England Journal of Medicine* Vol. 292 (1975): 78–80. © 1975 Massachusetts Medical Society. Reprinted with permission of the Massachusetts Medical Society.

ACTIVE AND PASSIVE EUTHANASIA

JAMES RACHELS

The distinction between active and passive euthanasia is thought to be crucial for medical ethics. The idea is that it is permissible, at least in some cases, to withhold treatment and allow a patient to die, but it is never permissible to take any direct action designed to kill the patient. This doctrine seems to be accepted by most doctors, and it is endorsed in a statement adopted by the House of Delegates of the American Medical Association on 4 December 1973:

> The intentional termination of the life of one human being by another—mercy killing—is contrary to that for which the medical profession stands and is contrary to the policy of the American Medical Association.
>
> The cessation of the employment of extraordinary means to prolong the life of the body when there is irrefutable evidence that biological death is imminent is the decision of the patient and/or his immediate family. The advice and judgement of the physician should be freely available to the patient and/or his immediate family.

However, a strong case can be made against this doctrine. In what follows I will set out some of the relevant arguments, and urge doctors to reconsider their views on this matter.

To begin with a familiar type of situation, a patient who is dying of incurable cancer of the throat is in terrible pain, which can no longer be satisfactorily alleviated. He is certain to die within a few days, even if present treatment is continued, but he does not want to go on living for those days since the pain is unbearable. So he asks the doctor for an end to it, and his family joins in the request.

Suppose the doctor agrees to withhold treatment, as the conventional doctrine says he may. The justification for his doing so is that the patient is in terrible agony, and since he is going to die anyway, it would be wrong to prolong his suffering needlessly. But now notice this. If one simply withholds treatment, it may take the patient longer to die, and so he may suffer more than he would if more direct action were taken and a lethal injection given. This fact provides strong reason for thinking that, once the initial decision not to prolong his agony has been made, active euthanasia is actually preferable to passive euthanasia, rather than the reverse. To say otherwise is to endorse the option that leads to more suffering rather than less, and is contrary to the humanitarian impulse that prompts the decision not to prolong his life in the first place.

Part of my point is that the process of being 'allowed to die' can be relatively slow and painful, whereas being given a lethal injection is relatively quick and painless. Let me give a different sort of example. In the United States about one in 600 babies is born with Down's syndrome. Most of these babies are otherwise healthy—that is, with only the usual pediatric care, they will proceed to an otherwise normal infancy. Some, however, are born with congenital defects such as intestinal obstructions that require operations if they are to live. Sometimes, the parents and the doctor will decide not to operate, and let the infant die. Anthony Shaw describes what happens then:

> When surgery is denied [the doctor] must try to keep the infant from suffering while natural forces sap the baby's life away. As a surgeon whose natural inclination is to use the scalpel to fight off death, standing by and watching a salvageable baby die is the most emotionally exhausting experience I know. It is easy at a conference, in a theoretical discussion to decide that such infants should be allowed to die. It is altogether different to stand by in the nursery and watch as dehydration and infection wither a tiny being over hours and days. This is a terrible ordeal for me and the hospital staff—much more so than for the parents who never set foot in the nursery.[1]

I can understand why some people are opposed to all euthanasia, and insist that such infants must be allowed to live. I think I can also understand why other people favour destroying these babies quickly and painlessly. But why should anyone favour letting 'dehydration and infection wither a tiny being over hours and days'? The doctrine that says a baby may be allowed to dehydrate and wither, but may not be given an injection that would end its life without suffering, seems so patently cruel as to require no further refutation. The strong language is not intended to offend, but only to put the point in the clearest possible way.

My second argument is that the conventional doctrine leads to decisions concerning life and death made on irrelevant grounds.

Consider again the case of the infants with Down's syndrome who need operations for congenital defects unrelated to the syndrome to live. Sometimes, there is no operation, and the baby dies, but when there is no such defect, the baby lives on. Now, an operation such as that to remove an intestinal obstruction is not prohibitively difficult. The reason why such operations are not performed in these cases is, clearly, that the child has Down's syndrome and the parents and the doctor judge that because of that fact it is better for the child to die.

But notice that this situation is absurd, no matter what view one takes of the lives and potentials of such babies. If the life of such an infant is worth preserving what does it matter if it needs a simple operation? Or, if one thinks it better that such a baby should not live on, what difference does it make that it happens to have an unobstructed intestinal tract? In either case, the matter of life and death is being decided on irrelevant grounds. It is the Down's syndrome, and not the intestines, that is the issue. The matter should be decided, if at all, on that basis, and not be allowed to depend on the essentially irrelevant question of whether the intestinal tract is blocked.

What makes this situation possible, of course, is the idea that when there is an intestinal blockage, one can 'let the baby die,' but when there is no such defect there is nothing that can be done, for one must not 'kill' it. The fact that this idea leads to such results as deciding life or death on irrelevant grounds is another good reason why the doctrine would be rejected.

One reason why so many people think that there is an important moral difference between active and passive euthanasia is that they think killing someone is morally worse than letting someone die. But is it? Is killing, in itself, worse than letting die? To investigate this issue, two cases may be considered that are exactly alike except that one involves killing whereas the other involves letting someone die. Then, it can be asked whether this difference makes any difference to the moral assessments. It is important that the cases be exactly alike, except for this one difference, since otherwise one cannot be confident that it is this difference and not some other that accounts for any variation in the assessments of the two cases. So, let us consider this pair of cases:

In the first, Smith stands to gain a large inheritance if anything should happen to his six-year-old cousin. One evening while the child is taking his bath, Smith sneaks into the bathroom and drowns the child, and then arranges things so that it will look like an accident.

In the second, Jones also stands to gain if anything should happen to his six-year-old cousin. Like Smith, Jones sneaks in planning to drown the child in his bath. However, just as he enters the bathroom Jones sees the child slip and hit his head, and fall face down in the water. Jones is delighted; he stands by, ready to push the child's head back under if it is necessary, but it is not necessary. With only a little thrashing about, the child drowns all by himself, 'accidentally,' as Jones watches and does nothing.

Now Smith killed the child, whereas Jones 'merely' let the child die. That is the only difference between them. Did either man behave better, from a moral point of view? If the difference between killing and letting die were in itself a morally important matter, one should say that Jones's behaviour was less reprehensible than Smith's. But does one really want to say that? I think not. In the first place, both men acted from the same motive, personal gain, and both had exactly the same end in view when they acted. It may be inferred from Smith's conduct that he is a bad man, although that judgement may be withdrawn or modified if certain further facts are learned about him—for example, that he is mentally deranged. But would not the very same thing be inferred about Jones from his conduct? And would not the same further considerations also be relevant to any modification of this judgement? Moreover, suppose Jones pleaded, in his own defence, 'After all, I didn't do anything except just stand there and watch the child drown. I didn't kill him; I only let him die.' Again, if letting die were in itself less bad than killing, this defence should have at least some weight. But it does not. Such a 'defence' can only be regarded as a grotesque perversion of moral reasoning. Morally speaking, it is no defence at all.

Now, it may be pointed out, quite properly, that the cases of euthanasia with which doctors are concerned are not like this at all. They do not involve personal gain or the destruction of normal healthy children. Doctors are concerned only with cases in which the patient's life is of no further use to him, or in which the patient's life has become or will soon become a terrible burden. However, the point is the same in these cases: the bare difference between killing and letting die does not, in itself, make a moral difference. If a doctor lets a patient die, for humane reasons, he is in the same moral position as if he had given the patient a lethal injection for humane reasons. If his decision was wrong—if, for example, the patient's illness was in fact curable—the decision would be equally regrettable no matter which method was used to carry it out. And if the doctor's decision was the right one, the method used is not in itself important.

The AMA policy statement isolates the crucial issue very well; the crucial issue is 'the intentional termination of the life of one human being by another.' But after identifying this issue, and forbidding 'mercy killing,' the statement goes on to deny that the cessation of treatment is the intentional termination of a life. This is where the mistake comes in, for what is the cessation of treatment, in these circumstances, if it is not 'the intentional termination of the life of one human being by another'? Of course it is exactly that, and if it were not, there would be no point to it.

Many people will find this judgement hard to accept. One reason, I think, is that it is very easy to conflate the question of whether killing is, in itself, worse than letting die, with the very different question of whether most actual cases of killing are more reprehensible than most actual cases of letting die. Most actual cases of killing are clearly terrible (think, for example, of all the murders reported in the newspapers), and one hears of such cases every day. On the other hand, one hardly ever hears of a case of letting die, except for the actions of doctors who are motivated by humanitarian reasons. So one learns to think of killing in a much worse light than of letting die. But this does not mean that there is something about killing that makes it in itself worse than letting die, for it is not the bare difference between killing and letting die that makes the difference in these cases. Rather, the other factors—the murderer's motive of personal gain, for example, contrasted with the doctor's humanitarian motivation—account for different reactions to the different cases.

I have argued that killing is not in itself any worse than letting die; if my contention is right, it follows that active euthanasia is not any worse than passive euthanasia. What arguments can be given on the other side? The most common, I believe, is the following:

The important difference between active and passive euthanasia is that, in passive euthanasia, the doctor does not do anything to bring about the patient's death. The doctor does nothing, and the patient dies of whatever ills already afflict him. In active euthanasia, however, the doctor does something to bring about the patient's death: he kills him. The doctor who gives the patient with cancer a lethal injection has himself caused his patient's death; whereas if he merely ceases treatment, the cancer is the cause of death.

A number of points need to be made here. The first is that it is not exactly correct to say that in passive euthanasia the doctor does nothing, for he does do one thing that is very important: he lets the patient die. 'Letting someone die' is certainly different, in some respects, from other types of action—mainly in that it is a kind of action that one may perform by way of not performing certain other actions. For example, one may let a patient die by way of not giving medication, just as one may insult someone by way of not shaking his hand. But for any purpose of moral assessment, it is a type of action none the less. The decision to let a patient die is subject to moral appraisal in the same way that a decision to kill him would be subject to moral appraisal: it may be assessed as wise or unwise, compassionate or sadistic, right or wrong. If a doctor deliberately let a patient die who is suffering from a routinely curable illness, the doctor would certainly be to blame for what he had done, just as he would be to blame if he had needlessly killed the patient. Charges against him would then be appropriate. If so, it would be no defence at all for him to insist that he didn't 'do anything.' He would have done something very serious indeed, for he let his patient die.

Fixing the cause of death may be very important from a legal point of view, for it may determine whether criminal charges are brought against the doctor. But I do not think that this notion can be used to show a moral difference between active and passive euthanasia. The reason why it is considered bad to be the cause of someone's death is that death is regarded as a great evil—and so it is. However, if it has been decided that euthanasia—even passive euthanasia—is desirable in a given case, it has also been decided that in this instance death is no greater an evil than the patient's continued existence. And if this is true, the usual reason for not wanting to be the cause of someone's death simply does not apply.

Finally, doctors may think that all of this is only of academic interest—the sort of thing that philosophers may worry about but that has no practical bearing on their own work. After all, doctors must be concerned about the legal consequences of what they do, and active euthanasia is clearly forbidden by the law. But even so, doctors should also be concerned with the fact that the law is forcing upon them a moral doctrine that may be indefensible, and has a considerable effect on their practices. Of course, most doctors are not now in the position of being coerced in this matter, for they do not regard themselves as merely going along with what the law requires. Rather, in statements such as the AMA policy statement that I have quoted, they are endorsing this doctrine as a central point of medical ethics. In that statement, active euthanasia is condemned not merely as illegal but as 'contrary to that for which the medical profession stands,' whereas passive euthanasia is approved. However, the preceding considerations suggest that there is really no moral difference between the two, considered in themselves (there may be important moral differences in some cases in their *consequences*, but, as I pointed out, these differences may make active euthanasia, and not passive euthanasia, the morally preferable option). So, whereas doctors may have to discriminate between active and passive euthanasia to satisfy the law, they should not do any more than that. In particular, they should not give the distinction any added authority and weight by writing it into official statements of medical ethics.

READING ENDNOTE

1. Shaw, Anthony, 'Doctor, Do We Have a Choice?' *The New York Times Magazine*, 30 Jan. 1972, p. 54.

QUESTIONS

1. If the consequences of active and passive euthanasia are the same, namely the death of the patient, can a utilitarian identify a morally relevant difference between them?

2. Are (1) withholding or withdrawing life support treatment and (2) giving a patient a lethal injection equally describable as "the intentional termination of the life of one human being by another," as Rachels insists?

3. Rachels' article points out that 'doing nothing' (omissions) are equally subject to moral assessment as actions (commissions) are. This was a point insisted upon by Bentham as well. Is it right? Can you imagine cases where a failure to act is as bad as acting to bring about the same result? Do all the cases involve duties to aid or provide for others?

4. Doctors are usually thought to have two primary duties: to care for their patients and to do no harm. In cases of decisions to terminate life support or actively bring about death, are these duties in conflict?

5. Does anything in Rachels' argument depend upon the special relationship between doctors and patients?

6 If we allowed active euthanasia, Rachels says, we would alleviate needless suffering among the terminally ill. Can you imagine any other morally relevant consequences of allowing this practice that a utilitarian would need to consider in determining whether or not we should follow Rachels' advice? Be careful not to commit any fallacies in answering this question.

7. The Smith and Jones case is designed to show that the distinction between killing and letting die is arbitrary even in cases not involving physicians and their patients. In that example, one crucial assumption is that they both act from the same (selfish) motive. What role can consideration of motives play in utilitarian reasoning?

✦ ✦ ✦

Douglas P. Lackey, Missiles and Morals: A Utilitarian Look at Nuclear Deterrence

Douglas P. Lackey examines the issue of nuclear deterrence from a utilitarian perspective. Taking preference satisfaction as the subjective measure of value, he examines a country's efforts to maintain first strike capability, maintain equal nuclear arms capability with rival states, or to unilaterally disarm from both a prudential and moral perspective. Lackey suggests that a prudential calculation will take the preferences of your own country's population into account, while a moral calculation will take all preferences into account. Importantly, arguing about the effects of nuclear policies appeals to incomplete information: no one knows what will happen in many nuclear situations, or what the odds are that any imagined outcome will in fact occur. We simply have not had enough experience with nuclear wars. Decisions about policy are made under conditions of uncertainty. In cases of certainty, or in cases which involve risk, rational (prudential) decision making is well understood—to choose rationally under certainty, one must detail all the certain outcomes of each possible course of action, discover, and then sum their utility. The course of action with the highest utility is then chosen. In cases of risk, where the outcomes of an action occur with a known probability, one must simply list all of the outcomes of each possible course of action, discover the utility of each, multiply each utility by the possibility of occurrence, and sum the results. The course of action with the highest expected utility is then chosen. Under uncertainty, however, you do not know all of the possible results of each course of action, or you do not know how likely each result is. Calculation under incomplete information (uncertainty) is problematic. Indeed, one of the values of Lackey's paper is that it illustrates the level of complexity involved in assessing the likely consequences of various acts or policies at the national and international levels.

Various principles have been proposed to rectify the problem of uncertainty. Lackey examines three principles designed to circumvent this problem: Minimax, Dominance, and Expected Value Maximization.* Minimax is a risk avoidance principle. It suggests that the rational choice to make is the one whose worst outcome is at least as good as any other option's worst outcome. Morally speaking, Minimax suggests that disarmament is the moral alternative, as only in this way can you avoid a two-sided nuclear war (which is the worst outcome possible). Prudentially the case is less clear, due to Lackey's acknowledgement that it is difficult to decide how many people in one country will prefer two-sided nuclear war to being the target of a one-sided nuclear attack. The Dominance principle suggests that one should choose the principle that has a result that cannot be improved upon, no matter what your opponent might do. Lackey finds that choosing equal capability is prudentially preferable

---

* In fact, Lackey considers four possible strategies for choice in the full version of the paper. We have left out his discussion of the Disaster Avoidance Principle because it does not apply to the nuclear deterrence case and so is beside the point of the paper for our purposes.

to nuclear disarmament, while nuclear disarmament is morally preferable to equal capability. Lackey also attempts to mimic choice under risk and apply the Expected Value principle, by simply appealing to general categories of risk and attempting to calculate the expected value of each possible policy. He concludes that both morally and prudentially, equivalence is superior to nuclear superiority, and that disarmament is both morally and prudentially superior to equivalence.

We observe here one of the major stumbling blocks for utilitarianism. Under two of the proposed decision rules, prudence and morality suggest different courses of action. Of course this is not surprising: if what is in our interest were also always the right thing to do, we would have no need for morality. But utilitarianism is a particularly demanding theory. If utilitarians suggest that we must forego prudence and disarm, that is one thing. But what of personal sacrifices? If we see a grenade thrown into a room, are we morally obligated to throw ourselves on it to save the rest of the people in the room? Are there limits to the sacrifices that utilitarianism may require of us, and if so, on what are they based?

✦ ✦ ✦

Douglas P. Lackey, "Missiles and Morals: A Utilitarian Look at Nuclear Deterrence," *Philosophy and Public Affairs* 11:3 (Summer 1982): 189–231. © 1982 Princeton University Press. This is a shorter version of the complete paper. Reprinted with permission of Princeton University Press.

Missiles and Morals: A Utilitarian Look at Nuclear Deterrence

D O U G L A S P . L A C K E Y

Though American foreign policy since 1945 has oscillated between conciliation and confrontation, American military policy at the strategic level has remained firmly tied to the notion of nuclear deterrence. After Hiroshima and Nagasaki, it was apparent that the effects of nuclear weapons were so terrible that their future use could never be condoned. But the threat to use nuclear weapons need not require their use, and such threats, in themselves, might prevent great evils. For those worried about Soviet expansion, a credible threat to use nuclear weapons might hold Soviet power in check. For those worried about future nuclear wars, the threat to use the bomb in retaliation might prevent nuclear wars from beginning. For an American public eager for demobilization, nuclear threats provided an appealing substitute for foot soldiering on foreign soil.[1] The stance of deterrence, of threat without use, appeared to both liberals and conservatives to command an overwhelming moral and prudential case. Small wonder, then, that after several abortive, perhaps deliberately abortive,[2] attempts at the internationalization of atomic weapons, the United States opted for unilateral development of nuclear weapons and delivery systems. Whatever residual qualms policy makers felt about the possession of nuclear arms were effectively silenced by the explosion of the first Soviet bomb in 1949. That the Soviets should possess nuclear weapons when the United States did not was politically unthinkable. Thirty-two years and ten thousand American nuclear weapons later, it still is.

Nevertheless it was arguable almost from the first that the case for deterrence was weaker than it seemed. The effectiveness of nuclear threats as a deterrent to Soviet aggression or Communist expansion was and remains barely credible. If the threat to use nuclear weapons did not prevent the subversion of Czechoslovakia, the blockade of Berlin, the collapse of Chiang Kai-shek, the fall of Dienbienphu, or the invasion of Hungary, all of which occurred before the Soviet Union could effectively deter an

American nuclear strike with nuclear weapons and missiles of its own, how much less effective must nuclear threats have been towards deterring the Soviet invasion of Czechoslovakia in 1968 and the invasion of Afghanistan in 1979, and how little effect could such threats have as a deterrent to the much discussed but little expected invasion of West Germany by forces of the Warsaw pact?[3]

Since there have been no uses of nuclear weapons in war since 1945, the case for nuclear threats as a deterrent to first uses of nuclear weapons seems a bit stronger. Nevertheless the role that nuclear deterrence has played in keeping the world free of nuclear war is a matter for debate. In the case of wars in progress, nuclear weapons have not been introduced in many cases because they cannot be effectively deployed relative to overall military objectives. The Israelis cannot use nuclear weapons on the Golan for fear of polluting the Kennerit; the Iraquis could not use them against Jerusalem without destroying the mosques they seek to liberate. The United States could not use nuclear weapons in South Vietnam without contaminating the countryside of our own allies; the Soviets could not use them against Prague and Budapest without destroying the industries they seek to exploit. As for the prevention through deterrence of large-scale nuclear war, it can be argued that every decrease in the chance of a nuclear first strike that results from fear of a retaliatory second strike is matched by an increase in the chance of a nuclear first strike that results from accident or mistake, human or mechanical failure; that every decrease in the chance that innocent millions will die from an undeterred first strike is matched by an increase in the chance that innocent millions will die from a nuclear second strike that cannot be stopped after the initial deterrence has failed. To these dangers we should add the consideration that the American argument, "the United States must have the bomb if the Soviet Union has one," is replicable by every nation state, producing pressure for proliferation which in turn increases the chance of war, and the consideration that no degree of threat can deter a nuclear terrorist who prefers to be dead rather than blue, or red, or green, and who has built his bomb with the help of weapons technology developed by states that are sworn "to deterrence only." There is little, at least in a preliminary survey of the evidence, that supports the idea that the construction of nuclear weapons for the purpose of issuing nuclear threats has contributed to the prevention of nuclear wars since 1945, or will contribute towards preventing them in the future. Whatever the game theorists say, the common sense view that you cannot prevent wars by building bombs still has some weight.

The argument that nuclear deterrence can replace the war of soldiers on the ground with a war of threats in the air has also seen hard sledding since 1945. The need for retaining conventional forces has been apparent since the Berlin blockade, and the effect that reliance on nuclear deterrence has had on the quality of conventional forces is by now well known. It is no accident that the last successful American military operation (Inchon) precedes the development of ICBMs, and the increasing ineptitude of American conventional forces exhibited in the successively botched Son Tay, Mayaguez, and Iranian rescue attempts is too obvious to bear comment. There is no necessary connection between nuclear strength and conventional weakness, but in a world of limited resources the development of strategic forces has twisted military budgets in favor of high technology, and the result has been complicated guns that won't shoot and complicated planes that can't fly.[4] The idea that the nation's "first line" of defense consists of radar towers and missiles rather than men on the battlefield must inevitably weaken the morale of the Army and the Marines. However plausible it may have seemed to John Foster Dulles, there is little support now for the view that nuclear threats can substitute in any way for the painful sacrifices of conventional war.

The moral and prudential case for deterrence seems overcome by events. But there is a rejoinder to these criticisms that many find decisive: deterrence is bad, but disarmament is worse. Elected officials remember well that the only Presidential candidate since 1945 with a kind word for nuclear disarmament was humiliated in 1972 and voted out of the Senate in 1980. Fortunately moral philosophers do not stand for election and are free to examine all the options regardless of practical constraints. This is what I propose to do, with the important limitation that the moral systems I shall bring to bear upon the subject are all utilitarian systems. In normal circumstances one may have one's doubts about utilitarianism, but if nuclear war is among the results of policies under consideration, the gravity of the consequences carries all else before.

I. Four Decision Rules

The agreeable utilitarian idea that the moral worth of acts and policies is to be measured in the value of their consequences has been troubled from the beginning by the problem that the consequences of policies are often uncertain. Suppose that Policy 1 will produce either A or B, that Policy 2 will produce either C or D, and that by some accepted standard of value A is better than C but B is worse than D. The rule that the best policy is the one with the best consequences will not tell us which policy to choose, and there is no consensus among utilitarian theorists as to how the general rule should be modified in order to generate the morally right choice. Nevertheless there are many ingenious suggestions about how to deal with choice under uncertainty, and in this essay we will deploy four different principles of choice: Minimax, Dominance, Disaster Avoidance, and Expected Value Maximization. Each principle will be used twice over, first, for the utilitarian calculation, which we will call the moral calculation; second, for a prudential calculation, which will indicate, from the standpoint of the United States, what the prudential course of action might be.

Each prudential and moral calculation requires a standard of value, and in the essay the usual standard of value will be the satisfaction of preferences. In the utilitarian calculation, we will consider outcome A to be better than outcome B if the vast majority of persons in this and in several future generations would prefer A to B. In the prudential calculation, we will consider outcome A to be better than outcome B if the vast majority of Americans in this and in several future generations would prefer A to B. Given the subject matter of nuclear war, for many problems value can be equated with human lives, and outcome A can be considered better than outcome B if fewer people are killed by war in A than are killed by war in B. But considering that at least some Americans are on record as preferring being dead to being red, and since many Americans (I think) would prefer a small chance of nuclear attack to a very large chance of Soviet world domination, the equation of value with human lives cannot always be relied upon, especially in the prudential calculation.

In all four models of choice we confine our inquiry to just two nations—the United States and the Soviet Union. These are the primary protagonists in the nuclear drama, and we will argue in a later section that conclusions reached about the bilateral case can also be applied straightforwardly to the multilateral case. Furthermore, we will apply our four models of choice to just three strategies, *Superiority*, *Equivalence*, and *Nuclear Disarmament*. Though there are many strategies for nuclear armament, these three have been at the center of the strategic debate at least since the late 1950s:

> S: Maintain second strike capacity; seek first strike capacity; threaten first and second strikes ("Superiority").

> E: Maintain second strike capacity; do not seek first strike capacity; threaten second strikes only ("Equivalence").

> ND: Do not seek to maintain second strike capacity ("Nuclear Disarmament").

In the statement of these strategies the terminology is standard: Nation A is presumed to have *first-strike capacity* against B if A can launch a nuclear attack on B without fear of suffering unacceptable damage from B's subsequent counterstrike; nation A is said to have *second-strike capacity* against B if A is capable of inflicting unacceptable damage on B after having suffered a nuclear first strike by B.

✦ ✦ ✦ ✦ ✦

II. MINIMAX

Considering the hundreds of billions of dollars the United States has spent on strategic weapons since 1945, it is remarkable how little anyone knows about what would happen should these weapons be used. In an unsettling account of the present state of national defense James Fallows writes:

> There has never been a nuclear war, and nobody knows what a nuclear war would mean. . . . No one knows how these weapons would perform if they were fired; whether they would hit the targets at which they are aimed; whether human society would be set back for decades, centuries as a result. . . . Most strategic arguments (are) disputes of faith rather than fact.[5]

Fallows's gloomy judgment is confirmed by a report presented to Congress in 1979 by the Office of Technology Assessment:

> The effects of nuclear war that cannot be calculated are at least as important as those for which calculations are attempted. Moreover even these very limited calculations are subject to large uncertainties. . . . This is particularly true for indirect effects such as deaths resulting from injuries and the unavailability of medical care, or for economic damage resulting from disruptions and disorganization rather than direct disruption.[6]

Fallows and the OTA do not exaggerate. To date no Minuteman missile has been test-fired from an operational silo; no American ICBM has been properly tested on a North-South trajectory, and missile accuracy reports are a guessing game subject to vagaries of wind, gravitational anomaly, and fratricidal interference from other "friendly" missiles. On top of all this, the entire defense communications network and all electronic guidance systems may be disrupted by the electromagnetic pulses that emanate from thermonuclear blasts.[7]

Anyone who accepts such estimates of the depth of our ignorance about nuclear war will be encouraged to use a principle of choice that does not require knowledge of the probabilities that a given nuclear policy will produce a given result. Of such principles, perhaps the most widely used in both prudential and moral calculation is the Minimax Principle:

> Choose any policy the worst outcome of which is at least as good as the worst outcome of any other policy.

Let us do the Minimax moral calculation first. The worst outcome of both the Superiority Strategy and the Equivalence Strategy is a large scale thermonuclear exchange in which both sides launch as many of their missiles as possible. The worst outcome of the Nuclear Disarmament Strategy is a unilateral nuclear strike on the United States by the Soviet Union followed by whatever increases in Soviet power such a strike might bring. (I list a unilateral Soviet nuclear attack as an outcome of ND not because ND makes such attacks likely but because they are physically possible given ND. Minimax pays no heed to probabilities.) Since the vast majority of persons (especially Russian persons) in this and several future generations would prefer a one-sided attack on the United States to an all-out nuclear war between the United States and the Soviet Union, the utilitarian Minimax Principle declares that the morally right policy is Nuclear Disarmament.

The prudential calculation is not so straightforward. Americans as a group will agree with people at large as to the worst outcome associated with each policy. But it is not so clear that Americans will agree that an outcome in which the Soviet Union attacks an unresponding United States is preferable to an outcome in which the Soviet Union attacks and the United States responds. A reasonable survey of prevailing American sentiments would probably report (a) that a substantial number of Americans would prefer one-sided destruction to two-sided destruction, even if the destroyed side happens to be the American side, on grounds that more lives are saved if only one side is destroyed, and (b) that a substantial number of Americans would prefer two-sided destruction to one-sided destruction, on the grounds that if the Soviet Union attacks the United States, the Soviet Union deserves to be punished. If these are the genuine American preferences, the Minimax Principle yields no verdict in the prudential case. For the record, we might also note that Minimax reasoning fails to distinguish, either morally or prudentially, between the Equivalence Strategy and the Superiority Strategy, since the same disaster is the worst outcome in either case.

III. DOMINANCE

Like Minimax, Dominance is a principle of choice under uncertainty which makes no reference to probabilities of outcomes:

> Choose a policy (if any) yielding results which cannot be improved, no matter what the opposition or nature may choose to do.

Obviously such policies are rarely found, but many writers feel that such a dominant strategy is available in the arena of nuclear choice. For simplicity, let us consider only the Equivalence Strategy and the Nuclear Disarmament Strategy, and let us assume that the only variable in the environment is the Soviet choice between E and ND. Since each side has two options, there are four outcomes:

1. The United States arms; the Soviet Union disarms;
2. The United States and the Soviet Union both disarm;
3. The United States and the Soviet Union both arm; and
4. The United States disarms; the Soviet Union arms.

If we suppose (as most students of strategy do) that the vast majority of American people prefer these outcomes in the order in which they are presented, then prudentially the United States should remain armed, no matter what the Soviet Union does.[8] By the Dominance Principle, then, the United States should stick with Equivalence.

Since these ratings are made from the national point of view, the conclusion thus far is strictly prudential. The moral argument yields surprisingly different results. Presumably a large majority of people in the world prefer 2 to 1, that is, they prefer neither side having nuclear arms to one side having them. This suffices to show that Equivalence does not dominate from the moral point of view. Furthermore, if we assume that a large majority of people in the world, fearful of all-out nuclear war, prefer that the United States practice ND even if the Soviet Union does not, it is Nuclear Disarmament that dominates from the moral point of view.

We have the consistent but disagreeable result that, if we follow Dominance, prudence dictates one policy while morality dictates another. We could challenge this conclusion by making different assessments of preferences. But there are other grounds which might lead us to conclude that the real problem here is not the assessment of preferences but the Dominance Principle itself.

IV. Conceptual Problems

Both the Minimax and the Dominance Principles are examples of game-theoretical strategic principles that treat each outcome as the result of equally permissible and equally possible moves in a gamelike situation. Rapoport, Green, and others in the past have criticized certain aspects of the game-theoretical approach;[9] its tendency, for example, to treat situations of nuclear strategy as zero sum games in which cooperation is impossible, rather than as constant sum games in which it can be prudent to cooperate. But the game-theoretical approach is inadequate in a way that cannot be remedied by shifting to broader principles and a wider range of games. In the standard logic of games each alternative is taken as given, and there is no room for calculating how the threat to make one move will influence the chance that another move is made, a consideration which is at the heart of the argument for deterrence. Consider the following argument, which proceeds on the basis of fixed alternatives: "The logical possibilities are that either the Soviets will attack or they will not attack. If they attack, there is no point in threatening to counterattack, since the whole point of the threat was to prevent the attack. If they do not attack, there is no point in threatening to counterattack, since there is no initial attack for the threat to deter: we conclude, therefore, nuclear threats are futile, or they are otiose." The notion that threats might diminish the chance of attack goes by the board. Perhaps we should dispense with deterrence, but the argument for dispensing with it cannot be this easy!

Even worse difficulties can be generated by combining information about outcomes with the dominance principle. Suppose that Americans prefer outcomes 1 through 4 as stated in the previous Section, and suppose that it is given information that (a) whenever the United States arms, the Soviet Union will arm, and that (b) whenever the United States disarms, the Soviet Union will disarm. Since Americans prefer mutual disarmament to mutual armament, the preferred strategy in the light of the given information is for the United States to disarm. But game-theoretical reasoning still insists that the preferred strategy is to remain armed. Even if the Soviets will disarm when the United States disarms, it remains true that they will either arm or disarm. If they arm, it is better for the United States to arm. If they disarm, it is better for the United States to arm. Therefore the United States should arm in any event. The result will be mutual armament, a situation worse than that which could confidently be achieved by the choice of disarmament. It is not possible here to review all the systems devised in recent years by game theorists attempting to cope with this problem. Suffice it to say that there is a consensus that something must be done but no consensus about what to do, and the state of the field is sufficiently unsettled to warrant serious investigation of more information-sensitive decision principles.[10]

✦ ✦ ✦ ✦ ✦

VI. Expected Value

Perhaps the most natural of all responses to the problem of uncertainty is to discount the weight of consequences by whatever chance there is that they will not occur. To compute the "expected value" of a policy, then, we should consider each possible outcome of the policy, multiply the utility of that outcome by the probability that it will occur, and take the sum of all these products. In the area of nuclear strategy we cannot supply precise numbers for the probabilities of the outcomes, nor can we attempt to supply precise figures for the corresponding utilities. Nevertheless, we *do* have much more information about these subjects than the orderings of probabilities to which we were restricted in the Disaster Avoidance model, and what imprecision there is in our information can be respected by stating the information in the form of approximations. For example, we can classify the probability of outcomes as "negligible," "small but substantial," "fifty-fifty," "very likely," and "almost certain," and we can classify outcomes as "extremely bad," "bad," "neutral," and so forth. In considering the products of utilities and outcomes, we can neglect all outcomes of negligible probability, and all outcomes of small but substantial probability *except* those classified as extremely good or extremely bad. In many cases, use of such estimates will yield surprisingly definite results.

Now, what are the "outcomes" the probabilities of which we ought to consider? Given the traditionally assumed goals of deterrence, we should certainly consider the effects of each policy on the probability of nuclear war, the probability of Soviet non-nuclear aggression, and the probability of Soviet nuclear blackmail. As we have noted, in considering the probability of nuclear war, it is essential to distinguish the probability of a one-sided nuclear strike from the probability of all-out nuclear war. Among other outcomes, we will consider only the effects of nuclear strategies on military spending, since the impact of policies on spending can be determined with little controversy. Since we have four outcomes and three policies to consider, the probabilities can be represented on a three-by-four grid (see Table 1). Each probability assessment will be defended in turn.

Table 1

	One-sided Strike*	All-out Nuclear War	Soviet Aggression	Very High Military Spending
Superiority	Fifty-fifty [a]	Fifty-fifty [b]	Small [c]	Certain [d]
Equivalence	Small [e]	Small [f]	Small [g]	Fifty-fifty [h]
Nuclear Disarmament	Small [I]	Small [j]	Small [k]	Small [l]

* A "one-sided strike" is a first strike that may or may not be answered by a second strike. A comparison of the probability of one-sided strikes and two-sided strikes in a given row indicates that a first strike will lead to an all-out nuclear war.

Value of the Superiority Strategy

[a] Strategists disagree about the probability of Soviet or American first strike under the Superiority Strategy. All students of the subject rate it as having at least a small but substantial probability. I believe that it is more reasonable to rate the probability as fifty-fifty within a time frame of about fifty years, since (1) every real or presumed step towards first strike capacity by either side raises the chance of a preemptive first strike by the side falling behind; (2) the concentration on technological development prompted by the Superiority Strategy raises that chance of a technological breakthrough that might destabilize the balance of power; (3) the increasing technological complexity of weapons required by the Superiority Strategy raises the chance of a first strike as a result of accident or mistake; (4) the constant changes of weaponry required by the Superiority Strategy creates pressure for proliferation, either because obsolete weapons are constantly disposed of on the international arms market or because wealthy developing countries, dazzled by new weapons, make buys to keep up with appearances.

[b] Under Superiority, the chance of an American second strike—given a Soviet first strike—is practically the same as the chance of a Soviet first strike. Though it is always possible that the President or his survivor will not respond to a Soviet first strike, the military and technological systems installed under the Superiority Strategy are geared for belligerence. Accordingly the chance of an American failure to respond is negligible.

[c] Even in the face of the Superiority Strategy, the chance of Soviet nonnuclear aggression (an invasion of West Germany or Iran, for example) must be rated as small but not negligible. The prospect of an American first strike in response to a Soviet conventional attack may not be taken seriously by the Soviets, especially if Soviet military personnel think that they can deter any American first strike with the prospect of a massive Soviet second strike.

[d] The sums of money required to sustain the Superiority Strategy are staggering. The Reagan administration's rejection of SALT and its apparent acceptance of the Superiority Strategy will produce an increase in the fraction of the American gross national product devoted to defense from five to six and one-half percent: an increase of over $150 billion per year over the Carter projections, which were largely keyed to the Equivalence Strategy.

Value of the Equivalence Strategy

[e] Most students of strategy agree that the chance of an American or Soviet first strike under the Equivalence Strategy is small but substantial. The peculiar pressures for a first strike listed under the Superiority Strategy are absent, but there is still the chance of a first strike through accident, mistake, human folly, or a suicidal leadership.

[f] Since the chance of a first strike is less under Equivalence than under Superiority, there is less chance of an all-out nuclear war under Equivalence than under Superiority. The chance of a first strike under Equivalence is small, and the

chance of all-out war following a first strike is smaller still. Since the primary aim of the Equivalence Strategy is not to "defeat" the Soviet Union or to develop a first-strike capacity, but to deter a Soviet first strike, it may be obvious to the President or his survivor that once a Soviet first strike is actually launched, there is no point whatsoever in proceeding with an American second strike. If the chance that the President will fail to respond is substantial, the chance of an all-out war under Equivalence is considerably less than the chance of a first strike under Equivalence.[11] On the other hand, the credibility of the American deterrent to a first strike depends on the perception by Soviet planners that an American second strike is inevitable once a Soviet first strike is launched, and the President and his defense strategists may decide that the only convincing way to create this perception is to make the American second strike a *semi-automatic* response. Thus it might be difficult to stop an American second strike even if the President wished to forgo it. On balance, it seems reasonable to rate the chance of the second strike as greater than one-half the chance that the Soviet first strike will be launched. This would make the chance small but still substantial.

[g] Over the years two arguments have been proposed to show that Superiority provides a more effective deterrent against Soviet aggression than does Equivalence.

(1) The Superiority Strategy requires constant technological innovation, and technological innovation is an area in which the United States possesses a relative advantage. If the United States presses forward with strategic weapons development, the Soviet Union will be so exhausted from the strain of keeping up with the United States that it will have little money or energy left over for nonnuclear aggression. In the end, the strain such competition will exert on the Soviet economy might produce food riots like those in Poland in 1970, and might even bring down the Soviet socioeconomic system.

But since "the strain of keeping up" did not stop the Soviets from invading Hungary, Czechoslovakia, and Afghanistan, the level of expenditure needed to produce truly effective strain is unknown. Furthermore, the assumption of *relative* economic stress is undemonstrated: at least one economist who has seriously studied the subject has argued on various grounds that a unit of military spending by the United States disrupts the American economy far more than the equivalent military spending by the Soviet Union.[12]

(2) It is occasionally argued that the Soviets will take the possibility of an American second strike more seriously under the Superiority Strategy than under the Equivalence Strategy, since the Superiority Strategy gives the United States something closer to first-strike capacity and therefore something less to fear from a Soviet second strike.

But in the game of nuclear strategy one cannot "almost" have first-strike capacity; one either has it or one doesn't. There is no reason to think that the Superiority Strategy will ever yield first-strike capacity, since the Soviet Union will feel forced to match the United States step for step. The Soviets know that the President will never be confident enough in American striking capacity to risk the survival of the United States on a nuclear response to Soviet nonnuclear aggression. Consequently, there is no reason to think that Superiority provides a better deterrent against Soviet aggression than does Equivalence. The chance of serious nonnuclear Soviet aggression under Equivalence is small.

[h] In the presence of serious efforts at arms control, expenditures for strategic weapons will be much less under Equivalence than under Superiority. If efforts at arms control fail, then expenditures will remain very high. The chance of very high expenditures under Equivalence would best be put at about fifty-fifty.

Value of the Nuclear Disarmament Strategy

[i] Most strategists are agreed that the chance of a Soviet first strike under the Equivalence Strategy is small. I believe that the chance of a Soviet first strike is small even under the strategy of Nuclear Disarmament.

(1) Since under Nuclear Disarmament at most one side retains nuclear arms, the chance of nuclear war occurring by accident is reduced at least by one half, relative to the Equivalence Strategy. Since only half the technology is deployed, there is only half the chance of a mechanical malfunction leading to war.

(2) Since at most one side remains armed, there is considerably less chance under Nuclear Disarmament that a nuclear war will occur by mistake. The principal mistake that might cause a nuclear war is the mistake of erroneously thinking that the other side is about to launch a nuclear attack. Such mistakes create enormous pressure for the launching of preemptive strikes, in order to get one's weapons in the air before they are destroyed on the ground. There is no chance that this mistake can occur under Nuclear Disarmament. The side that remains armed (if any) need not fear that the other side will launch a nuclear attack. The side that chooses to disarm cannot be tempted to launch a preemptive strike no matter what it believes the other side is doing, since it has no weapons with which to launch the strike.

(3) Even the opponents of Nuclear Disarmament describe the main peril of nuclear disarmament as nuclear blackmail by the Soviet Union. Opponents of disarmament apparently feel that after nuclear disarmament, nuclear threats are far more probable than nuclear disasters.

(4) Though nuclear weapons are not inherently more destructive than other sorts of weapons, conceived or actual (the napalm raids on Tokyo in March 1945 caused more deaths than Hiroshima or Nagasaki), nuclear weapons are universally *perceived* as different in kind from nonnuclear weapons. The diplomatic losses a nation would incur upon using even tactical nuclear weapons would be immense.

(5) A large scale nuclear attack by the Soviet Union against the United States might contaminate the American and Canadian Great Plains, a major source of Soviet grain imports. The Soviets could still turn to Argentina, but the price of grain after the attack would skyrocket, and no combination of Argentinean, Australian, or other grain sources could possibly compensate for American or Canadian losses.

(6) The Soviets will find it difficult to find actual military situations in which it will be practical to use atomic weapons against the United States, or against anyone else. Nuclear weapons proved superfluous in the Soviet invasions of Hungary and Czechoslovakia, and they do not seem to be practicable in Afghanistan, where the human costs of the Soviet attempt to regain control are high. If the Soviets did not use nuclear weapons against China between 1960 and 1964 in order to prevent the development of Chinese nuclear capacity, it is hardly likely that they could use them against a nonnuclear United States. Of course it is always *possible* that the Soviet Union might launch a nuclear attack against a nonnuclear United States, perhaps as an escalatory step in a conventional conflict, but it is also *possible* that the Soviet Union will launch a nuclear attack on the United States *right now*, despite the present situation of the Equivalence. The point is that there is no such thing as a guarantee against nuclear attack, but the probability of an actual attack is small under either strategy.

[j] The chance of all-out nuclear war under the Equivalence Strategy is slight, but the chance of all-out nuclear war under Nuclear Disarmament is zero. There cannot be a two-sided nuclear war if only one side possesses nuclear arms.

[k] In considering the threat of Soviet nonnuclear aggression under Nuclear Disarmament, we must consider Soviet nuclear threats—usually called "nuclear blackmail"—as well as possible uses of conventional arms by the Soviets.

(1) Suppose that the United States unilaterally gives up second-strike-capacity. What are the odds that the Soviet Union would attempt to influence American behavior through nuclear threats? Obviously, one's views about the chances for successful nuclear blackmail depends on one's views about the chances of a Soviet first strike against a nonnuclear United States. If the chances of a Soviet first strike are slight, then the chances of successful blackmail will also be slight. We have already argued on a variety of grounds that chances of a Soviet strike under ND are small. I would suggest that the ability of the Soviet Union to manipulate a nonnuclear United States would be the same as the ability of the United States to manipulate the Soviet Union from 1945 to 1949, when strategic conditions were reversed. Anyone who reflects on events from 1945 to 1949 will conclude that nuclear threats have little effect on nations capable of acting with resolve.

There is always the chance that the Soviet Union will carry out its nuclear threats, but there is always the chance that the Soviet Union will carry out its threats even if the United States retains nuclear weapons. There is no device that provides a guarantee against nuclear blackmail. Consequently it cannot be argued that Equivalence provides a guarantee against blackmail that Nuclear Disarmament does not.

The foregoing dismissal of nuclear blackmail violates conventional strategic wisdom, which is concerned with nuclear blackmail almost to obsession. Numerous authors, for example, cite the swift fall of Japan after Hiroshima as evidence of the strategic usefulness of nuclear weapons and nuclear threats. The case of Japan is worth considering. Contrary to the canonical view certified by Secretary Stimson in his famous (and self-serving) *Harper's* article in 1947,[13] I believe that the bombings of Hiroshima and Nagasaki had almost no effect on events leading to the surrender of Japan. If so, the force of the Japanese precedent, which still influences strategic thought, is greatly attenuated.

Obviously the bombings of Hiroshima and Nagasaki had no effect on the popular desire for peace in Japan, since the Japanese public did not know of the atomic bombings until the war was over. What is more surprising is that the bombings do not seem to have influenced either the Emperor or the military command in making the decision to sue for peace. The Emperor, as is now well known, had decided for peace as early as January 1945, and if he was set on peace in January, he did not need the bombings of August to make up his mind. The military, on the other hand, do not seem to have desired peace even after the bombs were dropped; the record shows that the military (a) correctly surmised that the United States had a small supply of these bombs, (b) debated improved antiaircraft measures to prevent any further bombs from being delivered, and (c) correctly inferred that bombs of this type could not be used to support a ground invasion, which they felt they could repulse with sufficient success to secure a conditional surrender. What tipped the political scales so that the Emperor could find his way to peace was not the bombing of Nagasaki on 9 August, but the Russian declaration of war on 8 August. Unaware of Stalin's commitment at Yalta to enter the war against Japan, the Japanese had hoped through the spring and summer of 1945 that the Soviets would mediate a negotiated settlement between the United States and Japan rather than send the Red Army into a new theater of war. When the Russians invaded Manchuria on 9 August, Premier Suzuki, according to reports, cried, "The game is over," and when the Emperor demanded surrender from the Council of Elders on 10 August, he never mentioned atomic bombs as the occasion of his demand for peace.[14] Little can be inferred from such evidence about the effectiveness of nuclear threats.

(2) The strategy of Nuclear Disarmament does not forbid uses of conventional arms in response to acts of aggression. Since there is no reason to believe that adoption of the strategy of Nuclear Disarmament by the United States will make acts of Soviet aggression any more palatable than they are at present, in all probability the American government under ND will appropriate funds for conventional arms sufficient to provide a deterrent to Soviet aggression roughly comparable to the deterrent provided by nuclear arms under S and E. This argument assumes that the deterrent effects of the American strategic nuclear arsenal (whatever they are) can be obtained with a developed arsenal of modern conventional weapons. A review of the difficulties involved in the use of strategic nuclear weapons in concrete situations may convince the reader that conventional weapons can match the deterrent effect of nuclear weapons. Indeed, the whole development of "flexible response" systems during the McNamara era testifies to the widespread recognition that strategic nuclear weapons provide little leverage to nations who would seek to control the flow of world events.

[1] Since it is impossible to predict how much money must be spent on conventional forces in order to supply a deterrent equal to the present (nuclear) deterrent against Soviet nonnuclear aggression, it is possible that levels of military spending

under ND will be greater than levels under E. But it is also possible that the levels of spending will be much less. The technical equipment to maintain E is fantastically expensive, but the labor costs of training and improving conventional forces can also be staggering. All things considered, it is still likely that spending will be less under ND than under E, especially if the draft is revived.

Comparison of Superiority and Equivalence

The chance of a Soviet first strike is greater under Superiority than under Equivalence, and the chance of all-out nuclear war is greater under Superiority than under Equivalence. The ability of Equivalence to deter Soviet nonnuclear aggression is equal to the ability of Superiority to deter such aggression, and the Equivalence strategy costs less. Thus Equivalence is preferable to Superiority from both the prudential and the moral point of view.

Comparison of Equivalence and Nuclear Disarmament

We have argued that Nuclear Disarmament and Equivalence are equal in their ability to deter Soviet nonnuclear aggression. In the category of military spending Nuclear Disarmament is preferable to Equivalence. In the category of "all-out war" ND is clearly superior to E, and in the category of "first strikes," ND seems to be about equal to E. Thus we have what seems to be a decisive prudential and moral argument in favor of Nuclear Disarmament: in every category, ND is either equal to or superior to E.

✦ ✦ ✦ ✦ ✦

VIII. Multilateral Considerations

The preceding conclusions resulted from arguments limited to relations between the United States and the Soviet Union. Do these results change if we consider the present multilateral situation? Is unilateral disarmament still preferable when many nations have bombs? The expansion of the nuclear club does seem to have adversely affected the political movement for nuclear disarmament, which flourished in the late 1950s and early 1960s. If only two nations have nuclear weapons, nuclear disarmament by one may provoke nuclear disarmament in the other, producing the ideal result of general nuclear disarmament. But if many nations possess nuclear weapons, disarmament by one can hardly be expected to provoke disarmament by all of the others, and each armed nation, considering the fact that at least some other nations will continue to retain nuclear arms, may feel compelled to keep its weapons in order to deter the hard-core non-cooperators. Even the most ardent supporters of disarmament become disheartened when they consider the difficulties of arranging a simultaneous surrender of nuclear weapons by seven or more independent nation states.

None of the arguments of the preceding sections, however, depends on the assumption that the Soviet Union will disarm if the United States arms, nor do they depend on the assumption that nuclear disarmament by the United States will increase the probability that the Soviet Union will disarm. Since the geographical situation of the Soviet Union makes Soviet disarmament contingent upon disarmament by both NATO and the Chinese, and since it is generally believed by the Soviet leadership that "backwardness" has been the source of Russian catastrophes across the centuries, it is highly unlikely that the Soviet Union will disarm *no matter what* the United States does. The fact remains that there are fewer expected deaths, and fewer expected American deaths, under ND than under E.

There are several considerations which show that the case for disarmament in the multilateral situation is as strong as or stronger than the case for disarmament in the bilateral situation. The case for Nuclear Disarmament is *at least as strong* in the multilateral situation because the multilateral case can legitimately be decomposed into a set of bilateral cases. The main reason why ND is preferable to E in the bilateral case is that the costs of war, if it occurs, are much higher under E than under ND, making ND preferable even if the chance of *a* war is higher under ND than under E. This argument makes no use of special information about the United States and the Soviet Union, and, if it is sound at all, it is also sound for the U.S.-China case, the China-U.S.S.R. case, the U.S.S.R.-NATO case, and all of the other cases that in sum make up the multilateral problem.

The case for ND in the multilateral situation is *stronger than* the case for ND in the bilateral situation if one considers the import of Richard's theorem, proved in the 1930s, that *if every pair of a triplet of nations is stable, the triplet itself may still be unstable.*[15] For example, even if relations between the United States and the Soviet Union, the Soviet Union and China, and China and the United States are relatively stable, it is possible that the ensemble of these three nations is unstable, producing an arms race, and perhaps even a war. On the other hand, relative stability can be restored by any nation in the triplet that unilaterally withdraws from the nuclear club. Thus unilateral disarmament reduces the chance of war among those nations that do not choose to disarm, a result that recommends itself both prudentially and morally. In sum, if a nation is better off with Nuclear Disarmament in the bilateral case, it is even better off with Nuclear Disarmament in the multilateral case.

IX. FROM MORALS TO POLITICS

Nuclear Disarmament, Superiority, and Equivalence are the nuclear strategies most discussed by theorists, and other strategies are largely variants or specifications of these three. If utilitarianism favors Nuclear Disarmament over Superiority and Equivalence, it favors Nuclear Disarmament *tout court*. For utilitarians, ND is morally right, and ought to be adopted.

It remains to consider whether it is also morally right to *advocate* or *support* Nuclear Disarmament. Support is logically distinct from adoption, and acts of support have their own sets of consequences. It is possible, and by no means paradoxical, that within the utilitarian framework support for the morally right policy may be morally wrong.

The commonest situation where support for the right leads to the wrong is a three-way election in which support for the best candidate will elect the worst, while support for the second best outcome will defeat the worst. Moderate liberals whose support for Charles Goodell over Richard Ottinger led to the election of James Buckley in 1972 and whose support for Jacob Javits over Elisabeth Holtzman led to the election of Al d'Amato in 1980 found themselves in each case with their least preferred candidate. In such situations utilitarianism joins hands with a Weberian ethic of responsibility and calls on moral agents to support the second best.

It is often alleged that the competition between S, E, and ND is rather like the Senate races in New York in 1972 and 1980, and many who agree that ND is morally superior to E fear that open advocacy of ND will drain support from E and lead to victory for the Superiority Strategy. The flaw in this reasoning is to compare a three-way election with winners determined by votes to a three-way policy choice with winners determined by the ultimate vector of political pressure. With candidates and votes, support for the extreme steals votes from the center. With policies and pressures, pressure from one extreme helps support the center against pressure from the other. In choosing platforms and policies, Americans have traditionally shied away from extremes, and a three-way race between S, E, and ND places E in the central position historically favored by the American people. A two-way race, which places the "center" between Equivalence and Superiority, allows the supporters of Superiority to argue that their strategy is no more extreme than Equivalence. If the moral principle which evaluates support of strategic policies (as opposed to the policies themselves) determines that support should be exercised in the way most likely to defeat Superiority, there is as much a case for public support of Nuclear Disarmament as there is for Nuclear Disarmament itself.

READING ENDNOTES

The author would like to thank the National Endowment for the Humanities for fellowship support during the period of time in which this article was written. Thanks are also due to Mrs. Esther Gutenberg for her help and patience.

1. In the sequence of these things, the idea of nuclear threats as a deterrent to nuclear war seems, oddly, to have come first. As early as 1946, Bernard Brodie wrote:

   The first and most vital step in any American security program for the age of atomic bombs is to take measures to guarantee to ourselves in case of attack the possibility of retaliation in kind. The writer in making this statement is not for the moment concerned about who will win the next war in which atomic bombs have been used. Thus far the chief purpose of our military establishment has been to win wars. From now on its chief purpose must be to avert them. It can have almost no other useful purpose (Bernard Brodie, ed., *The Absolute Weapon* [New York: Harcourt Brace, 1946], p. 76).

But the idea of nuclear retaliation as a deterrent to nonnuclear aggression followed soon after, and to this date the United States has persistently and repeatedly refused to announce a policy of "no first use."

2. The case that the 1946 Baruch Plan for the internationalization of atomic weapons was deliberately designed to be nonnegotiable is persuasively made by Gregg Herken, *The Winning Weapon: The Atomic Bomb in the Cold War* (New York: Knopf, 1980). According to Herken the earlier Acheson-Lilienthal plan might have been negotiable.

3. Nigel Calder in *Nuclear Nightmares: An Investigation into Possible Wars* (New York: Viking, 1980), p. 42 notes that the NATO concept of deterring a Warsaw pact invasion of West Germany with NATO nuclear retaliation assumes that NATO will not be deterred from this nuclear first strike by the thought of a massive Soviet second strike in return. Calder correctly observes that this is odd thinking, since the possibility of an American second strike is supposed to be the threat which deters a Soviet first strike. Apparently the tacticians believe that the thought of destruction of Russian cities will deter the Soviets in a way that the thought of the destruction of American cities will not deter NATO. Since this belief is very probably false, we have a paradox: either nuclear deterrence will deter nonnuclear aggression but not nuclear aggression or it will deter nuclear aggression but not nonnuclear aggression. Thus deterrence in the European theater cannot simultaneously do the two jobs for which it was originally designed: deterring Soviet aggression, and deterring nuclear war.

4. The gun is the M-16 and the plane is the F-111. For the tragic history of the M-16 see James Fallows, *National Defense* (New York: Random House, 1981), chap. 4.

5. Fallows, *National Defense*, pp. 139–40.

6. "The Effects of Nuclear War," U.S. Congress, Office of Technology Assessment, 1979, p. 3.

7. On the electromagnetic pulse or EMP, see Janet Raloff, "EMP: A Sleeping Dragon," *Science News*, 9 May 1981, pp. 300–302, and 16 May 1981, pp. 314–15.

8. Technically, it might be possible to develop a prudential case for nuclear disarmament as follows: (a) take all alleged preferences for two-sided destruction, (b) subtract from these all preferences based on the idea that a second strike against Russia is needed to deter their first strike; this idea is illicit since the preference poll in all cases assumes that the first strike has already occurred, and (c) subtract all preferences based on considerations of retributive justice on the grounds that these are political preferences rather than personal evaluations of the utility present in the situations judged. (For the distinction between political preferences and personal preferences see Ronald Dworkin, "What is Equality? Part 1: Equality of Welfare," *Philosophy & Public Affairs* 10, no. 3 [Summer 1981]: 197–98.) The residue of support for nuclear retaliation might be small enough for us to judge that the American people prudentially prefer disarmament.

9. For criticisms of the zero-sum approach to nuclear strategy see Anatol Rapoport, *Strategy and Conscience* (New York: Harper & Row, 1964); and Philip Green, *Deadly Logic* (Columbus, OH: Ohio State University Press, 1966).

10. For approaches which attempt to break out of the static analyses which have prevailed since von Neumann and Morgenstern see Nigel Howard, *Paradoxes of Rationality* (Cambridge, MA: The M.I.T. Press, 1971); Michael Taylor, *Anarchism and Cooperation* (New York: John Wiley & Sons, 1976); and Steven Brams and Donald Wittman, "Nonmyopic Equilibria in a 2 × 2 Games" (forthcoming). Howard, Taylor, and Brams and Wittman all note that the prudential argument for armament presented here for the United States will lead Soviet strategists to the same result, and thus individual prudence produces a collective result (mutual armament), which is less liked by each side than mutual disarmament. In sum, all these authors assume that nuclear arms races are Prisoners' Dilemmas. Howard's theory of metagames, Taylor's theory of supergames, and the Brams/Wittman theory of moves all try to show that a proper theory of games will establish that the mutually preferred solution is an equilibrium from which prudent players will not depart. I find it impossible to connect Howard's metagame equilibria with the psychology of the players; see, *contra* Howard, John Harsanyi, "Communication," *American Political Science Review* 68 (1974): 729-31; 1692–95. Taylor's supergame equilibria require repeated plays of the game, and for obvious reasons repeated plays of games involving nuclear war have little relation to reality. Furthermore, Taylor's equilibria require low discount rates, and in most thought about nuclear

war, long run payoffs are highly discounted in favor of such short run results as political intimidation or war prevention. Bram's theory of moves is not affected by discount rates, but it provides no clue as to how to move to the cooperative solution when history has trapped players in a noncooperative equilibrium. A far better approach to escaping the Prisoners' Dilemma is to never enter into it, and I have suggested ("Ethics and Nuclear Deterrence," in *Moral Problems* 2d ed., ed. James Rachels [New York: Harper & Row, 1975], pp. 332–45) that nuclear arms races in particular are not Prisoners' Dilemmas if the payoffs are properly evaluated.

11. The thought that an American President may lack the nerve to destroy civilization depresses the military mind. In stating the requirements of deterrence, General Maxwell Taylor writes, "So understood, deterrence depends essentially on an assured destruction capability, a strong communications net, and a strong President unlikely to flinch from his responsibility.... Such reflections emphasize the importance of the character and will of the President as a factor adding to the deterrent effect of our weapons. Since the attitude of the President will be strongly influenced by that of the people whom he represents, national character also participates in the effectiveness and stability of deterrence.... In addition to the moral [*sic*] qualities of the President and the nation there are a number of other factors which may stabilize or undermine deterrence" (Maxwell Taylor, *Precarious Security* [New York: W.W. Norton, 1976], pp. 68–69). On the other hand, some military figures, at least in their public statements, are entirely confident that the President will respond and launch the second strike. General George Seignious, former director of the joint staff of the Joint Chiefs of Staff, testified in 1979, "I find such a surrender scenario irresponsible—for it sends the wrong message to the Soviets. We have not built and maintained our strategic forces—at the cost of billions—in order to weaken their deterrent impact by telling the Russians and the world that we would back down—when, in fact, we would not" (quoted in Herbert Scoville, *MX: Prescription for Disaster* [Cambridge, MA: The M.I.T. Press, 1981], p. 82).

12. See Seymour Melman, *Our Depleted Society* (New York: Holt, Rinehart & Winston, 1965), and *Pentagon Capitalism* (New York: McGraw-Hill, 1970).

13. Stimson's "The Decision to Use the Atomic Bomb" appeared in the February 1947 *Harper's Magazine*, pp. 97–107. Typical of Stimson's *post hoc ergo propter hoc* is:

> We believed that out attacks struck cities which must certainly be important to the Japanese military leaders, both Army and Navy, and we waited for a result. We waited one day.

14. For the Emperor's active attempts to obtain peace see Herbert Feis, *The Atomic Bomb and the End of World War II* (Princeton: Princeton University Press, 1966), p. 66. For the military response to the atomic bombings see Hanson Baldwin, *Great Mistakes of the War* (New York: Collins-Knowlton-Wing, 1950), pp. 87–107. For Suzuki's remark that "The game is over" see W. Craig, *The Fall of Japan* (New York: Dial, 1967), p. 107. One interesting suggestion about the special effectiveness of the atomic bomb against Japan is found in a remark made by General Marshall to David Lilienthal in 1947, "We didn't realize its value to give the Japanese such a shock that they could surrender without loss of face" (quoted in Feis, *The Atomic Bomb*, p. 6). Marshall's remark is prima facie reasonable, but I can find nothing in the documents on the Japanese side that supports it.

15. Lewis Fry Richardson, *Arms and Insecurity* (Chicago: Quadrangle, 1960), chap. 9. See also E. Gold's "biographical preface" in L.F. Richardson, *Statistics of Deadly Quarrels*, ed. Quincy Wright and C.C. Lienau (Chicago: Quadrangle, 1960), p. xxv.

DEFINITIONS AND EXPLANATIONS

Expected utility: In calculating utility under conditions of uncertainty, we use the measure of expected utility. Expected utility is a function of two variables: the utility of an outcome and the probability that it will result from your choice. Thus computing expected utility involves this simple calculation: the utility of an outcome $\times$ the probability that it will occur = expected utility.

Game theory: Game theory is a fairly recent off-shoot of rational choice theory. Rational choice theory is designed to explain what makes a given choice rational when an agent's choice is the only factor that determines which outcome will be brought about. Many people have accepted that individual utility maximization is the correct principle of rational choice for individuals. Often, however, we face what are called strategic choice situations, where the outcome that will eventually be brought about is not determined just by the choice of one agent, but by the combined choices of at least two people. In such cases, what is rational for one person to do depends, in part, upon what they expect the other person to do, and vice versa. But neither knows for sure what the other will do. Suppose, for example, that I am trying to avoid you and you are trying to meet me. We both know that a mutual friend has invited the other to a party. What should I do: go to the party or stay home? The answer will depend, in part, on whether I think you will go to the party or not. Supposing I really do not want to see you, then if I think there is even a small chance that you are going to go, I should stay home. But since you want to meet me, you are likewise likely to try to guess whether I will go or not in trying to decide what you should do. Such situations, where the outcome brought about (we meet contrary to my wishes or we don't contrary to your wishes) depends on the choices of both of us, is a strategic choice situation. Game theory is the theory of rational choice under such conditions. Because the situation with respect to choices involving nuclear armament or disarmament is likewise a strategic situation, between two or more nations, game theory has been applied to try to determine which possible strategy it is rational for countries to adopt.

Nuclear deterrence: All deterrence involves the use of threats to try to modify the behaviour of another person. Criminal law uses the threat of legal punishment, for example, to try to ensure that anyone who might be tempted to break the law does not do so. The threat is supposed to make it more likely that people will do as the law requires. In the case of nuclear deterrence, one state or political group threatens to use nuclear weapons as a deterrent to nuclear war. That is, one state says to all others that it will use nuclear weapons if any of the other states does. The hope is that by doing so the other states will be more likely not to use nuclear weapons first. Like all deterrence strategies, the likelihood that such a threat will be effective in deterring the behaviour it is meant to deter depends in part on the credibility of the threat: it must be fairly believable.

Post hoc ergo propter hoc: Latin, meaning after this, therefore because of this. This is the name of a fallacy. The mistake is in thinking that just because one thing or event followed another, that the first caused the second. It is to infer a causal connection between two events, just because one followed the other. In the case of nuclear deterrence, the common mistake is to assume that just because one state has adopted the policy of nuclear deterrence (has armed and threatened to use nuclear weapons if attacked), that policy must be responsible for the subsequent fact that they have not been attacked. In other words, it is to assume that the threat has caused the absence of nuclear war. This is a mistake, because there may be many other explanations for why states have not used nuclear weapons.

QUESTIONS

1. What is the Minimax principle of choice? Can you imagine a situation in which it is the rational principle to follow?

2. What is the Dominance principle of choice? Can you imagine a situation in which it is the rational principle to follow?

3. What is the principle of Expected Utility Maximization? Can you imagine a situation in which it is the rational principle to follow?

4. How does the policy of deterrence lead to a proliferation of weapons?

5. Lackey argues that Minimax supports nuclear disarmament as the moral choice (even if it is unilateral, one-sided disarmament). Why would most people prefer ND to S or E on Minimax grounds? What is Lackey's argument?

6. Lackey argues that Dominance supports nuclear disarmament as the moral choice (even if it is unilateral, one-sided disarmament). Why would most people prefer ND to S or E on Dominance grounds? What is Lackey's argument?

7. Lackey argues that Expected Value Maximization supports nuclear disarmament as the moral choice (even if it is unilateral, one-sided disarmament). Why would most people prefer ND to S or E on Expected Value Maximizing grounds? What is Lackey's argument?

8. When Lackey wrote this paper in 1982 the international community was quite different than it is today. Which of his assumptions or conclusions have been supported by developments over the past twenty years?

9. Why should we fear a nuclear war beginning by mistake more than we should fear an intentional use of nuclear weapons? Are those reasons stronger or weaker today than they were when Lackey wrote?

10. Does the increased use of terrorism in the international arena undermine any of Lackey's assumptions for the moral superiority of nuclear disarmament?

11. If it would be immoral to actually use nuclear weapons in a first strike situation, is it also immoral to threaten to use them in this way? What could a utilitarian say about this?

✦ ✦ ✦

Susan Dimock and Christopher Tucker, Affirmative Action and Employment Equity in Canada

Susan Dimock and Christopher Tucker argue that affirmative action policies are not justified. They first briefly consider justice-based arguments. They consider the suggestion that those who have been adversely discriminated against in the past now deserve to be compensated for those past wrongs as a matter of corrective justice, or that those who currently face diminished life prospects because of past discrimination must be advantaged now as a matter of distributive justice. They reject both sets of arguments from justice.

The main portion of Dimock and Tucker's paper focuses on the consequences of affirmative action policies. Such policies have been justified by arguing that the instantiation of such policies will likely lead to better consequences than the lack of them. Affirmative action policies designed to promote a multicultural workforce have been argued to better serve the needs of a multicultural community. Such policies have also been argued to reduce prejudice, which leads to inefficient judgements, and to increase such historically disadvantaged group members' self esteem, by presenting them with relevant role models in the workforce. Dimock and Tucker respond to each in turn.

Their main focus, however, is on the role that affirmative action might be thought to play in the elimination of prejudicial attitudes that are the main cause of discrimination. It is shown that this psychological case for affirmative action is in even worse shape than the justice-based ones. There are several psychological studies that strongly suggest that affirmative action policies do not lead to a less prejudiced population, but instead more firmly entrench prejudiced attitudes. Further, the very existence of affirmative action policies lead people to perceive women as less suited for their jobs. Finally, studies indicate that affirmative action policies will not lead to greater self-esteem for the relevant group members. Affirmative action policies, thus, are not justified on utilitarian grounds.

We observe that these unexpected results reveal the limit of theory: sometimes the obvious inference in a classroom is not what happens in real life. Affirmative action policies designed to give women a chance to prove themselves seem to obviously be able to demonstrate to people the error of their previous sexist beliefs. Having a strong woman role model in the professional world ought to help other women see what is possible for themselves. Affirmative action can be reasonably expected to help achieve this end. These plausible assumptions have been disconfirmed by psychological study. Armchair philosophy must occasionally give way to empirical research.

✦ ✦ ✦

Affirmative Action and Employment Equity in Canada

SUSAN DIMOCK AND
CHRISTOPHER TUCKER

I. INTRODUCTION

Canada is a country committed to the principle of legal equality amongst its citizenry. This principle is enshrined, among other places, in the fundamental law of the land: the Canadian Constitution. In particular, the *Canadian Charter of Rights and Freedoms* (1982) lays down in s. 15(1) that "Every individual is equal before and under the law and has the right to the equal protection and equal benefit of the law without discrimination and, in particular, without discrimination based on race, national or ethnic origin, colour, religion, sex, age or mental or physical disability." Notwithstanding this commitment to equality, the subsection of the *Charter* immediately following this allows for the implementation of affirmative action programs. Thus s. 15(2) states that "Subsection (1) does not preclude any law, program or activity that has as its object the amelioration of conditions of disadvantaged individuals or groups including those that are disadvantaged because of race, national or ethnic origin, colour, religion, sex, age or mental or physical disability."

The affirmative action programs which s. 15(2) permits may take a number of forms. They may be adopted by educational institutions, employers, financial institutions, landlords, insurance companies and many other institutions that are in a position to award benefits within society; depending upon the benefit in question, the specific details of the affirmative action plan will vary, of course. Moreover, even within a single sector there is considerable variation as to the steps that an institution might take by way of adopting affirmative action policies. Take, for example, affirmative action programs within the area of employment. It may be decided that the best way to ameliorate the disadvantages of those discriminated against in the past is to adopt a tie-breaking mechanism: if two candidates are otherwise equally qualified for a job, but one is from a disadvantaged group, then the company will hire that person. Or the company may decide that, because of past discrimination, persons from disadvantaged groups cannot compete on a fair footing with those from more privileged groups, and so it may adopt a policy of ranking applicants which gives minority candidates extra credit, as it were, just for being a member of the minority group. Alternatively, a company might decide that more aggressive measures are needed to attract persons from previously disadvantaged groups into their workforce. Thus it might adopt a policy whereby certain positions are set aside for members of minority groups, or it might adopt a quota system which sets hiring targets for specific groups. Though many people think that the exact nature of the program adopted matters to its justification (typically people tend to think that tie-breaking measures are easier to justify than quota systems, for example), we shall not be concerned with the differences between these approaches in what follows. For we believe that all affirmative action programs stand or fall together.

Our concern in this paper is with the justification of affirmative action programs. That they stand in need of justification can be seen from a number of different perspectives. First, the allowance (and in some cases requirement) that educational institutions, employers and others adopt affirmative action programs seems problematic in a society committed to equality. For such programs clearly privilege some over others; they treat people unequally. Secondly, it would seem that affirmative action policies must be inefficient in a certain way. For such programs allow that a candidate may or must be admitted to the institution or hired even though he or she is not the most qualified for the position, because he or she belongs to an historically disadvantaged group. Finally, for every person who is benefited by an affirmative action plan, there is another person who is disadvantaged by it. Those who would have received the benefit on the basis of merit in the absence of affirmative action seem to have some legitimate grievance: they have been adversely discriminated against. Those who view affirmative action programs in this light tend to refer to them as policies of "reverse discrimination." Whatever we call it, though, it is clear that affirmative action stands in need of justification for these reasons.

We shall concentrate on affirmative action as it applies only to employment in what follows. Our concern will be to examine the arguments that are offered in favour of affirmative action policies in hiring, particularly those which have played an important role in setting Canadian policy and law on matters of affirmative action and employment equity. We shall conclude that the reasons typically offered in defence of affirmative action are inadequate.

The basic argument will proceed as follows. Those who wish to defend the use of affirmative action programs typically do so on one of two importantly different grounds. The first general approach to justifying affirmative action programs is to argue that they are required by justice. The second approach is to argue that they produce good consequences for society. We shall argue that the arguments from justice are problematic, and that only consequentialist reasons seem capable of providing a defensible justification of affirmative action. But whether a particular policy like affirmative action actually produces good consequences is an empirical matter. So while we can agree with those consequentially-minded philosophers and legal theorists that *if* affirmative action programs produced significant goods for society then they could be justified, we shall question whether they actually do produce such goods. And we shall find that most of the goods which it is suggested are made available by affirmative action programs not only are not produced by such programs, but are actually retarded by them. Thus the second approach to defending affirmative action policies is also unsuccessful.

II. Justice-Based Defences of Affirmative Action

Those who wish to argue that affirmative action programs are justified because they are required by justice have two routes available to them, and both have had numerous followers. They each correspond to the kind of justice that affirmative action is supposed to serve: compensatory justice or distributive justice.

II.1 Compensatory Justice

The first argument from justice has it that affirmative action is required as a matter of *compensatory* justice. The idea is this: members of the groups that are now to be favoured by affirmative action have in the past been adversely discriminated against. As a result of that discrimination, they now occupy a significantly disadvantaged position relative to those who were not discriminated against in the past. Because the past discrimination was unjustified, based on attributed rather than actual characteristics, it was unfair. Therefore, the resulting advantages for some and disadvantages for others were equally unfair; some benefited unjustly at the expense of others. As a matter of justice, then, we must right this wrong.

Now this argument has been subject to considerable attack. Most important, we think, is that it is incompatible with the actual way in which affirmative action programs must work. For affirmative action programs identify those who are to be favoured by group membership. Thus, for example, the Canadian Employment Equity Act which was passed in 1986 identified four designated groups whose members were to be advantaged via affirmative action programs: women, aboriginal peoples, persons with disabilities, and persons who are, because of their race or colour, in a visible minority in Canada. If we adopted the compensatory justice model for defending such legislation we should have to say that every member of these groups has been disadvantaged relative to others who are not members of these groups, such that those who were not disadvantaged gained benefits unfairly at the expense of those who were disadvantaged. And this is precisely the position that the courts have in fact taken in Canada. Group membership alone is taken as sufficient evidence that a person has been discriminated against or is entitled to affirmative action assistance. Under s. 15(2) of the Charter, "The court would be spared assessing the situation of every individual covered by an ameliorative program to determine whether he or she were entitled to be included in the class of *disadvantaged* persons. Every member of the disadvantaged group would be assumed to have been disadvantaged and thereby entitled to the benefit of the program…"[1]

But of course the presumption that every member of a disadvantaged group has thereby been disadvantaged is highly implausible! We cannot assume that just because an individual belongs to an historically disadvantaged group, that that individual has been disadvantaged and so deserves compensation. It may be true, for example, that women as a group have been discriminated against to their detriment in employment, but that surely does not alone entitle someone like Princess Diana or Jackie Kennedy-Onassis to compensatory benefits. For they simply have not suffered from adverse discrimination and so have no claim to compensation. The point of all this is a general one, though: because we cannot identify individual victims of past discrimination on the basis of group membership alone, affirmative action programs which make entitlements to compensatory benefits available just on that basis cannot be justified. They will extend benefits to those who do not deserve them. Furthermore, they are unlikely to benefit those who are most entitled to compensation on this model because, even with affirmative action programs that grant them extra points or that reserve positions for members of their group, those individuals who have been most severely disadvantaged by past discrimination will not be able to compete for valuable employment positions; they will lack the skills needed to compete even for an affirmative action position.

A similar problem arises if we concentrate, not on the beneficiaries of affirmative action, but on those who lose out as a result of such programs. According to the compensatory justice approach, we may disadvantage those who belong to groups that have benefited from past discriminatory practices (white, abled, non-aboriginal males, in particular). The reason given for this is that they have gained unfair benefits at the expense of others, and so must now provide compensation for their ill-gotten gains. But the group problem re-emerges here: not every white, abled, non-aboriginal man has participated in discriminatory practices or benefited from them. Just as we cannot identify the victims of discrimination by group membership alone, neither can we identify the beneficiaries of discrimination in that way.

Consideration of those who are to be relatively disadvantaged by affirmative action programs on compensatory grounds raises a further concern. The discrimination at issue is an historical event, which has produced significant disadvantages for those in the designated groups. But the people who have participated in that discrimination are long since dead; they are certainly not the same people who are now told that they must suffer losses in order to compensate those who have been historically disadvantaged. But is this not a case of "the sins of the father being visited upon his sons"? In other words, is this not a clear case of holding the descendants of those who have committed past wrongs responsible for those wrongs, even though they in no way participated in them or had control over them? And do not societies committed to justice abhor such practices?

Whatever the deficiencies of the compensatory justice argument for affirmative action may be and whether its advocates can meet the challenges raised here need not concern us any longer, however, for this argument has not been particularly important in Canada (unlike the United States). It certainly has not been a significant influence in the development of our legislative programs, at least, and since we are concerned with assessing the reasons that have actually been given in support of our affirmative action policies and laws, we can safely move along.

II.2 Distributive Justice

A second argument founded on justice is offered by those in favour of affirmative action as well. In this approach affirmative action is defended as a matter of *distributive* justice. Those in the designated groups have been unjustly deprived of opportunities and benefits in the past, which make them unable to compete now on the same terms with others who have not been similarly disadvantaged. The result is distributively unjust, because some have a vastly greater share of the goods which society makes available than others do, through no fault of their own. This injustice in the distribution of society's benefits has to be rectified, and affirmative action is one way to do that.

It is frequently taken as evidence of past discrimination, on this view, that different groups are under-represented in various positions in society relative to their percentage of the population at large. Thus, for example, the fact that only 7% of upper management positions in the public sector are held by women, despite the fact that women make up just over 50% of the total population, is taken as evidence of discrimination against women in employment and career advancement. Not surprisingly, then, the goal of affirmative action which defenders of this view usually adopt is that of having in all sectors of employment a level of representation for each group which is equal to their proportion of the general population.

As with the previous argument from justice, however, this approach faces some very serious challenges. Problems of identifying individuals solely by group membership arise again here, for example, though in a different form. For individuals are not typically identifiable as members of a single group. Is a disabled woman who occupies a managerial position to count as increasing the representation of one group or two?

More importantly, this argument rests upon two very dubious assumptions. The first is that, in the absence of past discrimination, there would in fact be participation in all sectors of the economy equal to representation in the population. This is very unlikely. Given that some differences are genetic, some are a contingent feature of such circumstances as geography, and others are cultural without being based on discrimination, it is unlikely that people will be drawn to or excel at different occupations proportionately with their share of the general population.

The second problem is that this approach assumes that the just distribution of economic positions in society will be equal across groups. This is a controversial moral judgement; those who wish to defend it must show that a distribution of the economic rewards of society which maintains an equality between a group's percentage of the population and their participation in all sectors of society is better than (more just than) alternative principles of distributive justice. Such alternatives include principles which hold that economic rewards should be distributed according to merit, need, virtue, contribution, etc. Though we cannot enter into the debate concerning the proper conception of distributive justice here, we need not; for again, such arguments have not played a central role in the development of Canadian public policy and law.

Though these arguments from justice have occupied much of the attention of philosophers and other theorists in thinking about affirmative action, they are at best highly contentious and they have failed to generate any consensus concerning the permissibility of such programs. Indeed, for every defender of affirmative action on the grounds that it is required by justice (compensatory or distributive), one can find opponents who insist that it is a subversion of justice. It subverts justice, moreover, in exactly the same way that discrimination of the type to be resisted does, because it makes benefits available to people on such arbitrary grounds as skin colour or gender, rather than on relevant grounds such as merit.

Those who think that affirmative action is in fact discriminatory against those who have been privileged in the past may nonetheless think that it is justified, as a necessary means to eliminating the gross inequality that characterizes our society and as a way of providing those who have been previously disadvantaged with a fair opportunity of bettering their fortunes. To take this kind of line, however, is to adopt a very different approach to the justification of affirmative action, one which looks not to its justice but to its good social consequences.

III. Consequentialist Justifications of Affirmative Action

Those who argue that affirmative action is justified because it will lead to significant social benefits are offering a consequentialist position. Consequentialism is the view that an action, policy, law or what have you is justified when it produces good consequences. The best action is that which, of the alternatives available, produces the best consequences. The most common consequentialist position is typically some form of utilitarianism, which holds that the consequences that matter are those affecting the welfare, happiness, well-being or utility of all those affected by the action, policy or law in question. Utilitarianism then says that the right thing to do, or the morally justified thing to do, is whatever, among the alternatives, will maximize the welfare, happiness, well-being or utility of all those affected by the choice. This has been the route adopted by most Canadian philosophers who have sought to defend affirmative action, as well as by our legislators in setting public policy and developing laws designed to achieve employment equity and eliminate discrimination in the workplace.

Now those who wish to defend affirmative action on the grounds that it will produce good social consequences (and that nothing less invasive of freedom will do so) must explain what good consequences are to be expected from such policies. A number of good consequences have been proposed in this regard.

III.1 To Better Serve the Needs of Minority Cultures

It is frequently claimed in support of affirmative action that the needs of minority cultures are unique in important ways, and that the best way of ensuring that those needs are met in a way that is sensitive to their differences is to have representatives from the minority cultures themselves providing the services. This is typically taken to require affirmative action programs specifically designed to increase the spaces available to members of the minority cultures in advanced educational and training programs, rather than affirmative action designed to achieve employment equity in all sectors of the economy.

This argument may be able to provide a limited defence of affirmative action programs, particularly in relation to fields such as medicine in which cultural differences are often very significant and dictate a different approach to the physician/patient/family relationship, death, medical procedures, consent and patient autonomy, etc. A similar case may be made with respect to the legal profession. In such cases it may be plausible to conclude that medical and legal services provided by members of one's own community would be better than those provided by others from outside of one's cultural group.

This argument faces some serious challenges, however. First, it is simply not possible to ensure that members of the various ethnic, racial, linguistic and cultural groups that constitute Canada's diverse population be served by professionals drawn from their own communities exclusively or even primarily. The resources that would be required to implement such a system are simply not available. Most communities can only support a small number of specialized professionals, whether they are medical, legal or financial specialists, for example. Furthermore, if one were to attempt to increase the participation of various minority cultures' members in the different professions as a means of providing better service to those groups, one would not only have to adopt affirmative action policies to ensure that training was available to these individuals, but one would then also have to ensure that they practised their professions in centres whose population is made up of a sufficient number of the minority group's members. This would be a significant invasion into the freedom of those who are to be the beneficiaries of such programs, and it is certainly not a policy that has received political support or expression in Canada. Finally, such an argument seems to run a serious risk of isolating minority communities, of maintaining their distinctiveness and homogeneity at the price of cutting them off from other communities and their members. This model seems ill-suited to achieve the Canadian vision of a multi-cultural society, in which distinct and diverse peoples come together, not into a melting pot which eliminates their differences, but into a mosaic where each piece of the pattern is unique but related to all the rest in a way that renders the result unified and beautiful. The Canadian vision of multi-culturalism depends upon interaction between peoples, which will give rise to knowledge and tolerance of differences. Any policy which presupposes that individuals in minority cultures can only receive adequate service from members of their own group flies in the face of our national ideal.

Thus while increasing the participation of various minority groups within such professions as medicine and law would, perhaps, improve the quality of service available to members of those groups, this approach provides only a very limited defence of affirmative action programs at best. For the good that such a policy would make available can be provided to only a few groups, likely in large urban centres, and even there members of minority groups would still have to receive a considerable amount of service from non-member specialists. Furthermore, this good cannot be achieved by affirmative action programs alone but must be conjoined with restrictive requirements designed to ensure that those who receive the professional training use their skills in the service of their minority group; this is a serious cost which may offset any good that such a policy might make possible. Finally, this approach runs the risk of isolating and marginalizing the groups it is designed to assist. For these reasons, this consideration is not sufficient to justify the wide-spread use of affirmative action programs in society at large.

This case does, however, raise an issue that permeates our discussion of the various consequentialist defences that are offered in favour of affirmative action programs: those who wish to employ consequentialist arguments must consider *all* of the consequences a policy is likely to achieve. For it is not enough to establish that a policy would have some good consequences, if those are vastly outweighed by bad consequences that would also attend it. Furthermore, this case, like those to follow, should serve as a warning. In particular, philosophers are notorious for speculating about the likely consequences of various proposals, without much empirical investigation. Thus while a good consequence of affirmative might on first glance seem plausible in the abstract, the details often belie the suggested benefit. When discussing empirical matters, it is best to get out of our armchairs and consult the experts in the field, as we shall see.

III.2 To Promote Diversity

Affirmative action policies are often advocated on the grounds that they will promote diversity in employment situations. Philosophers and other academics are often among those who advance diversity as a reason for adopting affirmative action programs. It is likely that this is a case in which a specific good for a very unique profession has been inappropriately applied to others where it fits less well. For there may indeed be good reason to think that universities and other centres of research and learning benefit from a diversity of views, cultural influences, histories, etc. It is not surprising, therefore, that professional philosophers and other academics should promote diversity as a value in its own right; within their professions diversity is a significant good. But it would be problematic to conclude from this that affirmative action as a general program in society is justified, for it is not at all clear that diversity is a value in its own right. Rather, it seems vastly more likely that diversity is promoted as a good because people believe that it will be instrumental in achieving other goods: tolerance, understanding, an undermining of the racist/sexist/ablist attitudes that produce the invidious discrimination in the first place, different groups will then have role models available upon which their members can draw, etc. These goods, which diversity in the population of various employment sectors is supposed to generate, all depend on diversity itself leading to some fundamental changes in attitudes, both by those who are to be the beneficiaries of affirmative action and those who are thereby forced not to discriminate against those whom they otherwise would discriminate against. Since the effect on attitudes has occupied a central place in Canadian justifications of affirmative action, both in the political and academic arena, we shall examine this claim closely in what follows.

III.3 Attitudinal Changes and the Reduction of Prejudice

Those who adopt a consequentialist approach to affirmative action typically relate the good consequences that they anticipate from affirmative action programs ultimately to a change of attitudes among the members of society. This is not surprising, of course, since the discrimination that affirmative action policies is supposed to ameliorate ultimately stems from prejudicial attitudes based on arbitrary characteristics of persons such as race, ethnicity, gender, physical disabilities, etc. If these attitudes are fundamentally responsible for discriminatory practices, then policies aimed at eliminating these attitudes seem the best approach to eliminating discrimination. It would seem, furthermore, that changing attitudes is really behind the more specific consequentialist arguments that are advanced in favour of affirmative action: that it will promote diversity, lead to better service for minority groups, provide role models for members of groups which have been previously disadvantaged because of prejudice and the like are all held out as good because they will lead to greater tolerance and understanding between groups. Those who have been prejudiced against in the past will come to be seen as competent and contributing members of their professions, both by those who previously undervalued them and by themselves. Through participation previously disadvantaged groups will gain not only the esteem they deserve from others, but self-respect as well. As prejudicial attitudes are eroded, people from previously disadvantaged groups will be increasingly able to simply compete on a fair basis with others, for they will no longer have to overcome the arbitrary biases against them that racism, sexism, etc. put in their way in the past. The end result of this process, consequentialists hope, is a society in which people are judged and rewarded purely on the basis of merit. When such a state is reached affirmative action programs will no longer be needed, a state which all who take a consequentialist approach represent as the final goal; affirmative action is at best a temporary means to overcoming the prejudice that denies some people the opportunities they deserve, and once those prejudicial attitudes have been overcome affirmative action commitments can simply whither away.

Now these are some very sweeping generalizations about what all or most consequentialists think on the matter of affirmative action. They are borne out, however, by an examination both of the writings of our most prominent philosophers and of our legislators and policy makers. Take, for example, the work of L.W. Sumner. Sumner argues that affirmative action, or positive discrimination as he calls it, cannot be defended on grounds of corrective or compensatory justice. He does think that it can be defended on consequentialist grounds, however, and he rests his argument on using affirmative action as a means of overcoming certain prejudicial attitudes. Concentrating just on the use of affirmative action policies that favour women in employment, Sumner argues that affirmative action programs are needed principally to combat the effects of sexism, and ultimately to eliminate sexist attitudes themselves. He identifies two forms of sexism: primary (direct or overt) sexism, and more importantly what he calls "secondary sexism," which consists in a host of attitudes by which the abilities or commitment of female candidates for employment or promotion are undervalued because of prejudicial attitudes about women. Secondary sexist attitudes include such things as the belief that women will be less committed to their jobs because of family responsibilities, that a female candidate will not be able to fit into a male dominated work environment, etc. Now Sumner thinks that secondary sexism is "one of the main mechanisms whereby employment practices continue to discriminate against women"[2] and that affirmative action programs must discriminate in favour of women in order to neutralize the immediate effects of such sexist attitudes and thereby ultimately eliminate those attitudes. "The centrepiece of the consequentialist argument is the claim that introducing a measure of discrimination against men will be the most effective means of eliminating discrimination against women, and thus of minimizing discrimination in the long run."[3]

Likewise, Thomas Hurka believes not only that sexist attitudes lead to discrimination against women in employment but that changing those attitudes is one of the principal benefits of affirmative action. Indeed, he thinks that affirmative action will produce positive changes not only in men's attitudes toward women but also in women's attitudes towards themselves.

> If the belief that women are inferior persists in Canada, either consciously or subconsciously, it's partly because women aren't sufficiently prominent in Canadian life. Moving them quickly into important jobs can help dispel that belief and the many harms it does.

Equally important are the changes in women's attitudes. What you aspire to in life depends on what you think you can do, which depends on what people like you have done before. Women in prominent jobs can be role models, encouraging young women to work for similar success. If the young women achieve success this will benefit both them and society, which now wastes much of their potential.[4]

In this quotation we find Hurka appealing to two of the consequentialist reasons discussed above—increasing the representation of a given group in a particular field and the role model argument—though his reason for doing so is not that these benefits alone are sufficient to justify affirmative action but that they will lead to the change in attitudes that will ultimately eliminate discrimination based on the prejudicial belief that women are inferior to men.

Let us turn now to an examination of the legal literature supporting affirmative action, and particularly employment equity. The Supreme Court of Canada, for example, has made it clear in a number of rulings that the purpose of s. 15 of the Charter, as well as the various Provincial Human Rights Codes, is to prevent the deleterious effects of discrimination. In so doing, they have adopted a consequentialist position at two levels. First, whether a particular law, labour practice, insurance provision or what have you is discriminatory depends upon its effects, not the intent of those who have adopted it. No intent to discriminate or other foul motive is necessary in order to establish that discrimination has occurred. Secondly, they have attributed to anti-discrimination and equity legislation a consequentialist justification or purpose: to remove the negative effects of prejudice.[5]

The Supreme Court's position is not unique in this respect. Indeed, as we shall see, the approach taken by the members of our legal community has been thoroughly consequentialist, with the goal of changing prejudicial attitudes as a means of reducing discrimination occupying a prominent position in their deliberations about the justification of affirmative action policies. This concentration on creating a climate in which attitudes of fellow-feeling, respect, inclusivity and mutual understanding replace those of prejudice, ascriptions of inferiority upon whole groups and exclusion of those who are different than oneself, as a means of effecting greater equality within society, is reflected in virtually all of the Provincial and Territorial Human Rights Codes. Thus we read in the Preamble to the Human Rights Code of Ontario, for example, that "WHEREAS it is public policy in Ontario to recognize the dignity and worth of every person and to provide for equal rights and opportunities without discrimination that is contrary to law, and having as its aim the creation of a climate of understanding and mutual respect for the dignity and worth of each person so that each person feels a part of the community and able to contribute fully to the development and well-being of the community and the Province...."[6] The Canadian commitment to affirmative action and employment equity must be understood against the backdrop of this more sweeping commitment to equality and the goal of creating a society free of invidious prejudice.

In 1986 the federal Government of Canada passed the Employment Equity Act. In that Act four groups of persons were identified as victims of prejudicial discrimination in employment and designated as groups for whom employment equity was immediately needed: women, aboriginal peoples, persons with disabilities, and persons who are, because of their race or colour, in a visible minority in Canada. It is clear from writings related to this Act that its framers intended it to have the effect of increasing the participation of members of the designated groups in employment situations from which they had traditionally been excluded on grounds that they belonged to one of the designed groups. "Employment Equity is a result-oriented program which seeks evidence that employment situations for the designated groups are improving, indicated by their greater numerical representation in the workforce, improvement in their employment status, occupations, and salary levels in jobs for which they are available and qualified."[7]

Now the government of Canada clearly recognizes that the factors contributing to the relative employment disadvantage of persons in the designated groups are diverse. Many which they identified in discussing the Employment Equity Act might be categorized as structural, involving the way employment activity is structured: thus lack of day-care facilities for women, lack of ramps and elevators for disabled persons, the organization of the work-day into standard eight-hour shifts and the like present barriers to certain groups. These can be easily remedied, however, and the Supreme Court of Canada has made it clear that the equality guaranteed to all Canadians under the law requires that employers take reasonable steps to accommodate workers with special needs.[8] Much more important for our purposes are the attitudinal causes which the government identified as leading to the under-representation of the designated groups in the workforce, particularly at the managerial or professional levels. For these attitudes are not only a barrier in and of themselves, but they retard the willingness or ability of employers to see the value of making the needed structural changes. Among those attitudes, identified in the Government of Canada Background Paper to the proposed Employment Equity Act, are the following: "Foremost is the attitude of many non-disabled persons: there is a widespread misunderstanding and under-rating of the abilities of disabled persons." And in relation to aboriginal peoples, "Native people face attitudinal and cultural barriers to their equitable participation in the economy. Racial intolerance and misunderstanding" are chief amongst them. Likewise, "Research attests to the existence both of prejudicial attitudes to non-whites and systemic discrimination based on racial factors."[9] It is clear from these and similar claims that the authors of the Background Paper believe that prejudicial attitudes play a crucial role in the perpetuation of discrimination against the designated groups, and insofar as they adopted employment equity (affirmative action) as their response to such discrimination, that they believe that affirmative action policies can (help to) eliminate those pernicious attitudes.

The perceived relation between prejudicial attitudes and discrimination in employment was perhaps no where more clearly articulated than in the report of the Royal Commission on Equality in Employment, headed by Judge Rosalie Abella. In their report the members of the Royal Commission made it clear that they understood both discrimination and equity to essentially involve certain attitudes. Thus "the goal of equality is more than an evolutionary intolerance to adverse discrimination. It is to ensure, too, that the vestiges of these arbitrarily restrictive assumptions do not continue to play a role in our society."[10] And as to their understanding of discrimination, they characterized it this way: "Discrimination in this context means practices or attitudes that have, whether by design or impact, the effect of limiting an individual's or a group's right to the opportunities generally available because of attributed rather than actual characteristics."[11]

Group membership and prejudicial attitudes based on group membership are central in the approach adopted by the Royal Commission on Equality in Employment: "Remedial measures of a systemic and systematic kind are the object of employment equity and affirmative action. They are meant to improve the situation for individuals who, by virtue of belonging to and being identified with a particular group, find themselves unfairly and adversely affected by certain systems or practices. System remedies are a response to patterns of discrimination that have two basic antecedents:

a) a disparate negative impact that flows from the structure of systems designed for a homogeneous constituency; and

b) a disparately negative impact that flows from practices based on stereotypical characteristics ascribed to an individual because of the characteristics ascribed to the group of which he or she is a member."[12]

Judge Abella does not believe that voluntary programs can effect a significant reduction in employment discrimination; mandatory programs are necessary. "Given the seriousness and apparent intractability of employment discrimination, it is unrealistic and somewhat ingenuous to rely on there being sufficient public goodwill to fuel a voluntary program."[13] Apparently coercion will effect an end of discrimination even in the absence of a change of attitude (increase of goodwill), contrary to everything else that we have seen!

IV. THE REAL CONSEQUENCES
OF AFFIRMATIVE ACTION

In the introductory paragraph of the last section, we suggested that if it is believed that prejudiced attitudes are responsible for the discriminatory practices, then any policy designed to eliminate these attitudes seems to be the best way to eliminate discrimination. We then went on to make clear that affirmative action policies, at least in Canada, have been traditionally defended on the grounds that the increased representation of target groups in the workforce would eliminate these prejudiced attitudes, as well as arrest (or at least retard) the discriminatory hiring practices which result from them.

The appropriateness of these policies, then, must be evaluated by how effectively they serve their ends. In other words, these affirmative action policies may only be deemed appropriate responses to discriminatory acts and prejudiced attitudes if they serve to eliminate these acts and attitudes; insofar as the former largely stem from the latter, moreover, the efficiency with which affirmative action eliminates those prejudiced attitudes will determine whether it can be justified on consequentialist grounds.

As we have argued above, that the elimination of prejudiced attitudes is of paramount import to the Canadian philosophical and legal communities is clear: Sumner focuses primarily on the importance of changing sexist attitudes, while Hurka believes that the overcoming of prejudiced attitudes is one of the principal benefits of affirmative action. The Ontario Human Rights Code states explicitly that creating a prejudice free environment in which its citizens can live is one of its principal aims. Canada's Employment Equity Act, likewise, must be understood as an attempt to overcome prejudicial attitudes.

So, then, affirmative action policies may be viewed as appropriate responses to discriminatory hiring practices only insofar as they can be thought to aid the overcoming of prejudiced beliefs. Unfortunately, as we shall see, there is no good reason to believe that these policies serve this end. The psychological literature on the subject indicates that affirmative action policies would actually frustrate efforts geared towards the elimination of prejudiced attitudes held by persons against others because of their membership in historically disadvantaged groups, building resentment in prejudiced individuals, and further entrenching their previous discriminatory behaviours. This literature also fails to indicate that the "role model" approach to overcoming negative attitudes that disadvantaged persons hold regarding their own social group is served by affirmative action.

IV.1 The Alteration of Other's Attitudes

It is easy to understand why someone would suppose that a workforce that well represents minorities at large would be one in which prejudiced attitudes dwindle off and die. A bigot, prejudiced against each and every type of person who is different than himself, when at work would be forced to get to know people of type X, Y, and Z, and, through continued interaction with these persons, would then come to respect them, or at least tolerate them. After watching presentation after presentation by persons of groups X, Y and Z, the bigot would have to reason to the conclusion that he was wrong after all, and that these groups are not lazy and stupid (to take common prejudiced beliefs). After sharing a change room with them, the bigot would be forced to conclude that they did not smell. And after a very long time, it may even be the case that the bigot is forced to reason to the conclusion that all the members of these groups are not out to get him, and do not even hate him *en masse*. This is a fairly persuasive presentation, and no reasonable person would ignore its power. Unfortunately, there is data available to justify supposing that the bigot is not appropriately described as being "reasonable."

Persons with no prejudice imagine themselves in the situation just described, and come to the conclusion that they would end up as unprejudiced persons. They then hastily conclude that anyone in that situation, whether previously prejudiced or not, would likewise come to judge people from minority groups fairly upon getting to know them better. But the results of imposing affirmative action programs upon non-prejudiced people is not particularly telling, since all it amounts to is this: those who are not already prejudiced will not become so if they are forced through affirmative action to interact in the workplace with members of previously disadvantaged groups. But this is not the group that affirmative action must reform in order to eliminate discrimination. What reaction can we expect to our scenario from those who are prejudiced?

People with prejudice need not find the evidence undermining their prejudiced beliefs compelling, and it is far from clear that the imagined scenario would have the desired effects. Persons with prejudiced attitudes have incentive to reason to entirely different conclusions than non-prejudiced persons when confronted with a workplace enhanced by affirmative action policies. In fact, there is ample evidence to suggest that workplaces affected by affirmative action policies would have negative, rather than positive or even negligible, consequences on the bigot's opinions. There is evidence that suggests that affirmative action policies, and indeed "politically correct" (PC) environments more generally, lead to the entrenching of a bigot's disposition, and lead to more radical, but perhaps less obvious, discriminatory behaviours.

For the last several decades, it has been recognized by several psychologists that transgressing a personal standard or conviction creates mental costs for the transgressor. If you maintained all your life that John Denver's songs were all a bit cheesy, and then actually heard a song which you said you quite liked, and were then informed that it was by John Denver, you would experience some mental discomfort (and some razzing). It is also recognized quite generally (indeed, it is sometimes treated as a tautology) that one avoids discomfort when one can. To tie this together to the point at hand: if a racist was forced to admit that race X was not so bad after all, then he would experience some psychological costs. Further, if a racist was going to experience some psychological harm, then he would have reason to avoid it if it were possible.

It turns out that in the case in question—the discomfort associated with coming to the conclusion that being a racist is wrong—it is possible to avoid the harm. Ziva Kunda has presented us with a compelling argument which suggests that a person's choice of rules of inference to reason with depends upon the conclusion desired.[14] While there are limits to how wild the reasoning may be, if there is a seemingly plausible argument which may be constructed that allows for the conclusion desired to continue to be endorsed, then it will continue to be endorsed. Bigots, then, are able to construct an argument which allows them to maintain that their racist attitude is warranted, and thus avoid the psychological discomfort which would result from coming to the conclusion that their racist attitudes are incorrect, and must be changed. We certainly recognize these types of rationalizations: "I have to work with an X, but *he's not like the others, he …*," or "You're O.K., for a skirt," or the somewhat more disturbing, "I wonder who she's getting assistance from, and why?" It is worth noting that the stronger one's racism is, the more discomfort may be expected to obtain after realizing that one's personal opinions regarding race X are incorrect. Deeply racist persons would have stronger motivation to avoid coming to the conclusion that their attitudes are inappropriate.

Interestingly enough, it was likely the recognition of the desire to minimize the discomfort associated with an action that contravened one's ideology which led people to the conclusion that affirmative action policies were a good idea to begin with. It was previously thought that by forcing one to say that something was the case, one would then modify one's previous position with regard to the opinion in question. To turn back to our previous example, upon being told that the song played was by John Denver, one may then modify one's previous position and say "Well, at least *that* wasn't cheesy, like his earlier material" or something similar which allows you to maintain some form of consistency. In the case of affirmative action, then, once forced to the conclusion that the co-workers from group X aren't lazy/stupid/smelly, etc., the bigot would then be motivated to conclude that Xs overall aren't that bad, really. Unfortunately, this is not how cognitive dissonance is believed to actually work. The discomfort associated with expressing something that is inconsistent with one's personal values only arises when one freely chooses to engage in the expression.[15] Forced expressions of non-prejudiced sentiments do not result in a bigot being motivated to become less bigoted.

Being forced to publicly endorse non-racist/sexist sentiments, and to recognize that one is apt to react in a way that society at large prohibits, leads to stress of quite another type, as well. Bigots who recognize that they are living in a PC environment are likely to alter their public behaviours to appear to conform to PC standards, and feel threatened and fearful. E. Ashbly Plant and Patricia Devine have recently run several tests which measure the degrees to which people have adopted anti-racist attitudes due to personal endorsement of non-prejudiced beliefs, compared with others who have adopted anti-racist behaviours due to external pressure.[16] Their findings indicate that people who "cave in" and conform to anti-racist behaviours in response to external pressure do not thereby internalize anti-racist sentiments. Racists can retain their racist sentiments, and feel threatened and fearful, in proportion to how deep the racism runs—the more racist, the more threatened they feel.

Plant and Devine write:

> We are much less sanguine about the likelihood that threat-related feelings, in the absence of guilt, will lead to prejudice reduction ... simply avoiding situations in which non-prejudiced social pressure is experience and/or situations involving contact with outgroup members would be effective strategies to remove the anticipated threat. ... [17]

When possible, then, it is likely that these racist individuals would engage in antisocial behaviour, or band together in closed communities. It is not always possible to avoid members of a given group, or a PC society, especially when in the workforce, and especially in a workforce in which affirmative action policies are implemented. What then of the results of the tension created by a racist's fear?

It seems plausible that such resentment could ultimately culminate in these people lashing out against the . . . norms . . . of even outgroup members . . . under anonymous conditions . . . .[18]

Incidents of a group of masked individuals gathering and beating members of minority cultures/lifestyles are certainly not rare enough to make this chilling speculation as implausible as one may desire.

The very existence of affirmative action programs has also been shown to lead to a devaluing of women's contributions in the workplace. Madeline E. Heilman highlights another unexpected effect of affirmative action on sex discrimination: the knowledge that a workplace has adopted affirmative action policies leads to a further devaluing of the women who work within it.[19] Studies have shown that there are no different aptitudes between women and men in the upper levels of business, yet the belief that there are such differences persists. Heilman suggests that women's underrepresentation in the upper levels of business arise from the beliefs in the existence of these differences, and the lack of fit between these perceived differences and people's expectations about what it takes to succeed in upper-management. Women are undervalued because of inaccurate perceptions, and affirmative action was supposed, in part, to dispel such beliefs by giving women a chance to prove that they are capable of being at least as effective as men in traditionally male-dominated occupations. Heilman shows, however, that Affirmative Action does not have this result. Through a series of studies, Heilman finds evidence that suggests that the very perception of the existence of affirmative action remedies in a business environment leads to a further devaluation of women in the workplace. A woman in a workplace characterized, at least in part, by affirmative action policies is thought to be less capable than that same woman in that same workplace without an affirmative action policy. This result certainly gives one pause.

To summarize, then: If one consults the psychological literature of the day, affirmative action policies cannot be thought to result in a change of attitude of the racist/sexist/ablist. All that they can reasonably be thought to result in is increased hostility towards already disadvantaged groups. This is not a result to be applauded, nor even tolerated. And insofar as the purpose of affirmative action policies is to change the dispositions of the racists/sexists/ablists at large, these policies must be thought to utterly fail.

IV.2 Changing Attitudes about Oneself

Even if affirmative action cannot change the attitudes of racists/sexists/ablists, does it not still have value insofar as it provides role models for members of disadvantaged groups and raises their self-esteem? Certainly changing the attitudes of members of previously disadvantaged groups about themselves has been seen as integral to the purpose of affirmative action in Canada. Hurka, for example, explicitly mentions the inspiring of individuals to achieve as one of the goals of such programs. So, while failing to justify affirmative action policies on the grounds that they would lead to the eradication of racist attitudes, advocates may still find grounds to justify affirmative action because of the positive effects a role model could have to the members of the relevant group.

Members of disadvantaged groups, having been raised in a culture that inculcates the belief that they cannot achieve success in a given field, do not attempt to do so, even if they have the desire. To this extent we can agree with Hurka. In order to overcome this belief, and realize their dreams, it is thought that a role model in the given field would allow disadvantaged persons to come to the conclusion that they, too, could achieve such success. A successful group member in the field of figure-skating could provide the necessary example for a member of a disadvantaged group to say to himself, "That person is an X, and he is a good figure-skater. Therefore people who are from group X can figure-skate. I am an X, and therefore, despite what I previously thought, I can probably figure-skate too."

Unfortunately, it turns out that this is a simplistic expectation. It is generally accepted in the literature that *relevant* others are necessary to inspire. An aspiring academic is not inspired by a successful football-player of the same group, for example; to be relevant the role model must have achieved success in the same particular field as the person to be inspired desires success in. By hypothesis of affirmative action supporters, it is also necessary that the role model be relevant in another respect, namely, be of the same group membership. This is also supported by the literature on the subject of how relevance is determined.

The existence of even relevant role models may nonetheless fail to inspire others or boost their self-esteem. Penelope Lockwood and Ziva Kunda have presented strong evidence that suggests that when another person is perceived as relevant, that person will only inspire if his or her success is seen as achievable by the person engaging in the comparison.[20] An aspiring football-player from group X, seeing a quite successful football-player of the same group membership, will not be inspired if the star player's success is due to the fact that he weighs 325 pounds, and the football-player-to-be weighs only 165 pounds, and has little chance at gaining the weight necessary to achieve the success of the role model in question. In fact, if the role model's success is seen as unattainable, the person whom one hopes would be inspired is likely to be discouraged, insofar as the comparison is seen to be relevant. Whatever the profession, the message is the same: only perceivably attainable success will inspire, while perceivably unattainable success will deflate.

This has disastrous consequences for the advocate of affirmative action. Each role model must be successful in order for him or her to inspire anyone at all. This success will be seen as attainable by some, unattainable by others, according to how highly they value their own potential. For those who do not think that they can achieve the same level of success, this example will deflate, leaving them worse off than before. For affirmative action to have as a goal the raising of certain people's self-esteem, it must be thought that these people have low self-esteem. If they have low self-esteem, it is then more likely that they will perceive the role model's success as unattainable, which would then deflate their feelings of self-worth. We are not claiming that all members of group X will find the success of any relevant role model unattainable; we are merely claiming that it is likely that *most* of the members of this group X, interested in achieving success at activity Y, will find that success unachievable because of their low self-esteem. If this is the case, overall affirmative action policies would be causing more harm than good on their supporters' own terms.

It may be argued that people's self-esteem is not *so* low, and that overall they feel that they can achieve the success showcased by the relevant role model. But that being the case, the need for affirmative action policies to raise the self-esteem of the members of these groups is puzzling, to say the least.

Lastly, to consider the middle ground, it could be suggested that the group's self-esteem is low enough to warrant an attempt to have it raised, yet high enough to make it the case that a typical role model will, overall, have a positive effect on the group in question. In this case, we would have to weigh the relative success of affirmative action in achieving both of its stated objectives—changing the opinions of bigots, sexists, and ablists on the one hand, and inspiring members of the disadvantaged groups to reach for their dreams on the other. We would then have to suggest that it fails to achieve the first objective, indeed it achieves quite the opposite effect, and would only marginally achieve the second. When looked at in this light, then, it seems to us that the conclusion to draw is that affirmative action programs are not justified on their stated grounds, and ought to be rescinded.

V. Conclusion

We have argued that none of the common defences of affirmative action programs are successful. Employment equity policies are not required by justice, and they fail to significantly reduce the prejudice that produces invidious discrimination against the members of identifiable groups within society. Given that such policies have the significant costs outlined in the introduction of this paper, their failure to provide significant counter-balancing benefits requires that we declared them unjustified. This is not to say, of course, that racism/sexism/ablism must be countenanced nor that those who are committed to eradicating prejudice and the discrimination it inspires should relax their efforts. But to those who suggest that, while not perfect, affirmative action is the only solution we have, we suggest turning instead to focus their efforts on education, paying particular attention to the young, in order to ensure that racist/sexist/ablist attitudes fail to obtain in our society.

READING ENDNOTES

1. Report of the Commission on Equality in Employment, *Employment and Immigration Canada* 1984 (Supply and Services, Canada); reprinted in Wesley Cragg, ed., *Contemporary Moral Issues* 3rd edition (Toronto: McGraw-Hill Ryerson Ltd, 1992). Hereafter cited as Abella, for its chief author: Judge Rosalie Abella; page numbers refer to Cragg, p. 191.

2. L.W. Sumner, "Positive Sexism," *Contemporary Moral Issues* 3rd edition, ed. Wesley Cragg (Toronto: McGraw-Hill Ryerson Ltd., 1992), p. 221; originally published in *Social Philosophy and Policy* 15:1. He takes the term "secondary sexism" from Mary Anne Warren, "Secondary Sexism and Quota Hiring," *Philosophy and Public Affairs* 6:3 (1977).

3. *Ibid.*, p. 223.

4. Thomas Hurka, "Affirmative Action: How Far Should We Go?" *Contemporary Moral Issues* 3rd ed. Cragg *op. cit.*, p. 209; originally published in *The Globe and Mail.*

5. *Cf.* Law Society of B.C. et al *v* Andrews et al, Supreme Court of Canada (1989) 1 S.C.R. 143; Ontario Human Rights Commission et al and Simpson-Sears Ltd., Supreme Court of Canada (1985) 2 S.C.R. 536; Brooks *v* Canada Safeway Ltd., Supreme Court of Canada (1989) 1 S.C.R. 1219.

6. Preamble to the Human Rights Code of Ontario 1990, Chapter H.19.

7. Government of Canada Paper, "Outline of the Employment Equity Act," reproduced in *Ethical Issues: Perspectives for Canadians*, ed. Eldon Soifer (Toronto: Broadview Press, 1992), p. 418.

8. *Cf.* Ontario Human Rights Commission et al and Simpson-Sears Ltd., Supreme Court of Canada (1985) 2 S.C.R. 536.

9. Government of Canada Background Paper, "Employment Equity and Economic Growth," reproduced in *Ethical Issues*, ed. Soifer *op. cit.*, p. 420.

10. Abella *op. cit.*, p. 185.

11. *Ibid.*

12. *Ibid.*, p. 189.

13. *Ibid.*, p. 192.

14. Ziva Kunda, "The Case for Motivated Reasoning," *Psychological Bulletin*, Vol. 108, No. 3, pp. 480–498.

15. *Ibid.*, p. 484.

16. Plant, E.A. & Devine, P.G. "Internal and external motivation to respond without prejudice," *Journal of Personality and Social Psychology,* 75 (1998), 811–832.

17. *Ibid.*, p. 826.

18. *Ibid.*, p. 826.

19. Madeline E. Heilman, "Sex Discrimination and the Affirmative Action Remedy: The Role of Sex Stereotypes," *Journal of Business Ethics*, 16 (1997), pp. 877–889.

20. Penelope Lockwood and Ziva Kunda, "Superstars and Me: Predicting the Impact of Role Models on the Self," *Journal of Personality and Social Psychology*, 73:1, pp. 91–103.

DEFINITIONS AND EXPLANATIONS

Affirmative action: Affirmative action policies and programs are designed to remedy unjust discrimination suffered by certain groups in the past, where that past discrimination makes it the case that members of the groups do not now enjoy full equality of opportunity with others who have not been discriminated against in the past. In Canada, affirmative action policies have been adopted for women, members of visible minorities, aboriginal persons, and persons with disabilities. Affirmative action must be distinguished from anti-discrimination policies, which cover a much greater number of people. We may not adversely discriminate against people on the bases of sex, disability, race, ethnicity, age, religion, sexual orientation, family status, etc. Whereas anti-discrimination policies are designed to ensure that individuals are not unjustly denied benefits or opportunities they are entitled to on arbitrary grounds (like sex or age), affirmative action policies are designed to privilege or provide an advantage to the members of the target groups. So, for example, a certain number of college or university spaces might be reserved specifically for applicants from the target groups, or employers may have to ensure that they hire members of the target groups if they are qualified for a position.

Empirical: Relying or based solely on experience, experiment, or observation. 1. An empirical fact is a fact discoverable through experience. 2. Empirical knowledge is gained only through experience and observation; it is acquired *a posteriori*, which is the contrary of *a priori*. Empirical claims include those about the physical world (e.g., the earth is flat), history (e.g., Aristotle was an ancient Greek philosopher), psychology (all people strive after an unlimited amount of power), etc. Our empirical beliefs are always, in principle, capable of being wrong; they are never necessarily true, because they concern contingent facts about the way that the universe actually is. In order to know whether an empirical claim is true or not, one must do some experiment or make some observations "in the world." Some empirical claims may be true universally (e.g., that all people desire their own happiness), but they still are merely contingent rather than necessary; we can imagine them being false without contradiction or we can imagine the world (in this case human nature) being different so that this true universal claim would be false.

QUESTIONS

1. Given their clearly laudable goal, why do affirmative action programs need to be justified?

2. What is compensatory justice? How might it be thought to require affirmative action for historically disadvantaged groups?

3. Why do arguments from compensatory justice make group membership morally relevant? Why is this problematic?

4. What is wrong with holding the descendants of some people responsible for the wrongs of their forbearers?

5. What is distributive justice? How might it be thought to require affirmative action for historically disadvantaged groups?

6. What problems arise from using group membership in arguments for affirmative action on the grounds of distributive justice?

7. What two objections are raised against the distributive justice justification for affirmative action? How strong are they?

8. How likely is it that affirmative action will result in the provision of better services to minority cultures? Why can such benefits only provide a limited defence of affirmative action?

9. Even if we cannot now provide a morally required good to some people (because of scarce resources) does that mean that we have no duty to try to do so?

10. What practical difficulties are there in trying to ensure that minority cultures can be served by professionals from their own groups?

11. Is diversity in and of itself a value in the workplace? Is it, instead, merely an instrumental value because it makes other goods possible?

12. Why is it initially plausible to think that affirmative action would result in attitudinal changes that would undermine prejudice and ultimately discrimination? Why must changing attitudes be the fundamental goal?

13. Why must we hope that affirmative action becomes unnecessary in the future? What does this tell us about the moral status of affirmative action?

14. How does secondary sexism rest on prejudicial attitudes about women?

15. Why are intentions to discriminate unnecessary to the moral wrongness of discriminatory practices, in consequentialist thinking?

16. What psychological mechanisms operate so as to make prejudice self-reinforcing?

17. Why does the role-model argument have only limited success in justifying affirmative action?

18. Is the position taken by Dimock and Tucker compatible with maintaining anti-discrimination policies in society?

19. How strong is this case against affirmative action? How strong can any consequentialist argument be? Is the fact that a moral judgement is questionable itself a good reason to dismiss it?

20. Is it legitimate to restrict discussion of a moral issue to a particular country on utilitarian grounds?

CHAPTER THREE

KANTIAN DEONTOLOGY

INTRODUCTION

Immanuel Kant was a German contemporary of the British philosopher Jeremy Bentham, yet in many ways Kant's ethical writings were a response to the utilitarian turn in English speaking philosophy. Kant objected, in particular, to what he considered to be three central mistakes made by the early utilitarians. First, he rejects any subjective theory of the good as sufficient for the grounding of morality. Rather than locating the foundation of morality in what we happen to care about (what makes us happy, what satisfies our preferences), Kant insists that reason is the basis of morality. Second, he rejects consequentialism, on the grounds that consequences of any act will be variable and changing, depending upon circumstances, but morality must be universal and the same in all circumstances. To see the problem here, we must return briefly to the distinction between act and rule utilitarianism. Recall that if we accept act utilitarianism, then the right action will be whichever produces the best consequences in the circumstances. But we can readily imagine circumstances in which many seemingly immoral actions would have the best results: lying in the example we gave previously, but many other immoral actions might be justified within utilitarianism. If you and your children are starving and have no other way to feed yourselves than by stealing food from a farmer's field, then doing so might have the best consequences overall. If, on the other hand, we develop rule utilitarianism then a different problem arises. Once we discover the moral rules which, if everyone followed them, would have the best consequences, we must consider what to do in exceptional circumstances. For surely there will arise situations in which following the rule will clearly not have the best consequences. Sometimes we can do more good by breaking the rule than by following it. Consider, for example, the rule against the intentional killing of persons. Suppose that you had had it in your power to kill Adolf Hitler in the late 1930s or early 1940s. Surely you would have done more good by killing him than by following the rule against taking human life. In such cases the utilitarian faces a dilemma. Either she says we should follow the rule anyway, in which case the justification for doing so cannot be consequentialist (since we are imagining cases in which following the rule will not produce the best results), or she says that we ought to treat the case as an exception to the rule (in which case it loses all moral force as a rule). Kant will argue, by contrast, that some actions are wrong *per se*, universally and necessarily. Third, he inverts the order of moral thinking. Rather than beginning with a theory of value, and building a theory of the right upon it, Kant instead begins with a theory of the right and of duty.

Kant begins with a theory of duty rather than a theory of value because he believes that it is a conceptual truth that a valid moral law must bind all rational wills. All genuine moral laws must be universal and be necessarily binding on every rational creature. This requires Kant to adopt a very different method from that of the utilitarians in determining what our duties are. Whereas different people may care about different things, moral duty must be the same for all. But if all rational creatures are necessarily bound by the moral law, then no empirical investigation of human value would be sufficient to discover the basis of moral duty. Not only is there considerable variability and difference in human values, but there may be other rational creatures besides human beings. As we will never be able to poll all rational wills, to see what they care about, we can only be sure of a necessary connection between rational wills and moral duty if moral duty is based on something other than human values. We must find a basis for duty that is shared, necessarily, by all rational wills. Kant finds that basis in rationality itself. As a result, he will begin his moral theorizing with an analysis of the basic concepts of rationality itself. Thus Kant insists that conceptual analysis alone will uncover the truth about morality.

> Since I am here primarily concerned with moral philosophy, the foregoing question will be limited to a consideration of whether or not there is the utmost necessity for working out for once a pure moral philosophy that is wholly cleared of everything which can only be empirical and can only belong to anthropology. That there must be such a philosophy is evident from the common idea of duty and of moral laws. Everyone must admit that if a law is to be morally valid. i.e., is to be valid as a ground of obligation, then it must carry with it absolute necessity. He must admit that the command, 'Thou shalt not lie,' does not hold only for men, as if other rational beings had no need to abide by it, and so with all the other moral laws properly so called. And he must concede that the ground of obligation here must therefore be sought not in the nature of man nor in the circumstances of the world in which man is placed, but must be sought a priori solely in the concepts of pure reason; he must grant that every other precept which is founded on principles of mere experience—even a precept that may in certain respects be universal—insofar as it rests in the least on empirical grounds—perhaps only in its motive—can indeed be called a practical rule, but never a moral law.[1]

Thus Kant employs a very different methodology than did the utilitarians. We explain each of these in more detail in what follows.

A Good Will

Kant famously rejects all subjective theories of value when he declares that there is nothing that is good without qualification except a good will. All of the internal traits of character and mind—intelligence, wit, judgement, courage, resolution, and perseverance—are not good without qualification, since they may be used for evil ends. The same is true of external advantages that many call good—power, riches, honour, and even health; all may be perverted into evils when enjoyed by the vicious, vain, or proud. Even happiness itself, says Kant, is not good in all cases. When an evil person is happy and enjoys all the comforts and contentments of life, this is a bad thing rather than a good thing. "Thus a good will seems to constitute the indispensable condition of being even worthy of happiness."[2] Having thus rejected all other possible candidates, Kant concludes that the only thing that is necessarily and always good is a good will.

Kant goes on to make it clear that a good will is good quite independently of any consequences it does or is expected to have.

> A good will is good not because of what it effects or accomplishes, nor because of its fitness to attain some proposed end; it is good only through its willing, i.e., it is good in itself. … Even if, by some unfortunate fate…, this will should be wholly lacking in the power to accomplish its purpose; if with the greatest effort it should yet achieve nothing, and only the good will should remain…, yet would it, like a jewel, still shine by its own light as something which has its full value in itself.[3]

But just what is it that a good will wills? How do we know that a will is good, independently of the consequences it brings about? Kant's answer is that a good will is one that wills to do its duty for duty's sake. There are two components to this answer. First, a good will acts in conformity to duty. But, further, a good will does so precisely out of respect for duty, rather than from any independent motive. Obviously the first requirement is that a person with a good will always does her duty; a good will can never act contrary to duty. But the second adds the requirement that the reason for doing her duty is respect for duty itself. And this adds quite a bit. For we often have independent reasons to do what duty requires. We might have selfish reasons to do our duty, when doing so serves our interests. Thus the reason a business person treats her customers honestly might be because doing so is a good business practice and serves her interest in staying in business. Likewise, Kant thinks we have a duty not to kill ourselves. Most people refrain from suicide for reasons that are independent of that duty, however, because they enjoy living. Likewise most parents care for their children because they love them and want them to thrive and be happy, rather than out of duty to do so. In such cases there are independent motives or inclinations that lead to actions that conform to duty, though they are not done from duty. The true test of a good will, then, arises from situations in which a person does not want to do her duty, when inclination or self-interest inclines against duty. Kant's example is of a person who suffers from adversity and hopeless sorrow to such an extent that he no longer desires to go on living. Should he, despite all other motives, refrain from committing suicide, he shall have acted from duty alone. And, Kant says, only then does his action have moral worth. Only actions willed out of respect for duty itself have true moral worth.

Categorical Imperative

What does it mean to act from duty alone? Kant has ruled out the moral value of actions undertaken to produce good consequences, for oneself or others, from love and other affections, from natural inclination, and from self-interest. Rather, a good will respects the moral law itself. It subordinates itself to the law as a necessity. Law is here conceived of as necessarily binding objective principles of pure practical reason. Such objective principles are commands of reason, and the formula of such commands are called imperatives. All such imperatives are expressed by "ought" statements, and represent the relation of an objective law of reason to a will. Such imperatives determine those with a good will.

But what sort of law can that be thought of which must determine the will without reference to any expected effect, so that the will can be called absolutely good without qualification? Since I have deprived the will of every impulse that might arise for it from obeying any particular law, there is nothing left to serve the will as principle except the universal conformity of its actions to law as such, i.e., I should never act except in such a way that I can also will that my maxim should become a universal law.[4]

From this basic description of imperatives as commanding the will, Kant develops the first formulation of the Categorical Imperative (the moral law).

- Categorical Imperative as Universalizability

  Act only according to that maxim whereby you can at the same time will that it should become a universal law.[5]

This formulation of the categorical imperative is often called the Universalizability Principle. It requires that we be willing to universalize the maxim upon which we propose to act. If you are not willing or able to universalize your proposed maxim, the action cannot be in conformity with the moral law. Two types of cases present themselves. First, there seem to be some cases in which you cannot coherently universalize your maxim, because doing so generates an inconsistency in the conception of your maxim. (This is often called the incoherence in conception test of universalizability.) Consider Kant's own example first, that of giving a false promise (a promise that you know, when making it, you intend not to keep). This is an unfortunately common experience, of course, but what we want to know is why it is wrong. Kant's answer here is that it is wrong because it rests on a maxim that cannot be coherently universalized. The maxim is something like "I may give a false promise (which is a species of lying) whenever it is necessary for some end I have." I may promise, for example, to repay a sum of money I wish to borrow from another, knowing that when the time comes to repay the money I will be unable to do so. I may indeed be able to will such a maxim for myself, as an exception to the general moral rules requiring truth-telling and promise-keeping. But I cannot will that this become a universal law. For to universalize the rule that everyone can make false promises and lie when it serves their interests to do so would undermine the very practice of promise making itself. Promise making as a practice depends upon trust that those making the promise will follow through, and are telling the truth about their intentions to do so. Such a practice would break down if we could not rely upon the word of others, and this would be the result of a universal law that allowed everyone to give false promises. A similar argument could be mounted with respect to many other immoral actions, which share this feature of making exceptions to the general rules just for oneself. Consider, for example, the case of cheating in university or on your taxes.

A second kind of incoherence might arise from violations of the categorical imperative. There may be some maxims that you cannot universalize because you cannot will the result. (This is the contradiction in the will test of universalizability.) Kant's example here is of a person who considers not giving aid to someone in serious need. Suppose you see someone in serious need of aid, which you can provide at little cost to yourself. You might think that you have no duty to provide the aid, because you can will the maxim that "no one gives aid to anyone else." There is nothing incoherent in the conception of such a practice, whereby everyone simply looks out for themselves. But, says Kant, there is still a problem, because you cannot will that others not come to your aid when you are in need. You will want their help yourself if you are in distress, and so you cannot universalize a law that allows everyone to withhold mutual assistance.[6]

Kant has now provided an answer to the question what a good will can will. It can only will maxims that can coherently be universalized as universal laws. It can only will categorical imperatives. He has not yet established a necessary connection between the categorical imperative and the idea of a rational will, however, such that a rational will must always follow the categorical imperative. He has not yet established that there is a practical principle requiring all rational beings always to judge their actions in the way laid down in the universalizability test. To understand how Kant establishes that all rational creatures ought to act from a good will, ought to act only on maxims that can be universalized, we need to say something briefly about rational action.

All rational action is for an end. All rational action, in other words, is purposeful, and involves agents selecting the most efficient and effective means to some end they are trying to realize, goal they are trying to satisfy or purpose they are trying to fulfil. Since all rational action is for an end, what Kant needs here is an end that is necessarily shared by all rational beings as such and that fulfilling that end requires all rational beings to will in accordance with the categorical imperative itself. He claims to find such an end, one that is given by reason alone and so is equally valid for all rational creatures, and which is of absolute worth as an end in itself: rational being itself.

> If then there is to be a supreme practical principle and, as far as the human will is concerned, a categorical imperative, then it must be such that from the conception of what is necessarily an end for everyone because this end is an end in itself it constitutes an objective principle of the will and can hence serve as a practical law. The ground of such a principle is this: rational nature exists as an end in itself. In this way man necessarily thinks of his own existence; thus far is it a subjective principle of human actions. But in this way also does every other rational being think of his existence on the same rational ground that holds also for me; hence it is at the same time an objective principle, from which, as a supreme practical ground, all laws of the will must be able to be derived. The practical imperative will therefore be the following:

- Categorical Imperative as Respect for Persons

   Act in such a way that you treat humanity, whether in your own person or in the person of another, always at the same time as an end and never simply as a means.[7]

Kant believes that the universalizability and respect for persons characterizations of the categorical imperative are two articulations of the same basic principle. The categorical imperative is the moral law by which all good wills are determined and the foundation from which are derived all specific moral duties.

To say that all good wills are determined by the categorical imperative might raise in the mind of readers two related questions at this point. Both concern the degree to which people have free will on Kant's view. What does it mean to say that all good wills are necessarily bound by the moral law? Does it mean, first, that every one must obey the dictates of morality? Can we ever choose to act immorally? Obviously Kant's theory had better make immoral actions possible, since we know that people act immorally quite often. So we must not interpret his claim that there is a necessary connection between rational willing and moral willing to rule out the possibility of immoral behaviour. In fact, Kant can easily recognize and accept that people act immorally as a matter of fact. This is because people are not only subject to objective practical principles, such as the categorical imperative, but subjective ones as well. Individual desires, inclinations and the like provide practical principles for the agent whose desires and inclinations they are. When a person acts on such principles, she may be practically rational. That is, she may be acting appropriately given her subjective ends. But if the case involves a conflict between the person's subjective principle and the objective principle of morality, then she must subordinate her subjective ends to her rational ends, that is, the only rational action for her will be the moral choice. If she nonetheless chooses to act immorally she will also be acting irrationally. In this way Kant says that rational wills will be determined by the categorical imperative, though not every person will act rationally in all instances.

There is a second way in which we might be bothered by the notion that all rational wills must be determined by the moral law, however. We might worry that if the moral law is universal and objective then it offends human autonomy and dignity. For it imposes constraints upon rational agents that are not just independent of what they happen to care about but it demands that people subordinate their individual concerns to the dictates of morality when the two come into conflict. Kant has an answer to this worry as well. Because the categorical imperative is based on respect for human rationality itself, treating persons as ends in themselves and never merely as means or things, and because it involves duties that can be willed by persons themselves as universally binding laws, individuals find themselves subordinate to the moral law in such a way that their autonomy and dignity are respected. It is not a law imposed upon people from the outside, but an articulation of a law that must bind all rational natures as such. Therefore Kant also provides the following alternative explication of the categorical imperative.

- Categorical Imperative as a Principle of Autonomy

  From this there now follows the third practical principle of the will as the supreme condition of the will's conformity with universal practical reason, viz., the idea of the will of every rational being as a will that legislates universal law.

  According to this principle all maxims are rejected which are not consistent with the will's own legislation of universal law. The will is thus not merely subject to the law but is subject to the law in such a way that it must be regarded also as legislating for itself and only on this account as being subject to the law (of which it can regard itself as the author).[8]

In this way Kant reconciles human freedom with subordination to the moral law, and reinforces the view that rational nature (the only kind which can set law for itself) is the ultimate value. Without such a reconciliation, subjecting an autonomous will to an objective law would seem to contradict the recognition of a rational nature as being of ultimate value (the only thing which is an end in itself).

Hypothetical Imperatives

Categorical imperatives are distinguished by Kant from merely hypothetical imperatives. Whereas categorical imperatives represent actions as objectively necessary in themselves (as commands of pure reason), hypothetical imperatives represent the necessity of an action only as a means for attaining something else that one wants. Categorical imperatives take the form "You ought to do x." They are binding on every rational will. Hypothetical imperatives, by contrast, must always refer to the end for which they ought to be done. They have this form: "If you want y, you ought to do x." Here you ought to perform some action as a means to an end which you have. The imperative is conditional, as a practical directive of reason, on you actually having that end. Generally what hypothetical imperatives individuals are bound by depend upon what their individual ends or goals happen to be. For this reason hypothetical imperatives are generally not binding on all rational agents as such.

There is one exception that Kant allows to this, when he acknowledges that it is a fixed feature of human nature that all people want to be happy. All people have as one of their ends, by a kind of natural necessity, the desire to be happy. As such, all human beings will be subject to the hypothetical imperatives of prudence, which command that they take the necessary means to attain their own happiness. This is so because Kant considers it analytic that "Whoever wills the end, wills (so far as reason has decisive influence on his actions) also the means that are indispensably necessary to his actions and that lie in his power."[9] Yet even in this case Kant denies to the resulting imperatives the kind of objective necessity that belongs to the commands of morality. He does so on the grounds that we cannot know completely what will make us happy, and so we cannot know with certainty what prudence requires. As a result, he says, prudence issues at most general counsels rather than specific commands. Further, because such imperatives depend on the prior purpose of achieving happiness, they remain hypothetical.

Kant's view is that any moral theory that attempts to ground moral duty or moral law in contingent (even if universal) facts about human beings (including that they desire to be happy, that they have certain preferences, that they value certain activities or any other subjective states about which we can know only empirically, by experience), such as utilitarianism, must remain inadequate. For such theories cannot show morality to be anything more than hypothetically binding upon people; such a theory cannot capture the inescapable and universal force of morality.

[T]he categorical imperative alone purports to be a practical law, while all the others may be called principles of the will but not laws. The reason for this is that whatever is necessary merely in order to attain some arbitrary purpose can be regarded as in itself contingent, and the precept can always be ignored once the purpose is abandoned. Contrariwise, an unconditional command does not leave the will free to choose the opposite at its own liking. Consequently, only such a command carries with it that necessity which is demanded from a law.[10]

Thus Kant denies that utilitarians, or any other theorists, who make a subjective conception of human good the foundation of their theories, can provide an adequate account of morality.

Duties

Kant believes he can derive from the categorical imperative a complete catalogue of duties. He begins by dividing duties into two general categories: duties to self and others, and perfect and imperfect duties. Perfect duties are those without exceptions; they hold in all circumstances. Imperfect duties are those that either allow exceptions in the interest of inclination, or permit the person who owes the duty considerable choice in how to fulfil it; such duties do not determine a unique action in each and every circumstance. There are both perfect and imperfect duties to both self and others, which results in a four-fold division. The following are Kant's examples of each.

Perfect duty to oneself: Self-preservation; the duty not to commit suicide.

Perfect duty to others: Keeping promises and telling the truth.

Imperfect duty to oneself: Developing one's natural talents.

Imperfect duty to others: Charity and the rendering of aid to those in need.

Kant claims to be able to derive these duties from the Categorical Imperative directly, using the universalizability standard of morality. We leave it to the reader to figure out why we cannot universalize maxims that contradict these duties, using the incoherence in conception and contradiction in will tests.[11] We also leave it to the reader to determine in what way violating the duties set out contravene the respect for persons principle, that is, why violating our duties treats humanity as a mere means and not as an end in itself.[12]

Dignity and Price

Kant distinguishes between things that have a price and things that have dignity. All things that have a price can be replaced by something else as an equivalent, because they are means to the satisfaction of human needs, inclinations, or tastes. Their worth depends upon the contingencies of human desires and affections, and external circumstances. They are valued for their effects and the advantages they provide. As such, things with a price can be elements in hypothetical imperatives only. By contrast, things with dignity cannot be so replaced. Only things that can be ends in themselves, of intrinsic worth, have dignity. Thus, for reasons that should be clear by now, Kant believes that only rational natures have dignity. And the foundation of that dignity is the very power that makes morality and freedom jointly possible for us, as legislators of the moral law, namely, rational autonomy.

✦ ✦ ✦

Onora O'Neill, Ending World Hunger

Onora O'Neill, while recognizing that Kantianism cannot give specific advice regarding how one ought to fulfil one's moral duties, nevertheless presents a compelling example of how to reason about which particular obligations one has. Focusing on Kant's imperative that one may never treat anyone merely as means, but instead as ends in themselves, O'Neill explains how this imperative entails a duty to relieve world hunger and poverty. People are treated as mere means when their autonomy is undercut. When coerced to perform an action or to agree to certain terms, or lied to for the same (or other) ends, people are not able to act autonomously. Refraining from force and fraud are not the only requirements of treating people as ends in themselves. Respecting people as ends in themselves also requires sustaining their autonomy when it is in jeopardy. Autonomy, for O'Neill, is a matter of degree, and when it is threatened, respect for autonomous agency requires others to defend it (imagine an attempt to universalize the rule that no one aids another when his or her autonomy is threatened). Insofar as we understand hunger and poverty to undercut autonomy, then we have a duty to give aid to the hungry and the poor.

O'Neill also takes some time to examine Kantianism along side both utilitarianism and libertarianism on such issues as respect for life and the duty to aid the poor. Kantianism seems to compare quite favourably against such theories on these issues given many of our moral judgements. Such comparisons are essential when reasoning about which general moral principles might lie behind our particular moral judgements. But we must be cautious about giving up a possible moral rule too quickly in the face of a single counter-intuitive result. Our particular moral judgements are up for revision as well. It is only after we see how well each theory does in capturing our moral judgements, and which revisions to our moral judgements we then find acceptable, that we may come to a well-reasoned conclusion regarding any possible moral rule.

✦ ✦ ✦

Kant's Formula of the End in Itself and World Hunger

Onora O'Neill

A Simplified Account of Kant's Ethics

Kant's theory is frequently and misleadingly assimilated to theories of human rights. It is, in fact, a theory of human obligations; therefore it is wider in scope than a theory of human rights. (Not all obligations have corresponding rights.) Kant does not, however, try to generate a set of precise rules defining human obligations in all possible circumstances; instead, he attempts to provide a set of *principles of obligation* that can be used as the starting points for moral reasoning in actual contexts of action. The primary focus of Kantian ethics is, then, on *action* rather than either *results*, as in utilitarian thinking, or *entitlements*, as in theories that make human rights their fundamental category. Morality requires action of certain sorts. But to know *what* sort of action is required (or forbidden) in which circumstances, we should not look just at the expected results of action or at others' supposed entitlements but, in the first instance, at the nature of the proposed actions themselves.

When we engage in moral reasoning, we often need go no further than to refer to some quite specific principle or tradition. We may say to one another, or to ourselves, things like "It would be hypocritical to pretend that our good fortune is achieved without harm to the Third World" or "Redistributive taxation shouldn't cross national boundaries." But when these specific claims are challenged, we may find ourselves pushed to justify or reject or modify them. Such moral debate, on Kant's account, rests on appeals to what he calls the *Supreme Principle of Morality*, which can (he thinks) be used to work out more specific principles of obligation. This principle, the famous Categorical Imperative, plays the same role in Kantian thinking that the Greatest Happiness Principle plays in utilitarian thought.

A second reason why Kant's moral thought often appears difficult is that he offers a number of different versions of this principle, which he claims are equivalent but which look very different. A straightforward way in which to simplify Kantian moral thought is to concentrate on just one of these formulations of the Categorical Imperative. For present purposes I shall choose the version to which he gives the sonorous name, *The Formula of the End in Itself.*

The Formula of the End in Itself

The Formula of the End in Itself runs as follows:

> Act in such a way that you always treat humanity, whether in your own person or in the person of any other, never simply as a means but always at the same time as an end.

To understand this principle we need in the first place to understand what Kant means by the term 'maxim.' The maxim of an act or policy or activity is the *underlying principle* of the act, policy, or activity, by which other, more superficial aspects of action are guided. Very often interpretations of Kant have supposed that maxims can only be the (underlying) intentions of individual human agents. If that were the case it would limit the usefulness of Kantian modes of moral thought in dealing with world hunger and famine problems. For it is clear enough that individual action (while often important) cannot deal with all the problems of Third World poverty. A moral theory that addresses *only* individual actors does not have adequate scope for discussing famine problems. As we have seen, one of the main attractions of utilitarianism as an approach to Third World poverty is that its scope is so broad: it can be applied with equal appropriateness to the practical deliberations of individuals, of institutions and groups, and even of nation states and international agencies. Kantian ethical thinking can be interpreted (though it usually isn't) to have equally broad scope.

Since maxims are *underlying* principles of action, they may not always be obvious either to the individuals or institutions whose maxims they are, or to others. We can determine what the underlying principles of some activity or institution are only by seeing the patterns made by various more superficial aspects of acts, policies, and activities. Only those principles that would generate that pattern of activity are maxims of action. Sometimes more than one principle might lie behind a given pattern of activity, and we may be unsure what the maxim of the act was. For example, we might wonder (as Kant does) how to tell whether somebody gives change accurately only out of concern to have on honest reputation or whether he or she would do so anyhow. In such cases we can sometimes set up an "isolation test"—for example, a situation in which it would be open to somebody to be dishonest without any chance of a damaged reputation. But quite often we can't set up any such situation and may be to some extent unsure which maxim lies behind a given act. Usually we have to rely on whatever individual actors tell us about their maxims of action and on what policymakers or social scientists may tell us about the underlying principles of institutional or group action. What they tell us may well be mistaken. While mistakes can be reduced by care and thoughtfulness, there is no guarantee that we can always work out which maxim of action should be scrutinized for purposes of judging what others do. On the other hand, there is no problem when we are trying to guide our own action: if we can find out what duty demands, we can try to meet those demands.

It is helpful to think of some examples of maxims that might be used to guide action in contexts where poverty and the risk of famine are issues. Somebody who contributes to famine-relief work or advocates development might have an underlying principle such as, "Try to help reduce the risk or severity of world hunger." This commitment might be reflected in varied surface action in varied situations. In one context a gift of money might be relevant; in another some political activity such as lobbying for or against certain types of aid and trade might express the same underlying commitment. Sometimes superficial aspects of action may seem at variance with the underlying maxim they in fact express. For example, if there is reason to think that indiscriminate food aid damages the agricultural economy of the area to which food is given, then the maxim of seeking to relieve hunger might be expressed in action aimed at *limiting* the extent of food aid. More lavish use of food aid might *seem* to treat the needy more generously, but if in fact it will damage their medium- or long-term economic prospects, then it is not (contrary to superficial appearances) aimed at improving and securing their access to subsistence. On a Kantian theory, the basis for judging action should be its *fundamental* principle or policy, and superficially similar acts may be judged morally very different. Regulating food aid in order to drive up prices and profit from them is one matter; regulating food aid in order to enable local farmers to sell their crops and to stay in the business of growing food is quite another.

When we want to work out whether a proposed act or policy is morally required we should not, on Kant's view, try to find out whether it would produce more happiness than other available acts. Rather we should see whether the act or policy is required if we are to avoid acting on maxims that use others as mere means and act on maxims that treat others as ends in themselves. These two aspects of Kantian duty can each be spelled out and shown to have determinate implications for acts and policies that may affect the persistence of hunger and the risk and course of famines.

Using Others as Mere Means

We use others as *mere means* if what we do reflects some maxim *to which they could not in principle consent*. Kant does not suggest that there is anything wrong about using someone as a means. Evidently every cooperative scheme of action does this. A government that agrees to provide free or subsidized food to famine-relief agencies both uses and is used by the agencies; a peasant who sells food in a local market both uses and is used by those who buy the food. In such examples each party to the transaction can and does consent to take part in that transaction. Kant would say that the parties to such transactions use one another but do not use one another as *mere means*. Each party assumes that the other has its own maxims of action and is not just a thing or prop to be used or manipulated.

But there are other cases where one party to an arrangement or transaction not only uses the other but does so in ways that could only be done on the basis of fundamental principle or maxim to which the other could not in principle consent. If, for example, a false promise is given, the party that accepts the promise is not just used but used as a mere means, because it is *impossible* for consent to be given to the fundamental principle or project of deception that must guide every false promise, whatever its surface character. Those who accept false promises *must* be kept ignorant of the underlying principle or maxim on which the "undertaking" is based. If this isn't kept concealed, the attempted promise will either be rejected or will not be a *false* promise at all. In false promising, the deceived party becomes, as it were, a prop or tool—a *mere means*—in the false promisor's scheme. Action based on any such maxim of deception would be wrong in Kantian terms, whether it is a matter of a breach of treaty obligations, of contractual undertakings, or of accepted and relied upon modes of interaction. Maxims of deception *standardly* use others as mere means, and acts that could only be based on such maxims are unjust.

Other standard ways of using others as mere means is by violence or coercion. Here too victims have no possibility of refusing what is done to them. If a rich or powerful landowner or nation destroys a poorer or more vulnerable person, group, or nation or threatens some intolerable difficulty unless a concession is made, the more vulnerable party is denied a genuine choice between consent and dissent. While the boundary that divides violence and coercion from mere bargaining and negotiation varies and is therefore often hard to discern, we have no doubt about the clearer cases. Maxims of violence destroy or damage agents or their capabilities. Maxims of coercion may threaten physical force, seizure of possessions, destruction of opportunities, or any other harm that the coerced party is thought to be unable to absorb without grave injury or danger. For example, a grain dealer in a Third World village who threatens not to make or renew an indispensable loan without which survival until the next harvest would be impossible, unless he is sold the current crop at pitifully low prices, uses the peasant as mere means. The peasant does not have the possibility of genuinely consenting to the "offer he can't refuse." In this way the outward form of some coercive transactions may *look* like ordinary commercial dealings: but we know very well that some action that is superficially of this sort is based on maxims of coercion. To avoid coercion, action must be governed by maxims that the other party can choose to refuse and is not forced to accept. The more vulnerable the other party in any transaction or negotiation, the less that party's scope for refusal, and the more demanding it is likely to be to ensure that action is noncoercive.

In Kant's view, acts done on maxims that endanger, coerce, or deceive others, and thus cannot in principle have the consent of those others, are wrong. When individuals, institutions, or nation states act in ways that can only be based on such maxims, they fail in their duty. They treat the parties who are either deceived or coerced unjustly. To avoid unjust action it is not enough to observe the outward forms of free agreement, cooperation, and market disciplines; it is also essential to see that the weaker party to any arrangement has a genuine option to refuse the fundamental character of the proposal.

Treating Others as Ends in Themselves

For Kant, as for utilitarians, justice is only one part of duty. We may fail in our duty, even when we don't use anyone as mere means, if we fail to treat others as "ends in themselves." To treat others as ends in themselves we must not only avoid using them as mere means but also treat them as rational and autonomous beings with their own maxims. In doing so we must also remember that (as Kant repeatedly stressed, but later Kantians have often forgotten) human beings are *finite* rational beings in several ways. First, human beings are not ideal rational calculators. We *standardly* have neither a complete list of the actions possible in a given situation nor more than a partial view of their likely consequences. In addition, abilities to assess and to use available information are usually quite limited. Second, these cognitive limitations are *standardly* complemented by limited autonomy. Human action is limited not only by various sorts of physical barrier and inability but by further sorts of (mutual or asymmetrical) *dependence*. To treat one another as ends in themselves such beings have to base their action on principles that do not undermine but rather sustain and extend one another's capacities for autonomous action. A central requirement for doing so is to share and support one another's ends and activities to some extent. Since finite rational beings cannot generally achieve their aims without some help and support from others, a general refusal of help and support amounts to failure to treat others as rational and autonomous beings, that is, as ends in themselves. Hence Kantian principles require us not only to act justly, that is, in accordance with maxims that don't injure, coerce, or deceive others, but also to avoid manipulation and to lend some support to others' plans and activities. Since hunger, great poverty, and powerlessness all undercut the possibility of autonomous action, and the requirement of treating others as ends in themselves demands that Kantians standardly act to support the possibility of autonomous action where it is most vulnerable, Kantians are required to do what they can to avert, reduce, and remedy hunger. They cannot of course do everything to avert hunger: but they may not do nothing.

Justice and Beneficence in Kant's Thought

Kant is often thought to hold that justice is morally required, but beneficence is morally less important. He does indeed, like Mill, speak of justice as a *perfect duty* and of beneficence as an *imperfect duty*. But he does not mean by this that beneficence is any less a duty; rather he holds that it has (unlike justice) to be selective. We cannot share or even support *all* others' maxims *all* of the time. Hence support for others' autonomy is always selective. By contrast we can make all action and institutions conform fundamentally to standards of nondeception and noncoercion. Kant's understanding of the distinction between perfect and imperfect duties differs from Mill's. In a Kantian perspective justice is more than the core of beneficence, as in Mill's theory, and beneficence isn't just an attractive but optional moral embellishment of just arrangements (as tends to be assumed in most theories that take human rights as fundamental).

Justice to the Vulnerable in Kantian Thinking

For Kantians, justice requires action that conforms (at least outwardly) to what could be done in a given situation while acting on maxims that use nobody. Since anyone hungry or destitute is more than usually vulnerable to deception, violence, and coercion, the possibilities and temptations to injustice are then especially strong. They are often strongest for those who are nearest to acute poverty and hunger, so could (if they chose) exploit others' need.

Examples are easily suggested. I shall begin with some situations that might arise for somebody who happened to be part of a famine-stricken population. Where shortage of food is being dealt with by a reasonably fair rationing scheme, any mode of cheating to get more than one's allocated share involves using some others and is unjust. Equally, taking advantage of others' desperation to profiteer—for example, selling food at colossal prices or making loans on the security of others' future livelihood, when these are "offers they can't refuse"—constitutes coercion, uses others as mere means, and so is unjust. Transactions that have the outward form of normal commercial dealings may be coercive when one party is desperate. Equally, forms of corruption that work by deception—such as bribing officials to gain special benefits from development schemes, or deceiving others about these entitlements—use others unjustly. Such requirements are far from trivial and are frequently violated in hard times; acting justly in such conditions may involve risking one's own life and livelihood and may require the greatest courage.

It is not so immediately obvious what justice, Kantianly conceived, requires of agents and agencies who are remote from destruction. Might it not be sufficient to argue that those of us fortunate enough to live in the developed world are far from famine and destruction, so if we do nothing but go about our usual business will we successfully avoid injustice to the destitute? This conclusion has often been reached by those who take an abstract view of rationality and forget the limits of human rationality and autonomy. To such people it seems that there is nothing more to just action than non-interference with others. But once we remember the limitations of human rationality and autonomy, and the particular ways in which they are limited for those living close to the margins of subsistence, we can see that mere "noninterfering" conformity to ordinary standards of commercial honesty and political bargaining is not enough for justice toward the destitute. If the demands of the powerful constitute "offers that cannot be refused" by the government or by the citizens of a poor country, or if the concessions required for investment by a transnational corporation or a development project reflect the desperation of recipients rather than an appropriate contribution to the project, then (however benevolent the motives of some parties) the weaker party to such agreements is used by the stronger.

In the earlier days of European colonial penetration of the now underdeveloped world it was evident enough that some of the ways in which "agreements" were made with native peoples were in fact violent, deceptive, or coercive—or all three. "Sales" of land by those who had no grasp of market practices and "cession of sovereignty" by those whose forms of life were prepolitical constitute only spurious consent to the agreements struck. But it is not only in these original forms of bargaining between powerful and powerless that injustice is frequent. There are many contemporary examples. For example, if capital investment in a poorer country requires the receiving country or some of its institutions or citizens to contribute disproportionately to the maintenance of a developed, urban "enclave" economy that offers little local employment but lavish standards of life for a small number of (possibly expatriate) "experts," while guaranteeing long-term exemption from local taxation for the investors, then we may doubt that the agreement could have been struck without the element of coercion provided by the desperation by the weaker party. Often enough the coercers in such cases are members of the local as well as the international elite. Or if a trade agreement extracts political advantages (such as military bases) that are incompatible with the fundamental political interests of the country concerned, we may judge that at least some leaders of that country have been "bought" in a sense that is not constant with ordinary commercial practice.

Even when the actions of those who are party to an agreement don't reflect a fundamental principle of violence, coercion, or deception, the agreement may alter the life circumstances and prospects of third parties in ways to which they patently could not have not consented. For example, a system of food aid and imports agreed upon by the government of a Third World country and certain developed states or international agencies may give the elite of that Third World country access to subsidized grain. If that grain is then used to control the urban population and also produces destitution among peasants (who used to grow food for that urban population), then those who are newly destitute probably have not been offered any opening or possibility of refusing their new and worsened conditions of life. If a policy is imposed, those affected *cannot* have been given a chance to refuse it: had the chance been there, they would either have assented (and so the policy would not have been *imposed*) or refused (and so proceeding with the policy would have been evidently coercive), or they would have been able to renegotiate the terms of trade.

Beneficence to the Vulnerable in Kantian Thinking

In Kantian moral reasoning, the basis for beneficent action is that without it we will fail to treat others of limited rationality and autonomy as ends in themselves. This is not to say that Kantian beneficence won't make others happier, for it will do so whenever they would be happier if (more) capable of autonomous action, but that happiness secured by purely paternalistic means, or at the cost (for example) of manipulating others' desires, will not count as beneficent in the Kantian picture. Clearly the vulnerable position of those who lack the very means of life, and their severely curtailed possibilities for autonomous action, offer many different ways in which it might be possible for others to act beneficently. Where the means of life are meager, almost any material or organizational advance may help extend possibilities for autonomy. Individual or institutional action that aims to advance economic or social development can proceed on many routes. The provision of clean water, of improved agricultural techniques, of better grain storage systems, or of adequate means of local transport may all help transform material prospects. Equally, help in the development of new forms of social organization—whether peasant self-help groups, urban cooperatives, medical and contraceptive services, or improvements in education or in the position of women—may help to extend possibilities for autonomous action. While the central core of such development projects will be requirements of justice, their full development will also demand concern to treat others as ends in themselves, by paying attention to their particular needs and desires. Kantian thinking does not provide a means by which all possible ways of treating others as ends in themselves could be listed and ranked. But where some activity helps secure possibilities for autonomous action for more people, or is likely to achieve a permanent improvement in the position of the most vulnerable, or is one that can be done with more reliable success, this provides reason for furthering that way of treating others as ends.

Clearly the alleviation of need must rank far ahead of the furthering of happiness in other ways in the Kantian picture. I might make my friends very happy by throwing extravagant parties: but this would probably not increase anybody's possibility for autonomous action to any great extent. But the sorts of development-oriented changes that have just been mentioned may *transform* the possibilities for action of some. Since hunger and the risk of famine are always and evidently highly damaging to human autonomy, any action that helps avoid or reduce famine must have a strong claim on any Kantian who is thinking through what beneficence requires. Depending on circumstances, such action may have to take the form of individual contribution to famine relief and development organizations, of individual or collective effort to influence the trade and aid policies of developed countries, or of attempts to influence the activities of those Third World elites for whom development does not seem to be an urgent priority. Some approaches can best be undertaken by private citizens of developed countries by way of lobbying, publicity, and education; others are best approached by those who work for governments, international agencies, or transnational corporations, who can "work from within" to influence the decisions and policies of these institutions. Perhaps the most dramatic possibilities to act for a just or an unjust, a beneficent or selfish future belongs to those who hold positions of power or influence within the Third World. But wherever we find ourselves, our duties are not, on the Kantian picture, limited to those close at hand. Duties of justice arise whenever there is some involvement between parties—and in the modern world this is never wholly lacking. Duties of beneficence arise whenever destitution puts the possibility of autonomous action in question for the more vulnerable. When famines were not only far away, but nothing could be done to relieve them, beneficence or charity legitimately began—and stayed—near home. In an interconnected world, the moral significance of distance has shrunk, and we may be able to affect the capacities for autonomous action of those who are far away.

The Scope of Kantian Deliberations about Hunger and Famine

In many ways Kantian moral reasoning is less ambitious than utilitarian moral reasoning. It does not propose a process of moral reasoning that can (in principle) rank *all* possible actions or all possible institutional arrangements from the happiness-maximizing "right" action or institutional downward. It aims rather to offer a pattern of reasoning by which we can identify whether proposed *action or institutional arrangements* would be just or unjust, beneficent or lacking in beneficence. While *some* knowledge of causal connections is needed for Kantian reasoning, it is far less sensitive than is utilitarian reasoning to gaps in our causal knowledge. It may therefore help us reach conclusions that are broadly accurate even if they are imprecise. The conclusions reached about particular proposals for action or about institutional arrangements will not hold for all time, but be relevant for the contexts for which action is proposed. For example, if it is judged that some institution—say, the World Bank—provides, under present circumstances, a just approach to certain development problems, it will not follow that under all other circumstances such an institution would be part of a just approach. There may be other institutional arrangements that are also just; and there may be other circumstances under which the institutional structure of the World Bank would be shown to be in some ways unjust.

These points show us that Kantian deliberations about hunger can lead only to conclusions that are useful in determinate contexts. This, however, is standardly what we need to know for action, whether individual or institutional. We do not need to be able to generate a complete list of available actions in order to determine whether proposed lines of action are not unjust and whether any are beneficent. Kantian patterns of moral reasoning cannot be guaranteed to identify the optimal course of action in a situation. They provide methods neither for listing nor for ranking all possible proposals for action. But any line of action that is considered can be checked to see whether it is part of what justice and beneficence require—or of what they forbid.

The reason this pattern of reasoning will not show any action or arrangement of the most beneficent one available is that the Kantian picture of beneficence is less mathematically structured than the utilitarian one. It judges beneficence by its overall contribution to the prospects for human autonomy and not by the quantity of happiness expected to result. To the extent that the autonomous pursuit of goals is what Mill called "one of the principal ingredients of human happiness" (but only to that extent), the requirements of Kantian and of utilitarian beneficence will coincide. But whenever expected happiness is not a function of the scope for autonomous action, the two accounts of beneficent action diverge. For utilitarians, paternalistic imposition of, for example, certain forms of aid and development assistance need not be wrong and may even be required. But for Kantians, who think that beneficence should secure others' possibilities for autonomous action, the case for paternalistic imposition of aid or development projects without the recipients' involvement must always be questionable.

In terms of some categories in which development projects are discussed, utilitarian reasoning may well endorse "top-down" aid and development projects that override whatever capacities for autonomous choice and action the poor of a certain area now have in the hopes of securing a happier future. If the calculations work out in a certain way, utilitarians may even think a "generation of sacrifice"—or of forced labor or of imposed population-control policies—not only permissible but mandated. In their darkest Malthusian moments some utilitarians have thought that average happiness might best be maximized not by improving the lot of the poor but by minimizing their numbers, and so have advocated policies of harsh neglect of the poorest and most desperate. Kantian patterns of reasoning are likely to endorse less global and less autonomy-overriding aid and development projects; they are not likely to endorse neglect or abandoning of those who are most vulnerable and lacking in autonomy. If the aim of beneficence is to keep or put others in a position to act for themselves, the emphasis must be placed on "bottom-up" projects, which from the start draw on, foster, and establish indigenous capacities and practices for self-help and local action.

UTILITARIANS, KANTIANS, AND RESPECT FOR LIFE

Respect for Life in Utilitarian Reasoning

In the contrasting utilitarian and Kantian pictures of moral reasoning and of their implications for hunger, we can also discern two sharply contrasting pictures of the value of human life.

Utilitarians, since they value happiness above all, aim to achieve the happiest possible world. If their life plans remain unclear, this is because the means to this end are often unclear. But one implication of this position is entirely clear. It is that if happiness is the supreme value, then anything may and ought to be sacrificed for the sake of a greater happiness. Lesser possibilities of happiness and even life itself ought to be sacrificed to achieve maximal happiness. Such sacrifices may be required even when those whose happiness or lives are sacrificed are not willing. Rearing the fabric of felicity may be a bloody business. It all depends on the causal connections.

As our control over the means of ending and preserving lives has increased, utilitarians have confronted many uncomfortable questions. Should life be preserved at the cost of pain when modern medicine makes this possible? Or will happiness be greater if euthanasia is permitted under certain circumstances? Should the most afflicted be left to starve in famine situations if the happiness of all, and perhaps the average happiness, will be greater if those whose recovery is not likely to be complete are absent? Should population growth be fostered so long as total (or again perhaps average) happiness is increased, even if other sorts of difficulties arise? Should forced labor and enforced redistribution of income across national boundaries be imposed for the sake of a probably happier world? How far ought utilitarians to insist on the sacrifice of comforts, liberties, and even lives in order to "rear the fabric of felicity"?

Utilitarians do not deny that their moral reasoning raises many questions of these sorts. But the imprecision of our knowledge of consequences often blurs the answers to these questions. As we peer through the blur, we can see that on a utilitarian view lives must be sacrificed to build a happier world if this is the most efficient way to do so, whether or not those who lose their lives are willing. There is nothing wrong with using another as mere means, provided that the end in view is a happier result than could have been achieved any other way, taking account of the misery the means may have caused. In utilitarian thinking, persons are not ends in themselves. Their special moral status, such as it is, derives from their being means to the production of happiness. But they are not even necessary means for this end, since happiness can be located in nonhuman lives. It may even turn out that maximal happiness requires the sacrifice of human for the sake of animal lives.

In utilitarian thinking life has a high but derivative value, and some lives may have to be sacrificed for the sake of greater happiness or reduced misery in other lives. Nor is there a deep difference between ending others' lives by not helping (as some Malthusians suggest) and doing so as a matter of deliberate intervention or policy.

Respect for Life in Kantian Reasoning

Kantians reach different conclusions about human life. They see it as valuable because humans have considerable (but still quite incomplete) capacities for autonomous action. There may be other beings with more complete capacities, but we are not acquainted with them. Christian tradition speaks of angels; Kant referred to hypothetical beings he called Holy Wills; writers of science fiction have multiplied the varieties. There are certainly other beings with fewer capacities for autonomous action than humans standardly have. Whether we think that (some) animals should not be used as mere means, or should be treated as ends in themselves, is going to depend on the particular picture we have of partial autonomy and on the capacities we find that certain sorts of animals have or are capable of acquiring. This is a large question, around which I shall put some hasty brackets. It is quite an important issue in working out the famine and development implications of Kantian thinking, since development strategies have different implications for various animal species. For the moment, however, I shall consider only some implications of human capacities for (partially) autonomous action in Kantian thinking on respect for human life in contexts of acute vulnerability, such as destitution and (threatened) hunger.

The fundamental idea behind the Categorical Imperative is that the actions of a plurality of rational beings can be mutually consistent. A minimal condition for their mutual consistency is that each, in acting autonomously, not preclude others' autonomous action. This requirement can be spelled out, as in the formula of the end in itself, by insisting that each avoid action that the other could not freely join in (hence avoid violence, deception, and coercion) and that each seek to foster and secure others' capacities for autonomous action. What this actually takes will, as we have seen, vary with circumstances. But it is clear enough that the partial autonomy of human beings is undermined by life-threatening and destroying circumstances, such as hunger and destitution. Hence a fundamental Kantian commitment must be to preserve life in two senses. First, others must not be deprived of life. The dead (as well as the moribund, the gravely ill, and the famine-stricken) cannot act. Second, others' lives must be preserved in forms that offer them sufficient physical energy, psychological space, and social security for action. Partial autonomy is vulnerable autonomy, and in human life psychological and social as well as material needs must be met if any but the most meager possibility of autonomous action is to be preserved. Kantians are therefore committed to the preservation not only of biological but of biographical life. To act in the typical ways humans are capable of we must not only be alive, but have a life to lead.

On a Kantian view, we may justifiably—even nobly—risk or sacrifice our lives for others. When we do so, we act autonomously, and nobody uses us as a mere means. But we cannot justly use others (nor they us) as mere means in a scheme that could only be based on violence, deception, or coercion. Nor may we always refuse others the help they need to sustain the very possibility of autonomous action. Of course, no amount of beneficence could put anyone in the position to do all possible actions: that is not what we need to be concerned about. What we do need to be concerned about is failure to secure for others a possibility of some range of autonomous action.

Where others' possibilities for autonomous action are eroded by poverty and malnutrition, the necessary action must clearly include moves to change the picture. But these moves will not meet Kantian requirements if they provide merely calories and basic medicine; they must also seek to enable those who began to be adequately fed to act autonomously. They must foster the capabilities that human beings need to function effectively. They must therefore aim at least at minimal security and subsistence. Hence the changes that Kantians argue or work for must always be oriented to development plans that create enough economic self-sufficiency and social security for independence in action to be feasible and sustainable. There is no royal road to this result and no set of actions that is likely to be either universally or totally effective. Too many changes are needed, and we have too little understanding of the precise causal connections that limit some possibilities and guarantee others. But some broadly accurate, if imprecise, indication of ranges of required action, or ranges of action from which at least some are required, is possible.

NEARBY HUNGER AND POVERTY

Hunger and Welfare in Rich Countries

So far we have been considering how we might think about and respond to the poverty, hunger, and famine that are characteristic of parts of the developing world. However, both poverty and hunger can be found nearer home. Poverty in the developed world is nowhere so widespread or acute as to risk famine; but it is well documented. Hunger in the developed world is doubly hidden. As always, it shows more in the blighting of lives and health than in literal deaths. However, in contrast to Third World poverty, poverty in rich countries is a minority problem that affects parts of the population whom not everybody meets. Perhaps the most visible aspect of this poverty-amid-wealth in the 1990s is the number of homeless people now to be found on the streets of great and once-great cities in some of the richest societies of the world. In the warmer climates of the Third World, the need for warm and decent housing is also often unmet—but homelessness is nowhere a worse experience than in the colder parts of the developed world. Although the homeless of the rich world may be able to command money that would constitute wealth in a very poor country, its purchasing power where they are is not enough for minimal housing, decent hygiene, and clothing and may not be enough for adequate food. Apart from the highly visible homeless there are many others in the richer countries who for one reason or another go hungry.

The utilitarian and Kantian ways of thinking considered in this chapter have clear implications for responses to nearby hunger. For utilitarians there will be no doubt that this hunger too produces misery, and should be ended by whatever means will add to the total of human happiness. Many of the strategies that have been used successfully to eradicate hunger in some developed countries have been strongly influenced by this utilitarian thinking. For example, in many western European states social welfare systems guarantee basic welfare, including health care for all, and minimal income. The public policies of these welfare states are funded by taxation, and there would be wide public agreement that these policies produce a greater total happiness than would *laissez-faire* policies, which would leave the poor without a publicly funded "safety net." Opposition to welfare state policies, which can reliably reduce poverty and end hunger, is not likely to come from utilitarians. On the contrary, utilitarian activism has been one of the major forces behind the emergence of welfare states.

Opposition to a welfare state has, however, been vocal among some sorts of human rights thinkers. They articulate the worry that a welfare state, like foreign aid or food aid, is unjust to those who are taxed to provide the funds, and damaging to those who become dependent on what they often disparagingly call welfare handouts.

The objection to redistributive taxation has been part of a long-standing polemic between advocates of "equality" and of "liberty" during the period of the Cold War. Some of the advocates of liberty (often called libertarians) have adopted an extreme view of the demands of liberty, and argue that unrestricted rights to property-without-taxation are a human right. They conclude that the welfare state is an attack on human liberty. Equally, some advocates of equality have argued for a very strong imposition of material equality, which would indeed make heavy inroads into individual liberty. The underlying arguments for both extreme positions, and for their favored interpretations of human rights, are quite unconvincing. In practice, societies have to strike some balance between liberty and equality. Good social welfare policies are an attractive way of accommodating liberty and equality because they ensure that nobody is so vulnerable that their liberty is wholly eroded, but they do so without a heavy reduction of liberty of those who pay the necessary taxes. The even-handed collection of just taxes leaves richer citizens very great liberty to lead their lives as they will, and enables poorer citizens to reach a minimally decent standard of living that secures their capabilities for leading their lives with dignity. The real issues for social policymakers in the area of taxation have to do with questions about the containment of costs, the fairness of taxation, and the efficiency of its collection rather than with illusory attempts to create societies that embody liberty without equality, or equality without liberty.

The second of these worries, that welfare creates dependence, is a rather implausible objection to policies that end hunger: nothing damages autonomy and creates vulnerability and dependence as much as debilitating hunger and demeaning homelessness. A lack of welfare systems perhaps guarantees that the poor do not depend on the state, but it increases rather than ends their dependence. Worries about dependence have a limited appropriate role in considering *what sort* of welfare policies to pursue. Should welfare payments be in cash or in kind? How far is means testing needed? Should support go to families or to individuals? Do some welfare systems damage the incentive to work? These detailed questions, rather than ideological defense either of unrestricted liberty or of unrestricted equality, are the real issues for social policymakers today.

The Kantian position presented here stresses the importance of not using others as mere means and of treating them as ends in themselves. This position demands commitment to institutions that enable people to become and remain autonomous agents. Hence Kantians would be particularly concerned to prevent the extremes of poverty that lead to hunger and homelessness. The hungry and homeless are particularly vulnerable to every sort of injustice, and above all to violence, coercion, and deception, all of which use people as mere means. On the other hand, this same commitment to autonomy would lead Kantians to demand that welfare policies leave welfare recipients as much in charge of their lives as possible. They would argue that welfare policies (e.g., minimum wage, health care, unemployment pay, child benefit, and many others) can all be structured to enhance rather than restrict the autonomy of those who receive benefits or payments. Good welfare policies manifest rather than damage respect for persons. Kantians do not, of course, advocate justice alone, but also insist that beneficence is important and should be manifested in support and concern for particular others and for their projects. The commitment would also be relevant to actions to relieve poverty, hunger, and homelessness. A society that manages not to use any of its members as mere means, and funds adequate levels of welfare payment, can either succeed in treating its more vulnerable members as ends in themselves, whose particular lives and plans must be respected, or fail to do so by leaving them to the undermining and humiliating procedures of an ill-trained welfare bureaucracy. Because Kantians are concerned for justice and beneficence, they would never see beneficence alone as an adequate response to poverty, homelessness, and hunger at home or abroad. Mere charity is too capricious to secure for the poor capabilities to lead their own lives. Equally, unlike persons with rights-based sorts of ethical thinking, they would never see justice alone as a morally adequate response to human vulnerability.

Whether poverty and hunger are in the next street or far away, whether we articulate the task in utilitarian, in Kantian, or in other terms, the claims of justice and of beneficence for the two cases are similar. What may differ in the two cases are our opportunities for action. Sometimes we have far greater possibilities to affect what goes on in the next street than we do to affect what goes on on distant continents. Since nobody can do everything, we not only *may* but *must* put our efforts where they will bear fruit. This, however, provides no license for injustice to distant others. Nearby neighbors need justice, but they are not entitled to justice at the expense of those who are far away. Hence legitimate concern for justice and welfare for those who are nearby fellow-citizens has always to work with and not against the vast efforts of countless agents and institutions across the world and across the generations of mankind to put an end to world hunger. In a world in which action affects distant others, justice cannot be stopped at local or national boundaries: there is no such thing as social justice in one country. It is only our activism, and not our thinking or concern, that can legitimately be local. If we act by the ecologist's slogan "Think globally, act locally" not only in protecting vulnerable environments but in protecting vulnerable humans, we may, however, become part of the solution rather than part of the problem of world hunger . . . .

DEFINITIONS AND EXPLANATIONS

Laissez-faire: French, meaning to leave alone, or let do. 1. Often taken to represent a broadly liberal political perspective in which people are to be left alone to pursue their own values and desires as they see fit, free from government interference in private affairs. 2. Also used, more specifically, to represent the attitude of classical liberals and libertarians to the free market under capitalism, in which the market is to be left free of government intervention and regulation. Prices are to be determined just by market factors such as supply and demand.

Malthusian: Named after Thomas Malthus (1766–1834), who believed that we must limit population growth because if we did not we would face severe food shortages and ultimately famine. Neo-Malthusians follow Malthus in believing that population controls are necessary if we are to have a sustainable and adequate food supply.

QUESTIONS

1. Why is consent a good test for determining whether someone is being used as a *mere* means to another's ends?

2. If consent is the test, does that not validate every voluntary transaction, contract or mode of interaction, such as those between a prostitute and her john, an organ seller and buyer, or a pusher and a junkie?

3. What does it mean to be able "in principle" to consent to the maxim under which another acts toward you?

4. O'Neill argues that we cannot consent to be used in ways that involve deception, violence, or coercion. In each case, the reason is slightly different, however. What is wrong with each of these modes of interaction, such that people cannot consent to be used deceptively, violently, or coercively? What is the common thread among the answers?

5. O'Neill says that the respect for persons principle involves two distinct duties: of justice and beneficence. What does each require? Are they perfect or imperfect duties?

6. O'Neill's discussion of the limits of human rationality and autonomy implies that they are matters of degree rather than kind, that they can be had more or less, rather than in an all-or-nothing fashion. What are the implications of this understanding for possible duties that we might owe to animals, children, and the senile?

7. From the various examples O'Neill gives of actions that can be expected to extend or expand possibilities for autonomous action, can you develop a general sense of what she means by "autonomy"?

8. Why is alleviating need more important than other ways of furthering happiness for Kantian beneficence?

9. Why do Kantians need less complete causal knowledge than utilitarians to decide what is morally required of them?

10. Why must Kantians generally favour local involvement of communities in solving problems like hunger and sustainable development?

11. Is O'Neill's treatment of utilitarianism a charitable or fair one? Would it have to be modified if she took the alleviation of pain to be as important as the promotion of happiness within utilitarianism, as both Bentham and Mill insisted upon?

12. O'Neill speaks about people in the developed world "who for one reason or another go hungry." But does it matter why people go hungry in affluent societies? If it is because of their own poor choices, their own criminal conduct, etc., why do we have a duty to aid them? Or if (as is actually the case in places like Canada), most homeless people suffer from addiction or mental illness, or both, what does Kantianism counsel, given that they have diminished rationality and autonomy?

13. O'Neill's discussion of why violence, deception, and coercion are wrong may be extended to explain why many forms of interaction between the developed and developing worlds are wrong; consider, for example, drug testing on poor populations by Western pharmaceutical companies; resource depletion in the Third World; the high costs of HIV/AIDS retroviral drugs, etc. Does Kantianism provide the resources to think through the morality of such practices?

14. How do we draw the line between exploitation and coercion?

15. Is the vagueness of Kantianism a strength or a weakness?

16. If the poor far away and the local poor are both "poor," why does the imperfect duty to aid dictate that we must help both, as O'Neill suggests? What would be wrong with just helping the local poor?

✦ ✦ ✦

J. Skidmore, Duties to Animals: The Failure of Kant's Moral Theory

James Skidmore argues that a Kantian cannot incorporate direct duties to animals into Kant's moral theory. Kant grounds the duty to refrain from cruelty to animals in a duty to humanity, suggesting that abuse of animals disposes the abuser to mistreat people. Since we have a duty not to mistreat people, we ought not to abuse animals. The contingency of this duty to animals does not sit well with some, for if it were to turn out that abusing animals relieved stress, so that we could better interact with people, Kant would presumably support a duty to abuse animals! Skidmore presents us with many plausible attempts to reconcile a direct duty to animals with Kant's contention that autonomy grounds both dignity and obligation, but ultimately finds them all lacking. It is only rational wills that are owed consideration. Kant cannot accept these formulations that attempt to extend his theory to include direct duties to animals.

No one has seriously contended that animals are autonomous agents, and this unlikely claim seems to be the step that is necessary in order to ground a direct duty to animals. O'Neill offers one possible middle ground—that autonomy is a matter of degree. Perhaps some animals are semi-autonomous. We have some reason to argue that this is the case, for if not, it seems that Kant cannot account for a direct duty to children or the mentally challenged either. While O'Neill has shown that utilitarianism has no necessary respect for even autonomous life, Skidmore has shown that Kant values only rational life, and other life only indirectly (at best).

✦ ✦ ✦

Duties to Animals: The Failure of Kant's Moral Theory

J. SKIDMORE

Contemporary Kantians have faced a particular challenge when attempting to develop plausible applications of Kant's moral theory to concrete moral problems: How do we avoid some of Kant's own infamous conclusions? With respect to such issues as lying, suicide, and punishment, proponents have worked hard to show that Kant's theory can be separated from his own specific applications of it.[1] This is important, since most of us have come to see many of his moral views as implausible.

In this spirit, two contemporary Kantians, Allen Wood and Christine Korsgaard, have attempted to separate Kant's theory from yet another of his own applications: his conclusions regarding the moral status of non-human animals. Kant is well known, by now, for insisting that our duties to animals are merely, "indirect duties towards humanity."[2] In short, he argues that if we develop a habit of treating animals cruelly this will damage our character and ultimately lead to inappropriate treatment of other human beings.

Kant's indirect approach seems inadequate as an account of the moral consideration at least some animals deserve, as Wood and Korsgaard agree. Wood, for example, questions Kant's dependence on such a psychological contingency, highlighting in particular one of its most counterintuitive consequences:

> if it happened to be a quirk of human psychology that torturing animals would make us that much kinder toward humans (perhaps by venting our aggressive impulses on helpless victims) then Kant's argument would apparently make it a duty to inflict gratuitous cruelty on puppies and kittens so as to make us that much kinder to people.[3]

Most of us are convinced, along with Wood, that cruelty toward animals would be wrong even if it did not lead to similar insensitivity toward human beings. Thus, what Korsgaard and Wood each attempt to provide is an alternative Kantian explanation of the way in which morality constrains our treatment of animals. Neither of these approaches succeeds, however, and there is no other obvious Kantian alternative to fill the gap. Thus, Kantians may not be able to separate Kant's theory from his own account of our duties to animals as indirect duties to human beings.

1.

The question that provides the challenge to a Kantian is clear: Can we separate Kant's conclusions regarding animals from his theory in the way some philosophers have argued that we can separate his conclusions regarding lying, suicide, or punishment? Even a brief look at his development of the categorical imperative in the *Groundwork for the Metaphysics of Morals* suggests that the task is difficult. His conclusions regarding animals seem much more obviously to be a straightforward application of the categorical imperative in at least two of its formulations.

Consider the formulation that commands us to act "in such a way that you treat humanity, whether in your own person or in the person of another, always at the same time as an end and never simply as a means."[4] Questions have been raised as to just what Kant means by "humanity" or *Menschheit*. While some philosophers have suggested that this formulation simply commands us to treat human beings as ends and never merely as means, most agree that with "humanity" Kant refers not to human beings as such, but to a particular feature of them, rational agency.[5] Meanwhile, no one has supposed that the term "humanity" refers also to animals lacking rationality. It has been taken for granted that a command to treat the humanity in persons as an end has no direct application to non-human animals.[6] Thus, this formulation of the categorical imperative appears simply to ignore all or most non-human animals, those that cannot plausibly be said to possess rational nature in Kant's sense.

This is made particularly clear in the discussion leading up to this formulation. Kant establishes first that if there were a moral imperative, it would have to command categorically. He then argues that the possibility of such a categorical imperative depends on the existence of ends whose value is absolute or unconditional:

> But let us suppose that there were something whose existence has in itself absolute worth, something which as an end in itself could be a ground of determinate laws. In it, and in it alone, would there be the ground of a possible categorical imperative?[7]

Why does a categorical imperative need an unconditional end? Since Kant argues that all action involves the pursuit of an end which is taken to be good, the possibility of an imperative that commands action unconditionally depends upon an end whose value is likewise unconditional. In this way, a categorical imperative exists if and only if an end of unconditional worth exists as well.[8]

Kant immediately goes on to argue that there is such an unconditional end, and it is none other than "man, and in general every rational being."[9] It is a person's existence as a rational being which has unconditional worth. This leads swiftly to the second formulation of the categorical imperative, namely, the command to treat the rational agency in a person for what it is, an end in itself. Kant concludes that all other beings have only a conditional worth. He says that beings "whose existence depends not on our will but on nature have, nevertheless, if they are not rational beings, only a relative value as means and are therefore called things."[10]

It seems clear that Kant's development of the second formulation of the categorical imperative divides living beings into two groups for the purposes of morality. First, there are rational beings, or persons, who have an unconditional worth which he calls dignity, and as such they must be treated as ends in themselves. Second, there are all other beings, non-rational beings who have only conditional worth and thus take on the moral status of things that may be treated merely as means. This suggests that Kant's later conclusion that there are no direct duties to animals can be seen as a simple and direct application of the formula of humanity and the reasoning that leads up to it.

The same can be said of the formulation of the categorical imperative that appeals to a kingdom of ends. Kant claims that "all maxims proceeding from [an agent's] own legislation ought to harmonize with a possible kingdom of ends as a kingdom of nature."[11] Two features of the ideal kingdom are crucial. First, according to Kant, members of such kingdom are rational agents and only rational agents: "A rational being belongs to the kingdom of ends as a member when he legislates in it universal laws while also being himself subject to these laws."[12] Second, Kant maintains: "In the kingdom of ends everything has either a price or a dignity."[13] Only the legislating members in such a kingdom have the incomparable worth of dignity. All other beings have only conditional worth, worth as a means to some end, and are thus accorded not dignity but price.

This brief look at two of Kant's formulations of the categorical imperative suggests that Kant's later conclusions regarding animals may prove difficult to disentangle from the theory itself. The claim that we have no direct duties to animals seems to follow immediately from the system of value that is present in the two formulations and the reasoning behind them. It is a system in which the source of all value is rational agency itself. It is rational agency, and only rational agency, which possesses the incomparable worth of dignity; and it is the ends of such agency that determine the price of everything else. Thus, as Christine Korsgaard says, on "Kant's view it is human beings, with our capacity for valuing things, that bring to the world such value as it has."[14] Indeed, he can claim later that without "men the whole creation would be a mere waste, in vain, and without final purpose."[15] It is this conception of value from which his later skeptical conclusions regarding duties to animals seem to follow so clearly. Far from mere prejudices, they appear to be a simple and direct application of his categorical imperative and the system of value that accompanies it.

2.

These arguments are not conclusive, but they do serve to shift the burden of proof onto the proponents of Kantian theory to show just how it can establish anything more than Kant's indirect duties regarding animals. It is this burden that contemporary writers have recently begun to take up. In a recent article, Allen Wood devotes considerable attention to it. Wood acknowledges the apparent difficulty that a Kantian theory is in with regard to animals. He agrees that most animals do not possess rational nature in Kant's sense. They are not autonomous beings, and thus would seem not to fall under the categorical imperative's injunction to treat beings with such nature as ends.

According to Wood, the source of Kant's difficulty is his commitment to what Wood calls the personification principle: "This principle specifies that rational nature is respected only by respecting humanity *in someone's person*, hence that every duty must be understood as a duty to a *person* or persons."[16] Thus, Kant was committed to the idea that any duty we have is a duty to some specific rational being, and this leads to the categorical imperative's emphasis on treating the humanity in persons as an end. Since most animals simply do not possess rational natures in Kant's sense, commitment to this principle forces him to explain apparent duties to animals in terms of indirect duties toward other persons.

Wood suggests that if we abandon the personification principle we will discover a more plausible Kantian explanation of our duties regarding animals. By rejecting the personification principle, we are no longer committed to the claim that respecting rational nature always involves respecting an instance of it in a person. Instead, we can argue, as Wood does, that "we should *also* respect rational nature *in the abstract*."[17] This allows us to acknowledge duties regarding non-rational animals and humans provided that "they bear the right relations to rational nature."[18] Such relations, Wood claims, include possessing "fragments" of rational nature, necessary conditions of it, and potential for it.[19] He argues that we cannot treat beings with these sorts of relations to rational nature callously without thereby showing disrespect for rational nature itself. Thus, by rejecting the personification principle and acknowledging a duty to respect rational nature as such, we can establish clear duties regarding non-rational animals, and human beings, that are related to rational nature in relevant ways.

Whether Kant is in fact committed to the personification principle, or whether Kantians ought to reject it, will no doubt be controversial; however, even if we accept Wood's suggestion and allow duties to rational nature in the abstract, questions remain regarding the plausibility of the connections he draws between such rational nature and the capacities of animals. For example, he claims that many animals possess fragments of rational nature. One example he points to is the capacity many animals have to experience pain and pleasure.[20] While many animals clearly seem capable of such experience, the connection to rational nature is difficult to see. Is the capacity really part of rational nature itself? Pain and pleasure, after all, would seem in the end to be experiences, conscious mental states. Just as certain animals are capable of perceiving light within a certain range of frequencies, so are certain animals capable of perceiving states of their own body in part through experiences of pain and pleasure. Is vision then a fragment of rational nature, part of what it is to be rational? This would seem to stretch rational nature well beyond a reasonable interpretation of its scope; yet it is not clear how the capacity to experience pain and pleasure differs from these other sensory capacities. If it does not, then it will not be a plausible candidate for a fragment of rational nature.

A better case can be made for Wood's other example, the capacity of animals to have desires.[21] Desires are intentional states that seem to go hand in hand with beliefs, and it is not clear that we can make sense of the possession of beliefs and desires independently of at least minimal rationality. Thus, the capacity for desire, if not itself a fragment of rationality, does seem to suggest the presence of minimal rationality in any being who possesses it. Could a Kantian claim that respect for rational nature entails respect for animals insofar as they are capable of desire?

To answer this we must consider what it is about rational nature, according to Kant, that commands our respect. Is it, for example, the capacity for desire that confers dignity upon rational nature? It seems clear that for Kant it is not. Notice, for example, that his sharp distinction between persons and things in the kingdom of ends seems to depend on the idea that it is the autonomy of rational agency that confers dignity. For it is autonomy, the capacity to set ends and pursue them independently of desire, the capacity to obey categorical imperatives, that makes moral agency possible. It is autonomy that allows us to conceive of ourselves as legislators in a kingdom of ends. Other more rudimentary features of rational nature might be found in other animals, but if the dignity of rational nature extended to these creatures as well, then Kant could not draw the sharp distinction he does between persons and things. Thus, for Kant, "autonomy is the ground of the dignity of human nature and of every rational being."[22]

The claim that autonomy is the source of dignity is certainly nothing new. Almost every contemporary Kantian seems to accept it. Barbara Herman says that "the capacity to act for reasons all the way down is defining of rational agency. Kant calls it autonomy. It is what we respect in respecting a person as an end-in-herself."[23] Onora O'Neill makes a similar claim:

> Reason, by contrast [with desires], depends on nothing separable from the agent. It is merely autonomy in thinking and acting, considered in the abstract. Without autonomy there can be neither practical nor theoretical reasoning.[24]

More important, Wood himself seems to accept this view in a footnote:

> If it is *humanity*, in the technical Kantian sense of the capacity to set ends according to reason, which is an end in itself, then it is *personality*, or the capacity to give and follow objectively valid moral laws, which gives rational nature its dignity.[25]

Thus, Kant's claim that rational nature deserves respect as an end is essentially a claim that autonomous nature deserves such respect. This raises a problem for Wood's argument that animals deserve moral consideration insofar as they are capable of desire. Even if it is true that the capacity for desire is a fragment of rational nature, it is not a fragment of autonomy. It is therefore difficult to see why the Kantian command to respect autonomous nature, even in the abstract, entails a command to respect the capacity for desire that many animals possess. In short, while it may be true that many animals possess fragments of rational nature, most are not even partially autonomous, so that the command to respect even fragments of autonomous nature wherever they are found will still not have any direct application to them.

Similar problems arise for Wood's claim that animals deserve consideration insofar as they possess some of the "infrastructure" for rational nature, certain necessary conditions for it. For example, Wood points out that many animals have what Tom Regan calls "preference autonomy," which Wood suggests "is a necessary condition for rational autonomy and part of its structure."[26] It is no doubt true that preference autonomy is necessary for rational autonomy in this way, but it is not clear why respect for the dignity of rational autonomy entails respect for any being possessing some of its necessary conditions. After all, there are any number of necessary conditions for such autonomy in human beings: consciousness, the capacity to metabolize oxygen, the ability to digest food, and the ability to maintain a body temperature between thirty and forty degrees Celsius, to name a few. While all of these capacities are part of the infrastructure of autonomy in human beings, no one could claim that all of them deserve moral consideration wherever they are found. Thus, the fact that animals possess certain capacities, such as preference autonomy, that are necessary conditions for autonomy does not show that the animals deserve moral consideration; for it is clearly possible to respect autonomous nature, even in the abstract, without respecting each of its necessary conditions wherever it is found.

What respect for rational autonomy does entail is respect for its necessary conditions in beings who are actually, or perhaps potentially, autonomous. This is why we must be concerned to preserve the lives of persons and respect their preferences. But the concern will not apply in the case of animals, for in them the capacities for life and preferences do not facilitate rational autonomy at all; most animals are not rationally autonomous and never could be. While respecting the dignity of rational autonomy does entail concern for the conditions that make it possible, this has no application to the large majority of animals for whom such autonomy is simply not possible.

Wood's account, then, while drawing interesting connections between rationality and certain capacities that many animals possess, does not succeed in explaining why Kantian respect for rational nature, even in the abstract, entails respect for certain capacities of animals. Once it becomes clear that, for Kant and his followers, it is the autonomy of rational nature that confers dignity, and that in most animals such autonomy is wholly absent, it appears that Kantian respect for such autonomy need not involve any direct constraints on our treatment of such animals.

3.

In her recent book, *The Sources of Normativity*, Christine Korsgaard examines this difficulty briefly and offers her own solution. She develops a counterpart to the Kantian argument for the status of rational nature as an end in itself in order to establish that life is similarly an end in itself. This comes in connection with her analysis of pain as the perception of a reason to act, rather than an intrinsically bad experience:

> A living thing is an entity whose nature it is to preserve and maintain its physical identity. It is a law to itself. When something it is doing is a threat to that identity and perception reveals that fact, the animal finds that it must reject what it is doing and do something else

instead. In that case, it is in pain. Obligation is the reflective rejection of a threat to your identity. Pain is the *unreflective* rejection of a threat to your identity. So pain is the *perception* of a reason, and that is why it seems normative.[27]

From here she argues that this reason, the perception of which is pain, is a public reason even in the case of animals.

> When you pity a suffering animal, it is because you are perceiving a reason. An animal's cries express pain, and they mean that there is a reason, a reason to change its condition. And you can no more hear the cries of an animal as mere noise than you can the words of a person. Another animal can obligate you in exactly the same way another person can. It is a way of being *someone* that you share. So of course we have obligations to animals.[28]

Korsgaard's claim that the pain of animals provides a reason that obligates us depends on an analogue to the Kantian argument for why we must respect the rational agency of others. It is consistency that demands it, given that we necessarily value it in ourselves. Korsgaard constructs an analogous appeal to consistency in the case of valuing not rational nature but animal nature:

> It is not just as human but considered as sensible, considered as an animal that you value yourself and are your own end. And this further stretch of reflection requires a further stretch of endorsement. If you don't value your animal nature, you can value nothing. So you must endorse its value.[29]

From here, consistency demands that we value animal nature not only in ourselves but wherever it is found. Regardless of the being in question, the reasons that such animal nature gives rise to can obligate us. "So the reasons of other animals are also reasons for you."[30]

If successful, this account would provide a Kantian with a strong foundation for direct duties toward animals. There are difficulties, however. Korsgaard's discussion seems to lay great emphasis on a teleological conception of life, suggesting that living things are, by their very nature, oriented toward certain goals or ends, such as self-preservation. Setting aside questions about the adequacy of such a conception, it is unclear how it automatically gives rise to reasons. Korsgaard suggests that the teleological orientation of animals creates reasons for them to do certain things, such as avoid the threats that pain signals. But it seems implausible to attribute reasons independently of any ability to act for reasons.

Consider plants. We might say that certain plants, by their very nature, are oriented toward certain ends. They may strive to grow toward sunlight and establish a root system for nourishment and stability, for example. Does it follow that plants have reasons to pursue such ends? It is hard to imagine what this could mean. Plants simply are not the kinds of things that can have reasons to do anything at all, and this may also be true of most animals. Given their nature, most animals just instinctively try to avoid the conditions that give rise to pain. Human beings have these same instincts, but in our case we attribute to ourselves a reason to avoid such conditions because of our ability to set ends. We set ends for which our continued physical well-being is a necessary means, and this provides us with a reason, not just an inclination, to promote it. Since it is not at all clear that many animals can set ends in this way, it is not clear that their pain-avoiding instincts provide them with reasons to act in certain ways.

There are also difficulties with Korsgaard's claim that valuing our own animal nature forces us, on pain of inconsistency, to value such nature wherever we find it. It may well be true that in your case, as a human being, if "you don't value your animal nature, you can value nothing."[31] But is this because such animal nature is an end in itself, possessing the unconditional worth of dignity? Or is it because such nature is necessary for the presence of rational autonomy, which alone is an end in itself? It would seem that a Kantian is committed to the second alternative. Given that we must value our autonomy as an end, it does not follow that we must value in ourselves the conditions that make it possible. This entails valuing our animal nature and the capacities that make it up, just as it entails valuing our existence as living things or as warm-bodied things. We must value all of the properties and capacities that together make our autonomy possible.

But, again, it does not follow from this that we must value the animal nature of other animals any more than it follows, from the fact that we must value our lives and our body temperatures, that we must value all living things or all things of a certain temperature. In the case of animals such nature does not make possible the capacity for autonomy, just as in the case of plants or rocks, their status as living things or warm things does not enable autonomy. For a Kantian, the reason we must value animal nature in human beings, its connection to rational autonomy, does not serve as a reason to value similarly its presence in other animals in whom rational autonomy is simply absent. In short, respect for autonomy does not entail respect for all of its necessary conditions wherever they are found. While such conditions must be respected where autonomy is actually or potentially present, it is not clear why they must be respected even in beings with no capacity for autonomy at all.

The argument that Wood and Korsgaard make to establish moral duties regarding animals fail in that, while Wood and Korsgaard draw certain connections between the capacities of many animals and rational nature itself, they do not draw the sort of connections that a Kantian needs. Rational nature indeed includes or depends upon a wide variety of capacities, from the ability to pursue the satisfaction of desires to the mere ability to digest food and stay alive; but the Kantian account of the dignity of rational nature, its unconditional worth, finds its source in the capacity for autonomy. Once this is clear, it becomes apparent that the Kantian command to respect such rational nature as an end, whether in persons or in the abstract, will not itself entail any moral constraints on our treatment of beings in whom such autonomy is wholly absent.

4.

The failure of Wood's and Korsgaard's attempts to establish more direct duties toward animals may give us further reason to think that Kantians will have to settle for something like Kant's own indirect account of such duties. There is, however, at least one further avenue Kantians might pursue. This far we have neglected Kant's first formulation of the categorical imperative, in which he commands us to act only on maxims that we could will to become universal laws.[32] It seems initially that this crucial notion of the universalizability of maxims might be relevant to questions regarding the moral concerns animals deserve; for to the extent that animals are capable of suffering, for example, in the same ways we are as human beings, we might think that the maxims for some of our actions toward animals are not universalizable.

Such a Kantian approach is at least hinted at by Gunther Patzig. In discussing our moral duty not to inflict unnecessary suffering on animals, Patzig argues that

> [e]ach of us knows what pain and suffering are, and each of us expects others to respect his vital interest in avoiding suffering. Since for moral reasons one can only demand of others what one is prepared to abide by oneself, the same rule binds me with respect to those who are my equal, that is, with respect to all humans. But it would be unreasonable to insist on a radical distinction between humans and non-humans as long as the latter behave in such a way that we must acknowledge their similar ability to experience pain and suffering, pleasure and misery. So the principle forbidding infliction of arbitrary suffering and callous neglect extends beyond the realm of humans to that of non-humans.[33]

This seems to appeal to something like Kantian universalizability. The idea is that since we have reason to think that animal suffering is similar to human suffering in significant ways, we cannot consistently demand that others respect our ability to suffer and at the same time refuse to respect an animal's similar ability. This seems analogous to the appeal Kant makes to inconsistency in the moral assessment of maxims of non-beneficence. In attempting to will a universal law of non-beneficence, my will comes into conflict due to the fact that I must at the same time will that others come to my aid if I find myself in need of assistance.[34]

Difficulties arise, however, when we pursue this strategy to cases of animal mistreatment. The crucial question is, what maxim lies behind my intention to mistreat an animal? For example, if I formulate the maxim as, "I will inflict suffering on a non-human animal when it serves my purposes," or, "I will inflict suffering on this non-human animal for my entertainment," then it seems possible to will this as a universal law. I can will that everyone inflict suffering on non-human animals when it suits her without any conflict, for I am not a non-human animal and never will be.

We quickly realize that the attempt to employ the formula of universal law to establish duties to animals encounters the traditional problem associated with that formulation: How do we specify the relevant maxim to be universalized? Of particular importance here is how we exclude from the maxim facts that seem morally arbitrary. For example, if a slaveholder may properly formulate his maxim as, "I will enslave black people in order to use their labor," then it is not clear that it will be impossible for him to will this as a universal law; if he is not black, such a universal law would present no threat to him. A Kantian must find some way of explaining why morally arbitrary features must not be included in the properly formulated maxim. She must find some way to mimic the effect of a veil of ignorance, as developed by John Rawls, which prevents individuals from using irrelevant knowledge of their own circumstances in order to tailor principles of justice in their favor.[35]

One prominent account of the way in which maxims are appropriately formulated is due to Onora O'Neill. Acknowledging that an act may be described as involving any number of intentions, O'Neill argues that the relevant maxim for a particular action is the most general or fundamental intention involved, the intention which informs or makes sense of the other intentions involved in the act. She considers an example involving the welcoming of a guest:

> In making a new visitor feel welcome I may offer and make him or her some coffee. As I do so there will be innumerable aspects of my action that are intentional—the choice of mug, the addition of milk, the stirring—and there will also be numerous aspects of action that are "below the level of intention"—the gesture with which I hand the cup, the precise number of stirs, and so on. But the various specific intentions with which I orchestrate the offer and preparation of coffee are all ancillary to the underlying principle. *Maxims are those underlying principles or intentions by which we guide and control our more specific intentions.*[36]

Thus, O'Neill suggests that the relevant intention for the purposes of the formula of universal law is the intention a person has at the deepest level, the underlying maxim which informs the more detailed intentions involved in carrying the action out.

It is not clear, however, that this account gets past the difficulties raised by the example of the slaveholder. Suppose we consider what the underlying intention of the slaveholder might be. Is it impossible that his most basic intention is to enslave black people, or take advantage of their enslavement for various purposes? Certainly his intention is not simply to enslave human beings as such, which he clearly could not will to be a universal law; for he may have no intention of enslaving white people like himself.

Similarly, what is the intention at bottom of the person who mistreats animals for amusement? Might it not be to inflict suffering on animals? Certainly it need not be simply to inflict suffering on sentient beings, for he may have no intention of inflicting suffering on another person. These cases seem to show that O'Neill's account of maxim formulation will not succeed in excluding the kinds of maxims that must be excluded in order for the formula of universal law to generate duties to animals.

Barbara Herman provides an alternative to O'Neill's conception. Herman notices, like O'Neill, that any act will have an indefinite number of possible descriptions, "most of which omit the aspects of the action that raise moral questions."[37] The difficulty with O'Neill's account is that there is no guarantee that by focusing on the most basic intention of an act, the intention that underlies all others, we will capture all of the morally relevant features of the act. Herman attempts to solve this difficulty by appeal to what she calls rules of moral salience, rules that guide the agent in locating the features of an act which are morally relevant. They are rules, for example, which specify that while the fact that an act is a speech act is never morally relevant, the fact that an act is a lie is always morally relevant.

How are such rules developed? What guides us in choosing a set that will succeed in locating the morally relevant features of our acts? Herman appeals to what she takes to be the most fundamental conception in Kant's ethics: rational agency as an end in itself:

> I think of the RMS as an interpretation, in rule form, of the respect for persons (as ends-in-themselves) which is the object of the Moral Law. Their function is to guide in the recognition of those areas where the fact that persons are moral persons ought to instruct agents' deliberations and actions . . . . The *ground* of the RMS is in the conception of a person as moral agent (or end-in-himself) that comes from the experience of the Moral Law as a Fact of Reason. So, while the RMS are not a product of the CI procedure, their role and their subject matter are a product of the Moral Law.[38]

In developing the appropriate rules of moral salience, then, we are guided by the fundamental conception of a moral agent as an end in herself.

Returning to our earlier examples, it appears that with this account we can do a better job of explaining how the formula of universal law can exclude maxims involving slavery. While it may be true that a slaveholder's deepest level intention is that he will enslave black people for certain purposes, it remains true that in doing so he is missing what is undeniably a moral salient feature of the practice: the fact that it involves enslavement of people, of rational beings. An appropriate set of rules of moral salience will reveal that any description of his action that omits this fact is inadequate. Such rules will show that the proper maxim, for the purposes of the formula of universal law, will include it, and once this is done it becomes clear that the maxim is not universalizable. The slaveholder could not will the enslavement of people as a universal law.

It is not so clear, however, that rules of moral salience can be employed equally well in the case of the agent who mistreats animals. The question here is whether such rules can be used to establish, say, the general moral salience of suffering. Given Herman's description of them, it is clear that we will be able to develop rules that emphasize the moral salience of the suffering of moral agents. Given the way in which such suffering tends to interfere with rational agency, for example, its infliction will normally be inconsistent with the commitment to such agency as an end in itself. But will we be able to generate rules that establish the general moral relevance of suffering, including that of non-rational beings? It appears that this will be impossible, for according to Herman the source of these rules is the fundamental conception of moral agency as an end in itself, which she suggests lies behind all formulations of the categorical imperative. If so, then there would seem to be no way to generate rules which establish the relevance of all suffering. Only rules establishing the relevance of the suffering of moral agents will be legitimate. Thus, even with an appropriate set of rules of moral salience in place, we would not be able to show the impermissibility of maxims of inflicting suffering on non-rational beings to suit our purposes. Such maxims would not include the sort of suffering that the rules would have us identify as morally salient, and thus such rules would not be of help in raising problems with such maxims.

It may seem that the only remaining option for a Kantian is to appeal to the fact that we might ourselves one day lose our rational agency and be subject to the kind of non-rational suffering that animals experience. Suppose this is possible, and suppose it is the case that we will, presently, that if we were to fall into such a state, others should not inflict suffering on us as it suits them. At this point we do seem to have the material for a conflict in the will when applying the formula of universal law; for we cannot consistently will both that everyone inflict non-rational suffering as they wish and also will that no one inflict non-rational suffering on us if we ever become vulnerable to it. If this is the way in which we must apply the formula of universal law in this case, then it looks as if we have Kantian grounds for a moral duty not to inflict suffering on non-rational animals simply to suit our purposes.

This strategy may hold some promise, though it has not been pursued by anyone in print. Still, it could not succeed without first overcoming serious difficulties. First, in order for this approach to be successful, a Kantian must explain to us why we cannot be indifferent about how people should treat us were we to lose our rational agency. In order to generate a contradiction of will in the universalization process it is necessary that we must will that others not inflict unnecessary suffering on us if we ever lose our rational agency. If it is even rationally possible for us to be indifferent to this, then no conflict is generated when we universalize our maxim of inflicting suffering on non-rational beings when it suits us.

It is helpful to look to the example of Kant's duty of beneficence. In the *Groundwork for the Metaphysics of Morals*, Kant argues that a maxim we might set of never helping others when they are in need cannot be universalized without a conflict of will; for he claims that we cannot will that no one assist us if we are ever in need of help. To explain this claim, Barbara Herman has pointed to the fact that as rational agents there are ends that we necessarily must set, ends that are necessary to our very existence as rational beings. Moreover, given our vulnerability as human beings, we can never rule out the possibility that we may one day need assistance in pursuing such ends.[39] It follows from this that we must will, insofar as we are rational, that if such a situation arises we do in fact receive the help we need.

This line of reasoning will not carry over to the case of inflicting suffering on non-rational beings. We cannot infer from the ends we must have as rational agents any conclusions about what we must will regarding a scenario in which we lose such agency. Once we lose our rational agency we no longer set the ends necessary to sustain it, nor are we capable of setting any ends at all in Kant's sense. Thus, it seems that our indifference to how others should treat us were we to lose our rational capacities would not conflict with any end that we necessarily have as rational agents. This makes it more difficult to explain why we could not be indifferent in just this way, and thus be perfectly consistent in willing the universal law that everyone inflict suffering on non-rational animals as they wish.

In fact, there would seem to be only one explanation for why we could not rationally be indifferent to our own non-rational suffering, and this is that suffering itself is an intrinsic evil. If we could acknowledge that even non-rational suffering is bad in itself, then we might argue that we cannot rationally be indifferent to the prospect of our own non-rational suffering. If suffering is intrinsically bad, then it is bad for us whether we are rational or not, and we must never be indifferent to its occurrence. Without such an appeal to suffering as an intrinsic evil, there is no apparent way to explain why it is irrational to be indifferent in just this way.

Thus, it seems that a Kantian must be able to acknowledge suffering as an intrinsic evil in order to establish that the maxim in question violates the formula of universal law. But can we accept this within a Kantian framework? A closer look at the Kantian conception of value suggests that the answer must be no. Consider, for example, the Kantian account of the good developed by Christine Korsgaard in her article, "Two Distinctions in Goodness." On Korsgaard's interpretation, a Kantian conception of value involves a crucial distinction between what is conditionally and unconditionally good. "A thing is unconditionally good," she says, "if it is good under any and all conditions, if it is good no matter what the context."[40] Something is conditionally good, on the other hand, if its goodness depends on certain conditions being met.

One of Korsgaard's central conclusions is that things which are conditionally good can nevertheless be objectively good, provided simply that the relevant conditions are met. But it is a different question that concerns us here: What is it, for Kant, that is unconditionally good? The answer, according to Korsgaard, is the good will, and only the good will, as Kant himself famously claims in the first sentence of the *Groundwork of the Metaphysics of Morals*. This suggests that suffering itself will not be considered intrinsically bad on a Kantian conception of value.

There are further difficulties. According to Korsgaard, not only is the good will the only thing that possesses unconditional value, it is thereby the condition for the goodness of everything else:

> Since the good will is the only unconditionally good thing, this means that it must be the source and condition of all the goodness in the world; goodness, as it were, flows into the world from the good will, and there would be none without it.[41]

Given Kant's definition of the good will as a rationally autonomous will, committed to acting in accordance with the categorical imperative, it follows that on a Kantian conception of value, something has value only insofar as it is connected to the rational ends of a moral agent.[42]

This raises difficulties when we return to the scenario in which we have lost our rational agency. The question is, must we regard the suffering of a non-rational being as a bad thing? The answer seems to be no, for such pain is not connected to the ends of any rational agent. No rational agent is setting an end of avoiding the suffering, and thus on a Kantian theory it is difficult to see how it could be considered bad. This suggests that as Kantians we could indeed be indifferent to whether others inflict suffering on us were we to lose our rational agency. Indeed, as Kantians it would seem strange to be anything but indifferent to it. With the loss of our rational agency, we no longer set an end to avoiding the suffering, and it thereby ceases to be bad. If it is not bad, it is perfectly reasonable to be indifferent to its occurrence.

A Kantian thus finds herself in something of an ironic circumstance. It is clear that most of us are not in fact indifferent to the prospect of our own future suffering, even if that suffering were to take place after we had lost our rational agency. This suggests that most of us could not consistently universalize a maxim of inflicting arbitrary suffering on non-rational beings. However, the Kantian conception of value itself undermines this by challenging the attitude toward the prospect of our own non-rational suffering. On this conception of value, indifference to such suffering, far from being ruled out, seems perfectly reasonable because the suffering is no longer a bad thing. Thus, it looks as if a Kantian theory cannot accommodate the conception of value required to show that a maxim of inflicting arbitrary non-rational suffering violates the formula of universal law.

5.

What are we permitted to conclude regarding the prospect of more direct constraints on the treatment of animals within the framework of Kantian moral theory? If the conclusions above are correct, the outlook appears bleak. The examination of each of Kant's formulations of the categorical imperative suggests that there is no obvious way that any of them can be used to establish more direct constraints. None of the explicit attempts on the part of Kantians to establish such constraints has succeeded. Most important, the difficulty in each case arises from a feature of Kant's theory that is central to it: the dignity of rational autonomy. Kant's rejection of direct duties to animals appears to follow straightforwardly from this core feature of the theory. If this is correct, then Kantians will be left with the alternative of adopting some version of Kant's own view that apparent duties to animals are in fact indirect duties to other people or ourselves.

Of course, we have not yet shown that such an indirect account cannot succeed. Perhaps Kant's view is not so implausible after all. In a recent article in the *Journal of Value Inquiry*, for example, Dan Egonnson has argued that Kant's indirect account can establish a duty not to kill animals for food, and Lara Denis argues that Kant's account can justify significant constraints on our treatment of animals.[43] If they are right, then Kantians may not need to improve upon Kant's own view. However, without examining this alternative in detail, there are good initial reasons to doubt whether such an approach could on its own provide a plausible account of constraints on our treatment of animals.

First, there is the counterfactual worry that Allen Wood raises for an indirect account. Kant's view depends crucially on the existence of a strong contingent relation between our treatment of animals and our treatment of human beings. It relies on the claim that brutal or callous treatment of animals leads to or reveals a tendency toward morally inappropriate treatment of human beings. While such a relation may in fact hold, it is certainly not analytic. We can imagine people who are able to treat animals callously without becoming callous toward each other. A proponent of Kant's indirect duties must admit that if we had this ability, callous treatment of animals would be generally unobjectionable. In turn, a proponent would have to admit that if there are some people who actually do have this ability, indirect duties do not apply to them, and they are free to treat animals as they please. To Wood, and most of us, this result is deeply inadequate. We are convinced, for example, that even if animal torture did not lead to cruelty toward human beings, it would still be wrong. A proponent of Kant's indirect duties account would have to deny this.

There is a more serious initial problem for an indirect account, however. Again, such a view depends crucially on the truth of some contingent relationship between our treatment of animals and our treatment of human beings. While such a relation may hold, it is not clear that a proponent of an indirect duties account can provide a plausible explanation of why it holds. If this cannot be done, then such an approach will collapse, unable to account for a crucial premise on which it depends.

On Kant's view, animals in principle have the status of mere things. If not for the contingent relationship between our treatment of animals and our treatment of human beings, it would be no more objectionable to abuse animals than to abuse baseballs with bats. For such a theory, then, there is in principle a crucial moral distinction between the suffering of human beings and the suffering of animals. Human suffering is morally significant in a way that animal suffering is not. But the existence of this clear moral distinction would seem to render the truth of the appropriate contingent relation mysterious. If there is a clear moral distinction between animals and human beings, then why does callous treatment of animals lead to similar treatment of human beings?

We do not typically think that abusing baseballs leads to abusive treatment of people. Most of us are perfectly capable of grasping the fact that abusing people matters morally and abusing baseballs does not. Why, then, on Kant's indirect account, can we not implement the similar distinction between animals and human beings in order to prevent our callous treatment of animals from leading to callous treatment of human beings? If there is a perfectly obvious moral distinction between non-human animals and human beings, why can we not see this and prevent our ill treatment of the non-human animals from leading to ill treatment of people?[44]

There are two possible explanations a Kantian might offer. A Kantian might argue that moral agents are generally incapable of grasping this moral distinction. We simply lack the moral sophistication to understand the sharp moral distinction between animals and human beings. But this is clearly implausible. Most of us are not so unsophisticated. Just as we can grasp the distinction between abusing baseballs and abusing human beings, we could certainly grasp the moral distinction between animal and human suffering if it were equally sharp.

Alternatively, a Kantian might argue that, while we are capable of grasping the distinction, we are not capable of putting it into practice. Through some failure of will, we might not be capable of implementing the distinction in order to prevent our callous treatment of animals from leading to callous treatment of human beings. Yet this seems implausible as well. Some of us have stronger wills than others, but most of us seem clearly capable of acting on moral distinctions we take to exist. If we became thoroughly convinced that animal suffering was not itself morally relevant, most of us could adjust our behavior accordingly, minimizing the effects that certain callous treatment of animals might have on our treatment of other people.

If approaches along neither of these lines is plausible, then Kant's indirect duties account cannot succeed. While such a view depends upon a strong contingent connection between our treatment of animals and our treatment of human beings, it may have no plausible explanation for the existence of such a connection. This brief examination is of course far from conclusive; however, it suggests that Kantians should be wary of avoiding the problem of justifying more direct duties to animals by falling back upon Kant's own indirect account. If Kantian theory cannot establish direct duties to animals, there is no guarantee that Kant's indirect duties provide a plausible alternative.

The problem that animals present for a Kantian theory is thus potentially much more serious than has often been assumed. While the applied philosophical literature on animal issues has typically been dominated by controversial questions of whether or not animals have rights, and whether practices of experimentation and meat-eating are morally acceptable or unacceptable, the challenge for the Kantian is more basic: Can the theory justify any significant moral constraints at all on the treatment of animals? It appears that the answer may be no.[45]

READING ENDNOTES

1. See Barbara Herman, *The Practice of Moral Judgment* (Cambridge, Mass.: Harvard University Press, 1993), esp. pp. 132–158; Thomas Hill, *Dignity and Practical Reason in Kant's Moral Theory* (Ithaca, N.Y.: Cornell University Press, 1992), pp. 67–75; and Thomas Hill, *Autonomy and Self-respect* (Cambridge, England: Cambridge University Press, 1991).
2. Immanuel Kant, *Lectures on Ethics*, Louis Infield, trans. (New York: Harper and Row, 1963), p. 373.
3. Allen W. Wood, "Kant on Duties Regarding Nonrational Nature," *Proceedings of the Aristotelian Society* 72 (1998, suppl.) p. 194.
4. Immanuel Kant, *Grounding for the Metaphysics of Morals* (Indianapolis: Hackett Publishing, 1981), p. 429.
5. See Thomas Hill, "Humanity as an End in Itself," *Dignity and Practical Reason in Kant's Moral Theory*, p. 39, and Christine Korsgaard, "Formula of Humanity," *Creating the Kingdom of Ends* (Cambridge, England: Cambridge University Press, 1996) p. 110.
6. See William Wright, "Treating Animals as Ends," *Journal of Value Inquiry* 27 (1993).
7. Kant, *Grounding for the Metaphysics of Morals*, p. 428.
8. See Korsgaard, *op. cit.*, pp. 114–119.

9. Kant, *Grounding for the Metaphysics of Morals*, p. 428.
10. *Ibid.*
11. *Ibid.*, p. 436.
12. *Ibid.*, p. 433.
13. *Ibid.*, p. 434.
14. Korsgaard, *op. cit.*, p. 131.
15. *Ibid.*
16. Wood, *op. cit.*, p. 196.
17. *Ibid.*, p. 198.
18. *Ibid.*, p. 197.
19. *Ibid.*
20. *Ibid.*, p. 200.
21. *Ibid.*
22. See Kant, *Grounding for the Metaphysics of Morals*, p. 446.
23. Herman, *op. cit.*, p. 228.
24. Onora O'Neill, *Constructions of Reason* (Cambridge, England: Cambridge University Press, 1989), p. 64.
25. Wood, *op. cit.*, p. 208.
26. *Ibid.*, p. 200.
27. Christine Korsgaard, *The Sources of Normativity*, (New York: Cambridge University Press, 1996), p. 150.
28. *Ibid.*, p. 153.
29. *Ibid.*, p. 152.
30. *Ibid.*, p. 153.
31. *Ibid.*, p. 152.
32. Kant, *Grounding for the Metaphysics of Morals*, p. 421.
33. Günther Patzig, *Ökologische Ethik—innerhalb der Grenzen bloßer Vernunft*, my trans. (Göttingen: Vandenhoeck & Ruprecht, 1983), p. 14.
34. See Barbara Herman, *op. cit.*, pp. 45–72.
35. See John Rawls, *A Theory of Justice* (Cambridge, Mass: Harvard University Press, 1971), esp. pp. 136–142.
36. O'Neill, *op. cit.*, p. 84.
37. Herman, *op. cit.*, p. 75.
38. *Ibid.*, pp. 86–87.
39. *Ibid.*, p. 54.
40. Christine Korsgaard, "Two Distinctions in Goodness," *Creating the Kingdom of Ends*, p. 178.
41. *Ibid.*, p. 181.
42. See Kant, *Grounding for the Metaphysics of Morals*, p. 437.
43. Dan Egonnson, "Kant's Vegetarianism," *Journal of Value Inquiry* 31 (1997): and Lara Denis, "Kant's Conception of Duties Regarding Animals: Reconstruction and Reconsideration," *History of Philosophy Quarterly* 17 (2000).
44. See Robert Nozick, *Anarchy, State, and Utopia* (New York: Basic Books, 1974), p. 36.
45. I owe thanks to several people. Norman Dahl and Sarah Holtman provided invaluable feedback on earlier drafts, and I benefited as well from comments made by Dale Jamieson and an anonymous reviewer for the *Journal of Value Inquiry*.

DEFINITIONS AND EXPLANATIONS

Reductio ad absurdum: Latin, meaning reduced to absurdity. This is a common way of arguing against a position, in which a person shows that a given position leads to such absurd results that the original position must be rejected.

Teleology, teleological conception of life: The theory that everything (some thing) has a final end or function, and that one cannot understand it unless one knows its end or function. This was a common view in ancient Greek philosophy. It is usually part of a world view that attributes a design to nature or the universe (natural or divine) that directs things to their proper ends. A person may be a teleologist about some things but not others. One might think that human beings have a final end (to know God, or do good, or seek knowledge) but deny that rocks or planets have such an end. Human beings may have a final end, simply as human beings, while rocks and planets may not; if so, we could not understand human nature without knowing the end appropriate to our nature, but we could understand rocks and planets. A teleological conception of life is one that attributes some end to life without which we cannot understand it, without which we cannot make sense of a whole range of human behaviour; in this case the end is self-preservation.

Veil of ignorance: This is an idea made famous by John Rawls in his immensely important book, *A Theory of Justice* (1971). Rawls wanted to discover which principles of justice it would be most fair to adopt in society. He constructed an elaborate thought experiment to answer this question, which involved imagining people choosing between possible principles of justice for the distribution of rights and freedoms, opportunities and income. Among the possible principles he considers are a principle of strictly equal distribution, distribution based on need, or on the greatest happiness principle. Because he wanted to ensure that the principles chosen would be fair, he imposed what he called a veil of ignorance on the choosers, so that they had to make their choice without knowing any arbitrary facts about themselves: their sex, their talents, whether they were rich or poor, their race, their health status, whether they suffered from disabilities, and what their particular conception of the good life might be. Because the choosers were ignorant of such details about themselves, they could not try to skew the choice of principles to favour their particular characteristics. If you did not know what race or sex you are, for example, you would not choose principles of justice that favoured one race or sex over others.

QUESTIONS

1. To what extent must Kantians (or any other theorists) be consistent with the actual positions defended by the founders of their philosophical positions?

2. Kant says that we have duties not to act cruelly to animals, but they are indirect, based ultimately on the possibility of harm to humans. How important is it that a theory not only gives the right answer on a specific issue (we ought not to torture animals) but that it does so for the right reason?

3. Is it plausible to think that what is wrong with torturing animals is the potential harm to people such actions might result in? Is torturing animals ultimately a wrong done to people, or to the animals themselves?

4. The respect for persons principle seems to be restricted just to "humanity" understood as beings capable of rational autonomous agency. As such, it seems to leave animals out of the domain of moral concern or duty. What or who else would it leave out?

5. What could it mean to respect "rational nature *in the abstract*," as separable from respecting rational nature in actual persons?

6. What does "autonomy" mean for Kant?

7. Christine Korsgaard develops an argument from consistency that is designed to show that we have direct duties to animals: because we must recognize pain in ourselves as a reason to change our condition, we must also see pain in anything else as a reason to change its condition. What is Skidmore's argument against this extension of Kant's view?

8. What value does our own well-being as animals have on the Kantian picture?

9. If it is the capacity for autonomy that confers dignity upon persons and grounds the requirement of respect, what does this imply about the status of children, irreversibly comatose adults, the senile, and the insane?

10. Consider the attempt to derive a duty not to inflict suffering on animals from the universalizability formulation of the categorical imperative. How would such an argument go? What does the discussion here show about the difficulty of actually determining what the relevant "maxim" is?

11. Why is the relevant maxim for the universalizability test not "I can inflict suffering on sentient creatures just for fun?" Why could I not universalize such a maxim? If the issue only involves the infliction of pain, why is sentience not the only morally relevant feature of the situation?

12. Consider the following analogy with Kant's example of a person not now in need but who cannot will a general practice of non-aid because, *if* he were in need he would will that he be given aid. Though not now deprived of rationality, *if* I were to lose my rational agency I would will that no one inflict suffering upon me. Why does this not serve to ground a duty not to inflict suffering on the non-rational? Why does Skidmore reject the analogy?

13. Given that we all have a desire to be happy (a contingent but universal fact about people), can we not ground a duty not to inflict suffering on people on that basis, even if they are not capable of rational agency?

14. Skidmore argues that a Kantian must conclude that we should be indifferent to our own suffering if we lose our capacity for rational agency. How does the argument go? Is it a *reductio ad absurdum* of Kantianism?

15. To what extent do Skidmore's arguments depend upon treating autonomy or rational agency as an all-or-nothing concept, rather than a matter of degree along a continuum? Which conception of autonomy and rationality is more plausible?

✦ ✦ ✦

Mario Morelli, Commerce in Organs: A Kantian Critique

Commerce in organs has always been a contentious issue. Something inside us rebels at the thought of a person selling his liver or even his kidney in an open market. It seems less troubling to us for persons to give one of their organs away, however. These reactions cannot be easily squared with a consequentialist theory of morality. Mario Morelli thinks that a Kantian moral theory can do a better job. Morelli argues that Kant reasons that treating all humanity as an end, never simply as a means, implies that we can never treat anyone as an object, nor instrumentally, nor alienate our own bodies. This seems straightforwardly to imply that Kant thought we could never sell or give away our bodies. Morelli argues that this only seems to follow if we do not attend to the fact that Kant said that the duty of nonalienation is not absolute but is rather *prima facie*. Kant explicitly allows that we can remove organs or limbs in an effort to preserve our life. Alienation is only wrong if it devalues humanity. It seems obvious that selling an organ, then, would be treating something with dignity (a person) as if it had a price and so would devalue humanity. Alternately, however, if we attend to the reason why one would give away an organ, no such illegitimate motive presents itself. Giving an organ away will be motivated by a desire to save another's life. This is surely an instance of protecting the autonomy of another, and therefore is a wholly legitimate way to fulfil our duty to aid. And thus are our intuitions squared with Kantianism.

Much depends here on our acceptance of the nonalienation requirement that Kant imposes. However plausible it is that the categorical imperative entails that we may not objectify or use others solely as instruments of our will, it is questionable in the extreme whether a respect for autonomy requires the inalienability of our bodies. Rejecting that value requires a separation of rationality from body that seems to allow for the possibility of permissible commerce in organs. Morelli ably indicates this, and other, limitations of the argument. In doing so, he also personifies the critical moral attitude. One can never over-state the case being made, and must be guided by reason.

Mario Morelli, "Commerce in Organs: A Kantian Critique," *Journal of Social Philosophy* 30:2 (Summer 1999): 315–324. © 1999 Blackwell Publishers. Reprinted with permission of Blackwell Publishers.

Commerce in Organs: A Kantian Critique

M A R I O   M O R E L L I

In this paper, I want to examine some ethical issues involved with commerce in organs. Buying and selling organs is one possible option for the procurement and allocation of human organs for transplantation. In particular, I shall focus on the question of the permissibility of commercial sale of organs by a living person, with delivery while the person is still alive (e.g., the sale of a kidney). I want to address the issues from the perspective of Kantian ethics, with its emphasis on respect for humanity, in oneself and in others, including respect for bodily integrity. It is understandable that Kant himself has very little to say, at least directly, about the topic. A Kantian perspective, however, is both pertinent to the issue and also potentially fruitful. Its emphasis on respect for persons and its view of human persons as embodied human beings hold out promise for understanding and defending the often-expressed concerns about the possible exploitativeness of some organ procurement practices, and for countering the insufficiency of consequentialist theories to justify adequate constraints on such practices.

I. ORGAN TRANSPLANTATION ISSUES

"Whether alive or dead, every body stands today as a potential source of therapeutic benefit to the body of every other human."[1] This statement, made by Russell Scott in his 1981 book *The Body as Property,* expresses (with its clever play on the word "body") the enhanced value of human organs and tissues made possible by medical success in transplantation. Exploiting the value and achieving the benefit give rise to questions of ethical judgment, public policy, and legal regulation, so that the terms under which transplantation is carried out are acceptable to the society in which it occurs. Scott properly takes note of the reason for a cautious and deliberate approach in this difficult area: "[T]he laws on this subject authorize drastic invasions of the human body. A society that seeks access to the bodies of its citizens for the removal of their contents obviously enters a highly sensitive personal area."[2] Fully achieving the benefits in this medical development—of helping the sick by the use of human tissues and organs—involves deep human sentiments and values concerning the treatment of the dead, the memory of human slavery, and the control of the individual by the state.

In the United States, the legal framework that has evolved is represented by the Uniform Anatomical Gift Act (UAGA), which provides for the donation of human organs either by the individual before death or by the family or legal guardians after the individual's death. Living donors may also donate kidneys or bone marrow with appropriate informed consent. The UAGA was silent on the matter of organ sales, with different interpretations given to that silence. The National Organ Transplant Act, however, prohibits sale and purchase of human organs for "valuable considera-tion." This applies only to interstate commerce; several states expressly forbid sale of organs. Sales of certain human tissues and materials, such as blood and semen, are permitted. I might mention that a number of countries have adopted a third approach to organ procurement, different from donation and sale, which is variously called sal-vaging, conscription, or presumed consent. Under this approach, organs may be taken from a decedent, usually with the stipulation that they not be taken if an objection has been registered by the decedent or by the family.

There are various considerations in favor of the gift or donation approach favored by the UAGA. Concerns have arisen, however, primarily due to the continuing shortage of organs. The other approaches, although rejected early on as policy options, have had and continue to have proponents. In a 1968 paper by Alfred Sadler and Blair Sadler the argument was made that the UAGA is a desirable policy option because it respects the right of the individual to control the disposition of his or her body after death.[3] It also balances the other interests involved, those of the family, physicians, and society. Further, it encourages and facilitates donation and thus helps to increase the supply of organs and tissues available for transplantation as well as medical research. Sadler and Sadler pointed out the deficiencies of then existing statutes and the inadequacies of common law doctrines. With respect to the latter, in early English law, a "no property" doctrine was accepted: "[I]n keeping with the tra-ditional Western emphasis on the dignity and sanctity of the individual, the body was considered incapable of being owned in a commercial sense, and thus, could not be bought or sold. This resulted in the refusal of early common-law decisions to recog-nize any property rights in the body of a deceased person."[4] In time, courts, especially in the United States, formulated the idea of a "quasi-property right" that family had in the body of a deceased individual; this typically included a duty to dispose of the body property and a right against mistreatment of the body such as mutilation. The UAGA was presented as the approach that conforms to and promotes widely shared values in American society, whereas the other alternatives, sale and salvaging, run counter to, or threaten to undermine, some of those values. The values in question include respect for the individual, autonomy, generosity, and beneficence.

Although I shall be focusing on one type of objection to the sale of organs, it is useful to keep in mind the other approaches to organ procurement. Routine salvaging (or presumed consent) and commercial sale are advocated on the grounds that they are likely to increase the supply of organs and with that the saving of lives. Commercial sale is also defended on grounds of enhancing autonomy or liberty of individuals. Among the variety of criticisms made of commerce in organs, the one that is the focal point of my concern is sometimes called the commodification problem. This kind of criticism has been made in connection with other current issues, especially commercial surrogacy and commercial sex, including prostitution and pornography. Although there are similarities in the type of criticism, there are significant differences in the application of commodification concerns in these areas in contrast to organ sales. Although Marxist uses of the concept of commodification are better known, I shall instead, as mentioned earlier, draw on the lines of argument in Kantian tradition. I shall try to distinguish some of the different issues or problems covered under the idea of commodification.

II. KANTIAN RESPECT FOR HUMANITY

The most apt Kantian principle for the discussion of the commodification problem is the famous second formulation of this categorical imperative found in Kant's *Foundations of the Metaphysics of Morals:* "Act so that you treat humanity, whether in your own person or that of another, always as an end and never as a means only."[5] The appeal of this as a moral directive, especially when applied to issues such as organ procurement, has several sources. The most obvious one is the strong rejection of using or exploiting another person for one's own purposes. Closely related to this is its requirement that we respect the humanity or dignity of another. A third one is the expression it gives to the significance of respecting one's own humanity. Actions and activities may be morally impermissible because they are degrading or dehumanizing or abusive of the agent. Similarly, even consent of the other person may defeat the claim of violating another's dignity. Although there is an obvious vagueness to the principle, making its precise application and import unclear, it is easy to see how it might apply to the issue of organ procurement. Salvaging might be seen as using people as mere means, selling organs might be regarded as degrading, and purchasing organs as exploitative in one or more ways. Of course, even these judgments are tentative, requiring fuller development and qualification.

I would like to proceed by distinguishing several ways in which this Kantian precept of respect for persons can be linked to the broader issue of commodification, and the more specific one of organ sales. One can find these in some application of the principle by Kant. In considering the topic of suicide, Kant denies that suicide is consistent with the idea of humanity as an end. He says: "Man, however, is not a thing and thus not something to be used merely as a means; he must always be regarded in all of his actions as an end in himself. Therefore, I cannot dispose of man in my own person so as to mutilate, corrupt, or kill him."[6] Immediately following this passage, Kant adds that this basic principle needs more careful qualification, citing cases such as amputation of limbs to save one's life, or exposing one's life to danger in order to protect it. In the passage itself there are two related ideas, one which can be called "objectification" (treating a person as a thing or object) and the other "instrumentality" or "exploitation" (using a person once objectified as a means or instrument). In another work, *The Metaphysical Principles of Virtue*, Kant classifies various duties; in one classification, there are perfect duties one owes to oneself as an animal or physical being as well as a moral being. There are three goods or goals people so viewed aim at: preservation of life, preservation of the species, and preservation of capacities for purposive use of their faculties. Each has its vice or vices, with suicide as the vice associated with the aim of preservation of life. Kant also, however, described partial suicide: "To deprive oneself of an integral part or organ (to mutilate oneself), for example, to give away or sell a tooth so that it can be implanted in the jawbone of another person, or to submit oneself to castration in order to gain an easier living as a singer, and so on, belongs to partial self-murder."[7] Again though, it is important to recognize the qualification Kant adds to this statement, which makes clear the relevance of motive and circumstance. "But this is not the case with the amputation of a dead organ, or one on the verge of mortification and thus harmful to life."[8] These passages from Kant are more closely related to the issue of organs as commodities. There is an explicit mention of selling for gain and thus the reference to the idea of a commodity, not simply as a useful or serviceable thing, but one that is subject to market exchange. Kant also expresses another idea relevant to the formula of respect for humanity, namely, the integrity of the body. One's humanity for Kant included one's body, and the destruction or alienation of one's body, in whole or in part, is a violation of the principle, at least in most cases. Thus, in addition to the concepts of objectification and instrumentality mentioned earlier, Kant also employs the idea of alienation of the body, of destroying bodily integrity. Treating humanity as an end in itself and not merely as a means seems to involve one or more of these features. These are also features that figure prominently in the commodification problem. To these might be added the specific issue tied to commodification, namely, buying and selling, or market exchange. Kant, in a discussion of another formulation of the categorical imperative, distinguishes between dignity and price, including market price. Humanity has dignity, a special kind of value or worth, "exalted above all price" that "admits of no equivalent."[9] People can have a market price in the sense that their qualities, like skill and diligence, can relate to satisfying general human inclinations and needs. In some of the current discussions of commodification, especially in connection with commercial surrogacy contracts, the label "market-alienability" has been given to this.[10]

III. COMMODIFICATION AND BODILY INTEGRITY

Margaret Jane Radin has made several useful points about market-inalienability (and market-alienability), noting that there are differences in types (e.g., by legal rule or by moral rule) and in degree (e.g., unrestricted open trading on some good, or restrictions on sellers, on buyers, or on prices). She suggests that a legal rule providing for complete market-inalienability is often an expression of the desire for noncommodification of the good.[11] One further observation she makes is that market-inalienability is compatible with other forms of alienability, such as gift or donation. Various aspects of the Kantian view I have been discussing seem attractive as ways of justifying market-inalienability of human organs. In particular, they seem to provide a way of judging commercial sale as simply wrong, not for the bad consequences that might result, such as decreasing donations and possibly reducing the number of organs available, or leading to the exploitation of the poor, who would most likely serve as organ sellers. One major difficulty is that a consistent application of the Kantian perspective seems to rule out organ gifts as well as organ sales. This difficulty was encountered in an earlier quoted passage from Kant in which he criticized the "giving away or sale of a tooth." The difficulty can also be found in a Kantian argument presented by Charles Fried in his book *Right and Wrong*. Fried begins by posing several questions: "But should persons be selling kidneys? Even though they may not be compelled to donate them, should they not be donating them freely? Do not all of the arguments I made against compelling donations—arguments about the priority of bodily integrity to tradable and distributable goods—do not all of these arguments compel the conclusion there should not be a trade in body parts, perhaps for the same reason that there should not be a trade in sexual gratification (prostitution)?"[12] Fried maintains that given the primacy of bodily integrity, no one except a desperately poor person would want to sell his or her organs, and we as a society would not want anyone to do so, for we would want him or her to share our moral convictions. He concedes that it would not violate anyone's rights for individuals to sell their kidneys. Fried also seeks to distinguish selling one's body and body parts from selling one's talents and labor. The latter involve effort and choice. He then states: "True, choices are intimate and personal, but when a man sells his body he does not sell what is his, he sells himself. What is disturbing, therefore, about selling human tissue is that the seller treats his body as a foreign object . . . . The shame of selling one's body is that it splits apart an entity one knows should not be split. It is thus not the sale itself which is disturbing, but the treatment of the body as a separate, separable entity."[13]

Careful attention to Fried's discussion reveals the difficulty mentioned before: respect for the value of personal integrity, an aspect of Kantian respect for humanity, precludes the taking or compulsory donation of organs and the sale of organs. But then the voluntary donation of organs, identified by Fried as the acceptable approach, seems to involve the same "treatment of the body as a separate, separable entity." This is precisely what Fried finds disturbing about organ sales. Gerald Dworkin cites this very problem as the main objection to Fried's argument, which he calls the "alienation" argument (which is one of several versions of the commodification argument against the sale of organs). As Dworkin notes, if selling organs is bad, then so is donation: "For if selling organs splits apart an entity one knows should not be so split, so does donating it. One treats one's body just as much as a foreign object if one gives away a kidney as if one sells it."[14] No reason is given by Fried why the apparent alienation of the body in organ donation either does not really occur with donation or is not an objectionable kind of alienation.

I think that Fried's argument can be salvaged, in the sense of being made more consistent and plausible, by returning to its Kantian source. Fried properly identifies what I take to be the key element of the argument, namely, that selling one's body is selling oneself. Fried, however, is anxious to avoid any criticism of market exchange as inherently shameful, and to insist that people should be able to sell their labor and talents as commodities in the market. In allowing for this, Fried need not back off his judgment that selling oneself is objectionable. Expressed in another way, people's talents can be commodified or made market-alienable while still regarding people's bodies as market-inalienable.

Kant, in a discussion of prostitution in *Lectures on Ethics*, states what I cited above as the key element in Fried's argument: "Man cannot dispose over himself because he is not a thing; he is not his own property; to say that he is would be self-contradictory; for in so far as he is a person he is a Subject in whom the ownership for things can be rested, and if he were his own property, he would be a thing over which he could have ownership . . . . Accordingly, a man is not at his own disposal. He is not entitled to sell a limb, not even one of his teeth. But to allow one's person for profit to be used by another for the satisfaction of sexual desire, to make oneself an Object of demand, is to dispose of oneself as over a thing and to make of one a thing on which another satisfies his appetite, just as he satisfies his hunger upon a steak."[15] This passage clearly shows Kant's rejection of what is sometimes called the "self-ownership" view of the body, just as Fried had rejected it.[16] In this discussion Kant mentions selling a body part, again a limb or tooth, unlike earlier passages in which he condemned even giving away a body part. The question that needs to be addressed is why, on a Kantian view, selling a body part is not respecting one's humanity, whereas donating an organ may not be objectionable, at least sometimes. The short answer is, I think, that selling oneself or part of oneself is always treating oneself as a mere means. It is treating oneself as an object with a market price, and thus a commodity. The transaction, the selling, is done for the receipt of the money to be obtained. One's humanity, one's body, is being treated only as a means and not as an end in itself. It is not simply the giving up of a body part that is objectionable: it is giving it up for the reason of monetary gain. However, there are forms of alienation of the body, such as donation of a kidney to save another's life, that would not violate the principal. The Kantian principle of treating humanity as an end in itself provides a ground for an imperfect duty of beneficence. One is not using oneself as a mere means if one donates a kidney for such beneficent purposes. The giving up of a body part for other reasons, as in Kant's example of the individual who does so to more easily gain employment, is violating humanity in his person. Further support for this reading can be found in the casuistic questions accompanying Kant's discussion of these issues, such as whether it is permissible to sever a diseased limb that poses a threat to one's life, or to innoculate oneself with a vaccine that is itself a risk to one's life. These are open questions for Kant, suggesting that partial suicide is not always wrong. It is wrong only when it "devalues one's humanity," which will depend on the reasons for which the action is done and circumstances in which it takes place.[17] Obviously with the medical advances making transplantation of organs such as kidneys a possibility, the reason for donating a body part to another can be a beneficent one.

One can find in this Kantian perspective a consistent line of argument for organ donation and against organ sales. It reflects intuitions deeply held by many, even some who favor commodification of body parts. Some of the latter favor restricted forms of market-alienability, so that only the individual can sell his or her body organs or tissues, or that no one should be permitted to sell vital organs, or that only the state may be the purchaser of organs, with free distribution based on nonmarket criteria.[18] These restrictions on market-alienability are efforts to avoid some types of treatments of humans that are deemed too exploitative or degrading. The salient difference is that, unlike a Kantian perspective, treating the body or body parts as commodities or salable goods is not regarded in any way as a denial or devaluing of one's humanity.

In closing, I want to acknowledge three limitations of the Kantian argument against commodification of the body that I sought to develop and clarify. The first is that the line of argument does not apply, at least in a direct way, to the sale of organs of decedents. It may be reconstructed or supplemented to do so, but it would need additional premises to explain just how it is that respecting one's humanity extends to use of one's body and body parts after one's death. The second point is related to the first. It has sometimes been proposed that individuals be allowed to sell their body parts, with delivery after the death of the individual (assuming the organs are usable). Here again the same sort of additional premises would be needed to extend the argument to the use of the body and body parts after death. Obviously, there is the salient difference between the two cases in that if there is a violation of the principle of respect for humanity in the sale of the body parts of a decedent, in the first case it is the family showing disrespect for the humanity of the decedent, whereas in the second case it is the individual violating her or his own humanity. The third point has to do with the difficulty of providing a satisfactory defense of the Kantian value I have identified as bodily integrity. It seems to me unquestionably present in Kant's writings, but it is one aspect of his moral theory that a number of moral philosophers, Kantian and non-Kantian, have found objectionable. They have understandably had reservations about its centrality in a theory that emphasizes rationality, autonomy, and freedom as features of moral personality. Obviously for Kant, the physical embodiment of such features is an inescapable and significant aspect of human beings. The nature and degree of significance this aspect has is, in large part, what makes the ethical issues in organ procurement so difficult and controversial. This is especially true of the more specific issue, sale of human organs, on which I have focused in this paper. I think that a reasonably strong case can be made for the value of bodily integrity in terms of the Kantian principle of respect for persons, insofar as human persons are embodied. After all, it is undeniable that our existence as rational and autonomous beings and the exercise of our powers of rationality and autonomy are dependent to a considerable extent on our physical well-being. To take the extreme case, Kant objects to suicide as violative of respect for our humanity, at least in general; typically, the preservation of our rationality and autonomy requires the preservation of our lives.[19] Beyond this extreme case of taking one's life, however, it can be argued in a parallel way that what we do to or with our bodies can also constitute or contribute to the impairment of our capacities for rationality and autonomy. The development and exercise of those capacities require care and restraint in the treatment of one's body. For example, Thomas Hill suggests that the Kantian principle of respect for humanity "tends to oppose drug use which seriously impairs a healthy person's capacities to think and take charge of his life."[20] Just as suicide may be condemned as generally wrong, so too many other actions (or omissions) that endanger one's health and well-being or that impair faculties or powers important to the exercise of one's autonomy. Again, as I argued earlier, the reasons for which one does any of these things are of crucial significance.

There are several difficulties with this line of argument in favor of bodily autonomy. It is not clear that all forms of "bodily integrity" are closely linked to the preservation of autonomy and rationality. Some of the examples cited by Kant, for example, a person selling a tooth, or the selling of one's hair (which Kant distinguishes from the case of teeth, describing hair as part of the body but not a bodily organ). The loss or sale of a tooth, hair, or even a kidney are neither life-threatening nor potentially destructive of a person's autonomy or rationality. I think that some Kantian and perhaps non-Kantian replies to this problem are in order. Even if some body parts are less central to a person's identity as a moral being and to a person's physical health and well-being, the highly personal and intimate nature of the body (as one's person) renders the very project of distinguishing among body parts in terms of their alienability and salability a suspect one. There are also so-called slippery slope concerns with allowing any body parts to be objects for sale: if sharp lines cannot be drawn between central and incidental body parts, then it may be best not to risk creating a category of incidental body parts that may be bought and sold.

There is an even more serious difficulty for the Kantian value of bodily integrity, namely, what exactly is wrong with the sale of a body part, whether it is a tooth or a kidney? Does treating body parts as commodities for sale or exchange involve a denial of respect for the humanity of the person whose body part is commodified? Perhaps this should instead be considered an expression or exercise of a person's autonomy with respect to his or her body, rather than a showing of disrespect to one's embodied humanity. David Richards, in a paper dealing with commercial sex rather than commerce in organs, presses this line of attack.[21] Richards notes that for Kant, autonomy is the basis of moral personality, with autonomy understood as "the capacity to order and choose one's ends as a free and rational being."[22] According to Richards, in Kant's discussion of sexual morality the person (or moral personality) is illicitly identified with the body, so that "the body acts as an absolute and inexplicable limit on autonomous freedom." It is wrong to surrender one's autonomy, "[b]ut Kant conflates this valid moral idea with the unrelated idea that one's body parts are not alienable."[23] Richards insists that donation and sale of body parts, including organs, are not only consistent with respect for one's humanity, but are valid exercises of one's autonomy, at least under certain circumstances.

I have argued in the paper that it is possible within a Kantian perspective to distinguish between donation and sale of organs. Richards is, in effect, raising the question why is it important to do so. I think that several lines of argument are available in responding to the question posed by Richards and others, such as Gerald Dworkin.[24] At the personal level, there are always present concerns about the reasons a person may have for selling an organ and the voluntariness of the consent given by that person. The generic reason captured by the expression "for money" often disguises more than it reveals. Additionally, the buyer's transaction with the seller may be one in which the seller is seen merely as a means. Although the offer of a "fair payment" may show a respect for the seller's humanity, it may raise troubling problems about whether it constitutes an undue inducement or influence on the seller, so that the fully voluntary character of his consent to the transaction is compromised.

At the institutional level, more powerful objections to commercial sale can be cited. Kant, of course, would condemn as immoral any system of property that views human beings and human bodies as things that may be owned and thus subject to buying and selling. Even if, following Richards, we do not accept Kant's identification of the person (moral personality) with the body and allow for the possibility of the sale of a body part as an exercise of autonomy and thus as compatible with respect for humanity, a society may still be reluctant to institutionalize commercial exchange of human organs. At a practical level, a society would face a dilemma: should a free market be allowed to operate to set prices, conditions of sale, and so on, or should there be substantial social regulation, through legislation, administrative bodies, or public or quasi-public agencies? The more reliance there is on free markets, the greater is the risk of inadequate protection of genuine autonomy and the overextension of commodification of bodies. The less reliance there is on impersonal market forces to shape the character of such commercial transactions, the more a society would have to involve itself in making collective decisions about which body parts may be sold, by and to whom, at what prices, and under what conditions. Unless a surprising consensus emerged, such judgments would become subject to processes of political bargaining and compromise in which concern for respect for humanity and autonomy might be submerged. Furthermore, a society's endorsement of a commercial system of exchange of body parts might be interpreted symbolically as a commitment to a view of human beings whose worth is in part determined by their commercial value. It is difficult enough for capitalist societies to give expression to the equal worth of persons; the commodification of human organs would exacerbate this difficulty. At this point, the commodification objection to the sale of body parts leads into what is usually called the "exploitation" objection. Given differences between the rich and poor in almost all human societies, commercial schemes for human organ procurement will typically lead to the poor as sellers and the rich as buyers, on terms set by the latter and favorable to their interests. Not only will there be a danger of exploitation of the poor by such schemes, but their ability to secure organs when they are in need will be diminished, unless the society makes a determined effort to provide health care on roughly equal terms to all of its citizens. Permitting commerce in organs would provide further inroads of commercial practices into the provision of medical and health care services. Of course it is incumbent on a decent society to do more than discourage and prohibit commerce in human organs in order to show respect for the dignity and equal worth of its members; it must seek to provide opportunities for work and other means of livelihood, so that selling one's organs is not a last resort or even an option worthy of consideration.

READING ENDNOTES

1. Russell Scott, *The Body as Property* (New York: Viking Press, 1981), 51.
2. Scott, 80.
3. Alfred Sadler and Blair Sadler, "Transplantation and the law: The need for organized sensitivity." *Georgetown Law Journal*, 57 (1968–69), 9.
4. Sadler and Sadler, 11.
5. Immanuel Kant, *Foundations of the Metaphysics of Morals*, trans. Lewis White Beck (Indianapolis, IN: Bobbs-Merrill, 1959), 47.
6. Kant, 47.
7. Immanuel Kant, *The Metaphysical Principles of Virtue*, trans. James Ellington (Indianapolis, IN: Bobbs-Merrill, 1964), 84.
8. Kant, *Metaphysical Principles*, 84.
9. Kant, *Foundations*, 53.
10. Margaret Jane Radin, "Market-inalienability," *Harvard Law Review*, 100 no. 4 (1987), 1845–1937.
11. Radin, 1855.
12. Charles Fried, *Right and Wrong* (Cambridge: Harvard University Press, 1978), 142.
13. Fried, 142.
14. Gerald Dworkin, "Markets and morals: The case for organ sales," in Gerald Dworkin (ed.), *Morality, Harm, and the Law* (Boulder, CO: Westview Press, 1994), 160.
15. Immanuel Kant, *Lectures on Ethics*, trans. Louis Infeld (New York: Harper and Row, 1963), 165.
16. See, for example, Courtney Campbell, "Body, self, and the property paradigm," *Hastings Center Report*, 22 (1992), 34–42, esp. 39–40.
17. Thomas Hill, "Humanity as an end in itself," in *Dignity and Practical Reason in Kant's Moral Theory* (Ithaca, NY: Cornell University Press, 1992), 38–57.
18. See, for example, Lori Andrews, "My body, my property," *Hastings Center Report*, 16 no. 5 (1986), 28–38; and Susan Rose-Ackermann, "Inalienability and the theory of property rights," *Columbia Law Review*, 85 no. 4–5 (1985), 931–69.
19. Consider Kant's remarks in *The Metaphysical Principles of Virtue*: "To destroy the subject of morality in his own person is tantamount to obliterating from the world, as far as he can, the very existence of morality itself; but morality is, nevertheless, an end in itself. Accordingly to dispose of oneself as a mere means to some end of one's own liking is to degrade the humanity in one's own person, which, after all, was entrusted to man to preserve" (83–84).
20. Thomas Hill, "Self-regarding suicide: A modified Kantian view," in *Autonomy and Self-Respect* (Cambridge: Cambridge University Press, 1991), 99.

21. David A. J. Richards, *Sex, Drugs, Death, and the Law* (Totowa, NJ: Rowman and Littlefield, 1982), chap. 3.
22. Richards, 109.
23. Richards, 109–10.
24. See note 14.

DEFINITIONS AND EXPLANATIONS

Prima facie: Latin, meaning at first view. 1. A conclusion drawn upon a first examination of a subject, which stands until further evidence is discovered, but which is subject to revision upon closer inspection; 2. When applied to moral categories such as rights or duties, the qualification of *prima facie* implies that the right or duty holds, unless it is overridden or defeated by some contrary consideration, such as a competing right of another person or a duty of greater priority. Thus, for example, we have a duty not to maim ourselves, but that duty can be overridden by the more basic duty of self-preservation in cases where the only way to save our life is to amputate a damaged limb or remove a diseased organ. Thus the duty against maiming ourselves is only *prima facie.* The contrast in the case of *prima facie* rights and duties is with those rights and duties that are **absolute.** No competing moral claim or consideration can defeat an absolute right or duty; it holds without exception and in every case. For Kant, the duty of self-preservation, i.e., the duty not to commit suicide, is an absolute duty.

QUESTIONS

1. Morelli suggests that there are a number of considerations that support the UAGA approach to organ donation over other alternatives. How many of them are Kantian, or can even be considered morally relevant by Kantians?

2. What is "the commodification problem?"

3. What does Morelli think are the principal strengths of the respect for persons principle?

4. How does the sale of organs by live donors violate the prohibitions against "objectifying" and "instrumentalizing" persons?

5. Morelli says that Kant includes the notion of bodily integrity as part of one's humanity, and so he objects to the alienation or destruction of the body as contrary to the duty to respect humanity. But if bodily integrity is part of humanity, does this give us a way to value our own freedom from pain (*contra* Skidmore)?

6. What does it mean to say that organs should be market-inalienable? Why should organs have this status when, by contrast, our bodily labour and our talents and skills do not?

7. Let us grant for the sake of argument that "selling one's body is selling oneself" and so incompatible with respect for our own humanity. Why is selling a bit of our body like an organ treated as equivalent to selling the body itself? Is selling a kidney equally selling "oneself"? What about selling our blood, sperm, hair, DNA sequence, or ova?

8. What is the relevance of Kant's discussion of prostitution to the question of organ donations or sales?

9. What is the morally relevant difference between allowing another to use your body temporarily for their sexual ends and allowing another to use your muscles cutting their grass or moving their furniture? Don't both equally treat the body as a commodity, as a means to make money by the seller?

10. What is the significance of giving away a body part *for money*? Why does money matter? Suppose you give it for a promotion, or to show your love for another, or to make people think that you are altruistic. Are these actions any better than straightforward sale?

11. How is giving an organ away compatible with bodily integrity, while selling it is not?

12. Does the notion of "partial suicide" make sense?

13. If we think that some actions are inherently wrong, can we make sense of the claim that the reasons why it is done and the circumstances under which it is done are morally relevant to its assessment (as Morelli says in trying to distinguish between donation and sale)?

14. How can bodily integrity be important to Kant at all? Consider what Kant says about the goodness of a good will here. It is true, but only contingently, that human beings require bodily integrity to exercise their autonomy. How can a universal law rest on contingent facts for Kant?

15. If the sale of organs is wrong because it threatens our capacity for rational agency, shouldn't we allow the use of organs from incompetent humans?

16. O'Neill grounds a Kantian duty to relieve extreme poverty and hunger in the need for minimal physical well-being as a condition of autonomy. You might think that we have a duty to respect bodily integrity for the same reason: because bodily integrity is necessary for autonomy. But can that reason ground a duty not to sell body parts the loss of which in no way impedes human functioning or the capacity for autonomy? Can it ground a duty not to prostitute oneself?

17. Are Morelli's practical concerns about the societal implications of allowing commercial sale of organs convincing? Are they Kantian?

18. What would Kant's understanding of the relation between persons and their bodies imply about the following practices?

    1. the use of cosmetics and other surface "beauty" products.

    2. the use of cosmetic surgery.

3. the growing phenomena of self-mutilation (which ranges from piercing and tattooing, to splitting the tongue, to the amputation of healthy limbs).

4. the use of fetal tissue for bio-medical experimentation.

5. the use of sexual reassignment surgery for transgendered persons (who believe that the sex they were born with does not match their gender and who feel trapped in the wrong body).

19. If, as O'Neill suggests, we have an imperfect duty to aid in supporting the autonomy of others, and we can do so by donating a non-vital organ to someone who will die without it, is it more Kantian to follow Kant's own words prohibiting the donation or to make the donation?

◆ ◆ ◆

J. Baird Callicott, The Pragmatic Power and Promise of Theoretical Environmental Ethics: Forging a New Discourse

J. Baird Callicott, the prominent American environmental philosopher, has two over-riding objectives in this paper. The first is to re-examine the notion of intrinsic value in such a way as to overcome some of the more worrying failures of Kant's moral theory, so that it can play a central role in environmental ethics. Second, he wants to insist, *contra* many contemporary pragmatists, that it important for environmental theorists to remain committed to theory.

Kant grounds the intrinsic value of a being in its having a rational nature. Familiar from Singer's article are the twin problems of this kind of grounding: it seems unable to accommodate animals and non-rational humans. Gorillas and children, for example, are not easily afforded moral value on this construction. Responding, as some are tempted to do, that children and gorillas are *somewhat* rational goes some way to alleviating these particular concerns, but does not go nearly far enough for many environmentalists. This extension of rationality to gorillas and children will never stretch far enough to cover members of the plant kingdom, which are not rational in any traditional sense. Nor will it ever cover groups, such as ecosystems, which are not individuals in any traditional sense.

Callicott's alternative is to suggest that we re-examine what it means for something to have value. There is no value, Callicott claims, without a subject who values. The distinction between the instrumental or intrinsic value of objects (to speak generally) is not an argument about a quality that objects have, but an argument about how objects are regarded by valuing subjects such as us. An object has intrinsic value if it is valued by someone independently of any use that object has as a means to some other end. An object has instrumental value if it is valuable to someone because it helps them as a means to some other end. There are people who value ecosystems, gorillas, and children noninstrumentally (not just as means to some other end they have), and so they have intrinsic value. A Kantian theory of intrinsic value can, on this reading, extend moral worth to such objects.

Callicott then develops an argument that highlights the importance of engaging in what might seem like abstract moral theorizing. He takes as his opponents those who insist that it makes no difference *how* we value nature, and so debates about whether nature has intrinsic or instrumental value, and what exactly these mean, are largely or wholly beside the important point. The fact that we do value nature is agreed upon, and so we ought to act to protect it as best we can. These activists claim that theory is simply taking valuable resources away from the fight to save the environment. In response, Callicott shows that thinking of environments as intrinsically valuable has wide-ranging practical consequences, which serve the goals of protecting non-human entities and systems. Environmental protection is served by the view that non-human entities have intrinsic and not merely instrumental value in a number of ways. The concept of intrinsic value forms the core of a discourse that transforms how we think about the relationship between human beings and the environments of which they are a part. And that transformation in our thinking serves the practical causes that environmental activists seek to promote.

One lesson of Callicott's paper might be this: theory matters. Even when ethical theorizing seems abstract and general, dense and complex, and far removed from the actual concerns of moral agents living their lives and trying to decide what to do, we should not abandon it. Ethical theories can change the world for the better.

✦ ✦ ✦

J. Baird Callicott, "The Pragmatic Power and Promise of Theoretical Environmental Ethics: Forging a New Discourse," *Environmental Values* 11 (2002): 3-25. Reprinted with permission of the publisher, The White Horse Press, Cambridge UK.

The Pragmatic Power and Promise of Theoretical Environmental Ethics: Forging a New Discourse

J. BAIRD CALLICOTT

INTRODUCTION

In one of the most ancient and venerable sources of Chinese philosophy, the *Analects*, a disciple asks Confucius what he would do first were he to become the prime minister of the State of Wei.[1] Without question, Confucius replies, first I would rectify names. His disciple was puzzled by this saying; and for a long time so was I. But no more, for I am coming to appreciate the power of names, and of discourse, more generally, in the formation of environmental policy.

The true answer to Juliet's question, 'What's in a name?' in Shakespeare's play, is 'Really, quite a lot.' Consider various names for women—'chicks,' 'babes,' 'broads,' 'ladies.' The feminist movement has made us keenly aware that what we call someone or something—what we name him, her, or it—is important. A name frames, colours, and makes someone or something available for certain kinds of uses . . . or abuses. Even the name 'lady' is freighted with so much baggage that it is not worn comfortably by many women. A major effort of feminist politics has been the rectification of names for women, and more generally, the rectification of gender discourse.

Self-styled Pragmatist environmental philosophers have complained that environmental philosophy has been bogged down in ivory-tower theorising to little practical effect.[2] Here I argue that theoretical environmental philosophy has had and is having a profound, albeit indirect, practical effect on environmental policy. It has done so by creating a new discourse that environmental activists and environmental professionals have adopted and put to good use. At the heart of this new discourse is the concept of intrinsic value in nature. I sketch the history of this concept and its associated discourse, and indicate how it is practically impacting environmental policy.

ENVIRONMENTAL PHILOSOPHY MORE THEORETICAL THAN APPLIED

Environmental philosophy has been less an 'applied' subdiscipline of philosophy than some of the other applied subdisciplines with which it is often lumped—biomedical ethics, business ethics, and engineering ethics, for example. Environmental philosophy has, more particularly, been more involved with reconstructing ethical theory than with applying standard, off-the-rack ethical theories to real-world environmental problems.

In large part that is because standard ethical theory had been so resolutely—even militantly—anthropocentric that it seemed inadequate to deal with today's environmental problems. In scope and magnitude, contemporary human transformation of the environment is unprecedented. Gradually, the impact of human activities on non-human nature became almost ubiquitous in scope and unrelenting in intensity, so much so that by the mid-twentieth century, the existence of an environmental *crisis* was widely acknowledged. And the contemporary environmental crisis seems morally charged. For example, the current orgy of human-caused species extinction seems wrong—morally wrong. And not just because the anthropogenic extinction of many species might adversely affect human interests or human rights. Most first-generation environmental philosophers, therefore, took the task of environmental ethics to be constructing a nonanthropocentric theory of ethics that would somehow morally enfranchise nonhuman natural entities and nature as a whole—directly, not merely indirectly to the extent that what human beings do in and to nature would affect human interests and human rights.

This was the burden of the first academic paper in the field, 'Is There a Need for a New, an Environmental Ethic?', by Australian philosopher Richard Routley, presented to the Fifteenth World Congress of Philosophy in Varna, Bulgaria in 1973.[3] A similar task was set by Norwegian philosopher Arne Naess (1973) in his paper, 'The Shallow and the Deep, Long-range Ecology Movements: A Summary.'[4] In the first paper on environmental ethics by an American philosopher, Holmes Rolston III argued that the central task of environmental philosophy is to develop a 'primary,' not a 'secondary,' 'ecological ethic.'[5] Animal rights theorist Tom Regan reiterated Rolston's understanding of the enterprise—that a proper environmental ethic was 'an ethic *of* the environment,' not an 'ethic for the use of the environment,' which he called a mere 'management ethic.'[6]

THE KANTIAN CONCEPT OF INTRINSIC VALUE

Central to the theoretical challenge of developing a direct, a primary ethic *of* the environment is the problem of intrinsic value in nature. Although the early twentieth-century English philosopher G. E. Moore[7] wrote much about intrinsic value, Immanuel Kant's modern classical concept of intrinsic value and the way it functioned in his ethics most influenced the thinking of contemporary environmental philosophers.[8] Central to Kant's ethic is the precept that each person be treated as an end in him- or herself, not merely as a means. Indeed, the second formulation of Kant's categorical imperative is this: 'Act so that you treat humanity, whether in your own person or that of another, always as an end and never as a means only.'[9] Kant justifies—or 'grounds'—this precept by claiming that each person has intrinsic value. That claim in turn is justified by finding in each person an intrinsic value-conferring property, which Kant identified as reason. Thus, rational beings, according to Kant, have intrinsic value, and should therefore be treated as ends in themselves and never as means only.

This Kantian approach to ethics appears at first glance to be unpromising for developing a *nonanthropocentric* environmental ethic, as Routley, Naess, Rolston, and Regan so unambiguously set forth the task. Why? Because Kant's intrinsic value-conferring property, reason or rationality, had long been regarded as a hallmark of human nature. At the dawn of Western philosophy, Aristotle declared that reason or rationality was the 'differentia' that distinguished 'man,' as a species, from the other animals. *Anthropos* is the uniquely 'rational animal,' according to Aristotle. Thus, Kant's approach to ethics appears to be a brief for anthropocentrism and to foreclose the possibility of nonanthropocentrism. Indeed, Kant[10] goes out of his way to exclude non-human natural entities and nature as a whole from ethical enfranchisement: 'Beings whose existence does not depend on our will but on nature, if they are not rational beings, have only relative worth as means and are therefore called "things"; on the other hand, rational beings are designated "persons" because their nature indicates that they are ends in themselves, i.e. things which may not be used as a means.' For Kant, human beings are ends; beings whose existence depends on nature are means.

EXTENDING THE KANTIAN CONCEPT OF
INTRINSIC VALUE TO (SOME) ANIMALS

But look again. In the *Foundations of the Metaphysics of Morals*, Kant himself is quite careful to avoid speciesism—analogous to racism and sexism—the *unjustified* or *ungrounded* moral entitlement of one's own kind and the exclusion of other kinds. Not being human, but being *rational* is that in virtue of which a human being has intrinsic value. Kant consistently holds open the possibility that there may be other-than-human rational beings. He never more specifically identifies who such non-human rational beings may be. Some passages suggest Kant might be thinking of God and the heavenly host; others that he might be thinking of rational beings on other planets that inhabit very different bodies and therefore have very different desires and inclinations than do human beings. In the passage just quoted, he seems to hold open the possibility that there may be non-human rational beings found in terrestrial nature. It is in this orthodox Kantian moral climate that so much ethical significance was recently attached to proving that chimpanzees and gorillas could master rudimentary language skills, and could, via American Sign Language or some other surrogate for spoken language, express themselves creatively.[11] For Descartes had insisted that the ability to use language creatively—not merely rotely as he believed parrots to do—was an indication of rationality.[12]

Proving that chimpanzees and gorillas are minimally rational does undermine anthropocentrism, but only a little. It certainly does not take us very far in the direction of an expansive environmental ethic—however much it may help ethically rehabilitate our primate relatives and spare them the indignities and outrages of the zoo trade and biomedical research. Kant's conceptual distinction between humanity and rationality was, however, also exploited theoretically in another way, which proved to be more powerful and transformative. Not all human beings are minimally rational. The so-called 'marginal cases' are not.[13] Infants, the severely mentally handicapped, and the abjectly senile are the usual suspects. They are thus in the same boat with all the other '[b]eings whose existence ... depend[s] on nature ... i.e., things which may be used merely as a means,' to quote Kant once more. Let's get specific: if we equitably applied Kant's ethical theory, we could justifiably perform the same painful and destructive biomedical experiments on unwanted non-rational infants that we inflict on non-rational nonhuman animals; we could open a hunting season on the severely mentally handicapped; and we could make pet food out of the abjectly senile.

Such abhorrent implications of Kant's moral philosophy provided nonanthropocentric theorists with an opportunity to propose retaining Kant's form of moral argument—which has, after all, been so compelling in Western ethical thought—but revising its specific conceptual contents, so as to include the marginal cases in the class of persons and rescue them from the class of things. The form or ethical architecture that was retained is Kant's close linkage of moral ends, intrinsic value, and a value-conferring property. Thus to be a moral end, and not a means only, you must have intrinsic value, but making rationality the value-conferring property, appears, in light of the 'Argument from Marginal Cases' to be too restrictive. Various alternatives to rationality have been proposed, selected to justify the theorist's personal ethical agenda. Regan who was content to limit 'moral considerability' to warm, furry animals, proposed being the 'subject of a life' as the intrinsic value-conferring property.[14] Subjects of a life have a sense of self, remember a personal past, entertain hopes and fears about the future—in sum, enjoy a subjective state of being, which can be better or worse from their own point of view. Peter Singer who wanted to extend 'moral considerability' a bit more generously, proposed sentience, the capacity to experience pleasure and pain, as the intrinsic value-conferring property.[15] That move reached a much wider spectrum of animals—how wide is not completely clear—but, clearly, it left out the entire plant kingdom.

EXTENDING THE KANTIAN CONCEPT OF INTRINSIC VALUE TO ALL LIVING BEINGS

To reach out and touch all living beings with moral considerability, several theorists proposed having *interests* as a plausible and defensible intrinsic value-conferring property.[16] A living being—a tree for example—can have interests in the absence of consciousness. This basic idea was variously expressed. A living being has a good of its own, whether or not it is good for anything else. Unlike complexly functioning machines, such as automobiles, whose ends or functions are determined or assigned them by their human designers to serve human ends, living beings have ends, goals, or purposes—*teloi*, in a word—of their own. They are, in Paul Taylor's terminology, 'teleological centres of life.'[17] In Warwick Fox's, they are *autopoietic*—self-creating and self-renewing.[18]

PROBLEMS WITH BIOCENTRISM AND THEIR PROPOSED SOLUTIONS

The main problem, theoretically speaking, with biocentrism—as this modified or expanded Kantian approach to nonanthropocentric environmental ethics has come to be called—is that it seems to stop with individual organisms. At once biocentrism both too broadly *and* too narrowly distributes intrinsic value.

As to the former, granting each and every organism moral considerability makes ethical space way too densely crowded, rendering our most routine and vital human actions ethically problematic. Surely, it is perfectly possible to refrain from ill-using our fellow primates as objects of amusement and subjects of medical experimentation, with little human inconvenience. Equally possible—and with only a little more mindfulness, abstemiousness, and inconvenience—we might give up eating meat and using other products made from animals, our fellow sentient beings. But we have to eat something, slap mosquitoes and other annoying insects, rid ourselves and our domiciles of vermin, weed our flower gardens—all of which are morally questionable if every living being has intrinsic value and should be treated as an end in itself, not a means only.

On the other hand, biocentrism too narrowly distributes intrinsic value in nature because it does not provide moral considerability for what environmentalists most care about. Frankly, environmentalists do not much care about the welfare of each and every shrub, bug, and grub. We care, rather, about preserving *species* of organisms, *populations* within species, *genes* within populations—in a word we care about preserving biodiversity. We care about preserving communities of organisms and ecosystems. We also care about *air* and *water* quality, *soil* stability, and the integrity of Earth's stratospheric *ozone membrane*. None of these things appear to have interests, goods of their own, ends, purposes, or goals, and thus none has intrinsic value, on this account.

Solutions to both biocentric distribution problems have been proposed. A solution to the too-broad distribution problem is to distribute intrinsic value unequally or differentially.[19] Grant all organisms base-line or minimal intrinsic value. Thus, when our own interests are not at stake, we should leave them alone to pursue their own ends, to realise their own *teloi*, each in its own way. Additional intrinsic value is distributed to sentient organisms, yet more to subject-of-a-life organisms, and more still to rational organisms.[20] Thus, because we human beings, as rational, sentient subjects of a life, have the most intrinsic value, we are entitled to defend it and cater to it by doing bad things to other organisms with less intrinsic value—but only if we conscientiously deem it to be necessary. That seems plausible enough, although rather conventional, leaving us human beings at the top of the moral pyramid where we have always been. The difference is that in traditional Western ethics the pyramid was low and squat. Nonhuman organisms were mere things, with no intrinsic value at all. They were thus available for any human use at all, however fatuous. Differential biocentrism extends the moral pyramid's height and mass to much greater proportions, albeit leaving human beings at the pinnacle.

A solution to biocentrism's too-narrow distribution problem is less plausible. Lawrence Johnson has seized upon somewhat dated, minority views in evolutionary biology and ecology to argue that species and ecosystems have interests.[21] Some biologists have argued that species are not collections of organisms capable of interbreeding, but supra-individuals that are protracted in space and time.[22] If so, we may convince ourselves they have interests, and therefore intrinsic value, and therefore moral considerability. And there is a long, albeit fading, tradition in ecology that conceives ecosystems to be superorganisms to which individual organisms are related as cells and species as organs.[23] And if so, again, we may believe they have interests, and therefore intrinsic value, and therefore moral considerability. But these are big ifs. Rolston takes a different approach.[24] He points out that the most fundamental end of most organisms is to realise their genetic potential—to represent ('re-present') their species and to reproduce ('*re-produce*') it. They have a good of their own—*which is their species*. Thus does Rolston try to convince us that species per se may plausibly be said to have intrinsic value. For organisms to flourish, even to live at all, they must live in an ecological context or habitat. Thus does Rolston try to justify finding intrinsic value in biotic communities and ecosystems.

THE SUBJECTIVIST ACCOUNT OF
INTRINSIC VALUE IN NATURE

This mainstream line of argument in environmental ethics, which begins with a Kantian superstructure, works through animal liberation, and terminates in biocentrism, assumes that intrinsic value supervenes or piggybacks on some objective property. Thus intrinsic value, albeit supervenient, itself therefore appears to be an objective property in nature. Indeed, the adjective 'intrinsic' seems logically to require that *intrinsic* value, if it exists at all, exist as an objective property. It is intrinsic to the being that has it. Kant himself appears to think that intrinsic value is something objective: 'Such beings [rational beings] are not merely subjective ends whose existence as a result of our action has a worth for us, but are objective ends, i.e., beings whose existence in itself is an end.'[25] But the idea that value—or worth—of any kind can be objective seems to fly in the face of a shibboleth of modern Western philosophy: René Descartes' division of the world into the *res extensa* and the *res cogitans*, the subjective and objective domains, respectively, and David Hume's ancillary distinction between fact and value. *All* value is, from the most fundamental modern point of view, subjectively conferred. No valuing subject, no valuable objects. That is, without the existence of valuing subjects, no value of any kind would exist in the world—from a modern point of view.

Nevertheless, some nonanthropocentric environmental philosophers—I among them—have argued that a robust account of intrinsic value in nature can be provided even within the severe constraints of the allied object-subject/fact-value distinctions.[26] From a modern point of view, 'value' is first and foremost a verb. Value, more technically put, is conferred on an object by the intentional act of a valuing subject. If so, 'instrumental' and 'intrinsic' may be regarded as adverbs, not adjectives. Thus one may value (verb transitive) some things instrument*ally*—our houses, cars, computers, clothes, and such. Similarly, one may value (verb transitive) other things intrinsic*ally*—ourselves, our spouses, children, and other relatives. If we have learned our religion and moral philosophy well, we may intrinsically value all other human beings. Indeed, it is logically possible to value intrinsically anything under the sun— an old worn out shoe, for example. But most of us value things intrinsically when we perceive them to be part of a community to which we also belong, because we are evolved to do so.[27]

'Perceive' here is the key word, for perception can be trained and redirected. Much of the suasive environmental literature aims to train and redirect our perception of nature such that we see it as the wider community in which all our other communities are embedded. Aldo Leopold's *A Sand County Almanac* is an outstanding example. In the Foreword, Leopold writes, 'We abuse land because we regard it as a commodity belonging to us. When we see land as a community to which we belong, we may begin to use it with love and respect.'[28] Most of the remainder of the book is devoted to persuading us that ecology 'enlarges the boundaries of the community to include soils, waters, plants, and animals, or collectively the land.'[29] When that happens, people will have 'love, respect, and admiration for land, and a high regard for its value ... [and b]y value I mean something far broader than mere economic value; I mean value in the philosophical sense'—intrinsic value, in other words.[30]

THE CRYPTO-SUBJECTIVISM OF ALLEGEDLY
OBJECTIVIST ACCOUNTS OF INTRINSIC VALUE

How could Kant, a thoroughly modern philosopher, and a close student of Hume, actually think that intrinsic *value* is an objective property (of rational beings)? A closer reading of Kant himself indicates that in fact he does not think it is. Kant writes, 'Man necessarily *thinks* of his existence this way'—that is, as an end-in-itself, some-thing of intrinsic value—'thus far, it is a *subjective* principle of human action.'[31] Kant is intellectually honest; he is fully aware that—given the constraints of the Cartesian *res cogitans/res extensa* and ancillary Humean fact/value distinctions—value is not objective, in the same sense that a rock is objective, something existing independently of the intentional act of a valuing subject in the *res extensa*. Kant goes on, however: 'Also every other rational creature *thinks* of his own existence by means of the same rational ground which holds also for myself, thus it is at the same time an *objective* principle from which, as a supreme practical ground, it must be possible to derive all laws of the will.'[32] The meaning of 'objective,' in the above-quoted fragment from Kant, is 'universal,' not 'existing independently of the intentional act of a valuing sub-ject.' In other words, Kant uses the concept of objectivity in its epistemological, not in its ontological sense. Each organism should be an unconditional end for all moral agents, because for itself it is an unconditional end-in-itself.

A closer reading of Rolston—the most subtle thinker of the purportedly objec-tivist school of intrinsic-value-in-nature theorists—also shows that he follows Kant in effecting an unmarked shift from the ontological to the epistemic sense of 'objective' and back again. We human beings self-consciously value ourselves, as well as other things, intrinsically. But lemurs, Rolston notes, also demonstrably value themselves intrinsically, though perhaps not self-consciously.[33] So do warblers. What Rolston does is find in nature a wide spectrum of non-human reflexively valuing subjects.[34] He begins with human subjects, then moves on to our close relatives, phylogenetically speaking, and on from there, to subjects more distantly related and arguably less acutely conscious than lemurs and other primates—birds, reptiles, insects—all in some sense self-valuing subjects. Finally, Rolston posits the existence of valuing subjects stripped of all subjectivity: 'Trees are also valuable in themselves,' Rolston writes.[35] But why? How? Because, as he explains, they are 'able to value themselves.' In what sense? Is Rolston going beyond conventional science and claiming a secret, inner life for plants? Not at all: 'Natural selection picks out whatever traits an organism has that are valuable to it, relative to its survival. When natural selection has been at work gathering these traits into an organism, *that organism is able to value* on the basis of those traits. *It is a valuing organism*, even if the organism is not a sentient valuer . . . .'[36] So, clearly, although the valuing subject may lack sentience, indeed consciousness of any kind—that is, the valuing subject may, paradoxically, lack subjectivity—Rolston agrees with the subjectivists that the value of any object, a value*ee*, depends, in the last analysis, on the existence of a valuing subject, a valu*er*.

For Rolston, the ethical payoff of this analysis is characteristically Kantian. Rolston's environmental ethic follows the Kantian pattern, but broadens the 'subjective principle' to the maximum extent possible. Reflexive self-valuing is not confined to 'man,' nor to 'rational creatures,' nor even to sentient or conscious creatures, but to any and all evolved creatures. And, just as Kant, Rolston argues that because they value themselves intrinsically, we should value them intrinsically as well. That makes the principle 'objective,' but in a different sense of the word, which neither Kant nor Rolston marks.

THE PRAGMATIST CRITIQUE OF THEORETICAL ENVIRONMENTAL PHILOSOPHY

As this brief summary will indicate—and, believe me, it is brief, sketchy, and incomplete, given the voluminous literature on subject—mainstream environmental philosophy has been preoccupied with a very abstruse and arcane theoretical project. A growing cadre of environmental philosophers, identifying themselves as Pragmatists of one kind or another, has begun to protest against this preoccupation with theory, especially the theoretical problem of intrinsic value in nature.[37] They variously, but basically, argue that it makes no difference to environmental practice and policy whether we think of nature as having intrinsic value or only instrumental value. Whether we value nature as a means to human ends or an end in itself, we still value it—and therefore will save it. Norton calls this the 'convergence hypothesis.'[38] Because the concept of intrinsic value in nature makes no difference to environmental practice and policy, debate about it is a waste of time and intellectual capital that could better be spent on something more efficacious. Further, lay people cannot understand the jargon-ridden, abstract discourse of theoretical environmental philosophy. If they do get an inkling of what it is about, they will be alienated from it, because most lay people are uncritically anthropocentric. Worse, nonanthropocentrism and the concept of intrinsic value in nature is divisive, setting environmental philosophers at odds with one another, occasioning endless, unbecoming bickering between shallow and deep theorists, and, among the deep, between subjectivists and objectivists.

Instead, the Pragmatist contingent contends, environmental philosophers could better spend their time and intellectual capital helping lay people clarify their actual environmental values—as opposed to speculating about some newfangled value which they would then try to impose on lay people—and helping lay people sort out what to do in the context of specific problems or issues.[39] Often we may find that conflicting values support the same policy—as, for example, when those who value waterfowl for hunting and those who value it for watching can support waterfowl habitat preservation and restoration policies—and philosophers can help lay people figure that out.[40] This is characterised as a more bottom-up, rather than top-down approach to environmental philosophy.[41] Begin with something specific and local—a scheme to develop a forested landscape or to dam a stream and create a lake, or a plan to reha- bilitate an abandoned mine site or to reintroduce an extirpated predator. The role of environmental philosophers in environmental policy and decision-making processes is to bring the tools of conceptual analysis, values clarification, and, yes, ethical theory, to bear on the problem—but only to the extent that theory is familiar (and thus con- ventional), easily understandable, and illuminating, and to the extent that the problem itself determines what theories are useful to its solution.

THE PRACTICAL EFFICACY OF THEORETICAL ENVIRONMENTAL PHILOSOPHY

I have no quarrel whatever with the bottom-up approach to environmental philos- ophy. I myself was a recipient of a three-year grant from the bi-national Great Lakes Fishery Commission to work with an ichthyologist and an aquatic community ecolo- gist to re-envision fishery management policy in the Great Lakes for the new millen- nium. My role was precisely to clarify such fuzzy conservation concepts as biological integrity, ecosystem health, ecosystem management, ecological restoration, ecological rehabilitation, ecological sustainability, sustainable development, and adaptive man- agement; and to examine the values that have driven, drive, and will drive fishery management in the Great Lakes in the past, present, and future.[42] I do have a quarrel, however, with the representation of the bottom-up, Pragmatic approach as a compet- itive alternative to theoretical environmental philosophy and to the invidious com- parison that environmental Pragmatists make between the two, virtually insisting that theorists should stop their pointless and pernicious theorising.[43] I believe that the two—theory and practice—should be complementary, not competitive. Further, I think that theoretical environmental philosophy is powerfully pragmatic; that theory does make a difference to practice.

What difference? First, the convergence hypothesis—which Norton[44] confesses is merely 'an article of environmentalists' faith'—is not a credible article of faith because it is hard to believe that all Earth's myriad species, for example, are in some way useful to human beings.[45] Many may represent unexplored potential new pharmaceuticals, foods, fibres, and fuels. But many more may not.[46] Many species that have no actual or potential resource value are critical agents in ecological processes and/or perform vital ecological functions or 'services.' But many more do not.[47] Many non-resource, non- ecological-service-provider species are, nevertheless, objects of aesthetic wonder and/or epistemic curiosity to the small percentage of the human population that is aesthetically cultured and scientifically educated. But such amenity values that endangered non- resource, non-ecological-service-provider species have for a tiny human minority afford them little protection in a world increasingly governed by market economics and majority-rule politics. In short, conservation policy based on anthropocentrism alone—however broadened to include potential as well as actual resources, ecosystem services, and the aesthetic, epistemic, and spiritual uses of nature by present *and future* people—is less robust and inclusive than conservation policy based on the intrinsic value of nature.[48]

Second, in setting forth the 'convergence hypothesis,' Norton focuses exclusively on the content of anthropocentric and nonanthropocentric (or intrinsic) values and the environmental policies they support.[49] But if we focus instead on the formalities, as it were, or structural features of the policy discourses involving, on the one hand, claims of intrinsic value in nature and those, on the other, that only involve anthropocentric value claims, a hypothesis contrary to the 'convergence hypothesis' is suggested. Perhaps it should be called the 'divergence hypothesis.'

Broad recognition of the intrinsic value of human beings places the burden of proof on those who would over-ride that value for the sake of realising instrumental values. For example, an intrinsically valuable human being not wishing to sell a piece of property at any price may refuse any offer to buy it. Their intransigence, however, may be trumped if benefits to the public rise beyond a certain threshold. If, for example, the recalcitrant owner's property stands in the way of an urban light-rail train track, then the property may be 'condemned,' and the owner paid fair market value for it, whether he or she is willing to sell it or not. If nature were also broadly recognised to have intrinsic value the burden of proof would shift, *mutatis mutandis*, from conservators of nature to exploiters of nature.[50] If something has only instrumental value, its disposition goes to the highest bidder. If that something is some subsection of nature—say, a wetland—conservationists must prove that an economic cost-benefit analysis unequivocally indicates that it has greater value as an amenity than it has, drained and filled, as a site for a proposed shopping mall. But if the intrinsic value of wetlands were broadly recognised, then developers would have to prove that the value to the human community of the shopping mall was so great as to trump the intrinsic value of the wetland. The concept of intrinsic value in nature functions politically much like the concept of human rights. Human rights—to liberty, even to life—may be over-ridden by considerations of public or aggregate utility. But in all such cases, the burden of proof for doing so rests not with the rights holder, but with those who would override human rights. And the utilitarian threshold for over-riding human rights is pitched very high indeed. As Fox puts it:[51]

> The mere fact that moral agents must be able to justify their actions in regard to their treatment of entities that are intrinsically valuable means that recognizing the intrinsic value of the nonhuman world has a dramatic effect upon the framework of environmental debate and decision-making. If the nonhuman world is only considered to be instrumentally valuable then people are permitted to use and otherwise interfere with any aspect of it for whatever reasons they wish (i.e., no justification is required). If anyone objects to such interference then, within this framework of reference, the onus is clearly on the person who objects to justify why it is *more useful* to humans to leave that aspect of the nonhuman world alone. If, however, the nonhuman world is considered to be *intrinsically valuable* then

the onus shifts to the person who wants to interfere with it to justify why they should be allowed to do so: anyone who wants to interfere with any entity that is intrinsically valuable is morally obliged to be able to offer a *sufficient justification* for their actions. Thus recognizing the intrinsic value of the nonhuman world shifts the *onus of justification* from the person who wants to protect the nonhuman world to the person who wants to interfere with it—and that, in itself, represents a fundamental shift in the terms of environmental debate and decision-making.

THE PRAGMATIC POWER OF THE RIGHTS DISCOURSE

Mention of human rights leads to my third and last point about the pragmatic power and practical difference of theoretical environmental philosophy and its preoccupation with the concept of intrinsic value in nature. Human beings have shoes, teeth, kidneys, thoughts, and rights. Human shoes and teeth are out there for anyone to see. Human kidneys may be observed during surgery or autopsy. We are privy only to our own thoughts and infer the thoughts of others from what they do, what they say, and what they write. However open to view or hidden away, human shoes, teeth, kidneys, and thoughts are all things of this world. But 'human rights' is a name for nothing; it is but an idea—a fiction—created by Western moral philosophers.[52] Theoretical moral philosophers created, more generally, a rights *discourse* in the West.[53]

When it was fresh and new, other moral philosophers tried to silence that discourse, for various reasons. For example, in the eighteenth century Jeremy Bentham, infamously, dismissed the idea that human beings have rights as 'nonsense on stilts.'[54] But the human-rights discourse survived its political and philosophical naysayers. It was institutionalised in the West by the adoption of the Bill of Rights, the first ten amendments to the Constitution of the United States, in 1789. It was globalised by the adoption of the Universal Declaration on Human Rights by the United Nations General Assembly in 1948, now translated and published in 300 languages.[55] Presently, the United Nations International Bill of Human Rights consists of the Universal Declaration plus other human-rights measures adopted during the 1950s and '60s—the International Covenant on Economic, Social and Cultural Rights, and the International Covenant on Civil and Political Rights and its two Optional Protocols, one on civil and political rights, one on the abolition of the death penalty.[56] The United Nations maintains an active (and geopolitically important) Commission on Human Rights and an office of 'High Commissioner for Human Rights.' Human-rights discourse, throughout the latter half of the twentieth century and the beginning of the twenty-first has had enormous pragmatic effect worldwide as an instrument of criticism and political reform.[57] In the name of human rights, we condemn everything from 'female circumcision' in parts of Muslim Africa to the Tienamen Square massacre in China, and reform of everything from the political status of American Indians in the United States to that of brides in India.

Especially in the subjectivist version that I endorse, the concept of intrinsic value of nature, like the concept of human rights, designates less a substantive thing than a pragmatic limit on policies driven by aggregate utility. Practically by definition, the *adjective* 'intrinsic' entails that the character or property it modifies exists objectively in the entity to which it is attributed. Indeed, often the adjective 'intrinsic' means that the character or property it modifies is the very essence of the entity to which it is attributed. For example, transporting oxygen to tissues in organisms is intrinsic to haemoglobin; competition is intrinsic to sport; volatility is intrinsic to the gaseous state of matter. In environmental philosophy, however, 'intrinsic value' has also been consistently implicitly defined, *via negativa*, as the antonym of 'instrumental value.' What value remains—if any does—after all something's instrumental value has been accounted for is its intrinsic value. Personally, I want to be useful to my family, friends, colleagues, neighbours, fellow citizens, and to my various human communities, and to the biotic community. But when the time comes, if it should come, because of age, infirmity, or both, that I cease to be of instrumental value, I shall still value myself intrinsically and expect others to value me that way as well (or at least treat me as if they did). Thus to value something intrinsically—as we shift from the adjectival-objective to the adverbial-subjective form—is to value something for itself, as an end-in-itself (to reinvoke the Kantian mode of expression), not merely as a means to our own ends, not merely as an instrument. From this perspective, there is no objective property in entities to which the noun 'value' corresponds. Rather we subjects value objects in one or both of at least two ways—instrumentally or intrinsically—between which there is no middle term.

THE PRAGMATIC EFFICACY OF THE INTRINSIC-VALUE-IN-NATURE DISCOURSE

Pragmatist philosophers now carp and cavil against the concept of intrinsic value in nature as still more nonsense on stilts. Bryan Norton, for one, has carried on a virtual jihad against the idea.[58] But environmental activists—for example, Dave Foreman, founder of Earth First!, the most radical group of environmental activists in the United States—have appreciated its practical efficacy. A while ago, Foreman wrote, 'Too often, philosophers are rendered impotent by their inability to act without analysing everything to absurd detail. To act, to trust your instincts, to go with the flow of natural forces, *is* an underlying philosophy. Talk is cheap. Action is dear.'[59] Later, Foreman changed his tune.[60] He identified four forces that are shaping the conservation movement at the dawn of the new millennium. They are, and I quote, first 'academic philosophy,' second, 'conservation biology,' third, 'independent local groups,' and fourth, 'Earth First!' That's right, 'academic philosophy' heads the list. This is some of what Foreman has to say about it:

> During the 1970s, philosophy professors in Europe, North America, and Australia started looking at environmental ethics as a worthy focus for discussion and exploration. . . . By 1980, enough interest had coalesced for an academic journal called *Environmental Ethics*

to appear . . . . An international network of specialists in environmental ethics developed, leading to one of the more vigorous debates in modern philosophy. At first, little of this big blow in the ivory towers drew the notice of working conservationists, but by the end of the '80s, few conservation group staff members or volunteer activists were unaware of the Deep Ecology–Shallow Environmentalism distinction or of the general discussion about ethics and ecology. At the heart of the discussion was the question of whether other species possessed intrinsic value or had value solely because of their use to humans [and] . . . what, if any, ethical obligations humans had to nature or other species.[61]

Notice that for the discourse of intrinsic value and, more generally, environmental ethics to have practical effect, it was not necessary for 'working conservationists' to follow the ins and outs of the 'big blow in the ivory towers.' Such philosophical niceties as what property justifies or grounds the intrinsic value of nature, which natural entities possess intrinsic value and which do not, and whether intrinsic value is an objectively existing supervenient property or is subjectively attributed and defined negatively as opposed to instrumental value, was not of the least importance. All that was important was that working conservationists were aware of the anthropocentric –nonanthropocentric distinction and the fact that there was a 'general discussion about ethics and ecology,' going on among environmental philosophers, 'at the heart' of which 'was the question of whether other species possessed intrinsic value or had value solely because of their use to humans.' Note the parallel with human-rights discourse. Few human rights advocates and activists are conversant with the debate among moral philosophers about whether human rights are natural, God-given, or the wholly artificial product of a 'social contract.' It is the general idea under philosophical discussion that fires up the imaginations of lay people, morally inspires them, and reorients their perception of the world—the social world in the case of human rights, the natural world in the case of nonanthropocentric environmental ethics.

The intrinsic-value-in-nature discourse soon spread from 'conservation group staff members and volunteer activists' to professional natural resources managers. For example, in my work for the Great Lakes Fishery Commission, I found 'intrinsic value'—by that name—attributed to the fishes of Lake Superior in a management plan produced by the Minnesota Department of Natural Resources. In a recent review of the philosophical debate about intrinsic value in nature, Christopher Preston points out the various domains of discourse that the concept of intrinsic value in nature has now penetrated.[62] In addition to that of environmental activists and government-agency environmental professionals, it crops up in the discourse of the new field of ecocriticism—in discussions of nature poets, such as William Wordsworth, Robinson Jeffers, and Gary Snyder, and of nature writers, such as Edward Abby, Annie Dillard, and Barry Lopez. According to Preston, the concept of intrinsic value in nature is 'latent' in some U. S. environmental laws—the Wilderness Act of 1964, the 1973 Endangered Species Act, for example—and in some international declarations and treaties, such as the 1982 World Charter for Nature and the Global Biodiversity Treaty, signed by 160 countries (not including the United States) at the Earth Summit in Rio de Janeiro in 1992.[63]

THE EARTH CHARTER: A UNIVERSAL
DECLARATION OF INTRINSIC VALUE IN NATURE

Preston concludes that '[t]here is plenty of evidence to suggest that belief in intrinsic value in nature is playing an increasingly prominent role in the formation of environmental attitudes *and policies* worldwide.'[64] One might protest that that depends on what is meant by 'worldwide.' If Preston means that the concept is pragmatically efficacious worldwide because belief in intrinsic value in nature is playing an increasingly prominent role in the formation of environmental attitudes and policies in North America, Western Europe, Australia, and New Zealand, he is surely correct. But if he means also to suggest that it is pragmatically efficacious in such countries as China and India, the world's two largest, some may have reason to doubt his claim. I have no experience in India, nor in the People's Republic of China, but I have been invited to lecture extensively in the Republic of China (Taiwan) and so can say from personal experience that many Taiwanese environmental NGOs partially cast their activities in the discourse of the intrinsic value of nature. As to India, the evidence is contradictory. Ramachandra Guha, in a justly famous article, argued that although 'the transition from an anthropocentric (human-centered) to a biocentric (humans as only one element in the ecosystem) view in both religious and scientific traditions is to be welcomed . . . this dichotomy is, however, of little use in understanding the dynamics of environmental degradation.'[65] By implication, presumably, it would thus be of little use in opposing the dynamics of environmental degradation. Vandana Shiva, on the other hand, in a justly famous book, argues that in popular traditional Indian belief, nature is an active subject, not a passive object, as in modern Western thought.[66] Neither Guha or Shiva focus their discussions specifically on the concept of intrinsic value in nature, though Guha's somewhat equivocal discussion of 'biocentrism' and Shiva's approving discussion of nature as active subject could, by implication, be understood as bearing on it.

There is another piece of evidence supporting the worldwide currency of the concept of intrinsic value of nature not mentioned by Preston that is much less problematic. After more than a decade of worldwide 'consultations' with thousands of people representing millions of constituents in hundreds of interest groups and political-identity groups, the Earth Charter Commission issued a final draft of an 'Earth Charter' in March, 2000. The idea of an Earth Charter was first conceived during preparations for the 1992 United Nations Conference on Environment and Development (a.k.a. the Earth Summit). Afterward, the Commission was formed to draft a document that would be circulated throughout the world for comment and revision, finally to be submitted to the United Nations for endorsement by the General Assembly in 2002, on the tenth anniversary of the Earth Summit. The very first principle of the Earth Charter reads: '1. Respect Earth and life in all its diversity. a. Recognize that all beings are interdependent and *every form of life has value regardless of its worth to human beings.*'[67]

The *phrase* 'intrinsic value' does not appear in the final draft of the Charter—although it did in preliminary drafts, including the penultimate one. The *concept* seems to remain, however, in the statement that 'every form of life has value regardless of its worth to human beings.' A diehard environmental Pragmatist opposed to the concept of intrinsic value in nature and determined to suppress it could argue that these words of the Earth Charter should be interpreted to mean that every form of life may have instrumental value for forms of life other than human beings, but such would be a tortured interpretation. Such an interpretation implicitly assumes, moreover, that if not 'every' then some nonhuman forms of life have intrinsic value—else why must we care about what is of instrumental value to them? Further, arguments, such as those of Ehrenfeld, that many forms of life, often those most at risk of extinction, are 'non-resources'—whether for human or other kinds of being—implies that, as a matter of fact, not every form of life has instrumental value.[68] In any case, the principal architect of the Earth Charter provides decisive comments on the proper interpretation of the words in question in response to my inquiry about the absence of the phrase 'intrinsic value' in the final version of the document after it had appeared in all the previous ones:

> In your letter you express some concern about what may have been the anthropocentric orientation of some of our constituencies. You also identify the critical points in the text [those just quoted] where the ecocentric orientation of the Charter is made explicit. Throughout the document you will find that we have made a consistent effort to make clear that the moral community to which human beings belong extends beyond the human family to include the entire larger living world. In line with this outlook, the first principle, from which all the others flow, affirms respect for 'Earth in all its diversity.'[69]

I think that if the Earth Charter is eventually endorsed by the United Nations General Assembly, the result may well be comparable to the adoption of the Universal Declaration of Human Rights by the same body in 1948. The U.N. Universal Declaration of Human Rights was not a binding law or international treaty. But it did put the concept of human rights at play on the world stage. In effect, it globally institutionalised the discourse of human rights. Similarly, the Earth Charter may institutionalise and globalise the discourse of environmental ethics with its most potent concept of the intrinsic value of nature. In comparison with this achievement of theoretical environmental philosophers—the creation and dissemination of such a transformative discourse—the programme of bottom-up environmental ethics recommended by Pragmatists appears quite modest and unambitious. Certainly, the energy and intellectual capital of theoretical environmental philosophy should not be redirected into such yeoman (and yeowoman) work; on the contrary it should be redoubled.

THE ENVIRONMENTAL PRAGMATIST CAPITULATION TO THE CONCEPT OF INTRINSIC VALUE IN NATURE

Minteer has recently argued that Pragmatists need not eschew the concept of intrinsic value in nature, after all.[70] He even demonstrates that Norton himself, the most ardent opponent of the concept of intrinsic value of nature, actually endorses it, although he still refuses to use the term 'intrinsic value' because it is 'tainted'.[71] This is ironic because the only reason it may seem to be tainted is because environmental Pragmatists, and especially Norton, have conflated the various not-so-subtly differing theories of intrinsic value (reviewed here) into one grotesque caricature, in their zeal to stamp out intrinsic-value theorising in environmental philosophy. Minteer, who apparently relies on Norton to characterise (that is, caricature) intrinsic value theory in nature thinks that Rolston and I hold more or less the same theory while, as clearly noted here, our theories differ dramatically (my attempt to argue that Rolston is a crypto-subjectivist notwithstanding). Minteer insists, for example, on 'the universalist and foundationalist uses of the concept by such theorists as Callicott and Rolston'.[72] According to Minteer, Norton finds us guilty of 'disengaged ontological and meta-physical solutions for environmental quandaries' and 'of abstraction and ideological dogmatism among other vices'.[73] Among these other vices are 'foundationalism,' 'Cartesianism,' and being 'universalistic,' 'monistic,' and even 'intellectualistic.' Minteer never explains just what these vices amount to, however. What, for example, is foun-dationalism? What does it mean to offer 'ontological and metaphysical solutions for environmental quandaries' and why is this a vice? All Minteer does is sling these words around and rhetorically condemn them. Further, I have repeatedly tried to explain in what sense I advocate monism in environmental ethics and in what sense I do not.[74] All such niceties, however, are simply ignored by Minteer, who, despite my express declaration to the contrary, insists that I am 'reductionist' on a 'quest for a universal master principle.'[75]

Had Minteer read what Rolston and I have actually written about intrinsic value in nature, rather than relying on Norton's caricature, he might have discovered that the kind of Pragmatist theory of intrinsic value that he recommends and seems to believe that he is articulating for the first time is more or less the same as I have long espoused. He writes, 'I do think we can, as pragmatists, accommodate noninstru-mental values in our justifications of environmental policy. [W]e may value non-human nature noninstrumentally.' And he insists 'human's "do" the valuing, which may or may not be instrumental.' That is pretty much what I have been arguing all along, with the proviso that lots of other forms of life can also 'do' a bit of valuing. All value, in short, is of subjective provenance. And I hold that intrinsic value should be defined negatively, in contradistinction to instrumental value, as the value of some-thing that is left over when all its instrumental value has been subtracted. In other words, 'intrinsic value' and 'noninstrumental value' are two names for the same thing.

Minteer frankly acknowledges that 'we pragmatists have tended to neglect and often besmirch the worth and validity of intrinsic value claims in our enthusiastic embrace of a wide and deep instrumentalism, even if the former resonate with large segments of the public.'[76] He even goes so far as to acknowledge that 'intrinsic value arguments might be the most powerful and effective in certain circumstances.' But he also claims that intrinsic-value-in-nature theorists 'disparage instrumental values.' This is certainly not true. For example, I have written the following topic sentence for a chapter in a textbook on conservation biology and then have gone on to fully and sympathetically flesh out each topic: 'The anthropocentric instrumental (or utilitarian) value of biodiversity may be divided into three basic categories—goods, services, and information.'[77] Because some conservation biologists have confused it with intrinsic value, I go on to cautiously note that 'The psychospiritual value of biodiversity is possibly a fourth kind of anthropocentric utilitarian value,' which I also then fully flesh out.[78] The taxonomy of 'value in nature' that Rolston develops is even more elaborate; in the abstract of one article he lists '(1) economic value, (2) life support value, (3) recreational value, (4) scientific value, (5) aesthetic value, (6) life value, (7) diversity and unity values, (9) dialectical value, and (10) sacramental value.'[79] In the abstract of another, he 'itemize[s] twelve types of value carried by wildlands[:] economic, life support, recreational, scientific, genetic diversity, aesthetic, cultural symbolization, historical, character building, therapeutic, religious, and intrinsic.'[80] Rolston thinks that appeal to *all* of them—and all but one are anthropocentric/instrumental—by those wishing to preserve wildlands is both effective and legitimate. Thus it is anti-intrinsic-value-in-nature Pragmatists, not us more inclusive pro-intrinsic-value-in-nature theorists who are 'locking out those citizens from the moral debate who choose to speak about the value of nature in ways that' Norton and other Pragmatists 'can[not] philosophically abide.'[81]

Minteer is no more specific about Norton's arguments against intrinsic value in nature than he is about the nature of foundationalism or universalism.[82] He vaguely refers to 'the epistemic problems regarding the justification of intrinsic values as well as the metaphysical status of noninstrumental claims' discussed by Norton, but provides no summary. What Minteer does provide, however, is some insight into Norton's motives. Norton, he says, is 'primarily motivated by his desire to speak clearly and effectively to practical matters of environmental management and problem solving.'[83] Thus he 'concluded early on,' according to Minteer, that intrinsic value theory was a pragmatic 'dead end and that a weak anthropocentric approach and a broad instrumentalism could deliver the goods.'[84] But intrinsic value theory just would not go away as Norton wished it would. I am grateful to Minteer for documenting that Norton, despite his campaign against the concept of intrinsic value in nature, occasionally forgets himself and acknowledges its pragmatic power in supporting what Minteer calls 'good environmental policy.'[85] More importantly, I am also grateful to Minteer for candidly acknowledging, what Norton has persistently denied, that the notion that nature has noninstrumental value is increasingly part of 'the public's everyday intuitions and sentiments regarding nonhuman nature.'[86] My main point in this essay is that the public might not now have so commonly valued nature noninstrumentally had the work of environmental philosophers not created a new discourse—the discourse of intrinsic value in nature, a new, positive, and inspiring name, as opposed to the essentially privative term 'noninstrumental'—in which the public's everyday intuitions and sentiments regarding nonhuman nature might be powerfully articulated.

CONCLUSION

We sometimes forget, I think, that we live, move, and have our human being in a world of words, as well as in a physical world beyond words. For all its importance—which above all environmental philosophy affirms and celebrates—that world beyond human words is only accessible through the portal of human discourse. In conclusion, therefore, we must agree with Confucius that the first order of business in any policy arena is to rectify names, so that our policies and practices are framed in terms of the most efficacious and transformative discourse. The way Confucius would rectify names is by adminstrative fiat. In a democracy we do so by means of the free and sometimes technical philosophical discussion of frequently controversial and some-times new and radical ideas. While that discussion, especially if it is carried on largely in the academy, may seem far removed from the fray of public policy debate and hopelessly impractical, in multiple and diffuse ways it seeps out of the ivory tower into the public domain, and finally funds the formation of public policy and practice. That has, demonstrably, been the case with theoretical environmental ethics and its central idea, the intrinsic value of nature.

READING ENDNOTES

1. Hall, D. L. and R. T. Ames. 1987. *Thinking Through Confucius.* State University of New York Press, Albany.
2. Norton, B. G. 1992. 'Epistemology and Environmental Values.' *The Monist* 75: 208–226.
3. Sylvan, R. 2001. 'Is There a Need for a New, an Environmental Ethic?' In M. E. Zimmerman, J. B. Callicott, G. Sessions, K. J. Warren, and J. Clark (eds.) *Environmental Philosophy*, 3nd edition. Upper Saddle River, New Jersey: Prentice-Hall.
4. Naess, A. 1973. 'The Shallow and the Deep, Long Range Ecology Movements: A Summary.' *Inquiry* 16: 95–100.
5. Rolston III, H. 1975. 'Is There an Ecological Ethic?' *Ethics* 85: 93–109.
6. Regan, T. 1982. 'The Nature and Possibility of an Environmental Ethic'. *Environmental Ethics* 3: 19-34.
7. Moore, G. E. 1903. *Principia Ethica.* Cambridge: Cambridge University Press.
8. Kant, I. 1959 (1785). *Foundations of the Metaphysics of Morals.* L. W. Beck (trans.) New York: Library of Liberal Arts. (*Grundlegung zur metaphysic der Sitten.* Leipzig: Felix Meiner.)
9. Kant, I. 1959 (1785), p. 39.
10. Kant, I. 1959 (1785), p. 46.
11. Savage-Rumbaugh, S., S. G. Shanker, and T. J. Taylor. 1998. *Kanzi: The Ape at the Brink of the Human Mind.* New York: Oxford University Press, 1998.
12. Descartes, R. 1950 (1637). *Discourse on Method.* New York: Liberal Arts Press. 1637. *Discours de la méthod.* Paris: Michaelem Soly.
13. Regan, T. 1979. 'An Examination and Defense of One Argument Concerning Animal Rights'. *Inquiry* 22: 189–219.
14. Regan, T. 1983. *The Case for Animal Rights.* Berkeley: University of California Press.
15. Singer, P. 1977. *Animal liberation: A New Ethics for Our Treatment of Animals.* New York: Avon.

16. Goodpaster, K. E. 1978. 'On Being Morally Considerable'. *Journal of Philosophy* 75: 308–325; Johnson, L. E. 1991. *A Morally Deep World: An Essay on Moral Significance and Environmental Ethics*. Cambridge: Cambridge University Press; Taylor, P. W. 1986. *Respect for Nature: A Theory of Environmental Ethics*. Princeton: Princeton University Press.

17. Taylor, P. W. 1986.

18. Fox, W. 1990. *Toward a Transpersonal Ecology*. Boston: Shambhala Publications.

19. Goodpaster, K. E. 1978.

20. Rolston III, H. 1988. *Environmental Ethics: Duties to and Values in the Natural World*. Philadelphia: Temple University Press.

21. Johnson, L. E. 1991. *A Morally Deep World: An Essay on Moral Significance and Environmental Ethics*. Cambridge: Cambridge University Press.

22. Ghiselin, M. T. 1974. 'A Radical Solution to the Species Problem'. *Systematic Zoology* 23: 536–544; Hull, D. 1976. 'Are Species Really Individuals?' *Systematic Zoology* 25: 174–191.

23. McIntosh, R. P. 1985. *The Background of Ecology: Concept and Theory*. Cambridge: Cambridge University Press.

24. Rolston III, H. 1988.

25. Kant, I. 1959 (1785), p. 46.

26. Callicott, J. B. 1999. *Beyond the Land Ethic: More Essays in Environmental Philosophy*. Albany: State University of New York Press; O'Neill, J. 1992. 'Varieties of Intrinsic Value. *The Monist* 75: 119–1137; Routley, R. and Routley, V. 1980. 'Human Chauvinism and Environmental Ethics'. In D, Mannison, M. McRobbie, and R. Routley (eds.) *Environmental Philosophy*.

27. Callicott, J. B. 1999.

28. Leopold, A. 1949. *A Sand County Almanac, and Sketches Here and There*. New York: Oxford University Press, p. viii.

29. *Ibid*, p. 204.

30. *Ibid*, p. 223.

31. Kant, I. 1959 (1785), p. 47, emphasis added.

32. *Ibid*, p. 47, emphasis added.

33. Rolston III, H. 1994. *Conserving Natural Value*. New York: Columbia University Press.

34. *Ibid*.

35. Rolston III, H. 2002. 'Naturalizing Callicott'. In W. Ouderkirk and J. Hill (eds.) *Land, Value, Community: Callicott and Environmental Philosophy*. Albany: State University of New York Press, p. 118.

36. *Ibid*, p. 119.

37. Light A. 1996a. 'Compatibilism in Political Ecology'. In A. Light and E. Katz (eds.) *Environmental Pragmatism*. New York: Routledge, 161–184; Light, A. 1996b. 'Environmental Pragmatism as Philosophy or Metaphilosophy?' A. Light and E. Katz (eds.) *Environmental Pragmatism*. New York: Routledge, 325–338; Norton, B. G. 1984. 'Environmental Ethics and Weak Anthropocentrism'. *Environmental Ethics* 6: 131-148; Norton, B. G. 1991. *Toward Unity Among Environmentalists*. New York: Oxford University Press; Norton, B. G. 1992. 'Epistemology and Environmental Values'. *The Monist* 75: 208–226; Norton, B. G. 1995. 'Why I am Not a Nonanthropocentrist: Callicott and the Failure Monistic Inherentism'. *Environmental Ethics* 17: 341–358; Weston, 1985. 'Beyond Intrinsic Value: Pragmatism in Environmental Ethics'. *Environmental Ethics* 7: 321–339.

38. Norton, B. G. 1991. *Toward Unity Among Environmentalists*. New York: Oxford University Press.

39. Light, A. 1996b.

40. Norton, B. G. 1991.

41. Norton, B. G. 1991; Weston, 1985. 'Beyond Intrinsic Value: Pragmatism in Environmental Ethics'. *Environmental Ethics* 7: 321–339; Weston, 1992. 'Before Environmental Ethics'. *Environmental Ethics* 14: 321–338; Minteer, B. A. 2001. 'Intrinsic Value for Pragmatists?' *Environmental Ethics* 23: 69.

42. Callicott, J. B., L. B. Crowder, and K. Mumford. 1999. 'Current Normative Concepts in Conservation'. *Conservation Biology* 13: 22–35.

43. Norton, B. G. 1992. 'Epistemology and Environmental Values'. The Monist 75: 208–226; Minteer, B. A. 1998. 'No Experience Necessary?: Foundationalism and the Retreat from Culture in Environmental Ethics'. *Environmental Values* 7: 333–347.

44. Norton, B. G. 1991. *Toward Unity Among Environmentalists.* New York: Oxford University Press.

45. Ehrenfeld, D. 1976. 'The Conservation of Non-resources'. *American Scientist* 64: 647–655; Ehrenfeld, D. 1988. 'Why put a value on biodiversity?' In E. O. Wilson (ed.) *Biodiversity.* Washington: National Academy Press, 212–216.

46. Ehrenfeld, D. 1976.

47. Ehrenfeld, D. 1988.

48. Ehrenfeld, D. 1976; Ehrenfeld, D. 1988.

49. Norton, B. G. 1991.

50. Fox, W. 1993. 'What Does the Recognition of Intrinsic Value Entail?' *Trumpeter* 10: 101.

51. *Ibid*, p. 101.

52. Nickel, J. W. 1992. *Human Rights.* In L. C. Becker and C. B. Becker (eds.) *Encyclopedia of Ethics,* volume 1. New York: Garland. Pages 561–565 i

53. Gewirth, A. 1992. 'Rights'. In L. C. Becker and C. B. Becker (eds.) *Encyclopedia of Ethics.* New York: Garland. Pages 1103–1109.

54. *Ibid.*

55. United Nations. 1996. Fact Sheet No. 2 (Rev.1), The International Bill of Human Rights. Geneva: United Nations.

56. *Ibid.*

57. *Ibid.*

58. Norton, B. G. 1984. 'Environmental Ethics and Weak Anthropocentrism'. *Environmental Ethics* 6: 131-148; Norton, B. G. 1991. *Toward Unity Among Environmentalists.* New York: Oxford University Press; Norton, B. G. 1992. 'Epistemology and Environmental Values'. *The Monist* 75: 208–226; Norton, B. G. 1995. 'Why I am Not a Nonanthropocentrist: Callicott and the Failure Monistic Inherentism'. *Environmental Ethics* 17: 341–358.

59. Foreman, D. 1983. 'More on Earth First! and The Monkey Wrench Gang'. *Environmental Ethics* 5: 95–96.

60. Foreman, D. 1991. 'The New Conservation Movement'. *Wild Earth* 1 (2): 6–12.

61. *Ibid*, p. 8.

62. Preston, C. 1998. 'Epistemology and Intrinsic Values: Norton and Callicott's Critiques of Rolston'. *Environmental Ethics* 20: 409–428.

63. *Ibid.*

64. *Ibid*, p. 411, emphasis added.

65. Guha, R. 1989. 'Radical American Environmentalism and Wilderness Preservation: A Third World Critique'. *Environmental Ethics* 11: 71–83.

66. Shiva, V. 1989. *Staying Alive: Women, Ecology, and Development.* London: Zed Books.

67. Earth Charter Commission. 2000. *Earth Charter Briefing Book.* The Hague: Earth Council. Emphasis added.

68. Ehrenfeld, D. 1976; Ehrenfeld, D. 1988.

69. Rockefeller, S. C. 2000. Letter to author, July 12, 2000.

70. Minteer, B. A. 2001. 'Intrinsic Value for Pragmatists?' *Environmental Ethics* 23: 69.

71. *Ibid*, p. 66.

72. *Ibid*, p. 61.

73. *Ibid*, p. 65.

74. Callicott, J. B., L. B. Crowder, and K. Mumford. 1999. 'Current Normative Concepts in Conservation'. *Conservation Biology* 13: 22–35.

75. Minteer, B. A. 2001, p. 65.

76. *Ibid*, p. 61.

77. Callicott, J. B. 1997. 'Conservation Values and Ethics'. In G. K. Meffe and C. R. Carroll (eds.) *Principles of Conservation Biology*, second edition. Sunderland, Mass.: Sinauer Associates, 29.

78. *Ibid*, p. 30.

79. Rolston III, H. 1981. 'Values in Nature'. *Environmental Ethics* 3: 113.

80. Rolston III, H. 1985. 'Valuing Wildlands'. *Environmental Ethics* 7: 23.

81. Minteer, B. A. 2001, p. 61.

82. *Ibid.*

83. *Ibid*, p. 62.

84. *Ibid*, p. 63.

85. *Ibid*, p. 71.

86. *Ibid*, p. 60.

DEFINITIONS AND EXPLANATIONS

Anthropocentrism: Greek, meaning, roughly, human centred. Anthropocentrism is the view that human beings are the most important thing in the universe, that human beings stand above everything else there is. It follows fairly directly from such a view that human beings are uniquely valuable, and that everything else has value only if and because it is useful to human beings or serves their interests. This has been the dominant view with respect to understanding the relation between human beings and their environments in Western societies, though it contrasts with the view adopted by others, such as many aboriginal communities. Anthropocentrism is contrasted with **non-anthropocentrism**, which is just the rejection of the centrality of human kind's place in the universe. There are many forms of non-anthropocentric thinking; which particular form it takes will be determined by what else is considered to have value and what relation is thought to hold between the value of humans and other things.

Biocentrism: Greek, meaning, roughly, life centred. This is a term often used to describe a particular kind of non-anthropocentric view of the world. It treats all life, or all living things, as having value and attempts to rethink human relations with nature. Human beings are merely one (albeit very destructive) species within nature, and their claim to be able to use nature for their own purposes must be rejected if we are to respect the value of nature itself.

Pragmatism: Pragmatism in philosophy is related to pragmatism in every day life. A pragmatic person is one who is guided by practical considerations, rather than by abstract and general principles or rules. A pragmatist focuses on results, and on trying to find solutions to concrete, specific practical problems. Likewise, a philosophical pragmatist tests the validity of all concepts by their practical results. If a distinction between two concepts (such as between intrinsic and instrumental value) makes no practical difference, pragmatists think the theoretical distinction should be abandoned as useless or even meaningless. More generally, those who adopt a pragmatic approach to philosophical questions tend to be indifferent at best, and hostile at worst, to abstract theorizing and system building. Because pragmatists, with regards to environmental questions, tend to think that the abstract principles offered within theoretical ethics (such as the principle of utility or the categorical imperative) are useless for solving concrete environmental problems, they tend to reject the relevance of such theories to their work, and so adopt an anti-theoretical stance.

QUESTIONS

1. What role does the idea of intrinsic value play in Kant's argument that we must always respect humanity as an end in itself?

2. What property grounds the intrinsic value of persons, according to Kant? Why would this naturally lead to an anthropocentric view of ethics?

3. How do the two cases of (1) non-human primates and (2) non-rational humans serve to indicate that we should modify Kant's own account of who has intrinsic value (which property confers intrinsic value) while maintaining the importance of the idea of intrinsic value itself?

4. What is the moral relevance of having interests? Can it be the property that confers intrinsic value on entities?

5. Why does Callicott think that a biocentrism that makes having interests the basis of intrinsic value will distribute value too broadly in one sense, and too narrowly in another?

6. What is Rolston's solution to the problems involved in distributing intrinsic value too broadly: differential biocentrism? How do we decide questions of different levels or amounts of intrinsic value?

7. How does Rolston try to extend the value of individual organisms to include biotic communities, species, and ecosystems? Is the argument plausible? Does it show that species and ecosystems have intrinsic value, or only instrumental?

8. Why does Callicott think that intrinsic value must be subjective rather than objective? What is to be gained by thinking of the difference between instrumental and intrinsic value as a difference in the way we value things rather than as an objective property of things?

9. How does evolutionary biology provide a kind of valuing activity that can be used to extend value even to entities that lack consciousness?

10. What is Norton's "convergence hypothesis"? Is it plausible to think that it will make no important difference to how we treat nature if we value it instrumentally rather than intrinsically?

11. Callicott argues that recognizing the intrinsic value of nature has pragmatic power that instrumental value does not. The argument hinges on where the burden of proof lies in debates about how to use nature for human benefit. How does the argument go?

12. What is the analogy between intrinsic value in nature and human rights?

13. Callicott discusses many kinds of instrumental value that he and Rolston believe nature may have. What are these values? How can he accept that nature can be valuable in these ways, as well as intrinsically?

14. Does Callicott's subjective and negative description of intrinsic value remove any "mysteriousness" it may seem to have in our scientific age?

15. In what way is Callicott's paper a vindication of moral philosophy? Can you think of other areas in which the work of moral philosophers has created new discourses that have had important transformative effects for real life and concrete moral issues?

16. Does Callicott's approach still leave us with troubling questions about how to balance the competing interests of the various things that have intrinsic value when they conflict? Does the analogy with human rights help answer some of these questions?

CHAPTER FOUR

LIBERTARIANISM

INTRODUCTION

Libertarianism is a philosophical theory of both morality and politics. Indeed, libertarians see morality and politics as being on a continuum, rather than as different kinds of normative systems. This is because they see both as constraining or limiting individual freedom. The only important difference between moral rules and political rules, especially laws, is in the methods of their enforcement. Whereas political rules are ultimately enforced by the state, including by systems of punishment, moral rules are enforced informally by the members of the community, and the penalty for breaking them is moral condemnation, criticism, and the like. At the core of all libertarian thinking, however, is the importance given to individual freedom or liberty, and the need to justify restrictions on such liberty.

Libertarianism enjoyed its heyday in the English Enlightenment of the seventeenth and eighteenth centuries, although it continues to have many adherents today. It will be useful to briefly outline the circumstances leading to libertarian thinking, as they shed considerable light upon its central elements as a theory. In particular, three remarkable developments in normative thinking happened during the Enlightenment. First, individuals, rather than larger social units (such as the community or the church), came to be seen as the primary locus of value. Individual interests were thus treated as primary, and for this reason libertarianism is an individualistic doctrine. Second, it came to be thought that political society was artificial and morality was ultimately conventional. Rejecting the view that there were natural rulers and natural subordinates, and that there was a comprehensive moral code set by nature or by God, libertarians believed instead that both moral and political constraints were the creation of people and for a particular purpose. That purpose was, roughly, to allow individuals to live together peacefully and productively. As a result of their conventionalism, libertarians came to insist that any particular political or moral system could be justified (could be worthy of support) only if it served the purposes for which it was established. Moreover, those purposes were tied to individual interests rather than the interests of the community, the church, or what have you, given the commitment to individualism. Thus libertarians adopted an **instrumental conception of normative justification**. Finally, the Enlightenment saw the recognition that different people have quite different and often incompatible values. Different people have different conceptions of a good life, and have different commitments, goals, interests, and ends. This **value plurality** meant that no single conception of the good could be imposed upon (a group of) individuals consistently with the belief that it is individuals that matter and that morality must serve each of their interests. Thus libertarians adopted a subjective theory of value, and together with their other commitments, especially the reasonable expectation of competing and conflicting values, this led them to develop a view of the proper limits of interference with individual freedom.

Individualism

Libertarians are not alone in developing an individualistic moral theory. Both utilitarian and Kantian ethics are also individualistic; it is the happiness of individuals that matter to the former, and the dignity of individuals that is important to the latter. But what exactly is the nature of libertarian individualism? First, it is the recognition that only individuals have interests. Collectives of any kind have interests only metaphorically, and based on the interests of the individuals who make up the collective, group, or association. Second, only individuals are able to make morally significant choices. Groups, societies, and other collectives do not make choices; only individuals do. Likewise for actions: only individuals act. Thus if morality is about making the right choices and doing the right things, then morality applies to individuals rather than to groups. Related to this last point, because it is only individuals who choose and act, only individuals can be morally responsible for their actions and choices. In other words, moral responsibility is also an individual matter. Finally, only individuals can be the bearers of moral and political rights and obligations. Because libertarianism is ultimately a theory of rights and corresponding duties, and only individuals can have rights and duties, libertarianism is individualistic.

Subjective Value and Value Plurality

Libertarians adopt a subjective theory of value. Things are valuable only because and to the extent that they are valued by individuals. Individuals have ends, goals, commitments, projects, preferences, and conceptions of a good life. These are, then, the values of the individual. They derive their status as values only by being valued by someone. Thus all value is ultimately subjective and contingent, being based on the subjective states of individuals.

Libertarians also recognize, as we said above, that different individuals value different things. People differ in terms of what they think a good life is. They give meaning to their lives by pursuing different projects and ends. One only has to compare the diverse value structures of persons, one of whom is committed to family compared to another who values career success, someone who pursues wealth and status compared to another who seeks religious enlightenment, a person who finds intellectual pursuits worthwhile compared to another who has as his end a life of intense pleasure, etc., to see the force of this insight. To acknowledge this fact is to accept value plurality as a fact of the human condition.

This descriptive fact about the world, that different people value different things, is properly called the fact of value plurality. It should not be confused with another notion, which goes by the name of **value pluralism**. Unfortunately, the distinction is not often marked, though it is of significance. Like all "isms," value pluralism is a substantive normative theory. It says that a plurality of things has value, and that such values cannot be reduced to a single source. It is an objective theory of value, which claims to provide a list of those things that are valuable. Moreover, its proponents insist that all such values must be equally respected, because they are valuable in themselves.

Value plurality and value pluralism are obviously related. But they are not the same. One is a descriptive claim and one is a normative claim. The mere fact of value plurality does not itself give rise to any substantive moral claim (like "the different values of people ought to be respected") without additional normative premises. In libertarianism, those additional premises are provided by individualism and the instrumental conception of justification. It is only because individuals matter, and moral and political constraints must be justifiable to them, that the fact of value plurality acquires moral significance. If individuals matter, then what they care about also matters. If we are to respect individuals, we must respect the various things that give meaning to their lives. If we are to justify any normative constraints on the freedom of individuals, we must do so in a way that takes into account the fact that they do not share a comprehensive set of values (even a set of values that includes a plurality of values). Rather, if individuals matter then we must impose only restrictions upon their freedom that they would each accept, that they themselves would see are in their own interests, despite the differences between them. Libertarians believe that the result of these commitments is a requirement that we respect the liberty of individuals to pursue their own good as they see it, subject only to such constraints as are necessary to achieve their common interests in non-violence and mutually beneficial cooperation.

Liberty

Libertarians believe that everyone ought to be free to pursue their own good as they see it, subject only to such restrictions as can be justified to them as individuals. Thus respect for individual liberty is the primary requirement within libertarian thinking. Although everyone accepts that the distinguishing feature of libertarianism is the place it gives to individual liberty, it is in fact notoriously difficult to say exactly how liberty functions as basic in libertarian thinking. Sometimes liberty is described as the basic value of the theory (but that will be difficult to reconcile with the subjective and pluralistic theory of value), sometimes as the basic right of individuals (which will be difficult to explain on a purely conventional theory of morality). We might sidestep some of the difficulties here in the following way. It will surely be allowed that everyone values his or her own freedom. This follows just from the fact that we are all rational and purposeful creatures who pursue ends. We all have goals we are trying to achieve, commitments we are trying to fulfil, and a conception of the good life that we are trying to realize. This is what it means to say that we are purposeful creatures: we have ends the pursuit of which we value. Moreover, we are instrumentally rational creatures. As such, as Kant noted, we must will the means to our ends. And freedom, everyone will agree, is a necessary means to the achievement of our ends. Thus we must all value our own freedom, since we all desire to realize our values, whatever they happen to be, and freedom to act in pursuit of our values is necessary as a means to that end. Moreover, since everyone so values his or her own freedom, the freedom of everyone matters equally. In this way, libertarianism is also egalitarian.

Of course, our liberty cannot be unlimited. I ought not to be free to kill you, maim you, rob you, lie to you, etc. How do we determine the legitimate limits to liberty? How do we decide which moral or legal limits to individual freedom are justified? The libertarian answer is, roughly, that everyone has an equal interest in having his or her liberty respected, and so everyone has an equal right to liberty. Thus the first set of restrictions on liberty that will be justified are those restrictions that are necessary to protect the liberty of all. In other words, I may not exercise my liberty in a way that violates your equal right to liberty. These mutual restrictions on individual freedom will include some of those most basic moral proscriptions: limits on killing and other forms of violence, force, and fraud. Beyond the rules that are necessary to protect the equal right to liberty of all, the only other limitations on liberty that are acceptable will be those that individuals voluntarily submit to. Such will include commitments based on promising, and contracting in general. Only limitations based on mutual restraint or individual consent can be justified to the individuals who are thereby restrained. Thus, if we take seriously the requirement that all restrictions on individual freedom must be justified to the individuals being restricted, we will be able to justify only restrictions that are in everyone's interests (and so instrumentally justified) or that the individuals in question consented to as a means to realizing their individual values.

The Harm Principle

The most famous statement of the libertarian sentiment comes from John Stuart Mill in his important essay "On Liberty." In this essay Mill seeks to set out the proper limits of individual freedom. Though his focus is on political restrictions of liberty, the extent to which society or government can coercively interfere with individuals pursuing their own good, his conclusions were meant to be relevant to assessing not only legal but also moral limits on interference. As he put it, "The subject of this Essay is … Civil, or Social Liberty: the nature and limits of the power which can be legitimately exercised by society over the individual."[1]

Now Mill was aware that there were two distinct threats to individual freedom in society. In previous generations, when people lived under the autocratic control of some individual or small group of individuals, the primary threat to individual freedom came from the government. The greatest threat to individual liberty was the power of the rulers (the minority) who held political power over the vast majority of subjects. This was the threat of the tyranny of the few. Mill further pointed out that there were really only two strategies available for resisting the power of rulers. First, a people could insist that there are certain political liberties or rights that governments could not breach without inviting resistance. That is, if the governed treated certain rights or liberties as being beyond the reach of government, and they were prepared to openly rebel should the government try to interfere with them, then they might have some practical protection against interference with those rights or liberties. Many populations have treated some matters as being beyond regulation in this way. Second, a population could impose constitutional checks on government power; these would require authorization by the majority for certain kinds of government action.

With the advent of modern democratic states, however, in which rulers have power from the people, revocable by the people, it might be thought that there is no longer a need to so limit government power. To see the error of this way of thinking, however, we must keep in mind that "the people" are always only some of the people. Power in democracies is held by (at most) majorities, and the majority may try to oppress minorities. This is the threat of tyranny of the majority. The tyranny of the majority is even more insidious than the tyranny of the few because it operates not only through political offices and institutions, but socially as well. "Protection, therefore, against the tyranny of the magistrate is not enough: there needs protection also against the tyranny of the prevailing opinion and feeling; against the tendency of society to impose, by other means than civil penalties, its own ideas and practices as rules of conduct on those who dissent from them; to fetter the development, and, if possible, prevent the formation, of any individuality not in harmony with its ways, and compel all characters to fashion themselves upon the model of its own."[2]

As we might put it today, individuals need protection not only from governments, but also from "the moral majority" and those moral busybodies who insist not only that they must be free to live as they know to be right, but free to compel everyone else to live as they think best as well. In resistance to this tendency, Mill defends the primacy of the individual over the majority. We quote him at length.

> The object of this Essay is to assert one very simple principle, as entitled to govern absolutely the dealings of society with the individual in the way of compulsion and control, whether the means used be physical force in the form of legal penalties, or the moral coercion of public opinion. That principle is, that the sole end for which mankind are warranted, individually or collectively, in interfering with the liberty of action of any of their number, is self-protection. That the only purpose for which power can be rightfully exercised over any member of a civilized community, against his will, is to prevent harm to others. His own good, either physical or moral, is not a sufficient warrant. He cannot rightfully be compelled to do or forbear because it will be better for him to do so, because it will make him happier, because, in the opinion of others, to do so would be wise, or even right. These are good reasons for remonstrating with him, or reasoning with him, or persuading him, or entreating him, but not for compelling him, or visiting him with any evil, in case he do otherwise. To justify that, the conduct from which it is desired to deter him must be calculated to produce evil to some one else. The only part of the conduct of any one, for which he is amenable to society, is that which concerns others. In the part which merely concerns himself, his independence is, of right, absolute. Over himself, over his own body and mind, the individual is sovereign.[3]

Mill makes it clear in what follows that he is only here talking about mature individuals of normal capacity and who are members of mature societies: those "capable of being improved by free and equal discussion," by "conviction or persuasion." In such cases, compulsion is not a legitimate means to their own good.

The harm principle insists that the only legitimate grounds for interfering with the liberty of individuals is to prevent them from harming others. In formulating it, Mill explicitly rejects two other possible grounds of interference: paternalism and moralism. Paternalism involves interfering with persons for their own good (to prevent people from harming themselves), while moralism involves interfering with others to ensure that they act as the person interfering believes to be morally right or good (to prevent people from doing what you believe is immoral). He also explicitly relies upon a general distinction between self-regarding and other-regarding actions. Self-regarding actions are those whose consequences fall only or primarily on the person performing the action. Private masturbation might be the paradigm of a self-regarding action. Other-regarding actions, by contrast, have consequences that significantly affect the interests or well-being of others, and so they are actions in which others have a legitimate say. We leave it to the reader to think through some of the difficulties in maintaining such a distinction.[4]

In order to actually apply the harm principle, we must be able to identify the kinds of harms to others that it permits interference with. After all, not just any harm will be sufficiently grave or serious to justify interference with the liberty of others. Most especially, even if others are upset or offended by what I propose to do (because they think it immoral, heretical, unnatural, or just plain disgusting), if it is a self-regarding action they must still refrain from interfering with me. Mere offence to others cannot count as the kind of harm Mill has in mind, if there is to be any scope for individual freedom. Rather, Mill thinks that the kinds of harm in question, the prevention of which can justify interfering with persons, involve the violation of rights. In particular, the harm must arise from the action of an identifiable person(s) and be such as to interfere with the legitimate exercise of a right by another identifiable person(s). Thus there can be no harms against society or groups in general, independently of harms to specific individuals. Moreover, you must be able to link the harm directly to the actions of a specific person. Finally, the harm must violate a right.

Rights for Mill are based in interests that are sufficiently important that the right-holder (the person who has the right) can legitimately demand the assistance of others in protecting. Rights, we might say, protect vital interests. Rights also arise from participation in society. Because we derive many benefits from living in society, but those benefits can only be enjoyed if all participate in certain practices and do or refrain from doing certain things, we all owe as our duty to others (and they have a right against us) that we act as expected so as to secure those benefits. Here is how Mill put it:

> [E]veryone who receives the protection of society owes a return for the benefit, and the fact of living in society renders it indispensable that each should be bound to observe a certain line of conduct towards the rest. This conduct consists, first, in not injuring the interests of one another, or rather certain interests which, either by express legal provision or by tacit understanding, ought to be considered as rights; and secondly, in each person's bearing his share (to be fixed by some equitable principle) of the labours and sacrifices incurred for defending the society or its members from injury and molestation. These conditions society is justified in enforcing at all costs to those who endeavour to withhold fulfillment. Nor is this all society may do. The acts of an individual may be hurtful to

others or wanting in due consideration for their welfare, without going to the length of violating any of their constituted rights. The offender may then be justly punished by opinion, though not by law. As soon as any part of a person's conduct affects prejudicially the interests of others, society has jurisdiction over it, and the question whether the general welfare will or will not be promoted by interfering with it becomes open to discussion. But there is not room for entertaining any such question when a person's conduct affects the interests of no persons besides himself, or need not affect them unless they like (all the persons concerned being of full age and the ordinary amount of understanding). In all such cases, there should be perfect freedom, legal and social, to do the act and stand the consequences.[5]

Negative Rights

Mill uses rights to mark the bounds of legitimate interference with individual liberty. His reasons for recognizing some interests as sufficiently important as to be protected by rights is, however, utilitarian. That is, he weighs the consequences of allowing people to make their own choices in self-regarding matters without interference, on the one hand, and the consequences of allowing some members of society to interfere with others, on the other hand. For reasons we will not go into here, he determines that society is significantly better off if it respects the liberty of its members. Other libertarians ground the right to liberty in a more basic commitment to respect for persons, and thus derive libertarianism from deontology. Still other libertarians, most notably John Locke, have attempted to ground libertarianism in a theory of natural rights. In Locke's case, he insisted that all people are born with the right to life, liberty and estate (property).[6] But the right to liberty need not be grounded in either a theory of natural rights, deontology, or in utilitarianism. In fact, it is established just by the original three premises with which we began this discussion. For if all people care about their own freedom, as a means to pursuing the good as they judge it, and if any restrictions on that freedom must be justified to the individuals in question, then it will be the case that we have against others (fellow citizens and governments) a right to liberty. That is, they will not be able to legitimately interfere with our liberty without our consent, except for the kinds of purposes Mill set out.

Libertarians are committed to a theory of rights, which are grounded in the value to each person of his or her own liberty. For Locke, as we have said, they are the rights to life, liberty, and property. Now it might be puzzling how we move from the right to liberty to the others on this list. While respecting the liberty of individuals no doubt requires that we also respect their right to life, how do we derive property rights from liberty? Again, different libertarians have developed the answer to this question in different ways. But for libertarians the connection between liberty and property rights is undeniable. What, after all, is the right to liberty? It is the right to do what you want, unimpeded by others, provided only you do not interfere with others pursuing their rightful liberty. Having such a right implies that others have a duty not to interfere with your pursuits.

How could another interfere with the exercise of your liberty? Well, they could physically block you, e.g., tie you up, lock you in a room, gag you, drug you, and kill you. In all these cases, they interfere with your liberty by interfering with your body. And the reason this is a good way to interfere with you is because in order to do anything, you require control over stuff in the world: at a minimum, you require control over your own mind and body. It is unsurprising, then, that all libertarians accept that we have property rights to our own persons, to our bodies and minds. This is so because property rights just are control over things in the world. To say that you have a property right to some thing (that you own it) is just to say that you enjoy a collection of powers with respect to it, that you can control it in various ways, and that others cannot use it or dispose of it without your consent. Consider what we mean when we say that you own, say, a television set. We mean to say that you exercise a bundle of powers with respect to that TV. You may use it, sell it, destroy it, give it away, etc. We also mean that no one else may use it, sell it, etc., without your permission. Obviously, then, since the only way we can exercise any liberty at all is if we control our own minds and bodies, we have a derivative right to property in ourselves based upon our right to liberty.

But how do we move from property rights in ourselves to property rights to external stuff (cars, TVs, books, land, or DVD players)? There is, after all, no natural connection between individuals and stuff, in the way that there is between individuals and their own bodies and minds. The answer comes in two parts. Consider, first, the situation in which there are individuals and they own things in the world, material goods like cars and stereos. Leave aside the question of how they come to own what they do. Surely we can interfere with peoples' freedom just as much by violating their property rights to what they own as we can by physically stopping them from acting as they wish. If you own a car and want to go for a drive, I interfere with your liberty by stealing your car (or otherwise denying you the control you rightfully exercise over it as your property). Likewise, if you own a book, I interfere with your liberty to read your book if I burn it, or glue all its pages shut. Both of those acts are violations of your property, and both interfere with your liberty to do as you wish. In this way, the commitment to liberty entails a commitment to respecting property rights.[7]

But now we have to return to the question we left to the side: how do we come to own anything at all? Most libertarians accept that a person can acquire property in one of two ways. First, they can acquire something that was previously unowned by what is called **initial acquisition**. The idea comes from Locke. Suppose there is some unowned stuff in the world. If I come along and take up that stuff, incorporating it into some purposeful action of mine, I thereby mix my labour with it and come to own it. For Locke, it is the act of mixing my labour (which I own) with other things (previously unowned) that establishes property to those things. But we need not accept precisely this account of initial acquisition.

Again, other libertarians have derived the right to property differently than Locke did. We could, for example, provide a utilitarian justification for property rights. If it could be established that the general happiness is better promoted under a system of private property rights than under alternative systems of property (such as a socialist one of common ownership, no ownership, or limited ownership rights) then we would have reason to allow some acts of initial acquisition to begin rights to property. There may be such good reasons to allow private ownership, given the greater level of investment people seem willing to make in improving their own property compared with property held in common. Just think, for example, of the relative levels of care taken by home owners of their own property, compared with the care taken by tenants of rented property and of users of common property such as parks. That privately owned property is often put to much more productive use than property held in common is a well documented phenomenon, and may in part explain the great affluence of Western societies compared with others. Such utilitarian arguments in favour of private property can be found in the writings of the early utilitarians, as well as in Locke's.

It is important to note, however, that once again the libertarian need not appeal to these more basic principles to support their notion of property rights. For the property right follows again simply from the liberty right. Suppose, for example, that I come across an unowned track of land. I plough a field, till the soil, and plant a crop. I tend my garden throughout the spring and summer, waiting eagerly for the bounty of my crop come harvest time. Now suppose that another person comes along, just before I am ready to pick my crop, and takes it all. Surely such a person has interfered with my liberty. What I was trying to do was cultivate a crop for my own use. When he comes along and takes it, he interferes with the action in which I was engaged as surely as he would have if he tied me up to prevent me from enjoying the fruits of my labours. The morally significant fact here is not actually my labour, however, but the interference with my plans and activities. This is a violation of my liberty. If such actions are prohibited, because they would be unjustified interferences with my liberty, then we have again derivatively established a property right to the land. For I may legitimately use it and others may not, which is just to say that I own it and others do not.

The second way in which a person can come to own something is by exchange. If I own something I may give it away, sell it, or exchange it with another. Through such acts people come to acquire property by **transfer**.[8] This is, of course, the most common method by which property rights are acquired in our own society, where the vast majority of stuff is already owned. And, again, we can see that the right to transfer property is inseparable from the right to liberty itself. For if I own a camera and I want to give it to my daughter, any action that would prevent me from doing so would be an interference with my liberty. I would not be free to do as I choose, free from interference by others, if I could not dispose of my camera as I see fit. Because of the connection between liberty and the transfer of property, libertarians are also committed to promoting and protecting the free competitive market. In the free market individuals exchange what they own for other things that they want more. Restrictions on free market activity interfere with their freedom, and so the right to liberty extends to the right to free market exchanges. It also protects the right to enter into free contracts, for the same reason. Now interesting questions arise as to the limits of these rights. Are we free to sell ourselves into slavery? After all, we do own our own bodies and minds, and we can generally transfer what we own to others by gift or sale. Can we bequeath property by inheritance? How can we exercise property rights once we are dead? And what does this theory of ownership and liberty imply about our rights to sell sex, organs, or to commit suicide?

Finally, Mill and other libertarians insist that the right to liberty also entails a number of what we might call civil liberties or rights. The right to freedom of conscience, liberty of thought and feeling, freedom of opinion on all subjects, freedom of expression and freedom to publish our views, liberty of tastes and pursuits, freedom to pursue our life plans as we see best, and freedom of association and peaceful assembly are all entailed by the right to liberty itself. These rights are often thought of as being held against governments, and they prohibit the use of state power to interfere with the activities in questions.

Before leaving the topic of rights within libertarian thinking we must note three things. First, the rights that libertarians insist upon are what are known as **claim rights**. They are rights that have corresponding duties. Thus the following expressions are necessarily linked: "x has a right against y to z" and "y has a duty to x not to interfere with x's doing z." As this general schema makes clear, all claim rights are held by individuals against other individuals. In the case of the right to liberty, and those rights deriving from it, libertarians believe that all mature people of normal capacities have the right (in virtue of the value of liberty to them as purposeful agents), and moreover the right is held against everyone else. Everyone has the corresponding duty not to interfere with the right-holder's exercise of her right. Other more specific rights and duties, arising from the voluntary transactions of individuals (through promising, contracting, etc.) might be more limited, binding only the individuals involved in the transaction, but the basic moral and political rights derivable from the right to liberty itself are universal.

Second, the conception of rights that libertarians rely upon is entirely negative. It protects the right-holder only against interference with the right by others. **Negative rights** require those who have the corresponding duties to refrain from actions that would violate the right. So, for example, if the right to life is understood negatively, it is simply the right not to be killed. The corresponding duty is simply the duty not to interfere with the right-holder's living, i.e., the duty not to kill the right-holder. If the right to liberty is negative, the corresponding duty is the duty not to interfere with the right-holder's exercise of liberty, i.e., not to prevent the right-holder from doing whatever she has a right to do. This is in contrast to a positive conception of rights. **Positive rights** entail duties to provide the right-holder with whatever he needs to secure or enjoy the right. If understood as a positive right, the right to life would be the right to whatever one needs to live. As we mentioned in Chapter 1, the corresponding duties on others might be very onerous. If what another needs to live is food, then a positive right to life would entail that I have a duty to provide the life-saving food if I am able. Morality involves rights and duties that are shared universally, moreover. As libertarians are quick to point out, this is not a problem if the duties are merely negative. I respect everyone's right to life, liberty, and property when I am asleep or just minding my own business. So long as I do not steal, kill, or otherwise interfere with the legitimate business of others I fulfil my millions of duties. If, on the other hand, our duties are positive, if we must ensure that everyone has the means to live and enjoy liberty and property, then our duties may be impossible to fulfil and crushing to attempt.

Finally, libertarians are committed to a very minimal state. Governments are not supposed to impose any particular moral or religious code upon the members of society. To do so would violate the right to freedom of conscience and opinion. They must not enact laws that punish people for merely self-regarding behaviour. They must not interfere with the property rights of individuals without their consent. This suggests serious restrictions on the ability of governments to impose taxes, which in turn ensures that they will not have the resources to become unduly large and intrusive into the lives of citizens. They must not interfere with legitimate freedom of contract or the market. Instead, they must maintain only enough of a state to protect the rights of individuals against interference from their fellows and from external forces. Any other exercise of authority will be justified only with the consent of each person whose liberty would be otherwise restricted by it.

Some Confusion About Names

We note in closing that the view we have called libertarianism is often referred to as "liberalism" or "classic liberalism." There is some justification for this, given the history. But there is reason to distinguish between libertarianism and liberalism, despite the fact that the latter is in many ways merely a modern extension of the former and the fact that the commitment to individual rights and liberties that informs libertarianism could be thought of as an important defining feature of what we now call liberal states such as Canada. We use the label libertarianism to mark the view that takes liberty to be basic in the ways we have sought to explain. And we distinguish that view from modern liberalism, because both as a philosophical doctrine and as it is embodied in modern liberal states, liberalism now includes much that not only cannot be derived from the commitment to liberty, but is inconsistent with the priority of liberty. We mention this here merely to avoid confusion in the readings that follow, because many of the authors whose views we will read in this section refer to the views they are discussing as "liberal" rather than "libertarian." What we are interested in is examining the resources of the harm principle as the basic principle of libertarianism to provide guidance on practical moral problems, regardless of the name given to the theory that takes the harm principle to be basic or central.

DEFINITIONS AND EXPLANATIONS

Claim rights: The title belongs to Wesley Newcomb Holfeld, who distinguished between various kinds of rights as the term is used in law. A claim right is distinguished from others because it always has a corresponding duty. A full statement of a claim right always includes (a) the person who has or holds the right, (b) what it is a right to do or have or be, (c) the person against who the right is held, or who has the corresponding duty. To say that the right and duty are correlated means, furthermore, that they have the same object. Take, for example, the right to be free from unjust discrimination. If this is a basic and universal moral right then we might say, "Everyone has a right against everyone else to be free from unjust discrimination." But we could equally well say, "Everyone has a duty not to unjustly discriminate against everyone else." They are equivalent expressions of a single moral relation, characterized as a claim right. Likewise, if I promise my friend Bob to meet him for a drink at a conference, then he has a claim against me that I fulfil my promise. Bob has a right against me that I meet him for a drink, and I have a corresponding duty to meet him for that drink. Typically, the only way in which a claim right can be respected is to fulfil the duty it imposes, and the only one who can release you from such a duty is the right-holder (provided the right is alienable).

Initial acquisition: A theory of the beginnings of property rights to external objects in the world, usually associated with John Locke. For Locke, the act by which people came to own external objects that were previously unowned was by mixing their labour with them.

Instrumental conception of normative justification: To say that a normative system, such as morality or law, is *instrumentally* justified is to say that it is justified because it serves some purpose or goal. It is justified as a means to some end. For a libertarian, the end is set by the interest every person has in being free to pursue her own good as she sees it. To say that it is *justified* is to say that it is worthy of support, or that it could be consented to or accepted by the individuals who are to be bound by its norms.

Negative rights: A negative right imposes a negative duty, i.e., a duty not to be interfered with in doing, having, or being whatever it is that you have a right to. It requires those who have the corresponding duty to refrain from acting so as to interfere with or block your ability to exercise your right, to do what you have a right to do. If, for example, you have a right to freedom of religion against your government, for example, then your government must refrain from action that would prevent you from acting on your religious convictions or exercising your religious preferences. The government could violate your right equally by imposing a religion upon you (requiring you to practice a religion against your will) or by prohibiting the practice of your religion (by making such practice illegal and subject to punishment). In either case you are not free from interference in deciding how to express your religious convictions as you choose. Generally negative rights are easy to respect, since all they require is that we refrain from actively interfering with others.

Positive rights: A positive right imposes a positive duty, i.e., a duty to assist or enable the right-holder to exercise or enjoy whatever he has a right to. It requires those who have a corresponding duty to act so as to assist the right-holder in exercising his right. If the right-holder requires no help in exercising his right, then mere non-interference may be all that is required to respect his right. But if he needs more, and the right is positive, then whomever the right is held against has positive duties to aid. Take the right to be free from political persecution, for example. For someone like us, living in Canada and without involvement in criminal or other illegal organizations, all that is necessary for us to enjoy this right is for our government not to persecute us. But for many other people in the world, regardless of whether they have done any wrong or not, merely being left alone by others is not enough if they are to enjoy this right. They need assistance from others—protection, intervention, asylum, etc.—in order to exercise their right. If it is a positive right, and if it is held against everyone and not just their own governments, then everyone else has a duty to aid if they can. It is important when people use the language of rights in moral and political discussions to be clear whether the right being claimed is negative or positive, as well as to know against who the right is supposed to be held (just the government, all fellow citizens, all people generally). Only if we know these things can we hope to be able to determine what, if any, justification could be given for such a right.

Transfer: Refers to ways in which ownership of things can change from one person to another. Methods of transfer recognized in many societies include sale, gift, and bequeath. What is actually transferred in the exchange of property is properly thought of as a series of entitlements, a bundle of rights to use, dispose, exclude, and the like.

Value pluralism: A normative claim that there is a plurality of objective values in the world, which cannot be reduced to one common factor or element, and that all such values are equally worthy of respect.

Value plurality: A factual claim that people have different and at least partially competing and incompatible subjective values; people differ from one another in what they value, what they find meaningful and worthy of pursuit, and in their conceptions of a good life.

✦ ✦ ✦

Adrian Alex Wellington, Why Liberals Should Support Same Sex Marriage

Adrian Alex Wellington provides us with a libertarian account of the state's duty to recognize same sex couples, if it recognizes marriage at all. Marriage, on Wellington's account, is a state sanctioned bonding of two people, which entails certain rights and duties. A state marriage does not require that the parties love each other, or that they aim to have children, or that they aim to have sex, or that they find each other desirable (and so two homosexuals of different genders may marry), but it does require that they be of different sexes. Since the state is committed to neutrality regarding different conceptions of the good life, Wellington suggests that it must be committed to the formal equality of its citizens. This entails that if a benefit is being provided by the state, it must be available for all citizens, all other things being equal.

This might seem to directly imply that if any are able to obtain the benefit of the state's recognition of their marriage, then all (including same sex couples) must be able to obtain that benefit. But this would discount the libertarian's commitment to the harm principle. If a significant harm resulted from the granting of same sex marriage recognition, then a libertarian would have grounds to refuse to recognize same sex marriage. Wellington examines two of the most likely candidates for harm that might be thought to result from the recognition of same sex marriage: harm to heterosexuality and harm to homosexuality. Key to her argument is that the harm must result from the recognition of marriage itself. Any harm to those who value heterosexuality and devalue homosexuality is ultimately attributable to attitudes toward homosexuality itself, and so cannot be used to assess the question at issue, which is not homosexuality but the recognition by the state of homosexual unions. She concludes that no ban on same sex marriage is legitimate. Alternatively, any harm to those who value homosexuality will ultimately be attributable to reactions based in homophobia, and so again no ban on same sex marriage is legitimate. The state, then, must recognize same sex marriage.

We must recognize that the paper takes the form of a consistency argument. *If you do X, then you must also do Y.* It would be entirely permissible to suggest, given this argument, that marriage ought not to be recognized by the state at all. What might lend support to Wellington's contention that we ought to resolve the inconsistency by expanding state recognition to include same sex relationships rather than restricting the recognition so that no one has it would be an application of the harm principle: married couples currently enjoy the benefits of marriage, and it would harm them should the state remove these benefits. This in turn depends on these benefits being permissible benefits to begin with. These benefits might be impermissible in two ways: they may not be neutral regarding conceptions of the good, or they may lead to harm. If one can suggest that the state's conferring such benefits on married couples fails to be neutral regarding the confirmed bachelor's conception of the good, for example, then there is some reason to suggest that the state ought not to recognize marriage at all. Alternately, if these benefits require some harm to others, for example by single people shouldering a larger share of the tax burden, then the state may not recognize marriage at all. This discussion depends on a state's being *obliged* to continue some benefit that it was *permissible* to give. Things would turn out quite differently if a state were merely *permitted* to continue some benefit that it was *permissible* to give. Does the harm principle obligate the state in this way?

✦ ✦ ✦

Adrian Alex Wellington, "Why Liberals Should Support Same Sex Marriage," *Journal of Social Philosophy* 26:3 (Winter 1995): 5–32. © 1995 *Journal of Social Philosophy*. Reprinted with the permission of Blackwell Publishers.

Why Liberals Should Support Same Sex Marriage

A D R I A N A L E X W E L L I N G T O N

This paper is about the state sponsorship of same sex unions, or about "family values, queer-style," as one commentator has put it.[1] The simple claim of this paper is that gays, lesbians, and bisexuals should have the right to legally marry if they so choose.[2] This simple claim can be characterized as a claim about formal equality—the same sex marriage bar is a denial of the formal equality rights of lesbians, gays,[3] and bisexuals. However, the simple claim does not adequately capture the complexity of the issue, either for those who argue against same sex marriage or for those who argue for it.

In this paper I will present a more complex version of the above argument in the context of contemporary secular liberalism. The argument can be broken down into the following components:

(A) In a liberal society, sexual relations between consenting adults is beyond the purview of the state—"the state has no business in the bedrooms of the nation."[4]

(B) It is not possible to justify anything other than a functional account of marriage in contemporary secular liberal society.

(C) If some relationships—namely opposite sex ones—are to be given state sponsorship, there must be rational reasons consistent with liberal principles to deny that sponsorship to analogous relationships.

(D) On a functional account of marriage same sex relationships are analogous to opposite sex relationships.

(E) As a matter of formal equality, same sex unions should be entitled to state sponsorship.

(F) Any other arguments against the provision of state sponsorship to same sex unions could only make claim to liberal principles by reference to some formulation of the harm principle.

(G) There is no valid argument against same sex marriage based on the grounds of harm consistent with the harm principle.

All of these claims taken together provide a compound argument for the claim that gays, lesbians, and bisexuals should have the right to participate in state sponsored same sex unions if they so choose. The policy claim that corresponds to my argument is that legislative reform would be required to ensure the provision of that right.

The main claim of this paper is that as a matter of social justice liberalism requires the provision of the opportunity for state sponsorship and state recognition of same sex couples. The paper is concerned with an issue of political philosophy— whether a commitment to liberalism entails a commitment to support the rights of lesbians, gays, and bisexuals to marry persons of the same sex, should they so desire. Whether gays, lesbians, and bisexuals should choose to exercise the option, if available, of marrying persons of the same sex is a separate issue. The position that liberalism must, as a matter of political philosophy, recognize the validity of same sex marriage as an option for gays, lesbians, and bisexuals as well as for heterosexuals (should any heterosexuals choose to marry persons of the same sex) is distinct from the position that state sponsorship of same sex marriages should be pursued as a strategy for achieving gay rights or gay liberation. One can acknowledge that liberalism entails the commitment to support state sponsorship of same sex marriage without insisting that lesbians, gays, and bisexuals should participate in, or even advocate the provision of the opportunity to participate in same sex marriages.

I

This paper begins with certain crucial assumptions about the basic claims of liberalism and the fluidity of human sexuality and emotional attachment. The first basic claim of liberalism as a broadly defined concept is the claim that each person in a liberal society should be able to determine for her/himself just what constitutes the "good life." Corollary to that claim is another basic claim that the state should be neutral between conceptions of the "good life." The third basic claim is that a liberal society not only need not, but actually should not, be based on any specific picture of "human nature." A liberal society is one in which there are many diverse conceptions of "human nature," as with conceptions of the "good life," and that none should be accorded primacy or specific state endorsement. The fourth basic claim is that legal intervention in the lives of the members of a liberal society should be constrained as far as possible by the notion of liberty contained in the formulation of the harm principle.[5]

The claims concerning human sexuality and emotional attachment are simpler, but probably no less contentious. These claims are that human beings as a species have a remarkably diverse range of potential sexual practices and emotional affiliations.

Even given tremendous levels of socialization aimed at producing compulsory heterosexuality, many people resist this socialization and choose to reject, partly or completely, heterosexuality. One can assume that many more people would adopt homosexuality or bisexuality in practice or identify with either by inclination if those socialization pressures were ameliorated. The picture of a traditional marriage is that of heterosexual adults taking on a pair bonding union sanctioned by religion and/or the state involving fidelity and reproduction. Yet, many, many people who enter into the state of marriage, who partake of the status of the social practice of marriage, actually do not adhere to that traditional picture. Many marriages do not rest upon fidelity, and many marriages do not result in procreation. Further, many marriages are between parties, or involve parties, who do not primarily perceive themselves as heterosexual.

It seems clear that a liberal conception of sexuality must be one that recognizes the contingency of heterosexuality. There may be many subcultures or segments of a liberal society—religious fundamentalists, certain kinds of anti-homosexual moralists—which do not accept the assertion of heterosexuality as contingent. These groups may wish to entrench heterosexuality socially, morally, and legally, yet the very fact that they seek to entrench it and to force compliance with the norm of heterosexuality itself attests to the very contingency of the norm. It is because some people are unwilling to live in compliance with the norm, and are able to resist the supposed necessity of the norm, that these groups wish to adopt harsh measures of policing and enforcement of the norm. These groups who categorically oppose the assertion of contingent heterosexuality, nevertheless, are only part of liberal society. Liberal society also includes those who wish to partake in homosexual or bisexual pair bonding unions as well as those who wish to, or at least are willing to, tolerate such unions.

A liberal society is one that rests upon the provision of choice for individuals to determine what sorts of people they want to be, as well as what sorts of lives they want to lead. Part of the choices that one undertakes during the process of self construction and life construction is whether, and to what extent, to participate in pair bonding unions. In a society which is premised upon the separation of religion and democratic governance, indicated by the institution of civil marriage, these unions must be interpreted in the context of liberal and not religious norms. Despite the holdover of religious notions in the wording of the marriage ceremony itself, it is clear that people can engage in the practice of marriage without any specific commitment to religious conceptions of marriage. Marriage thus becomes a state sanctioned pair bonding union, an affirmation of state endorsement of the pair bonding itself. There is no requirement that one engage in heterosexual practices with one's marriage partner, and no requirement that one attempt to produce children. The only conditions one need meet in order to undertake civil marriage are that the partners are of opposite sex, of sufficient age, legally sane, and not too closely related (consanguinity conditions).[6] Of course, the partners must be able to pay the required fee for the ceremony.

It is interesting to note that once the religious basis for marriage is removed or at least elided that there is no longer any rational reason—rational in the sense of related to the purpose of the practice—to insist that parties to a civil marriage be of the opposite sex. A civil marriage is a self-defining ceremony, intended to accord a certain social status. The state cannot require that marriage partners endorse and live up to the ideal of fidelity, or endorse and live by the norm of heterosexuality, or endorse and live in accordance with the intention to reproduce. The marriage union in a secular liberal society is one that is interpreted by the parties in the context of the purported absence of teleological conceptions of human nature and of state sanctioned conceptions of the good life. The parties themselves determine what marriage means to them, and shape the practice to their needs and wants. How then can the state insist upon the condition that parties must be opposite sexes in order to participate in that kind of practice?

Marriages are intended to be unions, unions which apparently automatically create "couples" and then "families." There are of course couples outside of marriage and marriage partners who do not perceive themselves to be couples. There are of course families outside of marriage and marriages which do not actually function like families. The point is that civil marriages produce a certain kind of coupling—state sanctioned coupling. Other than the requirement that the parties be adults and be of opposite sex, the civil marriage ceremony can be tailored by the parties to incorporate their values and beliefs and preferences. The parties can undertake civil marriage in order to attain the social status of marriage but intend to be "unfaithful" to one another sexually with persons of the opposite or same sex. The parties can intend to be celibate, to avoid procreation or to engage in procreation, to have sex only with each other, or to never have sex with each other. In other words, marriage does not depend upon any particular set of sexual or emotional practices. Why then does it depend upon an arbitrary condition of membership in the opposite sex to one's intended partner?

If a homosexual person can marry another homosexual person of the opposite sex or a heterosexual person of the opposite sex, or a bisexual person marry a homosexual or heterosexual person of the opposite sex, why should lesbians, gays, and bisexuals be excluded from marrying a homosexual or bisexual or heterosexual person of the same sex? Heterosexuals are also prevented from marrying a heterosexual or homosexual person of the same sex as well. If one looks at marriage in the context of a liberal conception of the practice, divorced from the religious interpretation of the practice and the historical background of the practice, these restrictions make no sense. Apart from social prejudice and discrimination, there is no reason to insist that individuals of the same sex cannot form couples in the same way that parties to marriage form couples. Civil marriage is a self-defining, self-obligating union. The parties will determine what the union provides for them, and what need they have for the state sanction—from expression of commitment to tax breaks. Same sex couples are no less capable of determining this than opposite sex couples.

One does not have to be able to recognize the capacity in oneself to respond sexually to persons of either sex or of the same sex in order to recognize that the capacity exists in many others. One does not have to be able to recognize the capacity in oneself to form emotional affiliations with persons of either sex or of the same sex in order to recognize that the capacity exists in many others. There is no biological, or psychological reason that human beings must have sex or emotional affiliations only with persons of the opposite sex. There are only political or social reasons that motivate people to insist that heterosexuality is natural, or normal. Liberals are predisposed to resist arguments of the form that it is only "natural" or "normal" for humans to be X or to do Y. On my reading of liberalism the central driving force behind the adoption of liberal political philosophy and policy historically was to counteract precisely those kind of arguments in favor of the divine right of monarchs or in favor of religious morality. Divorce is one of the clearest examples of the movement towards a secularization of social practices that were initially the exclusive preserve of religion.

It seems clear that secular liberal societies can no longer rely upon outdated and archaic religious notions about the purposes of coupling and specifically of marriage. The attempts of courts to deal with common law opposite sex coupling point to several interesting things about contemporary civil marriage. The courts in some cases have attempted to develop functional characterizations of "spouses" and thus functional definitions of "couples."[7] These definitions include factors like the following: Did the parties share a bank account? Did the parties own property in common? Did the parties visit each others' relatives? Did the parties purchase shared items? Did the parties entertain guests together? Did the parties divide up household chores between them? Did the parties share meals? Did the parties provide nurturance and caring for each other when ill?

It is obvious that all these factors apply equally to same sex couples as to opposite sex couples. Same sex couples share bank accounts, own property in common, visit each other's relatives, purchase shared items, entertain guests together, divide up household chores, share meals, and provide nurturance and care for each other when ill. And of course, same sex couples, like opposite sex couples, have sex with each other. Any functional characterization of a couple—which I would argue is the only kind that could be endorsed by a full-fledged liberalism—is going to apply equally to same sex couples as to opposite sex couples.

If functional definitions are appropriate to determine whether unmarried couples were or are effectively married, and thus fall under "common law" marriage provisions of family law, then would functional definitions not be appropriate to determine whether same sex couples are suitable candidates for characterizations of "spouses" and thus suitable candidates to be deemed effectively married as well? Same sex couples look indistinguishable from opposite couples on the basis of functional definitions—that is, the differences among particular opposite and same sex couples would be as great as differences between opposite and same sex couples. The only reason that same sex couples do not fall under "common law" marriage provisions of family law is that same sex couples cannot marry, and thus they cannot be "effectively married." I should point out that "common law" marriage designation has to do with both the division of property and family assets, and the custody of, and access to, children. Both of these factors can be relevant to same sex couples who may own property together, have been in a relationship of economic dependence and support, and have children together (not the children of both of them together, but the children of each of them who they parent together or the children they have adopted together or singly previously).

None of the criteria in a functional definition of "spouse"—a person with whom one may share a bank account, own property, visit relatives, purchase shared items, entertain guests, divide up household chores, share meals, and have sex, and for whom one may provide nurturance and care—are gender specific. All are functional and relational. The significant issue in the determination of "spouse" is whether the two people relate to each other, and think of each other, in the manner of a "couple." What is a couple then, on this account, is a provisional definition that is something along the lines of a "voluntary relation premised on intimacy and connection." This phrase is my choice of wording; similar ideas based on functional definitions are suggested by the wording found in domestic partnership provisions and in certain court decisions.[8] My functional definition of marriage explicitly excludes the requirement of procreation, or even intended procreation. It is inconsistent, I argue, with a liberal account of marriage to include such a requirement. Thus, there is no basis to the attempt to privilege procreative or potentially procreative heterosexual marriage to encourage reproduction. Such an attempt could not be justified on my account.

Of course, the phrase "voluntary relation premised on intimacy and connection" could apply to affairs, and special friendships, so what needs to be added is the clause intended to produce the union of coupling. Thus, it is self-defining. What is distinctive about "couples" is that two people self-identify as a couple, and then other people identify those two people as a couple. There is no reason, once the notion of "couple" is characterized as functional and self-defining, to restrict the notion to opposite sex couples. And then if marriage is simply the legitimation by state sanction of self-defined, functional couples, there is no reason to restrict civil marriage to opposite sex couples.

The argument might be made that a significant feature of marriage is that the status of marriage represents a certain expression of social approval for the union. Thus, the state provides for couples to marry to express social approval for opposite sex coupling. It is of course arguments like this that make advocates of gay rights argue that gays, lesbians, and bisexuals need to have the opportunity to marry in order to be accorded the expression of social approval for their unions. The idea is that marriage is a legitimating social practice—that the status of marriage legitimates the coupling. Therefore, some lesbians, gays, and bisexuals wish to have their same sex coupling legitimated. The counter argument then is that "society," whatever that is, does not wish to bestow social approval on same sex coupling. Therefore, same sex couples should not be provided with the option of legitimating state sanctioned marriage.

This counter argument does not work, for several reasons. One reason is that people who marry engage in myriad forms of coupling which are not socially approved by large segments of the population—for example, childless marriages (by choice), open marriages, adulterous marriages, opportunistic marriages or marriages of convenience (for immigration purposes, for example), tabloid marriages ("grandmother- or grandfather-aged person marries teen" type of thing). It simply is not the case that whatever unions result from opposite sex marriages would be subject to social approval. It is not simply by virtue of the fact that parties are of opposite sexes that civil marriage expresses social approval. Another reason is that many, many people do support the idea of state sanctioned social approval for same sex unions. Obviously, most if not all gays, lesbians, and bisexuals support the idea of state sanctioned social approval for same sex unions.[9] Whether or not all gays, lesbians, and bisexuals would actually want to participate in the practice of same sex marriages, they would nevertheless not want to endorse a continuation of a source of discrimination against gays, lesbians, and bisexuals. There may be some homosexuals who object to the campaign for gay marriage, but the basis of their denial of support may be something other than a wish to see discrimination against gays, lesbians, and bisexuals continued.

It is also the case that some heterosexuals who would not wish to have the option to undertake same sex marriages for themselves would still support the provision of state sanctioned same sex marriages to those who do want them. Liberals are notorious for arguing for the rights of people to do things that liberals themselves may not want to do, and that other people (non liberals) do not support for anyone. Why should same sex marriage be any different? A liberal society is one in which the fullest possible range of options for human flourishing is to be encouraged, consistent with the need for respect of the civil rights and liberties of individuals. One important civil liberty is the freedom to engage in a state sanctioned union. The only possible reason that a liberal could have for rejecting same sex marriage is that the practice would in some way violate the harm principle.

It is important to clarify why the harm principle is even relevant in this context. The harm principle purports to stipulate the conditions under which the state could legitimately interfere with the liberty of its citizens; it sets out the bounds of individual liberty which must be respected by a liberal government. The harm principle is clearly germane to the issue of whether (homosexual) sodomy should be subject to criminal prohibition.[10] It makes sense therefore to apply the harm principle to that issue, but it is less clear why the harm principle should be applied to the issue of same sex marriage. There are several reasons why the application may be problematic.

Criminal prohibitions against sexual activity between consenting adults obviously violate the liberty of those subject to them. Thus, these prohibitions could only be justified if there was sufficient reason to do so, reasons which satisfy the requirements of the harm principle. If it could be shown that some harm—harm of the sort envisaged by Mill—results from the activity, then the prohibition could be justified. It cannot be shown that any harm of the sort envisaged by Mill results from the activity, and thus the criminal prohibition of homosexual activity cannot be justified. Any justifications of such criminal prohibitions could only be based on illiberal principles and prejudices.

The question of permitting homosexual marriage does not involve any clear violation of liberty. It could be argued that marriage law is an instance of power-conferring and entitlement-allocating legislation. Marriage law determines which couples are entitled to state sanction for their unions, and which couples are not. Marriage constitutes "an affirmation by the state, a larger-than-life acknowledgment of one's relationship, a seal of approval."[11] The question of whether the state can legitimately deny same sex couples the right to marry seems thus to be a question of equality. Are same sex couples equal to opposite sex couples, such that they should be entitled to the same state sponsorship of their unions? I argue that on a functional account of marriage formal equality would dictate that same sex couples are entitled to the same state sponsorship as opposite sex couples. I also argue that a functional account of marriage is the only type of account consistent with contemporary secular liberal society.

It should be sufficient, then, to say that the same sex marriage bar violates the formal equality of gays, lesbians, and bisexuals. Yet, it is not sufficient because the literature addressing the issue of same sex marriage does not facilitate a straightforward treatment in terms of formal equality. To respond to the objections that have been raised by critics of homosexual marriage, it is necessary to depart from a neat and simple analysis of equality.

The critics of homosexual marriage (both straight and gay) are not satisfied with the characterization of the issue as one of formal equality. Those critics who object to homosexual marriage because they object to homosexuality will not accept the claim of equality between same sex couples and opposite sex couples. That claim is contentious for them, and their response to that claim is typically to point out some kind of harm that is imputed to homosexual marriage. Those critics who object to homosexual marriage, or at least raise concerns about the pursuit of state sponsorship, but who do not object to homosexuality *per se* are concerned with issues of substantive equality. To address same sex marriage in the context of substantive equality is to talk about benefit and disbenefit, it is to talk about harm to interests.

Some readers might wonder whether the kind of harm that is being discussed in this section of the paper is really the kind of harm that Mill would have had in mind when he proposed the Harm Principle. I have two responses to that potential interjection. Firstly, what Mill would have had in mind is not determinative of the articulation of harm to be covered by the Principle for contemporary society. The debates over hate literature, pornography, and the limits of free speech are not really foreshadowed in Mill's formulation, yet these issues have become an integral part of how the Harm Principle is understood in contemporary liberal society. Secondly, the kinds of harms that are covered by the term stigmatization include the loss of jobs, physical assaults ("gay bashing"), and other violations of the civil rights of gays, lesbians, and bisexuals. These are certainly the kinds of things Mill's own formulation would have been intended to cover.

On the usual reading of Mill's harm principle, preventing harm to others is the only justified rationale for state interference with the liberty of individuals.[12] I propose to apply a variant of the harm principle which can accommodate the concerns about putative harm raised by both sets of critics of same sex marriage, but still does justice to liberal principles. That variant is the following: the only justification for the denial by the state of a benefit required by formal equality is that the provision of that benefit would harm others in the society. Thus, as a mater of public policy, the state must sponsor power-conferring or entitlement-allocating legislation required by formal equality unless it can be shown that significant harm (of the kind covered by the harm principle) would result from that sponsorship. It could be argued that my formulation had departed so far from Mill's principle that it could not be included under the same label. Nevertheless, I think that the term harm is irreplaceable in this context—since it is harm that justifies the denial of state benefits. My version could be called the State Benefits Version of the Harm Principle.

The objections to same sex marriage which need to be countered involve conceptions of harm. I contend that in order to make sense of the objections, and in order to make a valid case for state sponsorship, it is necessary to respond to the assertions about putative harm. I have found that the most efficacious way to do so is examine the application of my proposed formulation of the harm principle in the context of the legitimation of homosexual marriage.

II

There are effectively two distinct sets of criticisms of same-sex marriage on the grounds of imputed harm resulting from state sanction. One set of criticisms includes several variations on the idea that allowing same-sex marriages will bring about a threat to the nuclear family, marriage in general, or even to society. This set of criticisms is based on a claim that I will call the Harm to Heterosexuality claim. The other set of criticisms includes several variations on the idea that advocating and pursuing state sponsorship of same sex marriage will bring about a threat to the goals and objectives of gay liberation. This set of criticisms is based on a claim that I will call the Harm to Homosexuality claim. The objection to same sex marriage can make use of conceptions of harm that are either symbolic or empirical, or both. In other words, the kind of harm that is imputed can be harm that can be determined and measured empirically or it can be symbolic harm that is simply perceived.

The Harm to Heterosexuality is supposed to consist in the threat that same sex marriages pose to opposite sex marriages, harm in the form of decline in the sanctity of the institution of marriage, inconsistency with traditional definitions of family, or even in the most extreme articulations of the position, harm in the form of a contribution to an overall breakdown in social order. People who make these kinds of criticisms are motivated by the rejection of gay rights and liberation, and often even a "fear and loathing" of homosexuality.

Many versions of the Harm to Heterosexuality position are premised upon religious conceptions of sex, family, and society. As such, the harm that is claimed tends to be more symbolic than empirical. Insofar as the Harm to Heterosexuality position is based upon religious conceptions of sex, family, and society, it is easily dispensed with in the context of a discussion of liberalism. Given that liberalism requires the separation of church and state, it cannot be argued that the state should outlaw same sex marriages because such marriages are inconsistent with religious morality. Insofar as the Harm to Heterosexuality position is based upon some empirical sounding claim about actual harm to the institutions of marriage and family, or to "society" itself, it is obvious that this would have to be based on some kind of evidence. What kind of evidence could one possibly produce to argue that same sex marriages would erode the institutions of marriage and family?

Someone who wants to claim that same sex marriages will produce some kind of distinct social harm has to be able to show what harm is caused by the state sponsorship of marriage that is distinct from the harm that is imputed to same sex relationships themselves. Same sex coupling will continue with or without state sponsorship, and even with or without criminalization of some of the acts that are targeted as part of an attempt to outlaw homosexuality. People who object to same sex marriage may also object to homosexuality, but the point is that to make any kind of a case for why a liberal society should not provide legal sanction for relationships that are already occurring, an argument specifically against state sponsorship of marriage is needed. If liberalism is based, as I want to argue, on the notions of privacy, autonomy, and individual liberty, no argument against homosexuality based on mere moral or social disapproval is acceptable. There has to be evidence of actual harm that will be experienced by members of the society that amounts to more than mere offense at the actions or choices of others. Therefore, the critics of same sex marriage cannot argue that they object to state sponsorship because they object to homosexuality and state sponsorship legitimates homosexuality.

What quickly becomes clear once one looks at the various articulations of the Harm to Heterosexuality position is that it is difficult to separate the objection to same sex marriage from the objection to homosexuality. It is of course important to be able to separate these objections, because the only basis a liberal could accept for outlawing, or denying legitimacy to, same sex relationships, is that those relationships will actually cause harm to others. If we recognize that the harm that can be considered is not harm that consists of mere offense, then the symbolic element of the objection is disallowed. That leaves the empirical element of the objection.

One candidate for the requisite kind of harm that is proposed is the potential for gay marriage to undermine the legitimacy of straight marriage. This claim can be understood in two ways: one in which the delegitimation consists of symbolic harm to the institution and the other in which the delegitimation consists of actual harm to the institution in the form of decreased participation. The notion of symbolic harm to the sanctity of heterosexual marriage rests upon illiberal commitments and concerns, and thus does not raise issues germane to the consideration of what liberals should support.

The notion of the latter form of harm, one of decreased participation, underlies the claim that the opportunity for gay marriage will weaken the institution of heterosexual marriage. Yet, as others have pointed out, this argument rests upon (at least one) fallacy. As one commentator puts it, "[g]ay marriage could only delegitimize straight marriage if it were a real alternative to it."[13] That is, it could only delegitimize it if those who would otherwise participate in straight marriage chose to participate instead in gay marriage. Obviously, heterosexuals will continue to marry other heterosexuals. The people who will no longer participate in straight marriages if offered the opportunity to participate in gay marriages will be gays, lesbians, and bisexuals. Assuming that some gays who marry straights do so in order to be married and to have families, and not simply to avoid social stigma, then they would continue to do so. Those gays who marry straights in order to stay closeted and to avoid social stigma would continue to do so as long as the social stigmatization continues. Of course, the legalization of gay marriage would contribute to the erosion of the social stigma surrounding homosexuality, which would in turn encourage lesbians, gays, and bisexuals to participate in gay marriage. None of this suggests that there would be any real threat to significantly decreased participation in heterosexual marriage.

It thus seems as if the objection to same sex marriage characterized in terms of harm rests solely upon the objection to homosexuality itself. There is no argument against marriage of same sex persons that is not an argument against homosexuality. I want to assert that there is no valid empirical evidence that same sex relationships, in and of themselves, cause actual harm to any other persons. The claim that these relationships are harmful to the participants—even assuming there could be shown to be a factual basis to this dubious supposition—is of course an irrelevant claim, given liberalism's *prima facie* commitment to nonpaternalism. It is particularly illegitimate when the paternalism is based on contentious moral, religious, or social conceptions of the "good" of the intended beneficiaries of the paternalism.[14]

The Harm to Homosexuality is supposed to consist in the threat that state sponsorship poses to the achievement of gay liberation and to the project of reconceiving heterosexuality, homosexuality, and relations between the sexes. People who make these kinds of claims are motivated by a commitment to gay liberation, and to some articulations of gay rights—ones that do not amount to presumption of the notion of "sameness" between gays and straights but rather assume the notion of "difference" between gays and straights. The position of those in gay, lesbian, and bisexual communities[15] who reject the pursuit of state sponsorship for same sex relationships, is not of course that there is anything wrong with same sex relationships. Their position is that there is something wrong with state sponsorship, and something wrong with marriage.

It should be pointed out that those in lesbian, gay, and bisexual communities who raise objections to the prospect of gay marriage do so largely on grounds of strategy and tactics. The debate over gay marriage within gay, lesbian, and bisexual communities is mainly a debate over the priority of different venues or policies for the allocation of resources and the expenditure of efforts. The discussion in much of the literature thus addresses the advisability of pursuing gay marriage as a strategy for gay activists, and raises concerns about the diversion of efforts and resources from other significant issues. These debates—whether putting too much effort into this one option will divert efforts from other options that may be more central to sexual liberation, whether the pursuit of domestic partnership legislation should take priority over removal of the same sex marriage bar,[16] whether the potential backlash from the pursuit of this particular option will have repercussions, or whether the gay, lesbian, and bisexual community is too divided over the option to make it a priority—could all be seen to involve questions about goals and strategies for queer activism.[17] For instance, some "regard domestic partnership agreement registration as a distraction from the need to gain full rights to marry with full access to benefits and protections," while others perceive that registration is better because it "recognizes alternative family structures."[18] These questions about which is the better target begin with the assumption that gays, lesbians, and bisexuals are entitled to equality and then move to the attempt to articulate and clarify the appropriate way to characterize and pursue that equality.

The point is that gays, lesbians, and bisexuals who call into question the desirability of gay marriage generally do not dispute the position that the opposite sex requirement of marriage laws is "socially discriminatory and offensive to the basic liberal principles that underlie human rights legislation."[19] Even those who raise objections to same sex marriage do not deny that the same sex marriage bar is illiberal. Yet, it is still possible to construct an objection to state sponsorship to same sex marriage that imputes some type of potential harm that would result from the policy. This objection could take several different forms:

(1) one based on an objection to perceived conformity to "straight standards;"[20]

(2) one based on an objection to the oppressive patriarchal nature of the institution of marriage; and

(3) one based on an objection to the involvement of the state in the regulation of lesbian, gay, and bisexual intimate relationships. These objections tend to overlap and are difficult to disentangle.

The first form of the objection, based on rejection of the perceived conformity to "straight standards" inherent in same sex marriage, implies that the pursuit of conformity on the part of some gays, lesbians, and bisexuals—namely those who would want to get married—could indirectly harm the interests of those who would not want to get married, and thus who do not conform. The harm would consist of further stigmatization of those lesbians, gays, and bisexuals who choose not to get married once the option becomes available.[21]

It is possible to construct the imputed argument along the following lines. Homosexual sex is stigmatized and a cause for oppression of gays, lesbians, and bisexuals. If homosexuals could marry, those who would already tend to benefit from certain social privileges (class, race, ethnicity, and so forth) will likely be the ones to exercise the option. Those homosexuals who do not marry will be further stigmatized and oppressed, relative to the otherwise more privileged homosexuals who will marry.[22]

It is difficult to determine in what sense there would be more stigmatization or oppression of the lesbians, gays, and bisexuals who choose not to marry—absolutely or in terms of perception of relative privilege. It is at least partly an empirical question. What is relevant to the issue in question is whether the provision of state sponsorship for same sex marriage would result in more harm overall, harm of the sort that is germane to liberalism.

The significant issue for the question of whether liberalism should support same sex marriage is whether the resulting "extra" stigmatization would result from the provision of same sex marriage itself, or would be an unintended byproduct of pre-existing homophobia.[23] It is unclear whether the stigmatization of non-married or single gays, lesbians, and bisexuals would be more after the option of state sponsored same sex marriage is available or whether it would be the same amount of stigmatization, but would seem more in relation to the other married gays, lesbians, and bisexuals. That is, it is unclear whether it would be extra stigmatization or simply continuing stigmatization. Either way, the "extra" stigmatization should be the focus of additional efforts to reduce and eventually overcome homophobic societal attitudes. Unless one could show that denying same sex couples the right to marry would, in and of itself, decrease the stigmatization, it is necessary to address the resulting harm by other measures than continuing the same sex marriage bar.

The first objection to same sex marriage can be presented still more abstractly, in terms of the "politics of validating difference,"[24] and a general critique of "rights discourse" and "rights claims." The presumption is that there is something one could identify as lesbian and gay identity and culture that resists assimilation. There is no denial, however, that some gays and lesbians as individuals do not resist, and even welcome, assimilation. The concern is that whenever society extends rights to some previously disenfranchised group of persons—in this case the lesbians, gays, and bisexuals who want to get married—then other members of the group who "forswear or forego such rights risk being even more marginalized than before."[25] The objection seems to highlight the tension between individual rights which would be asserted by the group of same sex couples who want to marry, and collective interests which would be represented by the interests of the remainder of the group, the non-marrying gays and lesbians.[26]

The second form of the Harm to Homosexuality objection is the claim that marriage is an oppressive institution which lesbians and gay men should condemn, rather than lobby to join.[27] There are two different aspects of characterizing the harm of marriage in this objection. One aspect concerns the patriarchal nature of marriage as a social institution.[28] The other aspect emphasizes the balance of benefits and burdens that marriage may provide for particular same sex couples. The latter aspect is related to the former in that the reason some couples would not realize the potential benefits of marriage would have to do with the underlying oppressive features, and structural constraints of society. What Nitya Duclos calls the "hierarchy of privilege" ensures that some couples—whether opposite sex or same sex couples—will benefit more from the bundle of benefits that constitute marriage.[29] The provision of state sponsored marriage for same sex couples will also have effects on cohabiting same sex couples that may or may not be welcomed by those cohabiting couples.

Both aspects of the second objection—the particular and the general—have in common the focus on marriage. It is marriage as a social institution that is an oppressive patriarchal institution. It is marriage as a particular legislative scheme that has better or worse effects for particular couples. The important point for the purposes of this paper is that the putative harm does not result from the provision of same sex marriage, but rather from marriage itself. For the liberal, the question is whether it is justifiable for the state to continue to deny to same sex couples the option that is available to opposite sex couples—to participate in the potentially undesirable, arguably harmful institution of marriage. The liberal rejection of paternalism entails that individuals should be allowed to choose for themselves whether or not to participate in activities that may be harmful to themselves. The issue is not the desirability of marriage, but the desirability of the right.[30]

Several feminists have argued for the position that while marriage may be oppressive in its present form, it need not always be that way. Marriage, the argument goes, is a creature of law dependent upon the power of the state; as such, it is an historically and culturally contingent institution.[31] The further claim is made that same sex marriage could have the potential to "disrupt both the gendered definition of marriage and the assumption the marriage is a form of socially, if not legally, prescribed hierarchy."[32] At the very least, same sex marriages would require the rethinking of the content of the marriage vows and the exercise of linguistic creativity to replace the "husband" and "wife" terminology. These improvements would have symbolic value, and would contribute to the larger project of reforming marriage as a social institution. Same sex marriage, then, would produce no distinctive harm and might even ameliorate the current harm produced by marriage.

What makes the issue complicated is that it is possible to characterize the benefits that would accrue to lesbians, gays, and bisexuals upon provision of the right to state sponsorship of same sex marriage in two ways. One way is to emphasize the benefits that would be realized by individual members of same sex couples who could participate in marriage. The other way is to emphasize the benefits that would be realized by all queers consisting of increased tolerance of homosexuality and increased legitimacy for same sex unions. Some advocates of state sponsorship of same sex marriage argue that it is actually the "issue most likely to lead ultimately to a world free of discrimination against lesbians and gay men."[33] The characterization of benefits—the determination of which benefits will result and who specifically will benefit—is addressed in the literature in the context of the identification of attendant harms— the determination of which harms will result and who specifically will be harmed.

It is important to distinguish between the claim that same sex couples should be entitled to equal treatment with opposite sex couples—whether through domestic partnership arrangements or civil marriage—and the claim that these legal measures should be the focus of advocacy and struggle for gay rights. It is also important to distinguish between the claim that the right to choose X—for example, the right to choose to marry—will benefit those for whom X is a likely option and the claim that the right to choose X is a benefit to only those who do choose X. There is a difference between the concern that gay activists should not direct their energies to the pursuit of marriage and domestic partnership arrangements because only some gays and lesbians would want to participate in these institutions and the claim that only those who (will) participate in those institutions will be benefited by the existence of the choice.

The objection to same sex marriage based on the rejection of conformity should properly locate the harm in homophobia. The objection to same sex marriage based on the suspicion of marriage should properly locate the harm in marriage itself. The objection to same sex marriage based on the perniciousness of state regulation of sexuality should properly locate the harm in the combination of homophobia and marriage itself. It is obvious why queers would be suspicious of any manifestation of state regulation of sexuality.[34] The question, however, is whether gays, lesbians and bisexuals would be worse off with the provision of state sponsorship for same sex coupling. It is hard to see how they would be. The problem rests with state initiatives that amount to the entrenchment of intolerance of homosexuality.

According to the third form of the Harm to Homosexuality objection, marriage simply presents yet another vehicle of state regulation of sexuality. Marriage, however, does present some potential for protection from state regulation and other benefits. Nitya Duclos lists four objectives of the advocates of gay and lesbian marriage:

(1) "to revolutionize marriage and force society to rethink its collective views of sex and sexuality;"

(2) to provide validation and legitimation of same sex relationships;

(3) to enable lesbian and gay families to partake in the range of socioeconomic benefits of marriage;

(4) to legitimate gay and lesbian relationships in the eyes of courts to help lesbians and gays keep their children.[35]

It is clear that merely removing the obstacles to same sex marriage is not going to be sufficient for the realization of these objectives.

State sponsorship of same sex coupling will entail toleration of homosexuality, but it alone will not provide for respect and full equality without other social, political, legal, and economic changes.[36] For example, changes in judicial attitudes and child custody legislation will be necessary for the achievement of the fourth objective.[37] The effect of marriage breakdown will cause same sex couples to come under the purview of courts under divorce legislation. Same sex couples who separate and divorce will be subject to provisions concerning division of property, support, and custody of children. For some people, that will be a benefit and for others that will be a burden. The point is that it is not same sex marriage that increases the points of contact but the legislative regime governing marriage and divorce. The fear of state regulation should not amount to a fear of same sex marriage, but rather a fear of homophobia and a fear of the potential effects of the legislative regime governing marriage and divorce. Thus, harm would result from homophobia and the effects of marriage and divorce, but not from same sex marriage itself.

The consideration of the Harm to Homosexuality objections points to the need to distinguish between formal and substantive equality. The conceptions of harm contained in the various forms of the objection indicate concerns of substantive equality. The question of whether same sex couples should be denied the state sponsorship available to opposite sex couples is really a question of formal equality. The position of this paper is that the same sex marriage bar is a clear denial of formal equality for gay, lesbians and bisexuals. It is important to make clear, then, the relation between formal equality and substantive equality on this issue, if there is any relation.

The opponents to same sex marriage who are motivated by some version of the Harm to Homosexuality objection could be making one of three different claims about the effects of same sex marriage on substantive equality. These three claims are:

(1) same sex marriage would increase substantive equality;

(2) same sex marriage would decrease substantive equality; or

(3) same sex marriage would neither decrease nor increase substantive equality.

On the basis of the above discussion it seems that the three forms of the Harm to Homosexuality objection—the rejection of conformity, the suspicion of marriage, and the fear of state regulation—all attempt to implicate same sex marriage in the charge of jeopardizing substantive equality.

I have tried to argue, however, that what actually jeopardizes substantive equality is not the possibility of same sex marriage in and of itself, but the effects of pre-existing inequalities resulting from homophobia, the legal regime governing marriage and divorce, and other social inequalities. I would contend then, that same sex marriage at the least could be said to neither decrease nor increase substantive equality. It may even increase substantive equality if the claims concerning the potential liberatory effects of same sex marriage upon the institution of marriage are viable. The provision of state sponsored same sex marriage would certainly further the pursuit of formal equality for homosexuals, and for that reason it is incumbent upon liberals to support it.

III

Richard Posner in *Sex and Reason* presents several other arguments against same sex marriage. Posner argues that there are significant differences between punishing sodomy and prohibiting homosexual marriage such that the former is not justifiable but the latter might be. Posner claims that the laws criminalizing sodomy are unjustifiable and should be repealed, but that the bar to same sex marriage is probably justifiable and should be upheld. He gives three reasons for his claim, but only one amounts to an argument.

The first reason seems to be that homosexual unions do not deserve state approval, although they do not deserve state condemnation either. This first reason involves multiple assertions:

(1) that permitting homosexual marriage would be interpreted as "placing a stamp of approval on homosexuality, while decriminalizing sodomy would not;"

(2) that permitting homosexual marriage is tantamount to declaring that "homosexual marriage is a desirable, even a noble, condition in which to live;"[38]

(3) that permitting homosexual marriage would "place government in the dishonest position of propagating a false picture of the reality of homosexuals' lives."[39]

What Posner is not saying explicitly is as significant as what he is saying. He is saying that most people do not think that homosexual marriage is a noble or a desirable condition in which to live. He is implying that homosexual marriage is not entitled to a stamp of approval. Posner does not specifically say why homosexual unions do not deserve a stamp of approval One can only assume that it has something to do with the claim that homosexual unions generate "unstable, temporary, and childless" marriages.[40] It is the pretense that they are otherwise that seems to constitute the false picture the government would be propagating if it permitted homosexual marriage.

Posner assumes that he has provided empirical evidence for his claims in the earlier part of the chapter, "Homosexuality: The Policy Questions." Yet, some homosexual unions include children, some are very stable, and some are very long lasting, as Posner himself recognizes. Posner is either making sweeping generalizations and then contradicting himself, or else he is not providing sufficient support for his argument. Posner seems to assume that the information that a certain couple is married gives the picture that the couple has a stable, long-lasting, and child-producing union. He then seems to claim on the basis of empirical studies that homosexual couples are statistically less likely to be stable or permanent than are heterosexual couples. Thus, he argues that the government would be propagating a false picture by permitting homosexual marriage.

Of course many heterosexual unions also generate "unstable, temporary, and childless" marriages. Thus, for many opposite sex couples the information that a couple is married gives, according to Posner's reasoning, a false picture. Posner even acknowledges this fact. He allows that the suggestion that heterosexual marriages and prospective homosexual marriages differ fundamentally along these lines comes to seem ever more implausible. This then leads him to suggest that the appropriate response is one of "chucking the whole institution of marriage in favor of an explicitly contractual approach that would make the current realities of marriage transparent."[41] Gay and lesbian sexual liberationists might support the proposal to get rid of marriage altogether, but it is difficult to imagine that this prospect is imminent. In the interim, as long as opposite sex couples can choose to marry Posner needs to explain why same sex couples cannot have that choice. Posner needs to explain why same sex unions do not deserve state approval.

If it is the case, as Posner assumes, that most people do not consider homosexual unions to be noble and desirable, then what would follow from that? Homosexual unions are obviously desirable to those who participate in them, and likewise same sex marriages would be desirable to those who would participate in them. Homosexual unions are not ignoble to those who participate in them and they are inherently no more or no less noble than heterosexual unions to those who are tolerant and respectful of them. Posner argues for the decriminalization of homosexuality on the grounds of toleration. For liberals, however, the issue is not merely whether the political value of liberty requires the tolerance and acceptance of homosexuals. The question is whether the political value of equality further requires the state to provide the stamp of approval for same sex unions. Posner needs to provide an argument for the violation of equality that the denial of state sponsorship represents.

The second reason seems to be inconclusive—he identifies both an information cost and an information benefit to the prospect of same sex marriage. The information cost is that the more inclusive the concept of marriage becomes the less information the word "marriage" conveys. But as Posner would recognize, this argument would apply equally to other expansions of the concept of marriage. Posner then goes on to point out that the label same sex marriage would convey more information about the particular same sex relationship. Thus, same sex marriage would also provide an information benefit. Since they cancel each other out, the information cost consideration counts neither for nor against his argument.[42]

The third reason that Posner provides for distinguishing between decriminalization of sodomy and the legalization of gay marriage concerns the entitlements of marriage. He points out that authorizing same sex marriage would confer certain benefits on some homosexual couples, and then simply asks whether society would want this. On the question of costs and benefits, I think it is important to point out that Posner does not deal with the issue of the social and moral costs of leaving state sponsored discrimination unchallenged.[43] If the question of state sponsorship of same sex unions is simply a matter of determining whether there is a violation of formal equality, then the issue of costs and benefits is incidental. It is because those who address the question do not simply view it as a matter of formal equality that these other issues—such as costs and benefits—continue to be raised.

Posner has not presented sufficient argument for the claim that homosexual marriages should not be given the stamp of approval. Posner himself admits that his arguments are inconclusive.[44] All Posner has succeeded in showing is that removing the bar on same sex marriage has somewhat different implications than decriminalizing (homosexual) sodomy. He has not succeeded in showing that there is anything actually wrong with same sex marriage that does not amount to either rejection of homosexuality or the illiberal claims about the threat to the sanctity of marriage.

IV

I am not making any claim of the sort that gays, lesbians, or bisexuals should want to get married in order to mimic opposite sex coupling.[45] I am only claiming that the benefits of state sanctioned civil marriage—from expression of commitment to employee benefits and tax breaks—should be available to any self-defined couple, whether same sex or opposite sex. Same sex marriages can facilitate the provision of "spousal" benefits and establish the basis for same sex couple adoptions. The status of marriage thus provides more opportunities for people, and liberals should endorse that, if nothing else, about same sex state sanctioned union. Opposite sex couples can choose to marry or to remain in common law relationships or to register as domestic partnerships. Why shouldn't same sex couples have those same choices? Opposite sex couples can have the "benefits" of pursuing extra-marital affairs (given that some people find a certain pleasure in transgressing the bounds of marriage). Opposite sex couples can have the "benefits" of legal provisions concerning division of property and family assets upon marriage breakdown. Why shouldn't same sex couples have these same options? As an issue of equality and fairness, liberals should insist that the same range of coupling options and their attendant benefits be available to same sex couples as are available to opposite sex couples.

There are larger questions, of course, of why people should and do identify themselves as "couples," and of why the state should provide legal, political, and social benefits upon that identification. Those questions are not relevant to the specific claim that if the state does provide these benefits and if coupling is self-defining, then same sex coupling should not be deprived the state sanction accorded to opposite sex coupling. The larger questions aside, it is a matter of social justice and equality and non-discrimination that same sex couples should have access to, and be entitled to, equivalent benefits and privileges as opposite sex couples.

READING ENDNOTES

I would like to thank Allan Greenbaum for detailed comments and suggestions on the paper, and Andrea Austen for encouragement.

1. Chris Bull, "Till Death Do Us Part," p. 41. As Bull and others point out gays and lesbians are "openly marrying, raising children, and demanding official recognition of their partners as spouses." Bull says that same sex marriage is the "new hot issue in the nation's [the United States] gay and lesbian community." See Michelangelo Signorile's article, "Bridal Wave," for an account of how the issue is developing in Hawaii, which may end up being the first United States state to legally recognize homosexual marriages.
2. Gays and lesbians have been participating in commitment ceremonies (also called bonding or union ceremonies) for some time, but these of course do not have the "stamp of approval" nor the legal consequences of state sponsored marriage. In Canada, several challenges to the exclusion of same sex couples from legal provisions concerning "spouses" are working their way through the courts. These challenges are typically based on equality claims involving Section 15 of the Canadian Charter of Rights and Freedoms. See Bruce Ryder's, "Equality Rights and Sexual Orientation: Confronting Heterosexual Family Privilege," for more on the specifics of the Canadian context.
3. As per common usage, I will assume that gay refers to gay men and lesbian refers to gay women. Some people take the term "queer" to refer to gay men, lesbian women, bisexual women, bisexual men, transsexuals, and transvestites collectively.
4. This is the gist of what then Prime Minister Pierre Elliot Trudeau said when recommending the decriminalization of any sexual activity between consenting adults in private. This claim is a prior assumption to my version of a functional definition of marriage.

5. Clearly, I am developing my formulation of liberalism and its basic assumptions and commitments in reliance upon certain exponents of the liberal tradition—namely John Stuart Mill in *On Liberty*, Ronald Dworkin in "Liberalism," from Hampshire, ed., *Public and Private Morality*, and Joel Feinberg in *Harmless Wrongdoing*. There is a vast literature on liberalism, but interestingly very little of that literature that I am aware of actually addresses the question of a liberal position on the state sponsorship of same sex marriages.

6. These are the usual conditions for marriage—there will likely be some variation among jurisdictions. Nitya Duclos, in "Some Complicating Thoughts on Same Sex Marriage," says the common bars to marriage include: "minimum age limits, insanity, absence of consent (mistake, duress, and fraud), prohibited degrees of affinity and consanguinity, and a prior existing marriage." Duclos, p. 44, fn. 48.

7. Nan Hunter, in "Marriage, Law and Gender: A Feminist Inquiry," points out that the functionalist approach—which posits the identification of objective criteria to determine which relationships are the functional equivalents to marriage—underlay the recognition of common law marriage. See Hunter, p. 21 ff.

8. The San Francisco Domestic Partnership law states, "[d]omestic partners are two adults who have chosen to share one another's lives in an intimate and committed relationship of mutual caring, who live together, and who have agreed to be jointly responsible for basic living expenses incurred during the Domestic Partnership." See Appendix A: San Francisco Domestic Partnership Ordinance (1990) in David Chambers' article, "Tales of Two Cities...," p. 204. The New York Court of Appeals found in *Braschi v. Stahl Associates* that a gay couple must be treated as a family in relation to New York's rent control law. The Court found that the couple satisfied the following criteria: "the exclusivity and longevity of the relationship, the level of emotional and financial commitment, the manner in which the parties have conducted their everyday lives and held themselves out to society, and the reliance placed upon one another for daily family services." Chambers provides an extended discussion of that case from p. 192 ff. See Hunter, *supra*, p. 23.

9. I should point out that the support is often a qualified support for a series of complicated reasons. I will touch briefly on some of those reasons in the section concerning the Harm to Homosexuality objection to same sex marriages below, but it will not be possible for me to do justice in this paper to the fascinating complexity of the debates over same sex marriage in the lesbian, gay, and bisexual community. For some sense of what the issues are see the papers by Nitya Duclos, Mary Dunlap, and Nan Hunter in the Symposium on Lesbian and Gay Marriage in *Law and Sexuality: A Review of Lesbian and Gay Legal Issues*, Volume 1, Summer 1991 and see the papers by Thomas Stoddard and Paula Ettelbrick in *Lesbian and Gay Marriage*, edited by Suzanne Sherman. See also Chris Bull, "Till Death Do Us Part" and Michelangelo Signorile, "Bridal Wave."

10. Laws in several states in the United States which criminalize sodomy do not distinguish between heterosexual and homosexual sodomy. Yet, in *Bowers vs. Hardwick* the Georgia law was challenged by a homosexual man and the court dealt with the issue as if the law were intended to outlaw homosexual sodomy. In Canada, the federal criminal code was amended in May 1969 to remove the criminalization of any sexual acts between consenting adults.

11. Harlon Dalton, "Reflections on the Lesbian and Gay Marriage Debate," p. 7.

12. This general conception covers both narrower and broader conceptions of the Harm Principle. See Lyons, "Liberty and Harm to Others," for a discussion of the debate over how narrowly or broadly Mill's principle—which he calls the Principle of Liberty—should be construed. Brown argues that the principle should cover only harm producing conduct and Lyons argues that the principle should be expanded to include harm preventing conduct, which may not itself be harm producing—for example, good Samaritan behavior and joint cooperation behavior. My conception differs from that of both of these versions in that I focus on the justification of the denial of state benefits rather than the justification of the interference with liberty.

13. Andrew Sullivan, in "Here Comes the Groom: A (Conservative) Case for Gay Marriage," p. 20. Catharine MacKinnon points out that "persons secure in their heterosexuality would not be threatened by the availability of this option," i.e., gay marriage. MacKinnon, p. 27.

14. Michael Levin, in "Why Homosexuality is Abnormal," for example, attempts to provide a teleo-logical account of the harm that homosexuality presents. If his argument were persuasive, then paternalism would seem to follow. Michael Ruse's discussion of the claim that homosexuality is unnatural in, "Is Homosexuality Bad Sexuality?" tends to undercut Levin's claims.

15. It would be inaccurate and inappropriate to speak of "the" gay, lesbian, and bisexual community; but it would be equally inaccurate and inappropriate to speak of "the" gay, "the" lesbian, or "the" bisexual community. There are communities, and communities within communities. It might be possible to speak of a community of communities, but even that might be misleading. One can get a sense of the remarkable range of conceptions of equality for gays, lesbians, and bisexuals and of the range of recommended strategies from reading Paul Berman's essay, "Democracy and Homosexuality," in *The New Republic*, and from the following books (two of which Berman reviews); Bruce Bawer, *A Place at the Table: The Gay Individual in American Society*; Mark Blasuis, *A Politics of Sexuality: The Emergence of a Lesbian and Bay Ethos*; Diana Fuss, *Essentially Speaking: Feminism, Nature and Difference*; Marshall Kirk and Hunter Madsen, *After the Ball: How America Will Conquer Its Fear and Hatred of Gays in the 1990s*; Shane Phelan, *Identity Politics: Lesbian Feminism and the Limits of Community*; Michelangelo Signorile's *Queer in America: Sex, the Media and the Closets of Power*. There are many more references that could be given, but this list is sufficient to cover the range from separatist liberation perspectives to conservative assimila-tionist perspectives. Chris Bull's article in the *Advocate*, "Till Death Do Us Part," and Michelangelo Signorile's article in *Out*, "Bridal Wave," give some indication of the range of posi-tions on same sex marriage among gays and lesbians.

16. See David Chambers, "Tales of Two Cities: AIDS and the Legal Recognition of Domestic Partnerships in San Francisco and New York." Domestic Partnership ordinances have been enacted by municipali-ties in various United States cities. The domestic partnership arrangements usually contain a require-ment that same sex couples register as partners—"two people who have chosen to share one another's lives in an intimate and committed relationship of mutual caring." Chambers, p. 185. The other fea-ture of the arrangements is the provision by public and private employers that those couples who have registered will be entitled to the benefits provided to "spouses." Domestic Partnership regimes in the United States have usually been open to both homosexual and heterosexual unmarried couples. See Dunlap, p. 94, and Posner, pp. 313–314, on the arrangements in Denmark and Sweden.

17. Many of the discussions of the issue by gay and lesbian activists focus on this aspect. For example, Michael Lowenthal, in "Wedding Bells and Whistles," says that "[w]inning domestic-partnership privileges won't lead to acceptance for all lesbians and gay men, only for those in domestic part-nerships." He than goes on to say: "[r]ather than lobbying for policies that will benefit only those who choose to register domestic partnerships, we should be fighting for the fundamental civil rights that will guarantee equal treatment for us all." See Lowenthal, p. 5.

18. Suzanne Sherman points to the divided opinion on the topic among the interviewees for her book, *Lesbian and Gay Marriage: Private Commitments, Public Ceremonies*. See p. 8.

19. Nitya Duclos, "Some Complicating Thoughts on Same Sex Marriage," p. 31. Paula Ettelbrick, one of those most strongly opposed to same sex marriages admits that: "[w]hen analyzed from a standpoint of civil rights, certainly lesbians and gay men should have a right to marry." Ettelbrick, "Since When Is Marriage a Path to Liberation?," p. 21.

20. Michael Lowenthal says, in "Wedding Bells and Whistles," that he was part of efforts to obtain legal recognition of domestic partnerships but came to realize that the administration of the col-lege where he worked "would accept us only to the degree that we conformed to straight stan-dards." Lowenthal, p. 5.

21. The objection is framed this way by Mary Dunlap in "The Lesbian and Gay Marriage Debate: A Microcosm of Our Hopes and Troubles in the Nineties," p. 78, and Nan Hunter in "Marriage, Law and Gender ...," p.12. Dunlap asks, "If Outlaws Can Have in-Laws Then Won't Those Without In-Laws Become Outer Outlaws?" Nitya Duclos discusses the issue several times in "Some Complicating Thoughts on Same Sex Marriage." Paula Ettelbrick says, "gay marriage, instead of liberating gay sex and sexuality, would further outlaw all gay and lesbian sex that is not performed in a marital context." See Ettelbrick, "Since When Is Marriage a Path to Liberation?," p. 23.

22. This is a reconstruction of the various positions presented in the papers by Hunter, Duclos, and Ettelbrick.

23. Homophobia has become a common term for the unjust denial of civil rights to homosexuals, as well as to the irrational fear and hatred of homosexuals and homosexuality. The term was initially used in psychiatric literature to refer to the "phobia" that one might be a homosexual oneself. The term has taken on a broader meaning, one which functions in many respects analogously to sexism, racism, ableism, and classism. The term heterosexism is often used in the same contexts as homophobia.

24. Nan Hunter, supra, p.11.

25. Harlon Dalton, "Reflections on the Lesbian and Gay Marriage Debate," p. 5. As Dalton points out, "legal rights would never be extended if the bare fact that a subset of the class might thereby be disadvantaged were deemed to constitute a sufficient ground for inaction." He goes on to say that it is still problematic to pursue policies which will have the unintended effects of favoring some class members over others.

26. While this conflict is most readily treated as a conflict between individual and collective interests, it can also be conceived as a conflict between different collective interests and thus competing versions of collective rights—the interests of assimilationists and the interests of anti-assimilationists respectively. C.f. Leslie Green, "Two Views of Collective Rights," p. 325.

27. Hunter, supra, p.11. Hunter identifies two arguments that opponents to same sex marriage within lesbian, gay, and bisexual communities have relied on: the one about assimilation and stigmatization and the other one about the oppressiveness of marriage. Duclos and Dunlap also provide extensive discussion of the claim concerning marriage.

28. See Duclos, Dunlap, and Hunter for extensive discussions of marriage as a patriarchal institution. Duclos points out that the provision of same sex marriage may serve to legitimate marriage, which would have bad consequences for heterosexually identified women. It is of course the legitimation of marriage that would have the bad consequences.

29. Dunlap. p. 86, reproduces the following list of rights enjoyed by persons who marry: the right to obtain health insurance, bereavement leave, and make decisions when the partner is incapacitated; the right to visit the partner in hospitals, jails, mental institutions, and other places restricted to family members; the right to claim dependency deductions and statuses; the right to claim estate and gift tax benefits; the right to file joint tax returns; the right of inheritance (particularly in case of intestacy); the right to sue for infliction of emotional distress by injury to the partner, for loss of consortium, wrongful death and other personal injuries; the right to claim marital communication privilege; the right to live in housing for married persons; and more. See Duclos, pp. 52–53, for a more extensive list. Duclos also sets out a list of burdens the marriage brings, which includes the following: "spouse in the house" rules for state welfare assistance; "spouse's" credit history taken into account in credit rating; disentitlement from government student loans on the basis of "spouse's" income; anti-nepotism rules in employment, and more. See Duclos, pp. 53–54 for the complete list.

30. Thomas Stoddard makes this point in "Why Gay People Should Seek the Right to Marry," p. 18.

31. Nan Hunter, p. 13. See also Dunlap and Duclos for similar arguments.

32. Hunter, supra, p.16. As Catharine MacKinnon puts it in "Not By Law Alone," from *Feminism Unmodified: Discourses on Life and Law:* "I do think it might do something amazing to the entire institution of marriage to recognize the unity of "two" persons between whom no superiority or inferiority could be presumed on the basis of gender." MacKinnon, p. 27.

33. Thomas Stoddard, "Why Gay People Should Seek the Right to Marry," p.17.

34. See Dunlap for an extensive discussion of the harmful effects of the *Bowers v. Hardwick* decision and other homophobic state measures.

35. Duclos, p. 42.

36. Nan Hunter suggests that more encompassing changes be based on "gender dissent," which she says does not connote identity based on sexual orientation but rather conveys an active intent to disconnect power from gender and conveys an adversary relationship to dominance. Hunter, pp. 29–30. She argues that the pursuit of domestic partnership laws should complement the pursuit

of legalizing lesbian and gay marriage, and that "neither strategy is complete without the other." Hunter, p. 26. For more, on domestic partnership agreements, see David Chambers, "Tales of Two Cities...."

37. It is interesting, and disconcerting, to note that the Danish government which provided the right to marry for same sex couples by an act of Parliament still restricted the right of lesbian and gay couples to adopt children. There would be no rationale for the continuing restriction on a liberal treatment of the issue such as I have been developing. See Dunlap, p. 94.

38. Posner is echoing the wording of the United States Supreme Court decision in *Griswold v. Connecticut.* The court said that marriage is "an association for as noble a purpose as any involved in our prior decisions." See *Sexual Orientation and the Law* by the Editors of the *Harvard Law Review*, pp. 95 ff. for further discussion.

39. Posner, pp. 311–312.

40. Posner, p. 312.

41. Posner, p. 312.

42. In fact it is difficult to understand why Posner even brings the point up, since it is inconclusive and the things he says, on his own admission, seem to represent a "trivial addendum." See Posner, p. 312. It seems as if he needed to find a way to bring in some economic concept, since the context of his discussion is his use of a "law and economics" approach.

43. Harlan Dalton raises this point. Dalton articulates five questions on the issue of lesbian and gay marriage as follows: (1) Can the state legitimately deny lesbian and gay couples the right to marry? (2) Were such a right to exist, would lesbians and gay men gain or lose? (3) Can anyone, gay or straight, who enters into the institution of marriage avoid its misogynist and proprietary taint? (4) What impact does the struggle to make lesbian and gay marriage an option have on the politics of lesbian and gay liberation? (5) What would be the effect of a successful struggle to legalize lesbian and gay marriage on the institution of marriage itself? Dalton, p. 3. I would argue that it is really only the first question which raises specifically philosophical issues, and thus it is that question which has been the focus of the present paper. The other questions are important questions, but they really concern matters of political strategy and political sociology. It should be clear from the discussion in this paper that it is necessary to address issues that arise as a result of asking the other questions, but it is not necessary to be able to provide definitive answers to those other questions to be able to provide an answer to the first question.

44. Posner, p. 313.

45. Nitya Duclos says: "[g]iven that a same-sex marriage bar is a bad thing for the state to impose, lesbians and gay men still need to ask whether marriage is a good thing for them to seek." Duclos p. 42. Her article raises many significant issues for lesbians and gay men to consider about the desirability of marriage.

QUESTIONS

1. What does it mean to say that the state should be neutral between conceptions of the good life and conceptions of human nature?

2. What does Wellington mean when she says heterosexuality is "contingent"?

3. Why must a liberal society adopt only a secular and not a religious conception of marriage?

4. Why does a liberal society adopt a functional definition of common law marriage? What could the alternative be?

5. Why must a liberal society not include the intention to procreate as part of its conception of marriage?

6. To apply the harm principle to cover denials of benefits (rather than the direct imposition of harms or restrictions of liberty) requires reformulating the principle. What is Wellington's reformulation?

7. Why is denying a state benefit in a way that denies formal equality always a harm to people who are denied the benefit?

8. Critics of same sex marriage often base their opposition to it on claims that it will harm heterosexual institutions and practices. Wellington refers to these harms as the Harm to Heterosexuality claim. What harms are covered by this claim?

9. What harms could be done to marriage, families or societies by granting state sanction to same sex coupling? Can any claims of harm be made out that do not rest ultimately upon homophobia and the belief that homosexuality is immoral or unnatural?

10. What is "symbolic harm"? Why are symbolic harms almost impossible to separate from conceptions of the good life and substantive values and commitments?

11. Why must a liberal reject mere offence as the kind of harm that the harm principle allows us to restrict liberty to prevent? If mere offence was allowed to count as harm, would there be any room left for the liberty of the individual at all?

12. People who develop arguments against same sex marriage on the grounds of Harm to Homosexuality object to seeking state sponsorship of same sex coupling or to marriage itself. What reasons do people give from within the gay liberation movement itself to seeking state recognition of same sex marriage?

13. Assume that some religious persons really do suffer extreme psychological harm at the thought of same sex marriage (believing, for example, that those who participate in or support such practices will be eternally damned). Do we not then face a conflict of harms: if we allow same sex marriage we harm the religious, but if we ban same sex marriage we harm same sex couples wishing to marry? Isn't it question-begging to decide in principle against the religious in this case?

14. In Canada, given recent court decisions, changing the status quo will harm same sex couples who wish to marry. In the United States, changing the status quo will harm the religious. Does this lead to different conclusions, for the libertarian, about what is morally required or permitted in the two countries?

15. Given the other harms that marriage may do, why isn't Wellington's conclusion that the state should not recognize any marriages at all?

16. Do the arguments here in favour of same sex marriage extend to other forms of marriage that are currently unrecognized, such as polygamy?

✦ ✦ ✦

Judith Jarvis Thomson, A Defense of Abortion

Judith Jarvis Thomson's famous article gives a strong libertarian defence for the permissibility of abortion while taking seriously a fetus's right to life. She takes it that the pro-life argument is: in the case in question a person's right to life (the fetus) is in conflict with a person's right to decide (the mother) how her body is made use of. The right to life outweighs the right to bodily integrity, and so abortion is not permissible. Granting that the fetus is a person, she nevertheless denies that it follows that this person's right to life outweighs a mother's right to choose.

Making excellent use of thought experiments, Thomson presents us with the case of the famous violinist. Imagine that you awake one morning, and find that you have been kidnapped and attached to a violinist, to whom you need to remain attached to in order that this violinist might live. It would be nice if you stayed attached, suggests Thomson, but are you morally required to remain attached? She thinks not. The point is that your right to bodily integrity precludes anyone's claims to it. It might be thought that this argument does not apply to cases of pregnancy due to voluntary sexual activity (rape being analogous to kidnapping), but Thomson argues that this does not square with our basic judgements regarding responsibility. Pregnancy is a foreseeable result of sexual activity, but a burglary is a foreseeable result of leaving your window open on a hot night, and we do not think that the burglar is therefore entitled to any goods purloined under such conditions.

Thomson's article has two primary strengths: a compelling use of thought experiments to show the implications of our judgements and force us to re-think them, and her granting much of her opponent's position while arguing for an opposed conclusion. Granting all premises inessential to the conclusion being argued for brings clearly to light the crux of the matter. Arguing over inessential details bogs down critical reasoning. Granting an opponent premises for the sake of argument need not imply a belief in the premises, or imply that you are not sharp enough to recognize all of the problematic assertions your opponent makes, but instead implies an ability to think clearly about the issue at hand, and recognize which claims are central to that issue.

✦ ✦ ✦

A Defense of Abortion[1]

JUDITH JARVIS THOMPSON

Most opposition to abortion relies on the premise that the fetus is a human being, a person, from the moment of conception. The premise is argued for, but, as I think, not well. Take, for example, the most common argument. We are asked to notice that the development of a human being from conception through birth into childhood is continuous; then it is said that to draw a line, to choose a point in this development and say "before this point the thing is not a person, after this point it is a person" is to make an arbitrary choice, a choice for which in the nature of things no good reason can be given. It is concluded that the fetus is, or anyway that we had better say it is, a person from the moment of conception. But this conclusion does not follow. Similar things might be said about the development of an acorn into an oak tree, and it does not follow that acorns are oak trees, or that we had better say they are. Arguments of this form are sometimes called "slippery slope arguments"—the phrase is perhaps self-explanatory—and it is dismaying that opponents of abortion rely on them so heavily and uncritically.

I am inclined to agree, however, that the prospects for "drawing a line" in the development of the fetus look dim. I am inclined to think also that we shall probably have to agree that the fetus has already become a human person well before birth. Indeed, it comes as a surprise when one first learns how early in its life it begins to acquire human characteristics. By the tenth week, for example, it already has a face, arms and legs, fingers and toes; it has internal organs, and brain activity is detectable.[2] On the other hand, I think that the premise is false, that the fetus is not a person from the moment of conception. A newly fertilized ovum, a newly implanted clump of cells, is no more a person than an acorn is an oak tree. But I shall not discuss any of this. For it seems to me to be of great interest to ask what happens if, for the sake of argument, we allow the premise. How, precisely, are we supposed to get from there to the conclusion that abortion is morally impermissible? Opponents of abortion commonly spend most of their time establishing that the fetus is a person, and hardly any time explaining the step from there to the impermissibility of abortion. Perhaps they think the step too simple and obvious to require much comment. Or perhaps instead they are simply being economical in argument. Many of those who defend abortion rely on the premise that a fetus is not a person, but only a bit of tissue that will become a person at birth; and why pay out more arguments than you have to? Whatever the explanation, I suggest that the step they take is neither easy nor obvious, that it calls for closer examination than it is commonly given, and that when we do give it this closer examination we shall feel inclined to reject it.

I propose, then, that we grant that the fetus is a person from the moment of conception. How does the argument go from here? Something like this, I take it. Every person has a right to life. So the fetus has a right to life. No doubt the mother has a right to decide what shall happen in and to her body; everyone would grant that. But surely a person's right to life is stronger and more stringent than the mother's right to decide what happens in and to her body, and so outweighs it. So the fetus may not be killed; an abortion may not be performed.

It sounds plausible. But now let me ask you to imagine this. You wake up in the morning and find yourself back to back in bed with an unconscious violinist. A famous unconscious violinist. He has been found to have a fatal kidney ailment, and the Society of Music Lovers has canvassed all the available medical records and found that you alone have the right blood type to help. They have therefore kidnapped you, and last night the violinist's circulatory system was plugged into yours, so that your kidneys can be used to extract poisons from his blood as well as your own. The director of the hospital now tells you, "Look, we're sorry the Society of Music Lovers did this to you—we would never have permitted it if we had known. But still, they did it, and the violinist now is plugged into you. To unplug you would be to kill him. But never mind, it's only for nine months. By then he will have recovered from his ailment, and can safely be unplugged from you." Is it morally incumbent on you to accede to this situation? No doubt it would be very nice of you if you did, a great kindness. But do you *have* to accede to it? What if it were not nine months, but nine years? Or longer still? What if the director of the hospital says, "Tough luck, I agree, but you've now got to stay in bed, with the violinist plugged into you, for the rest of your life. Because remember this. All persons have a right to life, and violinists are persons. Granted you have a right to decide what happens in and to your body, but a person's right to life outweighs your right to decide what happens in and to your body. So you cannot ever be unplugged from him." I imagine you would regard this as outrageous, which suggests that something really is wrong with that plausible-sounding argument I mentioned a moment ago.

In this case, of course, you were kidnapped; you didn't volunteer for the operation that plugged the violinist into your kidneys. Can those who oppose abortion on the ground I mentioned make an exception for a pregnancy due to rape? Certainly. They can say that persons have a right to life only if they didn't come into existence because of rape; or they can say that all persons have a right to life, but that some have less of a right to life than others, in particular, that those who came into existence because of rape have less. But these statements have a rather unpleasant sound. Surely the question of whether you have a right to life at all, or how much of it you have, shouldn't turn on the question of whether or not you are the product of a rape. And in fact the people who oppose abortion on the ground I mentioned do not make this distinction, and hence do not make an exception in case of rape.

Nor do they make an exception for a case in which the mother has to spend the nine months of her pregnancy in bed. They would agree that would be a great pity, and hard on the mother; but all the same, all persons have a right to life, the fetus is a person, and so on. I suspect, in fact, that they would not make an exception for a case in which, miraculously enough, the pregnancy went on for nine years or even the rest of the mother's life.

Some won't make an exception for a case in which continuation of the pregnancy is likely to shorten the mother's life; they regard abortion as impermissible even to save the mother's life. Such cases are nowadays very rare, and many opponents of abortion do not accept this extreme view. All the same, it is a good place to begin: a number of points of interest come out in respect to it.

1. Let us call the view that abortion is impermissible even to save the mother's life "the extreme view." I want to suggest first that it does not issue from the argument I mentioned earlier without the addition of some fairly powerful premises. Suppose a woman has become pregnant, and now learns that she has a cardiac condition such that she will die if she carries the baby to term. What may be done for her? The fetus, being a person, has a right to life, but as the mother is a person too, so has she a right to life. Presumably they have an equal right to life. How is it supposed to come out that an abortion may not be performed? If mother and child have an equal right to life, shouldn't we perhaps flip a coin? Or should we add to the mother's right to life her right to decide what happens in and to her body, which everybody seems to be ready to grant—the sum of her rights now outweighing the fetus' right to life?

The most familiar argument here is the following. We are told that performing the abortion would be directly killing[3] the child, whereas doing nothing would not be killing the mother, but only letting her die. Moreover, in killing the child, one would be killing an innocent person, for the child has committed no crime, and is not aiming at his mother's death. And then there are a variety of ways in which this might be continued. (1) But as directly killing an innocent person is always and absolutely impermissible, an abortion may not be performed. Or, (2) as directly killing an innocent person is murder, and murder is always and absolutely impermissible, an abortion may not be performed.[4] Or, (3) as one's duty to refrain from directly killing an innocent person is more stringent than one's duty to keep a person from dying, an abortion may not be performed. Or, (4) if one's only options are directly killing an innocent person or letting a person die, one must prefer letting the person die, and thus an abortion may not be performed.[5]

Some people seem to have thought that these are not further premises which must be added if the conclusion is to be reached, but that they follow from the very fact that an innocent person has a right to life.[6] But this seems to me to be a mistake, and perhaps the simplest way to show this is to bring out that while we must certainly grant that innocent persons have a right to life, the theses in (1) through (4) are all false. Take (2), for example. If directly killing an innocent person inside her is murder, and thus impermissible, then the mother's directly killing the innocent person inside her is murder, and thus is impermissible. But it cannot seriously be thought to be murder if the mother performs an abortion on herself to save her life. It cannot seriously be said that she *must* refrain, that she *must* sit passively by and wait for her death. Let us look again at the case of you and the violinist. There you are, in bed with the violinist, and the director of the hospital says to you, "It's all most distressing, and I deeply sympathize, but you see this is putting an additional strain on your kidneys, and you'll be dead within the month. But you have to stay where you are all the same. Because unplugging you would be directly killing an innocent violinist, and that's murder, and that's impermissible." If anything in the world is true, it is that you do not commit murder, you do not do what is impermissible, if you reach around to your back and unplug yourself from that violinist to save your life.

The main focus of attention in writings on abortion has been on what a third party may or may not do in answer to a request from a woman for an abortion. This is in a way understandable. Things being as they are, there isn't much a woman can safely do to abort herself. So the question asked is what a third party may do, and what the mother may do, if it is mentioned at all, is deduced, almost as an afterthought, from what it is concluded that third parties may do. But it seems to me that to treat the matter in this way is to refuse to grant to the mother that very status of person which is so firmly insisted on for the fetus. For we cannot simply read off what a person may do from what a third party may do. Suppose you find yourself trapped in a tiny house with a growing child. I mean a very tiny house, and a rapidly growing child—you are already up against the wall of the house and in a few minutes you'll be crushed to death. The child on the other hand won't be crushed to death; if nothing is done to stop him from growing he'll be hurt, but in the end he'll simply burst open the house and walk out a free man. Now I could well understand it if a bystander were to say, "There's nothing we can do for you. We cannot choose between your life and his, we cannot be the ones to decide who is to live, we cannot intervene." But it cannot be concluded that you too can do nothing, that you cannot attack it to save your life. However innocent the child may be, you do not have to wait passively while it crushes you to death. Perhaps a pregnant woman is vaguely felt to have the status of house, to which we don't allow the right of self-defense. But if the woman houses the child, it should be remembered that she is a person who houses it.

I should perhaps stop to say explicitly that I am not claiming that people have a right to do anything whatever to save their lives. I think, rather, that there are drastic limits to the right of self-defense. If someone threatens you with death unless you torture someone else to death, I think you have not the right, even to save your life, to do so. But the case under consideration here is very different. In our case there are only two people involved, one whose life is threatened, and one who threatens it. Both are innocent: the one who is threatened is not threatened because of any fault, the one who threatens does not threaten because of any fault. For this reason we may feel that we bystanders cannot intervene. But the person threatened can.

In sum, a woman surely can defend her life against the threat to it posed by the unborn child, even if doing so involves its death. And this shows not merely that the theses in (1) through (4) are false; it shows also that the extreme view of abortion is false, and so we need not canvass any other possible ways of arriving at it from the argument I mentioned at the outset.

2. The extreme view could of course be weakened to say that while abortion is permissible to save the mother's life, it may not be performed by a third party, but only by the mother herself. But this cannot be right either. For what we have to keep in mind is that the mother and the unborn child are not like two tenants in a small house which has, by an unfortunate mistake, been rented to both: the mother *owns* the house. The fact that she does adds to the offensiveness of deducing that the mother can do nothing from the supposition that third parties can do nothing. But it does more than this: it casts a bright light on the supposition that third parties can do nothing. Certainly it lets us see that a third party who says "I cannot choose between you" is fooling himself if he thinks this is impartiality. If Jones has found and fastened on a certain coat, which he needs to keep him from freezing, but which Smith also needs to keep him from freezing, then it is not impartiality that says "I cannot choose between you" when Smith owns the coat. Women have said again and again "This body is *my* body!" and they have reason to feel angry, reason to feel that it has been like shouting into the wind. Smith, after all, is hardly likely to bless us if we say to him, "Of course it's your coat, anybody would grant that it is. But no one may choose between you and Jones who is to have it."

We should really ask what it is that says "no one may choose" in the face of the fact that the body that houses the child is the mother's body. It may be simply a failure to appreciate this fact. But it may be something more interesting, namely the sense that one has a right to refuse to lay hands on people, even where it would be just and fair to do so, even where justice seems to require that somebody do so. Thus justice might call for somebody to get Smith's coat back from Jones, and yet you have the right to refuse to be the one to lay hands on Jones, a right to refuse to do physical violence to him. This, I think, must be granted. But then what should be said is not "no one may choose," but only "*I* cannot choose," and indeed not even this, but "*I* will not act," leaving it open that somebody else can or should, and in particular, that anyone in a position of authority, with the job of securing people's rights, both can and should. So this is no difficulty. I have not been arguing that any given third party must accede to the mother's request that he perform an abortion to save her life, but only that he may.

I suppose that in some views of human life the mother's body is only on loan to her, the loan not being one which gives her any prior claim to it. One who held this view might well think it impartiality to say "I cannot choose." But I shall simply ignore this possibility. My own view is that if a human being has any just, prior claim to anything at all, he has a just, prior claim to his own body. And perhaps this needn't be argued for here anyway, since, as I mentioned, the arguments against abortion we are looking at do grant that the woman has a right to decide what happens in and to her body.

But although they do grant it, I have tried to show that they do not take seriously what is done in granting it. I suggest the same thing will reappear even more clearly when we turn away from cases in which the mother's life is at stake, and attend, as I propose we now do, to the vastly more common cases in which a woman wants an abortion for some less weighty reason than preserving her own life.

3. Where the mother's life is not at stake, the argument I mentioned at the outset seems to have a much stronger pull. "Everyone has a right to life, so the unborn person has a right to life." And isn't the child's right to life weightier than anything other than the mother's own right to life, which she might put forward as ground for an abortion?

This argument treats the right to life as if it were unproblematic. It is not, and this seems to me to be precisely the source of the mistake.

For we should now, at long last, ask what it comes to, to have a right to life. In some views having a right to life includes having a right to be given at least the bare minimum one needs for continued life. But suppose that what in fact *is* the bare minimum a man needs for continued life is something he has no right at all to be given? If I am sick unto death, and the only thing that will save my life is the touch of Henry Fonda's cool hand on my fevered brow, then all the same, I have no right to be given the touch of Henry Fonda's cool hand on my fevered brow. It would be frightfully nice of him to fly in from the West Coast to provide it. It would be less nice, though no doubt well meant, if my friends flew out to the West Coast and carried Henry Fonda back with them. But I have no right at all against anybody that he should do this for me. Or again, to return to the story I told earlier, the fact that for continued life that violinist needs the continued use of your kidneys does not establish that he has a right to be given continued use of your kidneys. He certainly has no right against you that *you* should give him continued use of your kidneys. For nobody has any right to use your kidneys unless you give him such a right; and nobody has the right against you that you shall give him this right—if you do allow him to go on using your kidneys, this is a kindness on your part, and not something he can claim from you as his due. Nor has he any right against anybody else that *they* should give him continued use of your kidneys. Certainly he had no right against the Society of Music Lovers that they should plug him into you in the first place. And if you now start to unplug yourself, having learned that you will otherwise have to spend nine years in bed with him, there is nobody in the world who must try to prevent you, in order to see to it that he is given something he has a right to be given.

Some people are rather stricter about the right to life. In their view, it does not include the right to be given anything, but amounts to, and only to, the right not to be killed by anybody. But here a related difficulty arises. If everybody is to refrain from killing that violinist, then everybody must refrain from doing a great many different sorts of things. Everybody must refrain from slitting his throat, everybody must refrain from shooting him—and everybody must refrain from unplugging you from him. But does he have a right against everybody that they shall refrain from unplugging you from him? To refrain from doing this is to allow him to continue to use your kidneys. It could be argued that he has a right against us that *we* should allow him to continue to use your kidneys. That is, while he had no right against us that we should give him the use of your kidneys, it might be argued that he anyway has a right against us that we shall not now intervene and deprive him of the use of your kidneys. I shall come back to third-party interventions later. But certainly the violinist has no right against you that *you* shall allow him to continue to use your kidneys. As I said, if you do allow him to use them, it is a kindness on your part, and not something you owe him.

The difficulty I point to here is not peculiar to the right to life. It reappears in connection with all the other natural rights; and it is something which an adequate account of rights must deal with. For present purposes it is enough just to draw attention to it. But I would stress that I am not arguing that people do not have a right to life—quite the contrary, it seems to me that the primary control we must place on the acceptability of an account of rights is that it should turn out in that account to be a truth that all persons have a right to life. I am arguing only that having a right to life does not guarantee having either a right to be given the use of or a right to be allowed continued use of another person's body—even if one needs it for life itself. So the right to life will not serve the opponents of abortion in the very simple and clear way in which they seem to have thought it would.

4. There is another way to bring out the difficulty. In the most ordinary sort of case, to deprive someone of what he has a right to is to treat him unjustly. Suppose a boy and his small brother are jointly given a box of chocolates for Christmas. If the older boy takes the box and refuses to give his brother any of the chocolates, he is unjust to him, for the brother has been given a right to half of them. But suppose that, having learned that otherwise it means nine years in bed with that violinist, you unplug yourself from him. You surely are not being unjust to him, for you gave him no right to use your kidneys, and no one else can have given him any such right. But we have to notice that in unplugging yourself, you are killing him; and violinists, like everybody else, have a right to life, and thus in the view we were considering just now, the right not to be killed. So here you do what he supposedly has a right you shall not do, but you do not act unjustly to him in doing it.

The emendation which may be made at this point is this: the right to life consists not in the right not to be killed, but rather in the right not to be killed unjustly. This runs a risk of circularity, but never mind: it would enable us to square the fact that the violinist has a right to life with the fact that you do not act unjustly toward him in unplugging yourself, thereby killing him. For if you do not kill him unjustly, you do not violate his right to life, and so it is no wonder you do him no injustice.

But if this emendation is accepted, the gap in the argument against abortion stares us plainly in the face: it is by no means enough to show that the fetus is a person, and to remind us that all persons have a right to life—we need to be shown also that killing the fetus violates its right to life, i.e., that abortion is unjust killing. And is it?

I suppose we may take it as a datum that in a case of pregnancy due to rape the mother has not given the unborn person a right to the use of her body for food and shelter. Indeed, in what pregnancy could it be supposed that the mother has given the unborn person such a right? It is not as if there were unborn persons drifting about the world, to whom a woman who wants a child says, "I invite you in."

But it might be argued that there are other ways one can have acquired a right to the use of another person's body than by having been invited to use it by that person. Suppose a woman voluntarily indulges in intercourse, knowing of the chance it will issue in pregnancy, and then she does become pregnant; is she not in part responsible for the presence, in fact the very existence, of the unborn person inside her? No doubt she did not invite it in. But doesn't her partial responsibility for its being there itself give it a right to the use of her body[7]. If so, then her aborting it would be more like the boy's taking away the chocolates, and less like your unplugging yourself from the violinist—doing so would be depriving it of what it does have a right to, and thus would be doing it an injustice.

And then, too, it might be asked whether or not she can kill it even to save her own life: If she voluntarily called it into existence, how can she now kill it, even in self-defense?

The first thing to be said about this is that it is something new. Opponents of abortion have been so concerned to make out the independence of the fetus, in order to establish that it has a right to life, just as its mother does, and they have tended to overlook the possible support they might gain from making out that the fetus is *dependent* on the mother, in order to establish that she has a special kind of responsibility for it, a responsibility that gives it rights against her which are not possessed by any independent person—such as an ailing violinist who is a stranger to her.

On the other hand, this argument would give the unborn person a right to its mother's body only if her pregnancy resulted from a voluntary act, undertaken in full knowledge of the chance a pregnancy might result from it. It would leave out entirely the unborn person whose existence is due to rape. Pending the availability of some further argument, then, we would be left with the conclusion that unborn persons whose existence is due to rape have no right to the use of their mothers' bodies, and thus that aborting them is not depriving them of anything they have a right to and hence is not unjust killing.

And we should also notice that it is not at all plain that this argument really does go even as far as it purports to. For there are cases and cases, and the details make a difference. If the room is stuffy, and I therefore open a window to air it, and a burglar climbs in, it would be absurd to say, "Ah, now he can stay, she's given him a right to the use of her house—for she is partially responsible for his presence there, having voluntarily done what enabled him to get in, in full knowledge that there are such things as burglars, and that burglars burgle." It would be still more absurd to say this if I had had bars installed outside my windows, precisely to prevent burglars from getting in, and a burglar got in only because of a defect in the bars. It remains equally absurd if we imagine it is not a burglar who climbs in, but an innocent person who blunders or falls in. Again, suppose it were like this: people-seeds drift about in the air like pollen, and if you open your windows, one may drift in and take root in your carpets or upholstery. You don't want children, so you fix up your windows with fine mesh screens, the very best you can buy. As can happen, however, and on very, very rare occasions does happen, one of the screens is defective; and a seed drifts in and takes root. Does the person-plant who now develops have the right to the use of your house? Surely not—despite the fact that you voluntarily opened your windows, you knowingly kept carpets and upholstered furniture, and you knew that screens were sometimes defective. Someone may argue that you are responsible for its rooting, that it does have a right to your house, because after all you *could* have lived out your life with bare floors and furniture, or with sealed windows and doors. But this won't do— for by the same token anyone can avoid a pregnancy due to rape by having a hysterectomy, or anyway by never leaving home without a (reliable!) army.

It seems to me that the argument we are looking at can establish at most that there are *some* cases in which the unborn person has a right to the use of its mother's body, and therefore *some* cases in which abortion is unjust killing. There is room for much discussion and argument as to precisely which, if any. But I think we should sidestep this issue and leave it open, for at any rate the argument certainly does not establish that abortion is unjust killing.

5. There is room for yet another argument here, however. We surely must all grant that there may be cases in which it would be morally indecent to detach a person from your body at the cost of his life. Suppose you learn that what the violinist needs is not nine years of your life, but only one hour: all you need to do to save his life is to spend one hour in that bed with him. Suppose also that letting him use your kidneys for that one hour would not affect your health in the slightest. Admittedly you were kidnapped. Admittedly you did not give anyone permission to plug him into you. Nevertheless it seems to me plain you *ought* to allow him to use your kidneys for that hour—it would be indecent to refuse.

Again, suppose pregnancy lasted only an hour, and constituted no threat to life or health. And suppose that a woman becomes pregnant as a result of rape. Admittedly she did not voluntarily do anything to bring about the existence of a child. Admittedly she did nothing at all which would give the unborn person a right to the use of her body. All the same it might well be said, as in the newly emended violinist story, that she *ought* to allow it to remain for that hour—that it would be indecent in her to refuse.

Now some people are inclined to use the term "right" in such a way that it follows from the fact that you ought to allow a person to use your body for the hour he needs, that he has a right to use your body for the hour he needs, even though he has not been given that right by any person or act. They may say that it follows also that if you refuse, you act unjustly toward him. This use of the term is perhaps so common that it cannot be called wrong; nevertheless it seems to me to be an unfortunate loosening of what we would do better to keep a tight rein on. Suppose that box of chocolates I mentioned earlier had not been given to both boys jointly, but was given only to the older boy. There he sits, stolidly eating his way through the box, his small brother watching enviously. Here we are likely to say "You ought not to be so mean. You ought to give your brother some of those chocolates." My own view is that it just does not follow from the truth of this that the brother has any right to any of the chocolates. If the boy refuses to give his brother any, he is greedy, stingy, callous—but not unjust. I suppose that the people I have in mind will say it does follow that the brother has a right to some of the chocolates, and thus that the boy does act unjustly if he refuses to give his brother any. But the effect of saying this is to obscure what we should keep distinct, namely the difference between the boy's refusal in this case and the boy's refusal in the earlier case, in which the box was given to both boys jointly, and in which the small brother thus had what was from any point of view clear title to half.

A further objection to so using the term "right" that from the fact that A ought to do a thing for B, it follows that B has a right against A that A do it for him, is that it is going to make the question of whether or not a man has a right to a thing turn on how easy it is to provide him with it; and this seems not merely unfortunate, but morally unacceptable. Take the case of Henry Fonda again. I said earlier that I had no right to the touch of his cool hand on my fevered brow, even though I needed it to save my life. I said it would be frightfully nice of him to fly in from the West Coast to provide me with it, but that I had no right against him that he should do so. But suppose he isn't on the West Coast. Suppose he has only to walk across the room, place a hand briefly on my brow—and lo, my life is saved. Then surely he ought to do it, it would be indecent to refuse. Is it to be said "Ah, well, it follows that in this case she has a right to the touch of his hand on her brow, and so it would be an injustice in him to refuse"? So that I have a right to when it is easy for him to provide it, though no right when it's hard? It's rather a shocking idea that anyone's rights should fade away and disappear as it gets harder and harder to accord them to him.

So my own view is that even though you ought to let the violinist use your kidneys for the one hour he needs, we should not conclude that he has a right to do so—we should say that if you refuse, you are, like the boy who has all the chocolates and will give none away, self-centered and callous, indecent in fact, but not unjust. And similarly, that even supposing a case in which a woman pregnant due to rape ought to allow the unborn person to use her body for the hour he needs, we should not conclude that he has a right to do so; we should conclude that she is self-centered, callous, indecent, but not unjust, if she refuses. The complaints are no less grave; they are just different. However, there is no need to insist on this point. If anyone does wish to deduce "he has a right" from "you ought," then all the same he must surely grant that there are cases in which it is not morally required of you that you allow that violinist to use your kidneys, and in which he does not have a right to use them, and in which you do not do him an injustice if you refuse. And so also for mother and unborn child. Except in such cases as the unborn person has a right to demand it—and we were leaving open the possibility that there may be such cases—nobody is morally *required* to make large sacrifices, of health, of all other interests and concerns, of all other duties and commitments, for nine years, or even for nine months, in order to keep another person alive.

6. We have in fact to distinguish between two kinds of Samaritan: the Good Samaritan and what we might call the Minimally Decent Samaritan. The story of the Good Samaritan, you will remember, goes like this:

> A certain man went down from Jerusalem to Jericho, and fell among thieves, which stripped him of his raiment, and wounded him, and departed, leaving him half dead.

And by chance there came down a certain priest that way; and when he saw him, he passed by on the other side.

And likewise a Levite, when he was at the place, came and looked on him, and passed by on the other side.

But a certain Samaritan, as he journeyed, came where he was; and when he saw him he had compassion on him.

And went to him, and bound up his wounds, pouring in oil and wine, and set him on his own beast, and brought him to an inn, and took care of him.

And on the morrow, when he departed, he took out two pence, and gave them to the host, and said unto him, "Take care of him; and whatsoever thou spendest more, when I come again, I will repay thee."

(Luke 10:30-35)

The Good Samaritan went out of his way, at some cost to himself, to help one in need of it. We are not told what the options were, that is, whether or not the priest and the Levite could have helped by doing less than the Good Samaritan did, but assuming they could have, then the fact that they did nothing at all shows they were not even Minimally Decent Samaritans, not because they were not Samaritans, but because they were not even minimally decent.

These things are a matter of degree, of course, but there is a difference, and it comes out perhaps most clearly in the story of Kitty Genovese, who, as you will remember, was murdered while thirty-eight people watched or listened, and did nothing at all to help her. A Good Samaritan would have rushed out to give direct assistance against the murderer. Or perhaps we had better allow that it would have been a Splendid Samaritan who did this, on the ground that it would have involved a risk of death for himself. But the thirty-eight not only did not do this, they did not even trouble to pick up a phone to call the police. Minimally Decent Samaritanism would call for doing at least that, and their not having done it was monstrous.

After telling the story of the Good Samaritan, Jesus said "Go, and do thou like-wise." Perhaps he meant that we are morally required to act as the Good Samaritan did. Perhaps he was urging people to do more than is morally required of them. At all events it seems plain that it was not morally required of any of the thirty-eight that he rush out to give direct assistance at the risk of his own life, and that it is not morally required of anyone that he give long stretches of his life—nine years or nine months—to sustaining the life of a person who has no special right (we were leaving open the possibility of this) to demand it.

Indeed, with one rather striking class of exceptions, no one in any country in the world is *legally* required to do anywhere near as much as this for anyone else. The class of exceptions is obvious. My main concern here is not the state of the law in respect to abortion, but it is worth drawing attention to the fact that in no state in this country is any man compelled by law to be even a Minimally Decent Samaritan to any person; there is no law under which charges could be brought against the thirty-eight who stood by while Kitty Genovese died. By contrast, in most states in this country women are compelled by law to be not merely Minimally Decent Samaritans, but

Good Samaritans to unborn persons inside them. This doesn't by itself settle anything one way or the other, because it may well be argued that there should be laws in this country—as there are in many European countries—compelling at least Minimally Decent Samaritanism.[8] But it does show that there is a gross injustice in the existing state of the law. And it shows also that the groups currently working against liberalization of abortion laws, in fact working toward having it declared unconstitutional for a state to permit abortion, had better start working for the adoption of Good Samaritan laws generally, or earn the charge that they are acting in bad faith.

I should think, myself, that Minimally Decent Samaritan laws would be one thing, Good Samaritan laws quite another, and in fact highly improper. But we are not here concerned with the law. What we should ask is not whether anybody should be compelled by law to be a Good Samaritan, but whether we must accede to a situation in which somebody is being compelled—by nature, perhaps—to be a Good Samaritan. We have, in other words, to look now at third-party interventions. I have been arguing that no person is morally required to make large sacrifices to sustain the life of another who has no right to demand them, and this even where the sacrifices do not include life itself; we are not morally required to be Good Samaritans or anyway Very Good Samaritans to one another. But what if a man cannot extricate himself from such a situation? What if he appeals to us to extricate him? It seems to me plain that there are cases in which we can, cases in which a Good Samaritan would extricate him. There you are, you were kidnapped, and nine years in bed with that violinist lie ahead of you. You have your own life to lead. You are sorry, but you simply cannot see giving up so much of your life to the sustaining of his. You cannot extricate yourself, and ask us to do so. I should have thought that—in light of his having no right to the use of your body—it was obvious that we do not have to accede to your being forced to give up so much. We can do what you ask. There is no injustice to the violinist in our doing so.

7. Following the lead of the opponents of abortion, I have throughout been speaking of the fetus merely as a person, and what I have been asking is whether or not the argument we began with, which proceeds only from the fetus' being a person, really does establish its conclusion. I have argued that it does not.

But of course there are arguments and arguments, and it may be said that I have simply fastened on the wrong one. It may be said that what is important is not merely the fact that the fetus is a person, but that it is a person for whom the woman has a special kind of responsibility issuing from the fact that she is its mother. And it might be argued that all my analogies are therefore irrelevant—for you do not have that special kind of responsibility for that violinist, Henry Fonda does not have that special kind of responsibility for me. And our attention might be drawn to the fact that men and women both *are* compelled by law to provide support for their children.

I have in effect dealt (briefly) with this argument in section 4 above; but a (still briefer) recapitulation now may be in order. Surely we do not have any such "special responsibility" for a person unless we have assumed it, explicitly or implicitly. If a set of parents do not try to prevent pregnancy, do not obtain an abortion, and then at the time of birth of the child do not put it out for adoption, but rather take it home with them, then they have assumed responsibility for it, they have given it rights, and they cannot *now* withdraw support from it at the cost of its life because they now find it difficult to go on providing for it. But if they have taken all reasonable precautions against having a child, they do not simply by virtue of their biological relationship to the child who comes into existence have a special responsibility for it. They may wish to assume responsibility for it, or they may not wish to. And I am suggesting that if assuming responsibility for it would require large sacrifices, then they may refuse. A Good Samaritan would not refuse—or anyway, a Splendid Samaritan, if the sacrifices that had to be made were enormous. But then so would a Good Samaritan assume responsibility for the violinist; so would Henry Fonda, if he is a Good Samaritan, fly in from the West Coast and assume responsibility for me.

8. My argument will be found unsatisfactory on two counts by many of those who want to regard abortion as morally permissible. First, while I do argue that abortion is not impermissible, I do not argue that it is always permissible. There may well be cases in which carrying the child to term requires only Minimally Decent Samaritanism of the mother, and this is a standard we must not fall below. I am inclined to think it a merit of my account precisely that it does *not* give a general yes or a general no. It allows for and supports our sense that, for example, a sick and desperately frightened fourteen-year-old schoolgirl, pregnant due to rape, may *of course* choose abortion, and that any law which rules this out is an insane law. And it also allows for and supports our sense that in other cases resort to abortion is even positively indecent. It would be indecent in the woman to request an abortion, and indecent in a doctor to perform it, if she is in her seventh month, and wants the abortion just to avoid the nuisance of postponing a trip abroad. The very fact that the arguments I have been drawing attention to treat all cases of abortion, or even all cases of abortion in which the mother's life is not at stake, as morally on a par ought to have made them suspect at the outset.

Secondly, while I am arguing for the permissibility of abortion in some cases, I am not arguing for the right to secure the death of the unborn child. It is easy to confuse these two things in that up to a certain point in the life of the fetus it is not able to survive outside the mother's body; hence removing it from her body guarantees its death. But they are importantly different. I have argued that you are not morally required to spend nine months in bed, sustaining the life of that violinist; but to say this is by no means to say that if, when you unplug yourself, there is a miracle and he survives, you then have a right to turn around and slit his throat. You may detach yourself even if this costs him his life; you have no right to be guaranteed his death, by some other means, if unplugging yourself does not kill him. There are some people who will feel dissatisfied by this feature of my argument. A woman may be utterly devastated by the thought of a child, a bit of herself, put out for adoption and never seen or heard of again. She may therefore want not merely that the child be detached from her, but more, that it die. Some opponents of abortion are inclined to regard this as beneath contempt—thereby showing insensitivity to what is surely a powerful source of despair. All the same, I agree that the desire for the child's death is not one which anybody may gratify, should it turn out to be possible to detach the child alive.

At this place, however, it should be remembered that we have only been pretending throughout that the fetus is a human being from the moment of conception. A very early abortion is surely not the killing of a person, and so it is not dealt with by anything I have said here.

READING ENDNOTES

1. I am very much indebted to James Thomson for discussion, criticism, and many helpful suggestions.
2. Daniel Callahan, *Abortion: Law, Choice and Morality* (New York, 1970), p. 373. This book gives a fascinating survey of the available information on abortion. The Jewish tradition is surveyed in David M. Feldman, *Birth Control in Jewish Law* (New York, 1968), Part 5, the Catholic tradition in John T. Noonan, Jr., "An Almost Absolute Value in History," in *The Morality of Abortion*, ed. John T. Noonan, Jr. (Cambridge, Mass., 1970).
3. The term "direct" in the arguments I refer to is a technical one. Roughly, what is meant by "direct killing" is either killing as an end in itself, or killing as a means to some end, for example, the end of saving someone else's life. See note 6, below, for an example of its use.
4. Cf. *Encyclical Letter of Pope Pius XI on Christian Marriage*, St. Paul Editions (Boston, n.d.), p. 32: "however much we may pity the mother whose health and even life is gravely imperiled in the performance of the duty allotted to her by nature, nevertheless what could ever be a sufficient reason for excusing in any way the direct murder of the innocent? This is precisely what we are dealing with here." Noonan (*The Morality of Abortion*, p. 43) reads this as follows: "What cause can ever avail to excuse in any way the direct killing of the innocent? For it is a question of that."
5. The thesis in (4) is in an interesting way weaker than those in (1), (2), and (3): they rule out abortion even in cases in which both mother *and* child will die if the abortion is not performed. By contrast, one who held the view expressed in (4) could consistently say that one needn't prefer letting two persons die to killing one.
6. Cf. the following passage from Pius XII, *Address to the Italian Catholic Society of Midwives*: "The baby in the maternal breast has the right to life immediately from God.—Hence there is no man, no human authority, no science, no medical, eugenic, social, economic or moral 'indication' which can establish or grant a valid juridical ground for a direct deliberate disposition of an innocent human life, that is a disposition which looks to its destruction either as an end or as a means to another end perhaps in itself not illicit.—The baby, still not born, is a man in the same degree and for the same reason as the mother" (quoted in Noonan, *The Morality of Abortion*, p. 45).
7. The need for a discussion of this argument was brought home to me by members of the Society for Ethical and Legal Philosophy, to whom this paper was originally presented.
8. For a discussion of the difficulties involved, and a survey of the European experience with such laws, see *The Good Samaritan and the Law*, ed. James M. Ratcliffe (New York, 1966).

QUESTIONS

1. If we suppose for the sake of argument that the fetus is a person, then the abortion debate becomes one of how to balance competing rights: the fetus's right to life and the pregnant woman's right to decide what happens in and to her body. What is the violinist example supposed to show about the relative priority of those two rights?

2. What relevance does the "killing" versus "letting die" distinction play in arguments against abortion even to save the mother's life? Can such arguments work without the distinction?

3. In cases where the continuation of a pregnancy threatens the life of the mother, a choice has to be made between the right to life of the fetus and the same right of the woman. What is the difference between the moral options open to third parties here compared with the options of the woman herself?

4. If a pregnancy threatens the life of the woman, does she not have a right of self-defence? If so, what does this tell us about the duty not to kill innocent people (the right to life)? Is it absolute or *prima facie*?

5. How does the libertarian premise that individuals own themselves lead to the conclusion that if the right to life of the mother and the fetus are in conflict then both the mother and third parties can choose to kill the fetus?

6. What does the right to life entitle the right-holder to? What limits are there on the right?

7. Why should we understand the right to life as the right not to be killed *unjustly*? Does this understanding fit our judgements about the morality of killing in other contexts: in a just war, in self-defence, for profit, for revenge, as legal punishment?

8. Do your judgements about the cases considered in Question 7 depend in any way on the innocence or immorality of the person to be killed? Does it matter that the fetus is innocent, whereas the burglar in another of Thomson's examples is guilty? Do we have a right to kill someone who threatens our life even if the person is innocent?

9. How can persons acquire a right to use another person's body, so that denying or depriving them of that right would be unjust?

10. If a woman voluntarily becomes pregnant, does this give the fetus a right to use her body? What role does the woman's degree of responsibility in becoming pregnant play in determining the rights of the fetus?

11. Thomson distinguishes between what people ought to do for others (because to not do would be indecent, callous, mean, etc.) and what people have a right against others that they do (because to not do would be unjust). Can you think of instances where people blur this distinction, or cases in which it helps us in thinking about our rights and duties more clearly?

12. Thomson speaks of people "assuming" responsibility for others through their choices and actions. Are there any "natural" relations of responsibility between people, or are all such relations of responsibility for others a matter of choice? Does the requirement that we all be Minimally Decent Samaritans imply some level of responsibility that people have to one another that is independent of special ties between them or their own choices and actions?

13. If libertarian rights are all negative (except those that have been granted by individuals in promising, contracting, etc.), and Thomson thinks both that it would be monstrous to watch Kitty Genovese die and that we all have a duty to be Minimally Decent Samaritans, does this suggest that she is not a libertarian?

✦ ✦ ✦

Michael McDonald, Aboriginal Rights

Michael McDonald presents us with a test case for determining whether the affluent are arguing from self-interest or from sound moral reasons in certain circumstances. Suppose (as well we might) that the affluent desire to retain their privileged position in society, and as much of their wealth as possible. When considering the case of welfare, an affluent member of society, recognizing that she is likely to pay taxes to support such a system, may adopt a libertarian position in order to argue against its legitimacy. This reaction may also come from a genuine moral judgement regarding the legitimacy of such systems. Whether she is arguing from self-interest or from basic moral judgements may be unclear even to herself.

The issue may become clearer, however, when her reaction to aboriginal land claims is assessed. For McDonald contends that a libertarian code requires the recognition of such claims. Libertarians believe that property claims are legitimate provided that the initial acquisition and all subsequent transfers of the property were themselves just. Assuming that aboriginal initial acquisition was legitimate, the subsequent seizure of such land certainly was not, and so we ought to return such lands, (or duly compensate for their loss).

In considering questions regarding efforts to undermine the legitimacy of the original acquisition of the land, McDonald suggests that various inadequacies in the theory of initial acquisition suggest that it is incomplete, and inadequate as a moral theory. Nevertheless, insofar as Canada wishes to maintain the useful fiction that the theory of initial acquisition is not problematic, it therefore has to grant native land claims.

There are two things to note here. First, while politically expedient, McDonald's conclusion here cannot be acceptable to a critical moral reasoner. Prudence cannot dictate moral reasoning. Second, we must take care to distinguish between a difficulty in a particular formulation of a theory, and a problem inherent in the theory itself. Only the latter can point to the inadequacy of that proposed theory as a moral theory.

Note: This article was first published in 1981, and so refers to Indian and Inuit people of Canada, rather than members of First Nations. Despite the changes in terminology since it was written, however, the arguments remain centrally relevant, we believe, to determining what aboriginal persons in Canada are owed by non-aboriginals.

✦ ✦ ✦

Michael McDonald, "Aboriginal Rights," from *Contemporary Issues in Political Philosophy*, eds. William Shae and John King-Farlow (New York: Academic Publications Inc., 1981). Reprinted with permission of the author.

Aboriginal Rights

Michael McDonald

How would you respond to the question "What sorts of treatment do the native peoples of Canada deserve?"

Since native peoples are amongst the most underprivileged Canadians, you might respond on the basis of your attitude to the poor. Thus, if you believe that Canadians should have welfare rights, then you would claim that Indians like other Canadians should not be allowed to fall below some national standard of minimum welfare. You may believe that this is best done through providing a guaranteed annual income or through the provision of various goods (such as food and housing) and various services (such as medical care and job training). You would then find yourself in agreement with Prime Minister Trudeau who in 1969 said that native people

> . . . should become Canadians as all other Canadians and if they are prosperous and wealthy they will be treated like the prosperous and wealthy and they will be paying taxes for the other Canadians who are not so prosperous and not so wealthy whether they be Indians or English Canadians or French or Maritimers and this is the only basis on which I see our society can develop as equals.

On the other hand, another person might make a libertarian response and deny that anyone has a right to welfare. He might argue that no one deserves "free passage"— that everyone should work his own way. The debate would then be joined over a whole set of familiar issues. What are the relative merits of free enterprise and planned economies? What does "equal opportunity" involve? How much may the government interfere in citizens' lives? And so the argument will wend its way over time-worn paths until one or both of you get tired and change the subject.

A very effective way of changing the subject is changing it so that you both wind up on opposite sides of the original question with you arguing against any special treatment for "the poor Indians" and your libertarian opponent demanding that they receive significant advantages from white society. I think this reversal is likely to happen if you shift the topic from welfare rights to aboriginal rights. Topic shifts of this sort, those which get the attacker and defender of a particular *status quo* to change places, very often provide interesting material for the political philosopher. Such is the case with aboriginal rights.

I. Entitlement Theory

What is the reason for this reversal in position?

I would suggest that there is something different about the ways in which we ground welfare and aboriginal rights. That is, when we argue for someone's having a welfare right we usually base our arguments on quite different sorts of premises than when we argue for aboriginal rights. The initial problem is then to characterize these sorts of differences.

Fortunately, this task has been made easier by the recent publication of *Anarchy, State, and Utopia* (New York, 1974) by Robert Nozick, who defends Locke's libertarian political philosophy. He argues that neither more nor less than the minimum or night watchman state of *laissez-faire* economics can be justified. In the course of this argument, he has to explain how people may legitimately have the exclusive use of various things, i.e., how they may come to own things. It is this discussion of "justice in holdings" that sheds light on the salient differences between welfare and aboriginal rights.

According to Nozick there are two primary ways in which I can have a just holding. If the object is unowned, I may under certain conditions come to own it; this is called "justice in the original acquisition of holdings." If the object is owned, then its owner may under certain conditions transfer it to me; this is called "justice in the transfer of holdings." Thus, for example, if you want to find out if the Atlantic salmon in my freezer is mine, you would want to know how I came to have the fish in my freezer: if I caught it, stole it, bought it, received it as a gift, etc. In short, you would ask for a history of ownership. The fish is mine if its original acquisition was just, and all subsequent transfers, if any, are also just. Insofar as you can trace this history, you can determine if I have a *clear* title. To the extent that you cannot trace this history, it is not clearly mine, e.g., if all you know is that a friend gave it to me but you have no way of knowing how he got it, you can't say for certain that it really is mine.

If you get a clear history and then find that the original acquisition or one of the subsequent transfers was unjust, then you or someone else has the problem of deciding how to rectify this injustice in holdings. The rectification of injustice in holdings is the third part of Nozick's theory of just ownership. Thus, if you find out that my generous friend stole the salmon from a seafood store, you'll have to decide whether or not you should tell me to return it.

Now let us imagine that you decide to settle the question of my ownership of the salmon by using welfare principles solely. Let us assume that whatever welfare criterion you intend to use will only apply to the two of us in this case. First, you appeal to "need." You say that you are hungry and desperately short of protein, while I am not; since needs should be satisfied, you should have the fish. Say that I ignore that plea, so you try a hedonic appeal: you claim that you will enjoy eating the salmon much more than I will; hence, by the greatest happiness principle, you should have the salmon. It is not difficult in either appeal to imagine how I would have to respond to prove that

I have a better title to the fish according to the criterion used. I would argue that I am needier than you or that I would really enjoy it more than you. Further it is not difficult to imagine the two criteria coming into conflict: you need the protein, but I would enjoy the dinner more. Then we would have to sort out which criterion takes precedence, e.g., that needs take precedence over wants. It is also not difficult to foresee some of the problems we might have in applying these considerations: how can I compare my need or enjoyment with yours, how can we properly take into account the effects of giving the fish to you or to me on each of our future needs or enjoyments, how do we know what counts as a "need" as opposed to what counts as a "want"? These are all problems which make up the bulk of philosophical debate about utilitarianism.

In our argument about who has the better welfare claim to the fish we proceed in a quite different way than we did earlier in trying to decide if the fish was a just holding of mine. Then we asked if the salmon had been justly acquired by me or justly transferred to me; in short, we looked backwards in time to see how the fish came into my possession. In the second case, we applied welfare criteria by looking to our present and future conditions to decide the issue according to our relative positions on the scale of need or enjoyment. Two major differences in the determination of ownership stand out in these cases: these are different attitudes to (a) the past and the future, and (b) the characteristics of the affected parties. Both (a) and (b) require some further explanation.

Regarding (a), we have seen that what mattered in determining justice in holdings were the acquisitions and transfers of the object; that is to say, the principle for the determination of ownership was *historical*. In the use of welfare criteria, we looked only at present and future considerations, viz. the relative degrees to which my or your having the fish would meet present and future needs or yield present and future enjoyment. Here we decided who owned the salmon on the basis of *end-results*. Our approach in the second case was *a*historical.

Regarding (b), you will recall that in the application of the welfare criteria we were concerned with the degree to which each of us had or lacked certain characteristics: if you were needier or would enjoy it more, then the fish should be yours. We were concerned in this case with the resulting *patterns* of the alternative distributions. In the first case, however, we proceeded without reference to patterns. There were no characteristics (such as need) which I might or might not have that would be determinative of the question of my ownership. It mattered not why I caught the fish (e.g., eat it, throw it back in the stream, or use it for fertilizer). Nor did it matter why someone transferred it to me (e.g., because I paid for it, because I am his son, or because he simply felt like it). In fact it doesn't even matter if I have a freezer full of Atlantic salmon and you have none or even no food at all. Justice in holdings is *unpatterned* in that there is no natural dimension (what I call a "characteristic") or set of dimensions according to which the distribution of goods should take place.

II. ABORIGINAL RIGHTS

We can now see how Nozick's approach to justice in holdings, which he calls "entitlement theory," ties in with the topic of aboriginal rights. Aboriginal rights are none other than original acquisition rights which haven't been transferred to anyone else. To defend the aboriginal rights of Canada's native peoples necessarily involves us in presenting a theory of original acquisition. Moreover, we must be willing to defend our theory of original acquisition against not only rival theories of original acquisition, but also against non-entitlement theories of ownership.

At the beginning of this paper, the argument about providing help to native people was carried on between a person who held a non-entitlement theory of the distribution of goods and one who held an entitlement theory. As you recall, one argued that native people should be helped on the basis of need. This, we have just seen, is an argument based on end-results and patterns. The other disputant argued that native people were not entitled to help. This argument is essentially historical and unpatterned.

Introducing aboriginal rights into the argument forced a change in the disputants' positions because it introduced a historical and unpatterned basis for the native people's entitlement. Now it was possible for the libertarian defender of property rights to argue that the natives had been dealt a historic injustice which stands in need of rectification. The defender of welfare rights must reject this approach, not because native people shouldn't receive significant benefits, but because in his view the only true basis for the reception of benefits is need. That is, he was arguing that benefits should be distributed in a patterned way with a view to the end-results achievable.

Now it is important to realize that we cannot simply let the disputants "agree to disagree." In practical terms, we are talking about claims to at least half of Canada. According to Peter Cumming and Neil Mickenberg in the second edition of *Native Rights in Canada* (Toronto, 1972), aboriginal claims have been superseded by treaties for less than one half of Canada. This would leave standing aboriginal claims to British Columbia, Quebec, the Maritimes, the Yukon, and parts of the Northwest Territories. Think of what this means to established settlements and to plans for Northern development. Remember, too, that "the natives are restless": they have been pressing their claims in the courts (in 1973 the Supreme Court of Canada split four to three against admitting an aboriginal claim), over the bargaining table (in Quebec native people have received a large cash and land settlement for allowing the James Bay Project to proceed in a scaled down form), at the barricades (in British Columbia), and before a royal commission (Mr. Justice Berger is carrying out an investigation of the effect of the proposed Mackenzie Valley Pipeline on native peoples). The questions of aboriginal rights is a real, not an ivory-tower, question.

In my examination of this question, I do not intend to say much more about nonentitlement theories except by way of contrast to entitlement theories. I shall instead focus on various problems that I see in the application of Nozickian and

Lockean entitlement theories to the question of aboriginal rights in Canada. I will argue that some of the problems anticipated in such an application of entitlement theory can be adequately handled, but that other problems—particularly those at the core—are much more difficult and may well be insurmountable.

I shall proceed by presenting a number of objections to an entitlement defence of aboriginal rights. I shall first state the objection in the broad and general way it occurs in non-philosophical discussion. Here I have tried to draw upon statements made by politicians, lawyers, and native people, as well as from discussions I've had with students and colleagues. This response will consist, first, in sorting out various objections that have been confused and run together in the non-philosophical context. After that, I shall see what kind of reply can be made within an entitlement theory. I have tried to give each objection a name which suggests the sort of objection made and renders the arguments easier to remember. This mnemonic aid is important because the arguments are often interrelated and used together for or against aboriginal rights.

A. The Vandals Argument

This is the kind of argument that Trudeau has used:

> If we think of restoring aboriginal rights to the Indians, well, what about the French who were defeated at the Plains of Abraham? Shouldn't we restore rights to them? What about the Acadians who were deported—shouldn't we compensate for this? And what about the other Canadians, the immigrants? What about the Japanese Canadians who were so badly treated at the end [of] or during the last war?

A similar position was taken by many Americans in response to James Foreman's demand that American churches and synagogues pay $500 million as reparations for years of slavery. In his book, *The Case for Black Reparations* (New York, 1973), Yale law professor Boris Bittker cites the *New York Times* response to Forman: "There is neither wealth nor wisdom enough in the world to compensate for all the wrongs in history."

An objector might ask if the descendants of the Roman victims of the Vandals' sack of Rome in 453 A.D. should be able to sue the Vandals' descendants? Here, however, we see the need to distinguish two separate objections. The first is what I shall call "Historical Disentanglement," and the second "Arbitrariness."

A.1. Historical Disentanglement. The first objection rests on practical difficulties in sorting out historical issues. The problem is to find out who is a descendant of the victims of an injustice and who is a descendant of the perpetrators of that injustice. In the Vandals' case the problems seem well-nigh insuperable. Even if some sorting out is possible, there will probably be enough intermarriage to confuse most cases thoroughly. Intermarriage has been alleged a serious barrier to reparations to blacks in the United States.

In the case we are considering, however,—that of native Canadians—we can get some powerful assistance from the facts. A quarter of a million Indians are registered under the Indian Act of 1951 as members of recognized bands. While we may have problems with the fairness of some of the provisions of that Act (e.g., Indian women who marry non-Indian males are deregistered and non-Indian females who marry Indian males are automatically registered), the fact remains that we have an accurate, though somewhat incomplete, record of many descendants of the purported victims of injustice. The cases of the unregistered Indians and of the Metis are more difficult, but we have two important facts which will help disentangle matters. First, these people have regarded themselves as native people. And secondly, they have been regarded by white Canadians as natives insofar as they have been objects of the same informal extra-legal distinctions (including racial prejudices) as those under the Indian Act. It should not prove to be too difficult to arrive at a consensus on who is or is not a native person amongst the Metis and other unregistered claimants of this status.

This, of course, leaves the question of tracing the descendants of those purported to have violated aboriginal title. Here again the facts help us—in this case it is the legal fact that only the Crown could seize land. In the case of New France, we can regard the Crown as the inheritor of whatever title France had to aboriginal lands.

It is also possible that we might in hard cases make use of a test Nozick suggests for determining the descendants of victims and perpetrators on the grounds that *persistent* inequalities are most likely a result of historical injustice. (While Nozick does not suggest "persistency" as a criterion here, I think it might make his suggestion more plausible.)

A.2. Arbitrariness. The second distinct element in the Vandals Argument is that suggestion that the defender of aboriginal rights wants to make an arbitrary and invidious distinction between rectifying the injustices done to aboriginal peoples and the injustices done to nonaboriginal Canadians. This is, I think, what Trudeau was asking, namely, how could we defend rectifying the injustices done to the Indians and ignore the injustices done by our nation to the French, the Acadians, and Japanese?

Trudeau goes on to say that we cannot "redeem the past"; we can only be "just in our time." This seems to let us argue that if we can't wholly rectify all the injustices we have ever done, then we needn't rectify any. The most favourable interpretation that I can put on Trudeau's conclusion is that we may have to face a multiplicity of competing claims of all sorts including a number of competing claims for the rectification of past injustices. We may then not be able to do everything that we ought ideally to do; in an imperfect world we may have to pay our most morally pressing debts in full and make only token payments on the remainder. There need be no arbitrariness in the recognition of aboriginal rights, for we can still recognize other past and present injustices. We may not be able to fully satisfy all the claims for rectification, but that isn't arbitrary either—there is no obligation to do more than one can.

B. The Forefathers Argument

There is another way of taking Trudeau's conclusion that we cannot redeem the past, and that is to say that we are only responsible for our sins and not for the sins of our fathers. How can I be blamed for what my French-Canadian ancestors did to the Indians of New France? How can anyone do more than be "just in his own time?"

Let's sort out this argument.

B.1. Backwards Causation. The first thing to clarify is whether saying that I ought to rectify injustice X involves saying that I am one of X's causes. If my children ruin my neighbor's prize roses, may I not have an obligation to make reparations? If I do, it needn't be the case that in so doing I am admitting that it was I who tramped through the roses. I may not even have to admit that it was somehow my fault that my children were in the garden. I may have told my children to stay out of the garden. Moreover, I may have done the best I can to instill in them a sense of respect for others' property. Then there is nothing more I should have done. (After all, there are outward bounds like child abuse for determining how far a parent can go in instructing his children.) Indeed my children may not have acted deliberately, purposely, or even intentionally; it was an accident pure and simple, for which even they are not to blame. But there it is: the roses are ruined, and I am the one who should set it right.

The point is that "responsibility" can be used in a variety of way. Sometimes it is used to indicate causality, in which case contemporaneousness or precedence in time is essential. But in the rose garden case, it was used to indicate who was *liable* for damages. The concept of liability is most highly developed within the law, but we do use it outside the law in our ordinary attributions of moral responsibility. The question then is whether anyone today has liability for the past violations (if any) of aboriginal rights.

There is a further confusion in this argument. This is to claim that backwards causation must be involved because I can only have obligations of my own making. Thus, I could have an obligation to contemporary native peoples respecting aboriginal rights only if I had undertaken to respect these rights, i.e., if I made a promise to or contract with their ancestors. It will take only a moment's reflection, however, to see that many obligations we have are not entered into voluntarily (or involuntarily either), e.g., not to kill, to express gratitude for favours received, to be kind, and to be honest.

B.2. Benefits Received. In (B.1) I didn't really so much respond to the Forefathers Argument as clear the way for a response to it. That liability-responsibility is different from causal-responsibility is important; nevertheless, it does not tell us if Canadians today have liability-responsibility for violations of aboriginal title. Neither does knowing that all obligations are not of our own making tell us if the rectification of this putative injustice is our responsibility.

A much more telling response is an analogy with the receipt of stolen goods. If person *A* steals person *B*'s watch and then makes a present of it to *C*, do we think that *C* has an obligation to return it to *B* even though he had no idea that he was in receipt of stolen goods when he accepted the watch? Surely, the answer is "Yes!" We might go on to say that *A* owes *C* something (an apology at minimum) for inconveniencing and embarrassing him. We would, I think, give the same answer even if the thief *A* can't recompense *C* (say that *A* is now dead). It is worth noting here that no one is blaming *C* for *A*'s stealing *B*'s watch or even for unwittingly accepting stolen property. *C* needn't feel any guilt about either of these matters. He should, however, feel guilt if he doesn't return the watch to *B*. I see no reason to change our views about returning the watch if instead of talking about *B* and *C* we talk about their heirs. I would not extend this to *A*'s heirs, however, who presumably have not benefited either from *A*'s theft, itself, or the gift of the watch to *C*.

The parallels with the case of aboriginal rights should be fairly obvious. Non-Indians have in Canada benefited (albeit in very unequal degrees) from the noncompensated supersession of aboriginal title. This is not to say that non-Indians *today* refused to compensate native people for the loss of aboriginal rights *during* the last and preceding centuries. These non-Indians certainly can't be held responsible for being born into this society or for immigrating to it. In this respect, breast-beating over what has been done to the "poor native" is neither due nor appropriate. Guilt is appropriate only if nothing is done to remedy injustices in the treatment of native people including, in particular, the rectification of past injustices.

Of course, the case for reparations becomes more difficult if we change the analogy somewhat. For example, what, if anything, does *C* owe *B* if after *C* receives the watch he loses it? It would be different if *C* were keeping *B*'s watch in trust for *B*, for then he could well be responsible for not losing it. This problem posed by lost or ruined articles seems quite likely to occur with the passage of significant periods of time. If we are talking about *C*'s and *B*'s great-grandchildren, the odds are that by this time the watch has been lost or no longer works.

That is, I think, the kind of thing that Bittker has in mind when he says that there would be no case for reparations to blacks if in the period since the Civil War there had been an unbroken ascent up to a present state of genuine equality. That is, the argument here is that reparations are not due if the relative advantage seized by the act of injustice gets lost or equalized in the course of history, so that it no longer makes any difference. It is *not* crucial to this argument that *both* the benefits accruing to the oppressors and their heirs and the evils suffered by the victims and their heirs no longer remain. It is enough to have the first without the second.

B.3. Inheritance.   There is a way of taking the Forefathers Argument that avoids the reply just advanced (B.2.). There I argued that if you can inherit benefits, you can inherit burdens chargeable against those benefits. This is like having to pay estate taxes and creditors before receiving an inheritance. As we have just seen, if you inherit nothing, you do not have any obligation (save, perhaps, "a debt of honour") to pay any debts chargeable against the estate. This suggests that there would be no aboriginal rights if there were no rights to make bequests; that is, aboriginal rights disappear if no one may rightfully inherit anything.

Native people could use this as an effective *ad hominem* argument in pressing their case. They could say to the rich and powerful in our society that Indians and Inuit will give up their claims to aboriginal rights if the rich and powerful will surrender all the property that they have inherited. This would not mean the end of private property but only the aspect of it—which I call "bequeathability." Other aspects of private property would remain (viz. rights of alienability, exclusive use, security, management, income, and so forth) but these "standard incidents" of property would be limited to the life of the holder. (To make this suggestion effective, we would have to set a limit to the life of corporations, for under our laws these "artificial persons" can be immortal.)

C. The Double Wrong Argument

The objection here is that to rectify one injustice another will have to be done, so that in rectifying the injustice done to the native people an injustice will have to be done to non-native Canadians by taking away from them land or the profit therefrom which they have in good faith purchased and improved. Moreover, the settlement of aboriginal claims will impose an enormous burden on those who in some cases are already disadvantaged.

The main response to this has already been made in the Forefathers Argument (B.2.). No one has a right to receive and retain what is not another's to give. "Good faith" here excuses one from complicity in the original theft: one is not to blame for the theft, so one needn't feel guilty about it. It does not excuse one from returning the stolen goods or the equivalent. Remember that we are working within the context of entitlement theory; justice in holding demands justice in acquisition and transfers. To give weight to the claims of those who have unjust holdings is just the sort of thing end-result theorists would do.

Nevertheless, the entitlement theorist can reduce the practical force of this objection by pointing out that third party beneficiaries (here, non-Indian and non-Inuit property owners) must return what remains of that which was wrongfully transferred to them. Given the ravages of time, one may not have to surrender any of one's own goods in making this reparation because nothing of value remains. I say "may not" because among the benefits received from the stolen property is that there is less drain on one's own resources. Thus, in the watch analogy, C or his heirs may benefit from not having to purchase watches of their own because they have the use of the watch stolen from B. So if the watch breaks after a few years while in C's possession, B might ask for rent for the use of his watch over the years before it broke. If C is now bankrupt, there may be little B can get (unless it is the case that entitlement theory would demand that C work the rent off). If it is the case that in addition to bankruptcy C also dies, then B cannot demand that C's would-be heirs pay for it out of their own justly acquired resources (including working the debt off). Death without the transmission of a benefice would seem on the entitlement theory to end the case for repayment simply because the unjust holding no longer exists. Presumably, in this wealthy nation, most of the benefit has been transmitted to us.

A final remark on the plight of the small property holder. According to the principles of rectification of injustice in holdings, it surely must be the case that those who have benefited most from unjust holdings owe more than those who have benefited least. Keeping in mind the complications about inheritance discussed earlier, it should be the case that in a society like ours, in which most wealth—especially capital—remains concentrated in a few families, the wealthiest would have the most to lose by the recognition of aboriginal rights. Here I would think especially of those who have benefited most from the exploitation of natural resources (like gas, oil, and minerals) in the areas in question, particularly Alberta, the North, and B.C. Of course, it has already been argued (B.3.) that these same people have the most to lose by denying aboriginal claims for they would thereby undermine their own claims to inherited wealth.

D. The Sovereignty Argument

In an article in *The Globe and Mail* (21 February 1973), Cumming has suggested that one possible reason for the Government's reluctance to recognize aboriginal rights is the fear that in so doing there would be a recognition of aboriginal sovereignty over the lands in question, to wit, Trudeau's reference to the Plains of Abraham. This is evident, too, in the same speech when Trudeau says, "It's inconceivable, I think, that in a given society one section of society have a treaty with another section of society." Trudeau is not the only politician in Canada's history to express concern about holding the country together; this is a country which has been plagued by threats of separatism—from Quebec, the West, and the Maritimes.

If it is the case that the recognition of aboriginal rights would necessarily involve a recognition of a separate aboriginal nation or nations then it is not clear what an entitlement theorist like Nozick would say. Nozick's invisible hand explanation of the emergence of a dominant protection agency as the (minimal) state never comes to grips with the fact that there is more than one nation in this complicated world. The fact of nationalism should also have some effect on Nozick's proposal for utopia—allowing diverse experiments in types of communities *within* a single nation. Are nationalists entirely wrong when they think that they must have control over the state and not just over the community? Another interesting way of putting this question is to ask what sorts of self-determination (determination particularly of a group's identity) are not possible in a libertarian society. Leaving aside these complex and difficult questions, it is possible to argue that if sovereignty is an issue here, then surely we must talk about more than justice in holdings.

The simplest way of dealing with this objection is to deny, as Cumming does, that sovereignty and property rights are connected except in an indirect way. In ordinary disputes over land ownership, neither claimant is trying to set up an independent nation. The adjudication usually follows the laws of the nation in which the property is situated. Although in a few difficult cases there can be arguments about which of two nation's laws are applicable, the dispute is primarily about ownership and only secondarily about sovereignty. It should be pointed out that no less an entitlement theorist like Locke claimed that rights to property are quite independent of rights to rule, for he maintained that property rights should survive changes in government including violent changes brought about by war.

E. The Litigation Argument

The general argument here is that claims to aboriginal title are unlike ordinary property claims. They are not amenable to the usual sorts of tests used by the courts to decide property rights. In particular many aboriginal claims are such as to deny courts the use of a most effective procedure for deciding between rival claims in cases where due to the passage of time both records are missing and memories are uncertain, namely, "prescription" which is "the operation of time as a vestitive fact." If this is correct, then how can anyone maintain that aboriginal claims can be settled in the same way as ordinary disputes about ownership? Indeed, how can anyone maintain that they are property rights at all?

This argument can be taken in part as a necessary corrective to the oversimplified reply that I just advanced against the Sovereignty Argument. There I argued that sovereignty and property were different kinds of rights. This may have left the impression that all property rights are alike and that aboriginal rights are like other property-rights. Neither of these contentions is true.

I agree with A.M. Honore that "property" is probably best thought of in terms of a list of "the standard incidents of ownership." This would be a list of the rights which a property owner has in the standard, full-blown case. It would include rights of physical possession, use, derivation of profit and capital, security, management, and so forth. One would probably also have to say something about the duties of ownership as well, in particular the prohibition of harmful use. If some of these incidents are missing in a particular case, we could still talk about "property-rights." In fact all the Indian treaties deny Indians the liberty of converting their reserves into capital, i.e., they may not alienate their lands, only the Crown may. In this sense, reserves could be seen as belonging to a particular people in perpetuity, not just to its present-day occupants; thus, future generations would have patrimonial rights. Aboriginal land claims involve the same kind of arrangement. (I should add here that if a whole people, conceived as a group extending across time into the future, can have property rights, then such right might well play havoc with many of the positions that Nozick defends on the basis of actions in a free market.)

So part of my reply to this argument is that while aboriginal titles may lack some of the standard incidents of property it may well be possible to still think of them as property rights. To properly establish this reply would require a great deal more space than I presently have. I think more needs to be said, however, about this argument along somewhat different lines.

First, there is the issue of "prescription." In the law it is the case that the passage of time can extinguish or establish ownership. This is determined by time limits established by custom or statute. For example, in some jurisdictions if you have made use of part of someone else's land as a right-of-way for twenty years, then the courts will uphold your right to continue to do so and thus bar the landowner from preventing your passage. Thus time has given you a right you formerly did not have and extinguished a property-right that the landowner had. The point of prescription is quite straightforward: the passage of time is used as a conclusive evidence because it simplifies the work of the courts in determining ownership. Thus, the jurist Savigny said, "All property is founded in adverse possession ripened by prescription."

The problem for aboriginal claims is that in many cases the land claimed is not now and has not been occupied by the claimants at all or on an exclusive basis for many years more than the limits set by law for the extinguishments of title. Yet it seems unfair therefore to deny title even though it is fair to do so in ordinary cases. In ordinary cases the law protects the property-owner's exercise of his property-rights before the period of prescription has elapsed. That is, if he wants to prevent his title from lapsing, he need only take action. Thus, in the right-of-way case, the property-owner can put up a "no trespassing" sign before the twenty years are out; this completely extinguishes your claim to a legally guaranteed right-of-way. If it is illegal to post the sign, then using the passage of time to effect a transfer of title would be unfair. The parallel here is that native peoples have not been given an opportunity to present their aboriginal claims, either through the courts or directly to government.

Secondly, the Litigation Argument does raise important doubts about the appropriate *forum* for the determination of the value and extent of various aboriginal claims. Cumming says that "the court is by far the least appropriate forum for dealing with aboriginal rights" because "litigation is expensive, time-consuming, and abounds with technical difficulties." He proposes instead that there be direct negotiations between the government and native people. Thus, this is essentially a practical, not an in-principle concern.

Thirdly, the Litigation Argument hints at a problem which will concern us in the next and final section. The problem, as seen from the perspective of this Argument, concerns the relationship between particular property-rights and the existing legal system. One way of finding the general area of difficulty is to ask if there can be property without laws. If there cannot be property without laws (as has been argued by generations of contractarians, Kant among them), then is property merely a creature of law? If property-rights can only be created and destroyed by law, what must be said about the entitlement theorists' claim that we have a natural right to "estate" in addition to "life and liberty"? In the next section I will consider some of these questions.

F. The Acquisition Arguments

Thus far, in all the objections and replies, I have tried to apply entitlement theory to the question of aboriginal rights. If I am right, then a number of interesting and plausible objections to entitlement theory and its application can be answered. In neither the objections nor the replies have I asked if native people actually have a claim to these lands on the basis of just original acquisition; for the sake of argument I have assumed that they do, and then gone to ask whether such claims should be recognised. Obviously, if native people in general or in particular did *not* make a just original acquisition of the land, the whole case for aboriginal rights fails. This would not show that all the native people's claims to land ownership are null and void, but it would remove the most important and the largest claims.

There is more than this practical issue at stake here. The whole entitlement theory rests on original acquisition. If the justice of an original acquisition is called into question then so also, Nozick says, are all subsequent transfers. If *all* original acquisitions can be called into question, then, perhaps, all claims to property rights are challengeable. One way of calling all aboriginal acquisitions into question is to deny that sense can be made of the concept of "original acquisition." Another way would be to deny that original acquisition as imagined by entitlement theorists can be a basis for rightful ownership.

So now I will turn to the "keystone" issue. I should say that some of the sharpest criticisms of the original acquisition doctrine come from Nozick himself. He writes in an almost ironic, or shall I say, "contrapuntal" way that involves the reader and enlivens debate. I will present four objections and responses. The responses, I should indicate, are partial and do not, I think, save entitlement theory (though, curiously enough, they save aboriginal rights).

F.1. The Jus Tertii Argument.

One way of challenging aboriginal rights *within* the framework of entitlement theory is to deny that the Indians and Inuit had made original and just acquisition. This could be denied on the grounds that Indians and Inuit weren't the first human beings in Canada and that Indians and Inuit acquired the northern half of this continent by force. In any event, given the lack of records of property acquisition, it could be claimed that no one can know for certain if the native people's ancestors acquired the lands justly as either first possessors or as a result of just transfer. This would at the very least make aboriginal claims suspect.

The argument presented here rests on a claim like the following: if Bill's acquisition of Blackacres from Alice is unjust, then Chuck's acquisition of the land from Bill need not follow the rules of just transfer in order to get as good, or better, title than Bill has to Blackacres. The underlying contention is that if title is, so to speak, "spoiled" at any point the property is simply up for grabs. Here I am assuming that the just owner Alice is not laying claim to Blackacres and that Chuck is in no way acting on behalf of Alice. The question is not, then, one of Chuck's rectifying an injustice done to Alice by Bill. The objection rests on the contention that given Alice's not laying or transferring her claim to another, Bill's act of injustice returns Blackacres to an ownerless situation from which Chuck may claim it.

Before questioning this contention, I would note that even accepting this reasoning there still is a difference between showing that Bill's title is spoiled and raising a suspicion that it may not be clear. In some cases, it simply is impossible for a possessor to prove that he has clear title; however, this does not mean that others can prove that he does not. Surely the burden of proof rests on those who charge wrongful possession.

Now as to the argument itself, it is worth noting that the practice under common law is not to establish ownership *absolutely* but *only relatively*, i.e., to decide who has a *better* right to possess. It would, I believe, be the case that a court would hold that Bill has a better title to Blackacres than Chuck and Alice has a better title to Blackacres than Bill. Regardless of the court's decision, it is certainly more convenient for a court to decide matters in this relative way (adjudicating only between the rival claims presented to it) rather than trying to do this once and for all (which would involve ruling on every conceivable claim). In this case, the court would settle the dispute between Bill and Chuck leaving it to others such as Alice to bring suit separately.

Which approach should an entitlement theorist adopt—that unjust acquisition or transfer returns the object to an ownerless condition or that it simply "weakens" the possessor's title? I wonder if in answering this question we will have to fall back on utilitarian considerations, e.g., about which procedure would be the most orderly and least disruptive for a given society. I am not sure how this question would be decided on purely entitlement grounds. That is, I don't know what *natural* rights to the ownership of Blackacres are held by Bill as opposed to Chuck. I would suspect that this cannot be determined without a *policy* decision about the rules governing property. Entitlement theory does not say which is the appropriate way of deciding ownership in this case. If this is right then it indicates an important gap in entitlement theory, for it means that the theory of justice in holdings has to be patched up by resorting to utilitarianism.

Apropos the question of aboriginal rights, it would seem that if we proceed on the basis of who has better title rather than on the basis of who has absolute title, then native people's claims would seem to be stronger than those of successive possessors.

F.2. The Spoilage Argument. In *The Second Treatise of Government*, Locke presents an objection to his view of justice in original acquisition:

> That if gathering the Acorns, or other Fruits of the Earth, & c. makes a right to them, then any one may *ingross* as much as he will.

Locke says that this is not so; one may take "as much as one can make use of to any advantage of life before it spoils . . . Whatever is beyond this, is more than his share and belongs to others." Locke grounds this limitation of original acquisition on God's will: "Nothing was made by God for Man to spoil or destroy." Yet it is clear that God's will is not capricious, for as Locke says earlier:

> God, who hath given the World to Men in common, hath also given them reason to make use of it to the best advantage of Life and convenience.

Men then have a right to self-preservation which entitles them to take the means thereto, viz. by acquiring the necessaries of life. Self-preservation grounds appropriation and sets limits to it.

Now it could be argued that the spoilage provision sets the limits too widely in that it allows me to refuse to share my bounty with my starving neighbours so long as I can use that bounty for "the best advantage of [my] Life and convenience." Matters are weighted heavily in favour of the propertied and against those without property. But let us for the sake of argument accept spoilage as an outward limit of just original acquisition. We can then ask whether native peoples violated the spoilage principle in acquiring these lands. If they did and if the Europeans who came here could make use of the wasted portions, then aboriginal claims may be defeasible on the grounds of wastage.

If this question is answerable, it would have to be on the basis of historical evidence; however, it is fair for the philosopher to ask about the determination of the criteria for wastage and spoilage: by what marks do we identify something as waste? Here it is tempting to ask if the thing in question is used for anyone's benefit. But will any minute amount of incremental benefit suffice to justify ownership or must there be some standard margin of benefit for this use to count here for title? Must there also be standards of efficient use? Would there be a combined standard, e.g., "Makes the best use of X for the greatest benefit"? Any benefit or efficiency standard would seem to be hopelessly utilitarian and redistributivist. On the other hand, having no standards at all would effectively deny a right of self-preservation to those without property and the correlative duty to share for the propertied.

If we try to fix on some mid-point (i.e., having a spoilage provision which is compatible with entitlement theory), then the question is how to justify our selection of standards on an entitlement basis. This is a particularly troublesome question in the case of aboriginal rights. In many cases an advanced agricultural and industrialized economy came into contact with a hunting, fishing, and gathering economy. The patterns of resource use were bound to be different. What would appear as under-utilisation in one economy might appear as over-utilisation in the other. Clearly Canada's native peoples made ingenious use of the often harsh environment, but their uses could not support the numbers of people that present-day uses can. (In this paper I am being deliberately silent about how much longer we can continue our use-patterns.) However, if we move in the direction of giving title to the Europeans rather than the native peoples, then we would have to surrender our ownership claims to any society which could support more people here more efficiently. This seems quite obviously in direct opposition to the whole thrust of an *entitlement* theory: if I am entitled to something, if it's *mine*, then I should within the limit of non-harmfulness be able to use it as efficiently or as inefficiently as I wish for whosoever's advantage I choose. This would accord with Nozick's slogan: "From each as they choose, to each as they are chosen."

Tentatively, then, if we are willing to deny the right of self-preservation and more especially the correlative duty of sharing when necessary to provide it, then we can still hold the entitlement theory and so avoid the conceptual difficulties posed by the spoilage principle.

F.3. The "Proviso" Argument. Spoilage is not the only limit Locke sets to original acquisition; he also suggests what Nozick calls "the Lockean Proviso," namely that there be "enough and as good left in common for others." This Nozick says, "is meant to ensure that the position of others is not worsened." Thus, we can imagine a parallel argument to the Spoilage Argument being advanced against aboriginal rights on the grounds that aboriginal possession violated the enough-and-as-good proviso.

Factually, this is going to be a tricky argument to work out for not only must it be shown that the native people did not leave enough and as good to the immigrants, but also that the immigrants have taken just enough to rectify this violation of the proviso. This will be very hard to prove, given the relative wealth of natives and immigrants. At present, indeed, native people could justifiably argue that the immigrants haven't left enough and as good to them.

Here, as in the Spoilage Argument, there are serious conceptual problems in determining the appropriate criteria. Nozick advances two interpretations of the Proviso:

> Someone may be made worse off by another's appropriation in two ways: first by losing the opportunity to improve his situation by a particular appropriation or any one, and second, by no longer being able to use freely (without appropriation) what he previously could.

Nozick accepts the second or "weaker requirement" and not the first or "the stringent requirement." The difference between the two seems to be between characterizing the proviso as applying to appropriation (ownership) or to use. But then it must be remembered that earlier Nozick says that the central core of the notion of a property right in X is "the right to determine what shall be done with X." If I have a right to use X, then would I not have a property right in X?

Be that as it may, Nozick argues that those who are unable to appropriate (because everything is now owned) are likely to be compensated for this restriction on their liberty by having their prospects increased by a system which allows (virtually unlimited) private acquisition. Nozick says the free market will make up for their loss of acquisition and/or use rights. The point is to compensate these people enough for not being able to appropriate or use what they could have had they been born earlier. Nozick suggests that the level of compensation can be determined by getting "an estimate of the general economic importance of appropriation."

But this, I suggest, won't do for several reasons. First, if this isn't forcing on someone a kind of compensation that he doesn't want, then in the case of those who really want to make acquisitions the state will have to take something away from various property-owners. Secondly, as my colleague Jan Narveson has argued, the level of compensation will probably have to be set high enough to amount to a tidy guaranteed annual income. Thirdly, it isn't clear how much compensation is to be given to any particular propertyless person. Does he get as much as he would have been likely to get if he were in the position of the last person who acquired property or as much as if he were the first person to acquire property? In either case, the primary basis for distribution (his acquisitiveness) seems suspiciously patterned. Fourth, if the benefits of a free market economy really do provide enough compensation, then why does it seem so unlikely that anyone who has more than a little property, e.g., E.P. Taylor, would want to change places with one of these people who can't acquire any property because everything is owned?

All of which suggests that on a *pure* entitlement theory—one which is based on historical entitlement—there would be no room for the Proviso. On a pure entitlement theory if you are born after all the accessible and useful unowned objects have been taken up by your predecessors, you are simply out of luck. The denial of the Proviso would also seem to be in agreement with Nozick's criticisms of Rawls' contention that a system of natural liberties allows distribution on morally arbitrary grounds—that the distribution of natural talents is not on the basis of desert leads Rawls to design the social system to compensate for this "arbitrariness" by favouring (other things being equal) the least talented in the distribution of goods. Nozick criticizes this as a "manna-from-heaven" model that totally ignores who has made these goods, i.e., Rawls ignores the crucial fact of historical entitlement. Similarly, the Proviso seems to ignore the crucial fact of appropriation.

Finally, as in the Spoilage Argument, we can ask what it is to leave "enough and as good"? If the standard is *usability*, then do we adopt the native peoples' idea of what is usable or the non-native immigrants? If we defend the latter, then in effect we are denying native peoples their ways of life. According to the Proviso, this would seem to demand that we compensate the native peoples for that loss. Yet is that something for which adequate compensation is possible other than allowing them to maintain their standards of use and so their way of life? Would not "the base line for comparison" be very high indeed then?

F.4. The Invalid Acquisition Arguments.

In both the Spoilage and Proviso Arguments, aboriginal title was challenged on the grounds that Indians and Inuit had acquired too much, i.e., more than they were entitled to acquire. It is possible to raise a different objection by claiming that they failed to acquire anything or scarcely anything at all. The heart of this contention is that native peoples did not perform the appropriate acquisitive acts. We get a variety of objections of this kind based on different views of what is an appropriate act of acquisition, that is depending on what sorts of human actions bring things out of a state of ownerlessness into a state of property. Before trying to get this argument off the ground, it is worth noting that both Nozick and Locke start with the assumption that before individual acquisition things are in an ownerless condition (the *res nullis* doctrine); there is another school of thought that assumes that before private acquisition takes place, things are held in common by all men (the *res communae* doctrine).

The major problem in raising this objection is fixing on some kind(s) of action that can be plausibly regarded as acts of original acquisition, i.e., upon the *rites* that generate property *rights*. Nozick raises very serious problems about Locke's criterion for ownership, namely that one owns that with which one has mixed one's labour. He asks about the boundaries of such an acquisition:

> If a private astronaut clears a place on Mars, has he mixed his labour with (so that he comes to own) the whole planet, the whole uninhabited universe, or just a particular plot?

Nozick also asks why mixing one's labour with something isn't simply throwing one's labour away, and if it isn't, then why should one have title to more than the value (if any) added by one's labour? If "mixing labour" is the acquisitive act, then surely these and related questions must be convincingly answered if entitlement theory is to proceed.

We have already seen that if usage is made the standard there are serious problems in determining whose standard of use should prevail. In fact, it would seem that an entitlement theorist should shy away from recognising usage as the acquisitive action, for anyone could take your title to X away from you by finding a better use of X (if you are already using it) or putting it to use for the first time (if you haven't used it yet). I would think that an entitlement theorist should say that it is solely up to X's owner whether and to what use X shall be put. Yet it is Locke who denies that the Indians of America have any ownership rights beyond what they use for food and clothing; English settlers have rights to the land itself because they till it. In short, Locke denies aboriginal rights because the Indians don't use the land in the same way as the English immigrants.

Perhaps, then, it will be suggested that acquisitive actions are *conventional*—literally consisting in the conventions (customs or laws) of a particular people. Thus in one society you own only what you actually have in hand or on your person at the moment, while in another you own whatever bears your mark, and in still another society you own only those things entered in the central ownership registry. Of course, there will be problems when societies with different ownership conventions each want to make exclusive use of the same objects. Each society (assuming no overlap in conventions) can say that the other society's people haven't really acquired the goods in question because of a failure to follow the appropriate conventions. I do not see how an entitlement theorist can say which set of conventions (in part, presumably, adopted for non-arbitrary reasons having to do with different patterns of usage) should prevail on the basis of entitlement theory; it seems to me that he must resort to patterned and, in the end, possibly redistributivist considerations. I think it is on the basis of these considerations that our society will have to deal with the contention (if it can be proven) that the Indian treaties are invalid because the whites and the Indians had totally different conceptions of ownership.

CONCLUSIONS

First, I hope to have shown in my consideration of entitlement theory that a number of plausible objections to it (A) through (E), can be answered. These are essentially peripheral objections. Once we get to the core of the theory, however, serious and, I would maintain, insurmountable problems arise. The entitlement theory of original acquisition cannot be maintained without resort to non-entitlement considerations—patterns, end-results, and pure conventions. To cleanse entitlement theory of these additions will make it so unattractive that it cannot be accepted as a theory of justice in holdings.

Secondly, and somewhat surprisingly, I think that I have made out the case for aboriginal rights. I claim that this country ought to recognise aboriginal rights *on the basis of original acquisition.* Of course, this conclusion depends on the validity of my claim that the only rationale that is advanced and is plausible for the present system of holdings in Canada is entitlement theory. I contend that it is on the basis of entitlement theory alone, that we could ever hope to justify the way in which most holdings are distributed in Canada. Just because entitlement theory won't work does not mean that our society won't proceed as if it does. The argument for aboriginal rights is provisional. But it ought to obtain until we are willing to redistribute holdings in this country on a truly just basis.

QUESTIONS

1. What does it mean to say that Nozick's theory of justice in holdings is (a) historical and (b) unpatterned? In what way are welfare rights (a) ahistorical and (b) patterned?

2. What does McDonald think are aboriginal rights?

3. What are the three components of Nozick's entitlement theory of property rights (justice in holdings)?

4. What is the relation between initial acquisition, transfer, and rectification as applied specifically to aboriginal land claims?

5. What is "the Vandals argument" against aboriginal entitlement to rectification?

6. Is it possible to sort out the question of who the descendants of the past injustice are and who the descendants of the perpetrators of that injustice are with respect to Canada's aboriginal populations?

7. What is wrong with the "Arbitrariness" argument against rectifying the past injustice done to aboriginal groups?

8. What is the difference between causal-responsibility and liability-responsibility? What, if any, connection exists between them? What relevance do questions of causation have to the question of aboriginal entitlements?

9. Consider McDonald's example of A stealing a watch from B and giving it to C. He thinks it is obvious that when C comes to know about the theft that he should return the watch to A. But does it matter to our intuitions here if C bought the watch from B rather than receiving it as a gift? Why should C be out good money because B committed an unjust act?

10. Why is it relevant that non-natives have continued to receive benefits from the past injustices? Why isn't continuing disadvantage to natives the most important moral consideration?

11. Can we trace some benefits now enjoyed by non-natives to the injustice involved in denying aboriginal land titles?

12. Are aboriginal land claims property rights claims?

13. Why does McDonald think that, even if the justice of aboriginal initial acquisition is not fully clear, they probably have a stronger claim to the land than do any successive possessors?

14. What is the spoilage limitation to Lockean original acquisition? How does this apply to comparisons of aboriginal land and resource use with non-aboriginal current practices?

15. What is the Lockean Proviso? Whose patterns of use (natives or immigrants) should be used to set the baseline for determining whether "enough and as good" has been left for others? Given that immigrant patterns of use do not include the use of natural spaces as such, in contrast to aboriginal use, does using a different baseline make a difference to the justification of aboriginal title to land?

16. Aboriginal use of land is non-fungible (meaning that the land itself cannot be replaced with anything else; there is no substitute for land use that would be equivalent in value to aboriginal persons), whereas under immigrant practices land is fungible. What does this difference imply about the question whether we must rectify the past injustice done to aboriginals by actually recognizing their title to the land or by paying compensation for the injustice?

17. McDonald considers a possible objection to aboriginal title on the grounds that perhaps aboriginal use did not count as establishing original title. This raises questions about what kind of use or acquisitive act grounds entitlement. We need not be bound by Locke's own understanding that it is mixing our labour with unowned goods that establishes title to them, and indeed it seems that libertarians have a better one. The question is not, have you mixed your labour with something, but are you using it in ways that are necessary to fulfil your purposes? Would interfering with your use be an interference with your rights to life and liberty? If so, such interference is prohibited. Why is this a better ground for property rights from a libertarian perspective? Apply it to aboriginal use.

✦ ✦ ✦

Janet Radcliffe Richards, Nephrarious Goings On: Kidney Sales and Moral Arguments

Janet Radcliffe Richards presents us with a sustained argument that suggests that a market in kidneys procured from live donors is morally acceptable, notwithstanding our initial repugnance at the idea of such a practice. Taking the stance that we must first presume that people are at liberty to do what they wish, unless it can be argued that such choices ought not to be respected, the case seems clear. If we disallow organ sales, we take away from people (who would sell their kidney) their preferred choice, all things considered. We may not interfere in such choices unless they are non-autonomous, or violate the harm principle. She examines each possibility in turn.

Perhaps the choice to sell one's organ is non-autonomous due to ignorance. One ought not to be able to sell one's kidneys because one does not, or cannot, understand some relevant information. But the appropriate response to ignorance is surely to inform, not to forbid. Perhaps poverty leads to non-autonomous choice due to a severe restriction of viable options. But then the reasoning behind even further restricting the choices of the poor who would sell their organs seems opaque. Perhaps the amount of money offered for such a sale is irresistible, and thus coercive. However, coercion is objectionable due to a narrowing of choices, while this offer broadens the range of possibilities. It is concluded that this choice is autonomous. *Contra* that conclusion, however, Radcliffe considers what a paternalist would have to show to justly intervene regarding the decision to sell a kidney. It is not straightfor-wardly the case that if a decision would have been made non-autonomously, then its opposite must be the correct course of action. The paternalist would have to show that it is clearly not in the person's interests to have the offered money rather than the kidney. And this is a difficult case to make out.

Richards concludes by taking some time to examine our moral repugnance regarding the sale of kidneys, and considers its implications. Does it point to a basic moral truth (that such practice is evil) and thus reveal an insufficiency in libertarian thought (which cannot capture that evil)? Or is it instead an irrational reaction that we should disregard in light of critical moral reasoning? Richards concludes that it is the latter. There seems to be no feature of kidney sale that is generally condemned by our emotions. It seems then, that critical reflection counsels the rejection of our reaction to kidney sales as a legitimate moral judgement.

✦ ✦ ✦

Janet Radcliffe Richards, "Nephrarious Goings On: Kidney Sales and Moral Arguments," *The Journal of Medicine and Philosophy* 21 (1996): 375–416. © 1996 Kluwer Academic Publishers. Reprinted with permission of Kluwer Academic Publishers.

Nephrarious Goings On: Kidney Sales and Moral Arguments[1]

JANET RADCLIFFE RICHARDS

PART ONE—THE TRADITIONAL ARGUMENTS

I. The Situation and the Response

When evidence of the trade in transplant organs from live vendors first filtered through to Western attention a few years ago, the most remarkable aspect of the immediate response was its unanimity. From all points of the political compass, from widely different groups who were normally hard pressed to agree about anything, there came indignant denunciations of the whole business. It was a moral outrage; a gross exploitation of the poor by the rich, who were now taking the very bodies of those from whom there was nothing else left to take, and obviously intolerable in any civilized society.

It is significant that this indignation was not, in the first instance, directed at the supplementary horrors of which media-fuelled rumors soon began to grow. Stories about kidneys stolen during other operations, failure afterwards to pay the agreed price, flagrant profiteering, and even abduction and murder, later inflamed the outrage, but the trade in organs from live vendors was almost universally denounced as a moral scandal quite independently of any such embellishments, and such remarkable concord must suggest that the moral case for prohibition is unequivocal.

Nevertheless, the matter is nothing like as clear as it may seem. The case has some curious features that suggest a different explanation for this unusual meeting of minds, and shows the problem of organ sales in a rather different light.

I shall limit the discussion to kidneys—which, in being both paired and non-renewable, come in some sense midway between hearts on the one hand, and livers and blood on the other—and to the problem of live vendors. Conclusions reached about laws and policies appropriate to this case will not necessarily transfer to the sale of organs or tissues of other kinds and in other circumstances, but this case raises matters of principle that are central to all, and, indeed, to most other areas of medical ethics.

II. The Burden of Proof

Perhaps the most striking curiosity comes right at the beginning, in the way the situation is typically described. To hear the organ trade characterized in terms of the greedy rich and the exploited poor, you might think that the rich, tired of gold plating their bathrooms and surfeited with larks' tongues, had now idly turned to collecting kidneys to display with their Fabergé eggs and Leonardo drawings. But the rich in question here are *dying*, and desperately trying to save their lives; or, at the very least, to escape the crushing miseries of chronic illness and perpetual dialysis.[2] Most critics of the trade in organs would do all they could to find similar amounts of money if private medicine offered their only chance of escaping death or disability, and would not, in doing so, expect to be regarded as paradigm cases of greed. There is, if anything, less greed involved in spending money to save your life or to achieve your freedom than in keeping it to spend on luxuries before you become ill.

Add the attitude shown to the poor who are selling the organs is even odder. Consider, for instance, the case of the young Turkish father swept to everyone's television screen by the surge of outrage that followed the first revelations.[3] He was trying to meet the expense of urgent hospital treatment for his daughter. Presumably the prospect of selling his kidney, was, to say the least, no more attractive to him than it seems to us, but he nevertheless judged this to be his best available option. As we rush to intervene, therefore, saying how dreadful it is that he should be exploited in this way, we are taking away what he regards as his best option and leaving him in a situation he thinks even worse than the loss of a kidney. The same applies to other "desperate individuals" who advertise kidneys and even eyes in newspapers, or write to surgeons offering to sell them, "often for care of an ill relative."[4] The worse we think it is to sell a kidney or an eye, the worse we should think the situation in which we leave these people when we remove that option. Our indignation on behalf of the exploited poor seems to take the curious form of wanting to make them worse off still.

So, as we contemplate with satisfaction our rapid moves to thwart greed and protect the poor, we leave behind one trail of people dying who might have been saved, and another of people desperate enough to offer their organs thrust back into the wretchedness they were hoping to alleviate. And, furthermore, in a surprising contravention of our usual ideas about individual liberty, we prevent adults from entering freely into contracts from which both sides expect to benefit, and with no obvious harm to anyone else. Our intervention, in other words, seems in direct conflict with all our usual concerns for life, liberty, and the pursuit of happiness.

It is irrelevant to respond indignantly, as many people do, that no one should be in these desperate situations. Of course they should not; but even if there were any moral point in making rules for the world as we should like it to be rather than as it is, that would still provide no justification for prohibition. If we could eliminate poverty to the extent of removing all temptation for anyone to sell organs, prohibition would have nothing to do; and, conversely, as long as it has anything to do, some people must be at whatever level of desperation makes them see organ selling as their best option. Whatever the state of the world, prohibition either causes these harms or has no point at all.

Of course this is a long way from the end of the matter. The claim so far is that prohibition seems to cause various harms or to be undesirable in other ways;[5] but a hundred times a day we make choices that have some bad aspects, because we nevertheless judge the options that involve them to be best, all things considered.[6] To accept that some aspects of prohibition are intrinsically undesirable is compatible with claiming that it is still, all things considered, justified.

Nevertheless, when some course of action seems to involve positive harms, that does at least provide a clear direction of burden of proof. If you knew nothing more about some practice than that it involved sticking needles into children, your presumption, pending further evidence, would be that it should be stopped. You would (probably) withdraw your objections when you saw that nothing more sinister was going on than vaccination or the administration of anaesthesia, whose benefits far outweighed the intrinsic harm, but you would want the evidence first. The same applies here. Even if the conclusion can be reached that organ sales should be prohibited, the starting presumption must be the other way. Anyone wanting to forbid organ sales, therefore, must do one (or both) of two things: either show that there is something wrong with this account of the matter, and that prohibition does not involve any or all of these harms, or argue that they are outweighed by more important considerations on the other side.

It is difficult to separate these two elements in the debate, since the usual arguments against organ sales are not offered as replies to this particular challenge. Arguments that would, if successful, show that organ selling did not involve the evils alleged, are usually presented simply as arguments for prohibition. However, I shall use the distinction to determine the order of what follows. Sections III and IV contain discussions of arguments that would, if successful, undermine the claim that prohibition was a constriction of individual liberty and harmful to vendors and recipients. Section V analyses arguments which attempt to show that prohibition is justified in spite of such harms. Part 2 (sections VI–VIII) considers more generally what is shown by the way the debate has gone, and draws conclusions for the conduct of moral enquiry in this and other contexts.

III. Autonomy and Consent

Consider first the claim that prohibition prevents free contracts between consenting adults. Most people involved in the organs debate accept the fundamental tenet of Western liberalism that people should be allowed to control their own destinies as far as possible, but many claim that there can be no genuine, free consent to the sale of organs, and therefore (in effect) that there is no curtailment of liberty in preventing it. Since it is also claimed that genuine consent is an absolute requirement for any surgical procedure, the alleged impossibility of obtaining such consent under these circumstances is offered not merely as the removal of a *prima facie* objection to prohibition, but as a positive reason for demanding it. Several different arguments are produced to defend the claim that apparent consent to the sale of organs is not genuine. I shall discuss the three most familiar.

A. Incompetence Through Ignorance.

The most obvious way to argue that would-be organ vendors are not choosing freely is to claim that there is something about the people themselves that prevents their making genuinely autonomous choices. Enlightened Westerners will hesitate to suggest that Turkish and Indian peasants must be prevented from making their own decisions just because they are poor or foreign, but they may well argue that "since paid organ donors will always be relatively poor, and may be underprivileged and undereducated, the donor's full understanding of [the] risks cannot be guaranteed."[7] The requisite informed consent is impossible, and therefore organ sales should not be allowed.

This line of argument does get off to a reasonably promising start. It is plausible, though by no means uncontroversial, to claim that if people do not understand the implications of the various options open to them, the choices they make are in some sense not genuinely autonomous. It is probably also reasonable to think that people poor enough to be tempted by organ selling are likely to know little about the implications of the procedure. But even if both these matters were beyond controversy, there would still remain the question of how their conjunction with a commitment to the value of autonomy—to the intrinsic desirability of allowing rational beings to make their own choices about what happens to them—is supposed to support the conclusion that organ sales should be prohibited; and this is where the problems arise.

In the first place, no one committed to the value of autonomy would rush to institute a prohibition that would limit the freedom of *everyone*, just on the grounds that some, or even most, of the people most likely to be involved were incapable of making autonomous choices. At the very least, the first impulse should be to try to discriminate between people, and to interfere only with the ones who really are incapable of doing so. To justify a general prohibition it would be necessary to argue both that this could not be done, and that it would be worse to risk allowing the incompetent to choose than to curtail the freedom of the competent. I am not aware of anyone's having tried to make out such a case.

Second, ignorance as such is not an irremediable state. If ignorance is the obstacle to genuine choice, anyone concerned about autonomy will try to remove the ignorance before starting to foreclose options. In other context where we think it important that people should make considered decisions about risky and complicated matters (as in the case of other surgery, or abortion, or AIDS testing) we typically insist on counselling, both to check for ignorance and to provide information. Anyone who opposed giving the ignorant the chance to become informed would hardly be regarded as a respecter of autonomy.

And third, even if counselling were likely to be impracticable, or the ignorance of prospective organ sellers irremediable,[8] another problem would still remain. Respect for autonomy lies in the idea that *if* people are capable of genuine choice there is a presumption in favor of allowing their choices, but that implies nothing about what should happen if they are not. That is a quite separate question,[9] to which considerations of autonomy are *ex hypothesi* irrelevant.

Commitment to the intrinsic value of self-discrimination and fear that rational decisions about organ selling must be impossible for anyone who might be tempted by it, therefore, however unexceptionable in themselves, come nowhere near supporting the conclusion that organ sales should be prohibited. But even if the argument did work, it would still not do what is required in this context, because it would equally rule out a great many things that most objectors to organ sales have no intention of ruling out. In particular, it would preclude unpaid organ donation, at least in any population where kidney selling might be a temptation, since genuine consent would be impossible for the same reasons.[10] Whatever moral merits there may be in the giving of an organ, it can hardly be claimed as a miraculous remover of whatever intractable ignorance would have made genuine consent to its sale impossible, let alone one that works by backward causation.

This double criticism of the argument from ignorance—that its premises, even if plausible in themselves, do not support the conclusion that organ sales should be forbidden, and that even if they did they would equally support the unwanted conclusion of ruling out the unpaid donation of organs—sets a pattern that will soon be familiar.

B. Coercion by Poverty. Arguments about ignorance and incompetence concern what might be called internalities: characteristics of agents themselves that are supposed to make them incompetent to choose properly among whatever options are open to them. The most familiar arguments about autonomy and consent in the organs debate, however, are of a different kind. Most depend on the idea that would-be vendors are coerced by external circumstances, and that a coerced choice cannot count as genuine.

The commonest agent of alleged coercion is poverty. "Surely abject poverty . . . can have no equal when it comes to coercion of individuals to do things—take risks—which their affluent fellow-citizens would not want to take? Can decisions taken under the influence of this terrifying coercion be considered autonomous? Surely not . . ."[11] And, it is implied, since coerced consent is not genuine, the choice should not be allowed.

Once again, it is easy to see how this idea gets going. The poor would not be selling organs but for their poverty, so it may be reasonable to say that the poverty is coercing them into the sale. It is also widely taken for granted that decisions and agreements made under duress should not count, and it is easy to think of cases that support this idea. If some dealer in organs kidnaps me and threatens to take out one of my kidneys in some rat-infested cellar, without anaesthetic, unless I sign a document authorizing you to do the job properly in your modern hospital, of course I sign it; but equally of course, when I am delivered already anaesthetized to your operating theatre, and you are presented with this surprising document, you rightly suspect nefarious goings on and disregard my authorization. And when you do, nobody is likely to accuse you of gratuitously interfering with my decisions about how to run my life.

Nevertheless, illustrations like this are misleading, as can be shown by a slight change of scenario. Suppose the kidnapping went as before, but you knew that if you did not perform the operation the kidnapper could easily get me back and carry out his original intention. My consent would be just as coerced as before, but it would be preposterous for you to claim that respect for my autonomy obliged you to refuse to operate and leave me to the other fate. Coercion as such, therefore, cannot justify the disregarding of stated preferences.

This may seem surprising, but the matter becomes clear if, instead of going off into the metaphysics of true consent, we ask directly what it is about coercion that makes a defender of autonomy regard it as intrinsically undesirable. Coercion is a matter of reducing the range of options there would otherwise be. Deliberate coercers come and take away options until the best available is what they want you to choose; circumstances like poverty can, by extension, be regarded as coercive because they are also constrictors of options that make you choose what you otherwise would not.[12] This shows what it is about the first of the kidnapping cases that makes it right for anyone concerned about autonomy to ignore the coerced choice. The relevant point is not that my original consent was coerced, but that, having got me into your hands and away from the kidnapper, you are in a position to *remove the coercion* by restoring my original range of options. In the second case, by contrast, you cannot remove the coercion because the kidnapper can get me back, and if you disregard my wishes you will (in the extended sense that allows poverty as a kind of coercion) coerce me yet further, by precluding the best option even among the horribly limited range the original coercer has left me.

This is why it is quite wrong to say that the poor should be protected from selling their kidneys, "preferably, of course, by being lifted out of poverty," but otherwise by the complete prevention of sales.[13] It implies that prohibition and "lifting out of poverty" are unequally desirable variations on the same general theme, whereas the foregoing argument shows them to be, in the relevant sense, direct opposites. Protecting the poor from kidney selling by removing poverty works by increasing the options until something more attractive is available; prevention of sales, in itself, only closes a miserable range of options still further. To the coercion of poverty is added the coercion of the supposed protector, who comes and takes away (what the prospective vendor sees as) the best that poverty has left. This cannot be justified by a concern for freedom and autonomy.

What has happened, once again, is that an argument starting from intuitively acceptable beginnings—the idea that poverty is a kind of coercion, and that anyone concerned with freedom and autonomy should regard coercion as intrinsically undesirable—has veered off into confusion. The idea that coercion precludes proper consent depends on a confusion between the possession of a limited range of options and an inability to choose properly between whatever options there are. Anyone concerned with autonomy and liberty must be concerned about both of these individually, but must also take care not to run them together. If having a narrow range of choices (coercion, in this extended sense) is mistaken for incompetence to choose among the existing range (absence of true consent), and the coerced choice is prevented for that reason, the effect is to produce *exactly the opposite* of what *each* concern requires. The competent are prevented from making their own choices, and the already circumscribed are constricted still further.[14] The plausible premises are actually at odds with the conclusion they are supposed to support.

And, once again, even if the argument did work it could still make no distinction between sales and donations. If vendors can be said to be coerced by circumstances, then, for the same reasons, so can donors. If losing a kidney is intrinsically undesirable, it is just as undesirable for a donor as for a vendor, and chosen only because constricted circumstances have made it the best option all things considered. If coercion is a reason for not allowing organ sales, and poverty counts as a kind of coercion, coercion by threat of the death of a relative—quite a heavy kind of coercion, you would think—should equally rule out donation.[15] The logic is the same.

C. Coercion by Unrefusable Offers.

A different kind of argument is that tempting someone like the Turkish peasant with a payment of several hundred times his annual income amounts to making him an offer he cannot refuse, and coercing him in that way. Sells, for instance, objecting to any "externally applied construction of an individual's right to choose not to donate," includes in this category "all cases where a person sells one of his organs during life," because "here the financial benefits have such an impact on the life of the donor and his family as to be irresistible: the element of voluntariness of donation must be at least compromised, or, in extreme cases, abolished."[16]

It is once again easy to see how this idea might arise. The irresistible offer, like poverty, has the effect of making the intrinsically unattractive prospect of losing an organ part of the best all-things-considered option, and may therefore seem coercive in the same way. And, furthermore, there is a significant difference between this and coercion by poverty. You cannot improve the situation of the poor by cutting off the organ-selling option, because what needs to be removed is the poverty that is doing the coercing, not the best option poverty has left. But the irresistible offer is quite different, because it is itself the source of the alleged coercion. It may seem, therefore, that in this case ending the trade removes what is doing the coercing, and is genuinely liberating.

This argument, however, fails at a different point. The second premise is wrong: the unrefusable offer is not a form of coercion. It does indeed change the situation until the all-things-considered best option includes the intrinsically undesirable element of kidney loss, but it does so, not through the narrowing of options that is characteristic of coercion, but through a broadening of them. The original options are all still there, and if you choose the new one you presumably regard it as better, all things considered, than any you had before; and, furthermore, the more irresistible you find it, the more decisive your preference. Removing it is yet again a constriction of options, not an elimination of coercion, and therefore cannot be justified by arguments based on ideals of freedom and autonomy.

It is also worth noticing that a corollary of this argument, if it worked, would be that the less you offered—the more resistible the potential vendor found your offer—the less coercion you would be applying. It would be convenient to be able to show consideration for the poor by paying less for what they had to sell.

This is not the end of the arguments about coercion. It is also objected that organ selling can be indirectly coercive, in exposing people to coercion by relatives: if the option to sell organs is there, people may be put under pressure to take it. This is important, but it raises rather different issues. It will be discussed later (section V.E, below).

IV. Problems for Paternalists

A. Harm to the Vendor. It seems to be taken for granted, in this debate, that if it is impossible to get informed, autonomous consent for nephrectomy, that is enough to rule it out. This is what underlies all the attempts to justify prohibition by way of arguments that genuine consent is unobtainable. The assumption is, however, a rather surprising one, since it is quite at odds with out usual attitudes to consent in medical context. If a rational agent *withholds* informed consent that is usually thought to settle the matter, but if someone is incapable of giving consent for consent-requiring procedures such as surgery we do not automatically say that these cannot go ahead; we usually say instead that some guardian should make the decision. Even if we could show that some would-be organ vendors were incapable of deciding for themselves, therefore, that would justify only our taking the decision out of their hands. It would not, in itself, justify our deciding one way rather than another.

To take the next step, and say that a competent guardian must decide against the sale of organs, is to claim that this is what is best for the would-be vendor. This amounts, in effect, to disputing another of the apparent harms of prohibition: that it takes away the best option of the badly off. Someone who claims, for instance, that "state paternalism grounded in social beneficence dictates that the abject poor should be protected from selling parts of their bodies to help their sad lot in life" needs to explain why the poor are misguided in their judgment that organ selling is in their best interests.[17]

The issue the paternalist has to settle is one of rational risk taking. The potential harm of losing a kidney must be weighed against the potential benefits of whatever payment is received, and assessed against the probabilities that these harms and benefits will actually come about. This is obviously not easy. Probabilities are difficult to estimate and differ considerably between cases, and individuals have different views about the comparative merits of different outcomes. There is also great variation in individuals' willingness to take risks.

In spite of these difficulties, however, one conclusion does seem clear. Most prospective paternalists have no hope of claiming plausibly that the poor who want to sell their kidneys are obviously wrong about what is in their interests, because they cheerfully countenance, in other contexts, the running of risks that are quite objectively much less rational than this one. The dangers of hang gliding or rock climbing, or diving from North Sea oil rigs, are much greater than those of nephrectomy;[18] and even though it is impossible to generalize about the benefits of particular sums of money to individuals, it is plausible to say that the expected benefits will be much greater to the desperately poor, who see in selling a kidney the only hope of making anything of their wretched lives and perhaps even of surviving, than to the relatively rich.[19] If the rich who take risks for pleasure or danger money are not misguided, it is difficult to see why the poor, who propose to take lower risks for higher returns, should be regarded as so manifestly irrational as to need saving from themselves. You might rather think, *contra* Dossetor and Manickavel, that the poorer you were the more rational it would be to risk selling a kidney.

And once again, even if we could reach the general conclusion that kidney selling was bad for the vendors, the argument would apply equally to donors. If any aspect of organ selling is against the interests of the vendor, it is not (though this obvious fact seems to be overlooked most of the time) the getting of money but the loss of a kidney, and this is in principle identical for donor and vendor. There is no reason to presume that whatever the money is wanted for must matter less to the vendor than saving the life of a relative must to a donor; it all depends on how much the relative is valued and what the money is for.[20] Even if we discount the people who want to save sick relatives, and think only of the ones bent on paying off debts or educating children or finding dowries for sisters,[21] they may well be much more anxious to do these things than many a downtrodden wife has been to save her husband's life. The exchange of money is not even an indicator, let alone a determinant, of what is from the point of view of the vendor (and therefore the paternalist) the difference between reasonable and unreasonable risk.

B. Harm to the Purchaser. Given the way the organ selling issue is usually presented, you would expect the third claimed disadvantage of prohibition—harm to the prospective purchasers—to go uncontested. If what is complained about is the unfair advantage of the greedy rich, obviously the complainer wants to put a stop to that advantage.

It is therefore worth noticing for the sake of completeness, and for evidence of the scrambling that goes on in this debate, that the purchasers sometimes find themselves transformed from exploiters into the victims of unscrupulous middlemen, of substandard and profiteering clinics, and even—in what would in less serious circumstances be an entertaining reversal of the original position—of the poor themselves, who are likely to be suffering from all kinds of dreadful diseases, and who, in their eagerness to get their hands on the money, will probably lie about their health and infect the hapless recipient with hepatitis or AIDS.[22] It has also been alleged that the purchasers, like the vendors, cannot be said to have given the proper consent required for treatment, because the lack of donors in their own country leaves them with no real choice.[23]

However, the foregoing arguments about the poor show by implication the mistakes in both these lines of argument. Even though many of the claims about exploitative and careless clinics and less than candid vendors may be true, the question here is not of whether the purchasers are less well served than they ought to be, but of whether they would be better off without the trade at all. Clearly many, if not most, would not. Even if treatment carries a significant risk of disease, the alternative for most of the patients is certain death. And, furthermore, even if the risk were not worth taking in the present circumstances, that would still be an objection only to inadequacy of control, rather than to the trade as such.

The other claim, that the purchasers have not really given voluntary consent, is yet another case in which having a narrow range of choice is confused with an inability to make a fully informed choice among the options there are. Once again, you cannot show respect for people's autonomy by preventing them from taking the best option in a range you are arguing is already too narrow. If, on the other hand, the problem is an inability to make an informed choice because of inadequate information, that is a reason for supplying the information rather than for removing the option altogether.

V. Overriding Objections

The conclusion of the arguments so far, then, is that the original account of the situation must stand. Prohibition does interfere with the choices of competent adults, and it does typically harm would-be vendors and purchasers. If the case for prohibition is to be made out, therefore, it must be shown that these intrinsic disadvantages are outweighed by considerations of greater importance. Since opponents of organ sales have not on the whole even reached the stage of recognizing that prohibition has any disadvantages, not many arguments are presented as actually setting out to do this. There are, however, several in the field that might be offered for the purpose. This section considers an assortment of the most familiar.

A. Collateral Damage. The most obvious kind of objection to look for, if the vendors and purchasers themselves must on the whole be regarded as beneficiaries of the trade, is counterbalancing harm elsewhere. A first glance at possibilities, however, looks unpromising. Anecdotes and statistics are offered about harm to the principals that may have repercussions for their families; but if on the whole the principals can expect to benefit, so, typically, can their families. Help for the family is often the purpose of the sale. Increased wealth to individuals presumably also tends to benefit the surrounding community, and the process in general involves a transfer of wealth from the rich to the poor. And, indeed, *unless* the trade can be shown to be wrong—the point presently at issue—even depriving the despised middlemen and operators of clinics of their socially useful niche in lands of few opportunities must count as an unjustifiable harm. If anything, the first foray into the area of collateral harm suggests that even more harm is done by prohibition than appeared at first.

Perhaps that is why the dark predictions are usually about dangers less tangible and more amorphous, such as the corruption of sensibilities and general moral decline.[24] Rhetoric, however, is not enough to counterbalance such positive harms as death and destitution. It is necessary to be clear about exactly which evils are threatened, what evidence there is that that they would come about, and how bad it would be if they did. Most of the threats turn out to be ill equipped to withstand this kind of scrutiny.

For instance, there is the allegation that the trade is wrong because it commodifies the body. In this case the claim is clear enough—the trade involves treating parts of the body as a purchasable commodity—and since this is precisely what the trade is, rather than anything it does, the question of evidence does not arise. But so far this is just a restatement of the point at issue, not an argument for objecting to it, and the question remains of what the harm is supposed to be. "Commodification" carries derogatory overtones, of course, which is why it is used; but without further explanation the pejorative term simply begs the question. This one takes its force from our outrage at the idea of treating people themselves as commodities, but before the moral implications can be dragged over—before we approve the loaded word "commodification" in this context—we need to see whether the moral suggestion is justified; and obviously it is not. Treating people as commodities, with no say in their own destiny, is just about as different as it could be from letting them decide for themselves what to do with their own bodies, which is what is at issue here and might reasonably be regarded as the most fundamental issue of autonomy there was.

Commodification is also alleged to cause further harms. "It depreciates some of the fundamental professional and moral values of society by demeaning the dignity and autonomy of the human individual";[25] "By commodifying the body, mutual respect for all persons will be slowly eroded."[26] Those certainly sound like harms; but now there is the problem of evidence. Autonomy is not infringed by the trade, as has already been argued at length. And even though it may be degrading to be in a state where organ selling is the best option left, that does not imply that actually going through with the sale increases the degradation (as is usually thought about prostitution, for instance). On the contrary, Reddy claims that for many vendors a positive motive is given by the duties of Hindu ethics, and that respect and self-respect increase because of a duty done.[27] And even in Western cultures, if some of the unemployed could get a large sum of money and start again, supporting their families instead of living on the dole, would there by anything but a huge increase in their self respect, and the respect of others? This is an empirical question, but I defy any caviller to produce any evidence the other way, or even evidence of having looked for any.

It is also said that the trade "invites social and economic corruption . . . and even criminal dealings in the acquisition of organs for profit."[28] That too is a clear harm, but again there is the question of evidence. It is well known that when a commodity is in demand it is the illegality of trade that produces corruption, as happened during Prohibition in the United States. Many people now defend the legalization of drugs and prostitution on just these grounds.

Another idea is that the trade has adverse effects on the transplant programme itself. One claim is that if purchase is a possibility, related donors are more reluctant to come forward.[29] But if it is being claimed as a harm of the trade that vendors rather than donors are used, that once again begs the question at issue. *Unless* there is a reason for objecting to the trade it does not matter intrinsically that organs should come from vendors rather than from donors. If, on the other hand, the concern is that transplants from related donors are likely to be more successful than from vendors, the question arises of what the evidence is that the harm would occur. If relatives knew that their kidney would probably do better than a stranger's, that would presumably be a significant element in their calculations.

It is also said that if organs can be bought from living vendors there will be no incentive to overcome public resistance to a cadaver programme.[30] That would indeed be a drawback, since nobody doubts that it is desirable (other things being equal) to make as much possible use of the dead before resorting to the living, but there is the question of evidence again. The availability of purchased organs is certainly not the only or main reason for the shortage of cadaver organs, since there is a shortage where they are not available. It is said that people in positions of power will have no incentive to press for the programme if they can go and buy kidneys; but it might equally well be claimed that since these very people are the ones who respond with such disgust to the trade, its continuation might induce them to press even harder for change. This is a possibility, but in the absence of any proper research, nothing more; and, in the meantime, nobody who is seriously concerned about the supply of organs will rush to cut off one source of supply without positive evidence that doing so will open up better ones.

And so it goes on. Nearly all the objections that appeal to claims about harms caused by organ selling either beg the question, or treat mere possibilities as actual, or fly in the face of positive evidence. It is still possible that trade causes collateral harms substantial enough to outweigh the harms done by prohibition, but that has yet to be shown; and in the meantime the burden of proof continues to lie against prohibition.

B. Exploitation. An objection of a different kind is that the trade must be ended because it involves exploitation. Poverty may not make people irrational, it may be agreed, but it does not make them vulnerable to exploitation, and the vulnerable must be protected. The trade should therefore be stopped.

The problem about this argument lies in the way exploitation works, and, once again, in the crucial difference between coercion and inducement to do what is intrinsically unattractive. Coercion works by the removal of other options until the unattractive one is the best left; and in such cases it is possible, as already argued, to protect the victim by putting a stop to the coercer's activities. But exploitation does not take this form. It works the opposite way, by adding inducements until they just tip the balance, and the intrinsically unattractive option becomes part of a package that is, all things considered, the best available. What is bad about exploitation, and makes it different from the offering of inducements that is a normal part of buying and hiring, is that the exploiter seeks out people who are so badly off that even a tiny inducement can improve on their best option, and in that way can get away with paying less than would be necessary to someone who had more options available. (If this is exploitation, of course, it looks suspiciously like free market capitalism; there is nothing new in that idea.) But the fact remains that it works by inducement, and the logic of inducements still applies. Nobody can improve your position by removing an effective inducement, however small, because to do so is to take away your all-things-considered best option.[31]

Once again, in other words, we have an argument with unexceptionable premises—that the poor are vulnerable to exploitation, and that they should be protected—but whose conclusion does not follow. Although we can stop the exploitation by stopping the trade, to do so would be like ending the miseries of slum dwelling by bulldozing slums, or solving the problem of ingrowing toenails by chopping off feet. We put an end to that particular evil, but only at the cost of making things even worse for the sufferers. If our aim is the protection of the poor rather than just the thwarting of the exploiters,[32] and we lack either the will or the power to remove the poverty that makes them exploitable in the first place, the next best thing is (once again) to subject the trade to stringent controls. That is the only way of ending the exploitation that also protects the poor.

C. Altruism. Another kind of argument still is presented, like the voluntarism requirement, as a moral absolute overriding all weighings of harms and benefits. Financial inducements, it is said, are to be ruled out because they preclude altruism, and an absolute requirement of organ donation is that it should be altruistic.

Since this requirement is usually asserted rather than argued for, it is presumably taken to be self-evident. Nevertheless, it is surprising. At least the other arguments discussed so far have started with plausible moral concerns about such things as coercion and exploitation, and have foundered only in the transition between these and their conclusions. But in this case the principle itself, for all its supposed self evidence, seems positively at odds with all our usual attitudes. The world is, after all, full of transactions which the transactors see as being to their mutual benefit, and to which in principle we have not the slightest objection. We may particularly admire their one-way equivalents, when goods and services are given that would otherwise have to be bought, but it normally does not occur to us that unless some transaction can be guaranteed to be of this one-way kind it should not take place at all. It would normally be regarded as astonishing, and in the absence of explanation absurd,[33] to claim that it would actually be better that neither side should benefit than that both should.

Even if we accepted the principle, however, it would still have the usual problem of not supporting the required conclusion. Selling is not in itself at odds with altruism; it all depends on what the money is wanted for. It does not even matter exactly what definition of altruism is accepted. For any action that an opponent of sales would count as altruistic, it is easy to imagine a case of selling that would be altruistic by the same standards. If a father who gives a kidney to save his daughter's life is acting altruistically, then so, by the same criterion, is one who sells his kidney to pay to save his daughter's life; if it is altruistic to work long hours to earn money for your family, it is altruistic to sell your kidney for the same purpose.

And yet again, if a demand for altruism could form any part of an argument to rule out sales—if, for instance, it were claimed that organ sales should be prohibited because they *might* not be altruistic—it would rule out donations as well. For any gift or service that would count as non-altruistic in other contexts, an equivalent can be imagined for the donation of organs. If your hope of inheriting money deprives your visits to your rich great-aunt of altruistic content, it does the same for your similarly-motivated kidney donation. The distinction between the altruistic and the non-altruistic, however defined, is unrelated to the distinction between organ giving and organ selling.

D. Slavery. Another common line of objection works by appealing to other practices that most people would agree were intolerable, and attempts to derive an objection to kidney selling from a linking of the two. Slavery is the commonest of these. "It is sometimes argued that an individual should be free to sell his organs just as he sells his labor, and why should there be any objection? This argument, if taken to its conclusion, may easily be used to justify a return to allowing individuals to sell themselves into slavery, which is clearly unacceptable."[34] Similar lines of argument suggest that if kidneys can be sold, there can be no objection to the selling of vital organs such as hearts.

Arguments like this are not always clear, and particular versions may need spelling out before detailed replies can be given. But the usual intention seems to be to produce a *reductio ad absurdum;* anyone who thinks kidney sales are acceptable is committed to thinking slavery (or, as it may be, heart selling) is also acceptable; but since slavery is manifestly wrong, kidney sales must be wrong as well.

If this is the idea, the quotation above shows by implication where this strategy goes wrong. The argument does not show that the acceptability of kidney selling entails the acceptability of slavery, but only that *one particular justification* someone might offer for condoning organ sales—that people should be free to sell whatever is theirs—also entails the acceptability of slavery. The argument therefore works only *ad hominem,* against someone who offers that particular defence. Acceptance of one practice can never, in itself, logically commit anyone to acceptance of some other: it always depends on what the reasons are. The line of argument being developed here, for instance—depending on the claim that prohibition does definite harms, and therefore that there is a presumption against it until good arguments in its favor are produced—does not depend on the principle that people have an entitlement to sell what is their own, and is immune to this particular attack.[35]

Arguments of this kind exemplify yet again the now-familiar pattern. Most people are likely to agree that to allow slavery or the selling of hearts would obviously be wrong, but those premises are not enough to support the conclusion that kidney sales must therefore be wrong as well. And anyway, such an argument could not make the necessary distinction between sales and donations. People are not allowed to *give* themselves into slavery or give away their hearts, either, so if the argument did work we should have to conclude that the unpaid donation of kidneys should also be forbidden.

E. Higher-Level Preferences. This by no means exhausts the arguments, but the sound of barrel scraping increases with every new attempt, and enough of the familiar ground has been covered for the purposes of this essay. There is, however, one other kind of argument that should be mentioned, because although it hardly ever appears in the current debate—at least in a recognizable form—it is of an important general kind, and has a potential for success lacked by the candidates considered so far.

This is the possibility that lurks behind the idea that organ sales should be stopped because of the danger of pressure from relatives.[36] As it stands, this argument is as hopeless as the result of the repertoire, and for much the same reasons. If the risk of pressure to choose some option were enough on its own to justify the removal of that option altogether, it would lead to the conclusion that no one should have any options at all. (People should not be allowed to choose whom to marry, in case they were morally bullied into making an unwelcome choice.) And, in particular, it would rule out organ donations, since if the possibility of donations exist, so does the possibility of pressure to donate.

Nevertheless a potentially good kind of argument can be developed from these beginnings, which raises the possibility of bridging legitimately the gap between ideals of freedom and self determination, on the one hand, and conclusions that options should be restricted, on the other. This can be spelt out as a reply to the earlier arguments about coercion by unrefusable offers. The essence of the point is that it is too simple to presume that giving people a new opportunity must necessarily count as an extension of their options in any relevant way. What looks superficially like a straightforward addition to some range of choices, leaving all previous options intact, may really be nothing so simple. The addition may subtly change the existing range, removing possibilities that were there before; and if that happens, the choice of the new option is not enough to prove that it is preferred to anything previously available.

The pressure argument can be recast, schematically, in this form. As long as kidney selling is not a possibility you can keep at once your kidney, a clear conscience and family harmony. If a market develops you may feel you are being selfish for not taking the opportunity to benefit the family, or they may start dropping hints about how useful the money would be, and then your original option will have gone, and you will have to choose between keeping the kidney and satisfying the family. If you would have preferred the old situation to any of the options available in the new one, your range of choice has been *lessened* by the new one in the relevant sense of its having deprived you of a better option than it has introduced. Deciding in advance whether some new option is to be welcomed is once again a matter of deciding which risks should be taken. If you think the new option offers more dangers than benefits, and if in consequence you would prefer the present range of options to the new possibilities that would be opened up by the market in kidneys, anyone concerned for your freedom and autonomy would prefer to satisfy your higher-level preference to be without the new one.

This kind of recasting is important, because it shows how an argument starting with principles about the importance of autonomy might reach a conclusion that options should be curtailed, and explains how it might be rational to prefer to be without some option, even though it would have been chosen if it had been available. It also has another great advantage conspicuously lacked by other arguments considered so far, which is the potential for distinguishing between sales and donations. There may be good reasons for preferring to have one option open, but not the other. It depends on how the risks and benefits of each are assessed.

And, furthermore, this way of looking at the matter extends the range of possibly effective arguments for prohibition still further, because it shows that the risk of coercion is not the only reason there might be for preferring to be without a particular option. We have all kinds of reasons for preferring to be without options, many familiar from everyday life,[37] and others might arise in this context too.

One other possibility particularly worth mentioning is proposed (as part of a separate thesis, rather than as part of the organs debate) by the economist Robert Frank.[38] He argues that individuals are more concerned than is generally recognized about their relative, as opposed to absolute, position in the possession of various goods, and that one consequence of this is their agreeing to restrain competitions that would use considerable effort and resources, but leave relative positions much as they had been before.[39] He thinks this accounts for ways in which societies try to limit the role of money, and in particular for prohibitions on the sale of bodily parts. Although you can get ahead temporarily by selling yours, so can everyone else by selling theirs; and everyone will end up in the same relative position but with jeopardized health.

Frank presents this idea rather ambiguously between an *explanation* of why societies do this, and a *justification* of their doing it. The question here is about justification, and from this point of view the proposal is interesting for various reasons. It is like the foregoing argument about pressures in offering a justification in terms of higher-level preferences for removing a lower-level option, but it is different in several significant ways. One difference is that it contains, much more obviously than the pressure argument, the potential for distinguishing between sales and donations: organ giving does not offer a way for people to improve their social positions that could lead to a self-defeating competition, whereas organ selling might. But a more fundamental one is that it defends the conclusion that *everyone* in a particular society should be deprived of the option in question.

If the pressure argument considered earlier works, it is important that it works *for individuals*: any individual may decide, irrespective of what any others decide, that the danger of pressure to use some option may make it better to be without it. But it is the essence of the kind of case just considered that it is always a potential disadvantage to any individual, considered alone, to be without the option in question. It makes sense to want to be without it *only if you can get everyone else to agree to do the same*, and, it may be added, if the only way to get them to agree is for you to agree as well. (The best of all, from your own point of view, is to deprive everyone else, but not yourself, of the option.)[40] This difference has considerable implications for social policy, since in the first kind of case anyone concerned with individual liberty will try, as far as possible, to devise ways of giving different people their individual preferences, while in the second kind it is essential that the restriction should apply to whole communities. This possibility is therefore important for the question of which general prohibitions are compatible with concerns for freedom and autonomy.

However, it is essential to stress that, interesting as such possibilities are, they are still only possibilities. This is a kind of argument that *could* work, but only *if* it is actually the case that people do, or at least rationally should, have higher-level preferences to be without particular options, and so far none of the arguments seems compelling. Even the Frank proposal—the most interesting contender so far, and the only one I am aware of that actually recognizes the form of the problem and addresses it in that way—depends on accepting that most of the goods people want are for their positional rather than their absolute value, and that organ selling has the potential for runaway competition that would benefit nobody.[41] It seems far from clear that either of these is true. Even in affluent societies by no means all goods are wanted for their positional value, and in poor societies—the source of the vendors—even fewer of them must be. There is nothing in the least positional about the Turkish man's wish to save his daughter, nor in the desire of the abjectly poor to have the prospect of something other than a miserable grind for the whole of their short lives. Nor does organ selling have the runaway potential of the paradigm cases cited by Frank, since there is a fairly low limit to the number of kidneys that can be sold.

It is also significant that this line of argument works only from the point of view of potential vendors, and entirely overlooks the interest of recipients. People trying to decide whether it would be rational to be bound by rules of this kind would have to take into consideration the possibility not only that they might be tempted to sell organs, but also that they might need to buy them.

So although there are possibilities in arguments of this general form, no successful one seems yet to have been produced; and possibilities are not enough, because here is another context in which there seems to be a clear direction of onus of proof. A curtailment of options is just that, and must be presumed by anyone concerned with liberty an unjustifiable restriction of liberty until proved otherwise. Until a properly worked out argument is produced, the prohibition of organ sales remains without justification.

PART TWO—THE IMPLICATIONS FOR MORAL ENQUIRY

VI. A Series of Show Trials

The claim so far has been that the prohibition of organ sales seems to involve real harms of various sorts, and that none of the arguments offered by its defenders has succeeded in showing either that these are illusory, or that allowing the trade would cause even greater harms, or that there are overriding moral reasons of other kinds for concluding that they must be put up with. The conclusion at this stage must therefore be that there is no justification for prohibition, but only for trying to lessen whatever incidental harms are now involved in the practice.

The form the arguments have taken shows that this conclusion is only provisional. Someone may yet come along with good enough reasons to overcome the presumption in favor of organ sales; and, for what it is worth, I have a sneaking hope that this will happen, since I find the whole business as intuitively repugnant as does everybody else. But even if it does happen that will not affect the significance of the foregoing arguments, because the primary purpose of this paper is not to defend organ sales. Its purpose is to draw wide conclusions about the form of the debate; and to explain that it is necessary to go back and reconsider what has been going on so far.

A. The Form of the Arguments. An outsider, hearing that some essay had presented a defence of kidney selling, would probably presume that the argument was based on controversial libertarian principles about free trade and the rights of people to do what they liked with their own bodies, and—if unsympathetic—start raising moral or empirical objections to principles of that kind. But not only have the arguments offered here not depended on such principles; what is more significant is that they have not depended on controversial premises at all, either moral or empirical. They have depended almost entirely on logic and analysis, and have tried to show that the traditional arguments against organ sales fail not by the standards of some outside critic, but in their proponents' own terms.

There is, for instance, no sign that any opponent of organ sales would dispute the minimal moral starting point of this paper. There is nothing arcane about the idea that death, suffering, and the lessening of people's control over their own destinies are intrinsically undesirable and not to be tolerated without good reason. The fact that most opponents of organ sales accept this is shown by their attempts to prove that it is organ selling, rather than its prohibition, that results in such harms.

Conversely, hardly any of my own objections to the familiar arguments against organ sales have disputed the moral premises on which the arguments are based. I have not denied, for instance, that freedom and autonomy are good things, or that people should be protected from exploitation, or that it is dreadful for anyone to be driven by poverty into organ selling. Nearly all the criticisms made have been about the impossibility of reaching the conclusion that organ sales should be forbidden *given* the principles invoked by their proponents. The only principle that has been challenged is the altruism requirement, and even in that case the argument is based on the incompatibility of the requirement with what its proponents would accept in other contexts.

The criticisms have also not depended on controversial empirical claims. Most of them (about why unrefusable offers are not forms of coercion, for instance, or why the harm of exploitation cannot be prevented by the removal of the exploiters) have had nothing at all to do with empirical matters. But even in the exceptions, the arguments have not depended on positive empirical claims of my own, but on the negative claim that the arguments against organ sales themselves depend on empirical claims (for instance, about harmful consequences of the trade) for which their proponents have no evidence, or even, in some cases (as with the idea that legalization is likely to lead to corruption), have positive evidence against. Mere possibilities are being treated as facts, which is particularly unacceptable when the onus of proof goes the other way, and which nobody would regard as acceptable in an opponent's arguments.

The usual run of arguments against organ sales, therefore, fails not by the standards of some external critic who is producing rival empirical claims or offering different bases for moral judgment, but in terms of the very standards recommended by the proponents of the arguments themselves. The conclusions do not follow from the principles invoked in their support, either because the logic goes wrong or because the inference depends on invented facts. And it is worth noticing that this point is relevant to the familiar, last rest, all-purpose escape route of people driven into unwelcome corners by argument, which is the claim that logic must not be placed above moral intuitions. This line of argument cannot get off the ground because what logic demonstrates in cases like these is conflicts *of intuitions* (between, for instance, the importance of autonomy and impermissibility of organ selling) which the familiar arguments try to hide by presenting them as compatible or even necessarily connected. If there really is a conflict, so that one or the other must be given up or made subordinate to the other, it is *morally essential* that this should be faced.[42] Flailing at logic is not an appeal to a higher morality, but a refusal to attend to moral questions at all.

B. The Significance of the Failures.   The next significant point about the failures of the usual arguments is that they are not of an obscure kind, discoverable only by deep philosophical analysis, but mistakes that no one would be in any danger of making in less fraught contexts. This becomes apparent as soon as they are suitably transposed.

It is claimed, for instance, that concern for the vendor's autonomy demands the prohibition of organ sales, because the trade involves coercion by poverty or unrefusable offers, and true consent is therefore impossible. But if you reluctantly came to the conclusion that you must sell your great-grandmother's portrait, either because you were poor and threatened with eviction (coercion) or because Sotheby's had predicted it would fetch a million pounds at auction (unrefusable offer), no one would think it anything but a joke if friends expressing concern for your autonomy proposed to rush in to stop you on the grounds of coercion's precluding your true consent.[43]

Much the same applies to the rest of the arguments. It is argued that organ sales must be stopped because of exploitation and shoddy practices; but if the only shop in a neighborhood has been getting away with exploitatively high prices, or the only hospital with substandard treatment, it does not occur to anyone that simply closing them down, and leaving no services at all, is a useful way to protect the local population. Or it is argued that organ giving must be altruistic; but although we admire altruism, and are full of approval when aging parents are looked after by their children for love, we are not usually tempted to infer from this that people who have no relatives, or who are not loved by them, should do without care altogether rather than pay for it. Or it is said that organ selling involves unreasonable risks for the poor, but (as already argued) no one thinks twice about leaving well-off people to their own devices when they take greater risks for lower returns. And so on. In neutral contexts, these arguments would not deceive anyone for a moment.

This shows what is really going on. The familiar arguments against organ sales are rationalizations, and flagrant ones at that, of something already believed for other reasons. No one starting innocently from the beginnings of these arguments could possibly arrive at the conclusions to which they are supposed to lead. They seem to work only because their proponents are already, independently, convinced of their truth.

This is also suggested by many other aspects of the debate. It appears, for instance, in the speed of public reaction to the discovery of the trade, and the terms in which it was immediately condemned. If people had really been trying to work out whether this quite new activity was justified or not, they could hardly have overlooked so completely the obvious *prima facie* harms of prohibition, and would have been agonizing over the complexities of the problem rather than rushing into action. It appears in the way every demolished argument is immediately replaced by another, with ever weaker ones recruited to the cause as the early contenders fail. If the conclusion had been reached *by means of* some argument, refutation of that argument would be recognized as removing the reasons for accepting the conclusion. It also shows in the way assorted arguments of quite different and often incompatible kinds are heaped up together,[44] and in the flagrant invention of convenient facts. Both of these typically occur when deeply held convictions are being anxiously defended.

It is probably this deep conviction, furthermore, that underlies the ready characterizations (by people who probably know nothing of the matter) of all the surgeons and clinic organizers and middlemen involved as villains. There are horror stories about all these groups; but there are horror stories about most areas of commerce, and this does not tempt us to assume that all dealers must be scoundrels or all trade profiteering, or even to express outrage (as opposed to disquiet) in other contexts where vast profits are made from the practice of medicine. If it is assumed that anything earned through organ sales must be tainted, that suggests the trade is regarded as inherently, not merely incidentally, corrupt.

The moral of these arguments, therefore, is not just that the arguments offered for prohibition do not work, though that is important in itself. What is more significant is that there obviously exists a deep intuition about the unacceptability of organ sales, quite independent of, and fuelling, the curiously bad arguments pressed into its defence. That is why, even if a good argument for prohibition does appear later, it will not undermine the significance of the failure of the familiar set. The form of that failure proves the verdict of guilty to have been pronounced in advance, and the supposed debate merely a series of show trials.

VII. Repugnance as a Moral Guide

The fact that the intuitive resistance to organ sales exists quite independently of the arguments normally invoked to justify prohibition does not in itself prove that the intuition is misguided. Organ selling might still be something intrinsically evil, defying justification in terms of anything more fundamental. We do think there are such things; we must, if we think ethics is to get off the ground at all. Perhaps, then, all that can ultimately be said about the matter is caught by our rapid characterization of the whole business as *repugnant*—a word we tend to use when we are deeply averse to something, but find our feelings difficult to explain in terms of more obvious kinds of good and evil.

It is often said that such deep intuitions should be our ultimate moral authority: that "it is the emotional conviction which ultimately should determine where one makes one's stand."[45] But nobody seriously believes that all strong feelings of a moral kind are reliable guides to action. We are not even tempted to think so except in the case of our own; intuitions we do not share are seen as manifestations of irrationality and bigotry. And we should have doubts even about our own when we consider how passionately people may feel about matters that detached reflection suggests must be morally neutral, such as particular forms of the treatment of the dead,[46] or how many traditional reactions of deep repugnance to such things as interracial marriage, unfeminine women and homosexuality are now widely regarded as themselves repugnant. Mere strength of feeling cannot be taken to prove that moral bedrock has been reached.

How, then, can the moral reliability of this particular strong feeling be tested? If the idea is that whatever causes it is a fundamental evil in its own right, it is obviously irrelevant to test that claim by seeing whether it can be shown to be wrong in other terms. But anyone who is inclined to accept it as a moral guide can start by checking carefully exactly what circumstances prompt its appearance. Just as people are inclined to justify their wish to prohibit organ selling in terms of other kinds of moral concern, so, for obviously related reasons, they are inclined to explain their emotional response as arising in respect to exploitation, or inequality, or some other morally plausible generator of strong feelings. To test such claims, what is needed is a series of thought experiments. Organ sales and these other causes of moral concern can be imagined away from each other, to discover what really gives rise to the feelings of disgust. When that has been identified, it will be possible to look whatever it is squarely in the eye, and see whether reflection can endorse the idea that it is a fundamental evil.

So, for instance, it may be said that we find the trade repugnant because of the harm it does to the vendors; but if that were true, we should find the idea of making their situation worse by stopping the trade more repugnant still (worse that the

Turkish father should be forced to keep his kidney and watch his daughter die than that he should sell it and save her); and we should find donations repugnant in exactly the same way, since they do the same kind of harm.

We may claim to be disgusted that organs should be sacrificed for any other reason than love, or with less than complete willingness; but then we should find it no more repugnant that a father should sell his kidney to save his daughter than that he should give it to her directly, and we should feel just the same kind of repugnance at the thought that some reluctant relative should feel the heavy pressure of duty, or fear, and donate an organ without love.

We may say that what we find most repugnant about the trade is the abuse and exploitation; but in that case we should feel just as much disgust, of the same kind, about equal exploitation and abuse in other areas, and even more when these are worse (as, for instance, with the slave labor that produces cheap luxury goods for the affluent world). And, conversely, if the abuses were ended, and the trade properly regulated, the feelings of revulsion should go.

We may say that the disgust arises from the idea of cutting into, and damaging, a health body. If so, we should feel as much disgust about donations as about sales; and since no harm can be done by cutting into a dead body, there should be no disgust at the prospect of selling organs from the dead.[47]

We may claim that the source of the disgust is the unfairness of distribution: "wealthy people obtaining services not available to others."[48] If so, we should feel the same repugnance about any kind of private medicine (and, indeed about state-financed triple bypasses for citizens of the rich world whose cost would save thousands of lives elsewhere), and none if public agencies were to buy organs for general distribution.

Or we may say that the disgust is aroused by the desperate situation of the poor, and their being forced by circumstances to make such terrible decisions. If so, we should feel the same kind of disgust when desperation forces them to sell their labor at appallingly low prices (and more still if they can find no one to buy at any price and cannot alleviate their situation at all), and none at the idea that some reasonably well off person from a rich society might sell a kidney to achieve some non-necessary personal project, like travelling round the world or learning to fly.

Thought experiments like these make it clear to most people that when suffering and exploitation are imagined separately from the element of selling, the *peculiar kind of horror* aroused by the trade in organs does not appear. There may be other feelings of moral outrage, but not this one. And they also make it clear that in most cases—and probably, for most people, all cases[49]—the converse is also true. Take away these other elements that are claimed as the source of the disgust—consider organ selling in altruistic, non-exploitative, well-regulated circumstances—and the disgust obstinately remains. It really does seem to be the business of exchanging money for parts of the body, in itself and for no further reason, that catches our feelings in this distinctive way.

It is perhaps worth commenting that an indirect confirmation of this conclusion seems to lie in the only solution I have been able to think of to the mystery of the altruism requirement. There are many familiar contexts in which the contrast between giving and selling is described as between doing things for love—altruistically—and doing them for money. If this kind of contrast is (mistakenly) thought of as paradigmatic, the demand for altruism may get its apparent force from seeming to coincide with the absence of payment, while at the same time giving the appearance of offering justification because nobody doubts that altruism is a good thing. The altruism requirement, in other words, looks suspiciously like a mere restatement of the non-selling requirement, with spurious moral knobs on.[50]

If all this is true, and the emotional reaction really is to organ sales as such, irrespective of circumstances and consequences, is it possible to endorse it as a moral guide? Can the wrongness of organ sales be accepted as a ground-level moral fact, and one of such importance as to outweigh all our usual concerns about death, destitution and loss of liberty whenever they come into conflict?

When the matter is put as starkly as this it is hard to see how anyone could see it as a fundamental moral fact at all, let alone one of such overriding importance. Most people who react with repugnance to organ sales see nothing wrong in the exchange of money for goods in other circumstances, and see the donation of organs as positively commendable. Is it plausible that the combination of the two, in itself and for no further reason, can nevertheless be self-evidently and invariable evil? Can a sacrifice made with love and altruism be turned into a moral outrage just because payment comes somewhere into the matter, while an equal sacrifice made reluctantly or through vested interests is acceptable because it does not? Can the mere exchange of money transmute something inherently good into a transaction so appalling that it might even be better, as Broyer suggests,[51] to risk losing genuinely unpaid donations (and allow people to die in consequence) than allow even the *possibility* that payment might be involved? Presumably the feelings of repugnance can in principle be explained (perhaps in terms of Frank-type reasons), but it is hard to see how anyone could endorse them as moral guides.[52]

And as a matter of fact, it seems that nobody really does. Even if these arguments did not make it obvious that the prevention of organ selling *could* not plausibly be regarded as morally fundamental, it is nevertheless clear that it *is* not so regarded, because all the familiar arguments against organ sales try to explain its wrongness in other terms. Nobody says that it just is more important to prevent organ selling than any more obvious sort of harm, and leaves the matter there. Prohibition, it seems, must be justified, even if the only way to do it is to fudge connections and compatibilities with the very moral concerns that it overrides.

In fact, another thing that seems implied by the fragility of the familiar arguments is that the extreme strength of feeling underlying the resistance to organ sales runs with the recognition that it needs some defending. People do not resort to arguments as bad as these unless they think arguments are badly needed.

VIII. The New Form of the Problem

The situation then is this. When states enact laws forbidding the exchange of money for organs, or professional bodies pronounce their anathemas against it, they present their conclusions as arising from plausible moral concerns about autonomy, exploitation, and the interests of the poor. If my arguments have been right, however, this is not at all what is going on. In fact there is a strong, widely held and quite independent conviction that organ sales must be wrong, into whose defence has been pressed a motley array of arguments that could not have begun to persuade anyone who was really trying to work out the rights and wrongs of the issue from scratch. The prohibition of organ sales is derived not from the principles usually invoked in its support, but from a powerful feeling of repugnance that apparently numbs ordinary moral sensitivities and anaesthetizes the intellect, making invisible the obvious harms of prohibition, giving plausibility to arguments whose inadequacy would in less fraught contexts proclaim itself from the rooftops, and, in doing both these things, hiding the extraordinary force of its own influence.

And, furthermore, it exerts this force in a particularly sinister way. If we allow the feeling to direct our actions, the effect will be that we will try to get rid of whatever causes it. If it is not reliably connected to anything that ought, morally, to be eliminated, the *only* systematic benefit of removing its cause will be the elimination of the feeling as an end in itself. This is, of course, a great advantage to all those sensitive Westerners who suffer from it. Prohibition may make things worse for the Turkish father and other desperate people who advertise their kidneys, as well as for the sick who will die for lack of them; but at least these people will despair and die quietly, in ways less offensive to the affluent and healthy, and the poor will not force their misery on our attention by engaging in the strikingly repulsive business of selling parts of themselves to repair the deficiencies of the rich. But to place our own squeamish sensibilities above this real death or despair seems about as thoroughgoing an exploitation of the poor by the rich as any that has yet been discussed. If that is to be avoided, the influence of the feeling of repugnance must be eliminated from the analysis.

This is not, unfortunately, something that can be simply resolved on and done. It has been shown how thoroughly the deep opposition to organ sales can distort the arguments, and how invisible its influence can be even in the relatively straightforward cases discussed earlier. In complicated arguments about risks and probabilities, or individual preferences and social policies, it is inherently difficult for even the most unprejudiced enquirer to reach objective conclusions, and therefore all too easy to go through the motions of analysis and make the conclusion come out where the emotions have already determined that they should. On the other hand, once the problem and its manifestations have been recognized, there are various ways in which the danger may be lessened.

In the first place, if the failed arguments really do involve mistakes that would not be made in neutral contexts, one remedy is to be much more critical about the analysis of arguments in general, asking firmly of any candidate what we should think of its merits if we were really starting from the premises and asking, without any preconceptions, whether they supported the conclusion. Another technique is to use analogous arguments from other contexts as checks (as in the beginning of VI.B, above). Yet another is to regard with particular suspicion arguments whose conclusions come out the way we want them to.

It is also worth remembering that a favorite hiding place of old prejudices is in modified versions of absolute constraints. For instance, Dossetor and Manickavel (reluctantly) concede that there may sometimes be adequate justification for organ selling, but want to allow it only among certain populations, and even then hedged round with qualifications and restrictions. "For ethical acceptability potential kidney sellers must justify their desire on the grounds of 'indirect altruism' and potential buyers must be considered for the additional social obligation of 'mandated philanthropy' [essentially a tax to pay for transplants for members of the class from which the vendor came]—the decision being taken by a panel of society representatives."[53] Because dogma is being loosened and good causes supported this may sound liberal and benevolent, but the fact remains that purchasers and vendors are to be put through a series of hoops for which no justification is offered, and that the ones who stumble are left with the same unjustified harms as before. Why should vendors be made to prove altruistic intentions, rather than be allowed to judge their own best interests? Why should there be a tax on this surgical procedure, and this trade, but not others? Pretty obviously, there is still lurking in the background an assumption that the whole business is inherently shady, and that if it has to be allowed at all it must be severely restricted and purified by being forced to do other kinds of good. The feelings of repugnance are still working as hard as ever to distort the analysis, and the apparent concessions only slight lessenings of unjustified harm.

It is not only the details of the arguments, however, that have been distorted by the feelings of repugnance. More fundamentally, their influence has extended to the way the whole problem has been presented. The issue is usually seen as a "for and against" question, with two opposing sides. There is certainly an *against* side, in the sense that most of the opponents of organ sales seem to accept, as a moral absolute, the idea that organ sales are always and obviously wrong. But if you reject this idea—if you agree that the appearance of an absolute can be traced to a feeling of repugnance with highly dubious credentials—that does not mean you are *for* organ sales in the sense of supporting a corresponding absolute in favor of them, let alone in favor of an unfettered trade. To reject the absolute is, in itself, only to remove a constraint on the kind of answer that can be given to the wider question of how we can most acceptably procure organs for transplant, thereby opening the question up, and turning it (it has to be admitted) into the the kind of messy calculation of pros and cons that characterizes most moral decisions about public policy. And once the problem is recognized as taking this form, it becomes clear that there is no reason to expect a single answer to it, or to think of fixed and opposing sides at all.

In the first place, the answer may depend on all kinds of contingencies: on how many organs are needed, how many people are disposed to bequeath or donate them, the state of technology, the definition of death, social attitudes, the practicability of controls, the possibility of xenografting, and innumerable other matters. Changing circumstances may make prohibition desirable at some times but not at others.

Second, different answers may be appropriate in different places, even at a single time. Even if prohibition were thought desirable for one social group, it need not be for all. If (say) India came to a different conclusion from Britain—as an argument along the Frank lines might well imply, if one could be made to work—it would be a mistake to see that as a matter of India's accepting second class ethics.[54] Quite the contrary; if poor countries were put (or put themselves) under pressure to adopt policies appropriate only for richer ones, that would amount to yet another kind of oppression of the poor by the rich.[55] (This danger seems to lurk everywhere in this debate except where it is expected).

And third, whether the purchase of organs can be justified may depend not only on what the current circumstances are, but also on what arrangements we can devise within them. We might well decide that organ sales should be allowed if they could be arranged in certain ways (for instance with proper controls), but not in others (unbridled free enterprise). And when this is recognized, the issue of organ procurement changes its character completely, because instead of a simple question about whether this or that should be allowed, what appears is a choice between indefinitely many competing alternative policies. Total prohibition is only one option, to be compared with various kinds of local or temporary prohibitions, and every imaginable kind of arrangement for the controlling of sales. The question becomes permanently the general one of whether we can think of *better ways of arranging matters than at present*.

That, as it stands, leaves entirely open the question of the permissibility of organ sales. However, the fact also remains that nothing has yet dislodged the claim that the prohibition of organ sales harms both vendors and purchasers, and involves interventions in personal liberty. Nobody setting out in an unprejudiced way to improve some situation rushes to cause harm or restrict liberty. If there are abuses and dangers in the present trade, as there certainly are, the obvious way to improve the situation is to try to remove those. Only in circumstances where that turns out to be impossible, *and* there is good reason to think that the harms of organ trading outweigh the benefits, can prohibition be justified. Since the second has not been demonstrated, or the first even tried in any systematic way, the presumption must still be against prohibition.

There is also one further, positive, reason for keeping the trade in organs, which sounds perverse but is actually offered here more than half seriously. This is the very fact that most people do find it so profoundly shocking and distressing. It certainly is shocking; it is dreadful that people should be forced by distress and destitution into selling parts of themselves. Nevertheless, the fact remains that we seem quite capable of putting up with even worse distress as long as it is not forced on our attention in this peculiarly distasteful way. Many a Turkish peasant is now presumably worse off than before we banned the trade, and the potential recipients of their kidneys may be dead; but we are not clamouring about these desperate lives and ultimately deaths in the way we did about the evils of the trade. If we can be so unpleasantly reminded of the way things really are we may begin to take the despair of the poor and the dying more seriously: to make comparable outcries about the terms of third world trade, and give money to Oxfam, and leave kidneys to whoever needs them.

The sale of organs may perhaps be, as Broyer says, "a visible and intolerable symptom of the exploitation of the poor by the rich," but if so that is a reason for allowing it to continue.[56] If we are forced to suffer the intolerable symptoms, we shall less easily forget the disease.

READING ENDNOTES

1. An earlier version of some of these arguments appeared in Radcliffe Richards, J.: 1991, 'From him that hath not,' in W. Land and J.B. Dossetor (eds.) Organ Replacement Therapy: Ethics, Justice, Commerce, Springer-Verlag, Berling, New York: reprinted in C.M. Kjellstrand and J.B. Dossetor (eds.), Ethical Problems in Dialysis and Transplantation, Kluwer Academic Publishers, Dordrecht, 1992, pp. 53–60. I am grateful to members of the International Transplant Ethics Forum for helpful discussions of the present version.

2. Most sufferers from ESRD cannot be saved by dialysis, sometimes for physiological reasons, but in most cases because dialysis is simply unavailable. In India, for example, it is estimated that over 90% of sufferers die (see. e.g., Reddy, K.C., Thiagarajan, C.M., Shunmugasundaran, D., et al.: 1990, Unconventional renal transplantation in India: To buy or let die. Transplant Proceedings 22: 910), and the ones who buy kidneys in Bombay clinics would otherwise be among them; in Britain it is estimated that 2,000 patients a year die because of the unavailability of dialysis. Dialysis is also far more expensive than transplantation, in Britain costing about £25,000 *per year*, as opposed to a single cost of about £8,000 for a transplant (*The Sunday Times*, 30 July 1995). However much money were available for treatment, therefore, transplantation could save many times more lives than dialysis. Since there is an enormous shortage of organs available for transplant it must be presumed, in the absence of evidence to the contrary, that the purchase of organs does save lives and would, if more widely allowed, save many more.

   Dialysis is also incomparably less satisfactory from the point of view of quality of life. The patient in the *Sunday Times* report "felt as if his life had stopped" when renal disease forced him to give up his work and go on to dialysis. He found the experience "incredibly stressful," and expressed surprise that suicide was not more common among dialysis patients.

3. This happened in Britain in January 1989. The case was reported and discussed in all national newspapers between mid-January and early February, e.g., in *The Independent*, January 18.

4. Council of the Transplantation Society: 1985, 'Commercialization in transplantation: The problems and some guidelines for practice,' *The Lancet*, September 28, pp. 715–716.

5. This way of expressing the matter is meant to show that the argument is neutral between consequentialist and non-consequentialist approaches to ethics. Irrespective of whether interfering with people's choices about their own destinies is thought to *do them harm*, for instance, or to *deny their prima facie rights*, there is still a presumption against doing it, and a need for justification if it is to be done. Because nothing in the argument is affected by this distinction I shall ignore it from now on, and 'doing harm' should be taken as standing in for any kind of concern that provides a presumption against a particular action or policy.

6. The distinction between the claim that something is *intrinsically* bad (harmful or otherwise undesirable), and the quite different claim that it is bad *all things considered* and should not happen, will be crucial throughout this essay. It will not be practicable to hammer the point home on every occasion where their confusion would lead to misunderstanding.

7. Sells, R.A.: 1993, 'Resolving the conflict in traditional ethics which arises from our demand for organs,' Transplantation Proceedings 25 (6), December, pp. 2983–2984.

8. See, e.g., Broyer, 1991, p. 199: "It is far from sure that the donor would be able to understand fully the information about the sequelae of nephrectomy."

9. See the beginning of section IV, below.

10. Some people object to the use of live donors altogether, but for them the separate question of payment does not arise. This paper is specifically about whether the exchange of money can make unacceptable something that would otherwise have been acceptable. Anyone who has a general objection to the use of live donors can still consider the case of cadaveric organs, and the acceptability of payment for those. The arguments of this paper apply also to that problem, even though it is not directly discussed.

11. Dossetor, John B. and Manickavel, V.: 1992, 'Commercialization: The buying and selling of kidneys,' in C.M. Kjellstrand and J.B. Dossetor (eds.), *Ethical Problems in Dialysis and Transplantation*, Kluwer Academic Publishers, Dordrecht, p. 63. See also Abouna et al., 1991, p. 166: "A truly voluntary and noncoerced consent is also unlikely... The desperate financial need of the donor is an obvious and clear economic coercion."

12. This is how coercion differs from direct force: it depends on getting the person being coerced to make a choice. This is true even in extreme cases, although it may sound paradoxical. Before the kidnapper holds a gun to your child's head you can, technically, choose to keep your money and your child, or only the child (by giving away the money), or only the money (by abandoning the child). You do not think of these as a set of options only because it is so obvious which to choose, but they are all there. The kidnapper removes the first (best) option, leaving you to choose between the other two. This is also why it may be plausible to count poverty as a kind of coercion, even though there is no coercer trying to bring about a particular result: there are fewer choices than there would be if there were no poverty, so different choices are made. Note, however, that if this extended sense of the word is accepted it follows that we are coerced by circumstances whenever we do anything we find intrinsically undesirable, like paying the gas bill or having to work for a living. This makes coercion a matter of degree, and its complete absence impossible.

13. Dossetor and Manickavel, p. 63.

14. Note, however, a limiting case that may be the cause of some confusion: coercion may sometimes be so extreme as to remove the possibility of rational judgment. This is not a general truth about coercion, but it can happen (through torture or other extreme suffering). This may be partly what Dossetor and Manickavel have in mind. In cases where this can be established (and it certainly cannot be presumed true for all or even most organ vendors), the problem becomes the one discussed in the preceding section, of competence to consent.

15. Note also that this kind of coercion increases if other sources of organs are not available. Any curtailment of sales increases pressure on relatives to donate.

16. Sells, R.A.: 1991, 'Voluntarism of consent,' in W. Land and J.B. Dossetor (eds.), *Organ Replacement Therapy: Ethics, Justice, Commerce*, Springer-Verlag, Berlin, New York, p. 20.

17. Dossetor and Manickavel, p. 63.

18. It may be said that there are great dangers at the moment, because the trade is inadequately controlled. But if so the problem lies in the lack of control, not in the trade itself.

19. It is also alleged that the sudden rush of wealth will do the poor no good at all: that they are just at the mercy of friends and relatives who will rush in to scoop up whatever pickings they can, and will squander their substance in riotous living (see, e.g., Mani, M.K.: 1992, 'The argument against the unrelated live donor,' in C.M. Kjellstrand and J.B. Dossetor (eds.), *Ethical Problems in Dialysis and Transplantation*, Kluwer Academic Publishers, Dordrecht, p. 165). But to the extent that this is a significant danger that is a reason for recommending counselling, or perhaps payment by instalments, rather than for saying that the poor would be better off without the money.

20. The issue here is specifically the interests of vendors, not the objective value of a life.

21. See, e.g., Reddy, K.C.: 1991, 'Organ donation for consideration,' in W. Land and J.B. Dossetor (eds.), *Organ Replacement Therapy: Ethics, Justice, Commerce*, Springer-Verlag, Berlin New York, p. 176.

22. Abouna, G.M., Sabawi, M.M., Kumar, M.S.A., and Samhan, M.: 1991, 'The negative impact of paid organ donation,' in W. Land and J.B. Dossetor (eds.), *Organ Replacement Therapy: Ethics, Justice, Commerce*, Springer-Verlag, Berlin, New York, p. 167. Broyer, M.: 1991, 'Living organ

donation; the fight against commercialism,' in W. Land and J.B. Dossetor (eds.), *Organ Replacement Therapy: Ethics, Justice, Commerce*, Springer-Verlag, Berlin, New York, pp. 198–199.

23. Abouna *et al.*, p. 166.
24. See, e.g., Dossetor and Manickavel, 1992, p. 66; Broyer, 1991, p. 199; Abouna *et al.*, 1991, p. 169.
25. Abouna *et al.*, p. 170.
26. Dossetor and Manickavel, p. 66.
27. Reddy, p.176.
28. Abouna *et al.*, p. 171,
29. See, e.g., Abouna *et al.*, 1991, p. 167; Broyer, 1991, p. 199. It might also be added that this argument comes oddly from people who are anxious to establish the "true willingness" of people who volunteer organs for transplant. If there is difficulty in finding donors when vendors are available (see e.g., Broyer, p. 199), that suggests something less than true willingness on the part of the donors.
30. Broyer, p. 199.
31. People may be *deluded* into thinking that some inducement is in their interest, of course, but that is a different matter. Exploitation is often accompanied by deceit by the exploiter or misjudgment by the exploited, but it need not be.
32. Note, however, that according to this account the moral position of the so-called exploiters depends on their own means. If you are poor yourself, and cannot afford more than you offer, you are not exploiting. The higher the payment to the vendor, the richer the purchaser needs to be. A poor person suffering from kidney failure might non-exploitatively make a low offer for a kidney, but its not being exploitative would not help the vendor.
33. There are some context where payment is unacceptable because of the possibility of corruption, but these are quite unlike this case.
34. Abouna *et al.*, p. 169.
35. It may be replied that it is nevertheless vulnerable to a different attack of the same kind, since if slavery were the best option of the poor, there would, on the basis of this line of argument, have to be a presumption in its favor as well. That is true: if slavery really were someone's best option, and there were no overriding reasons to prohibit it, it would, by these arguments, have to be allowed. But this still would not show that there was anything wrong with allowing kidney sales. In the first place, if such an argument could be produced, it would show not that kidney selling must be rejected, but that slavery should be accepted. And anyway, second, the fact that it is proving difficult to find cogent objections to the trade in kidneys does not in the least suggest that it would be equally difficult in the case of slavery. One obvious difference between the two cases, for instance, is that if slavery is banned, employers who want laborers will have to hire the people they would otherwise have enslaved, whereas if kidney selling is banned the purchaser will have no reason at all to give money to the vendors. Organ selling also saves the lives of the purchasers; slavery has no corresponding benefits. And there may be comparable differences between the cases of vital and non-vital organs, which make it possible to find justifications for prohibition in the case of hearts but not of kidneys. The arguments discussed in section V.E are relevant to the matter of making distinctions of this kind; the overall line of argument being developed here leaves entirely open the extent to which it can be achieved.
36. This line of argument arises in many contexts, most familiarly in the case of voluntary euthanasia. It is also sometimes used against unpaid organ donation from live donors (see, e.g., *The Sunday Times*, 30 July 1995 [or back ref. to note 2]). The analysis given here applies to all issues of the same general kind.
37. For instance, some people would rather genetic counselling and amniocentesis were not available, so that they did not have to face decisions about starting families or terminating pregnancies. Game theorists also recognize the deliberate limiting of options as a strategic or bargaining ploy, in e.g., trade union negotiations or Cold War strategy (see, e.g., Schelling, Thomas C.: 1960, 1980, *The Strategy of Conflict*, Harvard University Press, Cambridge, p. 37 *et passim*).
38. Frank, R.: 1985, *On Choosing the Right Pond*, Oxford University Press, Oxford, chapter 10.

39. This is most familiar as the idea underlying arms control agreements, but Frank extends it to many unexpected areas of social life.
40. In other words, this is a characteristic solution to a problem of the Prisoner's Dilemma type.
41. This criticism of the Frank thesis applies only to its justificatory mode. It may still be correct as an explanation. Some evidence in favor of this seems to be offered by the fact that it is in the richer countries, and among the rich in the poorer countries—where positional goods are most important—that there is most opposition to organ selling. The poor do not seem to oppose it.
42. Dossetor and Manickavel (p. 71) say we should go by "reason informed by emotion." I should put it the other way round.
43. It is irrelevant to argue here that heirlooms are less important than organs. Even if they are (which presumably depends on the organ, the heirloom, and the values of the owner) this point concerns only the issue of autonomy, not the general advisability of doing either of these things.
44. As, for instance, when it is complained that vendors are exploited (paid too little), coerced by unrefusable offers (paid too much), and anyway should be altruistic (not paid at all); or when it is said that sales must be banned both because if people want to be paid that shows they must be less than fully willing (so failing to meet the voluntariness requirement), and because if organs can be bought relatives may be less willing to come forward to donate (in which case the relatives do not meet the requirement, and should be unacceptable on the same grounds).
45. Dossetor and Manickavel, p. 71.
46. As shown over 2,500 years ago by the well-known story from Herodotus, of Darius's experimental attempts to induce groups of Greeks, who buried their dead, and Callatians, who ate theirs, to treat their dead according to the other's customs. They both regarded the proposals with horror, and said no amount of money would induce them to do it.
47. If it is protested that the harm is to the people who have to sell their relatives' organs, rather than to the dead, the question changes to one of the earlier kind, about harm to the vendors themselves. One of the most significant indications that harm to the vendor is not the real source of most people's feelings is that the idea of exchanging money even for the organs of the dead seems to arouse disgust of much the same kind. It may be worth noting in passing that at the conference where an earlier version of some of these arguments was presented there was also a paper on the possibility of payment for organs from the dead (Cohen, L.R.: 1991, 'The ethical virtues of a futures market in cadaveric organs,' in W. Land and J.B. Dossetor (eds.), *Organ Replacement Therapy: Ethics, Justice, Commerce*, Springer-Verlag, Berlin, New York, pp. 302ff.). This was extremely well argued, but (I think it is true to say) pretty well ignored.
48. Land, W., and Dossetor, J.B. (eds.): 1991, *Organ Replacement Therapy: Ethics, Justice, Commerce*, Springer-Verlag, Berlin, New York, p. 231.
49. Since experiments like these are intended as self-diagnosis procedures, rather than arguments about justification, there is no reason to think everyone will come up with the same response. Some people may, for instance, find that their feelings of repugnance lessen, or perhaps even disappear, if the surrounding causes of disquiet are thought away. They may feel less disgust if organs are sold by the rich or bought for the poor, or if exploitation and carelessness are prevented. As long as the feelings do not appear in response to inequality or exploitation on their own, however, the selling is still the root cause of the disgust, even though that disgust may be lessened or removed by other mitigating circumstances.

    Some people, of course, may find that their responses of disgust are not correlated either way with organ selling; but these will not be the people who joined in the immediate cry for prohibition.
50. A variant on this phenomenon comes in the claim that organ sales must be prohibited because they are incompatible with true voluntariness. This idea trades on an equivocation between "voluntary" as meaning on the one hand something like "willing," and on the other "unpaid." If the two meanings are coalesced the willingness requirement seems to coincide with the non-payment requirement. See, for example, Sells's "altruistic voluntarism" (Sells, 1991, p. 22) as a requirement for organ donation.
51. Broyer, p. 198.

52. It may seem that the modified version of the feeling, which appears only when selling is combined with other grounds for moral disquiet, is not open to these objections. But that is an illusion resulting from the distracting impression that the response is to the other grounds for concern. The impulse it supports is still *to prohibit organ sales*, even if only in some cases rather than all, rather than to remove these other causes of disquiet. Furthermore, although the reaction may be to the worst cases, treating the feeling as a *guide to action* may often lead to harming the worst off rather than the better off. If organ selling by the poor, but not the rich, arouses this horror, the impulse will be to allow the rich to sell their organs to increase their pleasures, while intervening between the poor and their only hope. This is, in fact, a particularly dangerous form of the intuition, because its correlation with obvious causes of moral concern masks even more effectively what is really going on. That is why it is necessary to assess feelings of moral revulsion as guides to action, rather than more vaguely as expressions of moral concern.

53. Dossetor and Manickavel, p. 68. Contrast this proposal with other things that such panels might do, such as checking for informed consent and proper conditions of sale and treatment offering financial advice, and so on.

54. Abouna *et al.*, p. 170.

55. Note that this possibility does not depend on ideas of cultural relativism, or even on the lesser idea that societies ought to be allowed to decide for themselves. The point here is just that different circumstances may give rise to different rational conclusions; and although one element in those circumstances is people's actual beliefs and preferences, a simple difference of economic circumstances might be sufficient to bring about a difference of conclusion.

56. Broyer, p. 199.

DEFINITIONS AND EXPLANATIONS

Ad hominem: Latin, meaning against the person. 1. This is a fallacy, which typically involves dismissing or attacking the person with whom you are debating rather than addressing her reasons or arguments. It often takes the form of attacking your opponent on grounds of prejudice or some other bias, or on some personal characteristic. It is a fallacy because, even if the person taking a particular position is biased or un-educated or has some other "undesirable" characteristic (like being a woman, or gay, or black), this does not in itself imply anything about the position they are defending and it does not address the question at issue in any debate. 2. Less commonly, *ad hominem* is used to indicate that a person has developed an idiosyncratic view on some matter, such that in providing arguments against that view you will have defeated this specific opponent but not any moral general position to which it is related. In this sense, to develop an *ad hominem* argument is not mistaken, but very restricted in terms of its scope, really applying only to the specific person in question (and hence an instance of being against the person).

Nephrectomy: The surgical removal of a kidney. Note the interesting play on words in Richard's title now.

QUESTIONS

1. Is the exploitation of the poor who sell their organs a moral wrong on libertarian grounds? Do we violate their rights by preventing them from selling their organs?

2. In what way is a prohibition on organ sales a harm to the poor (potential sellers)? To the rich (potential buyers)?

3. Libertarians believe that competent adults should be able to enter into contracts with one another provided only that the contract does not harm others and that it is freely entered into. What is the usual test for determining whether a contract has been freely entered into?

4. Those opposed to organ sales argue that the poor who wish to sell their organs cannot give informed consent because they are too ignorant to understand the procedure and its possible consequences. Why does this argument fail to support a general prohibition on organ sales? Does it apply equally to organ donations and not just organ sales?

5. What is coercion? Does poverty necessarily subject those living in poverty to coercion, so that their choices are then non-free and non-autonomous? How can restricting options through prohibitions be a justified response to poverty?

6. Richards relies often on arguments from consistency to show that the arguments against organ sales would (if they worked) equally preclude donations. But consider a parent who wants to donate a kidney to save the life of his child. We must suppose that external factors (the child's illness, the lack of other suitable donors) have made this the best option open to him. Should we say that his choice is coerced because the only options he has are undesirable: lose a kidney or lose a kid? If not, why should we say poverty is coercive? Should we stop the father from choosing what he thinks is the best option open to him (donating the kidney)? If not, should we stop him from selling his kidney? Perhaps he needs the money to save his child's life by a different operation.

7. Even if one has severely restricted options (a choice only among various undesirable options), can one not autonomously choose among those options?

8. Are unrefusable offers necessarily coercive? Is there really such a thing? What is the difference between an unrefusable offer and an unrefusable threat?

9. Even if there are risks to the vendor involved in organ sales, can a libertarian consider those risks in banning such sales, given their stance on paternalism?

10. Do the poor necessarily misunderstand their interests if they think the risk of organ sale is worth taking for the benefit they will receive? Must such a choice be irrational?

11. If the risks of organ sales were sufficient to support a ban, would they not equally support a prohibition on donations?

12. How does coming at this issue from a libertarian perspective, with the presumption in favour of letting people decide for themselves what they will do with their own bodies, change the nature of the debate?

13. Does allowing organ sales open up new possibilities for families and others to coerce individuals into being vendors? Is that danger sufficient to off-set the certain benefits of organ sales, to venders, buyers, and their families? Does the danger apply equally to donations as it does to sales?

14. What role should strong feelings of repugnance play in our moral thinking?

✦ ✦ ✦

Danny Scoccia, Can Liberals Support a Ban on Violent Pornography?

Danny Scoccia presents us with reasons to suggest that libertarians may (not must) support a ban on violent pornography. He considers the weightiest reason to ban violent pornography is that it increases sexual assaults on women (harm to others). A libertarian might respond that this would be censorship, and that we do not ban free speech just because it causes someone to act on a viewpoint that is unacceptable. The commitment to neutrality towards conceptions of the good life requires as much. We may ban the harmful action, but not what leads up to the activity (see Wellington's insistence that we not ban homosexual marriage because of the homophobic reactions to it, but instead focus on banning suitably significant homophobic reactions). Scoccia responds that in this context the standard libertarian response is misguided. A libertarian's commitment to self-directed activity does not entail protecting free speech insofar as it non-rationally affects the mental states of those who hear it. Violent pornography is such a case of non-rational persuasion. Violent pornography, it is suggested, influences people via operant conditioning. In the typical case, it is supposed, the user of violent pornography views violent pornography, imagines being involved in similar acts of sexual violence, and these fantasies are coupled with the very powerful reinforcement of sexual arousal and masturbatory orgasm. This reinforcement then increases the chance of wishing to be engaged in such behaviour.

We feel it necessary to insist that cool deliberation, not heated disgust, rule the day. While Scoccia's paper leaves open the question of whether or not violent pornography should be banned, this is the logical next step in any examination of the issue. As repugnant as the idea of someone (perhaps a neighbour or friend) habitually viewing violent pornography might be, we must not allow that repugnance to overcome our rational faculties. Some find the idea of people engaging in homosexual activities, or interracial marriage, just as offensive. Violent pornography is a ticklish case for libertarians, and cool heads alone should determine if the facts bear out that violent pornography harms women in a way that would require a ban on pornography. Scoccia's argument suggests some powerful reasons for thinking that such a ban might indeed be justified.

✦ ✦ ✦

Danny Scoccia, "Can Liberals Support a Ban on Violent Pornography?" *Ethics* 106:4 (1996): 776–799. © The University of Chicago Press. Reprinted with permission from The University of Chicago Press and the author.

Can Liberals Support a Ban on Violent Pornography?

DANNY SCOCCIA

Proponents of a ban on violent pornography have defended their position in a number of different ways. One type of argument alleges that violent pornography harms women and that banning its production and distribution would prevent much of the harm. For example, some have claimed that it (as well as much nonviolent pornography) defames all women.[1] Another argument is that the abuse and degradation of women depicted in violent pornography is often real rather than simulated and inflicted on unwilling models or actresses afraid to report their victimization because of their vulnerability to further harm. This argument implies that we should ban violent pornography for more or less the same reasons that we currently ban child pornography. Yet another argument taps the resources of J. L. Austin's speech act theory in an attempt to show that violent (as well as much nonviolent) pornography performs a speech act with the illocutionary force of "subordinating" and the perlocutionary force of reinforcing women's subordinate sociopolitical status.[2] There are other harm arguments in addition to these, but perhaps the most popular of them is that violent pornography produces and/or strengthens in its male consumers desires to sexually assault women. Many of these consumers act on the desires, and the end result is an increased number of sexual assaults.

Without elaborating on the reasons why, I believe that this last argument is the one that poses the most serious challenge to defenders of free speech. Of course it invites some familiar objections. One is that there simply is not enough evidence to support the causal claim on which it rests. (I take that claim to be not that the consumption of violent pornography is by itself a causally necessary or sufficient condition of committing sexual assaults on women, but rather that there is a statistically significant connection between the two, such that curtailing the availability of the pornography would significantly reduce the total amount of sexual violence against women).[3] Still another objection is that even if violent pornography does lead many of its consumers to sexually assault women, that still would not justify a ban. For a ban enacted to prevent those assaults would violate a principle which lies at the heart of a liberal theory of free speech, namely, that it is seldom if ever permissible to censor speech on the grounds that it might or in fact does persuade hearers to accept and act on a bad viewpoint or noxious ideas.

I shall argue that this second objection is misguided. It is misguided not because the principle in question is incorrect, and not because it is not part of the most attractive version of a liberal theory (though I confess to being less than certain that it is), but because a ban on violent pornography enacted to reduce male violence against women is in fact quite consistent with it. The principle does not protect speech insofar as it nonrationally affects its hearers' mental states, and violent pornography affects its consumers in just that way. My thesis is not that liberals *must* support a ban on this material, but rather that their theory of free speech does not plainly forbid one. Whether or not liberals should support a ban turns on difficult empirical questions about which there is room for reasonable disagreement.

VIOLENT PORNOGRAPHY

Following Anthony Burgess, Joel Feinberg, and others, we may define "pornography" as representations, verbal or pictorial, whose function is to produce arousal in those who view or read them. As Burgess observes, "Such works encourage solitary fantasy, which is then usually quite harmlessly discharged in masturbation. A pornographic book, is then, an instrument for procuring a sexual catharsis, but it rarely promotes the desire to achieve this through a social mode, an act of erotic congress: the book is, in a sense, a substitute for a sexual partner."[4] Of course, if it is to fulfill its function, pornography will have to be "sexually explicit" to some minimal degree. But clearly representations can have a high degree of sexual explicitness without being for arousal (e.g., photographs of diseased genitalia in medical journals).

For our purposes it will help to distinguish the following categories of pornography:

a) Pornography which is not sexist or degrading to women; material which those feminists who regard "pornography" as a pejorative term prefer to call "nonsexist erotica"

b) Pornography which does not contain an explicit degradation or domination theme, but which is nevertheless sexist (e.g., portraying women as silly, stupid, and eagerly servile to men)

c) Nonviolent pornography which does contain an explicit degradation or domination theme (e.g., photos of a naked woman being urinated on, or on her hands and knees while wearing a dog collar and leash)

d) Violent pornography, containing depictions of women being raped, tortured, tied up, and so forth; in some of this material the victim is depicted as both enjoying and consenting to the sexual abuse she (or occasionally he) suffers, and in some as unwilling and terrorized[5]

The restrictions on pornography called for by the argument we are considering would cover only some of the material in *d* and perhaps *c*. They are narrower in scope than the Indianapolis antipornography ordinance coauthored by Catharine MacKinnon and Andrea Dworkin, which appears to be directed at all of the material in *b*, *c*, and *d*.[6] They are also narrower in scope than restrictions which apply to all graphic depictions of sexual violence. They would not cover *Toolbox Murders*, an R-rated "slasher" film which shows "a naked woman taking a tub bath, masturbating, then being stalked and killed with a power drill by a masked male," because it probably does not satisfy our definition of "pornographic."[7] It was R rated and, hence, almost certainly did not contain the unremittingly high level of sexual explicitness which men looking for a "substitute for a sexual partner" seem typically to want and which undoubtedly would have led to its receiving an X rating. On the other hand, the restrictions would apply to photographs of women having cigarettes extinguished on their breasts, in magazines with titles like *Black Tit and Body Torture*.[8] No doubt the lines between "violent" and "nonviolent" and between "pornographic" and "nonpornographic" are fuzzy. The fact that they are fuzzy generates worries about "chilling effects" which any thorough defense of a ban on violent pornography must address. I only claim that the typical R-rated "slasher" movie, however disgusting, violent, devoid of artistic merit, and socially harmful it may be, is not in the gray area which separates clear cases of the pornographic from clear cases of the non-pornographic. It is clearly nonpornographic and, thus, outside the scope of a ban which targets violent pornography.

THE PERSUASION PRINCIPLE AND VIEWPOINT-BASED RESTRICTIONS

Can liberals support such a ban? To what principles do they appeal in deciding whether or not to support this or any other restriction on speech? Perhaps the first and most important one is the "harm principle," which says that the only good reason to restrict speech (or conduct) is to prevent harm to vital social institutions or nonconsenting third parties. Liberals reject "pure legal moralism" (the view that the prevention of harmless immorality, if there is such a thing, is sometimes sufficient to justify restrictions on either conduct or speech), and further, they insist that there are types of harm (such as harm to which a person consents, and the frustration of external preferences) the prevention of which does not justify state coercion.[9]

The harm principle says that only speech which causes harm may be restricted. But is the fact that a type of speech causes much harm *sufficient* to justify restricting it? More precisely, if the expected good of restricting a category of speech exceeded the expected evil, would that make restrictions on it permissible? The liberal's answer would seem to be no. We have an interest in acquiring true beliefs and avoiding false ones. Since most of the more sensational stories in supermarket tabloids are patently false and even ridiculous (the "Elvis is alive; he was kidnapped by Martians" variety), but many of their readers still gullibly believe them, a ban on such journalism would prevent some of the harm these readers suffer when they accept the stories as true. But clearly the liberal cannot support such a ban. Because of the way this harm comes about—the reader's decision (for which he alone is responsible) to believe what is patently absurd—the liberal is unwilling to count its prevention as a good reason for limiting speech. In addition to the harm principle, the liberal theory of free speech seems to include what might be called the "persuasion principle," namely, that the prevention of a risk of harm created by the persuasive effects of speech does not ordinarily justify restricting that speech.

Ronald Dworkin, David Strauss, and (at one time) Thomas Scanlon have all embraced something like this principle.[10] What is more, they have rejected a defense of it based on an appeal to utilitarian or other consequentialist considerations and instead sought to derive it from the Kantian injunction to respect one's own and others' autonomy. Dworkin says, "Morally responsible people insist on making up their own minds about what is good or bad in life or in politics, or what is true and false in matters of justice or faith. Government insults its citizens, and denies their moral responsibility, when it decrees that they cannot be trusted to hear opinions that might persuade them to dangerous or offensive convictions."[11] We violate the autonomy of (or deny the status of full personhood to) adults when we censor speech because we regard them as so impressionable or feebleminded that they can be easily persuaded to act wrongly.[12]

In a way, Dworkin's remarks do not go far enough. Normative questions and "matters of faith" are not the only topics on which morally responsible people insist on forming their own judgments. Surely certain purely factual questions, such as whether the explanation of why black Americans as a group have a lower average IQ score than white Americans is largely genetic, or whether capitalism is more efficient than socialism, also belong in that category. The liberal theory of free speech is no less inimical to a ban on books like Charles Murray and Robert Herrnstein's *Bell Curve*, enacted to eliminate threats to racial harmony caused by false psychological and biological views, than it is to a ban on the advocacy of atheism or socialism. On the other hand, morally responsible people need not insist on judging for themselves all claims made by advertisers about the health benefits of their products. It seems consistent with remaining fully responsible and autonomous that one support a government ban on false advertising, FDA regulations requiring scientific evidence to back up claims about foods or medicines, and so on. It is not obvious what criteria distinguish factual claims that an autonomous person must judge for herself from those which she may defer to experts. But I assume that the persuasion principle as stated above can be amended so that it forbids a ban on false and racist biology but not false advertising.[13] Furthermore, if any pornography implicitly endorses factual claims about women, sexuality, or related matters, they will be in the category of claims the autonomous person must judge for herself. Hence, the amendment to the principle (whatever it is) will not put violent pornography's false claims about women (assuming it makes any), or the harm caused by men believing those false claims, outside the principle's scope.

Note that while the persuasion principle is probably best construed as a side constraint on laws which it is permissible for legislators to enact, it need not be regarded as an "absolute" one. That is, it need not be so strong as to protect even speech which it is highly probably will soon cause very great harm through its persuasive effects.[14] A nonabsolute persuasion principle thus affords no protection to specific and immediate incitements to criminal conduct (when the audience is suitably receptive to such calls, able to heed them, etc.), to false cries of "fire" in crowded theaters, nor, perhaps, to the vague advocacy of draft dodging in a society which finds itself in the dire circumstance of needing to mobilize an army of conscripts quickly, to repel a military invasion. The fact that it does not protect immediate incitements does not put violent pornography outside its scope, because this material clearly is not an immediate incitement to specific criminal conduct.[15]

Why think that a persuasion principle, so amended and circumscribed, lies at the heart of the liberal theory of free speech? Mainly because it helps to organize and explain many of the liberal's considered judgments about the permissibility of viewpoint-based restrictions, content-based but viewpoint-neutral restrictions, and content-neutral restrictions. A citywide ban on all billboards would be a content-neutral restriction, while a ban on billboards with commercial advertising would be content based but viewpoint neutral, and a ban on billboards with "pro-choice" or antiwar messages would be viewpoint based.[16] The main reason (though certainly not the only one) why this last restriction seems so clearly wrong is that it (or the rationale behind it) is bound to violate the persuasion principle. A nonabsolute version of the principle, permitting restrictions on speech which very probably causes great harm, implies that viewpoint-based restrictions must satisfy something like a "clear and present danger" test to be permissible. Such restrictions can seldom if ever pass that test.

A ban on "any public speech likely to elicit a violent audience response," though content neutral in formulation, seems clearly unacceptable, and the fact that it violates the persuasion principles explains why.[17] On the other hand, a ban on all billboards with commercial advertising, enacted in a quaint town whose members are strongly averse to urban blight, seems acceptable both because it is consistent with the principle (the harms it seeks to prevent are not caused via the targeted speech's persuasiveness) and because the belief that its benefits outweigh its harms is reasonable. The reasonableness of that belief would seem to be enough. Strong, quantifiable, "scientific" evidence that the aesthetic benefits outweigh the setback to economic efficiency seems unnecessary. While something like a "clear and present danger" test must be satisfied for viewpoint-based restrictions to be permissible, a weaker standard seems appropriate for viewpoint-neutral ones.

Nothing said so far implies that if a restriction is consistent with the persuasion principle, it is automatically acceptable to liberals. Consider a citywide ban on all large gatherings in public places, enacted to prevent excessive noise and litter. Though it is consistent with the principle, liberals will unanimously reject as misguided the belief that reducing these harms justifies such a broad restriction on free speech and assembly. It fails to recognize the inestimable importance of preserving many opportunities for public, political speech in a democratic society.

Would a ban on violent pornography be a viewpoint-based restriction that violates the persuasion principle? It would be a mistake to answer no either on the grounds that it does not explicitly state any viewpoint or on the grounds that there is reasonable disagreement about what viewpoint it implicitly endorses. A ban on flag burning is a clear instance of a viewpoint-based restriction, even though the act banned does not involve the explicit statement of a viewpoint and it will often be unclear what precise message the flag burner wishes to communicate. Of course the function or purpose of pornography is to arouse, not polemicize. But its having that function does not preclude it from implicitly endorsing a viewpoint as well. Many people have thought that violent pornography endorses violence against women, and it is not obvious that they are mistaken. It is not obviously wrong to interpret pornography in which, say, Asian women are bound and tortured, as implying that it is good to so treat some, many, or all Asian women. In any case I shall assume that violent pornography does condone misogynism in general and sexual violence against women in particular. To concede that it does is to concede that it contains or expresses a viewpoint, which in turn makes it harder to reconcile a ban on it with any theory which rejects viewpoint-based censorship, as the liberal theory does.

It also will not do to claim, as Cass Sunstein has, that a ban on violent pornography is viewpoint neutral if it is "directed to harm rather than at viewpoint" and it targets only this material, not all speech which explicitly or implicitly endorses violence against women.[18] Sunstein is wrong on both points, First, from the fact that some expressions of a viewpoint are tolerated, it does not follow that restrictions on other expressions of it are viewpoint neutral. If there is a ban on the oral advocacy of atheism but not Christianity, that is a viewpoint-based restriction (in statement and probably justification) even if it does not extend to the written advocacy of atheism (perhaps because the censors believe that only the illiterate can or need to be shielded from blasphemy). So even if violent pornography alone were banned, and the public speech of a quack psychoanalyst who holds that rape cures many female neuroses were tolerated, that by itself would not make the ban viewpoint neutral. Second, "harm rather than viewpoint" is a false dichotomy. Viewpoint-based censorship typically does not aim at the elimination of harmless immorality, but instead at the prevention of harms which it is thought statements of the viewpoint will cause. Often the fear is that gullible or easily corrupted listeners will be persuaded to accept a bad viewpoint, act on it, and harm others. A ban enacted with the aim of preventing harms so caused is still viewpoint based. And it will almost always be forbidden by the liberal's persuasion principle.

DISTINGUISHING PERSUASION FROM NONPERSUASION

The objection to the argument for a ban which we are considering is that it would be a viewpoint-based restriction of speech and thus in violation of the persuasion principle. The claim is that the liberal must judge it no less wrong than a ban on the speech of the quack psychoanalyst or on the speech of a fundamentalist minister who, citing the authority of Saint Paul, advocates the use by husbands of a stern discipline, including corporal punishment, in dealing with uppity wives who challenge their authority to rule the family. Though the persuasion principle is nonabsolute and so does not protect speech which via its persuasiveness poses a clear and present danger of substantial harm, speech which endorses or advocates a misogynistic viewpoint typically does not pose such a danger. That is why, according to the objection, the liberal theory of free speech protects all misogynistic speech, violent pornography included.[19]

But whether or not a ban on violent pornography violates the persuasion principle all depends on *how* it influences the psychological states of its users. The principle protects only persuasion, so if violent pornography alters its users' desires or beliefs by nonpersuasive means, a ban on it would not violate that principle. Of course, pornography clearly is not an attempt at persuasion in the sense of marshalling evidence, offering arguments, or citing reasons in support of its viewpoint. Neither are works of art like paintings or sculptures or acts of political protest like flag burning. Yet bans on flag burning and "decadent art" are clear examples of viewpoint-based restrictions which violate the persuasion principle. So the principle cannot rest on a narrow construal of persuasion in terms of offering reasons in support of an explicitly stated viewpoint. I suggest that the best way to distinguish persuasion from nonpersuasion, the one presupposed by the principle, sees them as two modes of influencing persons at the opposite ends of a continuum. At the extreme nonpersuasion or nonrational end would lie the following, if it were possible: oral speech with a certain pitch and modulation excites the aggression center in the brains of its listeners, causing in them strong urges to act violently even if they do not understand what is being spoken. At the other end lie most articles written by academics and published in scholarly journals. The speeches made by campaigning politicians to voters, in spite of the rhetorical tricks and fallacious arguments they frequently contain (ad hominem attacks, "straw man" caricature of an opponent's position, appeals to emotion, etc.), lie much closer to this pure persuasion end of the continuum. So too will be the speech of the quack psychoanalyst and the fundamentalist minister. On the other hand, a command which affects your behavior only if you understand its meaning, but which was given to you while you were drugged and under hypnosis, lies nearer the nonpersuasion end of it.

The key to determining where on the continuum an instance of speech belongs is not whether it influences its hearer against his will. If someone presents me with knockdown proof that a certain proposition is true, she affects my beliefs via persuasion, even if, having recognized her proof as cogent, I cannot help but assent to the proposition. The key seems to be the extent to which the speech allows in an idealized, "average" listener an appreciation of what he takes to be "good reasons" to shape whatever response (laughter, outrage, embarrassment, acceptance of a proposition, etc.) the speech leads him to have. If the speech causes the listener to have a certain mental state, and it either does not allow him to weigh reasons for and against having the state, or allows such deliberation to occur but somehow renders it impotent (so that he would have the mental state even if he judged it unreasonable, immoral, or whatever), then the speech is substantially nonpersuasive.[20] The listener of such speech is not responsible or to blame for whatever states it causes him to have.

The claim that there is a continuum here is consistent with the admission that nearly all speech has nonrational features which contribute to its ability to elicit a desired response from listeners. All that is being denied is that all speech contains or relies on them to the same extent. Speech at the far nonpersuasive end of the continuum relies on them to a greater extent than speech at the other end. The existence of a continuum implies that the persuasion principle can be understood in a number of different ways: for example, as covering only speech at the pure persuasion end or as covering all speech except that which lies at the far nonpersuasive end. Understanding it in the latter way seems more consistent with the Kantian injunction to respect autonomy from which Scanlon, Dworkin, and Strauss all wish to derive it. Surely it is a violation of the injunction to try to shield the average adult from speech which lies at the far rational end of the continuum. We would justifiably regard as insulting a ban on commercial endorsements by famous athletes or actors, enacted because it was supposed that we are so gullible, stupid, or easily manipulated that we need to be protected from their mildly insidious effects.

The criterion I have suggested for distinguishing persuasion from nonpersuasion no doubt implies that all pornography belongs closer to the nonrational or nonpersuasion end of the continuum as regards the way it produces arousal. Of course, judgment does mediate the arousal response to pornography in a certain way. Pornography is composed of pictorial or verbal representations, which can arouse only if one grasps their content or reference. In this respect it differs from both speech which causes aggression via its pitch or modulation and mechanical "sex aids." (The latter have no representational or semantic properties, and a fortiori, cannot produce arousal by anyone understanding them.)[21] The reason for saying that it causes arousal in a nonrational way is simply that the average person, exposed to sexually explicit depictions of the right sort, will be aroused even if she believes that she ought not be (e.g., because she judges arousal per se to be sinful).

But from the fact that pornography produces arousal in a nonrational way, it does not follow that a ban on some or all of it is consistent with the persuasion. Arousal per se is surely harmless. A ban on all pornography, enacted because it nonrationally causes what is claimed to be the harmless immorality of lusting for someone who is not one's spouse, would not violate the persuasion principle, but it would violate the harm principle. According to the argument for a ban which we are considering, the harm caused by violent pornography is increased sexual assaults against women. To reconcile a ban enacted to prevent that harm with the persuasion principle, what needs to be shown is that violent pornography causes misogynistic beliefs and/or desires, not just arousal, in a substantially nonrational way.

"SUBLIMINAL SUGGESTION"

Cass Sunstein has suggested in passing that violent pornography instills in its users an "ideology" through a process akin to "subliminal suggestion or hypnosis."[22] Subliminal suggestion, I assume, is the process whereby speech causes an unconscious mental state in the average person exposed to it, and it causes the mental state even if one consciously judges it unreasonable, imprudent, or immoral to have the state in question. Thus, subliminally suggestive speech belongs at the far nonrational end of the continuum. The claim that violent pornography affects its consumers' psychology in this or any other nonrational way of course does not imply that its producers intend it to do so. The pornographer surely does not intend to brainwash men into wanting to hurt women, if only because it is not in his interests. Quite the contrary: the sexual assaults committed by some of his product's users lead many to demand that the state shut down his business.

One problem with the subliminal suggestion hypothesis is that it seems hard pressed to explain why violent pornography is any more subliminally suggestive than misogynistic jokes or songs, or nonpornographic speech which condones sexual violence. Some studies have found that "favorable" rape depictions (the victim first resists but eventually appears willing and aroused) cause more "calloused" attitudes toward rape victims and a greater acceptance of rape myths (e.g., "no" really means "yes") than "unfavorable" ones. Presumably, rape myths are part of the ideology which Sunstein had in mind. But one of the studies found that nonpornographic movies containing similarly "favorable" rape depictions (e.g., "The Getaway," "Swept Away") had the same bad effects on viewers, and further, that the effects could be eliminated by a "debriefing session," in which the researchers conducting the experiment explained to the subjects why the myths are false.[23] These findings imply that violent pornography is no more subliminally suggestive with respect to rape myths than nonpornographic movies, and indeed, that neither communicate the myths in a way whose efficiency is unaffected by conscious consideration of objections to the myths.

Another problem with the subliminal suggestion hypothesis is this. A common objection to our argument for a ban is that its defenders face a dilemma: Either one can believe that his exposure to violent pornography caused this rapist to commit his crime, or one can believe that he has free will and is responsible for his actions; one can't have it both ways. Any reply to this objection will assume that compatibilism is a defensible position in the debate over free will and determinism. For the compatibilist it is only free will and certain kinds of causation (e.g., coercion by another) which are incompatible. As long as violent pornography does not affect its consumers' behavior in one of those responsibility-negating ways, the compatibilist insists that the consumers are morally and legally accountable for any sexual assaults they commit. But it seems that subliminal suggestion would have to count as one of those ways. To someone in whom a brainwashing has implanted strong but not irresistible urges to commit crimes, but not impaired his ability to engage in moral deliberation, it makes sense to say, "Your knowledge that it is wrong to act on those urges should have led you to resist them." But to someone in whom the brainwashing has gone much deeper, implanting false or immoral beliefs and anesthetizing his ability to hold them up to critical scrutiny, that cannot be said. We must excuse him for his wrong-doing.

Of course if one chooses to subject oneself to a brainwashing the foreseeable consequences of which include one's forming false or immoral beliefs, then one is fully responsible for having them, as well as for the actions one performs because one has them. But precisely because the subliminal suggestion hypothesis alleges that violent pornography causes misogynistic beliefs and values surreptitiously, it can hardly be "common knowledge" that it does so. So I conclude that the subliminal suggestion hypothesis is incompatible with the widely held and presumably correct belief that consumers of violent pornography who commit sexual assaults are fully responsible for their crimes.

CONDITIONING

Sunstein's hypothesis is not the only one which would put violent pornography at the far nonrational or nonpersuasive end of the continuum. Another—the one I wish to endorse—is that it produces new or reinforces preexisting desires or urges to harm women through a process akin to operant conditioning. Operant conditioning rests on the "law of effect," which says that rewarding or reinforcing a behavior x in circumstances y increases the probability that x and sufficiently similar behaviors will recur in y and sufficiently similar circumstances. Suppose, for example, that on many occasions, after a child has said "Thank you" to his mother for giving him a candy, she smiles at him and gives him another. That increases the probability not only of the child's uttering the same words to the same person in the same circumstances in the future, but also, via "response generalization," of his thanking others when they bestow on him similar favors. The child may learn to show his gratitude in nonverbal ways, with gestures or facial expressions that are very different in "topography" from the verbal behavior that was first reinforced.

There is some evidence that if one repeatedly thinks about drinking a cocktail and then conjures up thoughts of nausea, that diminishes the probability of one's actually drinking cocktails.[24] This suggests that response generalization can and does occur from contemplating an act to its actual performance and vice versa. Another more commonplace example of conditioning is advertising which makes no attempt to provide information about the product that a rational consumer might want, but instead merely tries to create an association in the consumer's mind between the product and something else the consumer finds desirable. Cigarette ads which portray smokers as especially gregarious, physically unblemished, or macho (the Marlboro man) do this using, perhaps, both classical and operant conditioning. Evidently, the ads are quite effective, causing many consumers to start smoking Marlboros and not just to look at more Marlboro ads or imagine being a Marlboro man. Obviously it does not have that effect on everyone who repeatedly views the ads—not every male who is already a cigarette smoker, or even every male for whom the thought of being macho is reinforcing. But it does have it on a sufficiently large number of consumers to make it rational for Marlboro executives to spend millions of dollars on it.

Turning now to violent pornography, we can distinguish the following behaviors:

1. Looking at sexually explicit pictures of someone else raping women
2. Fantasizing about raping women oneself
3. Looking at others pretending to rape women (e.g., in a live sex show)
4. Having perceptions of one's actually raping a woman

My claim is that the typical consumer of violent pornography frequently engages in behaviors 1 and 2, which are reinforced by the strong pleasures of arousal, masturbation, and orgasm. That creates not only an increased probability, stronger tendency, or (as I shall say henceforth) stronger *desire* to repeat 1 and 2 in the future, but also, via response generalization, a desire to engage in 4 (as well as 3). The response generalization required here seems neither different in kind nor greater in extent than that involved in aversion therapy for alcoholics or in Marlboro ads. Indeed, one difference between violent pornography and Marlboro ads tells in favor of the claim that the former is a more potent conditioner. What underlies the efficacy of the ads is pleasure at the thought of being a Marlboro man, whereas in the case of violent pornography there are the much stronger, more intense pleasure of sexual arousal and orgasm. The stronger the pleasure, the more potent the "reinforcer," other things being equal.

The conditioning hypothesis about violent pornography which I am defending would put it at the far nonrational end of the continuum only if a similar conditioning would have similar effects on the average male. It seems likely that it would. To claim as much is not to insult men or to suggest that they are all latent misogynists, but rather to recognize the potency of the reinforcer in question. If a vegetarian were forced repeatedly to look at pictures of steaks while neuroscientists stimulated pleasure centers in her brain, she would form a tendency to look at more pictures of steaks, look at real steaks, and perhaps even eat steaks. That does not mean that she will forsake her vegetarianism. If she firmly believes that there are strong prudential or moral reasons not to eat meat, she should succeed in resisting her steak urges (which presumably will be extinguished soon after the conditioning ceases). Similarly, if men who are not misogynistic (contra Andrea Dworkin, I assume there are many) were repeatedly forced by neuroscientists to view violent pornographic images while the pleasure centers of their brains were being stimulated, producing in them pleasures of the same intensity as those the consumer of violent pornography produces for himself via fantasy and masturbation, I surmise that they would eventually find themselves with urges or dispositions to sexual violence which they did not previously have, but which many of them would successfully resist owing to their belief that such violence is wrong.

A couple of objections may be raised to this conditioning hypothesis about violent pornography. First, granting that the repeated masturbatory use of it does have the conditioning and generalization effects described above, why think that it generates or reinforces a desire which can be satisfied only by actually harming women? Why not suppose instead that the desire which gets reinforced is one which can be satisfied either by the continued consumption of violent pornography or by actual sexual assaults on women? If the desire has that disjunctive structure, then women have little to worry about so long as the use of violent pornography remains a cheaper, more cost-effective way of satisfying it than actual sexual assaults. Its use would then be a sort of catharsis, and a ban on it would probably be counterproductive, increasing rather than decreasing harm to women. Second, it has already been admitted that some users may have the desire (i.e., the one which can be satisfied only by actual sexual assaults) but not act on it, because they have stronger, countervailing desires. For example, it could be the case that many of the men who fantasize about raping women who resist at first but then submit, enjoy, and give retroactive consent believe that it would be wrong to rape a woman who did not behave that way, believe that it would be okay to rape one who did, but realize that it is impossible to predict which women in the real world will behave the way they would like. And perhaps many other (fewer?) men, who enjoy the sadistic fantasy of raping women who look terrorized throughout, judge real sadistic rape so wrong that they never engage in it (in which case one would still expect them to feel some guilt for engaging in the fantasies). Indeed, the conditioning hypothesis about violent pornography is quite consistent with the possibility that none of its users hurt women, because all of them have stronger countervailing desires of some sort. The conditioning hypothesis is not identical to the causal claim that the consumption of violent pornography produces a significant increase in the total number of sexual assaults, nor does it entail it. Given this, is there any reason at all to believe that most users of violent pornography have no strong, countervailing desires, or that among those who do, their continued use of violent pornography will tend to weaken those desires?

These are fair questions. But they do not challenge the conditioning hypothesis per se. All I have claimed to this point is that if violent pornography leads to an increase in the total number of sexual assaults on women, that increase occurs because it has strengthened in its users a desire to assault women through a process of operant conditioning. It does not occur because violent pornography communicates a misogynistic viewpoint or ideology which its users decide to accept and act on. If the conditioning hypothesis is correct, acceptance of the viewpoint plays no role at all in the causal chain leading from consumption to sexual assaults on women. Hence, if violent pornography produces an increase in harm to women, it does so in a way that falls outside the coverage of the persuasion principle. The objections in the preceding paragraph do not cast doubt on that claim. Rather, they express doubts that violent pornography is responsible for any increase at all. I shall return to them shortly.

AN ADDITIONAL WORRY

Geoffrey Stone has noted that "it is too easy to characterize 'undesirable' ideas as insidious. The concept is too open-ended, too subject to manipulation to justify viewpoint-based discrimination."[25] He expresses a legitimate worry here. As the persuasion principle was stated earlier, it protects only speech which is not "substantially nonpersuasive." Clearly, the line between speech which is and speech which is not substantially nonpersuasive is not sharp, so there are cases which fall in a grey area, and courts would have to make tough decisions. Many groups would demand state interference with speech which they claim falls outside the protection of the persuasion principle and causes significant harm but which they really oppose only because it promotes a viewpoint they despise. (For example, some liberals are quick to label the sort of education that religious schools provide children as "indoctrination," but it seems to be the content of the teaching rather than the means by which it is imparted to which they really object.) Isn't the claim that the repeated masturbatory use of violent pornography gives rise to a kind of brainwashing really just a smoke screen for a viewpoint-based attack on misogynistic or sexist ideas? Wouldn't acceptance of the claim put us on a slippery slope which would make it increasingly difficult to resist calls for a ban on graphic nonpornographic depictions of sexual violence, sexist but nonviolent pornography, or even sexist TV commercials?

I do not see why it should. The conditioning hypothesis seems to me to succeed where the subliminal suggestion hypothesis failed, namely, in explaining why the masturbatory use of violent pornography affects the psychology of its user in a substantially more nonrational way than any of these other types of speech. Let us being with graphic, nonpornographic depictions of sexual violence. While the spectator of *Toolbox Murders* may enjoy watching the gore on the screen, he does little more than watch and enjoy watching. There is nothing comparable to masturbation in this case, no reinforcer of the behaviors of watching the violence or imitating it which approaches the strength of orgasm as a reinforcer. Slasher movies instead seem to produce their deleterious effects in other ways. On those spectators already strongly disposed to violence, they affect the timing and especially the manner in which violent crimes are committed. But there is no reason to believe that they inspire copycat crimes in an insidious way, one that circumvents the conscious, rational thought processes of these spectators. On minors and especially impressionable adults, "models" whom they strive to emulate, or through their "desensitizing" or "habituating" effects (i.e., their tendency to weaken inhibitions to acting violently). The worry that they have such corrupting effects on the young seems well founded and may justify restricting their viewership to adults. But it does not support the claim that graphic depictions of nonpornographic violence belong at the far nonrational end of the continuum and, thus, outside the scope of the persuasion principle.

Let us turn now to the question whether it is plausible to suppose that nonviolent but sexist pornography conditions its consumers to support patriarchy, accept the ideology of sexism (that men have a duty to display a condescending "gallantry" toward the "weaker" sex; it is "natural" for women to stay at home and raise children; women are too emotional to be entrusted with leadership responsibilities; etc.), or both.[26] That some pornography is sexist seems beyond doubt, though there seems to be much disagreement about which pornography is sexist and why. I assume that pornography is sexist if it features women who conform to an insulting, derogatory stereotype (e.g., the frivolous, empty-headed "bimbo"), and especially if it portrays women in positions of socioeconomic subordination happy to provide sexual services on command (e.g., a male executive orders a female secretary into his office to perform fellatio, and she dutifully and eagerly complies). Such pornography implicitly endorses a sexist viewpoint.[27] The question we need to consider is whether it conditions its users to accept that viewpoint.

Consider the following. Sexist pornography stimulates fantasies in which voluptuous but servile women satisfy the sexual desires of a man—presumably the one doing the fantasizing—on command. He masturbates, and the pleasure he receives reinforces a tendency to repeat such fantasy in the future. Through a first stage of response generalization, a tendency to control real women during sexual encounters, or perhaps to seek out slavish sexual partners, is also reinforced. Through a second state of it, the fantasy and arousal strengthen a desire to keep women politically and economically subordinate in the real world. Of course anyone who believes sexist pornography does all this can and should admit there are many other causes of that desire. Sexist pornography is a less important cause than traditional Judeo-Christian teachings about women, marriage, and family, and thus, it is far from being the linchpin of patriarchy, as some more radical feminists have claimed. But the advocacy of religious beliefs opposed to women's equality is clearly protected by the persuasion principle. Sexist pornography, if it affects its users in the way just described, would not be protected by it.[28]

But the suggestion that sexist pornography is just as potent a conditioner as violent pornography is implausible. It exaggerates how far response generalization can or normally does go. The conditioning hypothesis about violent pornography did not require anything like the second stage of response generalization described above. In the case of violent pornography, the acts which its users fantasize about are the very same acts as the ones they acquire urges to commit in the real world. This is not so in the case of sexist pornography: its users do not fantasize about keeping women at home to raise children or passing them over for job promotions in favor of less qualified male coworkers. A conditioning hypothesis about sexist pornography requires that generalization occur from behaviors of sexually dominating women to behaviors like opposing the Equal Rights Amendment or the legalization of abortion. Possibly it does occur to some degree. But the greater dissimilarity between these two types of behavior, as compared to fantasizing about raping and really raping, surely implies that if it occurs at all, it does so to a much lesser extent.

I do not deny that pornography with a sexist content will promote sexist attitudes in a nonrational way. Repeated exposure to any speech that depicts a class of persons in subordinate roles can habituate one (especially children) of the belief that it is natural for them to occupy such roles. I deny only that the masturbatory use of sexist pornography gives it a significantly greater ability nonrationally to promote patriarchy than the hearing or watching of sexist jokes or songs, sexist insults, televised beauty pageants, or the like, to do the same. Hence, I doubt that the reasons I have offered for believing that violent pornography lies outside the coverage of the persuasion principle apply with equal cogency to nonviolent but sexist pornography. A ban on sexist pornography, enacted to reduce the harm of subordinate socioeconomic status for women, cannot avoid violating liberalism's commitment to the persuasion principle.[29]

WHY LIBERALS CAN SUPPORT A BAN

To show that a ban on violent pornography is consistent with the persuasion principle is not (yet) to show that liberals can or should support it. To show that, one would also need to argue that they can or should accept the causal claim made by the argument for a ban. That claim, recall, is that the availability of violent pornography in our society causes a significant increase in the total number of sexual assaults on women. How high are the evidentiary standards that must be satisfied before we are entitled to accept that claim and base public policy decisions on it?

If violent pornography were protected by the persuasion principle, the theory of free speech which I have defended would permit a ban only if there were strong, indisputable evidence that its consumption causes an increase, that is, only if a ban could pass a "clear and present danger" test. This is the test to which Joel Feinberg and Fred Berger would subject a ban.[30] It is fairly obvious, I think, that the evidence of violent pornography's harmfulness does not and probably never will pass it. The idea that social science has or can provide hard evidence in support of the causal claim seems utterly misguided. Laboratory experiments which expose subjects to varying sexual/non-sexual and violent/nonviolent materials and then measure their responses will always be subject to the methodological objections that they create potentially significant causal conditions absent in the real world and that there are potentially significant conditions in the real world which cannot be replicated in the laboratory. (One such condition is that "outside the laboratory violence is not sanctioned, but inside the laboratory aggression is condoned, even encouraged, after the subject has viewed the violent material.")[31]

Because violent pornography falls outside the protection of the persuasion principle, the "clear and present danger" test is the wrong one to use. The weaker test to which we should subject a ban on this material is a purely consequentialist one which weighs its expected benefits against its expected costs. That test in turn implies that the lower those costs are, the less evidence is needed for causal claim on which the argument for a ban is based. The potential costs of a ban include the resources expended in enforcing it, the desire frustration which it would cause those violent pornography users who never commit acts of sexual violence, and the setback to various interests which free speech ordinarily promotes. Among those interests are the search for truth, the formation of autonomous beliefs and values, and the maintenance of a democracy in which the interests and ideals of different citizens are fully and fairly represented in debate over public policy. A ban could harm these interests either through reducing the availability of violent pornography, which might itself be thought to advance them, or through its "chilling effects" on other kinds of speech which certainly do advance them.

It seems to me that these evils are either avoidable or, to the extent that they are unavoidable, fairly minor. It can hardly be maintained that the availability of violent pornography is vital to the search for moral truths or that a ban on it would seriously impair autonomous belief and value formation (as a ban on the advocacy of atheism or socialism would). Nor is it plausible to claim that a ban is inconsistent with democratic ideals, because it would distort public debate about sexual violence, sexual equality, or the like. In this respect violent pornography seems no different from other pornography. It is precisely because restrictions on *any* pornography are much less likely to damage important free speech interests than restrictions on religious proselytizing, artistic expression, or political advocacy that it seems correct to regard pornography in general as a "low value" category of speech.[32]

A more serious objection to a ban is that it would set back these interests through its chilling effects on other, "high value" speech. It might be claimed that any ban would necessarily be couched in vague, sweeping terms and, as a result, would inhibit those who wish to include graphic depictions of sexual violence in nonpornographic works of art or political protest. A vaguely drafted ban could be exploited by Andrea Dworkin-type feminists intent on extirpating from the culture all "favorable" depictions of rape or sexual violence, even in nonpornographic works with serious artistic or political value. It would also be exploited by conservative prudes who wish to rid society of all erotica.

If a ban could not avoid such side effects, then its cost might well outweigh its benefits. But there is no good reason to believe that these slippery slope costs are unavoidable. While it may well require great care and skill to draft a ban which, unlike the Indianapolis anti-pornography ordinance, is not excessively vague or overly broad, there is no reason why it should be impossible in principle.[33]

Does the loss suffered by law-abiding violent pornography users who have been denied ready access to the material they desire provide a reason against a ban? To remain faithful to the harm principle, liberals must admit that it does. They cannot refuse to count as one of the costs of a ban the diminished satisfaction of users' desires to fantasize about raping women on the grounds that such fantasy is immoral even if it is never acted on. That would be legal moralism. Perhaps it can be argued that for many of these men a ban would be in their long-term self-interest. But even if it cannot be, it is hard to believe that it would impose a serious deprivation.

If a consequentialist test is the appropriate one to apply to a ban on violent pornography, and if the costs of a well-drafted ban are fairly minor, it would follow that fairly weak, speculative evidence in support of the causal claim is all that is needed. In response to the objection that the use of violent pornography may well be a catharsis, satisfying a desire with a disjunctive structure (for either more violent pornography or actual sexual assaults), I would advert to the cigarette advertising example used earlier. If the desire which Marlboro man ads produce in consumers were the disjunctive one (to smoke Marlboros *or* look at more Marlboro ads), the ads would not be so effective, since looking at more ads would be the cheaper way to satisfy it. Their effectiveness is evidence that the desire that they produce is the nondisjunctive one, simply to smoke Marlboros. Since the continued use of violent pornography involves the same nonrational, conditioning process, only with a more potent conditioner, it seems likely that it reinforces a similarly nondisjunctive desire. So violent pornography is unlikely to be a catharsis.

But, as has already been admitted, its reinforcing a desire that only sexual assaults can satisfy does not mean that it produces any increase in sexual assaults, much less a significant one, because it is possible that consumers of violent pornography have strong countervailing desires, beliefs, or personality traits. It must also be admitted, I think, that there is little reason to believe that the continued use of violent pornography is bound to weaken or eliminate such countervailing states in consumers who have them. But how many consumers are likely to have them? A sort of schizophrenic attitude toward women, involving gallantry toward "ladies" but hostility and a desire to dominate sexually independent women ("sluts"), seems prevalent and "normal" in some subcultures of our society. It seems to me at least reasonable to believe that those violent pornography users who were socialized within these subcultures will not have any strong countervailing desires.

Whether the above constitutes a strong enough reply to doubts that there is sufficient evidence to support the causal claim—and hence to doubts that a ban on violent pornography can satisfy even a test weaker than the "clear and present danger" test—seems to me to be a question about which there is room for reasonable disagreement. The liberal theory of free speech neither clearly forbids nor clearly requires a citywide ban on all billboards with commercial advertising, enacted to prevent excessive urban blight, because there is room for reasonable disagreement about whether its benefits (aesthetic) outweigh its cost (the setback to economic efficiency). The same is true of a ban on violent pornography.

READING ENDNOTES

I wish to thank Paul Sagal for his invaluable instruction on the topic of behavior conditioning.
1. See Helen Longino, "Pornography, Oppression, and Freedom: A Closer Look," in *Take Back the Night: Women on Pornography*, ed. Laura Lederer (New York: Morrow, 1980); and Judith M. Hill, "Pornography and Degradation," *Hypatia* 2 (1987): 39–54. For penetrating criticism of the argument, see Alan Soble, "Pornography: Defamation and the Endorsement of Degradation," *Social Theory and Practice* 11 (1985): 61–87; and Joel Feinberg *Offense to Others: The Moral Limits of the Criminal Law* (Oxford: Oxford University Press, 1985), pp. 147–49.

2. See Rae Langton, "Speech Acts and Unspeakable Acts," *Philosophy and Public Affairs* 22 (1993): 293–330.

3. A careful and well-informed discussion of the causal claim can be found in Frederick Schauer, "Causation Theory and the Causes of Sexual Violence," *American Bar Foundation Research Journal* (1987): 737–70.

4. Anthony Burgess, "What is Pornography?" in *Perspectives on Pornography*, ed. Douglas A. Hughes (New York: St. Martin's, 1970), pp. 4–8; quoted in Feinberg, *Offense to Others*, p. 130.

5. The *Final Report of the Attorney General's Commission on Pornography* (Washington, D.C.: U.S. Department of Justice, 1986) distinguished *c* from *d*. For further discussion of the distinction, see Schauer, pp. 741–42.

6. For a statement and defense of the ordinance, see Catharine MacKinnon, "Pornography, Civil Rights, and Speech," *Harvard Civil Rights–Civil Liberties Law Review* 20 (1985): 1–70. Included in the material which it would recognize as a civil rights violation are depictions of women "presented as sexual objects … through postures or positions of servility or submission or display." The sort of pornography typified by *Playboy* magazine centerfolds clearly "displays" women. If the ordinance is meant to include it, and if there is really nothing sexist or morally objectionable about it, then it targets more than just *b–d*.

7. *Final Report of the Attorney General's Commission on Pornography*, pp. 986–87; quoted in G. Hawkins and F. E. Zimring, *Pornography in a Free Society* (Cambridge: Cambridge University Press, 1988), p. 103.

8. Also, the "Beaver Hunters" advertisement in *Hustler* magazine, which "shows a nude woman strapped to the top of a car; the copy below the photograph states that the woman would be 'stuffed and mounted' as soon as the 'hunters' got her home." The example in the text and this quotation are taken from Cass Sunstein, "Pornography and the First Amendment," *Duke Law Journal* (September 1986): 589–627, p. 593.

9. I take the canonical liberal text to be John Stuart Mill, *On Liberty;* and Joel Feinberg's four-volume work *The Moral Limits of the Criminal Law* (vol. 1, *Harm to Others* [Oxford: Oxford University Press, 1984], and vol. 4, *Harmless Wrongdoing* [Oxford: Oxford University Press, 1988]) to be the most powerful elaboration and defense of the Millian position.

10. Thomas Scanlon, "A Theory of Freedom of Expression," *Philosophy and Public Affairs* 1 (1972): 204–26 (he calls it "the Millian principle"); Ronald Dworkin, "The Coming Battles over Free Speech," *New York Review of Books* (June 11, 1992), pp. 55–64; and David A. Strauss, "Persuasion, Autonomy, and Freedom of Expression," *Columbia Law Review* 91 (1991): 334–71 ("the persuasion principle"; I borrow this label from Strauss). Strauss claims that the persuasion principle has been respected in nearly all recent Supreme Court First Amendment decisions, with Puerto Rico Associates v. Tourism Company 478 US 328 (1986), which upheld a ban on casino advertising on the grounds that the state has a legitimate interest in shielding its citizens from encouragements to gamble, being a notable exception.

11. Dworkin, pp. 56–57.

12. The persuasion principle also implies that it is wrong to restrict speech either to spare an audience the shock or offense of hearing opinions they detest or to prevent possible violence against the speaker by an unsympathetic audience. But it is hard to see how restrictions enacted to prevent these two harms (at least the first one) would violate actual or potential listeners' autonomy. This is one reason for thinking that the persuasion principle cannot be defended on exclusively Kantian grounds.

13. The Millian principle defended by Scanlon in "A Theory of Freedom of Expression" had the counterintuitive implication that a ban on false advertising is impermissible. In a later article ("Freedom of Expression and Categories of Expression," *University of Pittsburgh Law Review* 40 [1979]: 519-50), Scanlon argued that the only way to avoid such implications is by rejecting the Millian principle (as derived from a "respect autonomy" side constraint) in favor of a thoroughly consequentialist theory of free speech. Though an acceptable consequentialism will recognize that we have a strong interest in being autonomous or making our own well-informed decisions, it will also require that the interest be balanced against other interests when they conflict.

14. For discussion of the notion of a "side constraint," see Robert Nozick, *Anarchy, State, and Utopia* (New York: Basic, 1974), pp. 28–33.
15. It seems to me doubtful that it is an immediate incitement to anything, but even if it were an incitement to sexual hatred, that would not make it an incitement to criminal conduct, because there is nothing criminal about sexual hatred per se. For further discussion, see Feinberg, *Offense to Others*, pp. 155–57.
16. See Geoffrey R. Stone, "Content Regulation and the First Amendment", *William and Mary Law Review* 25 (1983): 189–252, and "Comment: Antipornography Legislation as Viewpoint Discrimination," *Harvard Journal of Law and Public Policy* 9: 461–80. Sunstein (p. 615) argues that the distinction between viewpoint-based and content-based restrictions cannot be neutrally formulated, that is, drawn in a way that does not itself presuppose a contested normative viewpoint.
17. Stone, "Comment," p. 467, discusses this example. Though viewpoint neutral in statement, this restriction is likely to be viewpoint based in motivation (enacted by conservatives wishing to curtail the expression of controversial viewpoints opposed to the political status quo or critical of widely held moral beliefs). It would certainly have unequal effects on different political viewpoints, hampering the dissemination of controversial ones more than noncontroversial ones. But as nearly all restrictions are bound to have such unequal effects, that can hardly be an objection to it.
18. Sunstein, p. 612.
19. Stone seems to hold this view. His thesis in "Comment" is that broad antipornography restrictions of the sort exemplified by the Indianapolis ordinance are viewpoint based. But it seems clear that he would lodge the same complaint against narrower restrictions aimed only at violent pornography.
20. To use speech at the far nonrational end of the continuum in order to control the behavior of one's listener is, in effect, to use coercion, or to affect him via mere "causes" rather than "reasons." And that certainly violates the Kantian injunctions to respect others' autonomy and treat all persons as ends in themselves, never as mere means. But not all speech which violates these injunctions belongs at the nonrational end of the continuum. Though it is usually manipulative knowingly to give another bad or false reasons for acting, it is still to give reasons rather than merely to pull causal levers. Indeed, not even all coercive speech is nonrational in the sense at stake here. If it does not impede one's ability to deliberate about whether to accede to it, a threat belongs at the persuasion end of the continuum.
21. This seems to be the obvious reply to Frederick Schauer, "Speech and 'Speech'—Obscenity and 'Obscenity': An Exercise in the Interpretation of Constitutional Language," *Georgetown Law Journal* 67 (1979): 899–933, which argues that pornography is not really speech, because it functions no differently from sex aids.
22. Sunstein, pp. 607–08. This, together with the fact that it is meant to produce arousal, makes pornography "noncognitive" speech.
23. See Neil M. Malamuth and James V. P. Check, "The Effects of Mass Media Exposure on Acceptance of Violence against Women: A Field Experiment," *Journal of Research in Personality* 15 (1981): 436–46; on the efficacy of the debriefing sessions in counteracting the bad cognitive effects that viewing "favorable" rape depictions had on experimental subjects, see Neil M. Malamuth, "Rape Proclivity among Males," *Journal of Social Issues* 37 (1981): 138–57.
24. This example is mentioned by Richard Brandt. See *A Theory of the Good and the Right* (Oxford: Oxford University Press, 1979), p. 99, for citation of the relevant psychological literature. This example also serves to make the point that nothing in the law of effect requires that the behavior in question be publicly observable (thinking of drinking a cocktail is not). Also, one can accept the law without being a behaviorist and holding (as Skinner did) that all human behavior (apart from reflex behavior) is the product of operant conditioning. Finally, I take it that one can accept the law but reject the behaviorist's claim that talk of "behavioral tendencies" is always preferable to talk of "desires."
25. Stone "Comment," p. 478.

26. Appellants' brief to *ABA v. Hudnut* claims that it does: "By conditioning the male orgasm to female subordination, pornography … makes the subordination of women pleasurable and seemingly legitimate. Each time men are sexually aroused by pornography, they learn to connect a woman's sexual pleasure to abuse and a woman's sexual nature to inferiority. They learn this is their bodies, not just their minds, so that it becomes a natural physiological response. At this point pornography leaves no more room for further debate than does shouting 'kill' to an attack dog." Quoted by Nan D. Hunter and Sylvia A. Law, "Brief *Amici Curiae* of Feminist Anticensorship Task Force et al., in *ABA v. Hudnut*," reprinted in Patricia Smith, ed., *Feminist Jurisprudence* (Oxford: Oxford University Press, 1993), p. 474.

27. It is often claimed that *Playboy* magazine centerfolds are sexist because they "objectify" women, but it is unclear to me exactly what that is supposed to mean. No doubt the male consumer of such pornography has a purely carnal interest in the model posing. But why should taking a temporary, purely carnal interest in another person be any more objectionable than any of the many other ways in which people take a temporary, limited interest in one another? See Janet Radcliffe Richards, *The Skeptical Feminist* (Boston: Routledge & Kegan Paul, 1980), pp. 197–202.

28. Ronald Dworkin has argued, "It would plainly be unconstitutional to ban speech directly advocating that women occupy inferior roles, or none at all, in commerce and the professions, even if that speech fell on willing male ears and achieved its goals. So it cannot be a reason for banning pornography that it contributes to an unequal economic or social structure, even if we think it does" ("Liberty and Pornography," *New York Review of Books* [Aug. 15, 1991], pp. 12–15, p. 14). Someone who believes in the conditioning story about sexist pornography will reply that the reason for banning this pornography is not simply that it contributes to women's inequality, but rather that it does this in a way not protected by the persuasion principle.

29. MacKinnon, I take it, would agree. She appears to simply reject the liberal's commitment to no viewpoint-based censorship. More surprising is that *Hudnut* overturned the Indianapolis ordinance on the grounds that it was a viewpoint-based restriction forbidden by the First Amendment, and MacKinnon finds that decision legally flawed. She cites a number of cases in which the Supreme Court upheld restrictions on speech and claims that *Hudnut* was inconsistent with them. But since none of the restrictions in those cases was clearly viewpoint based, they are irrelevant to *Hudnut's* holding. See MacKinnon, pp. 24–25.

30. Feinberg endorses Berger's claim that "there must be strong evidence of a very likely and serious harm." See Feinberg, *Offense to Others*, p. 157; and Fred Berger, "Pornography, Feminism, and Censorship," in *Philosophy and Sex*, 2d ed., ed. R. Baker and F. Ellison (Buffalo, N.Y.: Prometheus, 1984), p. 341.

31. Daniel Linz, Steven D. Penrod, and Edward Donnerstein, "The Attorney General's Commission on Pornography: The Gaps between 'Findings' and Facts," *American Bar Foundation Research Journal* 81 (1987): 713–36, p. 722. Several other methodological problems are mentioned by the authors, who themselves have conducted several such experiments. In one they describe (p. 720), male college students are first angered and then shown one of four films: (*i*) "aggressive pornography," (*ii*) a film that was "X-rated but with no aggression or sexual coercion," (*iii*) a film that "contained scenes of aggression against women but without any sexual content," and (*iv*) a film with "neutral content." The men who viewed *i* "displayed the highest level of aggression against women," and those who viewed *iii* showed more aggression than those who viewed *ii*. Note that slasher movies like *Toolbox Murders*—R-rated movies which contain graphic sexual violence but not enough sexual explicitness to give them an X rating—belong to none of these categories, and hence, the results of this experiment do not support the claim that violent pornography is more harmful to women than this category of sexually violent speech. Both Deana Pollard ("Regulating Violent Pornography," *Vanderbilt Law Review* 43 [1990]: 125–59) and Sunstein (p. 593) misinterpret the social science research when they maintain that it does support such a claim.

32. For further discussion of the analysis of categories of speech as having low and high value, see Stone, "Content Regulation and the First Amendment," and Sunstein. The relatively low value of commercial speech seems to be an important part of the reason why the ban on billboards with

commercial messages is acceptable, while the relatively high value of political speech is the reason why the ban on all large gatherings in public parks, to prevent excessive noise and litter, is unacceptable.

33. One reason for not extending a ban to all pornography which contains an explicit degradation or domination theme (to the *c* category as well as the *d* category distinguished earlier) is that the difficulties in operationalizing 'violence' and 'pornographic' pale in comparison to the difficulties that beset any attempt to operationalize 'degradation.' Some of the latter difficulties are described in Berger.

QUESTIONS

1. What harms are involved in the production and use of violent pornography? Are they the kinds of harm that fall under the harm principle and so could be the basis for interfering with the liberty of those who make and consume such material through a general ban?

2. What are the two components that typically must be present before a libertarian will accept a restriction on freedom of speech?

3. What is the "persuasion principle" and why are libertarians committed to it?

4. What is the libertarian position on banning viewpoint-based speech, viewpoint-neutral speech and content-based speech? In what way are these positions required by acceptance of the persuasion principle itself?

5. Why must a "strong and present danger" test be met to justify restricting viewpoint-based restrictions on speech?

6. According to Scoccia, what is the viewpoint expressed by violent pornography?

7. The persuasion principle protects viewpoint-based speech even if it is reasonably likely that the viewpoint expressed is harmful (will produce harm to others). Why?

8. What is the difference between speech that causes people to adopt certain beliefs and attitudes by persuasion rather than by non-persuasive means?

9. In what way are non-persuasive influences upon our beliefs, attitudes, and desires incompatible with our autonomy, rationality, and responsibility? Can you think of other examples of non-persuasive forms of influence that a libertarian might want to ban?

10. In what way does violent pornography produce or reinforce desires or urges to harm women through a process akin to operant conditioning? Why is operant conditioning a non-persuasive mode of influencing people?

11. Why does Scoccia think that his conditioning hypothesis might support a ban on violent pornography but not on non-violent though still sexist and misogynist pornography?

12. Why does showing that violent pornography is not protected by the persuasion principle make it easier to justify a ban on it?

13. How plausible is the causal claim that viewing violent pornography actually leads to some increase in acts of violence against women? Should Scoccia, in speculating about this question, have looked at how many acts of violence actually occur in our society against women? Should we also consider the effects of other misogyny producing or reinforcing influences in society as well, since they will affect the degree to which people actually have the strong countervailing desires not to commit acts of violence that Scoccia talks about?

14. Scoccia leaves open the question whether violent pornography ought to be banned. What do you think? Why?

15. Are there other suitably strong reinforcers for violence available (other than orgasm) that would lead us to ban other materials once we start down this road of censorship? What is the dividing line between violent movies and violent pornographic movies? Or violent music and pornography?

16. Why, exactly, does Scoccia think that the strength of the reinforcer is the key to his argument, and his way of distinguishing between violent pornography, on the one hand, and other violent or sexist representations, on the other?

17. Why isn't it enough to overcome the presumption in favour of freedom of speech to establish that non-rational persuasion is used in some form of speech?

18. Can you apply Scoccia's reasoning here to other forms of speech that a libertarian might consider banning, such as hate literature?

19. Within libertarianism, we begin any discussion of a ban or prohibition on the activities of adults with the belief that such a ban or prohibition is *prima facia* wrong. Only if it can be shown that the activity would produce harm to others than the participants might we overcome the presumption in favour of individual freedom and so support the ban. In the case of activities like the making and viewing of violent pornography, does this presumption seem wrongheaded?

CHAPTER FIVE

LIBERALISM

———

INTRODUCTION

Modern liberalism (we will here concentrate on liberalism as it has developed in the last 50 years or so) is not a univocal view. There are many strands within liberal thought, and different proponents develop the view in different ways. But we shall try to capture some of the most common elements of the position, as well as those that make it an apt theory with which to try to resolve some of the more pressing moral problems of our times.

Liberalism draws on a large number of insights from the previous theories we have examined. First, it is still in many ways an individualistic view. Second, it takes from utilitarians the view that individual well-being is of fundamental importance. Third, it takes from Kant the insistence that personal autonomy is the foundation of ethics. And finally, like libertarians, liberals recognize that there is a plurality of values and that different people have different conceptions of the good life. They further accept that individuals have a right to choose for themselves how to live, and that the freedom to pursue their own conception of the good is vital to human flourishing. As a result, they accept the importance of the various civil liberties that libertarians have defended. Yet, as we shall see, in all of these cases the insights and commitments of previous thinkers are modified (sometimes fairly radically) within liberal thought.

Autonomy

Autonomy, the condition of self-rule or self-governance, played an important role in previous moral theories. In Kantianism, it is the condition that gives human beings dignity rather than mere price, and grounds the requirement that we treat all rational natures that are capable of living autonomously (setting the moral law for themselves) as ends in themselves and never as mere means to our ends. In Millian libertarianism, it is the condition that grounds the requirement that we allow individuals the liberty to choose for themselves their conception of a good life and the right to be free from interference in the pursuit of that conception. Autonomy comes to play an importantly different role within liberal thinking, however. Within liberalism, autonomy is no longer the precondition of rights and dignity, but rather it becomes the ultimate value. Allowing or enabling individuals to live autonomous lives—lives of their own choosing, directed to goals they find valuable—becomes the fundamental requirement of both politics and ethics.

This is a subtle but crucial shift in the use of autonomy within moral theorizing, and it has profound consequences. Suppose we accept for the moment that the point of moral rules and political institutions is to ensure that all people are able to live autonomous lives, as the liberal insists. This will enable us to make sense of many traditional liberal values and political principles. These include resistance to autocratic rule in favour of democratic institutions. Under the historic influence of liberalism, totalitarian and autocratic forms of government were condemned, because they do not allow sufficient scope for individual autonomy. This was especially so when the autocratic rule was also tied to a particular religion. Liberalism has always condemned the imposition of religion by the coercive apparatus of the state as one of the grossest violations of human rights. In their place, liberals have defended democratic institutions, in which the people have a significant say in the rules by which they will be governed. While autocratic governments pose a direct threat to the ability of individuals to live the lives they deem best, democratic institutions allow individuals to be (at least part) author of the rules that bind them and so do not pose a similar threat to individual autonomy. Likewise, liberalism had traditionally been associated with tolerance of diverse values and ways of life. Tolerance of different religions, cultural practices, individual values and commitments, sexual practices and the like are all hallmarks of liberal societies. And, again, the reason can be easily traced to the liberal commitment to the ultimate value of autonomy. Given the fact of value plurality (the fact that different individuals have very different sets of values and conceptions of a good life), a liberal state must tolerate a wide range of values and practices if it is to allow individuals to live lives that they find worthwhile and fulfilling. This requires tolerance of difference. And finally, as we said above, liberals' commitment to autonomy grounds extensive political and civil rights, such as the right to freedom of thought and expression, freedom of association and mobility, freedom of religion and political participation. The practical influence of such thinking has been profound, and the principles of liberalism can be readily seen to be embodied in such documents as the *Canadian Charter of Rights and Freedoms*.

Thus far it may seem that the commitment to autonomy as the fundamental value does not play a much different role within liberalism than it did within libertarianism. It grounds an extensive array of negative liberty rights. But this is only a part of the liberal picture. While liberals agree with libertarians that people need an extensive array of freedoms (areas of their lives over which they may exercise control unhindered by others, especially the state), liberals also recognize that there are threats to individual autonomy from many more sources than overt violations of negative liberty rights. That is, liberals recognize that if individuals are actually to lead autonomous lives then they need considerably more than just to be left alone. For poverty, ignorance and lack of education, severely restricted options, exploitation, illness, addiction, unfavourable social circumstances, prejudice and just plain bad luck can all impede the ability of individuals to actually lead lives that they find personally satisfying and worthwhile. Thus modern liberals believe that a commitment to the value of autonomy further entails an extensive array of positive rights. Those things that individuals need to actually exercise their autonomy in meaningful ways are then accorded the status of rights. Thus liberals recognize that individuals have a right to education, health care, freedom from discrimination and prejudice and the minimal material conditions needed to ensure that they have a suitably broad set of options and decent life prospects with which to exercise their right to autonomy.[1]

Perhaps an example will help make clearer the distinction between liberals and libertarians on this question of the proper scope of rights. Suppose you are a farmer and that you have planted a crop, investing considerable time and money into its development. It is almost harvest time. Now suppose that a bandit comes along and takes it. Perhaps he steals it under cover of darkness, or perhaps he puts a gun to your head and demands that you turn over the crop. In the first case you did not choose to give the crop to the thief, and even in the second your choice was utterly coerced and unfree. Libertarians will say that your liberty rights have been violated regardless of how the bandit acquires your crop, so long as it was without your free consent and against your will. They will also say that the bandit owes you compensation for the loss he unjustly inflicted upon you. Now suppose, to vary the case, it is not a bandit who takes off with your crop, but a swarm of locust. (Any natural disaster would do equally well.) Your crop is destroyed. A libertarian may commiserate with you for your loss. But she will not think that your liberty rights have been violated by the locust or the loss they inflicted. Nor will she think there is anyone who owes you compensation for the loss (though libertarians typically favour cooperative voluntary insurance schemes as a rational choice for many people engaged in risky behaviour like farming). A liberal, by contrast, denies that the two cases are so morally different. He will say that in both cases your autonomy is threatened by the loss you have suffered, and since we must protect and foster autonomy when it is threatened, that in both cases you should receive compensation (at least if the loss is significant enough to threaten your ability to live autonomously). Who is to pay the compensation is not settled, but if there is no other candidate in the offing then liberals typically say "the state" or "the government" ought to pay.[2] Such claims are familiar from farmers, fishers, beef ranchers, and numerous others in Canada today.

Primary Goods

Liberals accept that to a significant degree we must recognize the fact of value plurality, that people have different conceptions of a good life and different subjective values. And an adequate moral code or political system will have to give due weight to the subjective preferences of individuals. We will not fulfil the basic requirement of liberalism, which is to respect the rights of autonomous individuals, if we impose our conception of the good or our values upon others. Thus freedom and tolerance are required.

But liberals also recognize that there are serious limitations to this purely subjectivist approach to determining how we should treat others. The first problem is tied to what we said just above: people need more than negative freedom in order to be able to exercise their autonomy. But as soon as we try to say what else they need, we run the danger of imposing our values upon them. Consider, for example, the issue of education. We (the editors of this book) being educators and people who have dedicated themselves to the pursuit of knowledge might find it virtually impossible to imagine a worthwhile life that did not include opportunities of education and study. But if we took our judgement in this matter as a basis for saying that all people must receive an education, to some specified level at least, we would be imposing our values upon others who might not share them.[3] And it seems that a similar problem will plague every attempt to develop a list of basic needs that must be satisfied or to provide a list of basic goods that everyone should enjoy, as conditions of living an autonomous life. After all, what you need and what counts as a good to you will depend crucially on what you want to do, what projects you plan to pursue and what conception of the good life you are trying to realize. And yet if we are to move beyond mere negative liberty, it seems that we must be able to develop such a list of basic needs that must be met, basic interests that everyone has, or basic goods that all should enjoy so as to make possible autonomous lives. In moving in this direction we shall have to move beyond subjective preferences to an objective theory of value, needs, or interests.

Different liberals have articulated the conditions under which autonomy can be meaningfully exercised in different ways. One of the most influential characterizations comes from John Rawls. Though Rawls' theory of political liberalism is much more complex than we can go into here, we must mention one aspect of his view, namely, his list of "primary goods." These are goods that he supposes everyone wants, no matter what else they want. They are goods that satisfy needs that can be assumed to be shared by all free and equal citizens who have conceptions of the good that they are trying to realize in a context of value plurality. They are the necessary conditions of realizing the value of autonomy. Here is how Rawls first characterized his idea:

> Now primary goods . . . are things which it is supposed a rational man wants whatever else he wants. Regardless of what an individual's rational plans are in detail, it is assumed that there are various things which he would prefer more of rather than less. With more of these goods men can generally be assured of greater success in carrying out their intentions and in advancing their ends, whatever these may be.[4]

The actual list of primary goods that Rawls offers includes four general categories or types of goods:

1. rights and liberties;
2. opportunities and powers;
3. income and wealth; and
4. the social bases of self-respect.

Now Rawls thinks that he can advance this list of primary goods as shared because it presupposes only what he calls a "thin" theory of the good.[5] That is, these things can be seen as good no matter what an individual's "thick," comprehensive conception of the good is. They are goods that we can expect every rational person will want as much of as possible, because they will prove valuable to the pursuit of any conception of the good that individuals might subjectively hold.

Rawls' is only one possible objective list that a liberal might offer, by way of saying what more people need than bare liberty in order to lead autonomous lives. We leave it to readers to assess the adequacy of his list, or to think about possible additions to it. Rather than survey the other lists that have been offered, we turn now instead to some of the implications of the turn from a subjective to an objective theory of value. First, notice that the role of the state has been greatly expanded from that of the minimal state of libertarians. Presumably (and this is certainly Rawls' view), it will fall to the major political institutions of a society to ensure that all individuals enjoy a sufficiently high level of primary goods. Thus the state will now be charged not only with (1) providing and protecting the basic civil rights and liberties of citizens (such as the rights to freedom of expression, association, mobility, thought, etc.: the rights we noted were hallmarks of a liberal society); but it will also have to ensure that people have (2) adequate opportunities and powers (which for Rawls include educational and professional opportunities, and the opportunity to hold public office and participate in the political institutions of one's society, together with the exercise of whatever powers attach to those offices and positions); (3) sufficient income and wealth to have a reasonable chance of realizing their life plans (that will require significant redistribution of wealth in society through taxation and the maintenance of a welfare system); and (4) access to the social bases of self-respect (that will require the state to intervene when prejudice, lack of natural talents, bad luck, or low life prospects threaten to deprive persons of the bases of self-respect for morally arbitrary reasons). This is an extensive role for the state indeed. One way of summarizing the development within liberal thought of the need to move beyond negative rights to positive rights is to say that liberals endorse an objective conception of welfare. Welfare is some minimal level of well-being, assessed not only in terms of subjective states such as the degree to which one's preferences are satisfied or how happy one is, but also according to whether one enjoys a sufficient level of primary goods as to be able to live an autonomous life. The most egalitarian liberals insist, not that people are entitled to some minimal level of welfare, but that everyone must enjoy, so far as possible and subject only to their own autonomous choices, an equal level of welfare. While we have not yet moved to this wholesale egalitarian ideal, the concrete attempt to realize the goal of ensuring that all people enjoy an adequate (even if still unequal) level of welfare is what we call (not coincidently) "the welfare state."

Egalitarianism

Like the other theories we have considered, modern liberalism is in some sense or other an egalitarian theory. For liberals, every individual has an equal right to the conditions of autonomous agency. Again, of course, what exactly that comes to is a matter of dispute among liberals themselves. But some common themes can be identified. We will concentrate on two in this section: equal opportunities and distributive justice.

Liberals are committed to ensuring that all people enjoy equal opportunities to live a good life. They believe that no one should be disadvantaged by factors beyond their control. Such factors include obvious things like race and gender, but also include the social and economic status of one's parents and one's share of natural talents. Current social and political arrangements are such, of course, that these factors do significantly affect the life prospects of people. An individual in Canada born to poor black or First Nations' parents in fact has lower life prospects than an individual born to affluent white parents. But neither the poor nor the rich child deserves to have their life prospects determined by such factors, which are entirely beyond their control and (from their point of view) are simply a matter of luck. All liberals accept that some scheme must be adopted to erase, so far as possible, the influence of luck in determining the life prospects of persons. Many of the standard practices and institutions that we find in welfare liberal states, such as publicly funded and universal education and health care, are intended to minimize the effects of luck and provide the conditions by which individuals have an equal opportunity to achieve a good life for themselves. Although technically the commitment to making available to all the conditions of autonomous living probably only requires ensuring that everyone enjoys a minimal level of material well-being and a safety net to ensure that people's lives are not ruined through bad luck, liberals typically embrace a more robust egalitarianism than that. Instead, they have treated any of the material and social conditions that are important to realizing the goal of living autonomously as basic goods that everyone should enjoy, and enjoyment of these goods has been elevated to the status of positive rights. Everyone is entitled to have them, and if anyone cannot provide them for themselves then the right requires that others provide them.

Liberals further recognize that simply providing some basic goods to everyone as a starting point will not eliminate all of the barriers to equality of opportunity. In particular, they recognize that the effects of such things as racial prejudice and other forms of discrimination must also be removed if people are to have genuinely equal opportunities to participate fully in society, to succeed in realizing their goals, and to have fulfilling human lives. Liberals often, therefore, also endorse various schemes to eliminate the effects of past intolerance or prejudice (such as affirmative action programs targeted at disadvantaged minorities, especially with respect to educational opportunities and more highly valued social, political, and professional positions). And they advocate the imposition of anti-discrimination policies in the same areas, trying to ensure that those prejudices do not continue to lead to disadvantage for some.

Liberals also believe that the commitment to autonomy entails a theory of distributive justice. Justice refers to what people are due. So, for example, retributive justice provides a theory as to what wrong-doers, such as criminals, deserve and retributivists think that what criminals deserve or are due is punishment. Likewise, compensatory justice concerns what people are due if they have been injured or non-criminally harmed by another; it concerns what level of compensation is due to the victims of harm. Liberals may, and often do, have views about these questions of justice. And modern welfare states run courts that dispense both criminal and compensatory justice. They also undertake to provide compensation, from taxpayers' money, to many individuals who are harmed for reasons beyond their control (such as compensation paid to farmers in drought, to fishermen because of low fish stocks, to victims of flood or other natural disasters, and to cities faced with unforeseeable and unpreventable tragedies such as SARS). These practices follow the general liberal insistence that people should not suffer diminished life prospects for circumstances beyond their control (the compensation cases), but that they should be held responsible for the consequences of their unforced choices (which is why we can punish criminals). But more often liberals have concentrated on developing theories of distributive justice, that is, about how various goods should be distributed in society. We have seen that if the goods in question are thought to be primary goods or goods necessary in order to have an equal opportunity of living a good life or to off-set the effects of brute luck, then liberals believe they should be distributed equally. Beyond that, liberals disagree amongst themselves on the proper distributive principles. The most radical egalitarian would say that all social goods must be distributed equally, and merit or other personal and variable factors should have no role to play. Not many liberals take such a position, though Rawls comes close. He thinks that rights and liberties must be distributed equally, and that the vagaries of luck must be eliminated by ensuring genuine equality of opportunity. He also thinks that income and wealth should be distributed equally, with the following important caveat: if an unequal distribution of wealth would make the least well-off representative person in society better off than would a strictly equal distribution, then the inequality is permissible. So, for example, if there are some socially useful professions, such as that of physicians, that require (perhaps because of the stress involved in the job or because of the extensive training it requires) additional compensation in terms of income in order to induce people to enter them, and if even the least well off in society benefit from having them at the higher rate, then they may receive more than an equal share of income and wealth.[6]

Whatever the details of an individual liberal's conception of justice, and regardless of whether it is fully or only partially egalitarian, it must include the elements we have considered. It must be based on the belief that everyone is entitled to equal basic civil rights and liberties, it must provide the conditions of equality of opportunity, it must to a significant extent work to off-set the influence of luck on life prospects and it must provide everyone with the material conditions under which they have a reasonable chance of living an autonomous life.

Neutrality

Given their acceptance of the fact of value plurality and the requirement that governments in particular show equal respect for citizens, many liberals have further insisted that governments must be neutral between competing conceptions of the good. That is, liberals typically require that governments not act in such a way as to privilege any one conception of the good over others. They may not impose any religious beliefs or practices on their populations (the separation of church and state is yet another hallmark of liberal societies), but neither may they impose any particular moral code or ideal of the good life upon those who do not accept it. Beyond maintaining the conditions under which all citizens may equally enjoy their civil rights and liberties, equal opportunities and the material conditions of autonomy, governments must not direct the moral choices of their citizens. Just because the members of a government, or some significant portion of a population, finds some practice or value system to be immoral, disgusting, or otherwise misguided, they may not use the power of the state to prevent individuals from engaging in that practice.

This still, as we noted, leaves extensive scope for government action. Beyond those roles we have already mentioned, one other deserves attention before we move on. If the point of both morality and politics is to ensure that individuals are able to lead autonomous lives, there is considerable room for governments and others to directly interfere with the liberty of people, for their own good. Liberalism allows certain paternalistic interventions into the lives of individuals that libertarianism rules out. If there are behaviours that undermine the future ability of people to live autonomously, such as the use of mind destroying drugs, then on liberal grounds the state or others must be allowed to intervene with the choices of individuals to prevent such behaviour. It seems we may restrict people's autonomous choices now if doing so is necessary to protect their long-term autonomy in the future.

There is a related question here. It seems that liberals will sometimes have to make judgements about which choices are autonomous and which are not. After all, they insist that governments must respect the autonomous choices of their citizens and protect them from activities that threaten their ability to make such choices in the future. Thus we must be able to distinguish between autonomous and non-autonomous choices, and be able to recognize some activities as constituting a danger of diminishing or eliminating the autonomy of persons who engage in them. Can people, for example, autonomously choose to become drug addicts, or enter into prostitution? If we want to say no, are we not imposing our conception of the good upon them? Are we not led by the thought that such choices could never be made by any reasonable person, thereby denying to them the respect that they deserve? Lest this thought experiment seem too far fetched, consider that until quite recently homosexuality was treated as the kind of choice one could not autonomously make. The mechanism by which that result was accomplished was to deem homosexuality a mental illness. The mentally ill cannot make autonomous choices (at least with respect to some range of choices), and so by labelling the choice to engage in homosexual behaviour simply a sign of illness, its opponents removed the standard protection of it as a choice and implied that it did not need to be respected.

This last step is, in fact, a bit quick. Liberals are committed to protecting and fostering autonomous lives. By itself, that commitment says nothing about how we should treat the non-autonomous choices of individuals. The government may try to limit the incidents of such choices, by making force and fraud illegal, and by denying legal force to choice made under duress or ignorance. It might provide the social and material conditions that are thought most likely to enable people to make autonomous choices. And it might provide support to any number of activities that are designed to enable those not now capable of autonomy to develop it (drug rehabilitation, universal education, etc.). But in itself the commitment to autonomy does not tell us anything about how we should treat those who are permanently incapable of living autonomously (the senile, the irreversibly comatose or even severely brain damaged, animals, etc.).

Multiculturalism and Illiberal Cultures

The final topic we wish to discuss is one that is central to liberalism as it is understood and practiced in Canada specifically. Liberalism, as we have characterized it, is the view that all people should enjoy the freedoms, opportunities, and resources necessary to lead autonomous lives. That makes liberalism sound like a very individualistic view. But caution is needed here. It is true that what matters in liberal thinking are individuals and their ability to lead good lives of their own choosing. But it would be a mistake to think that we can talk meaningfully about what good human lives look like independently of the communities and cultures in which those lives are lived. This is a point made and explained in a series of important books by Canadian philosopher Will Kymlicka.[7] A person's values, as well as her sense of identity, are crucially shaped by the community in which she lives and the culture(s) with which she identifies. An individual's conception of the good life will be necessarily shaped by the culture in which she is embedded and through whose practices she understands both herself and the world.

Beyond merely recognizing the influence of cultures upon individuals' autonomy, however, we must also recognize that the well-being of individuals is often importantly dependent upon the well-being of their cultures and communities. People can only thrive if their communities are thriving. Thus the good of individuals will be intimately tied up with the good of the communities with which they identify. The most extreme example of the truth of this claim can be seen by examining the history of aboriginal peoples in this country: the destruction of culture has led to a profound loss of identity and meaning for the members of the communities that have been disrupted or destroyed. But the point holds more generally: the good of individuals is intimately dependent upon the well-being of their communities. In this sense, liberals need not be individualistic. That is, liberals can and should recognize the importance of culture to individuals.

Once the importance of cultures is recognized, however, a whole host of new questions and problems arise for liberals in multicultural societies such as Canada. Multiculturalism is both a fact of Canadian society—there is a multitude of minority cultures existing within the broader social and political framework of Canada—but it is also a national commitment. We value multiculturalism and are committed in the highest laws of our land to respecting minority cultures as such. Now it would take us too far from our main topic to develop anything like a comprehensive account of what makes a group a community or to defining a culture, but many of the common signs of a cultural community are a shared language, ethnicity, territory, history, and religion. But cultural communities are also made up of shared practices, ways of understanding the world and value systems. It is for this reason that we cannot typically talk of the values of an individual independently of the values and practices of his cultural community.

Now most people have rather superficially thought that liberalism, in a multicultural setting, simply requires neutrality on the part of governments. Governments must not actively promote or advantage any one culture over others, and all must be equally tolerated. Under the pressures of the cultural marketplace, some cultures will die out or be assimilated into the broader community over time while others may continue to thrive as minority cultures. But this will ultimately be an effect of the choices of individuals, and governments ought not to interfere with the natural processes by which cultural groups wax or wane. If we are to respect individuals, we must allow them to choose which cultural communities they identify with and want to support.

Canada has not always followed even this minimal liberal advice, of course. The government of Canada actively promotes Francophone culture, for example, and it has a sorry history of actively undermining native cultures. But even the ideal (never mind the reality of trying to live up to it) is not adequate. For if liberal states must show equal concern and respect for their citizens,[8] then it seems that governments must support minority cultures, given that individuals can only lead meaningful and autonomous lives within the context of such cultures. This is one of the dilemmas of our current liberal state. Kymlicka has argued that we must expand our notion of liberalism to include not only individual rights, but minority group's rights as well, but many other liberals have resisted this extension.

Multiculturalism raises another problem for liberalism as well. The problem is that many minority cultures are themselves painfully illiberal. That is, many minority cultures do not themselves show equal concern and respect for their members, they do not treat all their members as equals, they do not respect the rights of some of their members, they do not tolerate divergent values within the group, etc. The question of how liberal states should treat illiberal groups within their midst has long been a vexing one. Again, liberals seem to face a dilemma. If they must tolerate such differences among groups, maintaining government neutrality toward them and respecting the rights of members of the group to live as they judge best, then some members of the group will be denied the opportunity to lead a rewarding and autonomous human life. But then we have perhaps extreme limitations on the autonomy and rights of some in order to respect the autonomy and rights of others. Such sacrifices of some people for the good of others seem to be precisely what the egalitarian strands of liberalism are meant to rule out. The problem of illiberal minority cultures is even more problematic when the effects of its illiberal practices are designed to or in effect do preclude the development of autonomy for some or all of its members. Cultures that deny their members the right to leave, or deny educational opportunities to some of their members, or that impose limited and all-consuming indoctrination into a particular set of religious beliefs or values, for example, threaten the ability of individuals within the group to develop the capacity to form autonomous conceptions of a good life at all. Again the question of what we should do with respect to non-autonomous persons or choices arises, but now at the level of groups and whole ways of life. The problem in both cases may be the same, however: what are we to do if a person identifies with some group or values some activity, but that very group or activity retards the development or exercise of the person's autonomy itself. As we shall see, the tensions that arise for liberalism within multicultural societies are far-ranging.

✦ ✦ ✦

James Griffin, Welfare Rights

James Griffin argues that welfare rights are not simply political rights, but are more properly considered human rights (moral rights that people have simply in virtue of being human). He considers any formulation of human rights that restricts them to negative rights to be unduly minimal, given that the purpose of human rights is to protect agency. This is his *prima facie* case, which he then defends against objections. The first round of objections suggest that welfare rights do not have the proper form to be considered human rights: we give redress to welfare inequities locally, the minimal provisions necessary to live are simply *preconditions* of agency, and the idea of a "minimal level" of welfare is unclear. Human rights, alternatively, are of universal importance, are concerned with protecting agency itself, and are clearly demarcatable. He responds by observing that many moral duties depend on your location (such as the duty to give aid to a drowning child), that the right to life is also only concerned with a precondition of agency, and that ethics are full of unclear concepts. Secondly, he considers the idea that enforcing these rights contravenes other people's liberty or property rights. Giving to others necessarily leaves one with less. Griffin observes that taking away some of your property does not leave you any less able to lead a worthwhile life, and it is this ability to live a good life, ultimately, that is to be defended by liberty rights. The taking of property does not impinge on one's liberty. As to property, Griffin suggests that our own sentiments lead us to want to benefit those that we can, and these commitments balance against our right to property—we commit to others what, all things considered, we think we ought, up to a maximum of what we can.

Several cautions are necessary at this point. First, the idea that a right can be balanced off against other considerations is itself contentious. Rights typically demarcate the limit of permissible treatment of others, while pursuing social welfare or anything else. If someone has a right to life, it is *forbidden* to kill that person. The special ethical discourse involving rights has also typically been understood to clearly mark out such boundaries. If what we are talking about is not so clear, then perhaps some other ethical discourse than that of rights is appropriate. Griffin does not do justice to either of these features of rights when he suggests that they may be unclear, or traded off against other concerns (specifically social welfare). Care is also needed when examining Griffin's claim that taking away one's property does not lessen one's prospects of leading a valuable life. He may be making a logical point: liberty rights are not property rights. But one might also take him to mean that he assumes that taking a third of a person's income does not diminish that person's life prospects—this may or may not be the case, but it depends on that person's thoughts on the matter, not Griffin's, and not ours.

Lastly, Griffin suggests that it is our commitments that lead us to trade off our property rights against another's welfare rights. This is plausible in the single person case. If one person has property, and cares to see that another is benefited by some portion of it, then that person may legitimately transfer some of his goods to that other. However, in the case of groups this becomes trickier to argue for. Just because some people have these commitments, there seems no reason to be able to force others to share that commitment. Why not simply leave those that have that commitment free to donate to the furtherance of that cause, and leave the rest alone? If we are talking simply about commitments, does some person's commitment to fine art imply anything about my obligation to donate to the Art Gallery of Ontario? The point here is not that welfare is not worth defending, but that this worth cannot depend on the commitments of some.

✦ ✦ ✦

James Griffin, "Welfare Rights," *The Journal of Ethics* 4 (2000): 27–43. © 2000 Kluwer Academic Publishers. Reprinted with permission of Kluwer Academic Publishers.

Welfare Rights

JAMES GRIFFIN

1. THE HISTORICAL GROWTH OF RIGHTS

I want to try to clarify one of the most contentious rights, a right to welfare.

Welfare rights were very occasionally claimed in the eighteenth century.[1] But they gained currency only in the early and middle twentieth century. In 1936, the *Constitution* of the USSR granted rights to education, to work, to rest and leisure, to provision in old age, and to aid in sickness and disability. And, most importantly of all, the United Nations *Universal Declaration of Human Rights* of 1948 included all the major welfare rights. For example, Article 25 says:

> Everyone has the right to a standard of living adequate for the health and well-being of himself and his family, including food, clothing, housing and medical care and necessary social services, and the right to social security in the event of unemployment, sickness, disability, widowhood, old age, or other lack of livelihood in circumstances beyond his control.

Article 25 is a good example of how extensive—some would say lavish—proposed welfare rights have become.

Welfare rights are often classed as "positive" rights in contrast to "negative" rights such as not being prevented from choosing one's own goals (autonomy) and not being interfered with in their pursuit (liberty). Virtually all of the classical rights of the seventeenth and eighteenth centuries (what are sometimes called "first generation" rights) are, at least on the fact of it, negative—with the possible exception of the right to life (but more about that later). The welfare rights of the mid-twentieth century ("second generation" rights), being positive, seem to increase not only the number of rights but also the kinds. And if, as many philosophers think, duties not to harm are generally more stringent than duties to aid, welfare rights may constitute a less demanding kind of right—second rank as well as second generation. There are reasons, which I shall come to shortly, for doubting whether welfare rights can aspire to the status of *human* rights.[2]

It is plain that welfare rights exist, in some parts of the world, as *legal* rights. The question for us, however, is what sort of grounds those rights have. Are they also *ethical* rights? Are they, despite the doubts, *human* rights? It is not academic nicety that leads me to raise those questions. We have no clear picture of their grounds. And their grounds determine their content, their bearers, and in the end their authority.

What is more, our notion of a human right is practically without criteria for distinguishing between when it is used correctly and when incorrectly. So I must say something, even if only briefly, about how I think that the term is best understood. Unlike other animals, we humans can form pictures of what a good life is like and act to try to realize these pictures. This is our characteristically human way of life (the word "human" here needs an enormous amount of explanation, of course). And we value our status as humans especially highly, often more highly even than our happiness. Human rights are best seen as protections of one's human standing—one's *personhood*, as one might put it.

Now, there are two different ways of taking a personhood account of human rights. One can see it as justifying liberty rights, but giving no support at all to welfare rights. On this point of view, if human rights are protections of the essential components of agency, then they protect only our autonomous choice of a course of life and our not being stopped from pursuing it; nothing else is contained in the essence of agency. But I am inclined to interpret personhood differently. Rights, I should accept too, are protections of agency. But agency can be attacked from different sides. I can be stopped from choosing and pursuing my conception of a good life either by other persons' blocking me or by my suffering such deprivation that I cannot even rise to the level of agency. So I am inclined to describe the protection of agency as requiring, and human rights therefore as including, not only autonomy and liberty but also *minimum material provision*—that is, some sort of right to welfare.

2. A HUMAN RIGHT TO WELFARE: CONCEPTUAL DOUBTS

Why do so many people deny this? A human right is a claim of *all* humans, simply as humans, against *all* other humans. It is, in this way, doubly universal. At least, that is the way *liberty* rights work: all of us have a right not to be dominated or blocked, and the correlative duty falls on every other individual, on groups, on governments—in short, upon all agents. If there were a human right to welfare, it would therefore seem that all of us would have a claim to minimum provision that fell upon every other individual and group and government. But we do not think that. We think that only members of a particular group—say, citizens of a country—can claim welfare, and can claim it from only their *own* government. This suggests that welfare rights are, at most, ethical rights one has as a *citizen*. Carl Wellman, who has written as informatively about welfare rights as anyone else in our time, puts the point like this:

> The most obvious, and perhaps the most important, lesson to learn is that one should not conceive of our fundamental ethical rights to welfare benefits as human rights. These are not moral rights the individual has simply *as* a human being for they cannot be grounded in human nature or the general aspects of human existence *per se*. Our most fundamental welfare rights are at best civic rights, moral rights of the individual as a citizen holding against his or her state. Only in this way can the problems of scarce resources and pointless duplication be solved in theory and the responsibility for meeting human need fixed in practice.[3]

He explains these two problems in this way:

> The problem of scarce resources arises if one insists that the individual's right to have his or her life sustained is a universal human right. This virtually guarantees that the many demands imposed upon each agent will exceed the available resources or those that can be morally demanded of that party. Such excessive demands cannot be admitted as genuine ethical claims holding against that second part . . . The problem of pointless duplication arises if one assumes that any individual's right to have his or her life sustained holds against the world. If every person, private organization, and state government acted simultaneously to sustain the life of any individual claimant, their actions would largely duplicate one another . . . To avoid this pointless duplication, one must fix the responsibility for sustaining the life of any individual much more narrowly than upon everyone . . . Once more our conclusion must be that a significant ethical claim-right to have one's life sustained will be some sort of special right, not a general human right.[4]

It is better, the conclusion to this line of thought goes, to see whether there is a persuasive ethical case for admitting *special* moral welfare rights, or a persuasive political case for enacting some *legal* welfare rights.

In fact, some of the opponents of welfare rights understandably regard them as an entirely optional redistributive political programme trying to pass itself off as a non-optional matter of human rights—a twentieth century egalitarian wolf trying to pass itself off in seventeenth century libertarian sheep's clothing. If *everyone* had a right to basic education, health-care, and decent housing, then in virtually every present-day country there would have to be transfers from rich to poor. If the "minimum" provision fixed upon were fairly generous, the transfers would have to be substantial.

Besides the conceptual trouble with the notion of "a *human* right to welfare," there is also trouble with the idea of a "minimum provision." Does ethics provide any satisfactorily determinate notion of the "minimum?" Or is this instead a matter for political decision about what a particular government may wish, and can afford, to grant to its citizens? If the latter, then the content of the right to welfare is determined, not by universal human status, but by particular social conditions. Some have defined the minimum level as "subsistence"—enough to keep alive. (In Britain, the *Beveridge Report*, which greatly influenced the creation of the welfare state there, defined social security in terms of subsistence.) That would give the minimum a basis in universal human nature, in biological facts about what it takes to keep body and soul together. But the trouble with this definition is that no one (including the authors of the *Beveridge Report*) takes it literally. If it is taken literally, it is too ungenerous. It is certainly not generous enough to capture the notion of personhood; someone who spends all waking hours desperately scratching out an existence, without time for reflection, conversation, or learning, subsists, but does not rise to the status of personhood. If, however, the provision is more generous than mere subsistence, the problem of acute indeterminacy arises. What is that more generous level? For instance, how much education would the minimum provision require? Literacy? Enough to ponder the meaning of life? And what level of health? When life-expectancy is thirty years, or fifty, or seventy? Each society can, if it wishes, make these levels determinate, for instance by considering what is in its own general interests and within its capacities, but this would seem to yield a legal or a special ethical right, not a human one.

These conceptual doubts, it seems to me, can all be laid. A right to welfare cannot be a human right, it is said, because it is not grounded in human nature. But it is; it is grounded, in a way that I quickly sketched earlier, in personhood, in one's status as a human. What is true is that, whereas autonomy and liberty are *constituents* of personhood, minimum provision is only a necessary *condition* of it. But a necessary condition of personhood is still grounded in personhood. A right to life is regarded as one of the classic human rights, but it too is only a necessary condition of personhood.

A right to welfare cannot be a human right, another argument goes, because regarding it as such would allow all of us to have a certain claim against all the rest of us and, as Wellman put it in the passage I quoted, that would produce problems both of scarce resources and of pointless duplication. But these problems, too, seem to me soluble. In ethics, we accept a general obligation to help those in distress, at least if the benefit we can confer is great and the cost to us is small. That is almost universally agreed upon. For example, if I see a child fall into a pool, and I can save it just by wading in, and no one else is about, I must do it. But this is a claim that all of us make upon all the rest of us. Why, then, should it fall upon me in particular? Well, obviously because I happen to be the only one on the scene. Accidental facts such as being in a position to help can impose moral responsibilities—and nothing more special to the situation brings the responsibility than that. I need not be the child's father, or uncle, or fellow citizen. Of course, in many cases of need, it is one's own family, or local community, or central government that has the ability to help. At different periods in history, different agencies have had that ability. And, of course, the families of the needy have additional reasons to help them. Central governments may too, but mere ability, apart from any of the reasons arising from special relations, itself remains at least *one* reason-generating consideration. And ability provides a ground in the world as it is to distribute the burden to help along membership lines: a family to its members, a central government to its citizens. Ability also explains why, over time, the burden has shifted away from small groups to central governments. In the late Middle Ages and early modern period the church had the resources and the highly developed organization, the central government playing a much smaller role in society than it does now, and it fell upon the parish to provide alms houses and the like. Or, in the same period, it often fell upon the town government or the local squire to support the indigent.[5] Once we can find a rationale for assigning the responsibility, the problems of scarce resources and of senseless duplication no longer arise—that is, they are no greater than in fact we have them today.

I said a moment ago that mere ability is *one* reason-generating consideration in cases of aid. But moral life is complicated: many other considerations also shape moral norms—for instance, that a good life is a life of deep commitments to particular persons, causes, careers, and institutions; that deep commitments limit our wills in major ways; and that our powers of large-scale calculations about what maximizes good outcomes are also limited. Unless one stresses these other reason-generating considerations, my proposal that ability can fix who should give aid might look odd. A Rockefeller or a Getty has a great ability to help the needy. That ability, no doubt, means that they have above-average obligations to help. But the obligation upon them—and upon us, for that matter—does not go on until their—and our—marginal loss equals the marginal gain of the needy. The ethical story is far more complicated than that. The Rockefellers and the Gettys—and we—are allowed substantially to honour our own commitments and follow our own interests, and these permissions limit our obligations. All that I wish to claim is that mere ability is *one* consideration in fixing where to place the obligation to help.

What about the objection that the notion of the "minimum" is too indeterminate to constitute a feasible claim on others? The objection seems to rest upon a misconception of what human rights are. It assumes that human rights are constructed out of materials that are, in some way, purely moral, that human rights have fairly clear and simple lines drawn independently of the messy political decisions and arguments of a particular society. But not only are human rights not like that; moral norms in general are seldom like that. To make most moral norms determinate enough to serve as norms a particular society must make decisions much like those that legislators make—sometimes, indeed, they can actually be the decision of legislators that supply the needed determinateness. And human rights will not, in general, become determinate enough to serve as practically effective claims on others unless, to considerations of personhood, we add many considerations of a quite pragmatic social nature. This is true of human rights in general, and so true of liberty rights. There is nothing like the sharp difference between universally accepted liberty rights and the much challenged welfare right that these objections trade on. The supposed flaws in a welfare right are there too in liberty rights.

We, in this country, could get together and decide that what we would regard as "minimum" provision of food would be what kept known ailments away, that minimum education would be up to the age of sixteen, and so on. Of course, these decisions would, as implementations of the notion of personhood, be extremely rough and ready; to some extent they would be relative to the resources of our particular society. But messy practical considerations of the same sort enter into the definition of the domain of very many moral norms—say, of such norms as, Don't deliberately kill the innocent, and, Limit the loss of life. For instance, any norm governing euthanasia would have to take account of what we, with our particular moral traditions and level of education and so on, could manage without seriously undesirable consequences. For the same reasons, any norm governing charity would have to work with a picture of normal human capacities that is inevitably crude. Virtually all moral norms are rough, arbitrary, and to some degree relative to the society in which they arise (though this is hardly cultural relativism in its usual sense). Liberty rights to free speech, say, or to privacy exhibit the same features. Where do we place the line defining the sphere protected by a right to privacy? We should first have to consult the requirements of personhood. Any intrusion into one's life that prevented one from autonomously choosing a course through life and then pursuing it would be banned. There are such, but in the case of privacy they would have to be particularly gross actually to stop us from choosing and pursuing a course through life—a level of intrusion that has not often been achieved in human history. Would the right to privacy ban phone-taps, access to medical records, and having to produce identity cards on demand? Where, for the purposes of the right, privacy begins is no less rough, arbitrary, and influenced by one's estimate of the nature of one's society than where the minimum begins.

As we have seen, critics say welfare rights are at best *civic* rights, not *human* rights. But their theoretical reasons for saying so do not seem to stand up. Nor, I think, do governments in practice treat welfare rights *merely* as civic rights. For instance, the State of California has, in recent years, tried to deny various welfare services to illegal immigrants—that is, to people who are, in this particularly egregious way, non-citizens. In August 1996 the Governor, Peter Wilson, signed an executive order ending their access to a wide range of welfare benefits, including pre-natal care, long-term health care, and public housing.[6] But his order stopped short of denying them emergency health care. The Governor acted under a provision of a recently enacted federal law that makes illegal immigrants ineligible for all state and federal benefits, though with similar exceptions; the federal law also excludes services such as emergency medical care and disaster relief. And there is an obvious justification for those exceptions: there are some forms of aid that anyone able to give them owes to anyone in need of them—whether or not the two agents are related as government and citizen.

3. FEASIBILITY DOUBTS

I have already touched on doubts about the feasibility of a human right to welfare. Can we respect such a right? A human right to welfare is, on the face of it, a claim that everyone makes on everyone else. No individual and no government has the resources to meet so great a claim. But suppose that I am right in what I just said and that there are adequate reasons for assigning the claims to different agents: say, the claims of Britons to the British Government, of Argentines to the Argentine Government, and so on. But it is less and less likely that even rich nations can keep up with perfectly reasonably conceived welfare claims. Medical advances mean that one can do much more in the way of basic treatment, such as life-saving treatment, but at vast expense. Would a right to welfare, or to life, require a rich country to mount a crash pro-gramme, on the model of the Manhattan project, to find a cure for, say, AIDS? Governments are driven now to look for ways to limit benefits—for instance, to pay them for only a certain length of time.[7] And poorer countries may never, even in the future, be able to meet these claims. So the principle that "ought" implies "can" comes into play: one cannot make a duty of what is impossible. One would have a claim on welfare, only if others had a duty to supply it. And in many, perhaps most, cases those others cannot supply it. So there is no duty on them to supply it. And as there is no duty on them to supply it, there is no correlative right to claim it in the first place.[8]

Here the obvious answer seems to me the right one. Countries should meet wel-fare obligations to the extent that they can; more than that they are not obliged to do. Some opponents of welfare rights find this obvious answer unsatisfactory: these gov-ernments cannot meet the obligation (fully), the opponents say, so they cannot have the obligation. But it is hardly plausible to work on the principle that nothing can be a human right unless its claims can be met immediately and in full. Why should one ever accept such a restriction? Also, it is not, as many critics of welfare rights propose, that welfare benefits must be merely an ideal for some indeterminate future, merely a hope, and therefore not a right.[9] These critics say this because rights must, they think, make determinate claims, satisfiable now, upon governments and not merely gesture fondly towards an attractive future. But even for poorer governments the claims *are* determinate: namely, do what, with present resources, you can to raise your citizens to the minimum. Determinacy that comes only having consulted prevailing circum-stances is not indeterminacy.

The critics of welfare rights invoke the principle that "ought" implies "can." But once some sort of division of responsibility for the needy is, as it can be, worked out, it is much harder to say that richer governments cannot, on any plausible interpreta-tion of "cannot," help the needy. Whether they can, of course, depends partly upon how much help is demanded by the right, and I shall come to that in a moment.

Still, the principle that "ought" implies "can" is relevant here, so we must be clear about its interpretation. I have written about its interpretation elsewhere, and shall just summarize my view.[10] One cannot, in the sense relevant to obligation, meet a demand if the demand is beyond the capacity of the sort of people that on other espe-cially important grounds one would want there to be. A demand does not have to be entirely beyond the human frame; that is, it does not have to be the sort of demand that no human at all, no matter how it developed or was trained, could meet. The sort of people we want there to be, the sort of people able to meet the demands that are likely to be made upon them in the course of their lives, will be deeply committed to certain other persons by ties of love and affection. They must also be committed to certain goals and institutions and not others; otherwise, society will work badly. But such committed persons will be incapable of complete impartiality, incapable of treating everybody, their own children as well as a distant stranger, for one and nobody for more than one. Again, it is not that no humans are capable of this extreme impartiality; some very unusual people have in fact been. But we should not want to be like those people ourselves—the costs to a good life, both prudentially and morally, are far too great—nor should we dream of raising our own children to be like that either. And the people we should want there to be, people of deep commitments, cannot enter into and exit from these commitments as the utterly impartial promotion of good might demand. That, roughly put, is the strength of the "cannot" that implies "so it is not the case that one ought."

There are limits, therefore, to what one can demand of the sort of persons one would want there to be. Such persons will sacrifice themselves and their families only up to a point. Those limits would be difficult to place exactly, and anyone who tries to place them will have to put up with much roughness and arbitrariness. But these are, or at any rate should be, familiar problems in ethical life. This implies that there are limits to what any redistributive welfare programme can require. Its demands must stay within the capacities of the sort of people the society should want there to be. And that observation provides some resolution to an indeterminacy that I have just noted. I suggested a moment ago that in some cases the demand made by a right to welfare would be: Do what, with present resources, you can to raise your citizens to the minimum. That formula settles some indeterminacies while creating others: Do at what cost to oneself? The answer to that question is inevitably rough, but it is along these lines: At a cost within the capacities of the sort of persons we should want there to be. There are other restrictions as well, but this is a major one. It still leaves open the possibility of hefty claims on governments and, through taxation, on citizens to help the needy.

4. ETHICAL DOUBTS

Would not a human right to welfare, and perhaps even a special ethical right to welfare, be unacceptably damaging to other parts of our lives—to other rights and other values? Welfare rights would require substantial transfers of goods; they would allow each of us to keep back at least a minimum provision for ourselves, but they would lay claims to some of our surplus. But there is the familiar point that, by and large, goods do not appear on the scene like manna from heaven. For the most part, there is no wealth to transfer, unless it has first been created. It therefore comes into the world already owned. And it comes into the world, to some extent, *because* it can be owned. To put it in a rough, intuitive way, there is something odd, even at times morally wrong, in ignoring ownership.

That is a perfectly general point, to which Robert Nozick has given a well-known particular twist.[11] I have two kidneys and can survive on one: in that sense one of my kidneys is surplus to my minimum requirement. Yet most of us would regard it as a gross violation of my human rights if the government were to demand one of my kidneys for transplant. I may offer it, but it cannot be demanded. Much the same is true, Nozick thinks, of my property. Part of me is in it: my thought, my effort are all bound up with it. I may choose to give some of it to the needy, but if the government confiscates it, even for the same purpose, it violates my human right to liberty. To force redistribution of one's income, even for a worthy cause, is, in effect, to force me to work for a certain time for the state. It is forced labour; the government arrogates to itself partial ownership in my person. It thereby violates my human right to liberty, in the way that slavery does. It is, therefore, ruled out on moral grounds. But then the supposed human right to welfare is ruled out on the same moral grounds. Nozick's conclusion is farfetched, but there may be some less farfetched way of developing the general point. I shall come back to that possibility shortly.

Welfare rights bring about an expansion in the role of the state—an unhealthy expansion, critics maintain. Liberty rights seem very different; they impose only negative duties upon governments, which are met easily just by minding one's own business. They require no more than a minimal state apparatus that all countries would want to, and to be able to, supply: namely, police and courts. Welfare rights, in contrast, fall largely upon central governments, because they are the most effective and appropriate agents these days to discharge the duties. So welfare rights require a gigantic state apparatus. In the past, the needy were looked after (to the extent that they were) by civil society, by associations such as families, churches, local communities, and so on. But as more and more welfare work is pushed onto the central government, these smaller institutions intermediate to the individual and the centre wither—institutions that are more sensitive, more flexible, more efficient, and more economical than the central government that has supplanted them. These over-burdened economies stagnate, and the personalities of individual citizens decay. Welfare rights are destructive of the self-reliance on which all communities rest. There once was the notion, which we today associate with the harsher side of the nineteenth century, of the "deserving" poor, which has not been allowed to play a prominent role in the conceptual apparatus of the twentieth century welfare state. Some philosophers have written a restriction to the "deserving" poor into the right to welfare: the right is, says one,[12] "an ethical claim of the individual human being against his or her society to be provided with a minimal livelihood in the event that he or she lacks the means of sustaining life *because of circumstances beyond his or her control.*" But how can we derive that deservingness clause—"because of circumstances beyond his or her control"—from the concept of a *human* right to welfare? Human rights are claims that one has simply in virtue of being human, not in virtue of being a *deserving* human. That, indeed, is precisely the trouble that many find with a human right to welfare. Human rights are protections of personhood, and even undeserving persons are persons. Once welfare becomes a matter of human rights, as opposed, say, merely to special ethical rights, other ethical considerations, such as desert, seem to get squeezed out. We seem not to be *permitted* to introduce desert.

These ethical doubts seem to me much more substantial than the earlier ones. The recognition of welfare rights has, in our time, had very good and very bad consequences. We have gone from societies of a century ago with the evils of fear, insecurity, ignorance, malnutrition, and low life-expectancy to our present societies in the richer countries with the evils, on the personal level, of lack of self-reliance, self-respect, ambition and hope,[13] and, on the social level, of inefficient and costly central government and the undermining of valuable intermediate social institutions. There is no doubt that, with the best of intentions, we have cured one set of ills and produced another. But that is hardly new; this is the nature of social change. The sensible response to it is not to prevent change but to admit to the new ills as they appear and to try to cure them. The cures will in turn produce their own new ills, and so on forever. But one would have to be blackly pessimistic about human skills to think that all social cures are in the end worse than the ailments.

Nozick's particular version of the ethical objection seems to me to be getting at something important, although to exaggerate it greatly. His version has been replied to often and, to my mind, successfully.[14] I should myself wish to enter an objection to it at a very early stage. Nozick misunderstands what the political value of liberty is. Not every interference with what one wants to do is a violation of liberty. One violates someone's liberty only by stopping that person from pursuing what that person sees as a valuable life. For a government to tax someone's income, especially someone comfortably above the minimum level, would not stop that person from pursuing, or even living, a valuable life. My income's being taxed for redistributive purposes does not destroy my liberty, properly conceived, any more than my recognizing a moral obligation to give to charity does. Both are demanded of me—though in different ways—yet neither destroys my liberty. Neither is a form of, or tantamount to, slavery. If a slave manages to live a good life, on the slave's own conception of a good life, it is merely by lucky chance. But to have, say, one third of an ample income taken in tax does not stop one from pursuing, and having reasonable hopes of achieving, a worthwhile life.

Still, there is a strand in Nozak's thought that seems to me right. The goods that might be redistributed have, in general, to be created. Creating them confers a claim to them upon the creator. But at this point, instead of improperly citing liberty, I think that we can properly cite the pragmatic considerations I mentioned earlier. We are people of deep commitments, and it is a very good thing that we are. Our motivation is at its strongest when we ourselves, or the persons or causes about which we care, can be benefited. There are limits to how much self-sacrifice or sacrifice of what we most care about can be demanded in the name of ethics. The ultimate limit is the limit of the will of the sort of persons we should want there to be; if that limit is crossed, then the principle that "ought" implies "can" applies, and there is no moral obligation.

5. A Case for a Human Right to Welfare

The intuitive case for a *human* right to welfare goes something like this. Human rights are protections of human standing. We attach a high value to our living as agents—our autonomously choosing and freely pursuing our conception of a good life. Then it is not surprising that we should include among human rights, as indeed the tradition did from the start, not only a right to liberty but also a right to life. Can we value living in a characteristically human way without valuing the *living* as well as the *autonomy* and *liberty* that make it characteristically human? If human rights are protections of that form of life, they should protect life as well as that form. But if they protect life, must they not also ensure the wherewithal to keep body and soul together—that is, some minimum material provision?

That is the heart of the case. It appeals to our picture of human standing and argues that both life and minimum material provision, the former of which may be and the latter of which certainly is a welfare right, are integral to it. We shall not live autonomously and at liberty unless we *live*. Life is a necessary condition of being autonomous and free.

Of course, we should not want to include every necessary condition for autonomy and liberty in the class of human rights. It is also a necessary condition of my being autonomous and free that I was conceived, but one certainly would not want to grant me a human right to be conceived. We can stop the chain of necessary conditions from getting out of control by restricting human rights simply to a human agent as a going concern. That, no doubt, was what the early advocates of natural rights had in mind. They were trying to get some ethical purchase on relatively uncomplicated, normal human beings; it is hard enough to do that without at the same time covering all problem cases. But then why, as the tradition emphatically does, include *life* as a human right? If we are to assume, for the purposes of an account of human rights, that persons are going concerns, we have already assumed life. In a division between liberty rights and welfare rights, it is not easy to see on which side of the line life would come. Part, but only part, of the difficulty is the notorious indeterminacy of the right to life. Does it, as opponents of welfare rights are likely to say, include only a right not to be murdered? There is no doubt about the great importance of the norm, "Don't deliberately kill the innocent," but importance is not enough to make it a human right; all human rights are ethically important but not everything ethically important is a human right. I think that it would be a mistake to make the right to life a human right, yet restrict it just to the prohibition of murder. My reason is simply this: the rationale for human rights is not, on what seems to me the best account, a deontological prohibition. Its nature is quite different. It is centered on the high value that we attach to certain features that we sum up under the heading "personhood." One attacks the value of life if one wantonly discards it. And it would seem to be possible to discard it wantonly by more than just murder, for instance, by not bothering to throw a life-belt by one's side to someone drowning, or, in general, failure to save life when one can at little cost to oneself. If that is correct, if a human right to life must be at least that broad, then there is a human right to welfare. Certain forms of welfare are already included in the content of the right to life, on this somewhat ampler conception of it. If human rights are protective barriers around certain valuable things, then it is hard to see why we should accept some protections of them and reject others. This inclusive policy does not threaten to include too much—for example, a human right to be conceived. Conception, and other remote necessary conditions, introduce special moral questions that an account of human rights, quite properly, does not even try to answer.

The crux of the issue about a human right to welfare seems to me to be this: shall we have a more helpful way of talking about our social life if human rights are confined to liberty rights or if they also include a right to welfare? The first, narrower, conception is confined to a strict interpretation of the *constituents* of agency: autonomy and liberty. The second, broader, conception includes as well some of the *conditions* of agency: life, minimum material provision, and so on. Many writers have claimed (this is Isaiah Berlin's version of the remark) that "Liberty is one thing and the conditions for it are another."[15] Interpreted literally, this is too obvious to need saying; of course, there is a difference between a thing and a necessary condition for the thing. But I take it that the point is that, in the case of liberty, this distinction is often ignored. Too much, these writers suggest, is being smuggled into the notion of liberty in order to trade on liberty's undeniable rhetorical appeal. But I am not smuggling a right to welfare into the right to liberty. They are two distinct rights. My question is whether the right to welfare should be brought into the class of human rights. We could perfectly well stipulate the narrower sense for human rights. But I think that it is better to stipulate the broader. The narrower stipulation would give us too austere a consideration, too far removed from life as it has actually to be lived, so of too little use in regulation an actual society. It would have a certain theoretical purity, but little practical interest.

Let me explain this last point. What I have in mind when I speak of the "narrower" stipulation is one that restricts human rights to ones with correlative duties that are purely negative. It would say: "we must not dominate (deny autonomy to) or block (deny liberty to) other persons; but we do not have to aid them or facilitate things for them." But this distinction, already tenuous in theory, defines human rights so austerely as to make them irrelevant in the practice of actual human beings. Suppose the ruler of some country decides that he must not violate the autonomy of others; he must not take their decisions for them about how they will live. So he institutes votes on important issues.[16] He puts *one* ballot box in the entrance to the capitol building. "No matter," he says, "that most people are too poor to make the trip; no matter that, anyway, they are illiterate and cannot read the notice of the vote. To make them better off or literate is to aid or facilitate, and human rights do not require that. Their autonomy has been respected by the one ballot box in the capitol."

Now, on this austere account, one can fully respect a person's autonomy even if the person cannot actually achieve autonomy and, if things carry on like this, never will. There is a morally important distinction, though a conceptually troublesome one, between actively inflicting an evil, on the one hand, and omitting to confer a good, on the other.[17] Still, our interest in developing the language of human rights is not satisfied by tokens—for example, a single token ballot box that virtually no one can reach. Human rights are meant to back claims that actual people will make in the real world, so the right to autonomy cannot be satisfied by a ruler's offering only a token opportunity to vote. Our notion of autonomy requires a *real* opportunity. If we say that, then we shall have to go on to specify when an opportunity can be regarded as "real," but that is a demand that an account of human rights should be willing to accept. A real opportunity to express one's opinion requires widely distributed ballot boxes, explanation of the issues, and provisions for the illiterate. The human right to autonomy must be read as concerned not just with the possibility of autonomy but also with its realization.[18] So it requires certain facilitation: education, sufficient material resources to allow one's children enough time off to be educated, ballot boxes widely distributed, voting protected from intimidation and fraud, a press not only free but widely distributed, and so on. But then if the split between negative and positive duties is pushed as far as we were trying to do a moment ago, autonomy because unrealizable in the actual world and so unhelpful in political thought. Many of the negative duties correlated with human rights (for example, not denying autonomy) themselves involve positive duties (for example, ensuring conditions for the exercise of autonomy). This line of thought brings me back to my own substantive proposal about human rights: human rights are protections of our human standing—that is, of our actually possessing it. Does that not mean that human rights include a right to welfare?

READING ENDNOTES

1. Thomas Paine included minimum provision of education and welfare, and also a claim to a job, in *The Rights of Man* in 1792, and the French *Declaration* of 1793 (not the more famous one of 1789) included a right to education. But no welfare rights were included in the two most famous documents of the age, the American *Declaration of Independence* and the French *Declaration of the Rights of Man and of the Citizen*. Many governments did, in fact, make provisions for education and later for social security, but the provisions were made simply by legislation; they were merely political arrangements, not constitutional rights. Martin P. Golding says that "An explicitly recognized conception of welfare rights" existed in the nineteenth century, and in implicit form even in the Glossators' commentaries on Roman legal texts. See Martin P. Golding, "The Primacy of Welfare Rights," *Social Philosophy and Policy* 1 (1984), p. 124. I have drawn much of my account in this section from Carl Wellman, "The Development of Human Rights," *The Proliferation of Rights* (Boulder: Westview Press, 1999), Chapter 2.
2. "Third Generation" rights are the rights of the late twentieth century, rights not of individuals but of collectivities—say, of national or ethnic or linguistic groups. They are rights to national self-determination, the survival of one's culture, and so on. But my interest now is solely second generation rights.

   There is nothing surprising in the fact that welfare rights are second generation rights, that liberty rights antedated them. That in itself does not show that welfare rights are less central or authoritative. The natural rights doctrine was developed, especially in the seventeenth and eighteenth centuries, by middle class European and American men. Their chief concern was resistance to absolute monarchs, freedom to pursue their (largely commercial or agricultural) interests. They were in general economically secure; their relative wealth constituted an important part of the framework for their political thought—they simply took it for granted. The desperately needy had, at this time, scarcely found their voice; their poverty rendered them largely silent. The historical lateness in the appearance of welfare rights shows nothing about their importance, certainly not that they are dubious "accretions" to the "core" liberty rights. In our time, China is the main defender of welfare rights, against what they see as the one-sided advocacy of liberty rights by the

United States. They argue that welfare rights have to be satisfied before liberty rights are of much value, but it would be a confusion to think, as the Chinese government seems also to think, that welfare rights must be satisfied first in time; the work of various economists [e.g., Partha Dasgupta, *An Enquiry into Well-Being and Destitution* (Oxford: Clarendon Press, 1993), Chapter 5] has shown that the countries that most successfully avoid welfare disasters are the ones that have most political liberties. Welfare rights are indeed prior to liberty rights in the sense that they are the necessary condition for liberty rights' being of value to us; but that does not show that they are prior in the sense that they must be realized first.

3. Carl Wellman, *Welfare Rights* (Totowa, New Jersey: Rowman and Allanheld, 1982), p. 181. See also Maurice Cranston, "Human Rights: Real and Supposed," in D.D. Raphael (ed), *Political Theory and the Rights of Man* (London: Macmillan, 1967), pp. 50–51, for a similar argument.
4. Wellman, *Welfare Rights*, p. 163.
5. Ability also explains why we think that there may sometimes be international obligations to help. In 1996 the British Defence Secretary, Michael Portillo, told the House of Commons that Britain had a moral obligation to intervene in Bosnia to save refugees from starving because Britain was "one of the few nations on earth who have the military capability to help" (*Daily Telegraph*, 15 November 1996).
6. *New York Times*, 27 August 1996, p. 1.
7. There was (in 1996) consideration in the United States of a "five years and you're out" provision. And in New York John Marchi, a state senator, proposed an amendment that would alter the Constitution to say that the state "may" provide for the needy rather than "shall" provide for them (*New York Times*, 12 August 1996).
8. There is a good discussion in Wellman, *Welfare Rights*, pp. 31–41; see esp. p. 36.
9. E.g., Cranston, "Human Rights: Real and Supposed," p. 52.
10. James Griffin, *Value Judgement* (Oxford: Clarendon Press, 1996), pp. 89–92.
11. Robert Nozick, *Anarchy, State, and Utopia* (New York: Basic Books, 1974), pp. 169–172.
12. Wellman, *Welfare Rights*, p. 150; my italics.
13. This is a common theme in current right-wing political writing. In Britain, a right-wing think-tank, The Institute for Economic Affairs, republished Samuel Smiles' famous 1859 book, *Self-Help*, which describes "help from without" as "enfeebling." "Where men are subject to over-guidance and to over-government," he wrote, "the inevitable tendency is to render them comparatively helpless" (see report in *The Independent*, 20 October 1996).
14. See e.g., Jeremy Waldron, *Liberal Rights* (Cambridge: Cambridge University Press, 1993), pp. 18ff.
15. Isaiah Berlin, "Introduction," *Four Essays on Liberty* (Oxford: Oxford University Press, 1969), p. liii. See also John Rawls' distinction between the *extent* of liberty and its *worth* [*A Theory of Justice* (Oxford: Clarendon Press, 1972), p. 204] and his later comments on the distinction [in "The Basic Liberties and their Priority," in S. McMurrin (ed.), *Liberty, Equality, and Law: Selected Tanner Lectures on Moral Philosophy* (Cambridge: Cambridge University Press, 1987)].
16. I borrow the case from Susan Moller Okin, "Liberty and Welfare: Some Issues in Human Rights Theory," in J.R. Pennock and J.W. Chapman (eds.), *Human Rights, Nomos* XXIII (New York: New York University Press, 1981).
17. For my own view of its importance, see *Value Judgment*, Chapter VII, Section 9.
18. My argument here is similar, but not identical, to one by Golding, "The Primacy of Welfare Rights," esp. pp. 135–6.

DEFINITIONS AND EXPLANATIONS

"Ought" implies "can": This is a commonly appealed to principle of moral reasoning. It suggests that any true claim about what people ought to do (have a duty to do especially) logically implies that they can do (that it is within their capacities to fulfil their duty or do what they ought to do). The general point is that no defensible moral system would impose upon people duties that it is impossible (logically, physically or psycho-logically) for them to fulfil. Thus, if we accept this principle, we can know decisively that we do not and cannot have a duty to square a circle, fly unaided to the moon, or act against our own self-interest all of the time. Given the way we are constituted none of these things are possible for us, and so we cannot be duty bound to do them. In con-nection with rights theory, if recognizing a given right seems to imply that others have duties that it is impossible for them to meet (if the duties corresponding to a right cannot be fulfilled), then that is a decisive argument against recognizing the right so conceived. We cannot have rights against others that they do the impossible.

QUESTIONS

1. Against whom could the welfare rights listed in the United Nations *Universal Declaration of Human Rights* be held? Who has the corresponding duties? Against whom are human rights thought to hold?

2. Why does Griffin think that the value of personhood (autonomous agency) grounds rights to welfare as well as rights to liberty?

3. What two reasons does Carl Wellman give for thinking that welfare rights can be at most political or civil rights but not human rights? How does Griffin argue that these objections to treating welfare rights as human rights can be met?

4. What is the moral relevance of ability to help in assigning responsibility (duties corresponding to the right) to help?

5. Why are the obligations of those who can help limited in the way Griffin says they are? Does he give any argument for this conclusion?

6. How does the idea of "the sort of persons we should want there to be in society" help determine the level of aid required of people?

7. Nozick's point is that redistribution by forced taxation from the rich to the poor violates the property rights of the rich and forces them to work for others as slave labour. The idea is this. If I need a certain level of income to achieve my goals then I must work a certain amount of time (depending on market forces that price my labour and the material components of my goals). Suppose I work those hours and then the state comes and takes one-third of my income to give to others. That interferes with my liberty because I cannot now realize my goals and I have been forced to work some number of hours for others. What is "far-fetched" about these claims?

8. Griffin denies that compulsory taxation violates the liberty of the rich because it does not interfere with their ability to live a valuable life. Is this what libertarians like Mill were concerned with? And can this judgement be made without imposing a conception of what a good or valuable life is upon those who may disagree (contrary to the neutrality requirement of liberalism)?

9. What is the worry about big government that the critics of state welfare are concerned about? Is it plausible?

10. Why does the notion of a human right preclude considerations of desert and merit (what people deserve)? When we are thinking about what welfare assistance people need, are considerations of desert and why they are in need (their own choices or bad luck) not relevant?

11. Nozick points out that the goods to be redistributed under welfare schemes do not exist independently of the efforts of the people who make them. To make something with materials you have justly acquired, for Nozick, is to acquire property rights to the thing you made. To then have the government come and take it away without your consent is theft, and both a violation of your liberty (if you had plans to use it in other ways) and your property rights. Griffin argues against Nozick's conclusion on the basis of the kinds of commitments we have. What is the argument here? Does it actually address Nozick's point?

12. Griffin argues from the right to life to the right to welfare. Has Thomson shown such a step to be very problematic, even false?

13. Does Griffin treat the right to life as absolute?

14. If all human rights are "centered on the high value that we attach to certain features that we sum up under the heading 'personhood' " and are recognized because they protect personhood, does it follow that the irreversibly comatose, senile, insane, etc. lack any human rights?

15. Why, when he is talking about duties to rescue (picking a child out of a pool, throwing a life-belt to a drowning person), does Griffin always add the proviso "when we can aid *at little cost to oneself.*" Does this not suggest that what we have a right to be is just what Thomson said: that others be Minimally Decent Samaritans? How much more is required, even of someone who is materially comfortable, to give up one-third of his income continuously (as Griffin imagines would be fully acceptable to demand)? If we think of income as tied to work (as it is for the vast majority of taxpayers), does this make the requirement seem even more excessive?

16. Griffin thinks a purely negative (narrow) conception of rights that includes only autonomy and liberty would be impractical in real societies. But consider this: how much misery, need, and poverty is the result of violations of the negative rights to life, liberty, and property of people (including corruption and war when they violate those rights)? Why, in his example, are the people so poor and so illiterate that they cannot benefit from a right to vote? Now suppose that no negative rights violations happened over say, three generations within a given population. How much need would be left? Could we not in fact meet whatever level of need would exist just by being Minimally Decent Samaritans, through local charity and family aid?

17. Griffin insists that liberty rights and property rights are distinct, and then he uses this supposed distinction to argue against Nozick's claim that forced taxation violates liberty. Of course, Nozick and other libertarians reject the distinction. Since Griffin does not actually argue that the libertarians are wrong or that the distinction is real, what fallacy has he committed in his criticism of Nozick?

18. Even if we accept the distinction between liberty and property rights, we might still wonder if forced taxation violates property rights. If it does, why is Griffin so cavalier about that violation? Aren't rights violations morally serious?

✦ ✦ ✦

James P. Sterba, Abortion, Distant Peoples, and Future Generations

James P. Sterba presents arguments that suggest that if a liberal is committed to welfare rights of distant people and future generations, then she cannot support the right to abortion on demand, whether or not one considers the fetus a person. He takes the liberal commitment to welfare rights of both future generations and distant peoples for granted throughout his discussion. He first considers the fetus as a person. Using Thomson as a foil, Sterba suggests that if one argues that abortion is simply indecent but not a violation of a right that the fetus has then consistency demands the same conclusion for the welfare rights of distant peoples; to not aid distant peoples in dire need might be indecent but it is not a rights violation. Similarly, if one argues that property rights preclude the claim a fetus has regarding the right to life, then consistency demands the same conclusion regarding the welfare rights of distant peoples.

He next considers the fetus as a non-person. He suggests that the rights of future generations to a minimal level of welfare imply that we, at the very least, need to adopt a population policy. These arguments, in effect, imply a right for some future people not to be born (those who wouldn't have even their basic needs met). Then he searches for a way to distinguish between some future people having a right not to be born, and other future people having a right to be born, and comes up lacking. Without such a distinction, one cannot endorse a right not to be born, and fail to endorse a right to be born. Thus abortion on demand cannot be consistently endorsed, as some future people will have a right to be born.

Sterba's second argument is long and convoluted. We leave as an exercise for the reader to uncover why Sterba did not argue more directly for his conclusion. It is fairly straightforward to argue that endorsing welfare rights for future generations entails that potential people are properly the bearers of human rights. Fetuses are potential people, and therefore have human rights. Human rights include the right to life. Therefore fetuses have a right to life. This plausible enough looking argument is, nevertheless, fatally flawed.

✦ ✦ ✦

James P. Sterba, "Abortion, Distant Peoples, and Future Generations," *The Journal of Philosophy* 77:7 (1980): 424–440. © 1980 Journal of Philosophy, Inc. Reprinted with permission from The Journal of Philosophy, Inc.

Abortion, Distant Peoples, and Future Generations

James P. Sterba

Those who favor a liberal view on abortion and thus tend to support abortion on demand are just as likely to support the rights of distant peoples to basic economic assistance and the rights of future generations to a fair share of the world's resources.[1] Yet, as I shall argue, many of the arguments offered in support of abortion on demand by those who favor a liberal view on abortion are actually inconsistent with a workable defense of these other social goals. If I am right, many of those who favor a liberal view on abortion (whom I shall henceforth refer to as "liberals") will have to make an unwelcome choice: either moderate their support for abortion or moderate their commitment to the rights of distant peoples and future generations. I shall argue that the most promising way for liberals to make this choice is to moderate their support for abortion.

THE WELFARE RIGHTS OF DISTANT PEOPLES

It used to be argued that the welfare rights of distant peoples would eventually be met, as a by-product of the continued economic growth of the technologically developed nations of the world. It was believed that the transfer of investment and technology to the less developed nations of the world would eventually, if not make everyone well off, at least satisfy everyone's basic needs. Now we are not so sure. Presently more and more evidence points to the conclusion that without some substantial sacrifice on the part of the technologically developed nations of the world, many of the less developed nations will never be able to provide their members with even the basic necessities for survival. For example, it has been projected that in order to reduce the income gap between the technologically developed nations and the underdeveloped nations to 5 to 1 and the income gap between the technologically developed nations and the developing nations to 3 to 1 would require a total investment of 7200 billion (in 1963 dollars) over the next fifty years.[2] [For comparison, the Gross National Product of the United States for 1973 was about 922 billion (in 1963 dollars).] Even those who argue that an almost utopian world situation will obtain in the distant future still would have to admit that, unless the technologically developed nations adopt some policy of redistribution, malnutrition and starvation will continue in the less developed nations for many years to come.[3] Thus a recognition of the welfare rights of distant peoples would appear to have significant consequences for developed and underdeveloped nations alike.

Of course, there are various senses in which distant peoples can be said to have welfare rights and various moral grounds on which those rights can be justified. First of all, the welfare rights of distant peoples can be understood to be either "action" rights or "recipient" rights. An *action right* is a right to act in some specified manner. For example, a constitutional right to liberty is usually understood to be an action right; it guarantees each citizen the right to act in any manner that does not unjustifiably interfere with any other citizen's constitutional rights. On the other hand, *a recipient right* is a right to receive some specific goods or services. Typical recipient rights are the right to have a loan repaid and the right to receive one's just earnings. Secondly, the welfare rights of distant peoples can be understood to be either *in personam* rights or *in rem* rights. In personam rights are rights that hold against some specific namable person or persons, whereas in rem rights hold against "the world at large," that is, against everyone who will ever be in a position to act upon the rights in question. The constitutional right to liberty is usually understood to be an in rem right; the right to have a loan repaid or the right to receive one's just earnings are typical in personam rights. Finally, the rights of distant peoples can be understood to be either legal rights, that is, rights that *are enforced* by legal sanctions, or moral rights, that is rights that *ought to be enforced* either simply by moral sanctions or by both moral and legal sanctions. Accordingly, what distinguishes the moral rights of distant peoples from the requirements of supererogation (the nonfulfillment of which is never blameworthy) is that the former but not the latter can be justifiably enforced either by moral sanctions or by moral and legal sanctions. Since we will be primarily concerned with the moral rights of distant peoples to a certain minimum of welfare, hereafter 'right(s)' should be understood as short for 'moral right(s).'

Of the various moral grounds for justifying the welfare rights of distant peoples, quite possibly the most evident are those which appeal either to a right to life or a right to fair treatment.[4] Indeed, whether one interprets a person's right to life as an action right (as political conservatives tend to do) or as a recipient right (as political liberals tend to do), it is possible to show that the right justifies welfare rights that would amply provide for a person's basic needs.[5] Alternatively, it is possible to justify those same welfare rights on the basis of a person's recipient right to fair treatment. In what follows, however, I do not propose to work out these moral justifications for the welfare rights of distant peoples.[6] Rather I wish to show that if one affirms welfare rights of distant peoples, as liberals tend to do, then there are certain arguments for abortion that one in consistency should reject. These arguments for abortion all begin with the assumption that the fetus is a person and then attempt to show that abortion can still be justified in many cases.

DISTANT PEOPLES AND ABORTION

One such argument is based on a distinction between what a person can demand as a right and what is required by moral decency. Abortion, it is said, may offend against the requirements of moral decency, but it rarely, if ever, violates anyone's rights. Judith Jarvis Thomson[7] illustrates this view as follows:

> . . . even supposing a case in which a woman pregnant due to rape ought to allow the unborn person to use her body for the hour he needs, we should not conclude that he has a right to do so; we should conclude that she is self-centered, callous, indecent, but not unjust if she refuses (61).

In Thomson's example, the sacrifice the pregnant woman would have to make to save the innocent fetus-person's life is certainly quite minimal.[8] Yet Thomson and other defenders of abortion contend that this minimal sacrifice is simply a requirement of moral decency and that neither justice nor the rights of the fetus-person requires the woman to contribute the use of her womb even for one hour! But if such a minimal life-sustaining sacrifice is required neither by justice nor by the rights of the fetus-person, then how could one maintain that distant peoples have a right to have their basic needs satisfied? Obviously to satisfy the basic needs of distant peoples would require a considerable sacrifice from many people in the technologically developed nations of the world. Taken individually, such sacrifices would be far greater than the sacrifice of Thomson's pregnant woman. Consequently, if the sacrifice of Thomson's pregnant woman is merely a requirement of moral decency, then the far greater sacrifices necessary to meet the basic needs of distant peoples, if required at all, could only be requirements of moral decency. Thus liberals who want to support the welfare rights of distant peoples would in consistency have to reject this first argument for abortion.

Another argument for abortion that is also inconsistent with the welfare rights of distant peoples grants that the fetus-person has a right to life and then attempts to show that his right to life often does not entitle him to the means of survival. Thomson again illustrates this view:

> If I am sick unto death, and the only thing that will save my life is the touch of Henry Fonda's cool hand on my fevered brow, then all the same, I have no right to be given the touch of Henry Fonda's cool hand on my fevered brow. It would be frightfully nice of him to fly in from the West Coast to provide it. It would be less nice, though no doubt well meant, if my friends flew out to the West Coast and carried Henry Fonda back with them. But I have no right at all against anybody that he should do this for me (55).

According to Thomson, what a person's right to life explicitly entitles him to is not the right to receive or acquire the means of survival, but only the right not to be killed or let die unjustly.

To understand what this right not to be killed or let die unjustly amounts to, consider the following example:

> Tom, Dick, and Gertrude are adrift on a lifeboat. Dick managed to bring aboard provisions that are just sufficient for his own survival. Gertrude managed to do the same. But Tom brought no provisions at all. So Gertrude, who is by far the strongest, is faced with a choice. She can either kill Dick to provide Tom with the provisions he needs or she can refrain from killing Dick, thus letting Tom die.

Now, as Thomson understands the right not to be killed or let die unjustly, Gertrude's killing Dick would be unjust, but her letting Tom die would not be unjust because Dick has a greater right to his life and provisions than either Tom or Gertrude.[9] Thus killing or letting die unjustly always involves depriving a person of something to which he has a greater right—typically either his functioning body or property the person has which he needs to maintain his life. Consequently, a person's right to life would entitle him to his functioning body and whatever property he has which he needs to maintain his life.

Yet Thomson's view allows that some persons may not have property rights to goods that are necessary to meet their own basic needs whereas others may have property rights to more than enough goods to meet their own basic needs. It follows that if persons with property rights to surplus goods choose not to share their surplus with anyone else, then, according to Thomson's account, they would still not be violating anyone's right to life. For although, by their decision not to share, they would be killing or letting die those who lack the means of survival, they would not be doing so unjustly, because they would not be depriving anyone of his property.

Unfortunately, Thomson never explains how some persons could justifiably acquire property rights to surplus goods that would restrict others from acquiring or receiving the goods necessary to satisfy their basic needs. And Thomson's argument for abortion crucially depends on the justification of just such restrictive property rights. For otherwise the fetus-person's right to life would presumably entail a right to receive the means of survival.

It is also unclear how such restrictive property rights would be compatible with each person's right to fair treatment. Apparently, one would have to reinterpret the right to fair treatment so that it had nothing to do with receiving the necessary means of survival. A difficult task indeed.

But most importantly, accepting this defense of abortion with its unsupported assumption of restrictive property rights would undermine the justification for the welfare rights of distant peoples. For the same sort of rights that would restrict the fetus-person from receiving what he needs for survival would also restrict distant people from receiving or acquiring what they need for survival. Thus liberals who support the welfare rights of distant peoples would have an additional reason to reject this argument for abortion.[10]

Of course, many liberals cannot but be unhappy with the rejection of the two arguments for abortion which we have considered. For although they would not want to give up their support for the welfare rights of distant peoples, they are still inclined to support abortion on demand.

Searching for an acceptable resolution of this conflict, liberals might claim that what is wrong with the preceding arguments for abortion is that they both make the generous assumption that the fetus is a person. Once that assumption is dropped, liberals might claim, arguments for abortion on demand can be constructed which are perfectly consistent with the welfare rights of distant peoples. Although this line of argument initially seems quite promising, on closer examination it turns out that even accepting arguments for abortion on demand that do not assume that the fetus is a person raises a problem of consistency for the liberal. This is most clearly brought out in connection with the liberal's support for the welfare rights of future generations.

The Welfare Rights of Future Generations

At first glance the welfare rights of future generations appear to be on a par with the welfare rights of distant peoples. For, assuming that there will be future generations, then, they, like generations presently existing, will have their basic needs that must be satisfied. And, just as we are now able to take action to provide for the basic needs of distant peoples, so likewise we are now able to take action to provide for the basic needs of future generations (e.g., through capital investment and the conservation of resources). Consequently, it would seem that there are just as good grounds for providing for the basic needs of future generations as there are for providing for the basic needs of distant peoples.

But there is a problem. How can we claim that future generations *now* have rights that provision be made for their basic needs when they don't presently exist? How is it possible for persons who don't yet exist to have rights against those who do? For example, suppose we continue to use up the earth's resources at present or even greater rates, and, as a result, it turns out that the most pessimistic forecasts for the twenty-second century are realized.[11] This means that future generations will face widespread famine, depleted resources, insufficient new technology to handle the crisis, and a drastic decline in the quality of life for nearly everyone. If this were to happen, could persons living in the twenty-second century legitimately claim that we in the twentieth century violated their rights by not restraining our consumption of the world's resources? Surely it would be odd to say that we violated their rights over a hundred years before they existed. But what exactly is the oddness?

Is it that future generations generally have no way of claiming their rights against existing generations? Although this does make the recognition and enforcement of rights much more difficult (future generations would need strong advocates in the existing generations), it does not make it impossible for there to be such rights. After all, it is quite obvious that the recognition and enforcement of the rights of distant peoples is a difficult task as well.

Or is it that we don't believe that rights can legitimately exercise their influence over long durations of time? But, if we can foresee and control the effects our actions will have on the ability of future generations to satisfy their basic needs, then why should we not be responsible for those same effects? And if we are responsible for them, then why should not future generations have a right that we take them into account?

Perhaps what really bothers us is that future generations don't exist when their rights are said to demand action. But how else could persons have a right to benefit from the effects our actions will have in the distant future if they did not exist just when those effects would be felt? Those who exist contemporaneously with us could not legitimately make the same demand upon us, for they will not be around to experience those effects. Only future generations could have a right that the effects our actions will have in the distant future contribute to satisfying their basic needs. Nor need we assume that, in order for persons to have rights, they must exist when their rights demand action. Thus, to say that future generations have rights against existing generations we can simply mean that there are enforceable requirements upon existing generations that would benefit or prevent harm to future generations. Using this interpretation of the rights of future generations, it is possible to justify welfare rights for future generations by appealing either to a right to life or a right to fair treatment, but here again, as in the case of the welfare rights of distant peoples, I shall simply assume that such justifications can be worked out.[12]

The welfare rights of future generations are also closely connected with the population policy of existing generations. For example, under a population policy that places restrictions on the size of families and requires genetic screening, some persons will not be brought into existence who otherwise would come into existence under a less restrictive population policy. Thus, the membership of future generations will surely be affected by whatever population policy existing generations adopt. Given that the size and genetic health of future generations will obviously affect their ability to provide for their basic needs, the welfare rights of future generations would require existing generations to adopt a population policy that takes these factors into account.

But what population policy should existing generations adopt? There are two policies that many philosophers have found attractive.[13] Each policy represents a version of utilitarianism, and each has its own difficulties. One policy requires population to increase or decrease so as to produce the largest total net utility possible. The other policy requires population to increase or decrease so as to produce the highest average net utility possible. The main difficulty with the policy of total utility is that it would justify any increase in population—even if, as a result, the lives of most people were not very happy—so long as some increase in total utility were produced. On the other hand, the main difficulty with the policy of average utility is that it would not allow persons to be brought into existence—even if they would be quite happy—unless the utility of their lives were equal or greater than the average. Clearly what is needed is a policy that avoids both these difficulties.

Peter Singer has recently proposed a population policy designed to do just that—a policy designed to restrict the increase of population more than the policy of total utility but less than the policy of average utility.[14] Singer's policy justifies increasing a population of M members to a population of $M + N$ members only if M of the $M + N$ members would have at least as much utility as the population of M members had initially.

At first it might seem that Singer's population policy provides the desired compromise. For his policy does not seem to justify every increase in population that increases total net utility but rather justifies only those increases which do not provide less utility to members equal in number to the original population. Nor does his policy require increases in population to meet or surpass the average utility of the original population. But the success of Singer's compromise is only apparent. As Derek Parfit has shown,[15] Singer's policy shares with the policy of total utility the same tendency to increase population in the face of continually declining average utility.

For consider a population with just two members: Abe and Edna. Imagine that Abe and Edna were deliberating whether to have a child and they calculated that, if they had a child, (1) the utility of the child's life would be somewhat lower than the average utility of their own lives, and (2) the child would have no net effect on the total utility of their own lives taken together. Applied to these circumstances, Singer's population policy would clearly justify bringing the child into existence. But suppose further that, after the birth of Clyde, their first child, Abe and Edna were deliberating whether to have a second child and they calculated that, if they had a second child, (1) the utility of the child's life would be somewhat lower than the utility of Clyde's life, and (2) the child would have no net effect on the total utility of their own lives and Clyde's taken together. Given these circumstances, Singer's policy would again justify bringing this second child into existence. And, if analogous circumstances obtained on each of the next ten occasions that Abe and Edna consider the question of whether to bring additional children into existence, Singer's population policy would continue to justify adding new children irrespective of the general decline in average utility resulting from each new addition to Abe and Edna's family. Thus Singer's policy has the same undesirable result as the policy of total utility. It avoids the severe restriction on population increase of the policy of average utility but fails to restrict existing generations from bringing into existence persons who would not be able to enjoy even a certain minimum level of well-being.

Fortunately, a policy with the desired restrictions can be grounded on the welfare rights of future generations. Given that the welfare rights of future generations require existing generations to make provision for the basic needs of future generations, existing generations would have to evaluate their ability to provide both for their own basic needs and for the basic needs of future generations. Since existing generations by bringing persons into existence would be determining the membership of future generations, they would have to evaluate whether they are able to provide for that membership. And if existing generations discover that, were population to increase beyond a certain point, they would lack sufficient resources to make the necessary provision for each person's basic needs, then it would be incumbent upon them to restrict the membership of future generations so as not to exceed their ability to provide for each person's basic needs. Thus, if the rights of future generations are respected, the membership of future generations would never increase beyond the ability of existing generations to make the necessary provision for the basic needs of future generations. Consequently, not only can the welfare rights of future generations be justified on the basis of each person's right to life and each person's right to fair treatment, they also can be used to justify a population policy that provides the desired compromise between the policies of average and total utility.

FUTURE GENERATIONS AND ABORTION

Now the population policy that the welfare rights of future generations justify suggest an argument for abortion that liberals would be inclined to accept. The argument assumes that the fetus is not a person and then attempts to show that aborting the fetus is either justified or required if the fetus will develop into a person who lacks a reasonable opportunity to lead a good life. Most versions of the argument even go so far as to maintain that the person who would otherwise be brought into existence in these unfavorable circumstances has in fact a right not to be born, i.e., a right to be aborted. Joel Feinberg puts the argument as follows:

> . . . if, before the child has been born, we know that the conditions for the fulfillment of his most basic interests have already been destroyed, and we permit him nevertheless to be born, we become a party to the violation of his rights.
>
> In such circumstances, therefore, a proxy for the fetus might plausibly claim on its behalf, *a right not to be born*. That right is based on his future rather than his present interests (he has no actual present interests); but of course it is not contingent on his birth because he has it before birth, from the very moment that satisfaction of his most basic future interests is rendered impossible ("Is There a Right to Be Born? 354).

The argument is obviously analogous to arguments for euthanasia. For, as in arguments for euthanasia, it is the nonfulfillment of a person's basic interests which is said to provide the legitimate basis for the person's right to have his life terminated.

However, in order for this argument to function as part of a defense for abortion on demand, it is necessary to show that no similar justification can be given for a right to be born. And it is here that the assumption that the fetus is not a person becomes important. For if the fetus were a person and if, moreover, this fetus-person had a reasonable opportunity to lead a good life, then, it could be argued, this fetus-person would have a right to be born. Thus, proceeding from the assumption that the fetus is not a person, various arguments have been offered to show that a similar justification cannot be given for a right to be born.[16]

One such argument bases the asymmetry on a failure of reference in the case of the fetus that would develop into a person with a reasonable opportunity for a good life. The argument can be summarized as follows:

> If I bring into existence a person who lacks a reasonable opportunity to lead a good life, there will be a person who can reproach me that I did not prevent his leading an unfortunate existence. But if I do not bring into existence a person who would have a reasonable opportunity to lead a good life, there will be no person who can reproach me for preventing his leading a fortunate existence. Hence, only the person who lacks a reasonable opportunity to lead a good life can claim a right not to be born.

But notice that, if I do not bring into existence a person who would lack a reasonable opportunity to lead a good life, there will be no person who can thank me for preventing his leading an unfortunate existence. And, if I do bring into existence a person who had a reasonable opportunity to lead a good life, there will be a person who can thank me for not preventing his leading a fortunate existence. Thus, whatever failure of reference there is, it occurs in both cases, and therefore, cannot be the basis for any asymmetry between them.[17]

A second argument designed to establish the asymmetry between the two cases begins with the assumption that a person's life cannot be compared with his nonexistence unless the person already exists. This means that, if one allows a fetus to develop into a person who has a reasonable opportunity to lead a good life, one does not make that person better off than if he never existed. And it also means that if one allows a fetus to develop into a person who lacks a reasonable opportunity to lead a good life one does not make that person worse off than if he never existed. But what then justifies a right not to be born in the latter case? According to the argument, it is simply the fact that unless the fetus is aborted a person will come into existence who lacks a reasonable opportunity to lead a good life. But if this fact justifies a right not to be born, why, in the former case, would not the fact that unless the fetus is aborted a person will come into existence who has a reasonable opportunity to lead a good life suffice to justify a right to be born? Clearly, no reason has been given to distinguish the cases.

Furthermore, consider the grounds for aborting a fetus that would develop into a person who lacks a reasonable opportunity to lead a good life. It is not simply that the person is sure to experience some unhappiness in his life because in every person's life there is some unhappiness. Rather it is because the amount of expected unhappiness in this person's life would render his life not worth living. This implies that the justification for aborting in this case is based on a comparison of the value of the person's life with the value of his nonexistence. For how else can we say that the fact that a fetus would develop into a person who lacks a reasonable opportunity to lead a good life justifies our preventing the person's very existence? Consequently, this argument depends upon a denial of the very assumption with which it began, namely that the person's life cannot be compared with his nonexistence unless that person already exists.

Nevertheless, it might still be argued that an analogous justification cannot be given for a right to be born on the grounds that there is a difference in strength between one's duty to prevent a fetus from developing into a person who lacks a reasonable opportunity to lead a good life and one's duty not to prevent a fetus from developing into a person who has a reasonable opportunity to lead a good life. For example, it might be argued that the former duty is a relatively strong duty to prevent harm, whereas the latter duty is a relatively weak duty to promote well-being, and that only the relatively strong duty justifies a correlative right—in this case, a right not to be born. But, even granting that our duty to prevent harm is stronger than our duty to promote well-being, in the case at issue we are dealing not just with a duty to promote well-being but with a duty to promote *basic* well-being. And, as liberals who are committed to the welfare rights of future generations would be the first to admit, our duty to prevent basic harm and our duty to promote basic well-being are not that distinct from a moral point of view. From which it follows that, if our duty to prevent basic harm justifies a right not to be born in the one case, then our duty to promote basic well-being would justify a right to be born in the other.

Nor will it do to reject the notion of a right to be born on the grounds that if the fetus is not a person then the bearer of such a right, especially when we violate that right by performing an abortion, would *seem* to be a potential or possible person. For the same would hold true of the right not to be born which is endorsed by liberals such as Feinberg and Narveson: the bearer of such a right, especially when we respect that right by performing an abortion, would also *seem* to be a potential or possible person. In fact, however, neither notion necessarily entails any metaphysical commitment to possible persons who "are" whether they exist or not. For to say that a person into whom a particular fetus would develop has a right not to be born is to say that there is an enforceable requirement upon certain persons the violation of which would fundamentally harm the person who would thereby come into existence. Similarly, to say that a person into whom a particular fetus would develop has a right to be born is to say that there is an enforceable requirement upon certain persons the respecting of which would fundamentally benefit the person who would thereby come into existence. So understood, neither the notion of a right to be born nor that of a right not to be born entails any metaphysical commitment to possible persons as bearers of rights.

Of course, recognizing a right to be born may require considerable personal sacrifice, and some people may want to reject any morality that requires such sacrifice. This option, however, is not open to liberals who are committed to the welfare rights of future generations. For such liberals are already committed to making whatever personal sacrifice is necessary to provide for the basic needs of future generations. Consequently, liberals committed to the welfare rights of future generations cannot consistently reject a prohibition of abortion in cases involving a right to be born simply on the grounds that it would require considerable personal sacrifice.

But there is an even more basic inconsistency in being committed both to the welfare rights of future generations and to abortion on demand. For, as we have seen, commitment to the welfare rights of future generations requires the acceptance of a population policy according to which existing generations must ensure that the membership of future generations does not exceed the ability of existing generations to provide for the basic needs of future generations. Thus for liberals who assume that the fetus is not a person, this population policy would have the same implications as the argument we considered which justifies abortion in certain cases on the basis of a person's right not to be born. For if existing generations violate this population policy by bringing into existence persons whose basic needs they cannot fulfill, they would also thereby be violating the right not to be born of those same persons, since such persons would not have a reasonable opportunity to lead a good life. But, as we have also seen, accepting this argument which justifies abortion in certain cases on the basis of a person's right not to be born commits one to accepting also a parallel argument for prohibiting abortion in certain other cases on the basis of a person's right to be born. Consequently, commitment to the population policy demanded by the welfare rights of future generation will likewise commit liberals to accepting this parallel argument for prohibiting abortion in certain cases. Therefore, even assuming that the fetus is not a person, liberals cannot consistently uphold the welfare rights of future generations while endorsing abortion on demand.

There remains the further question of whether liberals who are committed to the welfare rights of distant peoples and future generations can make a moral distinction between contraception and abortion—assuming, that is, that the fetus is not a person. In support of such a distinction, it might be argued that, in cases where abortion is at issue, we can roughly identify the particular person into whom a fetus would develop and ask whether that person would be fundamentally benefited or fundamentally harmed by being brought into existence, whereas we cannot do anything comparable in cases where contraception is at issue. Yet, though this difference does exist, it does not suffice for morally distinguishing abortion from contraception. For notice that if persons do not practice contraception when conditions are known to be suitable for bringing persons into existence who would have a reasonable opportunity to lead a good life, then there will normally come into existence persons who have thereby benefited. Similarly, if persons do not practice contraception when conditions are known to be unsuitable for bringing persons into existence who would have a reasonable opportunity to lead a good life (e.g., when persons who would be brought into existence would very likely have seriously debilitating and ultimately fatal genetic defects), then there will normally come into existence persons who have thereby been harmed. On grounds such as these, therefore, we could certainly defend a "right not to be conceived" and a "right to be conceived" which are analogous to our previously defended "right not to be born" and "right to be born." Hence, it would follow that liberals who are committed to the welfare rights of distant peoples and future generations can no more consistently support "contraception on demand" than they can consistently support abortion on demand.

Needless to say, considerably more sacrifice would normally be required of existing generations in order to fulfill a person's right to be born or right to be conceived than would be required to fulfill a person's right not to be born or right not to be conceived. For example, fulfilling a person's right to be born may ultimately require caring for the needs of a child for many years whereas fulfilling a person's right not to be born may require only an early abortion. Therefore, because of the greater sacrifice that would normally be required to fulfill a person's right to be born, that right might often be overridden in particular circumstances by the rights of existing persons to have their own basic needs satisfied. The existing persons whose welfare would have priority over a person's right to be born are not only those who would be directly involved in bringing the person into existence but also those distant persons whose welfare rights would otherwise be neglected if goods and resources were diverted to bringing additional persons into existence. This would, of course, place severe restrictions on any population increase in technologically developed nations so long as persons in technologically underdeveloped nations still fail to have their basic needs satisfied. But for persons committed to the welfare rights of distant peoples as well as to the welfare rights of future generations, no other policy would be acceptable.

Obviously these results cannot but be embarrassing for many liberals. For what has been shown is that, with or without the assumption that the fetus is a person, liberals who are committed to the welfare rights of distant peoples and future generations cannot consistently endorse abortion on demand. Thus, assuming that the welfare rights of distant peoples and future generations can be firmly grounded on a right to life and a right to fair treatment, the only morally acceptable way for liberals to avoid this inconsistency is to moderate their support for abortion on demand.

READING ENDNOTES

Earlier versions of this paper were presented at a Symposium on Potentiality and Human Values sponsored by the American Society for Value Inquiry in 1978, at the Pacific Division Meeting of the American Philosophical Association in 1979, and at the Conference on Life Sciences and Human Values held at Geneseo, New York, in 1979. In the course of working through various versions of this paper, I have benefited from the comments of many different people, in particular, Janet Kourany, David Solomon, Jan Narveson, Gregory Kavka, Mary Ann Warren, and Ernest Partridge.

1. It is not difficult to find philosophers who not only favor a liberal view on abortion and thus tend to support abortion on demand, but also favor these other social goals as well. See Jan Narveson, "Moral Problems of Population," *Monist* LVII, 1 (January 1973): 62–86, and "Aesthetics, Charity, Utility and Distributive Justice," *ibid.*, LVI, 4 (October 1972): 527–551; Joel Feinberg, "Is There a Right to Be Born?" in James Rachels, ed., *Understanding Moral Philosophy* (Encino, Calif.: Dickenson, 1976), pp. 346–357, and "The Rights of Animals and Future Generations," in William Blackstone, *Philosophy and Environmental Crisis* (Athens: Univ. of Georgia Press, 1972), pp. 41–68; Michael Tooley, "Abortion and Infanticide," *Philosophy & Public Affairs*, II, 1 (Fall 1972): 37–65, and "Michael Tooley Replies," *ibid.*, II, 4 (Summer 1973): 419–432; Mary Anne Warren, "Do Potential People Have Moral Rights?", *Canadian Journal of Philosophy*, VII, 2 (June 1977): 275–289.

2. Mihajlo Mesarovic and Eduard Pestel, *Mankind at the Turning Point* (New York: New American Library, 1975), ch. 5.

3. Herman Kahn, William Brown, and Leon Martel, *The Next 200 Years* (New York: William Morrow, 1976), ch. 2.

4. For other possibilities, see Onora Nell, "Lifeboat Earth," *Philosophy & Public Affairs*, IV, 3 (Spring 1975): 273–292; Peter Singer, "Famine, Affluence and Morality," *ibid.*, I, 3 (Spring 1972): 229–243.

5. A person's basic needs are those which must be satisfied if the person's health and sanity are not to be seriously endangered.
6. For an attempt to work out these justifications, see ch. VI of my book, *The Demands of Justice* (Notre Dame, Ind.: University Press, 1980).
7. "A Defense of Abortion," *Philosophy & Public Affairs*, I, 1 (Fall 1971): 47–66.
8. Hereafter the term "fetus-person" will be used to indicate the assumption that the fetus is a person. The term "fetus" is also understood to refer to any human organism from conception to birth.
9. See her "Killing, Letting Die, and the Trolley Problem," *Monist*, LIX, 2 (April 1976): 204–217.
10. Notice that my critique of Thomson's arguments for abortion on demand differs from critiques that attempt to find an *internal* defect in Thomson's arguments. [For example, see Richard Werner's "Abortion: The Moral Status of the Unborn," *Social Theory and Practice*, III, 2 (Fall 1974): 210–216.] My approach has been to show that Thomson's arguments are *externally* defective in that a liberal who is committed to the welfare rights of distant peoples cannot consistently accept those arguments. Thus, Jan Narveson's telling objections to Werner's internalist critique of Thomson's arguments [see his "Semantics, Future Generations and the Abortion Problem," *ibid.*, III, 4 (Fall 1975): 464–466] happily do not apply to my own critique.
11. Donella H. Meadows, Dennis L. Meadows, Jorgen Randers, and William W. Behrens III, *The Limits to Growth* (New York: New American Library, 2d ed., 1974), chs. 3 and 4.
12. For an attempt to work out these justifications, see *The Demands of Justice*, ch. VI.
13. See Henry Sidgwick, *The Methods of Ethics* (London: Macmillan, 7th ed., 1907; Chicago: University Press, 1962), pp. 414–416; Narveson, "Moral Problems of Population," pp. 62–86.
14. "A Utilitarian Population Principle," in Michael Bayles, ed., *Ethics and Population* (Cambridge, Mass.: Schenkman, 1976), pp. 81–99.
15. "On Doing the Best for Our Children," in Michael Bayles, ed., op. cit., pp. 100–115. For additional problems with Singer's population policy, see R. I. Sikora, "Is It Wrong to Prevent the Existence of Future Generations?" in Sikora and Brian Barry, eds., *Obligations to Future Generations* (Philadelphia: Temple, 1978), pp. 128–132.
16. See Narveson, "Utilitarianism and New Generations," *Mind*, LXXVI, 301 (January 1967): 62–72, and "Moral Problems of Population," *op. cit.*
17. For a similar argument, see Timothy Sprigge "Professor Narveson's Utilitarianism," *Inquiry*, XI, 3 (Autumn 1968: 332-346), p. 338.

QUESTIONS

1. Is the distinction between action and recipient rights the same as the distinction between negative and positive rights?

2. How would the rights of distant people to welfare be grounded in the more basic rights to life or fair treatment?

3. In what way is Thomson's treatment of the rights of fetuses inconsistent with recognizing the right of distant peoples to welfare?

4. Does Sterba beg an important question against Thomson when he claims that she has not explained how some people may justifiably "acquire property rights to surplus goods that would *restrict* others from acquiring or receiving the goods necessary to satisfy their basic needs"? Is there any reason to suppose that the property rights of some restrict others from acquiring property rights? If such restriction is possible, is it necessarily unjust? Could the right to one's own body be anything but a restrictive property right?

5. What form of argument does Sterba use? What must we conclude from his argument about abortion and the welfare rights of distant peoples?

6. What rights does Sterba think future generations have? What duties do these rights impose on the present generation, i.e., us?

7. What are the three population policies that Sterba considers (from Sidgwick, Narveson, and Singer)? What is wrong with each of them?

8. What population policy does Sterba favour and why? How realistic is it to think we can now determine the level of population in the future whose basic needs we could provide? How many generations into the future do we have to consider?

9. What does the right not to be born amount to? What is the analogy with euthanasia? Does the right not to be born impose a duty on others to kill the fetus, or does it merely make such killing permissible?

10. When the right not to be born is coupled with considerations of "genetic health," as it is in Sterba's view, does this raise concerns about eugenics and judgements about which lives are worth living that those with disabilities would find problematic, perhaps even unjust?

11. Sterba argues that the same grounds that lead us to recognize that a fetus who lacks a reasonable opportunity to lead a good life has a right not to be born must also lead us to recognize that a fetus who has a reasonable opportunity to lead a good life has a right to be born. What implications does this have for our population policy in practice? Will only the well-off be permitted to have children? Would many aboriginal children be permitted to be born under this scheme, given the current state of some aboriginal communities? Would it reintroduce the spectre of forced sterilization of anyone not meeting the criteria of providing her offspring the opportunity of a good life?

12. Would the healthy, wealthy, and wise fall under a duty to reproduce against their will because future generations that have a reasonable opportunity to live a good life have a right to be born?

13. What is the inconsistency that Sterba thinks exists between a liberal commitment to a population policy that recognizes welfare rights of future generations and the liberal policy on abortion?

14. Why does Sterba think his argument can be extended to say that some people have a right to be conceived while others have a right not to be conceived? If Sterba's understanding of liberalism does imply that even the use of contraceptives is wrong in some cases, is this not a *reductio ad absurdum* of liberalism?

15. Does Sterba's article suggest that there may be an irresolvable tension between rights to life and liberty, on the one hand, and the rights to welfare, on the other? If so, does this show that liberalism is incoherent at base?

✦ ✦ ✦

Ruth Macklin, Ethical Relativism in a Multicultural Society

Ruth Macklin highlights some of the difficulties in a medical practitioner's efforts to respect the autonomy of patients. She first clears up some understandable, but nevertheless flawed, conclusions regarding what a duty to respect the autonomy of patients entails. It does not, for instance, imply an absolute duty to tell the truth (to say nothing of the whole truth). If a clinically incorrect description of a condition would have the effect of relaying more precisely the nature of that condition to a patient, then a respect for autonomy requires including that incorrect description. Some have thought that respecting the autonomy of individuals from other cultures requires acting as a doctor would in these environments, but Macklin rejects this interpretation of what is required of doctors in multicultural societies. Instead, she argues, one should always act in accordance with the wishes of the individual. A person in North America who would prefer a paternalistic doctor has his autonomy better respected if the doctor acts paternalistically, not if the doctor acts as the general consensus among North American doctors suggests she should. And so a respect for autonomy can lead one to ask about the individual's wishes regarding who they wish to be involved in the decision making process, and to what degree.

More problematic is the physician's commitment to informed consent. We seem to face a tri-lemma. On the one hand, if we withhold information from a patient, we cannot get *informed* consent. If, on another, we give patients all the information, we might do so against their wishes. Finally, if doctors make the decision for patients, then no consent, informed or otherwise, will have occurred. Macklin chooses the second of these options. What we may do, she suggests, is give the information in a manner appropriate to the patient. A statistician may be able to appreciate quantitative results best left unstated when dealing with a person who would become overwhelmed by such a statistical presentation. Respecting autonomy sometimes requires a principled editing of the relevant facts.

What respect for patient autonomy cannot require is respecting the traditions of another when harm to some third party is the result. If there is some potential for harm to a third part (a child, for example) a respect for autonomy does not mean saying nothing about the harms likely resulting from those traditions. A physician is expected to educate about dangers to health and life, and must do so, even at the expense of being less than respectful of another person's culture. Respect for culture is a derivative value at best. The professional obligation of a doctor is at the core of this last conclusion, and needs further comment. A professional is, in part, defined as an individual who has esoteric knowledge with the potential to significantly benefit others, where the potential beneficiaries can themselves not fully comprehend (due to lack of ability or the requisite learning) that body of knowledge. A professional, then, has a particular relationship with her client. She must strive to realize a good for that client who has no way of judging the various options available, or the appropriateness of the chosen course of action. A respect for autonomy requires that a professional educates (insofar as possible) her client regarding the options available, and substitutes her judgement for the client's insofar as that education is not possible. While the client cannot fully understand the particular profession, the professional cannot be said to fully understand her client either. Such substitutions of judgement with only imperfect information must always be undertaken with care.

✦ ✦ ✦

Ruth Macklin, "Ethical Relativism in a Multicultural Society," *The Kennedy Institute of Ethics Journal* 8:1 (1998): 1–22. © 1998 The John Hopkins University Press. Reprinted with permission of the John Hopkins University Press.

Ethical Relativism in a Multicultural Society

R U T H   M A C K L I N

Cultural pluralism poses a challenge to physicians and patients alike in the multicultural United States, where immigrants from many nations and diverse religious groups visit the same hospitals and doctors. Multiculturalism is defined as "a social-intellectual movement that promotes the value of diversity as a core principle and insists that all cultural groups be treated with respect and as equals."[1] This sounds like a value that few enlightened people could fault, but it produces dilemmas and leads to results that are, at the least, problematic if not counterintuitive.

Critics of mainstream bioethics within the United States and abroad have complained about the narrow focus on autonomy and individual rights. Such critics argue that much—if not most—of the world embraces a value system that places the family, the community, or the society as a whole above that of the individual person. The prominent American sociologist Renée Fox is a prime example of such critics: "From the outset, the conceptual framework of bioethics has accorded paramount status to the value-complex of individualism, underscoring the principles of individual rights, autonomy, self-determination, and their legal expression in the jurisprudential notion of privacy."[2]

The emphasis on autonomy, at least in the early days of bioethics in the United States, was never intended to cut patients off from their families by focusing monistically on the patient. Instead, the intent was to counteract the predominant and long-standing paternalism on the part of the medical profession. In fact, there was little discussion of where the family entered in and no presumption that a family-centered approach to sick patients was somehow a violation of the patient's autonomy. Most patients want and need the support of their families, regardless of whether they seek to be autonomous agents regarding their own care. Respect for autonomy is perfectly consistent with recognition of the important role that families play when a loved one is ill. Autonomy has fallen into such disfavor among some bioethicists that the pendulum has begun to swing in the direction of families, with urgings to "take families seriously"[3] and even to consider the interests of family members equal to those of the competent patient.[4]

The predominant norm in the United States of disclosing a diagnosis of serious illness to the patient is not universally accepted even among long-standing citizens comprising ethnic or religious subcultures. Moreover, "respect for autonomy" as an ethical principle continues to be misunderstood and perhaps even deliberately misrepresented. The following episode is illustrative.

An orthodox rabbi was invited to deliver a lecture on Jewish medical ethics at a medical school. The rabbi outlined some of the leading precepts of Jewish medical ethics and sought to compare them with their counterparts in contemporary secular bioethics. Understandably, given his commitment to Orthodox Judaism, he undertook to defend the precepts of Jewish medical ethics in those instances where they conflict with the secular version. The rabbi told the story of a man with an abiding fear of cancer who visited the doctor because he was worried about a small growth on his upper lip. The pair had a long-standing physician-patient relationship, and the doctor was aware of the patient's deep fear of cancer. When the patient paid a return visit following a delay in which the biopsy was examined, he said to the doctor: "It isn't cancer, is it?" The physician, after a brief hesitation, reassured the patient that he did not have cancer.

The rabbi commended the physician's action, saying that secular bioethics would insist on patient autonomy and require that the doctor tell the truth, thereby instilling great anxiety in the patient. The rabbi went on to say that the Jewish medical ethics does not place autonomy above all other values, noting that respect for autonomy has little place in Jewish medical ethics. Instead, the physician, as the person with medical expertise, has the obligation to do whatever is best for the patient, based on that expertise, and the patient—a layperson—does not have "a right to know" everything the doctor may discover. The impression the rabbi sought to convey was that secular bioethics mandates truth telling to patients even when it means inflicting unwanted information. In contrast, the more benevolent Jewish medical ethics allows for withholding diagnostic information and can support telling "white lies" in order to avoid harming the patient.

I am not concerned here to debate the general merits of the contemporary practice of disclosing a diagnosis of cancer. Nor do I intend to argue that a value placed on truth telling should prevail universally, inside medical practice as well as in the world at large. But I did object, when I listened to the rabbi's lecture, to his omission of a few critical pieces of information. He had taken the story of the patient fearful of cancer from an article in a medical journal written by the physician who also was a protagonist in the story. In the published article, the physician explained his action and sought to justify it, not by defending the tradition of medical paternalism but with a different rationale.

The physician believed he had an obligation to be truthful to his patients. He normally does disclose a diagnosis of cancer. However, reflecting in this case on the patient's extreme and irrational fear, the physician reasoned as follows. Although the patient did, indeed, have a form of cancer, it was a tiny growth confined to a small region of the skin, of a type that does not spread and could not have metastasized. The growth could be completely removed and there would be no further consequences. What this patient thought of as cancer—what he feared so deeply—was not the condition he actually had. So, the doctor reasoned, he could be conveying as much of an untruth by telling this man he had cancer, given the patient's conception of that disease. Telling the patient he did not have cancer was the doctor's way of saying that the man did not have what he most feared—a fatal illness. And that was being truthful.

One might quibble with the semantics of this little story: Did the doctor lie, or not? Wasn't it literally a lie? Or was the "larger" truth the physician intended to convey the "real" truth? Is it correct to say that the doctor was being truthful, even though he did not literally "tell the truth"? However those philosophical questions may be answered, the lessons that flow from the tale are several. The first lesson highlights the difference between an absolutist ethics and a universal ethics. An absolutist ethics contains exceptionless rules: "Never lie. Never break promises. Always tell the truth." Few people anywhere (rigid Kantians excepted) defend this form of absolutism. Every ethical rule has some exceptions, which can be justified in the usual manner by appealing to higher principles that would be violated if one adhered to the rule.

A universalist ethics, on the other hand, holds that fundamental ethical principles exist and can be used to justify specific rules. This brings us to the second lesson of the story: the fundamental principle that underlay the physician's response to the patient was the "respect for persons" principle. The rabbi who recounted the story sought to demonstrate the superiority of Jewish medical ethics because the beneficence of the physician's white lie was ethically defensible. And so it was.

Where the rabbi erred, however, was in his contention that secular medical ethics, with its reigning principle of "respect for autonomy," would require inflicting on the patient the unwanted information that he had cancer. The principle of "respect for persons" is broader than the principle of "autonomy" although the latter concept is often the relevant interpretation of what follows from "respect for persons." In this episode, the concept of autonomy played a different role from what usually follows from "respect for persons." This was a matter of the physician revealing to the patient the nature of his ailment, and describing it to him in a way that the patient would properly understand. In recognizing and being sensitive to the patient's fear of cancer, the physician showed respect for the patient's beliefs and values. The physician reasoned that this patient would misunderstand a diagnosis of cancer. Neither respect for persons nor beneficence mandates providing information that a patient would not fully comprehend.

The third lesson from this story is a reminder that the much-maligned principles of bioethics are often misused or abused by people conducting an ethical analysis. I neither know nor care whether the rabbi was intentionally distorting the application of the principle of "respect for autonomy" in order to demonstrate the beneficent nature of Jewish medical ethics. But it was simply a mistake to say that the principle of autonomy as employed in secular bioethics requires that doctors always "tell the truth" to patients, even when it may cause terrible harm.

PERSPECTIVES OF HEALTH CARE WORKERS AND PATIENTS

A circumstance that arises frequently in multicultural urban settings is one that medical students bring to ethics teaching conferences. The patient and family are recent immigrants from a culture in which physicians normally inform the family rather then the patient of a diagnosis of cancer. The medical students wonder whether they are obligated to follow the family's wish, thereby respecting their cultural custom, or whether to abide by the ethical requirement at least to explore with patients their desire to receive information and to be a participant in their medical care. When medical students presented such a case in one of the conferences I co-direct with a physician, the dilemma was heightened by the demographic picture of the medical students themselves. Among the 14 students, 11 different countries of origin were represented. Those students either had come to the United States themselves to study or their parents had immigrated from countries in Asia, Latin America, Europe, and the Middle East.

The students began their comments with remarks like, "Where I come from, doctors never tell the patient a diagnosis of cancer" or "In my country, the doctor always asks the patient's family and abides by their wishes." The discussion centered on the question of whether the physician's obligation is to act in accordance with what contemporary medical ethics dictates in the United States or to respect the cultural difference of their patients and act according to the family's wishes. Not surprisingly, the medical students were divided on the answer to this question.

Medical students and residents are understandably confused about their obligation to disclose information to a patient when the patient comes from a culture in which telling a patient she has cancer is rare or unheard of. They ask: "Should I adhere to the American custom of disclosure or the Argentine custom of withholding the diagnosis?" That question is miscast, since there are some South Americans who want to know if they have cancer and some North Americans who do not. It is not, therefore, the cultural tradition that should determine whether disclosure to a patient is ethically appropriate, but rather the patient's wish to communicate directly with the physician, to leave communications to the family, or something in between. It would be a simplistic, if not unethical response on the part of the doctors to reason that "This is the United States, we adhere to the tradition of patient autonomy, therefore I must disclose to this immigrant from the Dominican Republic that he has cancer."

Most patients in the United States do want to know their diagnosis and prognosis, and it has been amply demonstrated that they can emotionally and psychologically handle a diagnosis of cancer. The same may not be true, however, for recent immigrants from other countries, and it may be manifestly untrue in certain cultures. Although this, too, may change in time, several studies point to a cross-cultural difference in beliefs and practice regarding disclosure of diagnosis and informed consent to treatment.

One survey examined differences in the attitudes of elderly subjects from different ethnic groups toward disclosure of the diagnosis and prognosis of a terminal illness and regarding decision making at the end of life.[5] This study found marked differences in attitudes between Korean Americans and Mexican Americans, on the one hand, and African Americans and Americans of European descent, on the other. The Korean Americans and Mexican Americans were less likely than the other two groups to believe that patients should be told of a prognosis of terminal illness and also less likely to believe that the patient should make decisions about the use of life-support technology. The Korean and Mexican Americans surveyed were also more likely than the other two groups to have a family-centered attitude toward these matters; they believed that the family and not the patient should be told the truth about the patient's diagnosis and prognosis. The authors of the study cite data from other countries that bear out a similar gap between the predominant "autonomy model" in the United States and the family-centered model prevalent in European countries as well as in Asia and Africa.

The study cited was conducted at 31 senior citizen centers in Los Angeles. In no ethnic group did 100 percent of its members favor disclosure or nondisclosure to the patient. Forty-seven percent of Korean Americans believed that a patient with metastatic cancer should be told the truth about the diagnosis, 65 percent of Mexican Americans held that belief, 87 percent of European Americans believed patients should be told the truth, and 89 percent of African Americans held that belief.

It is worth noting that the people surveyed were all 65-years-old or older. Not surprisingly, the Korean and Mexican American senior citizens had values closer to their origin than did the African Americans and European Americans who were born in the United States. Another finding was that among the Korean American and Mexican American groups, older subjects and those with lower socioeconomic status tended to be opposed to truth telling and patient decision making more strongly than the younger, wealthier, and more highly educated members of these same groups. The authors of the study draw the conclusion that physicians should ask the patients if they want to receive information and make decisions regarding treatment or whether they prefer that their families handle such matters.

Far from being at odds with the "autonomy model," this conclusion supports it. To ask patients how much they wish to be involved in the decision making does show respect for their autonomy: patients can then make the autonomous choice about who should be the recipient of information or the decision maker about their illness. What would fail to show respect for autonomy is for physicians to make these decisions without consulting the patient at all. If doctors spoke only to the families but not to the elderly Korean American or Mexican American patients without first approaching the patients to ascertain their wishes, they would be acting in the paternalistic manner of the past in America, and in accordance with the way many physicians continue to act in other parts of the world today. Furthermore, if physicians automatically withheld the diagnosis from Korean Americans because the majority of people in that ethnic group did not want to be told, they would be making an assumption that would result in a mistake almost 50 percent of the time.

INTOLERANCE AND OVERTOLERANCE

A medical resident in a New York hospital questioned a patient's ability to understand the medical treatment he had proposed and doubted whether the patient could grant truly informed consent. The patient, an immigrant from the Caribbean islands, believed in voodoo and sought to employ voodoo rituals in addition to the medical treatment she was receiving. "How can anyone who believes in that stuff be competent to consent to the treatment we offer?" the resident mused. The medical resident was an observant Jew who did not work, drive a car, or handle money on the sabbath and adhered to Kosher dietary laws. Both the Caribbean patient and the Orthodox Jew were devout believers in their respective faiths and practiced the accepted rituals of their religions.

The patient's voodoo rituals were not harmful to herself or to others. If the resident had tried to bypass or override the patient's decision regarding treatment, the case would have posed an ethical problem requiring resolution. Intolerance of another's religious or traditional practices that pose no threat of harm is, at least, discourteous and at worst, a prejudicial attitude. And it does fail to show respect for persons and their diverse religious and cultural practices. But it does not (yet) involve a failure to respect persons at a more fundamental level, which would occur if the doctor were to deny the patient her right to exercise her autonomy in the consent procedures.

At times, however, it is the family that interferes with the patient's autonomous decisions. Two brothers of a Haitian immigrant were conducting a conventional Catholic prayer vigil for their dying brother at his hospital bedside. The patient, suffering from terminal cancer and in extreme pain, had initially been given the pain medication he requested. Sometime later a nurse came in and found the patient alert, awake, and in excruciating pain from being undermedicated. When questioned, another nurse who had been responsible for the patient's care said that she had not continued to administer the pain medication because the patient's brothers had forbidden her do so. Under the influence of the heavy dose of pain medication, the patient had become delirious and mumbled incoherently. The brothers took this as an indication that evil spirits had entered the patient's body and, according to the voodoo religion of their native culture, unless the spirit was exorcised it would stay with the family forever, and the entire family would suffer bad consequences. The patient manifested the signs of delirium only when he was on the medication, so the brothers asked the nurse to withhold the pain medication, which they believed was responsible for the entry of the evil spirit. The nurse sincerely believed that respect for the family's religion required her to comply with the patient's brother's request, even if it contradicted the patient's own expressed wish. The person in charge of pain management called an ethics consultation, and the clinical ethicist said that the brothers' request, even if based on their traditional religious beliefs, could not override the patient's own request for pain medication that would relieve his suffering.

There are rarely good grounds for failing to respect the wishes of people based on their traditional religious or cultural beliefs. But when beliefs issue in actions that cause harm to others, attempts to prevent those harmful consequences are justifiable. An example that raises public health concerns is a ritual practiced among adherents of the religion known as Santeria, practiced by people from Puerto Rico and other groups of Caribbean origin. The ritual involves scattering mercury around the household to ward off bad spirits. Mercury is a highly toxic substance that can harm adults and causes grave harm to children. Shops called "botánicas" sell mercury as well as herbs and other potions to Caribbean immigrants who use them in their healing rituals.

The public health rationale that justifies placing limitations on people's behavior in order to protect others from harm can justify prohibition of the sale of mercury and penalties for its domestic use for ritual purposes. Yet the Caribbean immigrants could object: "You are interfering with our religious practices, based on your form of scientific medicine. This is our form of religious healing and you have no right to interfere with our beliefs and practice." It would not convince this group if a doctor or public health official were to reply: "But ours is a well-confirmed, scientific practice while yours is but an ignorant, unscientific ritual." It may very well appear to the Caribbean group as an act of cultural imperialism: "These American doctors with their Anglo brand of medicine are trying to impose it on us." This raises the difficult question of how to implement public health measures when the rationale is sufficiently compelling to prohibit religious or cultural rituals. Efforts to eradicate mercury sprinkling should enlist members of the community who agree with the public health position but who are also respected members of the cultural or religious group.

BELIEF SYSTEM OF A SUBCULTURE

Some widely held ethical practices have been transformed into law, such as disclosure of risks during an informed consent discussion and offering to patients the opportunity to make advanced directives in the form of a living will or appointing a health care agent. Yet these can pose problems for adherents of traditional cultural beliefs. In the traditional culture of Navajo Native Americans, a deeply rooted cultural belief underlies a wish not to convey or receive negative information. A study conducted on a Navajo Indian reservation in Arizona demonstrated how Western biomedical and bioethical concepts and principals can come into conflict with traditional Navajo values and ways of thinking.[6] In March 1992, the Indian Health Service adopted the requirements of the Patient Self-Determination Act, but the Indian Health Service policy also contains the following proviso: "Tribal customs and traditional beliefs that relate to death and dying will be respected to the extent possible when providing information to patients on these issues."[7]

The relevant Navajo belief in this context is the notion that thought and language have the power to shape reality and to control events. The central concern posed by discussions about future contingencies is that traditional beliefs require people to "think and speak in a positive way." When doctors disclose risks of a treatment in an informed consent discussion, they speak "in a negative way," thereby violating the Navajo prohibition. The traditional Navajo belief is that health is maintained and restored through positive ritual language. This presumably militates against disclosing risks of treatment as well as avoiding mention of future illness or incapacitation in a discussion about advance care planning. Western-trained doctors working with the traditional Navajo population are thus caught in a dilemma. Should they adhere to the ethical and legal standards pertaining to informed consent now in force in the rest of the United States and risk harming their patients by "talking in a negative way"? Or should they adhere to the Navajo belief system with the aim of avoiding harm to the patients but at the same time violating the ethical requirement of disclosure to patients of potential risks and future contingencies?

The authors of the published studies draw several conclusions. One is that hospital policies complying with the Patient Self-Determination Act are ethically troublesome for the traditional Navajo patients. Since physicians who work with that population must decide how to act, this problem requires a solution. A second conclusion is that "the concepts and principles of Western bioethics are not universally held."[8] This comes as no surprise. It is a straightforward statement of the thesis of descriptive ethical relativism, the evident truth that a wide variety of cultural beliefs about morality exist in the world. The question for normative ethics endures: What follows from these particular facts of cultural relativity? A third conclusion the authors draw, in light of their findings, is that health care providers and institutions caring for Navajo patients should reevaluate their policies and procedures regarding advance care planning.

This situation is not difficult to resolve, ethically or practically. The Patient Self-Determination Act does not mandate patients to actually make an advance directive; it requires only that health care institutions provide information to patients and give them the opportunity to make a living will or appoint a health care agent. A physician or nurse working for the Indian Health Service could easily fulfill this requirement by asking Navajo patients if they wish to discuss their future care or options, without introducing any of the negative thinking. This approach resolves one of the limitations of the published study. As the authors acknowledge, the findings reflect a more traditional perspective and the full range of Navajo views is not represented. So it is possible that some patients who use the Indian Health Service may be willing or even eager to have frank discussions about risks of treatment and future possibilities, even negative ones, if offered the opportunity.

It is more difficult, however, to justify withholding from patients the risks of proposed treatment in an informed consent discussion. The article about the Navajo beliefs recounts an episode told by a Navajo woman who is also a nurse. Her father was a candidate for bypass surgery. When the surgeon informed the patient of the risks of surgery, including the possibility that he might not wake up, the elderly Navajo man refused the surgery altogether. If the patient did indeed require the surgery and refused because he believed that telling him of the risk of not waking up would bring about that result, then it would be justifiable to withhold that risk of surgery. Should not that possibility be routinely withheld from all patients, then, since the prospect of not waking up could lead other people—Navajos and non-Navajos alike—to refuse the surgery? The answer is no, but it requires further analysis.

Respect for autonomy grants patients who have been properly informed the right to refuse a proposed medical treatment. An honest and appropriate disclosure of the purpose, procedures, risks, benefits, and available alternatives, provided in terms the patient can understand, puts the ultimate decision in the hands of the patient. This is the ethical standard according to Western bioethics. A clear exception exists in the case of patients who lack decisional capacity altogether, and debate continues regarding the ethics of paternalistically overriding the refusal of marginally competent patients. This picture relies on a key feature that is lacking in the Navajo case: a certain metaphysical account of the way the world works. Western doctors and their patients generally do not believe that talking about risks of harm will produce those harms (although there have been accounts that document the "dark side" of the placebo effect). It is not really the Navajo values that create the cross-cultural problem but rather, their metaphysical belief system holding that thought and language have the power to shape reality and control events. In fact, the Navajo values are quite the same as the standard Western ones: fear of death and avoidance of harmful side effects. To understand the relationship between cultural variation and ethical relativism, it is essential to distinguish between cultural relativity that stems from a difference in values and that which can be traced to an underlying metaphysics or epistemology.

Against this background, only two choices are apparent: insist on disclosing to Navajo patients the risks of treatment and thereby inflict unwanted negative thoughts on them; or withhold information about the risks and state only the anticipated benefits of the proposed treatment. Between those two choices, there is no contest. The second is clearly ethically preferable. It is true that withholding information about the risks of treatment or potential adverse events in the future radically changes what is required by the doctrine of informed consent. It essentially removes the "informed" aspect, while leaving in place the notion that the patient should decide. The physician will still provide some information to the Navajo patient, but only the type of information that is acceptable to the Navajos who adhere to this particular belief system. True, withholding certain information that would typically be disclosed to patients departs from the ethical ideal of informed consent, but it does so in order to achieve the ethically appropriate goal of beneficence in the care of patients.

The principle of beneficence supports the withholding of information about risks of treatment from Navajos who hold the traditional belief system. But so, too, does the principle of respect for autonomy. Navajos holding traditional beliefs can act autonomously only when they are not thinking in a negative way. If doctors tell them about bad contingencies, that will lead to negative thinking, which in their view will fail to maintain and restore health. The value of both doctor and patient is to maintain and restore health. A change in the procedures regarding the informed consent discussion is justifiable based on a distinctive background condition: the Navajo belief system about the causal efficacy of thinking and talking in a certain way. The less-than-ideal version of informed consent does constitute a "lower" standard than that which is usually appropriate in today's medical practice. But the use of "lower" standard is justified by the background assumption that that is what the Navajo patient prefers.

What is relative and what is nonrelative in this situation? There is a clear divergence between the Navajo belief system and that of Western science. That divergence leads to a difference in what sort of discussion is appropriate for traditional Navajos in the medical setting and that which is standard in Western medical practice. According to one description, "always disclose the risks as well as the benefits of treatment to patients," the conclusion points to ethical relativism. But a more general description, one that heeds today's call for cultural awareness and sensitivity, would be: "Carry out an informed consent discussion in a manner appropriate to the patient's beliefs and understanding." That obligation is framed in a nonrelative way. A heart surgeon would describe the procedures, risks, and benefits of bypass surgery in one way to a patient who is another physician, in a different way to a mathematician ignorant of medical science, in yet another way to a skilled craftsman with an eighth grade education, and still differently to a traditional Navajo. The ethical principle is the same; the procedures differ.

OBLIGATIONS OF PHYSICIANS

The problem for physicians is how to respond when an immigrant to the United States acts according to the cultural values of her native country, values that differ widely from accepted practices in American medicine. Suppose an African immigrant asks an obstetrician to perform genital surgery on her baby girl. Or imagine that a Laotian immigrant from the lu Mien culture brings her four-month-old baby to the pediatrician for a routine visit and the doctor discovers burns on the baby's stomach. The African mother seeks to comply with the tradition of her native country, Somalia, where the vast majority of women have had clitoridectomies. The lu Mien woman admits that she used a traditional folk remedy to treat what she suspected was her infant's case of a rare folk illness.

What is the obligation of physicians in the United States when they encounter patients in such situations? At one extreme is the reply that in the United States, physicians are obligated to follow the ethical and cultural practices accepted here and have no obligation to comply with patients' requests that embody entirely different cultural values. At the other extreme is the view that cultural sensitivity requires physicians to adhere to the traditional beliefs and practices of patients who have emigrated from other cultures.

A growing concern on the part of doctors and public health officials is the increasing number of requests for genital cutting and defense of the practice by immigrants to the United States and European countries. A Somalian immigrant living in Houston said he believed his Muslim faith required him to have his daughters undergo the procedure; he also stated his belief that it would preserve their virginity. He was quoted as saying, "It's my responsibility. If I don't do it, I will have failed my children."[9] Another African immigrant living in Houston sought a milder form of the cutting she had undergone for her daughter. The woman said she believed it was necessary so her daughter would not run off with boys and have babies before marriage. She was disappointed that Medicaid would not cover the procedure, and planned to go to Africa to have the procedure done there. A New York city physician was asked by a father for a referral to a doctor who would do the procedure on his three-year-old daughter. When the physician told him this was not done in America, the man accused the doctor of not understanding what he wanted.[10]

However, others in our multicultural society consider it a requirement of "cultural sensitivity" to accommodate in some way to such requests of African immigrants. Harborview Medical Center in Seattle sought just such a solution. A group of doctors agreed to consider making a ritual nick in the fold of skin that covers the clitoris, but without removing any tissue. However, the hospital later abandoned the plan after being flooded with letters, postcards, and telephone calls in protest.[11]

A physician who conducted research with East African women living in Seattle held the same view as the doctors who sought a culturally sensitive solution. In a talk she gave to my medical school department, she argued that Western physicians must curb their tendency to judge cultural practices different from their own as "rational" or "irrational." Ritual genital cutting is an "inalienable" part of some cultures, and it does a disservice to people from those cultures to view it as a human rights violation. She pointed out that in the countries where female genital mutilation (FGM) is practiced, circumcised women are "normal." Like some anthropologists who argue for a "softer" linguistic approach,[12] this researcher preferred the terminology of "circumcision" to that of "female genital mutilation."

One can understand and even have some sympathy for the women who believe they must adhere to a cultural ritual even when they no longer live in the society where it is widely practiced. But it does not follow that the ritual is an "inalienable" part of that culture, since every culture undergoes changes over time. Furthermore, to contend that in the countries where FGM is practiced, circumcised women are "normal" is like saying that malaria or malnutrition is "normal" in parts of Africa. That a human condition is statistically normal implies nothing whatever about whether an obligation exists to seek to alter the statistical norm for the betterment of those who are affected.

Some Africans living in the United States have said they are offended that Congress passed a law prohibiting female genital mutilation that appears to be directed specifically at Africans. France has also passed legislation, but its law relies on general statutes that prohibit violence against children.[13] In a recent landmark case, a

French court sent a Gambian woman to jail for having had the genitals of her two baby daughters mutilated by a midwife. French doctors report an increasing number of cases of infants who are brought to clinics hemorrhaging or with severe infections.

Views on what constitutes the appropriate response to requests to health professionals for advice or referrals regarding the genital mutilation of their daughters vary considerably. Three commentators gave their opinions on a case vignette in which several African families living in a U.S. city planned to have the ritual performed on their daughters. If the procedure could not be done in the U.S., the families planned to have it done in Africa. One of the parents sought advice from health professionals.

One commentator, a child psychiatrist, commented that professional ethical practice requires her to respect and try to understand the cultural and religious practices of the group making the request.[14] She then cited another ethical requirement of clinical practice: her need to promote the physical and psychological well-being of the child and refusal to condone parenting practices that constitute child abuse according to the social values and laws of her city and country. Most of what this child psychiatrist would do with the mother who comes to her involves discussion, mutual understanding, education, and the warning that in this location performing the genital cutting ritual would probably be considered child abuse.

The psychiatrist would remain available for a continuing dialogue with the woman and others in her community, but would stop short of making a child-abuse report since the woman was apparently only considering carrying out the ritual. However, the psychiatrist would make the report if she had knowledge that the mother was actually planning to carry out the ritual or if it had already been performed. She would make the child-abuse report reluctantly, however, and only if she believed the child to be at risk and if there were no other option. She concluded by observing that the mother is attempting to act in the best interest of her child and does not intend to harm her. The psychiatrist's analysis demonstrates the possible ambiguities of the concept of child abuse. Is abuse determined solely by the intention of the adult? Should child abuse be judged by the harmful consequences to the child, regardless of the adult's intention? Of course, if a law defines the performance of female genital mutilation as child abuse, then it is child abuse, from a legal point of view, and physicians are obligated to report any case for which there is a reasonable suspicion. Legal definitions aside, intentions are relevant for judging the moral worth of people, but not for the actions they perform. This means that the good intentions of parents could exonerate them from blame if their actions cause harm to their children, but the harmful actions nevertheless remain morally wrong.

The second commentator, a clinical psychologist and licensed sex therapist, would do many of the same things as the child psychiatrist, but would go a bit further in finding others from the woman's community and possibly another support network.[15] Like most other commentators on female genital mutilation, this discussant remarked that "agents of change must come from within a culture."[16]

The third commentator on this case vignette was the most reluctant to be critical. A British historian and barrister, he began with the observation that "a people's culture demands the highest respect,"[17] On the one hand, he noted that custom, tradition and religion are not easily uprooted. But on the other hand, he pointed out that no human practice is beyond questioning. He contended that the debate over the nature and impact of female circumcision is a "genuine debate," and the ritual probably had practical utility when it was introduced into the societies that still engage in it. Of the three commentators, he voiced the strongest opposition to invoking the child abuse laws because it "would be an unwarranted criminalization of parents grappling in good faith with a practice that is legal and customary in their home country."[18] In the end, this discussant would approach the parents "much as a lawyer would address a jury," leaving the parents (like a jury) to deliberate and come to an informed decision. He would also involve the girls in this process, since they are adolescents, and should have input into the deliberations.

It is tempting to wonder whether the involvement of adolescent girls in deliberations of their parents would, in traditional Gambian culture, be even remotely considered much less accepted. The "lawyer-jury-adolescent involvement" solution looks to be very Western. If these families living in the United States still wish to adhere to their cultural tradition of genital mutilation, is it likely that they will appreciate the reasoned, deliberative approach this last commentator proposed?

Exactly where to draw the line in such cases is a difficult matter. Presumably, one could go farther than any of these commentators and inform the African families that since U.S. law prohibits female genital mutilation, which has been likened to child abuse, a health professional would be obligated to inform relevant authorities of an intention to commit child abuse. Conceivably, U.S. authorities could prevent immigrants from returning to this country if they have gone to Africa to have a procedure performed that would be illegal if done within the United States. But this is a matter of law, not ethics, and would involve a gross invasion of privacy since to enforce the ruling it would be necessary to examine the genitals of the adolescent girls when these families sought reentry into the United States. That would be going too far and probably deserves condemnation as "ethical imperialism." Since the cutting would already have been done, punitive action toward the family could not succeed in preventing the harm.

Another case vignette describes a Laotian woman from the Mien culture who immigrated to the United States and married a Mien man. When she visited her child's pediatrician for a routine four-month immunization, the doctor was horrified to see five red and blistered quarter-inch round markings on the child's abdomen.[19] The mother explained that she used a traditional Mien "cure" for pain, since she thought the infant was experiencing a rare folk illness among Mien babies characterized by incessant crying and loss of appetite, in addition to other symptoms. The "cure" involves dipping a reed in pork fat, lighting the reed, and passing the burning substance over the skin, raising a blister that "pops like popcorn." The popping indicates that the illness is not related to spiritual causes; if no blisters appear, then a shaman may have to be summoned to conduct a spiritual ritual for a cure. As many as 11 burns might be needed before the end of the "treatment." The burns are then covered with a mentholated cream.

The Mien women told the pediatrician that infection is rare and the burns heal in a week or so. Scars sometimes remain but are not considered disfiguring. She also told the doctor that the procedure must be done by someone skilled in burning, since if a burn is placed too near the line between the baby's mouth and navel, the baby could become mute or even retarded. The mother considered the cure to have been successful in the case of her baby, since the child had stopped crying and regained her appetite. Strangely enough, the pediatrician did not say anything to the mother about her practice of burning the baby, no doubt from the need to show "cultural sensitivity." She did, however, wonder later whether she should have said something since she thought the practice was dangerous and also cruel to babies.

One commentator who wrote about this case proposed using "an ethnographic approach" to ethics in the cross-cultural setting.[20] This approach need not result in a strict ethical relativism, however, since one can be respectful of cultural differences and at the same time acknowledge that there are limits. What is critical is the perceived degree of harm; some cultural practices may constitute atrocities and violations of fundamental human rights. The commentator argued that the pediatrician must first seek to understand the Mien woman in the context of her world before trying to educate her in the ways of Western medicine. The commentator stopped short of providing a solution, but noted that many possible resolutions can be found for cross-cultural ethical conflicts. Be that as it may, we still need to determine which of the pediatrician's obligations should take precedence: to seek to protect her infant patient (and possibly also the Mien woman's other children) from harmful rituals or to exhibit cultural sensitivity and refrain from attempts at re-education or critical admonitions.

A second pair of commentators assumed a nonjudgmental stance. These commentators urged respect for cultural diversity and defended the Mien woman's belief systems as entirely rational: "It is well grounded in her culture; it is practiced widely; the reasons for it are widely understood among the lu Mien; the procedure, from a Mien point of view, works."[21] This is a culturally relative view of rationality. The same argument could just as well be used to justify female genital mutilation. Nevertheless, the commentators rejected what they said was the worst choice: simply to tolerate the practice as a primitive cultural artifact and do nothing more. They also rejected the opposite extreme: a referral of child abuse to the appropriate authorities. The mother's actions did not constitute intentional abuse, since she actually believed she was helping the child by providing a traditional remedy. Here I think the commentators are correct in rejecting a referral to the child-abuse authorities, since a charge of child abuse can have serious consequences that may ultimately run counter to the best interests of the child.

What did these commentators recommend? Not to try to prohibit the practice directly, which could alienate the parent. Instead, the pediatrician could discuss the risk of infection and suggest safer pain remedies. The doctor should also learn more about the rationale for and technique of the traditional burning "cure." The most she should do, according to these commentators, is consider sharing her concerns with the local Mien community, but not with the mother alone.

There is in these commentaries a great reluctance to criticize, scold, or take legal action against parents from other cultures who employ painful and potentially harmful rituals that have no scientific basis. This attitude of tolerance is appropriate against the background knowledge that the parents do not intend to harm the child and are simply using a folk remedy widely accepted in their own culture. But tolerance of these circumstances must be distinguished from a judgment that the actions harmful to children should be permitted to continue. What puzzles me is the notion that "cultural sensitivity" must extend so far as to refrain from providing a solid education to these parents about the potential harms and the infliction of gratuitous pain. In a variety of other contexts, we accept the role of physicians as educator of patients. Doctors are supposed to tell their patients not to smoke, to lose weight, to have appropriate preventative medical checkups such as pap smears, mammograms, and proctoscopic examinations.

Pediatricians are thought to have an even more significant obligation to educate the parents of their vulnerable patients: inform them of steps that minimize the risks of sudden infant death syndrome, tell them what is appropriate for an infant's or child's diet, and give them a wide array of other social and psychological information designed to keep a child healthy and flourishing. Are these educational obligations of pediatricians only appropriate for patients whose background culture is that of the United States or Western Europe? Should a pediatrician not attempt to educate parents who, in their practice of the Santeria religion, sprinkle mercury around the house? The obligation of pediatricians to educate and even to urge parents to adopt practices likely to contribute to the good health and well being of their children, and to avoid practices that will definitely or probably cause harm and suffering, should know no cultural boundaries.

My position is consistent with the realization that Western medicine does not have all the answers. This position also recognizes that some traditional healing practices are not only not harmful but may be as beneficial as those of Western medicine. The injunction to "respect cultural diversity" could rest on the premise that Western medicine sometimes causes harm without compensating benefits (which is true) or on the equally true premise that traditional practices such as acupuncture and herbal remedies, once scorned by mainstream Western medicine, have come to be accepted side-by-side with the precepts of scientific medicine. Typically, however, respect for multicultural diversity goes well beyond these reasonable views and requires toleration of manifestly painful or harmful procedures such as the burning remedy employed in the Mien culture. We ought to be able to respect cultural diversity without having to accept every single feature embedded in traditional beliefs and rituals.

The reluctance to impose modern medicine on immigrants from a fear that it constitutes yet another instance of "cultural imperialism" is misplaced. Is it not possible to accept non-Western cultural practices side by side with Western ones, yet condemn those that are manifestly harmful and have no compensating benefit except for the cultural belief that they are beneficial? The commentators who urged respect for the Mien woman's burning treatment on the grounds that it is practiced widely, the reasons for it are widely understood among the Mien, and the procedure works, from a Mien point of view, seemed to be placing that practice on a par with practices that "work" from the point of view of Western medicine. Recall that if the skin does not blister, the Mien belief holds that the illness may be related to spiritual causes and a shaman might have to be called. Should the pediatrician stand by and do nothing if the child has a fever of 104° and the parent calls a shaman because the skin did not blister? Recall also that the Mien woman told the pediatrician that if the burns are not done in the right place, the baby could become mute or even retarded. Must we reject the beliefs of Western medicine regarding causality and grant equal status to the Mien beliefs? To refrain from seeking to educate such parents and to not exhort them to alter their traditional practices is unjust, as it exposes the immigrant children to health risks that are not borne by children from the majority culture.

It is heresy in today's postmodern climate of respect for the belief systems of all cultures to entertain the notion that some beliefs are demonstrably false and others, whether true or false, lead to manifestly harmful actions. We are not supposed to talk about the evolution of scientific ideas or about progress in the Western world, since that is a colonialist way of thinking. If it is simply "the white man's burden, medicalized"[22] to urge African families living in the United States not to genitally mutilate their daughters, or to attempt to educate Mien mothers about the harms of burning their babies, then we are doomed to permit ethical relativism to overwhelm common sense.

Multiculturalism, as defined at the beginning of this paper, appears to embrace ethical relativism and yet is logically inconsistent with relativism. The second half of the definition states that multiculturalism "insists that all cultural groups be treated with respect as equals." What does this imply with regard to cultural groups that oppress or fail to respect other cultural groups? Must the cultural groups that violate the mandate to treat all cultural groups with respect and as equals be respected themselves? It is impossible to insist that all such groups be treated with respect and as equals, and at the same time accept any particular group's attitude toward and treatment of another group as inferior. Every cultural group contains subgroups within the culture: old and young, women and men, people with and people without disabilities. Are the cultural groups that discriminate against women or people with disabilities to be respected equally with those that do not?

What multiculturalism does not say is whether all of the beliefs and practices of all cultural groups must be equally respected. It is one thing to require that cultural, religious, and ethnic groups be treated as equals; that conforms to the principle of justice as equality. It is quite another thing to say that any cultural practice whatever of any group is to be tolerated and respected equally. This latter view is a statement of extreme ethical relativism. If multiculturalists endorse the principle of justice as equality, however, they must recognize that normative ethical relativism entails the illogical consequence of toleration and acceptance of numerous forms of injustice in those cultures that oppress women and religious and ethnic minorities.

READING ENDNOTES

1. Fowers, Blaine J., and Richardson, Frank C. 1996. Why is Multiculturalism Good? *American Psychologist* 51: 609.
2. Fox, Renée C. 1990. The Evolution of American Bioethics: A Sociological Perspective. In *Social Science Perspectives on Medical Ethics*, ed. George Weisz, p. 206. Philadelphia: University of Pennsylvania Press.
3. Nelson, James Lindemann. 1992. Taking Families Seriously. *Hastings Center Report* 22 (4): 6–12.
4. Hardwig, John. 1990. "What About the Family?" *Hastings Center Report* 20 (2): 5–10.
5. Blackhall, Leslie; Murphy, Sheila T.; Frank, Gelya; Michel, Vicki; and Azen, Stanley. 1995. Ethnicity and Attitudes Toward Patient Autonomy. *Journal of the American Medical Association* 274: 820–25.
6. Carrese, Joseph, and Rhodes, Lorna A. 1995. Western Bioethics on the Navajo Reservation: Benefit or Harm? *Journal of the American Medical Association* 274: 826–29.
7. Carrese and Rhodes, p. 828.
8. Carrese and Rhodes, p. 829.
9. Dugger, Celia W. 1996. Tug of Taboos: African Genital Rite vs. U.S. Law. *New York Times* (28 December): 1.
10. Dugger, pp. 1, 9.
11. Dugger, 1996.
12. Lane, Sandra D., and Rubinstein, Robert A. 1996. Judging the Other: Responding to Traditional Female Genital Surgeries. *Hastings Center Report* 26 (5): 31–40.
13. Dugger, 1996.
14. Brant, Renée. 1995. Child Abuse or Acceptable Cultural Norms: Child Psychiatrist's Response. *Ethics & Behavior* 5: 284–87.
15. Wyatt, Gail Elizabeth. 1995. Ethical Issues in Culturally Relevant Intervention. *Ethics & Behavior* 5: 288–90.
16. Wyatt, p. 289.
17. Martin, Tony. 1995. Cultural Contexts. *Ethics & Behavior* 5: 290–92.
18. Martin, p. 291.
19. Case Study: Culture, Healing, and Professional Obligations. 1993. *Hastings Center Report* 23 (4): 15.
20. Carrese, Joseph. 1993 Culture, Healing, and Professional Obligations: Commentary. *Hastings Center Report* 23 (4): 16.
21. Brown, Kate, and Jameton, Andrew. 1993. Culture, Healing, and Professional Obligations: Commentary. *Hastings Center Report* 23 (4): 17.
22. Morsy, Soheir A. 1991. Safeguarding Women's Bodies: The White Man's Burden Medicalized. *Medical Anthropology Quarterly* 5 (1): 19–23.

QUESTIONS

1. What is multiculturalism?
2. How can multiculturalism be recognized as a value within an individualistic framework?

3. What is the connection between the value of patient autonomy and the medical practices of (1) full disclosure of information to patients and (2) informed consent?

4. What is the difference between absolutist and universalist ethics?

5. Medical ethics is often construed as involving four central principles: justice, beneficence, autonomy, and non-harm. How might all four be thought to flow from the "respect for persons" principle? Does having a common foundation guarantee that the four derived principles will never come into conflict?

6. What limit does Macklin support on respect for diverse religious and cultural practices?

7. Clitoral surgery is typically performed on minors, and so we might be inclined to try to prohibit it as a kind of child abuse. But, given that the mothers involved in the practice may believe that it is in the best interests of the child to have the surgery and so it is not abusive at all, can we make this judgement without imposing our Western values on her?

8. What does Macklin think are the basic duties of physicians, and especially pediatricians (specialists in child medicine)?

9. To what extent does Macklin advocate limits to the degree to which we must tolerate dangerous and harmful practices, even when they are supported by the values and belief systems of cultural groups?

10. Macklin raises the question we posed in our introduction to this chapter: what must liberal societies tolerate with respect to the practices of illiberal subcultures within them? Does she answer this question?

11. Why are multiculturalism and normative ethical relativism inconsistent?

12. Within liberal thinking, tolerance is thought of as a virtue. Is it a virtue to tolerate intolerance? Is it a virtue to tolerate intolerable practices?

13. Does Macklin's discussion suggest similar tensions that multiculturalism raises for other professionals besides medical practitioners?

✦ ✦ ✦

Sirkku Kristiina Hellsten, Pluralism in Multicultural Liberal Democracy and the Justification of Female Circumcision

Sirkku Kristiina Hellsten examines the tension for multicultural liberals between neutrality of the various conceptions of the good life, and the liberal commitment to the equality of all individuals. Liberals derive their commitment to neutrality towards conceptions of the good from their prior commitment to the idea that all individuals are equally worthy of respect. This prior commitment governs when one may legitimately interfere with the actions of another, namely, when those actions fail to respect the moral ideal that all individuals are equally worthy of respect. Constraints are right (legitimate) when they preserve the liberty and security of others. Female circumcision cannot be justified on these grounds, Hellsten argues, as it is harmful, and inegalitarian.

But there are still some worries about paternalistic interference that Hellsten wishes to assuage. Paternalism is only wrong if it defeats autonomy. We have to show that this interference is legitimate by showing that the young women subjected to it are not autonomous. Hellsten argues that these women are young, (mostly) poor, and subject to serious social coercion, and so their decisions to allow the procedure to be performed upon themselves or their daughters are not autonomous. Any commitment that these women have to the practice of female circumcision is therefore not autonomous, and interference is thus legitimate.

But, as Scoccia has argued, this is only one half of the argument for legitimate paternalistic interference. It now has to be shown that female circumcision is clearly not in these women's interest. Perhaps the case seems so obvious that no argument is deemed necessary. But this would only be the case if physical harm alone were considered. A rejection of this practice would likely lead to a devaluing of the young woman, ostracism by her family, and perhaps community. These are significant harms to one who, by hypothesis, is not autonomous. Closer argument seems called for, if this paternalistic interference is to be justified within a liberal framework.

✦ ✦ ✦

Sirkku Kristiina Hellsten, "Pluralism in Multicultural Liberal Democracy and the Justification of Female Circumcision," *Journal of Applied Philosophy* 16:1 (1999): 69–83. © Society of Applied Philosophy, 1999, Blackwell Publishers. Reprinted with permission of the Society for Applied Philosophy and Blackwell Publishers.

Pluralism in Multicultural Liberal Democracy and the Justification of Female Circumcision

S I R K K U   K R I S T I I N A   H E L L S T E N

FEMALE CIRCUMCISION AND WESTERN DEMOCRACIES[1]

In pluralistic Western European democracies the liberal principles of equality and freedom are in general widely respected. These countries now face a dilemma as immigrants or refugees from different cultures try to adapt to their new societies without losing their own cultural identity and traditions. On the one hand, liberal societies feel the danger of paternalism in interfering with the lifestyles and values of individuals from alien cultures. On the other hand, cultural practices which oppress individual equality and rights violate the very principles of equality and freedom.

One of these controversial traditional practices which has attracted much attention is female circumcision. It is a custom that is widespread in Africa north of the Equator, as well as in many African communities within Western societies.[2] However, history reveals that female circumcision of some kind has been practiced at one time or another on every continent. In Britain and in the USA during the last century, clitoridectomy was thought by some to be a remedy for all manner of 'ills,' from epilepsy and hysteria to nymphomania and masturbation.

In its most radical form, called infibulation, the operation involves amputation of the clitoris and the whole of the labia minora, and at least the anterior two-thirds and often the whole of the medical part of the labia majora. The two sides of the vulva are then stitched-together with silk catgut or thorns, and a tiny sliver of wood or a reed is inserted to preserve an opening for urine and menstrual blood.[3] There are no medical reasons for these types of mutilation of the female genitalia. In fact, the physical consequences of this practice are most harmful and will cause pain and illnesses for the rest of the victim's life. In the worst scenario the operation can lead to death.[4] However, even showing that the relevant medical, religious or sexual beliefs are false has not stopped the practice.

DEONTOLOGICAL LIBERALISM AND FEMALE CIRCUMCISION

The three core assumptions found in the liberal argumentation for value pluralism and tolerance relevant to the justification of female circumcision can be summarized as follows. Firstly, the liberal view is individualist in asserting or assuming the moral primacy of the person against the claims of any social collective. Every individual is seen as an autonomous moral agent capable of choosing his own values and way of life. This means that the right of an individual is always prior to any cultural claims. Secondly, liberalism is, at least on a minimum level, egalitarian because it confers on all such individuals 'the same moral status and denies the relevance to legal or political order of differences in moral worth among human beings.' Thirdly, it is universalistic because it affirms the moral unity of the human species and accords 'a secondary importance to specific historic associations and cultural forms.' Liberals then believe that all humans have something in common as human beings, even if our conceptions about a good life and values may vary.[5]

The demands for pluralism and tolerance in liberalism are based on the idea that a just society seeks not to promote any particular ends or goals, but enables its citizens to pursue their own ends, consistent with a similar liberty for all. It therefore must be governed by principles of justice that do not presuppose any particular conception of the good. A state must treat its citizens with equal concern and respect, and any individual's conception of the good life is not nobler or superior to another's.[6] Thus, the liberal response to the multiplicity of religious, cultural and moral traditions in modern society has been, as far as possible, to advocate toleration of different ways of living. Liberal principles of state neutrality and individual autonomy to choose one's values promote the freedom to choose one's culture, language, religion and traditions.[7] If individuals within a certain cultural minority wish to maintain their traditions, they should be able to do so.

However, even in liberal society freedom does not mean that individuals can do whatever they want to. They cannot, for instance, harm or suppress others. According to liberal principles, freedom can, and should, be restricted in order to promote equality. Constraints on one's liberty are justifiable when they protect the liberty and security of others.[8] What justifies the regulative principles is then not that they maximize the general welfare, or otherwise promote the common good, but rather that they conform to the concept of right. Right becomes a moral category given priority status over the good and is seen as independent of it. The claim that the right is prior to the good means that individual rights cannot be sacrificed for the sake of the general good. It also means that the principles of justice that specify these individual rights cannot be premised on any particular vision of the good life.[9]

If we now mirror female circumcision as a tradition against these core assumptions of liberalism, we can see that it cannot be justified by the liberal view. It causes harm to an individual and sacrifices her rights in the name of communal values. It also suppresses women as a group and violates the principle of equal respect.

However, even after these apparent violations against the liberal principles of equality and individual rights are recognized, the fear of paternalism often remains. Westerners are often accused of too easily underestimating the real autonomy of the primitive people in alien cultures and seemingly irrational and disgusting practices. If an individual insisted that holding on to certain cultural traditions is important for her life, could we deny this by convincing her that she would be more happy if she rejected these old customs of her culture? If we are to respect the liberal principles of equality and freedom, should we not allow a person to make up her own mind on her way of life?[10]

To solve this apparent dilemma between autonomy and the fear of paternalism we have to examine the elements of paternalism more closely. The best way to start is to return to Mill and quote his classic anti-paternalist statement in *On Liberty* (1859):

> The object of this Essay is to assert one very simple principle, as entitled to govern absolutely the dealing of the society with the individual in the way of compulsion and control, whether the means used be physical force in the form of legal penalties, or the moral coercion of public opinion. The principle is, that one sole end for which mankind are warranted, individually or collectively, in interfering with the liberty of action of any of their number, is self-protection. That the only purpose for which power can be rightfully exercised over any member of a civilized community, against his will, is to prevent harm to others. His own good, either physical or moral, is not a sufficient warrant. He cannot rightfully be compelled to do or forbear, because it will be better for him, because it will make him happier, because in the opinion of others, to do so would be wise, or even right. These are good reasons for remonstrating with him, or reasoning with him, or persuading him, but not compelling him, or visiting him with any evil in case he do otherwise. To justify that, the conduct from which it is desired to deter him, must be calculated to produce evil to someone else. The only part of the conduct of any one, for which he is amenable to society, is that which concerns others. In the part which merely concerns himself, his independence is, of right absolute. Over himself, over his own body and mind, the individual is sovereign.[11]

In this passage Mill manages to introduce most of the justificatory and conceptual problems thrown up by the issues of paternalism and autonomy. As Mill does, Gerald Dworkin also points out that in paternalism there are at least two principles involved: one asserts that harm to others is a relevant ground for restricting individual or collective freedom, and another asserts that harm to self is not. Thus, Dworkin characterises paternalism as 'interference with a person's liberty of action justified by reasons referring to the welfare, good, happiness, needs, interest or values of the person coerced.'[12] Joel Feinberg, however, sees (legal) paternalism 'as a liberty limiting principle that justified (state) coercion to protect individuals from self-inflicted harm, or in its extreme version, to guide them, whether they like it or not, towards their own good.'[13] Paternalism is then generally defined as the coercing of people primarily for what is believed to be their own good.[14] However, not all interventions in people's lives can be considered as paternalism, particularly if their purpose is to promote the realization of individuals' moral autonomy rather than to suppress it. There is a form of apparently paternalistic intervention which actually can be justified within a liberal society because it aims to 'free' individuals from suppressive systems of values, norms and practices which do not respect autonomy. It does this by helping them to gain independence and capacity for critical judgement.[15] This type of intervention is not necessarily paternalistic because it does contain coercion, constraint, violations of autonomy or other *prima facie* condemnable elements. Non-coercive intervention is usually autonomy-respecting and autonomy-promoting, and can thus be justified within the liberal society, if we can prove, first, that the recipient of the interventions is not at the relevant time capable of reasonable, voluntary decision-making and secondly, that the recipient would, without the intervention, inflict relatively grave harm on herself/himself or others. Thus, to condemn female circumcision in a pluralist and liberal society, we first have to show that this intervention is not paternalistic by proving that the individuals involved are forced to participate in this tradition by physical or social coercion rather than being able to choose their own values and traditions.[16]

Despite the apparent voluntariness of the victims involved, empirical study of the circumstances proves that female circumcision is mostly maintained by coercion in traditional societies. Firstly, female circumcision is usually associated with poverty, illiteracy and the low status of women. In patriarchal communities uncircumcised women are stigmatized and not sought in marriage, which helps to explain the paradox that the victims of this practice are also its strongest proponents. They can scarcely afford not to be. In these circumstances, women are reluctant to question the tradition or take an independent line lest they lose social approval. In poverty-stricken patriarchal communities struggling to survive, social acceptance and support may mean the difference between life and death.[17] Thus, women in these communities have no alternative but to go along with the practice. Their chances of leaving their community are also only hypothetical. When circumcision is required in order to guarantee a girl's chastity and fitness for marriage, and when getting married may be the only way to survive, the decision to follow the ritual is rational. If the only way to guarantee the future for your daughter is to circumcise her, the mother's decision is rational, even loving, given the circumstances. Thus, these women often defend the practice by appealing to the perilous and menacing practical consequences that would follow from abandoning the tradition. These decisions are not, however, independent or autonomous in the way a liberal view requires. If *de jure* autonomy, or right to self-determination which should not be violated, is interpreted as an option to check the validity of one's authorities and traditions whenever one feels it is necessary and rational, these women lack this option.[18] They live in circumstances which are coercive, oppressive and autonomy-violating. Since the development of human individuality and personal autonomy cannot occur in oppressive or coercive circumstances and since autonomy is, according to liberalism, what makes individuals valuable both to themselves and to their fellow creatures, oppression which thwarts individuality must be condemned by the liberal view.[19]

One might now point out that this may very well be the case in traditional communities, but how about multicultural liberal societies? Surely people living in liberal societies have more chances to change their life. However, we have to remember that even in the pluralistic societies some communities, whether religious or respecting other traditional norms, can be very coercive and violate autonomy by forcing (using physical, mental or social coercion) their members to accept the existing norms as moral truth. An even more telling argument to prove coercion and lack of autonomy in this case is the fact that female circumcision is generally carried out on small children, the age range being anywhere from one week to 14 years. Children of this age do not yet have an understanding of what is being done to them and why. Thus, they are not autonomous agents. Neither do they have any means of avoiding this physically and mentally violent and painful ritual.[20] This empirical evidence shows that this particular tradition is based on strong paternalism containing constraint, coercion and other prima facie condemnable autonomy-restricting elements and thus would have to be rejected by the liberal view.[21]

I shall now summarise the first part and restate why female circumcision cannot be defended as a cultural tradition by the principles of liberalism within liberal, multicultural societies. Firstly, female circumcision violates individual rights and harms individuals by causing pain and physical damage. Secondly, it violates the liberal principle of equal respect by suppressing women as a group. Since sexuality can be considered to be an important part of humanity, practicing this tradition denies women their sexuality, and subordinates women to the priorities and beliefs of men and thus denies part of women's value as equal human beings. Thirdly, and perhaps most importantly, women and children involved with this tradition cannot be considered to be autonomous decision-makers in the way liberal theory requires. Their decisions are rather based on ignorance, false beliefs and social pressure and leave these women in traditional societies no option but go along with the custom. This ritual victimizes little children with unnecessary violence and physical harm that will limit their opportunities to choose the best possible life for themselves in the future.

However plausible this argumentation is philosophically, it has still not convinced everyone living in a pluralist liberal democracy. In fact, what is interesting here is that it appears that those who most explicitly doubt this conclusion come from two totally opposite quarters; either they are radically subjectivist liberals who swear in the name of individual autonomy, disregarding the actual social suppression of this very same autonomy, or they are radically relativist traditionalists who still appeal to the argument for autonomy in order to promote the rights of minority cultures.

THE PROBLEMS OF THE RIGHTS OF MINORITY CULTURES

Next I want to move on from the liberal argument to the possible communitarian counter-arguments. I do this because many people, especially those from more traditional cultures, still see that political liberalism does not take its promise of multiculturalism and pluralism seriously, but instead comes down on the side of Western cultural imperialism. They see that liberal demands for equality and autonomy are in fact used to integrate all the other cultures into the dominant Western culture and that liberal pluralism is nothing but an illusion. In order to avoid this total cultural integration within liberal society there are still many people, whether immigrants or cultural traditionalists, who see that liberal pluralism and toleration mean that different cultural groups within a liberal society should be able to maintain their own cultural practices, whatever these practices might be, without any interference from the state. These groups could then attempt to justify the practice of female circumcision by, for instance, appealing to cultural rights and traditional values which individuals as members of particular social groups want to maintain.

Those people who promote tradition and established common values are often labelled as communitarians, because it is the communitarian theorists who have made the point that liberalism's individualist premises are unacceptable. Communitarians see that any conception of an individual always presupposes some view of society and community, since all individuals are social beings—and that ethical pluralism appears primarily in the practices of different communities rather than in the 'free choices' of individuals. The best-known communitarian critics of liberalism such as Alasdair MacIntyre, Michael Sandel, Charles Taylor and Michael Walzer, emphasise that all the values and norms we have chosen we have chosen as members of a particular community.[22] The Communitarians' claim that the principles of justice are apparently rooted in history, discourse and traditions of actual communities seem therefore to be legitimate. According to MacIntyre, a person's life can be understood only by looking at his actions within a story, a 'narrative.' Thus an understanding of oneself can be attained only in the context of the community that has shaped one's narrative. But MacIntyre's view of the form of these communities is generally limited to the family, the tribe, and the neighbourhood, and other 'communitarian' communities rather than to the state, the nation, class or other political communities. Indeed, the state, and particularly a liberal state, according to MacIntyre, exhibits a confusion of values, lacking even a shared understanding of the content of values. Therefore MacIntyre believes that a liberal state cannot hold any common moral beliefs; beliefs which are, however, necessary for a community to be genuine.[23]

Communitarians hit home in pointing out the problems the liberals have with the image of self. However, the communitarian model of a socially-embedded self has also its problems. The problem, though, is that it is equally abstract and leaves little space for the autonomous choices of individuals. For instance, Sandel's account of the constituted self has a risk of drowning the self in a sea of experience and circumstance. The danger is that the self becomes identical with the values, goals, and beliefs of community.[24] The communitarian image of the self also implies a conception of community which is in contrast to the individualist conception. The communitarian community is more than a mere association. It is a unity in which the individuals are members and it appears that this membership is neither artificial nor instrumental, but rather has its own intrinsic value. Michael Walzer describes community as community of character with a special sense of common life to be morally valuable and socially good. Thus, Walzer regards membership in a human community not only as a condition for participation in the state's provision of good, but also as a distributed good in itself; in fact, as a primary good that we can distribute to one another.[25] In general, the communitarian concept of community refrains from separating moral community, political community and cultural community from one another. It seems then that the communitarian view promotes nation states and small traditional communities. But if moral, political community and cultural community cannot be separated from each other, traditions such as female circumcision that oppress the weak may be accepted. As Amy Gutman has noted, a great deal of intolerance has come from societies of selves so confidently situated that they were sure repression would serve a higher cause. The common good of the Puritans of seventeenth century Salem commanded them to hunt witches; the common good of the Moral Majority of the twentieth century has commanded them not to tolerate homosexuals.[26] The apparent, morally unsatisfactory, practical consequences of communitarian politics could then lead to forms of cultural relativism.

Cultural relativism as an ethical stance assumes that there is no culture whose customs and beliefs dominate all others in a moral sense. If moral beliefs depend upon supporting existing social practices for their validity, there are standards by which to evaluate the cultural practices of different communities. When cultural relativism is taken to an extreme any practice of an indigenous society can be theoretically defended merely on the ground that it is a local custom, and outsiders' discussions of local violations of human rights, for instance, can be criticized as unwarranted, ideological interference. When taken to this absolutist extreme the term 'cultural relativism' implies that all cultures are morally or ethically equal and that there should be no judgements made of their cooperative, intrinsic worth. What is, and what ought to be, are the same thing. Radical, cultural relativism then holds that culture is the sole source of the validity of a moral right or rule.[27] Since cultures are not comparable, individual human rights are not universal, and no one, and particularly no Westerner, has the right to discuss ways in which other cultures could or should reorient their ethical or social systems. Thus, if cultural relativism could be seen as a consistent ethical stand, even inhuman traditions such as female circumcision could be justified by it.

The main question, then, is, *can* cultural relativism be seen as a consistent ethical stand by any one who promotes ethical pluralism? I shall next examine the tenability of two arguments, concerning alien traditions and practices which relativists have presented against pluralism which is based on the liberal universal moral standards of human rights. These arguments are also applicable in the case of female circumcision.

The relativists, for instance, claim that universalism is unattainable because, in practice, individual human rights are not protected worldwide. This argument implies a claim that something that one lacks is not meaningful. For countries that have not known peace and stability, civil and political rights have no meaning. Apparently, one is not capable of speculating on what the qualify of one's life would be if one had that which one lacks. Thus, circumcised women cannot miss the part of their sexuality and humanity which they never knew. This relativist argument, however, confuses the principles of universality with actual social practice, which is clearly not universal. This fallacy confuses the immediate existence of human rights with their possible legal and practical relevance.[28] One would not be likely to argue that the lack of access to nutrition means that starving people are indifferent to food. Quite the contrary. History shows that it is this lacking something that usually launches social movements for political change. People do envisage a life in which more of their rights are protected. To claim that what is not present is irrelevant, assumes that those who are denied rights do not have the intellectual capacity for autonomy and thus they cannot articulate their suffering and demand change.

The second relativist argument refers not to practice but to principle. Individual rights and human rights are untenable because in principle equal rights are not a universal cultural idea. This argument applies to the content of particular rights such as equality of sexes. The relativists may claim that because the belief that women are entitled to equal status as citizens is not universally accepted in African, Islamic or even Western societies, there are no valid grounds to believe that it *should* be accepted universally. However, at the same time the cultural relativist believes that cultural rights are universal, and thus the concept of right is universal, although its content varies among different societies. In fact, this radical cultural relativism could then be renamed cultural absolutism. This is a position according to which local cultural traditions, including religious, political, and legal practices, properly determine the existence and scope of civil and political rights enjoyed by individuals in a given society. But this is the key to the absolutist and universalistic perspective of the cultural relativists. For them, culture is the supreme value, more important than any other. Individual rights, in particular, should not be promoted if their implementation might result in a change in a particular culture. Instead the old values and customs should be respected. But the problem is then that the cultural relativists do not fully reject universalistic ethics as they claim to do.[29]

It appears to be clear that cultural relativism is not a logically consistent ethical stance. The fallacy of cultural relativism has been accurately pointed out by Bernard Williams in his *Morality* (1972). Williams claims that relativism consists of three propositions: that right can be coherently understood as meaning 'right for the given society'; that 'right for a given society' is to be understood in a functionalist sense; and that therefore it is wrong for people in one society to condemn and/or interfere with the values of another society. This view is clearly inconsistent, since it makes a claim in its third proposition, about what is right and wrong in one's dealings with other societies, which uses a nonrelative sense of right not allowed for in the first proposition.[30] Apart from its logically unhappy attachment of a non-relative morality of toleration or non-interference to a view of morality as relative, cultural relativism also has problems in identifying the relevant social unit. If culture, society or community is regarded as a moral unit, identified in part though its values, then it becomes bare tautology without any normative value: a necessary condition of the survival of a group-with-certain-values is that the group should retain those values. However, the survival of a society could also be understood in individualistic terms: as the survival of certain persons and their having descendants, in which case we would be led back to the liberal argumentation of pluralism.[31] This in fact is the case when cultural rights are promoted over individual rights. The conception of a right becomes even more vague if it is pinned on an abstract and evolving entity such as a culture. No social collective such as culture or community can be seen as a permanent entity. Culture characteristically changes and develops. And the development is attained by the work, interaction, and ideas of the individual members of the culture or cultures, in their striving for a more perfect society. Thus all social collectives are always composed of individuals, and can act only through the actions of their components. Whatever is said about any culture or community must at some stage be related and in some way reduced to discourse about the doings, beliefs, attitudes and dispositions of its individual components. Who actually did and thought what: and what led them to act and to think in the way they did, and not otherwise? The whole conception of cultural rights is then built on false premises and the only rights that maintain cultural pluralism are the rights of an individual as a member of a particular culture and community.

The central confusion of cultural relativism stems from its attempt to conjure out of the fact that societies have differing attitudes and values an a priori, non-relative principle to determine the attitude of one society to another. If we are going to say that there are ultimate moral disagreements between societies, we must include, in the matters that they can disagree about, their attitudes to other moral outlooks. Thus, we seem to have a universal *a priori* idea, at least about the existence of morality and its scope. It is also true that there are inherent features of morality that tend to make it difficult to regard a morality as applying only to a social unit. The element of universalisation which is present in any morality, but which applies under tribal morality perhaps only to members of the tribe, progressively comes to range over persons as such. It is essential to morality and its role in any society that certain sorts of reactions and motivations should be strongly internalised, and these cannot merely evaporate because one is confronted with human beings in another society.[32]

If the communitarians accept cultural relativism as an ethical stance they face the same contradiction which they accuse liberalism of in the case of subjectivism. If there are no criteria against which an individual can evaluate his or her values, communitarianism falls into the same Nietzschean nihilism with which it charges liberalism. If an individual embedded in society and its values and traditions is given no reason to question them, talking about moral judgments becomes irrelevant and meaningless. Thus, if social justice is any system practised in different cultures, why should we even talk about the moral value of pluralism, or morality in general?

Therefore, even if every community may have its own traditions and values, it is too much to say that every community has its own moral standards. As Williams notes, there is no reason for general acceptance of any rituals or traditions just because they are accepted in another culture. Adaptive reactions are not the only correct ones. When we are confronted with practices that are inhuman, there is no a priori demand for acceptance; quite the contrary. And as Williams has stated, it would be absurd to regard the disapproval of inhuman traditions as merely parochial or self-righteous. While societies develop and interact with one another they tend to adapt to the good features of the other societies. On the other hand, if adaptive reactions were the only correct ones, there would be no reason to condemn the liberal principles of individual rights as cultural imperialism either.

These logically unhappy conclusions are surely not what the communitarian argumentation set out to achieve. It seems to me that the communitarian criticism of liberalism is either deliberately or inadvertently misinterpreted by the collectivist traditionalists in order to defend their 'way of life' against the individualism and alienation that the liberal agenda is thought to imply. This normative aspect of the communitarianism which is, at its heart, actually quite liberal, is easily lost or misinterpreted by both the traditionalists and, even, by the radical liberals. However, this liberalism of the communitarians does not help them to avoid the problem of relativism. Their relativism derives from their reluctance to regard any particular culture or political system as the best, much as liberal subjectivism derives from the liberal reluctance to define any particular way of life as the model of the good life. It is also obvious that the communitarian critics of liberalism did not mean that any community with common beliefs and values is the best that there can be any more than the liberals meant that any values and any action of an individual can be considered. Rather, good communities are only those that leave space for the autonomy of individuals, and good individuals are those who build communities that leave space for autonomy. Liberals as well as communitarians then both think in terms of 'reflection,' 'critical scrutiny,' and 'corrections' of beliefs in communities which are engaged in the process of public debate and self-criticism. MacIntyre's mirror-model of the self, for instance, which sees the self as the reflection of its traditions, is not meant to drown the self in its traditions, but the complexity of traditions is rather seen as fostering an immanent critique.[33]

THE INFLUENCE OF CULTURE IN A PLURALIST SOCIETY

The liberal or communitarian demand for ethical pluralism is not meant to be relativist, either in a subjectivist or culturally relativist sense, even if in practice it is often interpreted as leading into a nihilist society in which 'anything goes.' Instead, it is a form of value pluralism which has an objectivist foundation in the promotion of individuals' moral autonomy, i.e., individuals' autonomy as moral agents.

In the liberal argumentation, however, this autonomy is often taken as a presumption, and thus the actual autonomy of individuals is often overestimated, while in the communitarian argumentation the social values are regularly given priority and the potential moral autonomy of an individual, is for its part, underestimated. Even in liberal societies, pluralism, which should be defined as the proper toleration of a diversity of ideas, is easily confused with relativism, which claims that in the end there are no right or wrong answers in ethics or religion. Proper pluralism, however, whether liberal pluralism or communitarian pluralism, requires respecting the right to hold divergent beliefs. It implies neither the relativists' acceptance of actions based on those beliefs nor his respect of the content of these beliefs, if the beliefs can be proven to be incoherent, controversial or harmful. Pluralism and tolerance are then rather related to the development of reasoned moral viewpoints and to the willingness to recognize the existence of other views, rather then their acceptance as such. Thus, tolerance is not blind acceptance of divergent views. Instead it means emphatic but also critical assessments of differing perspectives. Tolerance requires that different cultures and moral systems should be critically evaluated and assessed. This means questioning the basis and validity of different norms, beliefs and value systems. If we accept that the communitarian approach promotes critical ethical pluralism rather than cultural relativism in moral matters, it is obvious that it also promotes moral autonomy.

The central moral foundation of ethical pluralism is the realization of individuals' moral agency. This same point of view on autonomy can also be seen in the writings of such liberals as Mill and even Rawls as well as in the communitarian criticism of liberal subjectivism. For both liberals and communitarians it is important that people can become aware of the options available to them, and intelligently examine their value, only through having a rich and secure cultural structure. Thus, culture and cultural membership can be seen as having intrinsic value; not as having some moral status of their own, but as providing the context of choice.[34] Liberals however, often tend to fail to take into account that the social attachments which determine the self are not necessarily chosen by an autonomous agent and that membership of a particular cultural community is not necessarily voluntary.[35]

Therefore, in practice, the actual issues of social and cultural ties have always to be taken into account without one's ignoring the normative aspects of the pluralist ideal of autonomous moral agency. In attempting to find the limits for tolerance in a multicultural society, Mill's remark that 'there is need for protection also against the tyranny of the prevailing opinion and feeling, against the tendency of society to impose, by other means than civil penalties, its own ideas and practices as rules of conduct on those who dissent from them' should be kept in mind. The issue, then, is not merely political coercion, but social 'coercion' as well. Political liberties appear to be a necessary, but not a sufficient, condition for individuals to prosper. The challenge is then to create a cultural climate, not only a political system, in which humans can flourish and grow. The human faculties of perception, judgement, discriminative feeling, mental activity, and even moral preference, are exercised only in making choices. If a custom is followed just because it is a custom, a person makes no choice and gains no practice either in discerning or in desiring what is best.[36]

Whether we discuss an individual's choice as an autonomous and rational moral agent or as a member of a particular community, we can agree that even in, or rather, particularly in, a pluralist society, dubious and ambiguous ethical judgments can be criticized on at least the three following accounts in order to find out the best solutions. First, when practices such as female circumcision are defended by reference to cultural differences, one can always question the factual accuracy of this defence. This means that we can ask not only why certain traditions are considered desirable, but by whom and on what grounds. If the goals can in general be accepted and desired, we can further question whether these traditions are really the best means to the given ends.[37] If, for instance, we examine the reasons given to explain why female circumcision is practised, we shall find out the following. Even if the origins of this tradition have been impossible to trace, a variety of other reasons will be advanced by its adherents for continuing to support the practice today. Some say it is just a means of suppressing female sexuality and attempting to ensure chaste or monogamous behaviour; others believe that it was started long ago among herders as a protection against rape for the young girls who took animals out to pasture. It is also said to be the trademark of the Egyptian slavemarket. Circumcised female slaves were sold for a higher price, because they were less likely to be sexually active and get pregnant. Some Muslim people believe that circumcision is religiously ordained, even if the Koran does not support this assumption. Other adherents believe that intact female genitalia are 'unclean,' that an uncircumcised women is likely to be promiscuous and even that the operation improves the life chances of a woman's offspring. Others say it is a ritual initiation into womanhood.[38] It is clear that none of these given reasons bears close scrutiny. They are, in fact rationalizations for a practice that has woven itself into the fabric of some societies so completely that 'reasons' are no longer particularly relevant, since even invalidating them does not stop the practice. These reasons as such give no moral justification for the tradition. This tradition—as well as many other ones—is thus based on prejudice, false beliefs, and ignorance, not on critical judgement of its justification. As Mill notes, the problem is that customs are not often questioned by individuals involved in them, because 'people are accustomed to believe and have been encouraged in the belief that their feelings are better than reason, and render reasons unnecessary.'[39]

Secondly, without giving up on tolerance it is also possible to challenge the consistency of the practices, norms and prohibitions prevailing in a culture as a whole. If we can point out that the moral code of a society is self-contradictory, the requirement of consistency could be seen to prevent rational individuals from accepting the dictates of the system. One cannot, for instance, appeal to the protection of autonomy in order to maintain autonomy-suppressive traditions.[40] And finally, if these internally-oriented critiques prove to be ineffective, the moral system under consideration can be conceptually extended. While it is true that moral judgements are always relative to ethical theories or shared opinions, it is by no means the case that only existent socio-cultural entities could be studied by moral philosophy. There is no reason why cultural traditions should be equalised as to moral standards, even if we accept that our social environment affects our values.[41]

The reasoned critical rejection of old values and practices on the basis of new facts or new knowledge, or new understanding of old facts, is important for the good of the community as well as for the good of an individual. This chance for internal criticism is demanded by both the liberals and the communitarians. This criticism is based on a person's ability to separate the empirical reasons from the justifications of the tradition, and one's moral identity from one's cultural identity. This separation can only be made in a society which encourages reflective and critical thinking as an essential part of human flourishing.

Both the liberals and the communitarians see the capacity to form independent moral convictions as an important part of human flourishing.[42] However, as we have seen, their common normative aspect is easily lost when their incompatible methodological premises abstract the image of self from real-life situations. The communitarian emphasis on common values and social ties leaves the image of self without the capacity for autonomy, whereas the liberal emphasis on the meaning of rationality in order to derive the principles of justice builds an image of an already autonomous self. Thus, both approaches appear to be more descriptive than normative accounts of justice. Liberals succeed in describing the abstract nature of justice. Communitarians manage to describe how it works in real societies. What both approaches miss is the sensitivity to combine these perspectives into a normative theory of social justice, that would tell us how we, as real persons, should act in order to achieve the good life, and how we could build a just society which truly protects its members and promotes the development of human beings as autonomous moral agents.

CONCLUSION

Normatively, liberals and communitarians both promote ethical pluralism. Curiously enough, despite their methodologically different approaches they both face the problems of relativism. In its attempt to refrain from defining any particular way of life as the model of the good life, the liberal theory falls easily into subjectivism. Communitarians, for their part, refrain from defining any particular communal system as the most desirable, and are thus faced with cultural relativism. However, both liberals and communitarians imply that a good political and social system gives rise to the autonomy of its individual members. In other words, both liberals and communitarians consider individual autonomy more than a mere instrument. Rather, it has a value of its own. Both individual rights and communal values are to be seen as a means to attain autonomy rather than be defended as an end in themselves.[43]

The value of autonomy is in its role in the development of traits of intellect and moral character in individuals who guide the progress of societies. In a multicultural and democratic society the greatest good for a man is neither enjoyment nor passive contentment, but rather a dynamic process of growth and self-realisation. The highest social good is then the greatest possible amount of individual self-realisation and (assuming that different persons are inclined by their natures in different ways) the resultant diversity and fullness of life. Self-realisation consists in the actualisation of certain uniquely human potentialities, the bringing to full development of certain powers and abilities such as moral judgement. This in turn requires constant practice in making difficult choices among alternative hypotheses, policies, and actions. One does not realise what is best in oneself if social pressures to conform to custom lead one mindlessly along or when one is not given a choice in the first place, either 'because of being kept in ignorance or because of being terrorised by the wielders of bayonets.'[44]

When the normative requirement of pluralism is discussed in a multicultural democracy it is important to make a distinction between a belief or a tradition and its justification. It is apparent that most people go through life with a whole world of beliefs and adapt to practices that lack rational justification. Thus, the only way for a society to evolve and strive for the better is to question the justification of the existing practices and traditions. As even the communitarian forefather Aristotle noted, the old customs might sometimes be too simple and barbaric and thus they should be rejected, because 'In general, all human beings seek not the way of their ancestors, but the good.'[45] In short, I have attempted to show in this article that the ritual of female circumcision is one of these barbaric traditions and can have no moral justification in a pluralistic and multicultural society, whether we appeal to the liberal promotion of one's personal autonomy or to the communitarian promotion of common values.

READING ENDNOTES

1. In this context I have chosen not to discuss the moral justification of male circumcision which also has its horrors, particularly if operated in more severe versions than the relatively minor one adopted in Western societies. The reason for this exclusion is that for a male circumcision there is sometimes still a medical justification as in the uncommon event of problems such as phimosis, i.e. scarring of the foreskin and balanitis, i.e. infection of the foreskin. There are, however, no good medical reasons for female circumcision.

2. There are also two other types of female circumcision. 1. Circumcision proper, known in Muslim countries as sunna (which also means 'traditional'), is the mildest but also the rarest form. It involves the removal only of the clitoral prepuce. 2. Excision involves the amputation of the whole of the clitoris and all or part of the labia minora. In these milder forms female circumcision is reported from some countries in Asia, too. WHO (1986) A traditional practice that threatens health—female circumcision, *WHO Chronicle*, 40(I): pp. 31–36.

3. *WHO Chronicle* 40(I)(1986): pp. 31–36.

4. Adverse effects of the infibulation of physical health are as follows. The immediate dangers of the operation are haemorrhage and shock from acute pain, infection of the wounds, urine retention and damage to the urethra or anus. Gynaecological and genitourinary effects are haematocolpos, keloid formation, implantation dermoid cysts, chronic pelvic infection, calculus formation, dyspareimia, infertility, urinary tract infection and difficulty of micturition. Obstetric effects are perineal lacerations, consequences of anterior episiotomy e.g. blood loss, injury to bladder, urethra or rectum, late urine prolapse, puerperal sepsis, delay in labour and its consequences, e.g.: vesicovaginal and rectovaginal fistulae, fetal loss, fetal brain damage. *WHO Chronicle* 40(I)(1986): pp. 32–33.

5. Chandran Kukathas (1992) Are there any cultural rights? *Political Theory*, Vol. 20, No. 1, pp. 105–139; Will Kymlicka (1989) *Liberalism, Community and Culture* (Oxford, Clarendon Press); Will Kymlicka (1992) Response to Kukathas, *Political Theory*, Vol. 20, No. 1, pp. 140–146. For instance, the conception of human rights is based on the above presumptions. Human rights are considered in international law to be rights held equally by every individual by virtue of his or her humanity, and for no other reason: Rhoda Howard (1993) Cultural absolutism and the nostalgia for community *Human Rights Quarterly*, Vol. 15, No. 2, pp. 315–338.

6. This central assumption in John Rawls (1971) *Theory of Justice* (Cambridge, Harvard University Press) is taken from Kant's moral theory: see for example Immanuel Kant (1990) (orig. 1785). Social contract as an idea of reason in Michal Lessnoff (ed.) *Social Contract Theory* (Oxford, Basil Blackwell), pp. 124–137.

7. Kukathas, *Political Theory*, Vol. 20, No. 1, pp. 108, 118–109, Kymlicka, *op. cit.* 1989, 11–13, 164–166.

8. Ronald Dworkin (1977) *Taking Rights Seriously* (London, Duckworth); Joel Feinberg (1973) *Social Philosophy* (Englewood Cliff, Prentice-Hall) and Rawls *op. cit.*, p. 244.

9. See for example Rawls, *op. cit.*, pp. 3–22, 586–587; also in Michael Sandel (1982) *Liberalism and the Limits of Justice* (Cambridge, Cambridge University Press), pp. 1–14, 15–66.

10. Another concern is that rejecting harmful ritual like female circumcision outright could have ever more serious consequences. Ritual may simply be practised with greater secrecy and may result in even worse health complications.

11. John Stuart Mill (1986) *On Liberty* (orig. 1859) (New York, Prometheus Books) p. 16.

12. Gerald Dworkin (1972) Paternalism, *The Monist* 56: pp. 64–84.

13. Feinberg, *op. cit.*, p. 45.

14. Heta Häyry (1991) *The Limits of Medical Paternalism* (London, Routledge), pp. 54–55.

15. Häyry, *op. cit.*, pp. 19–77.

16. Coercion typically involves explicit or implicit threats and being conditionally structured: if you do not agree to do something unpleasant the coercer will see to it (or at least claim that he will see to it) that something even more unpleasant will happen to you or perhaps to somebody else (family, friends). A successful instance of coercion has occurred when the coercer (whether state or an individual) has managed to get you to do what he wants as result of a threat to interfere with your person, or your interests, either by positively attacking you (and your interests) or by withholding benefit from you. See the argumentation on this issue in Häyry, H., *op. cit.*, pp. 74-77.

17. *WHO Chronicle*, 40(I)(1986), p. 33.

18. Häyry, *op. cit.*, p. 75.

19. Feinberg, *op. cit.*, pp. 21-22, Rawls *op. cit.*, p. 261.

20. *WHO Chronicle*, 40(I)(1986): p. 32. The operation is usually performed by the traditional mid-wife, who carries out mutilation while a number of women, including the child's female relatives, hold the victim down to prevent her from fighting. It is only rarely that even local anaesthetics are used to ease the pain.

21. Liberals then would have not only a right but a duty to interfere, not only when this tradition consenting to physical harm is practised within a liberal society but also when it is practised in non-Western cultures which do not respect the equal moral status of all human beings. This interference itself should not be coercive, but it can be done by invalidating the reasons that maintain the practice by giving adequate information on the physical and sexual aspects involved and educating women in general. Helping women to achieve better living standards and improving their position gives them a better chance to make independent and well-grounded judgements about their own culture and its practices. After all, probably the best way to change unreasonable and inhuman traditions is reasoned critique from within the culture itself.

22. On communitarian criticism of liberalism in detail, see, for example, Sandel *op. cit.*, 1982; Alasdair MacIntyre (1984) *After Virtue* (London, Duckworth); Alasdair MacIntyre (1990). The privatization of good, an Inaugural Lecture, *The Review of Politics*, 4; Charles Taylor (1973) *Hegel and the Modern Society* (Cambridge, Cambridge University Press); Charles Taylor (1989) *Sources of the Self: The Making of Moral Identity* (Cambridge, Cambridge University Press); Michael Walzer (1990) The Communitarian critique of liberalism, *Political Theory*, Vol. 18, No. 1, pp. 6–23; Michael Walzer (1987) *Interpretation and Social Criticism* (Cambridge, Harvard University Press); and Michael Walzer (1983) *Spheres of Justice* (New York, Basic Books).

23. MacIntyre, *op. cit.*, 1990, pp. 346–352.

24. C. Fred Alford (1991) *The Self in Social Theory* (New Haven, Yale University Press), pp. 10–11.

25. Walzer, 1987, *op. cit.*, pp. 65–84.
26. Amy Gutman (1992) Communitarian critics of liberalism in Avineri & De-Shalit (eds.) *Communitarianism and Individualism* (New York, Oxford University Press), p. 132.
27. Howard, *Human Rights Quarterly, op. cit., loc. cit.*
28. *Ibid.*, p. 317.
29. *Ibid.*, pp. 318–319.
30. Bernard Williams (1972) *Morality* (Cambridge, Cambridge University Press), pp. 34–35.
31. Williams, *op. cit.*, p. 35.
32. Williams, *op. cit.*, p. 37.
33. Alford, *op. cit.*, pp. 16–17.
34. Kukathas, *op. cit.*, p. 119; Rawls, *op. cit.*, pp. 560–564.
35. Mill, *op. cit.*, pp. 65–67, for his part, sees the individual's capacity for autonomy as an essential but also a vulnerable feature of humanity. Mill points out that this vulnerability has to be taken into account when we discuss real-life situations and the justification of traditions. The sensitivity to the role of culture prevents Mill for overestimating a person's real autonomy, in the way in which Rawls's theory of justice does. It also prevents Mill from underestimating a person's capacity for autonomy, as the communitarians do. Mill's arguments promoting cultural plurality rest on human happiness, which requires intellectual and moral growth. Happiness and the good life, then, require not only freedom from interference, but also cultural diversity. This diversity provides concrete, living alternatives, life experiments that will facilitate intellectual growth and moral development.
36. *Ibid.*, p. 67.
37. Matti Häyry (1992) Moral relativism and the philosophical criticism of other cultures, *Science Studies* Vol. 5, No. 1, pp. 53–56.
38. *WHO Chronicle* 1986, p. 33.
39. Mill, *op. cit.*, p. 12.
40. Häyry, 1992, *op. cit.*, p. 55.
41. These three arguments for relative absoluteness of philosophical ethics appear in Häyry, *ibid., loc. cit.*
42. Kymlicka, *op. cit.*, pp. 164–165.
43. Häyry *op cit.*, p. 46. To further detect the instrumental value of freedom in liberal theory, we can interpret either how particular liberties or the sum of all liberties can be seen as prerequisites for attaining certain good and desirable things such as happiness or human flourishing. An essential part of this flourishing is to use autonomous reasoning and judgement to make one's choices and to lead one's own life. For instance, we can study a variety of freedoms and liberties such as freedom of expression: this has been defended referring to the value embodied in truth. Again, political liberties have been supported by reference to justice, equality, rationality and good government. All the goals referred to are valuable because they promote autonomy, which for its part is an essential part of human flourishing.
44. Feinberg, *op. cit.*, pp. 21–22.
45. Aristotle (1985) *Politics. The Complete Works of Aristotle: The Revised Oxford Translation,* Jonathan Barnes (ed.) (Princeton, Princeton University Press), 1258a39ff. Aristotle also criticizes Plato's idea that the state should be as much in unity as possible. Aristotle says, 'Plurality of numbers is natural in a state; and the farther it moves away from plurality towards unity, the less state (as democracy) it becomes.' Aristotle, *op. cit.*, 1261a10.

QUESTIONS

1. How does Hellsten characterize the core commitments of liberals to (1) individualism, (2) egalitarianism, and (3) universalism?

2. Why do these three core commitments support value pluralism and tolerance?

3. What are the moral limits on liberty within liberalism? Do these go beyond those recognized in libertarianism?

4. What does it mean to say that right is prior to the good within liberalism?

5. What three reasons are given for thinking that female circumcision violates liberal principles? Spell out the arguments.

6. What is the difference between general paternalism and non-paternalistic interventions that promote autonomy? Why does the distinction matter to liberals? Can it be made without taking a stand upon controversial claims about the good and conflicting values?

7. In what way are the conditions surrounding female circumcision coercive and oppressive? Do the same conditions raise similar concerns about the widespread practice of male circumcision in Western societies?

8. What moral relevance attaches to the fact that female circumcision is almost always practiced on girls when they are still children?

9. What is the communitarian critique of liberal individualism?

10. What theory of value is basic to communitarianism?

11. What is the danger implicit in the communitarian understanding of communities and their authority to set values for their members?

12. What is ethical relativism? Why is it inconsistent with a commitment to human rights, tolerance, and value pluralism? In what way is radical cultural relavism internally, logically incoherent?

13. Why does Hellsten reject the idea of cultural rights? What is the false premise she thinks they rest on?

14. What is the proper understanding of pluralism and tolerance, according to Hellsten? How do they have their foundation in the requirement to promote individual moral autonomy?

15. What status do the values of community and cultural membership have for liberals? Is it an unconditional value?

16. Why is it important to take the critical stance advocated by Hellsten in evaluating the traditional practices and rituals of cultures? What is the connection between this critical stance and critical moral reasoning?

✦ ✦ ✦

Barry Buzan, Who May We Bomb?

Although not couched in terms of liberalism, Barry Buzan's article is firmly grounded in the liberal tradition. Self-defence is a legitimate motive for action, even if it brings about harm to the aggressor. A man coming at you with a knife is likely bent on harming you, and you (or another) may use all due force to restrain that man to avoid that harm. However, not all lengths are legitimate. In general, innocent lives may not be (purposefully) sacrificed. Should you protect yourself by throwing another person in the knife-wielding maniac's path, you would be doing that person an injustice. Nowhere is the tension between legitimate self-defence and the harming of those who have done no wrong more visible than in the case of general war.

When thinking about war, the common response is to separate the civilian populations from the soldiers and the government; civilian immunity is the rule. Civilians are to be left alone, while the latter two are seen as legitimate targets (in a just war). This clear distinction dissolves, Buzan argues, when one considers whether or not a given population is responsible for their government. When people are not responsible for their government's actions, then this separation is clearly correct. The citizens of Iraq bear little responsibility for the actions of the recently removed heads of the Iraqi state. When the people are responsible for their government, and by implication for the government's actions, then the case gets trickier. If the population is responsible for the government, and thus for the harm it does, then it seems that simply removing the government does not remove the threat of harm. The population will reinstate mechanisms to bring about that harm again. In our example above, consider the possibility that there was a person behind the maniac's attack. Acting merely to neutralize the maniac does not remove the threat of harm. Self-defence seems to permit further action. Insofar as this is the case, people responsible for or supportive of a government that harms others are themselves legitimate targets.

Hard questions arise regarding how pre-emptive a strike may be. We need not wait until the maniac actually starts cutting before we begin to defend ourselves, but some legitimate limits are obviously going to be necessary. The magnitude of the potential harm and the likelihood of its being brought about are also going to have to be considered. While these types of considerations may seem overwhelming, a principled response is surely required given the magnitude of the decision to go to war.

✦ ✦ ✦

Barry Buzan, "Who May We Bomb?" from *Worlds in Collision: Terror and the Future of Global Order*, eds. Ken Booth and Tim Dunne (Hampshire: Palgrave Macmillan, 2002). © Barry Buzan 2002. Reprinted with permission of the author.

Who May We Bomb?

BARRY BUZAN

When war breaks out, who is a legitimate target?[1] The near-universal revulsion at the September 11 attacks shows that the civilians in the World Trade Center were not a legitimate target—even for those who oppose American power. The shift of the conflict to Afghanistan made the question of who may be bombed central to the legitimacy of the whole campaign against terrorism. Since the American war on terrorism is open-ended, the possibility of further American attacks on targets in Iraq, the Philippines, Somalia and Sudan, or in principle anywhere, remains on the agenda. The question can be fought over on both moral and legal grounds without any decisive answer resulting. But it is also a political and historical question, and it is that angle that I want to explore here. A political approach rests on the questions of how we (and by 'we' I mean the Western democracies) define who our enemies are, and what are we trying to achieve when we resort to war.

The idea that in war, peoples and their governments should be treated separately, has recently become something of a Western fetish, a way of asserting the West's claim to be civilized. In the war against Iraq, great efforts were made to avoid civilian casualties. Similarly, the air war against Serbia targeted the Milosevic regime and its supporting structures. The distinction between combatants and civilians has solid and valuable legal standing in the Geneva Conventions on the laws of war. But that distinction should not lead to the assumption, now becoming a centerpiece of the Western way in war, that all civilians are innocent and that only evil leaderships are the enemy. The Geneva Conventions are aimed at the protection of prisoners, the wounded and civilians, and they impose a range of restrictions on the conduct of war. But they do not outlaw war, nor do they solve the problem of how to distinguish between civilian and military actors.

The exclusion of civilians from definitions of 'enemy' contrasts markedly with the West's behaviour up until quite recently. During the Second World War there was far less concern to draw a distinction between peoples and governments, and both sides freely bombed each other's cities. The home front (production, logistics, conscription) was understood to be as much a part of the military enterprise as the fighting front. No clearer statement of the linkage between government and people could be made than the nuclear incinerations of Hiroshima and Nagasaki. The Cold War was more nuanced in its rhetoric, but much the same in practice. The West made communism the enemy rather than the Russian, the Chinese or the Korean people, but the nuclear arsenals would have obliterated their cities just the same. In Vietnam, as in all guerilla wars, drawing a civilian-military distinction was extremely problematic. As Mao Tse-tung understood, the whole point of guerilla strategy is to blend the fighters into a supportive population.[2] This blending bears some resemblance to the present dilemma about terrorists, who also hide in, and draw support from civilian populations. The idea that one has to make war on terrorists, opposed to dealing with them as criminals, is soberingly captured by the following remark attributed to Egyptian president Hosni Mubarak, 'Those who carry out terrorist acts have no claims to human rights.'[3] To understand wars, whether to fight them or to resolve them, it is vital to appreciate that they are conducted not just between groups of fighters but between groups of fighters and their networks of support. The distinction between military and civilian has to be understood in that context.

Three factors have contributed to the West's new policy of separating bad governments from their peoples. The first hinges on advances in technology. Since the 1970s, and increasingly over the past decade, it has become possible to deliver warheads with great accuracy to a target. Precision weapons now provide choices about what is and what is not targeted that were not available in earlier wars. This does make a difference, but one side-effect of the 'revolution in military affairs' (RMA) has been to establish unrealistic public expectations of precision in the use of force. Any collateral damage is used by Western critics, and even by target regimes, to cast moral doubt on military action.

The second factor is an evolution in public morality in the West which at least since the abolition of slavery has been increasingly committed to the idea that all peoples have the right to equal and decent treatment. By combining its technology and its values, the West is able to project its values by injecting an element of law and humanitarianism into the bloody business of war.

Third, Western governments calculate that narrowing the definition of enemy to evil leaderships is in their interests. In the mosaic of historically rooted cultural conflicts that replaced the big ideological divisions of the Cold War, separating peoples from their leaderships during war has many advantages. It moderates charges of cultural imperialism, of one civilization (usually the West) trying to impose its values on others, and it invites the overthrow of tyrants from within, thus keeping open the option of a people remaking itself and gaining quick re-entry into international society. If people can be made to do some or all of the work of removing their bad governments, then the West's casualties are reduced and the legitimacy of both the action and its outcome are increased.

These technological, moral and instrumental explanations for the West's separation of peoples and governments suggests that it is both morally desirable and efficient. But before accepting this view, one needs to return to the questions about how enemies are defined and what wars are fought for. A useful way into the issues is to ask, 'Do people get the governments they deserve?' During the Second World War, the Western answer was broadly 'Yes.' This understanding legitimized mass destruction attacks and the forced remaking of Japan and Germany under occupation regimes.

During the Cold War there was much more ambivalence about the linkage of governments and peoples and a tendency to assume that many of the peoples in the Eastern bloc did not get the governments they deserved. The populations of Eastern Europe definitely, and that of the Soviet Union more arguably, could be seen as victims of a coup, and thus as prisoners of their own governments. It is this position that has now been extended to most post-Cold War conflicts. There are some exceptions— conspicuously in US attitudes toward the Islamic revolution in Iran—but from North Korea through to Burma, Iraq, Libya, Serbia, and most recently to Afghanistan, the West's policy separates bad governments from their peoples and constructs its military strategy accordingly. Doing so supposes that people do not deserve their governments. Is this true?

At one end of the spectrum stand well-rooted democracies with traditions of individual rights, a broad franchise and regular elections. In democracies the demos consequently shares some responsibility for the government's foreign policy, whether people bother to vote or not. Citizens in democracies do deserve their governments. An extreme version of this link between people and government can be found in the Israel/Palestine confrontation. Arab radicals see no civilian sector in Israel. The Israelis have democracy, a large proportion of the Israeli adult population is in the military reserve and it is common for Israelis to carry, and use, guns. Israeli militants return the compliment by thinking of the Palestinians in much the same terms, as people united in the pursuit of terrorism. War is cast as an affair between peoples.

Also easy to determine are the cases at the other end of the spectrum, most obviously when countries have their governments imposed by an outside power. In the present international system, this condition is rare, though it might be claimed by Tibetans, Kurds, Kashmiris and other minorities who find themselves prisoners within states not of their own making. Most recently, it was exemplified by Eastern Europe under Soviet occupation. It is true that occupiers are usually assisted by parts of the local population, as the British were in India and the Nazis were in Europe. But as a rule, peoples under occupation are not responsible for their own governments.

The middle part of the spectrum is taken up by authoritarian governments of various sorts, which can be differentiated according to their degree of mass support. Just behind democracies come countries where mass revolutionary or nationalist regimes command wide support or acquiescence. These would include communist China, Vietnam, Cuba, Nazi Germany and Imperial Japan. Peoples in countries where the government has come to power through popular revolution, or has mass national support, do deserve the governments they get, and this explains the long political hangovers that still affect the Japanese and Germans in international society.

At the centre of the spectrum are countries with authoritarian regimes that command mass acquiescence rather than support. The commonest form of this is found in countries where military rule gains acceptance as a means of restoring stability. One thinks of cases such as Pakistan or, earlier, Nigeria, Brazil, Chile and Argentina. Acquiescence, of course, can be coerced, making the price of individual resistance high and allowing a minority who do support the government to rule over the rest. Such coercion is usually visible, allowing distinctions to be drawn between passive acceptance and terrorized obedience.

Toward the clearly undeserving end of the spectrum one finds blatant tyrannies such as in Burma, Iraq, Syria, Uganda under Amin, Haiti under the Duvaliers, and Zaire under Mobutu. The existence of repression may well be evident in its own right. It may also be shown when substantial sections of the population put up active resistance but fail to unseat the regime or secede from the state. Burma and Sudan are contemporary examples of such failed rebellions, as in some ways is Iraq.

This spectrum suggests a range of fairly clear answers to whether or not people deserve their governments. Yet there are cases where it is impossible to make a judgement. How can one tell whether the North Korean regime has mass support/acquiescence, or is just very efficient at repression and indoctrination? What does one do with split countries where the government is supported by one section of the population and opposed by another, as in Israel, Sudan, Sri Lanka, Turkey and, up to 1994, South Africa? Here one finds a combination of democracy for some of the population and repression for the rest. It would be difficult to argue that the Kurds in Turkey, the Palestinians in Israel or the southerners in Sudan get the governments they deserve.

Equally difficult questions arise about countries with strong structures of tribe and clan, such as Afghanistan, Congo, Libya, Somalia, Iraq, Indonesia and Saudi Arabia. In such places, the choice seems to be between dictatorship and chaotic political disintegration. In the case of Afghanistan, the US declared al-Qaeda and the Taliban to be the enemy. But how much support did the Taliban have amongst the population? They must have had some in order to take over most of the country as swiftly as they did, though they never eliminated armed opposition from the non-Pashtun areas. How much of that support represented real enthusiasm, and how much a simple desire to have any government in place of civil war? Democracy at the level of the state is almost impossible in places where the population is of multiple ethnicities/cultures and where there are not strong social structures shared by the people as a whole. If the state is not held together coercively, it falls apart. It is not clear, for example, that Libya or Iraq would end up with a different type of leadership than the ones they now have, if Gaddafi and Saddam Hussein were removed. In post-Taliban Afghanistan, this question is being put to the test. If it can be claimed that the social structures of a people lead with some certainty to dictatorship or anarchy, are the people who reproduce the cultures collectively responsible?

Culturalist approaches of this sort, or those that focus on ethnic or religious stereotypes, contain the danger of validating radical and xenophobic views, and of promoting 'clash of civilizations' thinking.[5] There is also the problem that any resort to such cultural generalizations has to be preceded by yet another question: what is the historical connection between people and the state they inhabit? In cases where the people have played a role in creating the state over time, the answer is clear.

Swedes, Haitians, Egyptians, Iranians, Chinese, Japanese, Americans, French and many other peoples would accept a close identity between themselves and the states they inhabit. But there are many cases where this link is weak or non-existent, most obviously in post-colonial countries.[6] States such as Congo, Iraq, Jordan, Nigeria and Syria have shallow traditions and artificial borders. Since decolonization, they have been held in place by the system of diplomatic recognition that makes them members of international society. Some post-colonial states have taken root and acquired legitimacy, especially those that corresponded in some degree to pre-colonial history, such as India and Vietnam. Many have not. The peoples who live in Sudan, Angola, Indonesia, Chad or Guyana cannot be held responsible for the states they occupy. Where the state itself has failed to take root amongst its people, this often determines what type of government they get.

In sum, the question of whether people get the governments they deserve can often be answered quite simply on the basis of day-to-day observations about the relationship between the demos and the government. This type of observation cannot always give a reliable answer, but is more useful than either sweeping generalizations about culture or simple assumptions that all civilians are innocent.

This brings us back to the question of whether the current Western habit of separating peoples from their leaders makes for better or worse war policy. There can be no doubt that it constrains the sort of military pressure that can be brought to bear. It forces the West into the curious posture, first seen in the war against Iraq, of worrying almost as much about enemy casualties as about its own; and risks undermining support for action when—as is inevitable—civilians are killed by mistake. There is a self-justifying humanitarian argument for keeping casualties to a minimum, as well as the legal constraint of the Geneva Conventions. There is also the instrumental case that such an approach helps to reduce the costs of conflict and makes political rehabilitation easier. Where people do not deserve the government they get, separating the two as far as possible must be imperative in any war policy.

But what of cases where peoples do deserve their governments? Here the questions are trickier. The problem is that if people really do deserve their government, and yet only the government is targeted, the country as a whole remains politically unreconstructed and thus a continuing danger to itself and to the international community. The crushing defeat of both states and peoples in Germany and Japan in the Second World War was instrumental in converting those countries into liberal democracies able to fit comfortably into the international community of the West. The remaking of the two countries is rightly regarded as a huge success and played a big role in the victory of the West in the Cold War.

To take a more recent case, what should the Western response have been during the air war against Serbia when civilians stood on the bridges to prevent them from being bombed? If they were there as a result of conspicuous coercion, then the bridges should not have been bombed. But if they were there as a demonstration of support for the Milosevic government then they made themselves legitimate targets. To delink people from their governments, when they are in fact closely linked, is to undermine the political point of resorting to war in the first place. In the end, war is about changing people's minds about what sort of government they want.

Looked at in this way of thinking, Afghanistan was a difficult case. It is not an arbitrary post-colonial construct, but neither is it a coherent self-made historical state. Afghan politics is typically fragmented and fractious, with many local chiefs commanding their own fighters. The Taliban certainly attracted many who actively backed it, but perhaps the bulk of its support was in the form of acquiescence, itself partly as a result of effective coercion. During recent decades there was also a great deal of foreign intervention in Afghanistan's domestic politics, which, by changing the internal balance of power, played a major role in determining what sort of government the Afghans got, whether they wanted it or not. Pakistan's role in bringing the Taliban to power was only the latest in a long line of interventions both by Afghanistan's neighbours and by interested great powers. And in a warrior culture like Afghanistan's (or Somalia's), where most men are armed and fighting is a way of life, distinguishing soldiers from civilians is deeply problematic. The picture was thus very mixed. Some Afghans clearly did deserve the government they got, and demonstrated this by supporting its policies and fighting on its behalf. Those who did so made themselves legitimate military targets. Many did not support the Taliban, and demonstrated that by their opposition or by flight. Many were in the middle, acquiescing either out of indifference or fear. Since the Taliban chose to make Afghanistan a danger to international society by allying itself with terrorists, its supporters, and up to a point those who acquiesced, were legitimate military targets. Only by dismantling its concentric circles of support and acquiescence could the Taliban, or any government, be overthrown, and space be created for a government that was more acceptable to both international society and to the Afghan people as a whole. Given the foreign, including US, interventions in its politics in the past, outsiders had a responsibility both to be quite selective in their violence, and to stay engaged in the process of building a new Afghanistan.

Unlike in Serbia, and arguably also Iraq, the West got it about right in Afghanistan. Those elements in the country that were enemies were spared to the extent feasible, given the limits of the technology and uncertainties about who was who. An interesting question that thankfully did not have to be answered was what the West should have done if events had unfolded such that Pakistan had begun to fall apart, and who might be in control of its nuclear weapons had come into doubt. Given the unbounded extremism of al-Qaeda, and the close relationship between Pakistan's intelligence service and the Taliban, the West would have had to make every effort to destroy Pakistan's nuclear arsenal, including, if necessary the use of nuclear weapons.

Looking ahead, the open-ended character of the war against terrorism poses several questions about who may be bombed. Given the unusual character of this 'war,' it may well not pose cases where questions about peoples and governments are a key feature in shaping military action. The main problem for the 'war against terrorism' will be the longstanding political ambiguity of 'terrorists' versus freedom fighters. If the enemy is defined as anyone using extreme methods of violence then the US will be dragged into endless domestic conflicts around the world. It will find itself in alignment with a variety of unsavoury governments, and without nearly all of its present coalition allies. If the war is against al-Qaeda, and any similar outfits (call them international terrorists) that have declared war on international society, then the campaign becomes more manageable. The use of violence against the bases of such organizations, and against any political authorities who support or tolerate them, would be politically legitimate.

Iraq, Somalia and Sudan have all been mooted as possible targets. How to deal with them depends on how terrorism is defined. On the narrow answer, these states only become targets if there is evidence that they are complicit in international terrorism, or that they themselves pose threats to international peace and security. The problem in Somalia is not the Afghan one of a government and/or people constructing itself as an enemy. Rather it is that Somalia has no coherent government, and this political chaos can allow space for international terrorists to operate autonomously. Military strikes there would have to be highly selective against the specific targets of international terrorism and their local supporters. Sudan appears to have been cooperative against al-Qaeda, so the question of military action may well not arise. At the moment there is almost no evidence against Iraq, and since US motives in relation to Iraq are poisoned by other issues, the evidence necessary for the US to attack Iraq under the aegis of the war on terrorism would have to be extremely compelling for the action to acquire political legitimacy. In many places, including within the West, the operations of international terrorists will be hidden within the social framework, and not obviously the knowing responsibility of either governments or citizens. Here the problem is not one of military strategy but one of policing and surveillance, and how these are kept in balance with civil liberties. Between war and police action lie military assistance operations, such as the one in the Philippines, where assistance is given to governments to fight 'terrorists' within their own territory.

Pacifists and the more dedicated type of humanitarians will find these arguments about applied violence unacceptable in principle. A case can be made that the answer to 'Who may we bomb?' should be 'Nobody.' The argument made above is only for those who believe that war still has a role to play in a complex, interdependent and conflictual world, and that the role needs to be both carefully constrained and fully considered. The military strategy and the political logic of war require careful specification of who the enemy is. A blanket assumption that all civilians are innocent will often not be justified. Whether or not people deserve their governments can be a tough question, but answers to it have to be found if ideas about humanitarian intervention are ever to acquire intellectual and political coherence.[7] International society has the right to confront governments and peoples that pose unacceptable threats to peace. If force is going to be used against a country in pursuit of civilizational objectives, the question of citizen responsibility has to be answered before appropriate military strategies can be devised. If the people clearly do not deserve the government they get, then military strategy must be devised as far as possible to target only the state and its army—as has been the case in recent Western interventions. But if people do deserve the government they get, and if the government is in gross breach of standards of civilization, then, as in the Second World War, the war should be against government and people.

READING ENDNOTES

1. An earlier version of this argument was presented in *Prospect* magazine, December 2001, pp. 38–41 (<www.prospect-magazine.co.uk>).
2. Mao Tse-tung, *On Guerrilla Warfare* (New York: Praeger, 1961).
3. *Economist*, February 2, 2002, p. 52.
4. Lawrence Freedman, 'The Revolution in Strategic Affairs', *Adelphi Paper 318*, London: IISS (1998).
5. Samuel P. Huntington, *The Clash of Civilizations and the Remaking of World Order* (New York: Simon and Schuster, 1996).
6. Bertrand Badie, *The Imported State: The Westernization of Political Order* (Stanford, CA: Stanford University Press, 2000).
7. James Mayall, *World Politics: Progress and Its Limits* (Cambridge: Polity Press, 2000); Nicholas J. Wheeler, *Saving Strangers: Humanitarian Intervention in International Society* (Oxford, Oxford University Press, 2000).

QUESTIONS

1. Is the war on terrorism different in kind than previous kinds of wars? Explain.

2. What are the three factors that Buzan believes explains the recent Western policy of separating evil governments (who are the enemy in war) from the civilian populations of target countries: the technological, moral, and instrumental?

3. Buzan links the following questions: "Who may we bomb?" and "Do people deserve their governments?" What is the connection between these two questions?

4. What is the difference between mass support and mass acquiescence for a government? In what way does it affect the degree to which a people deserve their government?

5. How do anarchy and dictatorship support each other?

6. Buzan's analysis supports the conclusion that the extent to which a people deserve their government is a matter of degree. Explain.

7. Why should we distinguish between civilian populations and governments in states where the people do not deserve their government? To what extent are questions of responsibility relevant to this issue?

8. Why should we not separate civilian populations from their governments in states where people do deserve their government? What are the instrumental reasons that Buzan gives for thinking that we should not? Are their also moral reasons for treating civilians as legitimate military targets in such cases?

9. What does Buzan think is the main point of war? Is this unduly narrow? Does it fit the history of warfare as you know it?

10. Is there a neutral way of distinguishing between terrorists and freedom fighters?

11. Must a government or a people pose a threat to international security before it can be a legitimate target of military action by outsiders?

12. Buzan's contention is that if a people do not deserve their government then military action should be confined to action against the government only, whereas if a people do deserve their government then the people become a legitimate target of military action along with their government. What does this imply about the legitimacy of military action against civilian populations in Western democracies? What does it imply about the legitimacy of the attack on the World Trade Center on September 11, 2001? What does it imply about the ability of the West to intervene in non-Western countries to repress international terrorism, civil war, or brutal dictatorships?

◆ ◆ ◆

Hugh Lafollette, Licensing Parents

Hugh Lafollette argues for the initially implausible claim that the state should require all parents to be licensed. Going even further, he suggests that parenting is one of the paradigmatic example of a practice that requires licensing. The argument proceeds via an examination of currently licensed practices. What makes it legitimate to license these practices (for example driving or performing surgery) is that engaging in these activities without a demonstrated level of competence entails an unacceptably high risk of harm to others. Nevertheless, with a demonstrated level of competence, such activities have a high value to society. Banning such activities if licensing is a viable option, then, seems an unduly harsh application of the harm principle. The lesson to draw from this, Lafollette suggests, is that if an activity is potentially harmful but the risk of that harm can be minimized by requiring a demonstrated competency, then that activity ought to be licensed. Examining the practice of parenting, it seems clear that it fits the bill. Parenting can be very harmful to children, but if you are even basically competent, this minimizes the risks to the child. Our intuitions regarding the legitimacy of investigating adoptive parents certainly supports Lafollette's claim: surely nothing about one's being either a birth parent or adoptive parent entails that a child is or is not due such caution. Objections to this line of thought are ultimately attributed to our (mistaken) belief that children are the property of parents. This property claim cannot stand up to critical examination.

Within the initially implausible claim that we ought to license parents we find one of the strengths of liberalism. In recognizing the value of autonomy, and a derivative duty to nurture autonomy, liberals come to value those who are not yet autonomous. Libertarians, by way of contrast, value only the autonomous, and have a great deal of difficulty in defeating the ownership model of parent/child relations.

◆ ◆ ◆

Hugh Lafollette, "Licensing Parents." *Philosophy and Public Affairs* 9:2 (Winter 1980): 182–197. © 1980 Princeton University Press. Reprinted by permission of Princeton University Press.

Licensing Parents

HUGH LAFOLLETTE

In this essay I shall argue that the state should require all parents to be licensed. My main goal is to demonstrate that the licensing of parents is theoretically desirable, though I shall also argue that a workable and just licensing program actually could be established.

My strategy is simple. After developing the basic rationale for the licensing of parents, I shall consider several objections to the proposal and argue that these objections fail to undermine it. I shall then isolate some striking similarities between this licensing program and our present policies on the adoption of children. If we retain these adoption policies—as we surely should—then, I argue, a general licensing program should also be established. Finally, I shall briefly suggest that the reason many people object to licensing is that they think parents, particularly biological parents, own or have natural sovereignty over their children.

REGULATING POTENTIALLY HARMFUL ACTIVITIES

Our society normally regulates a certain range of activities; it is illegal to perform these activities unless one has received prior permission to do so. We require automobile operators to have licenses. We forbid people from practicing medicine, law, pharmacy, or psychiatry unless they have satisfied certain licensing requirements.

Society's decision to regulate just these activities is not ad hoc. The decision to restrict admission to certain vocations and forbid some people from driving is based on an eminently plausible, though not often explicitly formulated, rationale. We require drivers to be licensed because driving an auto is an activity which is potentially harmful to others, safe performance of the activity requires a certain competence, and we have a moderately reliable procedure for determining that competence. The potential harm is obvious: incompetent drivers can and do maim and kill people. The best way we have of limiting this harm without sacrificing the benefits of automobile travel is to require that all drivers demonstrate at least minimal competence. We likewise license doctors, lawyers, and psychologists because they perform activities which can harm others. Obviously they must be proficient if they are to perform these activities properly, and we have moderately reliable procedures for determining proficiency.[1] Imagine a world in which everyone could legally drive a car, in which everyone could legally perform surgery, prescribe medications, dispense drugs, or offer legal advice. Such a world would hardly be desirable.

Consequently, any activity that is potentially harmful to others and requires certain demonstrated competence for its safe performance, is subject to regulation—that is, it is theoretically desirable that we regulate it. If we also have a reliable procedure for determining whether someone has the requisite competence, then the action is not only subject to regulation but ought, all things considered, to be regulated.

It is particularly significant that we license these hazardous activities, even though denying a license to someone can severely inconvenience and even harm that person. Furthermore, available competency tests are not 100 percent accurate. Denying someone a driver's license in our society, for example, would inconvenience that person acutely. In effect that person would be prohibited from working, shopping, or visiting in places reachable only by car. Similarly, people denied vocational licenses are inconvenienced, even devastated. We have all heard of individuals who had the "life-long dream" of becoming physicians or lawyers, yet were denied that dream. However, the realization that some people are disappointed or inconvenienced does not diminish our conviction that we must regulate occupations or activities that are potentially dangerous to others. Innocent people must be protected even if it means that others cannot pursue activities they deem highly desirable.

Furthermore, we maintain licensing procedures even though our competency tests are sometimes inaccurate. Some people competent to perform the licensed activity (for example, driving a car) will be unable to demonstrate competence (they freeze up on the driver's test). Others may be incompetent, yet pass the test (they are lucky or certain aspects of competence—for example, the sense of responsibility—are not tested). We recognize clearly—or should recognize clearly—that no test will pick out all and only competent drivers, physicians, lawyers, and so on. Mistakes are inevitable. This does not mean we should forget that innocent people may be harmed by faulty regulatory procedures. In fact, if the procedures are sufficiently faulty, we should cease regulating that activity entirely until more reliable tests are available. I only want to emphasize here that tests need not be perfect. Where moderately reliable tests are available, licensing procedures should be used to protect innocent people from incompetents.[2]

These general criteria for regulatory licensing can certainly be applied to parents. First, parenting is an activity potentially very harmful to children. The potential for harm is apparent: each year more than half a million children are physically abused or neglected by their parents.[3] Many millions are psychologically abused or neglected— not given love, respect, or a sense of self-worth. The results of this maltreatment are obvious. Abused children bear the physical and psychological scars of maltreatment throughout their lives. Far too often they turn to crime.[4] They are far more likely than others to abuse their own children.[5] Even if these maltreated children never harm anyone, they will probably never be well-adjusted, happy adults. Therefore, parenting clearly satisfies the first criterion of activities subject to regulation.

The second criterion is also incontestably satisfied. A parent must be competent if he is to avoid harming his children; even greater competence is required if he is to do the "job" well. But not everyone has this minimal competence. Many people lack the knowledge needed to rear children adequately. Many others lack the requisite energy, temperament or stability. Therefore, child-rearing manifestly satisfies both criteria of activities subject to regulation. In fact, I dare say that parenting is a paradigm of such activities since the potential for harm is so great (both in the extent of harm any one person can suffer and in the number of people potentially harmed) and the need for competence is so evident. Consequently, there is good reason to believe that all parents should be licensed. The only ways to avoid this conclusion are to deny the need for licensing *any* potentially harmful activity; to deny that I have identified the standard criteria of activities which should be regulated; to deny that parenting satisfies the standard criteria; to show that even though parenting satisfies the standard criteria there are special reasons why licensing parents is not theoretically desirable; or to show that there is no reliable and just procedure for implementing this program.

While developing my argument for licensing I have already identified the standard criteria for activities that should be regulated, and I have shown that they can properly be applied to parenting. One could deny the legitimacy of regulation by licensing, but in doing so one would condemn not only the regulation of parenting, but also the regulation of drivers, physicians, druggists, and doctors. Furthermore, regulation of hazardous activities appears to be a fundamental task of any stable society.

Thus only two objections remain. In the next section I shall see if there are any special reasons why licensing parents is not theoretically desirable. Then, in the following section, I shall examine several practical objections designed to demonstrate that even if licensing were theoretically desirable, it could not be justly implemented.

THEORETICAL OBJECTIONS TO LICENSING

Licensing is unacceptable, someone might say, since people have a right to have children, just as they have rights to free speech and free religious expression. They do not need a license to speak freely or to worship as they wish. Why? Because they have a right to engage in these activities. Similarly, since people have a right to have children, any attempt to license parents would be unjust.

This is an important objection since many people find it plausible, if not self-evident. However, it is not as convincing as it appears. The specific rights appealed to in this analogy are not without limitations. Both slander and human sacrifice are prohibited by law; both could result from the unrestricted exercise of freedom of speech and freedom of religion. Thus, even if people have these rights, they may sometimes be limited in order to protect innocent people, Consequently, even if people had a right to have children, that right might also be limited in order to protect innocent people, in this case children. Secondly, the phrase "right to have children" is ambiguous; hence, it is important to isolate its most plausible meaning in this context. Two possible interpretations are not credible and can be dismissed summarily. It is implausible to claim either that infertile people have rights to be *given* children or that people have rights to intentionally create children biologically without incurring any subsequent responsibility to them.

A third interpretation, however, is more plausible, particularly when coupled with observations about the degree of intrusion into one's life that the licensing scheme represents. On this interpretation people have a right to rear children if they make good-faith efforts to rear procreated children the best way they see fit. One might defend this claim on the ground that licensing would require too much intrusion into the lives of sincere applicants.

Undoubtedly one should be wary of unnecessary governmental intervention into individuals' lives. In this case, though, the intrusion would not often be substantial, and when it is, it would be warranted. Those granted licenses would face merely minor intervention; only those denied licenses would encounter marked intrusion. This encroachment, however, is a necessary side-effect of licensing parents—just as it is for automobile and vocational licensing. In addition, as I shall argue in more detail later, the degree of intrusion arising from a general licensing program would be no more than, and probably less than, the present (and presumably justifiable) encroachment into the lives of people who apply to adopt children. Furthermore, since some people hold unacceptable views about what is best for children (they think children should be abused regularly), people do not automatically have rights to rear children just because they will rear them in a way they deem appropriate.[6]

Consequently, we come to a somewhat weaker interpretation of this right claim: a person has a right to rear children if he meets certain minimal standards of child rearing. Parents must not abuse or neglect their children and must also provide for the basic needs of the children. This claim of right is certainly more credible than the previously canvassed alternatives, though some people might still reject this claim in situations where exercise of the right would lead to negative consequences, for example, to overpopulation. More to the point, though, this conditional right is compatible with licensing. On this interpretation one has a right to have children only if one is not going to abuse or neglect them. Of course the very purpose of licensing is just to determine whether people *are* going to abuse or neglect their children. If the determination is made that someone will maltreat children, then that person is subject to the limitations of the right to have children and can legitimately be denied a parenting license.

In fact, this conditional way of formulating the right to have children provides a model for formulating all alleged rights to engage in hazardous activities. Consider, for example, the right to drive a car. People do not have an unconditional right to drive, although they do have a right to drive if they are competent. Similarly, people do not have an unconditional right to practice medicine; they have a right only if they are demonstrably competent. Hence, denying a driver's or physician's license to someone who has not demonstrated the requisite competence does not deny that person's rights. Likewise, on this model, denying a parenting license to someone who is not competent does not violate that person's rights.

Of course someone might object that the right is conditional on actually being a person who will abuse or neglect children, whereas my proposal only picks out those we can reasonably predict will abuse children. Hence, this conditional right *would* be incompatible with licensing.

There are two ways to interpret this objection and it is important to distinguish these divergent formulations. First, the objection could be a way of questioning our ability to predict reasonably and accurately whether people would maltreat their own children. This is an important practical objection, but I will defer discussion of it until the next section. Second, this objection could be a way of expressing doubt about the moral propriety of the prior restraint licensing requires. A parental licensing program would deny licenses to applicants judged to be incompetent even though they had never maltreated any children. This practice would be in tension with our normal skepticism about the propriety of prior restraint.

Despite this healthy skepticism, we do sometimes use prior restraint. In extreme circumstances we may hospitalize or imprison people judged insane, even though they are not legally guilty of any crime, simply because we predict they are likely to harm others. More typically, though, prior restraint is used only if the restriction is not terribly onerous and the restricted activity is one which could lead easily to serious harm. Most types of licensing (for example, those for doctors, drivers, and druggists) fall into this latter category. They require prior restraint to prevent serious harm, and generally the restraint is minor—though it is important to remember that some individuals will find it oppressive. The same is true of parental licensing. The purpose of licensing is to prevent serious harm to children. Moreover, the prior restraint required by licensing would not be terribly onerous for many people. Certainly the restraint would be far less extensive than the presumably justifiable prior restraint of, say, insane criminals. Criminals preventively detained and mentally ill people forceably hospitalized are denied most basic liberties, while those denied parental licenses would be denied only that one specific opportunity. They could still vote, work for political candidates, speak on controversial topics, and so on. Doubtless some individuals would find the restraint onerous. But when compared to other types of restraint currently practiced, and when judged in the light of the severity of harm maltreated children suffer, the restraint appears *relatively* minor.

Furthermore, we could make certain, as we do with most licensing programs, that individuals denied licenses are given the opportunity to reapply easily and repeatedly for a license. Thus, many people correctly denied licenses (because they are incompetent) would choose (perhaps it would be provided) to take counseling or therapy to improve their chances of passing the next test. On the other hand, most of those mistakenly denied licenses would probably be able to demonstrate in a later test that they would be competent parents.

Consequently, even though one needs to be wary of prior restraint, if the potential for harm is great and the restraint is minor relative to the harm we are trying to prevent—as it would be with parental licensing—then such restraint is justified. This objection, like all the theoretical objections reviewed, has failed.

PRACTICAL OBJECTIONS TO LICENSING

I shall now consider five practical objections to licensing. Each objection focuses on the problems or difficulties of implementing this proposal. According to these objections, licensing is, (or may be) theoretically desirable; nevertheless, it cannot be efficiently and justly implemented.

The first objection is that there may not be, or we may not be able to discover, adequate criteria of "a good parent." We simply do not have the knowledge, and it is unlikely that we could ever obtain the knowledge, that would enable us to distinguish adequate from inadequate parents.

Clearly there is some force to this objection. It is highly improbable that we can formulate criteria that would distinguish precisely between good and less than good parents. There is too much we do not know about child development and adult psychology. My proposal, however, does not demand that we make these fine distinctions. It does not demand that we license only the best parents; rather it is designed to exclude only the very bad ones.[7] This is not just a semantic difference, but a substantive one. Although we do not have infallible criteria for picking out good parents, we undoubtedly can identify bad ones—those who will abuse or neglect their children. Even though we could have a lively debate about the range of freedom a child should be given or the appropriateness of corporal punishment, we do not wonder if a parent who severely beats or neglects a child is adequate. We know that person isn't. Consequently, we do have reliable and useable criteria for determining who is a bad parent; we have the criteria necessary to make a licensing program work.

The second practical objection to licensing is that there is no reliable way to predict who will maltreat their children. Without an accurate predictive test, licensing would not only be unjust, but also a waste of time. Now I recognize that as a philosopher (and not a psychologist, sociologist, or social worker), I am on shaky ground if I make sweeping claims about the present or future abilities of professionals to produce such predictive tests. Nevertheless, there are some relevant observations I can offer.

Initially, we need to be certain that the demands on predictive tests are not unreasonable. For example, it would be improper to require that tests be 100 percent accurate. Procedures for licensing drivers, physicians, lawyers, druggists, etc., plainly are not 100 percent (or anywhere near 100 percent) accurate. Presumably we recognize these deficiencies yet embrace the procedures anyway. Consequently, it would be imprudent to demand considerably more exacting standards for the tests used in licensing parents.

In addition, from what I can piece together, the practical possibilities for constructing a reliable predictive test are not all that gloomy. Since my proposal does not require that we make fine line distinctions between good and less than good parents, but rather that we weed out those who are potentially very bad, we can use existing tests that claim to isolate relevant predictive characteristics—whether a person is violence-prone, easily frustrated, or unduly self-centered. In fact, researchers at Nashville General Hospital have developed a brief interview questionnaire which seems to have significant predictive value. Based on their data, the researchers identified 20 percent of the interviewees as a "risk group"—those having great potential for serious problems. After one year they found "the incidence of major breakdown in parent-child interaction in the risk group was approximately four to five times as great as in the low risk group."[8] We also know that parents who maltreat children often have certain identifiable experiences, for example, most of them were themselves maltreated as children. Consequently, if we combined our information about these parents with certain psychological test results, we would probably be able to predict with reasonable accuracy which people will maltreat their children.

However, my point is not to argue about the precise reliability of present tests. I cannot say emphatically that we now have accurate predictive tests. Nevertheless, even if such tests are not available, we could undoubtedly develop them. For example, we could begin a longitudinal study in which all potential parents would be required to take a specified battery of tests. Then these parents could be "followed" to discover which ones abused or neglected their children. By correlating test scores with information on maltreatment, a usable, accurate test could be fashioned. Therefore, I do not think that the present unavailability of such tests (if they are unavailable) would count against the legitimacy of licensing parents.

The third practical objection is that even if a reliable test for ascertaining who would be an acceptable parent were available, administrators would unintentionally misuse that test. These unintentional mistakes would clearly harm innocent individuals. Therefore, so the argument goes, this proposal ought to be scrapped. This objection can be dispensed with fairly easily unless one assumes there is some special reason to believe that more mistakes will be made in administering parenting licenses than in other regulatory activities. No matter how reliable our proceedings are, there will always be mistakes. We may license a physician who, through incompetence, would cause the death of a patient; or we may mistakenly deny a physician's license to someone who would be competent. But the fact that mistakes are made does not and should not lead us to abandon attempts to determine competence. The harm done in these cases could be far worse than the harm of mistakenly denying a person a parenting license. As far as I can tell, there is no reason to believe that more mistakes will be made here than elsewhere.

The fourth proposed practical objection claims that any testing procedure will be intentionally abused. People administering the process will disqualify people they dislike, or people who espouse views they dislike, from rearing children.

The response to this objection is parallel to the response to the previous objection, namely, that there is no reason to believe that the licensing of parents is more likely to be abused than driver's license tests or other regulatory procedures. In addition, individuals can be protected from prejudicial treatment by pursuing appeals available to them. Since the licensing test can be taken on numerous occasions, the likelihood of the applicant's working with different administrative personnel increases and therefore the likelihood decreases that intentional abuse could ultimately stop a qualified person from rearing children. Consequently, since the probability of such abuse is not more than, and may even be less than, the intentional abuse of judicial and other regulatory authority, this objection does not give us any reason to reject the licensing of parents.

The fifth objection is that we could never adequately, reasonably, and fairly enforce such a program. That is, even if we could establish a reasonable and fair way of determining which people would be inadequate parents, it would be difficult, if not impossible, to enforce the program. How would one deal with violators and what could we do with babies so conceived? There are difficult problems here, no doubt, but they are not insurmountable. We might not punish parents at all—we might just remove the children and put them up for adoption. However, even if we are presently uncertain about the precise way to establish a just and effective form of enforcement, I do not see why this should undermine my licensing proposal. If it is important enough to protect children from being maltreated by parents, then surely a reasonable enforcement procedure can be secured. At least we should assume one can be unless someone shows that it cannot.

AN ANALOGY WITH ADOPTION

So far I have argued that parents should be licensed. Undoubtedly many readers find this claim extremely radical. It is revealing to notice, however, that this program is not as radical as it seems. Our moral and legal systems already recognize that not everyone is capable of rearing children well. In fact, well-entrenched laws require adoptive parents to be investigated—in much the same ways and for much the same reasons as in the general licensing program advocated here. For example, we do not allow just anyone to adopt a child; nor do we let someone adopt without first estimating the likelihood of the person's being a good parent. In fact, the adoptive process is far more rigorous than the general licensing procedures I envision. Prior to the adoption the candidates must first formally apply to adopt a child. The applicants are then subjected to an exacting home study to determine whether they really want to have children and whether they are capable of caring for and rearing them adequately. No one is allowed to adopt a child until the administrators can reasonably predict that the person will be an adequate parent. The results of these procedures are impressive. Despite the trauma children often face before they are finally adopted, they are five times less likely to be abused than children reared by their biological parents.[9]

Nevertheless we recognize, or should recognize, that these demanding procedures exclude some people who would be adequate parents. The selection criteria may be inadequate; the testing procedures may be somewhat unreliable. We may make mistakes. Probably there is some intentional abuse of the system. Adoption procedures intrude directly in the applicants' lives. Yet we continue the present adoption policies because we think it better to mistakenly deny some people the opportunity to adopt than to let just anyone adopt.

Once these features of our adoption policies are clearly identified, it becomes quite apparent that there are striking parallels between the general licensing program I have advocated and our present adoption system. Both programs have the same aim—protecting children. Both have the same drawbacks and are subject to the same abuses. The only obvious dissimilarity is that the adoption requirements are *more* rigorous than those proposed for the general licensing program. Consequently, if we think it is so important to protect adopted children, even though people who want to adopt are less likely than biological parents to maltreat their children, then we should likewise afford the same protection to children reared by their biological parents.

I suspect, though, that many people will think the cases are not analogous. The cases are relevantly different, someone might retort, because biological parents have a natural affection for their children and the strength of this affection makes it unlikely that parents would mistreat their biologically produced children.

Even if it were generally true that parents have special natural affections for their biological offspring, that does not mean that all parents have enough affection to keep them from maltreating their children. This should be apparent given the number of children abused each year by their biological parents. Therefore, even if there is generally such a bond, that does not explain why we should not have licensing procedures to protect children of parents who do not have a sufficiently strong bond. Consequently, if we continue our practice of regulating the adoption of children, and certainly we should, we are rationally compelled to establish a licensing program for all parents.

However, I am not wedded to a strict form of licensing. It may well be that there are alternative ways of regulating parents which would achieve the desired results—the protection of children—without strictly prohibiting nonlicensed people from rearing children. For example, a system of tax incentives for licensed parents, and protective services scrutiny of nonlicensed parents, might adequately protect children. If it would, I would endorse the less drastic measure. My principal concern is to protect children from maltreatment by parents. I begin by advocating the more strict form of licensing since that is the standard method of regulating hazardous activities.

I have argued that all parents should be licensed by the state. This licensing program is attractive, not because state intrusion is inherently judicious and efficacious, but simply because it seems to be the best way to prevent children from being reared by incompetent parents. Nonetheless, even after considering the previous arguments, many people will find the proposal a useless academic exercise, probably silly, and possibly even morally perverse. But why? Why do most of us find this proposal unpalatable, particularly when the arguments supporting it are good and the objections to it are philosophically flimsy?

I suspect the answer is found in a long-held, deeply ingrained attitude toward children, repeatedly reaffirmed in recent court decisions, and present, at least to some degree, in almost all of us. The belief is that parents own, or at least have natural sovereignty over, their children.[10] It does not matter precisely how this belief is described, since on both views parents legitimately exercise extensive and virtually unlimited control over their children. Others can properly interfere with or criticize parental decisions only in unusual and tightly prescribed circumstances—for example, when parents severely and repeatedly abuse their children. In all other cases, the parents reign supreme.

This belief is abhorrent and needs to be supplanted with a more child-centered view. Why? Briefly put, this attitude has adverse effects on children and on the adults these children will become. Parents who hold this view may well maltreat their children. If these parents happen to treat their children well, it is only because they want to, not because they think their children deserve or have a right to good treatment. Moreover, this belief is manifestly at odds with the conviction that parents should prepare children for life as adults. Children subject to parents who perceive children in this way are not likely to be adequately prepared for adulthood. Hence, to prepare children for life as adults and to protect them from maltreatment, this attitude toward children must be dislodged. As I have argued, licensing is a viable way to protect children. Furthermore, it would increase the likelihood that more children will be adequately prepared for life as adults than is now the case.

READING ENDNOTES

For helpful comments and criticisms, I am indebted to Jeffrey Gold, Chris Hackler, James Rachels, and especially to William Aiken, George Graham, and the Editors of the journal. A somewhat different version of this essay will appear in the Proceeding of the Loyola University (Chicago) Symposium, *Justice for the Child within the Family Context.*

Thanks are due to the directors of the symposium for kind permission to publish the essay in *Philosophy & Public Affairs.*

1. "When practice of a profession or calling requires special knowledge or skill and intimately affects public health, morals, order or safety, or general welfare, legislature may prescribe reasonable qualifications for persons desiring to pursue such professions or calling and require them to demonstrate possession of such qualifications by examination on subjects with which such profession or calling has to deal as a condition precedent to the right to follow that profession or calling." 50 SE 2nd 735 (1949). Also see 199 US 306, 318 (1905) and 123 US 623, 661 (1887).
2. What counts as a moderately reliable test for these purposes will vary from circumstance to circumstance. For example, if the activity could cause a relatively small amount of harm, yet regulating that activity would place extensive constraints on people regulated, then any tests should be extremely accurate. On the other hand, if the activity could be exceedingly harmful but the constraints on the regulated person are minor, then the test could be considerably less reliable.

3. The statistics on the incidence of child abuse vary. Probably the most recent detailed study (Saad Nagi, *Child Maltreatment in the United States*, Columbia University Press, 1977) suggests that between 400,000 and 1,000,000 children are abused or neglected each year. Other experts claim the incidence is considerably higher.

4. According to the National Committee for the Prevention of Child Abuse, more than 80 percent of incarcerated criminals were, as children, abused by their parents. In addition, a study of the *Journal of the American Medical Association* 168, no. 3: 1755–1758, reported that first-degree murderers from middle-class homes and who have had "no history of addiction to drugs, alcoholism, organic disease of the brain, or epilepsy" were frequently found to have been subject to "remorseless physical brutality at the hands of the parents."

5. "A review of the literature points out that abusive parents were raised in the same style that they have recreated in the pattern of rearing children. ... An individual who was raised by parents who used physical force to train their children and who grew up in a violent household has had as a role model the use of force and violence as a means of family problem solving." R. J. Gelles, "Child Abuse as Psychopathology—a Sociological Critique and Reformulation," *American Journal of Orthopsychiatry* 43, no. 4 (1973): 618–19.

6. Some people might question if any parents actually believe they should beat their children. However, that does appear to be the sincere view of many abusing parents. See, for example, case descriptions in *A Silent Tragedy* by Peter and Judith DeCourcy (Sherman Oaks, CA.: Alfred Publishing Co., 1973).

7. I suppose I might be for licensing only good parents if I knew there were reasonable criteria and some plausible way of deciding if a potential parent statisfied these criteria. However, since I don't think we have those criteria or that method, nor can I seriously envision that we will discover those criteria and that method, I haven't seriously entertained the stronger proposal.

8. The research gathered by Altemeir was reported by Ray Helfer in "Review of the Concepts and a Sampling of the Research Relating to Screening for the Potential to Abuse and/or Neglect One's Child." Helfer's paper was presented at a workshop sponsored by the National Committee for the Prevention of Child Abuse, 3–6 December 1978.

9. According to a study published by the Child Welfare League of America, at least 51 percent of the adopted children had suffered, prior to adoption, more than minimal emotional deprivation. See *A Follow-up Study of Adoptions: Post Placement Functioning of Adoption Families*, Elizabeth A. Lawder *et al.*, New York 1969.

   According to a study by David Gil (*Violence Against Children*, Cambridge: Harvard University Press, 1970) only .4 percent of abused children were abused by adoptive parents. Since at least 2 percent of the children in the United States are adopted (*Encyclopedia of Social Work*, National Association of Social Workers, New York, 1977), that means the rate of abuse by biological parents is five times that of adoptive parents.

10. We can see this belief in a court case chronicled by DeCourcy and DeCourcy in *A Silent Tragedy*. The judge ruled that three children, severely and regularly beaten, burned, and cut by their father, should be placed back with their father since he was only "trying to do what is right." If the court did not adopt this belief would it even be tempted to so excuse such abusive behavior? This attitude also emerges in the all-too-frequent court rulings (see S. Katz, *When Parents Fail*, Boston: Beacon Press, 1971) giving custody of children back to their biological parents even though the parents had abandoned them for years, and even though the children expressed a strong desire to stay with foster parents.

   In "The Child, the Law, and the State" (*Children's Rights: Toward the Liberation of the Child*, Leila Berg *et al.*, New York: Praeger Publishers, 1971), Nan Berger persuasively argues that our adoption and foster care laws are comprehensible only if children are regarded as the property of their parents.

QUESTIONS

1. Why is it not only permissible but required that liberal societies regulate potentially harmful activities, where the danger of harm is to others, through such things as licensing schemes?

2. In what way is parenting potentially dangerous to others? In what way does it require a range of competence to perform adequately (so as not to realize the harm that will result if done incompetently)?

3. Lafollette considers an objection to licensing parents that someone might raise on the grounds that people have a right to have children and a licensing scheme would violate that right. What does such a right amount to? Is it absolute or *prima facie*, negative or positive?

4. Why does Lafollette think that such a right must be conditional on the parent being competent and willing to not abuse or neglect the child and provide for its basic needs? Could it be anything else? Can you imagine taking seriously the claim of a would-be parent who said, "I have a right to have a child whom I intend to abuse, neglect and not provide for"?

5. What does this understanding of the right imply about women who take narcotics during pregnancy, or smoke cigarettes, or have HIV/AIDS?

6. Lafollette argues that the restraint of requiring potential parents to get a licence before having children is not very onerous compared with a number of other practices we engage in (such as locking up criminals and the insane). But why is this the comparison by which onerousness is tested, rather than how important being a parent is to people in terms of their overall life plans and conceptions of the good life?

7. Lafollette considers the practical objection to his recommended licensing scheme as that we cannot distinguish between good and bad parents. What is his response? Is it plausible?

8. Lafollette considers the practical objection to his recommended licensing scheme as that we cannot reliably predict who will be bad parents (abusive or neglectful). What is his response? Is it plausible?

9. Lafollette considers the practical objection to his recommended licensing scheme as that those who administer it would unintentionally abuse the system. What is his response? Is it plausible?

10. Does his response to the worry about abuse in the administration of a licensing scheme for parents adequately address the more systemic kinds of bias that operate in societies like ours: racial prejudice, homophobia, religious intolerance, ignorance, and fear of minority cultural traditions, etc.?

11. Lafollette considers the practical objection to his recommended licensing scheme as that the system would be unenforceable. What is his response? Is it plausible?

12. How strong is the analogy between licensing parents and our current regulations of adoption? Do the systemic biases that have plagued our adoption system (e.g., against same sex couples and single women) indicate that Lafollette must take the worries of abuse and unjust administration in the system more seriously than he does?

13. Could we achieve many of the desired results through a system of mandatory counselling and training in parenting skills for all women who become pregnant? Would this be less intrusive than a licensing scheme?

14. Do you agree with Lafollette's hypothesis that underlying our objections to restrictions of parental rights is an assumption that parents own or have sovereignty over their biological children? Does this explain a great many of our current practices with respect to parents, privacy, and decision-making authority for minors?

15. Why is the current attitude about the relationship between parents and children morally unacceptable? Do we need a liberation movement for children analogous to that for racial minorities, women, and animals?

CHAPTER SIX

FEMINISM

———

INTRODUCTION

As with many of the theories we have previously examined, feminism is not a single univocal view. There are many different feminist theories, as well as practical proposals for understanding and implementing feminist goals. But feminists are united by their acceptance of two simply stated claims, one descriptive and the other normative. The descriptive claim is this: all human societies, past and present, have been structured by **patriarchy**. Patriarchy is a complex system of beliefs, norms, social arrangements, political institutions, values, and practices that lead to and maintain the oppression of women by men. Such oppression, by which women are subordinated to men, is not just an accidental feature of existing social arrangements, moreover, but is a systemic feature of society. A complex of interconnected practices that make such subordination seem both natural and unproblematic, or simply invisible, maintains the oppression of women. So the descriptive empirical claim that all feminists accept is that existing societies are patriarchal. The normative or evaluative claim that all feminists accept is this: patriarchy is wrong. The subordination of women to men is morally unjustified and ought to be resisted. The goal is, ultimately, to overcome the inequality that currently exists between the sexes, to achieve what the well-known feminist Catharine MacKinnon calls genuine "sex equality."[1] Not all feminists share the same view of what genuine sex equality would look like, of course. Some think it will be achieved when women enjoy all the same liberal rights as men, in fact and not just formally or on paper. Others think it will be achieved when the roles and virtues traditionally associated with women and femininity (caring, mothering, nurturing, patience, benevolence) are valued equally with those traditionally associated with men and masculinity (economic and political activity, independence, justice). Still others think that real sex equality will not be achieved until society has moved away from its current gender-based roles and understandings to a state in which gender is undermined entirely, i.e., when members of both sexes experience the world and respond to each other in ways not describable as male or female. The goal here might be a state of androgyny.

Despite the differences between various schools of feminist thought, we shall try in what follows to provide a general overview of the theory as a whole that is faithful to the basic commitments of most feminists. Two things should be noted before we proceed. First, feminism has developed a unique methodology. Feminists believe that one of the reasons patriarchy has been so successful is because women have historically been denied a role in many of the most important institutions in society (politics, business, law, etc.). But women's exclusion goes deeper than that. Women have not been heard at all. Women have not been allowed to speak in their own voices. They have always been represented by men, if they have been considered at all. Men have defined what women's interests are and what their experiences mean. Feminists insist that women have a unique perspective, as the subordinates in a social and political system that subordinates them to men. Therefore, women must be able to speak in their own voices. Women must be able to define their own experiences and represent their own values. Thus feminists place a great deal of emphasis on empowering women to find their own voices, and they pay particularly close attention to personal histories, narratives, and other forms of first-person expression. Rather than beginning with sweeping claims about what human beings believe or value or need in general, feminist methodology begins at the local level in the unique and particular details of actual women's lives. For this reason, there are strong ties between feminist theorists in many different branches of study: anthropology, sociology, linguistics, as well as philosophy.

The second thing to note is that feminism has been largely a negative view, by which we mean it began as and continues importantly to be a method of critique and criticism. Thus much of feminist thinking is focused on revealing the patterns of thought and practice that lend themselves, even if only implicitly and unconsciously, to the support and continuance of patriarchy. Feminists spend a considerable amount of their time and energy exposing gender biases in traditional modes of thought, in the physical as well as the social sciences, in linguistic practices, in such fundamental social structures as the family, education, politics, the market, law, etc. But, more importantly for our purposes, feminist philosophers have also turned their critical attention to previous moral theories themselves. And they find within previous theories, like the ones we have looked at, much that contributes to the subordination of women to men. Thus feminism offers a critical examination of moral philosophy and moral thinking that must be taken seriously. It is with these criticisms of traditional moral theories that we will begin.

Masculine Values

Feminists point out that traditional moral theories are based on masculine values. Traditional moral theories take as basic the value of autonomy and rationality. This is certainly true of all the theories we have looked at, with the possible exception of utilitarianism. And feminists, as we shall see, have different concerns about it. Within Kantian deontology, libertarianism, and their modern offshoot welfare liberalism, the conditions of rationality and autonomy certainly do have pride of place. It is in virtue of the capacity of rational and autonomous agency that human beings are thought to have dignity, to be worthy of respect, and to be the bearers of rights. But rationality and autonomy are traits traditionally associated with men and masculinity. Men (the traditional and all-too-familiar story goes) are rational and autonomous, capable of setting their own rational plans of life. Autonomy entails a kind of independence, an ability to choose for oneself one's conception of a good life and the values one will pursue. But women are represented as being irrational, emotional, and dependent. Not only in representation but for millions of women in fact as well, they are not free to develop their own sets of values, or their own way of life. That is to a large extent set for them by others, by their cultural communities and by their biological status as child bearers.

Now it is not surprising that traditional moral theories reflect predominantly male values, given that they have been almost exclusively developed by men. But the feminist critique goes much deeper than that. The very questions with which traditional moral theories are concerned reflect a systemic gender bias. What are the legitimate limits of human freedom, what rights do people have, what duties do we owe to others just as rational agents? These questions make sense if we think of morality as concerned principally with what independent strangers can legitimately demand of one another. They are questions that reflect a conception of morality as applying in the first instance to interactions between those who are not bound together by existing ties of love or affection, family, or common cause. They concern how to protect the independence of individuals against unwanted intrusions. But these are not the typical concern of many women.

The work of psychologist Carol Gilligan began a new trend in thinking about moral problems.[2] She identified the kinds of concerns that are typical in traditional moral theories (concerns about rights and justice, as expressed in abstract and universal rules, principle or duties). She called this way of thinking about moral issues the "ethic of justice," and she found that it was the predominant attitude toward moral thinking exemplified by boys and men. But she also found a different voice, as she called it: a different attitude toward moral problems and a different set of moral concerns, which was more often exemplified in the way girls and women think about moral issues. Girls and women were less concerned with the application of abstract rights and principles to concrete moral problems, but instead sought ways to reconcile competing interests. They were concerned, not so much to ensure that their independence or autonomy were respected in situations of moral conflict, but rather with finding solutions that met the particular needs of the specific participants in the conflicts, and which allowed the relationships between the people involved to continue. She called this alternative attitude to thinking about moral matters an "ethic of care."

On the basis of Gilligan's work, many feminists have developed what is often called **relational feminism**, or the **care ethic**. It takes this name because women tend to see moral issues in the context of specific concrete relationships. They try to find solutions that meet the needs of others, express care for others, and maintain relationships. Given women's traditional roles as mothers and caregivers to others, who have primary responsibility to nurture and support those with whom they are in intimate relationships, as well as to maintain those relationships, it is not surprising that women see moral problems in a way that differs from the typical male response. Such differences are further reinforced through systemic patterns of socialization, in which girls are socialized to adopt a set of virtues and characteristics that support their role as nurturers in concrete relationships: virtues of caring, compassion, empathy, patience, and love. Girls are taught to think of needs of others, to see things from the point of view of others, and to serve others. Boys, by contrast, are taught to be independent, tough, and fair. Relational feminism accepts that there are these different patterns of moral thinking, and corresponding sets of virtues. Many think that the correct way to move forward, in light of these facts, is to work to ensure that both ways of thinking, and both sets of characteristics, are equally valued. Thus they do not want women to be assimilated into the male model of moral thinking, but rather want to bring about a state where the feminine perspective and feminine virtues are properly valued.

But the output of the ethic of care and the ethic of justice (of the feminine and masculine forms of moral thinking) are themselves very different, and that difference must also be examined. The ethic of justice produces rules and principles that are supposed to be general (indeed, universal) and impartial. They are supposed to govern the relations between all people, just as rational moral agents. But again this leaves out a great deal. Women do not deal with people just as rational moral agents. Women are mothers, wives, daughters, sisters, and friends. They often define themselves, and are defined within patriarchal societies, by their relationships with others. To say that morality is fundamentally about what we owe to each other as mere rational agents is to trivialize the moral concerns of women, or to deny that they are really moral concerns at all. For those concerns are particular rather than universal, and they are partial. They arise out of the concrete relationships in which women find themselves, and for which they have been assigned primary responsibility. They are thus not amenable to solution by the use of abstract and universal principles.

We must also note that traditional moral theories all begin with a conception of human beings as fully formed rational beings with the capacity of living good lives and autonomously pursuing their self-chosen ends. But human beings do not come ready formed. It takes years of care, love, sacrifice, and moral education to produce the agents that moral theories take for granted. By ignoring the role of women in raising children, and forming them for moral life, traditional moral theorists not only ignore this vital social task that women perform, but they ignore the morally significant elements of the practices by which it comes about.

Public and Private

One way of describing what is wrong, from a feminist point of view, with traditional moral theories is that they are moralities suitable only for regulating public activities. They are moralities that define the rules of politics, law, the market, property, and contracts. They define the legitimate relationship between individuals as public persons and between individuals and the state. But women have historically been denied the opportunity for full participation in public domains. They have been relegated to the private sphere of home and family. And the private sphere has traditionally been considered to be beyond the scope of morality. There is no need of rights or justice within the family. Indeed, many people would find absurd the idea of a family regulated purely by the requirements of justice. Family members who were concerned only with respecting the rights of fellow family members, and who were willing to press their own rights claims against other family members, would seem to many to be a perversion of family rather than its exemplar. Family structures and practices are also distinct from the public sphere by being protected as a domain of privacy. The flip side of saying that everyone has a right to privacy, and the state or others have no business interfering in private matters, has been that women have been excluded from the moral realm and left to the tyranny of their fathers, husbands, and brothers. As the saying goes, a man's home may be his castle, but for many girls and women that home is their prison. And their jailors exercise unfettered dominion over their prisoners, with no external review or constraint.

The relegation of women to the private sphere has led to other disadvantages for women. It makes them invisible. It makes them dependent on the men who represent them in the public domain, as well as economically dependent. And it has allowed their contribution to society to go entirely unrecognized and unvalued. Homemaking and mothering, caring for the elderly and the sick, providing the conditions in which men can thrive and succeed are not alternative careers, different but equally valued with those associated with public activity. Within patriarchal societies, they are not valued at all.

Early feminists thought that the solution to these problems was to ensure that women were extended equal rights to participate in the public sphere. These thinkers sought to have the basic rights identified within libertarian and liberal thought extended to women. They argued that, on liberalism's own terms, women had the same rights as men, and so the barriers that prevented them from living fully autonomous lives ought to be removed. The right to vote, the right to own property, the right to receive a higher education, the right to divorce, the right to hold public office and the right to be free from sex-based discrimination all followed. And under the influence of liberal feminism many gains for women were made. Most of the legal barriers to women's participation in public institutions were eliminated, and laws were enacted that made at least the grosser forms of violence against women criminal. The importance of such gains must not be underestimated, but it must also be recognized that they have been made only in a small number of states (modern liberal Western democracies, for the most part). And, even where formal equality rights have been extended to women, and they are free from legal barriers to participate in public institutions, women are still disadvantaged relative to men: they still bear primary responsibility for care of the children, the sick, and the elderly, and they still perform most of the other tasks associated with the private sphere. Even within the public sphere, the informal barriers to success faced by women are well documented. Women are more likely than men to work in service industries, to hold part-time or casual positions, to lack adequate benefits and pension packages, to suffer from discrimination, stereotyping, and face sexual harassment on the job. Women with full-time employment earn significantly less than men, and they are still dramatically underrepresented relative to their percentage of the population in the highest positions of power and social prestige (in law, in business, in higher education, in politics, in medicine, in science, etc.). In short, even with the extension of equal rights to women, our societies remain patriarchal. In liberal terms, we might say that the life prospects of women remain well below those of men, even though they enjoy equal rights and liberties, and formally equal opportunities. This is the injustice of patriarchy, because it denies to roughly half the population an equal chance of living a fully satisfying life on morally arbitrary grounds, namely sex.

But feminists have been concerned to undermine the dichotomy between public and private itself, and not merely to ensure that women may participate in public activities. The very distinction is problematic, because it denies the role of public institutions and practices, especially law, in creating a conception of the private that serves to reinforce the subordination of women. Consider, for example, the role of law in defining family structures. Through law a society defines what constitutes marriage, and until very recently that definition has been of a heterosexual union between a man and a woman. But law also defines or sets the rights of parents over their children, their responsibilities to their children, their rights in case of divorce, and who can be eligible for parental leave. It assigns responsibility for child care through its educational and day care policies. The list could be expanded indefinitely. Through legal and economic arrangements, societies structure the private. They define what counts as private, and what roles and responsibilities it involves. They also define its value. But given this interdependence between the private and the public, feminists insist that the distinction is bogus. It is not merely an artificially constructed division; it is one that works to reinforce the oppression of women. Thus it must be undermined. Once it is, the liberal conception of morality as applying just to the public sphere will likewise have to be rethought.

The Social Construction of Gender

Feminists have recently worried about the consequences of fully embracing the ethic of care. For it seems to reinforce certain essentialist assumptions about women, which themselves contribute to their subordination. In celebrating women's differences, and the feminine virtues, relational feminists seem to take for granted that there is a feminine and a masculine perspective, that the natural role of women is to be caregivers, and that relationships are worthy of maintenance independently of their moral qualities. All of these assumptions are deeply problematic.

Many feminists have increasingly come to think that gender is not a natural set of attitudes and characteristic, but a social construction. There is no natural or inevitable feminine or masculine perspective, but those perspectives are constructed by the social, economic, religious, moral, political, and other institutional structures and practices of a community. Because those perspectives have been formed within a social setting structured by patriarchy, moreover, gender as it is currently constructed is fundamentally influenced by men's power and women's subordination, by men's violence and women's passivity, by men's control and women's dependence. The result is, unsurprisingly again, the feminine virtues of care and the masculine virtues of strength. This issue, of the social construction of gender under patriarchy, has been most fully explored by **radical feminists** such as MacKinnon. As one commentator put it, "Overall, in the most general terms, the focus of radical feminism is on the domination of women by men through the social construction of gender within patriarchy. For them the solution to the oppression of women is to reverse the institutional structures of domination and to restructure gender, thereby eliminating patriarchy."[3] What gender would look like given such a profound change is a matter of some controversy, but that it would be a radical change is widely accepted. More importantly, if, as radical feminists think, gender is currently a product of patriarchy, then we must be cautious in following relational feminists in seeking to elevate the value of traditional feminine roles and virtues. For they are not only a product of patriarchy, but they also reinforce the subordination of women to men that made their construction possible.

Relational feminism might also be thought to rest on assumptions about the natural role of women. Such assumptions are widely shared, and have been taken for granted throughout virtually all of human history. Given the biological fact that women bear children, it has often been thought to follow that women must also naturally be caregivers. But we now know that child bearing and child rearing are not necessarily related activities. Children can be cared for by any competent adult or by communities as a whole. The fact that we have assigned primary responsibility for children to women, especially to their biological mothers, is no reason to think that this is the only or even the best arrangement for raising the next generation. Given rapidly changing family structures, to include adoptive parents, step-parents, homosexual parents, and the separation between genetic, gestational, and social parents made possible by new reproductive technologies, we may have a unique opportunity to rethink who should have primary care of children. Certainly we must at least accept that women are not naturally caregivers in any interesting sense. That, too, has been imposed upon women by patriarchy, and it serves to reinforce their continued subordination to and dependence upon men.

Finally, relational feminists note that central to the feminine perspective is the concern to maintain relationships. This concern is also problematic, because not all relationships are worthy of support. The tension between feminist goals and the desire to maintain relationships can be seen most clearly, of course, in cases of abusive relationships. Many women suffer violence at the hands of those with whom they are in intimate relationships. And many of these victims seem to want to stay in those relationships. They refuse to report the abuse, they resist the prosecution of their abusers, and they stay with or return to the men who victimize them. The complex phenomenon of the battered wife syndrome might help those of us who have not experienced such abuse to understand what leads women to so act, but surely a full explanation would also take into account the effects of the socially constructed role of women as the guardians of relationships. To say that maintaining relationships is valuable, independently of the quality of those relationship and their effects on the women who are in them, is dangerous in the extreme.

False Consciousness

One of the hallmarks of feminist methodology is consciousness raising. Because patriarchy is so pervasive, and because what is normal and natural has been defined by men from a position of absolute superiority, the oppression of women has appeared as either normal and natural, or it has been invisible. Because women have been socialized under patriarchy, they have often internalized the norms by which men exercise power over them. The socialization into gendered roles, of both boys and girls, plays a large part in this story. But so do the broader aspects of culture. The structure of family, education, work, language, law, and religion all play a role in making women's subordination invisible. Thus feminists believe that consciousness raising must be part of any agenda for social change.

This insight raises some serious issues, however. We considered the problem under liberalism of what we should do with respect to illiberal cultures within our society. Such cultures almost inevitably are especially bad for women. And yet the women within those cultures may fully identify with, and support, the very structures of thought, values, and practices through which they are oppressed. From a feminist point of view, such cultures are illegitimate and ought to be resisted and undermined. And yet, if we are to respect the women in question, and we acknowledge the importance of culture to individual well-being, it seems that we must not intervene in such a way as to destroy the culture. We seemingly face a dilemma: allow the continued oppression of women or disrespect what gives meaning to their lives. Neither option seems easy to take for feminists.

The problem raised by feminist treatments of illiberal cultures raises two further points of interest. One of the dominant effects of patriarchy is that it denies to women the ability to be fully autonomous agents. Women are not allowed to choose which values they will pursue, or to define for themselves what is a good and worthwhile life. They are socialized to have a limited range of options and a limited conception of the good. And while boys too are socialized under patriarchy, such socialization does not threaten their autonomy in the ways it does for girls. Boys are socialized to be independent, to accept that they have a wide range of options from which they may choose, and to develop the skills and attitudes that will enable them to set a rational and autonomous plan of life for themselves. Girls, by contrast, are taught that there are naturally imposed restrictions upon what they can do, and a natural range of activities in which they can find personal fulfillment. As women, they cannot radically remake themselves, reject the values and roles they have been assigned by their communities, without thereby abandoning those to whom they have special ties and responsibilities. In this way, patriarchy again operates in such a way that women are excluded from full moral status. Because their autonomy is limited, so is their dignity, and the requirement that we respect their choices is weakened. And feminism risks reinforcing this view, given the focus on false consciousness. If a woman's desires and commitments really are false (whatever exactly that means) then the reasons that traditional moral theories give us for respecting those commitments are diminished or extinguished. Thus we run the risk of some women (the enlightened feminists who have somehow managed to throw off the blinkers of patriarchy) who impose their values on all women in imperialistic fashion. This would run counter to the focus within feminist thought on the importance of hearing each woman's voice, in her own words as they have been shaped by her unique experiences.

But perhaps, it might be thought, utilitarianism can escape most of these worries. After all, utilitarianism does not require that one be a rational or autonomous agent to be worthy of moral concern. If patriarchy imposes unbearable hardships on women, and retards their ability to be happy in such a systemic way as feminists suggest, then we may condemn it. But we shall not be able to extend this line of thought far enough, if utilitarianism is based on a subject theory of value (such as pleasure, happiness, or preference satisfaction). For if feminists are right about the social construction of gender and the extent to which socialization under patriarchy has produced in women wide-ranging false consciousness, then we cannot take the happiness or preferences of women at face value, as it were. Even if women desire to live lives as traditional housewives and caregivers, for example, and desire to be dependent upon their husbands, those desires are based in false consciousness. From a feminist point of view, such desires must be undermined. But then, from a feminist point of view, there can be little value in satisfying those desires, even if the women in question will thereby be made happy. Thus feminism cannot be conjoined with subjective value-based utilitarianism to provide a better account of morality, for it can never accept that the basic values of individuals who have been raised under patriarchy are not themselves bad. It will be equally uncomfortable trying to embrace objective value-based utilitarianism. For if we are to provide a list of basic goods or objective values, we will have to engage in the kind of universal and abstract moral thinking of which feminism began as a critique. In fact, it seems that the only good that feminists themselves are united in recognizing is the good of promoting greater sexual equality. Thus feminism stands as a critique of all the traditional moral theories we have examined.

DEFINITIONS AND EXPLANATIONS

Patriarchy: 1. A form of social organization in which the father or eldest male is recognized as the head of the family or tribe, descent and kinship being determined through the male line. 2. Government by men. 3. Within feminist thought and now widely used, patriarchy refers to the pattern of social organization by which women are systemically and pervasively oppressed by men; a form of social organization characterized by radical differences in power enjoyed by men and women, by wideranging manifestations of sex inequality, in which women are relatively disadvantaged and men are advantaged.

Radical feminism: Radical feminists believe that patriarchy is sustained by socially constructed gender roles that give power to men and render women passive and dependent. Their goal is sex equality, which can only be achieved by a radical transformation of gender itself. Sex equality will not be achieved by ensuring that traditional feminine roles are properly valued, but by ensuring that power is equalized between the sexes.

Relational feminism: Inspired by the work of Carol Gilligan, relational feminists believe that we must rethink our traditional conception of morality so that it takes into account and duly values the traditional role of women as caregivers and as having primary responsibility for maintaining intimate relationships between people. This has given rise to a form of feminist moral theory sometimes called the **care ethic**, whose proponents celebrate the traditional caring roles of women in society and corresponding feminine virtues. Those who adopt a care ethic believe that women's oppression largely stems from the devaluing of the caring roles of women in society, and work to ensure that such roles and activities are more equally valued with traditionally male activities in the future.

✦ ✦ ✦

Lorenne Clark, Sexual Equality and the Problem of an Adequate Moral Theory: The Poverty of Liberalism

Lorenne Clark examines the liberal construction of what is permissible and finds it wanting. She notes that the public/private distinction has traditionally excluded family issues from moral evaluation, to the detriment of women who find themselves dominated by the patriarchal construction of the family. This moral blind spot, it is argued, suggests that a re-examination of the liberal conception of harm is in order. But it is clear to Clark that liberals have been unable to analyze the notion of harm in a way that is consistent with sexual equality. She takes as a case in point the liberal reaction to pornography. Liberals tend to argue that pornography is not harmful, and so no ban is necessary; feminists tend to disagree.

Feminists view pornography as hate literature. By falsely portraying women as willingly subservient to male fantasy, and as objects available for sexual use, pornography socializes men to accept women as such, which degrades and devalues them, diminishes male autonomy as well, and likely leads to men harming women. For all of these reasons, we ought to ban pornography. Clark thinks that pornography is inherently wrong, and that this fact alone ought to carry the day. But she does not rest her analysis on this simple statement of belief. She suggests a variety of wrongs that the permissibility of pornography would perpetrate. Men are wronged by such socialization because their autonomy is undermined by their acceptance of false beliefs. Women are wronged because their autonomy is undermined by the subservience forced upon them in a society created, at least in part, by the influence of pornography. Lastly, given common sense and the psychological studies done on patterns of recurring physical abuse (though notably *not* the studies done on the effects of pornography itself) we know that it is likely that the fantasy depicted in pornography will be acted out in the real world. For all of these reasons we ought to count pornography as harmful, and given liberalism's failure to support this conclusion, we ought to abandon liberalism as a moral theory as well.

Assuming that common sense and arguments by analogy persuade us that pornography really does cause such harm, and that autonomy is undermined by false beliefs, we still must grapple with the author's assertion that liberalism cannot accommodate a ban on pornography. Liberalism's commitment to the value of autonomy and to the harm principle seem to suggest that it can ban pornography if Clark's concerns are justified. The issue of false beliefs is also problematic. We have to seriously consider what is necessary for one group to be able to tell another that their beliefs are false. It is incredibly tempting to insist that every rational person ascribe to the beliefs we feel to be obviously correct. It is further tempting to suggest that those who do not so ascribe are non-autonomous. However, on what basis may we insist that our beliefs are superior? Women were once thought to be inherently irrational, and this observation was supported by the science of the time as well as common sense. What, other than hubris, allows us to be so sure of our position given the lessons that history has taught us?

✦ ✦ ✦

Lorenne Clark, "Sexual Equality and the Problem of an Adequate Moral Theory: The Poverty of Liberalism" from *In Search of the Feminist Perspective: The Changing Potency of Women*, eds. Mary Kathyrn Shirley and Rachel Emma Vigiers (Toronto: Resources for Feminist Research, Special Publication #5 (Spring 2001). Reprinted with permission of Resources for Feminist Research Publications.

Sexual Equality and the Problem of an Adequate Moral Theory: The Poverty of Liberalism

LORENNE CLARK

One of the fundamental principles endorsed by a liberal ethic is that there must be some areas of one's life in which one has the freedom to do what one wants, free from interference by others. It has been argued that there simply are some areas of life which are none of the law's business. For those familiar with the Wolfenden Report on Homosexuality in England, and the subsequent debate that this started both within and outside academic circles, this phrase, "none of the law's business," will have an all too familiar ring. Philosophically, this is reflected in debates about which areas of one's life should be essentially characterized by negative freedom, the ability to act free of restraints and scrutiny of others. Legally, it is reflected in debates about privacy, about the areas of one's life into which others should be legally prohibited from interfering.[1] There is virtually no one who would want to say that we should have no negative liberty or no privacy, but the debate still rages as to which areas of one's life should be guaranteed as areas of negative liberty through the creation of a legal right to privacy.

The difficulty is that no one has found a satisfactory method of drawing the boundaries between the private and other areas of life. In the past, the boundary was thought to be a *natural* one, based on the traditional distinction between the public and the private. The private just *was* "the private," and, as such should be guaranteed as an area of negative liberty and fully protected by means of a legally enforceable right to privacy. This was the basis of the argument in the Wolfenden Report. Here it was alleged that sexual relations between consenting adults simply are none of the law's business and the underlying rationale was that such behaviour should justifiably be left to the absolute discretion of individuals because it has effects on no one other than the participants. This was the rationale provided by John Stuart Mill in "On Liberty," and which was reiterated and defended by Herbert Hart in *Law, Liberty, and Morality*.[2] The best defence of this liberal tenet is the view developed by Mill that the law is justified in prohibiting actions if and only if doing them results in the inability of others to exercise rights of a similar kind. The underlying view is that rights should be distributed equally, which entails that no one can have rights the exercise of which would prevent others from exercising similar rights. The difficulty with the position is that it is virtually impossible to say with certainty of any action or pattern of behaviour that it has in principle no potential effects on others, either in terms of causing harm, or in terms of limiting the effective exercise of rights. Thus it is impossible *in principle* to draw a defensible boundary between the public and the private.

And certainly it has been indefensible to draw the legal boundary on the basis of the historical division between public and private. As is now abundantly clear, privacy functioned historically to protect those who were privileged to begin with. Privacy was a consequence of the ownership of private property, and, hence, was a commodity purchased with property. It has been a privilege accorded those of wealth and high social status. But more importantly from a feminist perspective, it protected not only the dominant class in the Marxist sense, but the dominant sex-class as well. The traditionally "private" was the sphere of the personal, home and hearth. And that area was the area within which women and children were forms of private property under the exclusive ownership and control of males. As the person in whom the absolute personality of family rested, male heads of households had virtually absolute rights over their wives and children. The family, clearly, was not and is not a partnership of equals. There is no mutuality in the marital relations and the rights and duties are decidedly one-sided.

Of course it is not the concept of privacy which is responsible for this state of affairs. But in drawing a boundary between the historically private and public, for the purpose of entrenching a legal right to privacy in the area of the traditionally private, it certainly functioned to condone and encourage the abusive and unjustified practices which were possible within this unequal relation. As is now clear, the family has been characterized by a great deal of physical violence. The legitimate basis of authority in the family is physical coercion, and it is and has been regularly relied on to secure to the male head of the house the attitudes and behaviours he wants. Women, much less children, had no right to protest such behaviour but were expected to suffer it, willingly, or otherwise. Thus, the last place feminists want to see a right to privacy is in the family. What possible sense can be made of the notion of being a consenting adult when one is in a relation in which one has no right to say no? Clearly, if we want privacy at all, where we do not want it is in the home.

The area of life most in need of regulation and control in the interest of creating more liberty and equality for women is the area of the traditionally private and personal. But greater liberty and equality for women can be purchased only at the cost of less liberty, and loss of status, for men. To the extent that women are given more rights within marriage, men are less able to do as they please; what was before permissible would now be either mandatory, as, for example, in making it a duty for men to share the housework and childcare, or prohibited, as for example in allowing a charge of rape between spouses. Within terms of the basic principle, such changes are justified. The past operation of the law has permitted many forms of behaviour which in fact caused physical and other direct and tangible harms to others, and which certainly prevented the effective exercise of like rights on the part of others. On the principle of like liberties for all, marriage must be turned into a relation of mutuality, and the relationships within it must be subject to regulation and control.

Why, then, has the demand for privacy centred so exclusively on preserving the traditional domain of male privilege? And why do the staunchest defenders of that view fail to see that in invoking these principles within a domain characterized by fundamental sexual inequality they are in fact both reinforcing that inequality and sanctioning its worst abuses? Thus, at the very least, adherents of the liberal ethic must acknowledge that there is no *natural* basis for deciding on what is private and what is public for the purpose of entrenching a legal right to privacy, and that the traditional area of the private is the area most in need of loss of privacy, in the name of promoting greater positive liberty and greater equality. How this fares on a purely utilitarian principle is of course problematic, for since men and women each make up roughly half the population, we cannot be sure that the benefits to women will in fact outweigh the losses to men.

In my view, the whole debate about privacy has been totally miscast because it has relied on the historical division between public and private. Thus, its liberal adherents continue to stress the need for privacy in just the areas where it is least defensible. Where we need the most protection, the legally enforceable right to prevent others from gaining access to information about us, and from disseminating that information to others without either our knowledge or our consent, is in the public world, the world of computers and charge-cards, credit ratings, and security forces. But this will mean much more regulation and control of the people and institutions which determine the structure and organization of the economic and social order. It will mean confronting the dominant class and the dominant sex in the public as well as the private sphere, and we should hardly be surprised to find that we are forced to part company with radical adherents of the liberal ethic. Equality cannot flourish without limiting the privileges some already have in both the private and the public spheres because the inequalities of the present system were a product of the unequal attribution of rights in the first instance; thus greater equality and liberty for those least advantaged under the present system necessitates placing restrictions on the privileged rights of those who are presently most advantaged. And since this must be done by creating obligations either to do or to forbear actions previously permitted, it can be accomplished only at the expense of negative liberty.

While the principles of the liberal ethic itself do not require the historical division between public and private, it has certainly been presupposed in liberal thinking about these issues. Recognition of the extent to which this has played a role must lead to a reappraisal of what it is that people should be at liberty to do, and it must find a basis for this which does not rest on traditional views of the different spheres of life, and the different roles of the sexes.

What is needed, at base, is a reappraisal of what is *harmful*. That, too, has historically been defined in terms of what the dominant sex and the dominant economic class find "harmful." An analysis of rape law demonstrates that point as well as anything could. Physically coerced sexual intercourse has been regarded as constituting a redressable harm if and only if the female victim was a dependent female living under either parental or matrimonial control, and in possession of those qualities which made her desirable as a piece of sexual and reproductive property available for the exclusive use of a present or future husband.[3] I dare say that when we start pressing for legal reform which will prohibit sexual harassment on the job we will find few adherents of liberalism rallying to our cause. It remains to be seen whether or not liberalism can survive and transcend the limitations of its own historical perspective, but in so far as it must renounce much of its accepted thinking about what sorts of actions individuals ought to be free to do, and must recognize that negative liberty must at least temporarily take a back seat to the promotion of equality, I cannot say I am hopeful about the outcome. But the ethics of liberalism will not do as the moral framework for the achievement of sexual equality unless it can meet this challenge.

But it is clear from a consideration of the issue of pornography that so far at least the ethics of liberalism has been unable to rethink its concept of harm in a way which is consistent with sexual equality. Feminists and civil libertarians are now at complete loggerheads over the issue. The trend among feminists is clear. More and more of them are coming to see that pornography is a species of hate literature.[4] To achieve its impact, it relies on depicting women in humiliating, degrading, and violently abusive situations. To make matters worse, it frequently depicts them willingly, even avidly, suffering and inviting such treatment. As is obvious to even the naivest of eyes, such recreations of heterosexual behaviour and relationships feed traditional male fantasies about both themselves and women.

Pornography is a method of socialization; it is the tangible, palpable embodiment of the imposition of the dominant sexual system which is a part of the dominant sex-class system. It is a vivid depiction of how to deploy male sexuality in just the way that will achieve maximum effect in maintaining the *status quo*. Pornography would be neither desired nor tolerated within any system other than one which sprang from the differential attribution of rights of ownership in which women and children are forms of sexual property, and in which they must either like it or quite literally lump it. It is the obverse of a morality which stresses female passivity and submissiveness, and it encourages the actualization of such states through active aggression and violence. Pornography has very little to do with sex, certainly with any conception of egalitarian sexual relations between the sexes, but it has everything to do with showing how to use sexuality as an instrument of active oppression, and that is why it is wrong. Some allege that it also feeds female fantasies about themselves and men, but that is certainly being questioned, at least in so far as it can be said that there is any hard empirical data to support it.[5]

That there should be no laws prohibiting the manufacture, sale, and distribution of pornography has traditionally and increasingly been defended as a freedom of speech, and freedom of press, issue. It is alleged that the reading or viewing of such material does not cause harm, or that if it does, it is harm only to those who willingly consent to it. The premise that it doesn't cause harm is defended by arguing that it relates only to the fantasy level and does not translate itself into interpersonal behaviour. And it goes further than this to argue that, indeed, it provides a healthy outlet, a cathartic effect, for those who might otherwise be tempted to act out their fantasies. Those who oppose pornography, particularly those who advocate its prohibition, are treated as Victorian prudes with sexual hang-ups. Women who object to it are seen as uptight, unliberated, and just not "with it" sexually speaking.

The general principle underlying the liberal view is of course that expressed by Mill in "On Liberty," who argued against any form of censorship on the ground that it was only through the free flow of information that the true and false could be separated. Prohibitions against the dissemination of any form of information functions to preserve the *status quo* and to prevent the development of a critically reflective morality which is itself necessary to pave the way for needed social change. The principle has much to be said for it. But that cannot change the fact that when it is uncritically made to apply within a domain characterized by inequality and by frankly abusive behaviour, a domain which is fundamentally shaped by a framework of social relations and institutions which makes all sexual relationships between men and women fundamentally coercive in nature,[6] it is bound to produce results which will be unacceptable because harmful to those who are in the pre-existing inferior position and who stand to be most affected by the attitudes and beliefs, as well as the practices, of those who use it.

The liberal argument has been that such material isn't harmful at all, and certainly cannot be seen as harmful to anyone other than the user, if harmful even to him. It isn't harmful because it functions merely to inflame male sexual desire. What is the harm if all it does is give a guy a bit of a rush? And it is right here that we must begin our critique. Surely we must acknowledge at least two things. First, it is not "normal" to get one's rushes from just anything. Secondly, if one gets desirable reactions from things which create a clear and substantial risk to others, then one can justifiably be prohibited from getting them that way. Persons who get their sexual stimulation from watching the atrocities perpetrated against the Jews during the Holocaust are not regarded as "normal," and rightly so. Furthermore, we do not feel that we are infringing any legitimate rights of others in preventing them access to material designed to provide sexual stimulation by this means. And the reasons for that are at least two-fold. First, as history has made all too clear, actions of this particular species do not remain at the level of mere fantasy. They have been acted out on the grand scale, so grand as to make any rational and reflective person aware that the possibility of a correlation between thought and action is at least strong enough to justify the imposition of prohibitions against material of this sort. Second, it stems from recognizing that even if the actual actions themselves are not acted out, the attitudes and beliefs of the persons enjoying them reflect attitudes toward the objects of the actions which are in themselves intrinsically bad and which are bound to produce practical effects in real life, if only to be expressed in bigoted and racist attitudes. All of the same arguments apply to material which depicts black people in degrading, humiliating, and abusive circumstances. Such material is, in itself, an affront to the dignity of the objects depicted, not least because they *are* being depicted purely as objects, dehumanized and depersonalized instruments for the satisfaction of someone else's perverted tastes.

The same case can be made with respect to heterosexual pornography.[7] As Camille Le Grand puts it, "pornography teaches society to view women as less than human. It is this view which keeps women as victims."[8] The typical way in which women are depicted in pornography certainly reflects a view of them as inferior to men, as inherently masochistic, and as primarily of value as instrument for the satisfaction of male lust. That is, in itself, intrinsically offensive to women, and is a straightforward objective affront to their dignity as equal persons. So on that ground alone, pornography ought to be prohibited just as we prohibit material depicting other social groups in such a fashion.

Of course, we could hardly argue within the parameters of our present culture that it is abnormal for males to react as they do to pornography. It is, unfortunately, all too normal, at least where we have any notion of statistical normality in mind. But neither is it unusual for rape victims to feel shamed, humiliated, and degraded by being raped; this is "normal" in the culture, but from any more rational perspective, it certainly is not "normal" in any normative sense. Much of recent efforts around the issue of rape have been designed specifically to change the perspective which rape victims have on that experience. Rape victims can come to see the assaultive behaviour perpetrated against them as legitimizing the anger which is appropriate to the nature of the attack. In short, it is possible both to identify the specific effects of socialization within a male supremacist and sexually coercive society, and to offset those effects with appropriate reconceptualization of the event. Women can come to identify the masochism and victimization into which they have been socialized, and can then act both to counteract it, and to be sublimely angry at a culture which socialized them into that mode. So, too, it should be possible for men to identify the sadism and attitudes of sexual aggressivity into which they are socialized and so act both to counteract them, and to be angry at a social system that produced that response. In short, *it is not a mark of personal depravity or immorality to be aroused by such material.* Given the cultural pattern of which it is a manifestation that is not at all surprising. Indeed, it is just what we would expect. But what must be recognized is that it is a socialized response, and that it is a response about which men should be both concerned and angry. And certainly, once its cultural roots are exposed, it is a response which should not be seen as needing or justifying the sale and distribution of the material which elicited it. Women must object to pornography because it both reflects and reinforces the patterns of socialization appropriate to a system based on the unequal status of the sexes, in which women are consistently regarded and treated as the inferiors, and the sexual property, of men. The socialization it brings about is *in itself* a limitation of the autonomy of women. Men ought to object to it for the same reason, and they ought to recognize that the socialization it brings about in terms of their self-images and internalized standards of conduct is also intrinsically undesirable given any commitment to the notion of sexual equality. To the extent that men are able to internalize the conviction that women and men are equal persons, they must recognize that the pleasurable responses they get from pornography are inappropriate to that conviction and are destructive to their ability to form self-images consistent with it. But that does not entail that they are in any sense to blame for those responses; they had as little choice about that as they did about their names. But we have, then, given strong arguments in support of the view that the eliciting of a pleasurable response is not in itself any reason to condone the sale and distribution of pornography, and that a proper understanding of the nature and causes of that response gives men as well as women solid grounds for objecting to the material which occasioned it. I believe that many more men would be able to understand and accept the feminist perspective on pornography if they could come to realize that they are not responsible for their sexual responses to it given the patterns of socialization which exist to mould us all into a set of social relations which institutionalizes male aggression and female passivity.

Thus, pornography is intrinsically harmful, both to women and to men. However, that does not end the argument with defenders of liberalism because their argument then moves on to the assertion that the harm to women is not direct enough to justify the legal prohibition of pornography. Frankly, I think that the argument that pornography is intrinsically offensive to the dignity of women ought to carry the day, but in the interests of completeness I want to go on to consider the other arguments that are brought to pornography's defence. Apart from this notion of an intrinsic harm and infringement of the rights of women, it will be argued that even if pornography is harmful to the user, it does not lead to direct harm to women, because the fantasies it supports remain fantasies, and it in fact prevents direct harm to women through its cathartic effect. I may say at the outset that I'm not at all impressed with either of these arguments. So far as the first is concerned, there is plenty of hard evidence available which supports the contention that modeling has a powerful effect on human behaviour. Studies of wife and child abuse consistently attest to the fact that there is a strong correlation between those who are abusers and those who come from family situations which were themselves abusive. The battered child becomes the battering parent; the son who witnessed his father battering his mother, and who was himself battered, becomes a battering husband.[9] Also, the evidence about the effect of violence depicted on television on the behaviour of children also points strongly in this direction.[10] People tend to act out and operationalize the behaviour that they see typically acted out around them. And surely that is hardly surprising. It is what has kept civilization going. If we weren't able to perpetuate the patterns of behaviour developed through cultural organization we wouldn't have come very far. So far as I know, however, there is no hard data to support the catharsis theory. It is a theory espoused by those who are looking for a rationale, though doubtless it has its roots in their awareness that they read pornography but don't rape and brutalize women. But raping and brutalizing women isn't the only harm that can be perpetrated against women. But so far there is little empirical support offered for the view that pornography feeds only the fantasy. Most psychiatric literature dealing with the "perversions" asserts that some people remain content with the fantasy while others do not.[11] But no one knows what differentiates the one who does actualize it from the one who doesn't. If this argument is going to be effective, it must be empirically demonstrated that this is so, and surely we cannot predict until the data are in that those who don't so outnumber those who do that we should, in the interests of an open society, tolerate the risk that some will. And since we are all imprisoned by the cultural stereotypes and the patterns of socialization appropriate to a society based on sexual coercion, how can those who do read it assert with certainty that they do not cause harm to women? They are hardly the best judges! As rape makes clear again, there is nowhere greater difference in perception than there is in the confusion surrounding rape and seduction. The men believe they are merely seducing, but the women perceive it as rape! And who is to judge? Certainly it is intrinsically unfair to permit only those who are the perpetrators of such behaviour to have a say in its interpretation.

While the liberal principle behind opposition to censorship is based on a recognition that desirable social change requires public access to information which challenges the beliefs and practices of the *status quo*, what it does not acknowledge is that information which supports the *status quo* through providing role models which advocate the use or threat of coercion as a technique of social control directed at a clearly identifiable group depicted as inferior, subordinate, and subhuman works against the interest both of desirable social change and of the members of the subgroup so identified. This has been clearly acknowledged in the case of violently anti-Semitic and other forms of racist literature. The same principles apply with respect to violently anti-female literature, and the same conclusion should follow. But this cannot come about until it is recognized and acknowledged that the dissemination of such material is itself a harm to the members of the group involved. It remains to be seen whether liberalism can accomplish this, but until it does, we cannot hope for its support on this issue.

In refusing to count as "harms" actions and practices which serve the interest of the dominant sex by reinforcing the patterns and effects of modes of socialization which support the sexist system, it renders itself incapable of changing that system and of promoting greater equality and positive liberty for women. Liberalism serves the interest of the dominant sex and the dominant class, though it contains within itself the potential for promoting greater equality and greater positive liberty for all. It can realize this potential, however, only by reconceptualizing harm in a way consistent with sex and class equality, and by recognizing that negative liberty must take second place to the promotion of equality at least until we have achieved a framework of enforceable rules which guarantees equality within both the public and the private spheres. When no one is allowed to do what is harmful to others, and/or what prevents them from effectively exercising liberty rights to autonomy and equality consistent with the equal attribution and effective exercise of like rights on the part of others, then we will have achieved a state in which liberty is concrete, and not a chimera which upholds the liberty of some at the expense of inequality to the rest. As women we are members of the disadvantaged sex. We are thus acting contrary to the interests of our sex in accepting any position which does not place the achievement of legally enforceable sexual equality at the forefront of its program.

That entails that we have to challenge traditional concepts of harm, and of liberty as the absence of restraint. We have been successful in removing most of the legal restraints which made both equality and liberty impossible, and that was the stage at which the ethics of liberalism served our purpose. But it has now outlived its usefulness to us. The achievement of *real*, rather than merely *possible*, equality and liberty now depends on placing effective, enforceable restraints on others; we can expect little support from liberalism as we move into this stage of our liberation.

READING ENDNOTES

1. A more detailed account of the relationship between the philosophical and legal debates, as well as a discussion of the complexity of the legal issue of privacy itself, is found in Clark, Lorenne M.G., "Privacy, Property, Freedom, and the Family," *Philosophical Law*, (Ed.) R. Bronaugh, Greenwood Press, Conn., 1978.
2. Hart, H.L.A., *Law, Liberty, and Morality*, O.U.P. London, 1963. This was Hart's answer to the objections raised by Lord Devlin to the recommendations and theory expressed in the Wolfenden Report. Devlin's position on this and other related matters is found in Devlin, Lord Patrick, *The Enforcement of Morals*, O.U.P., London, 1965.
3. For a discussion of the way in which the historical evolution and conception of rape law functioned to maintain the sexual *status quo*, and indeed continues to produce just the results we should expect to find with respect to the treatment and handling of rape cases within the criminal justice system, see Clark, Lorenne M.G., and Lewis, Debra J., *Rape: The Price of Coercive Sexuality*, The Women's Press, Toronto, 1977.
4. Among the articles that spring readily to mind are Morgan, Robin, "Theory and Practice: Pornography and Rape," *Going Too Far*, Random House, N.Y., 1977, Ch. IV. pp. 163–169; Russell, Diana, "Pornography: A Feminist Perspective," unpublished paper; Brownmiller, Susan, *Against Our Will*, Simon & Schuster, N.Y., 1975, pp. 394–396; and Shear, Marie, "Free Meat Talks Back," *Journal of Communication*, Vol. 26, No. 1, Winter, 1976, pp. 38–39.
5. For an excellent discussion of the way in which the empirical research that has been done on obscenity reflects a decidedly male bias, see McCormack, Thelma, "Machismo in Media Research: A Critical Review of Research on Violence and Pornography," *Social Problems*, Vol. 25, No. 5, 1978, pp. 544–555.
6. Clark and Lewis, *Rape: The Price of Coercive Sexuality*, Chs. 7 and 8 in particular.
7. Indeed, it is true of male homosexual pornography as well. But in the interest of not legislating in the interest of others, I am not advocating that we should prohibit this species of pornography. If men object to it, as in my view they should, whether homo- or heterosexual, it is up to them to express their opposition. Certainly I do not wish to infringe the rights homosexuals have to look at what they like, even though I cannot say with certainty that I am not adversely affected by it.

8. Quoted in Russell, Diana, "Pornography: A Feminist Perspective," *op. cit.*, p. 7, no reference given.

9. See, for example, Martin, Del, *Battered Wives*, Glide Publications, San Francisco, 1976, pp. 22–23; Pizzey, Erin, *Scream Quietly or the Neighbours Will Hear*, Penguin Books, England, 1974, Ch. 4; Van Stolk, Mary, *The Battered Child in Canada*, McClelland & Stewart, Toronto, 1972, pp. 23–27.

10. Bandura, A., Ross, D., and Ross, S.A., "Transmission of Aggression through Imitation of Aggressive Models," *Journal of Abnormal and Social Psychology*, 63, No. 3, 575–582.

11. Kraft-Ebbing, Richard von, *Psychopathia Sexualis*, 11th ed. rev. and enlarged, Stuttgard, 1901, pp. 94–95; Freud, S., *Introductory Lectures on Psycho-Analysis*, Standard Edition, 16:306.

DEFINITIONS AND EXPLANATIONS

Hate literature: Hate literature or hate propaganda is defined in Canadian criminal law as advocating or promoting genocide, inciting hatred or wilfully promoting hatred against an identifiable group. An identifiable group for these purposes includes any section of the public distinguished by colour, race, religion, or ethnic origin. The promotion of hate against members of identifiable groups is illegal in Canada. Notice that women are not an identifiable group for the purposes of this law.

QUESTIONS

1. Why is it impossible *in principle* to draw a defensible boundary between the private (in which people should have negative liberty) and the public (in which actions might be regulated)?

2. In what way has recognizing a right to privacy worked to support the subordination of women to men?

3. Can utilitarianism adequately explain what is wrong with pornography? Explain.

4. Why does Clark think that liberals need to rethink their conception of harm if liberalism is to be able to assist in achieving sex equality? What does her example of rape suggest about the way the conception of harm is influenced by sexism?

5. Is pornography a species of hate literature? Should the law be expanded to include women as an identifiable group?

6. In what way does pornography depict sexuality as an instrument of oppression?

7. Clark argues that, insofar as pornography reinforces the *status quo* in terms of sexual relations, it is harmful. If we still have a society structured by patriarchy, is it the case that anything that reinforces the *status quo* can be equally condemned as harmful to women?

8. Clark seems to say that all sexual relations between men and women are fundamentally coercive in nature. What implications does such a view have?

9. How strong is the analogy between someone who is sexually aroused by depictions of the atrocities committed against Jews in the Holocaust and someone who is sexually aroused by depictions of sexually explicit material? Even violent sexual material?

10. Clark insists that enjoying pornography reflects attitudes "which are in themselves intrinsically bad." Why? Can attitudes (divorced from actions) be intrinsically bad?

11. Does Clark confuse assessment of the attitude of enjoying pornography with what might be wrong with pornography itself, i.e., that it depicts women purely as objects for male gratification?

12. How can we distinguish "perverted tastes" from "normal" ones? Do at least some ways of marking the difference make pornography and responses to it normal?

13. Why is pornography necessarily an affront to the dignity of women?

14. In what ways are women treated as the sexual property of men?

15. In what way does pornography limit the autonomy of both men and women? How is it both a product of socialization under patriarchy and a reinforcer of sexual inequality?

16. How plausible is the claim that viewing pornography leads to direct harms (violence) to women? How strong are the analogies Clark draws between actual violence and further violence, on the one hand, and depictions of violence and actual violence, on the other? Does it become stronger when we attend to the systemic nature of patriarchy in society at large?

17. Why is Clark pessimistic about liberalism's ability to offer a conception of rights and harms that could work to achieve genuine sex equality for women?

✦ ✦ ✦

Susan Sherwin, Feminist Ethics and In Vitro Fertilization

Susan Sherwin compares and contrasts the reactions of theologians, deontologists, liberals, and feminists on the issue of the moral status of in vitro fertilization (IVF). Her main contention is that the feminist analysis allows for a more nuanced account of the moral status of IVF. Traditional moral theories are thought to analyze moral issues in isolation from the relevant cultural practices that surround them in an effort to see whether an action is to be universally forbidden, permitted, or required. Feminism, by way of contrast, requires judging the moral worth of activities relative to the culture in which they will be practiced.

In isolation, IVF seems to be a technology that would enhance the autonomy of women. Women who would not otherwise be able to reproduce, should they so desire, have that option available for them. While not being able to dismiss this benefit, feminists who look at our current culture see some reason to be less than wholly supportive of IVF procedures. In the first place, the procedure is controlled by medical staff, and so women have less control over this choice than one may have thought. Further, the medical institution does not gift every woman with this procedure, but instead only those both found worthy of the procedure (when Sherwin wrote the paper they had to be married, for example) and able to pay for it are accepted. Women are also seen to be under-informed about the procedure, have little choice with the clinics available to them, and may be faced with undue pressure to reproduce from both spouses and society at large. All of these concerns suggest that the desire to seek IVF is not an autonomous desire. Further, feminism must consider the re-enforcement of a woman's desire to find her self-worth in the act of procreation in a patriarchal culture. If this desire contributes to the subordination of women, and the availability of IVF contributes to the strengthening of this desire, then feminism finds itself even more hostile to IVF technology. It may be that feminists do have to be opposed to IVF right now, while undermining patriarchy, even at the expense of making some women less free than they could be otherwise.

And here one of the tensions in feminism comes out most strongly. On the one hand, a concern for a woman's autonomy suggests that the more options available to her the better. On the other hand, one needs to consider the legitimacy of desires that have the effect of keeping women subservient. Feminism may have to deny an independent, autonomous woman the choice of IVF (assuming that one grants that some women may autonomously choose to reproduce) for the greater good of undermining patriarchy, so that more women may be self-governing. But then feminism faces the same objection as utilitarianism: there is something objectionable in the idea that an individual may be sacrificed by others for the greater good. This may be particularly problematic for feminists who feel that women have been socialized under patriarchy to accept sacrificial roles.

✦ ✦ ✦

Susan Sherwin, "Feminist Ethics and In Vitro Fertilization," *Canadian Journal of Philosophy* Supplementary Volume 13 (1987): 265-284. © 1987 *Canadian Journal of Philosophy*. Reprinted with permission of the *Canadian Journal of Philosophy*, University of Calgary Press.

Feminist Ethics and In Vitro Fertilization[1]

S U S A N   S H E R W I N

New technology in human reproduction has provoked wide ranging arguments about the desirability and moral justifiability of many of these efforts. Authors of biomedical ethics have ventured into the field to offer the insight of moral theory to these complex moral problems of contemporary life. I believe, however, that the moral theories most widely endorsed today are problematic and that a new approach to ethics is necessary if we are to address the concerns and perspectives identified by feminist theorists in our considerations of such topics. Hence, I propose to look at one particular technique in the growing repertoire of new reproductive technologies, in vitro fertilization (IVF), in order to consider the insight which the mainstream approaches to moral theory have offered to this debate, and to see the difference made by a feminist approach to ethics.

I have argued elsewhere that the most widely accepted moral theories of our time are inadequate for addressing many of the moral issues we encounter in our lives, since they focus entirely on such abstract qualities of moral agents as autonomy or quantities of happiness, and they are addressed to agents who are conceived of as independent, non-tuistic individuals. In contrast, I claimed, we need a theory which places the locus of ethical concerns in a complex social network of interrelated persons who are involved in special sorts of relations with one another. Such a theory, as I envision it, would be influenced by the insights and concerns of feminist theory, and hence, I have called it feminist ethics.[2]

In this paper, I propose to explore the differences between a feminist approach to ethics and other, more traditional approaches in examining the propriety of developing and implementing in vitro fertilization and related technologies. This is a complicated task, since each sort of ethical theory admits of a variety of interpretations and hence of a variety of conclusions on concrete ethical issues. Nonetheless, certain themes and trends can be seen to emerge. Feminist thinking is also ambivalent in application, for feminists are quite torn about their response to this sort of technology. It is my hope that a systematic theoretic evaluation of IVF from the point of view of a feminist ethical theory will help feminists like myself sort through our uncertainty on these matters.

Let me begin with a quick description of IVF for the uninitiated. In vitro fertilization is the technology responsible for what the media likes to call 'test tube babies.' It circumvents, rather than cures, a variety of barriers to conception, primarily those of blocked fallopian tubes and low sperm counts. In vitro fertilization involves removing ova from the woman's body, collecting sperm from the man's, combining them to achieve conception in the laboratory, and, a few days later, implanting some number of the newly fertilized eggs directly into the woman's womb with the hope that pregnancy will continue normally from this point on. This process requires that a variety of hormones be administered to the woman—which involve profound emotional and physical changes—that her blood and urine be monitored daily, and then at 3 hour intervals, that ultrasound be used to determine when ovulation occurs. In some clinics, implantation requires that she remain immobile for 48 hours (including 24 hours in the head down position). IVF is successful in about 10-15% of the cases selected as suitable, and commonly involves multiple efforts at implantation.

Let us turn now to the responses that philosophers working within the traditional approaches to ethics have offered on this subject. A review of the literature in bioethics identifies a variety of concerns with this technology. Philosophers who adopt a theological perspective tend to object that such technology is wrong because it is not 'natural' and undermines God's plan for the family. Paul Ramsey, for instance, is concerned about the artificiality of IVF and other sorts of reproductive technology with which it is potentially associated, e.g. embryo transfer, ova as well as sperm donation or sale, increased eugenic control, etc.:

> But there is as yet no discernable evidence that we are recovering a sense for man [sic] as a natural object ... toward whom a ... form of "natural piety" is appropriate ... parenthood is certainly one of those "courses of action" natural to man, which cannot without violation be disassembled and put together again.[3]

Leon Kass argues a similar line in '"Making Babies" Revisited.'[4] He worries that our conception of humanness will not survive the technological permutations before us, and that we will treat these new artificially conceived embryos more as objects than as subjects; he also fears that we will be unable to track traditional human categories of parenthood and lineage, and that this loss would cause us to lose track of important aspects of our identity. The recent position paper of the Catholic Church on reproductive technology reflects related concerns:

> It is through the secure and recognized relationship to his [sic] own parents that the child can discover his own identity and achieve his own proper human development ...
>
> Heterologous artificial fertilization violates the rights of the child; it deprives him of his filial relationship with his parental origins and can hinder the maturing of his personal identity.[5]

Philosophers partial to utilitarianism prefer a more scientific approach; they treat these sorts of concerns as sheer superstition. They carefully explain to their theological colleagues that there is no clear sense of 'natural' and certainly no sense that demands special moral status. All medical activity, and perhaps all human activity, can be seen in some sense as being 'interference with nature,' but that is hardly grounds for avoiding such action. 'Humanness,' too, is a concept that admits of many interpretations; generally, it does not provide satisfactory grounds for moral distinctions. Further, it is no longer thought appropriate to focus too strictly on questions of lineage and strict biological parentage, and, they note, most theories of personal identity do not rely on such matters.

Where some theologians object that 'fertilization achieved outside the bodies of the couple remains by this very fact deprived of the meanings of the values which are expressed in the language of the body and in the union of human persons,'[6] utilitarians quickly dismiss the objection against reproduction without sexuality in a properly sanctified marriage. See, for instance, Michael Bayles in *Reproductive Ethics*: ' ... even if reproduction should occur only within a context of marital love, the point of that requirement is the nurturance of offspring. Such nurturance does not depend on the sexual act itself. The argument confuses the biological act with the familial context.'[7]

Another area of disagreement between theological ethicists and their philosophical critics is the significance of the wedge argument to the debate about IVF. IVF is already a complex technology involving research on superovulation, 'harvesting' of ova, fertilization, and embryo implants. It is readily adaptable to technology involving the transfer of ova and embryos, and hence their donation or sale, as well as to the 'rental of womb space'; it also contributes to an increasing ability to foster fetal growth outside of the womb and, potentially, to the development of artificial wombs covering the whole period of gestation. It is already sometimes combined with artificial insemination and is frequently used to produce surplus fertilized eggs to be frozen for later use. Theological ethicists worry that such activity, and further reproductive developments we can anticipate (such as human cloning), violate God's plan for human reproduction. They worry about the cultural shift involved in viewing reproduction as a scientific enterprise, rather than the 'miracle of love' which religious proponents prefer: '[He] cannot be desired or conceived as the product of an intervention of medical or biological techniques; that would be equivalent to reducing him to an object of scientific technology.'[8] And, worse, they note, we cannot anticipate the ultimate outcome of this rapidly expanding technology.

The where-will-it-all-end hand-wringing that comes with this sort of religious futurology is rejected by most analytical philosophers; they urge us to realize that few slopes are as slippery as the pessimists would have us believe, that scientists are moral people and quite capable of evaluating each new form of technology on its own merits, and that IVF must be judged by its own consequences and not the possible result of some future technology with which it may be linked. Samuel Gorovitz is typical:

It is not enough to show that disaster awaits if the process is not controlled. A man walking East in Omaha will drown in the Atlantic—if he does not stop. The argument must also rest on the evidence about the likelihood that judgment and control will be exercised responsibly ... Collectively we have significant capacity to exercise judgment and control ... our record has been rather good in regard to medical treatment and research.[9]

The question of the moral status of the fertilized eggs is more controversial. Since the superovulation involved in producing eggs for collection tends to produce several at once, and the process of collecting eggs is so difficult, and since the odds against conception on any given attempt are so slim, several eggs are usually collected and fertilized at once. A number of these fertilized eggs will be introduced to the womb with the hope that at least one will implant and gestation will begin, but there are frequently some 'extras.' Moral problems arise as to what should be done with these surplus eggs. They can be frozen for future use (since odds are against the first attempt 'taking'), or they can be used as research material, or simply discarded. Canadian clinics get around the awkwardness of their ambivalence on the moral status of these cells by putting them all into the woman's womb. This poses the devastating threat of six or eight 'successfully' implanting, and a woman being put into the position of carrying a litter; something, we might note, her body is not constructed to do.

Those who take a hard line against abortion and argue that the embryo is a person from the moment of conception object to all these procedures, and, hence, they argue, there is no morally acceptable means of conducting IVF. To this line, utilitarians offer the standard responses. Personhood involves moral, not biological categories. A being neither sentient nor conscious is not a person in any meaningful sense. For example, Gorovitz argues, 'Surely the concept of person involves in some fundamental way the capacity for sentience, or an awareness of sensations at the very least.'[10] Bayles says, 'For fetuses to have moral status they must be capable of good or bad in their lives ... What happens to them must make a difference to them. Consequently some form of awareness is necessary for moral status.'[11] (Apparently, clinicians in the field have been trying to avoid this whole issue by coining a new term in the hopes of identifying a new ontological category, that of the 'pre-embryo.')[12]

Many bioethicists have agreed here, as they have in the abortion debate, that the principal moral question of IVF is the moral status and rights of the embryo. Once they resolve that question, they can, like Englehardt, conclude that since fetuses are not persons, and since reproductive processes occurring outside a human body pose no special moral problems, 'there will be no sustainable moral arguments in principle ... against in vitro fertilization.'[13] He argues,

> in vitro fertilization and techniques that will allow us to study and control human reproduction are morally neutral instruments for the realization of profoundly important human goals, which are bound up with the realization of the good of others: children for infertile parents and greater health for the children that will be born.[14]

Moral theorists also express worries about the safety of the process, and by that they tend to mean the safety to fetuses that may result from this technique. Those fears have largely been put to rest in the years since the first IVF baby was born in 1978, for the couple of thousand infants reportedly produced by this technique to date seem no more prone to apparent birth defects than the population at large, and, in fact, there seems to be evidence that birth defects may be less common in this group—presumably because of better monitoring and pre and post natal care. (There is concern expressed, however, in some circles outside of the bioethical literature about the longterm effect of some of the hormones involved, in light of our belated discoveries of the effect of DES usage on offspring. This concern is aggravated by the chemical similarity of clomid, one of the hormones used in IVF, to DES.)[15]

Most of the literature tends to omit comment on the uncertainties associated with the effect of drugs inducing superovulation in the woman concerned, or with the dangers posed by the general anaesthetic required for the laparoscopy procedure; the emotional costs associated with this therapy are also overlooked, even though there is evidence that it is extremely stressful in the 85-90% of the attempts that fail, and that those who succeed have difficulty in dealing with common parental feelings of anger and frustration with a child they tried so hard to get. Nonetheless, utilitarian theory could readily accommodate such concerns, should the philosophers involved think to look for them. In principle, no new moral theory is yet called for, although a widening of perspective (to include the effects on the women involved) would certainly be appropriate.

The easiest solution to the IVF question seems to be available to ethicists of a deontological orientation who are keen on autonomy and rights and free of religious prejudice. For them, IVF is simply a private matter, to be decided by the couple concerned together with a medical specialist. The desire to have and raise children is a very common one and generally thought to be a paradigm case of a purely private matter. Couples seeking this technology face medical complications that require the assistance of a third party, and it is thought, 'it would be unfair to make infertile couples pass up the joys of rearing infants or suffer the burdens of rearing handicapped children.'[16] Certainly, meeting individuals' desires/needs is the most widely accepted argument in favour of the use of this technology.

What is left, then, in the more traditional ethical discussions, is usually some hand waving about costs. This is an extremely expensive procedure; estimates range from $1500 to $6000 per attempt. Gorovitz says, for instance, 'there is the question of the distribution of costs, a question that has heightened impact if we consider the use of public funds to pay for medical treatment.'[17] Debate tends to end here in the mystery of how to balance soaring medical costs of various sorts and a comment that no new ethical problems are posed.

Feminists share many of these concerns, but they find many other moral issues involved in the development and use of such technology and note the silence of the standard moral approaches in addressing these matters. Further, feminism does not identify the issues just cited as primary areas of moral concern. Nonetheless, IVF is a difficult issue for feminists.

On the one hand, most feminists share the concern for autonomy held by most moral theorists, and they are interested in allowing women freedom of choice in reproductive matters. This freedom is most widely discussed in connection with access to safe and effective contraception and, when necessary, to abortion services. For women who are unable to conceive because of blocked fallopian tubes, or certain fertility problems of their partners, IVF provides the technology to permit pregnancy which is otherwise impossible. Certainly most of the women seeking IVF perceive it to be technology that increases their reproductive freedom of choice. So, it would seem that feminists should support this sort of technology as part of our general concern to foster the degree of reproductive control women may have over their own bodies. Some feminists have chosen this route. But feminists must also note that IVF as practiced does not altogether satisfy the motivation of fostering individual autonomy.

It is, after all, the sort of technology that requires medical intervention, and hence it is not really controlled by the women seeking it, but rather by the medical staff providing this 'service.' IVF is not available to every woman who is medically suitable, but only to those who are judged to be worthy by the medical specialists concerned. To be a candidate for this procedure, a woman must have a husband and an apparently stable marriage. She must satisfy those specialists that she and her husband have appropriate resources to support any children produced by this arrangement (in addition, of course, to the funds required to purchase the treatment in the first place), and that they generally 'deserve' this support. IVF is not available to single women, lesbian women, or women not securely placed in the middle class or beyond. Nor is it available to women whom the controlling medical practitioners judge to be deviant with respect to their norms of who makes a good mother. The supposed freedom of choice, then, is provided only to selected women who have been screened by the personal values of those administering the technology.

Further, even for these women, the record on their degree of choice is unclear. Consider, for instance, that this treatment has always been very experimental: it was introduced without the prior primate studies which are required for most new forms of medical technology, and it continues to be carried out under constantly shifting protocols, with little empirical testing, as clinics try to raise their very poor success rates. Moreover, consent forms are perceived by patients to be quite restrictive procedures and women seeking this technology are not in a particularly strong position to bargain to revise the terms; there is no alternate clinic down the street to choose if a woman dislikes her treatment at some clinic, but there are usually many other women waiting for access to her place in the clinic should she choose to withdraw.

Some recent studies indicate that few of the women participating in current programs really know how low the success rates are.[18] And it is not apparent that participants are encouraged to ponder the medical unknowns associated with various aspects of the technique, such as the long term consequences of superovulation and the use of hormones chemically similar to DES. Nor is it the case that the consent procedure involves consultation on how to handle the disposal of 'surplus' zygotes. It is doubtful that the women concerned have much real choice about which procedure is followed with the eggs they will not need. These policy decisions are usually made at the level of the clinic. It should be noted here that at least one feminist argues that neither the woman, nor the doctors have the right to choose to destroy these embryos:

' … because no one, not even its parents, owns the embryo/fetus, no one has the *right* to destroy it, even at a very early developmental stage … to destroy an embryo is not an automatic entitlement held by anyone, including its genetic parents.'[19]

Moreover, some participants reflect deep seated ambivalence on the part of many women about the procedure—they indicate that their marriage and status depends on a determination to do 'whatever is possible' in pursuit of their 'natural' childbearing function—and they are not helped to work through the seeming imponderables associated with their long term well-being. Thus, IVF as practiced involves significant limits on the degree of autonomy deontologists insist on in other medical contexts, though the non-feminist literature is insensitive to this anomaly.

From the perspective of consequentialism, feminists take a long view and try to see IVF in the context of the burgeoning range of techniques in the area of human reproductive technology. While some of this technology seems to hold the potential of benefiting women generally—by leading to better understanding of conception and contraception, for instance—there is a wary suspicion that this research will help foster new techniques and products such as human cloning and the development of artificial wombs which can, in principle, make the majority of women superfluous. (This is not a wholly paranoid fear in a woman-hating culture: we can anticipate that there will be great pressure for such techniques in subsequent generations, since one of the 'successes' of reproductive technology to date has been to allow parents to control the sex of their offspring; the 'choice' now made possible clearly threatens to result in significant imbalances in the ratio of boy to girl infants. Thus, it appears, there will likely be significant shortages of women to bear children in the future, and we can anticipate pressures for further technological solutions to the 'new' problem of reproduction that will follow.)

Many authors from all traditions consider it necessary to ask why it is that some couples seek this technology so desperately. Why is it so important to so many people to produce their 'own' child? On this question, theorists in the analytic tradition seem to shift to previously rejected ground and suggest that this is a natural, or at least a proper, desire. Englehardt, for example, says, 'The use of technology in the fashioning of children is integral to the goal of rendering the world congenial to persons.'[20] Bayles more cautiously observes that 'A desire to beget for its own sake … is probably irrational'; nonetheless, he immediately concludes, 'these techniques for fulfilling that desire have been found ethically permissible.'[21] R. G. Edwards and David Sharpe state the case most strongly: 'the desire to have children must be among the most basic of human instincts, and denying it can lead to considerable psychological and social difficulties.'[22] Interestingly, although the recent pronouncement of the Catholic Church assumes that 'the desire for a child is natural,'[23] it denies that a couple has a right to a child: 'The child is not an object to which one has a right.'[24]

Here, I believe, it becomes clear why we need a deeper sort of feminist analysis. We must look at the sort of social arrangements and cultural values that underlie the drive to assume such risks for the sake of biological parenthood. We find that the capitalism, racism, sexism, and elitism of our culture have combined to create a set of attitudes which views children as commodities whose value is derived from their possession of parental chromosomes. Children are valued as privatized commodities, reflecting the virility and heredity of their parents. They are also viewed as the responsibility of their parents and are not seen as the social treasure and burden that they are. Parents must tend their needs on pain of prosecution, and, in return, they get to keep complete control over them. Other adults are inhibited from having warm, stable interactions with the children of others—it is as suspect to try to hug and talk regularly with a child who is not one's own as it is to fondle and hang longingly about a car or a bicycle which belongs to someone else—so those who wish to know children well, often find they must have their own.

Women are persuaded that their most important purpose in life is to bear and raise children; they are told repeatedly that their life is incomplete, that they are lacking in fulfillment if they do not have children. And, in fact, many women do face a barren existence without children. Few women have access to meaningful, satisfying jobs. Most do not find themselves in the centre of the romantic personal relationships which the culture pretends is the norm for heterosexual couples. And they have been socialized to be fearful of close friendships with others—they are taught to distrust other women, and to avoid the danger of friendship with men other than their husbands. Children remain the one hope for real intimacy and for the sense of accomplishment which comes from doing work one judges to be valuable.

To be sure, children can provide that sense of self worth, although for many women (and probably for all mothers at some times) motherhood is not the romanticized satisfaction they are led to expect. But there is something very wrong with a culture where childrearing is the only outlet available to most women in which to pursue fulfillment. Moreover, there is something wrong with the ownership theory of children that keeps other adults at a distance from children. There ought to be a variety of close relationships possible between children and adults so that we all recognize that we have a stake in the well-being of the young, and we all benefit from contact with their view of the world.

In such a world, it would not be necessary to spend the huge sums on designer children which IVF requires while millions of other children starve to death each year. Adults who enjoyed children could be involved in caring for them whether or not they produced them biologically. And, if the institution of marriage survives, women and men would marry because they wished to share their lives together, not because the men needed someone to produce heirs for them and women needed financial support for their children. That would be a world in which we might have reproductive freedom of choice. The world we now live in has so limited women's options and self esteem, it is legitimate to question the freedom behind women's demand for this technology, for it may well be largely a reflection of constraining social perspectives.

Nonetheless, I must acknowledge that some couples today genuinely mourn their incapacity to produce children without IVF and there are very significant and unique joys which can be found in producing and raising one's own children which are not accessible to persons in infertile relationships. We just sympathize with these people.

None of us shall live to see the implementation of the ideal cultural values outlined above which would make the demand for IVF less severe. It is with real concern that some feminists suggest that the personal wishes of couples with fertility difficulties may not be compatible with the overall interests of women and children.

Feminist thought, then, helps us to focus on different dimensions of the problem then do other sorts of approaches. But, with this perspective, we still have difficulty in reaching a final conclusion on whether to encourage, tolerate, modify, or restrict this sort of reproductive technology. I suggest that we turn to the developing theories of feminist ethics for guidance in resolving this question.[25]

In my view, a feminist ethics is a moral theory that focuses on relations among persons as well as on individuals. It has as a model an inter-connected social fabric, rather than the familiar one of isolated, independent atoms; and it gives primacy to bonds among people rather than to rights to independence. It is a theory that focuses on concrete situations and persons and not on free-floating abstract actions.[26] Although many details have yet to be worked out, we can see some of its implications in particular problem areas such as this.

It is a theory that is explicitly conscious of the social, political, and economic relations that exist among persons; in particular, as a feminist theory, it attends to the implications of actions or policies on the status of women. Hence, it is necessary to ask questions from the perspective of feminist ethics in addition to those which are normally asked from the perspective of mainstream ethical theories. We must view issues such as this one in the context of the social and political realities in which they arise, and resist the attempt to evaluate actions or practices in isolation (as traditional responses in biomedical ethics often do). Thus, we cannot just address the question of IVF per se without asking how IVF contributes to general patterns of women's oppression. As Kathryn Payne Addleson has argued about abortion,[27] a feminist perspective raises questions that are inadmissible within the traditional ethical frameworks, and yet, for women in a patriarchal society, they are value questions of greater urgency. In particular, a feminist ethics, in contrast to other approaches in biomedical ethics, would take seriously the concerns just reviewed which are part of the debate in the feminist literature.

A feminist ethics would also include components of theories that have been developed as 'feminine ethics,' as sketched out by the empirical work of Carol Gilligan.[28] (The best example of such a theory is the work of Nel Noddings in her influential book *Caring*.)[29] In other words, it would be a theory that gives primacy to interpersonal relationships and woman-centered values such as nurturing, empathy, and co-operation. Hence, in the case of IVF, we must care for the women and men who are so despairing about their infertility as to want to spend the vast sums and risk the associated physical and emotional costs of the treatment, in pursuit of 'their own children.' That is, we should, in Noddings' terms, see their reality as our own and address their very real sense of loss. In so doing, however, we must also consider the implications of this sort of solution to their difficulty. While meeting the perceived desires of some women—desires which are problematic in themselves, since they are so compatible with the values of a culture deeply oppressive to women—this technology threatens to further entrench those values which are responsible for that oppression. A larger vision suggests that the technology offered may, in reality, reduce the women's freedom and, if so, it should be avoided.

A feminist ethics will not support a wholly negative response, however, for that would not address our obligation to care for those suffering from infertility; it is the responsibility of those who oppose further implementation of this technology to work towards the changes in the social arrangements that will lead to a reduction of the sense of need for this sort of solution. On the medical front, research and treatment ought to be stepped up to reduce the rates of peral sepsis and gonorrhea which often result in the tubal blockage, more attention should be directed at the causes and possible cures for male infertility, and we should pursue techniques that will permit safe reversible sterilization providing women with better alternatives to tubal ligation as a means of fertility control; these sorts of technology would increase the control of many women over their own fertility and would be compatible with feminist objectives. On the social front, we must continue the social pressure to change the status of women and children in our society from that of breeder and possession respectively; hence, we must develop a vision of society as community where all participants are valued members, regardless of age or gender. And we must challenge the notion that having one's wife produce a child with his own genes is sufficient cause for the wives of men with low sperm counts to be expected to undergo the physical and emotional assault such technology involves.

Further, a feminist ethics will attend to the nature of the relationships among those concerned. Annette Baier has eloquently argued for the importance of developing an ethics of trust,[30] and I believe a feminist ethics must address the question of the degree of trust appropriate to the relationships involved. Feminists have noted that women have little reason to trust the medical specialists who offer to respond to their reproductive desires, for, commonly women's interests have not come first from the medical point of view.[31] In fact, it is accurate to perceive feminist attacks on reproductive technology as expressions of the lack of trust feminists have in those who control the technology. Few feminists object to reproductive technology per se; rather they express concern about who controls it and how it can be used to further exploit women. The problem with reproductive technology is that it concentrates power in reproductive matters in the hands of those who are not directly involved in the actual bearing and rearing of the child; i.e., in men who relate to their clients in a technical, professional, authoritarian manner. It is a further step in the medicalization of pregnancy and birth which, in North America, is marked by relationships between pregnant women and their doctors which are very different from the traditional relationships between pregnant women and midwives. The latter relationships fostered an atmosphere of mutual trust which is impossible to replicate in hospital deliveries today. In fact, current approaches to pregnancy, labour, and birth tend to view the mother as a threat to the fetus who must be coerced to comply with medical procedures designed to ensure delivery of healthy babies at whatever cost necessary to the mother. Frequently, the fetus-mother relationship is medically characterized as adversarial and the physicians choose to foster a sense of alienation and passivity in the role they permit the mother. However well IVF may serve the interests of the few women with access to it, it more clearly serves the interests (be they commercial, professional, scholarly, or purely patriarchal) of those who control it.

Questions such as these are a puzzle to those engaged in the traditional approaches to ethics, for they always urge us to separate the question of evaluating the morality of various forms of reproductive technology in themselves, from questions about particular uses of that technology. From the perspective of a feminist ethics, however, no such distinction can be meaningfully made. Reproductive technology is not an abstract activity, it is an activity done in particular contexts and it is those contexts which must be addressed.

Feminist concerns cited earlier made clear the difficulties we have with some of our traditional ethical concepts; hence, feminist ethics directs us to rethink our basic ethical notions. Autonomy, or freedom of choice, is not a matter to be determined in isolated instances, as is commonly assumed in many approaches to applied ethics. Rather it is a matter that involves reflection on one's whole life situation. The freedom of choice feminists appeal to in the abortion situation is freedom to define one's status as childbearer, given the social, economic, and political significance of reproduction for women. A feminist perspective permits us to understand that reproductive freedom includes control of one's sexuality, protection against coerced sterilization (or iatrogenic sterilization, e.g. as caused by the Dalkon Shield), and the existence of a social and economic network of support for the children we may choose to bear. It is the freedom to redefine our roles in society according to our concerns and needs as women.

In contrast, the consumer freedom to purchase technology, allowed only to a few couples of the privileged classes (in traditionally approved relationships), seems to entrench further the patriarchal notions of woman's role as childbearer and of heterosexual monogamy as the only acceptable intimate relationship. In other words, this sort of choice does not seem to foster autonomy for women on the broad scale. IVF is a practice which seems to reinforce sexist, classist, and often racist assumptions of our culture; therefore, on our revised understanding of freedom, the contribution of this technology to the general autonomy of women is largely negative.

We can now see the advantage of a feminist ethics over mainstream ethical theories, for a feminist analysis explicitly accepts the need for a political component to our understanding of ethical issues. In this, it differs from traditional ethical theories and it also differs from a simply feminine ethics approach, such as the one Noddings offers, for Noddings seems to rely on individual relations exclusively and is deeply suspicious of political alliances as potential threats to the pure relation of caring. Yet, a full understanding of both the threat of IVF, and the alternative action necessary should we decide to reject IVF, is possible only if it includes a political dimension reflecting on the role of women in society.

From the point of view of feminist ethics, the primary question to consider is whether this and other forms of reproductive technology threaten to reinforce the lack of autonomy which women now experience in our culture—even as they appear, in the short run, to be increasing freedom. We must recognize that the interconnections among the social forces oppressive to women underlie feminists' mistrust of this technology which advertises itself as increasing women's autonomy.[32] The political perspective which directs us to look at how this technology fits in with general patterns of treatment for women is not readily accessible to traditional moral theories, for it involves categories of concern not accounted for in those theories—e.g. the complexity of issues which makes it inappropriate to study them in isolation from one another, the role of oppression in shaping individual desires, and potential differences in moral status which are connected with differences in treatment.

It is the set of connections constituting women's continued oppression in our society which inspires feminists to resurrect the old slippery slope arguments to warn against IVF. We must recognize that women's existing lack of control in reproductive matters begins the debate on a pretty steep incline. Technology with the potential to further remove control of reproduction from women makes the slope very slippery indeed. This new technology, though offered under the guise of increasing reproductive freedom, threatens to result, in fact, in a significant decrease in freedom, especially since it is a technology that will always include the active involvement of designated specialists and will not ever be a private matter for the couple or women concerned.

Ethics ought not to direct us to evaluate individual cases without also looking at the implications of our decisions from a wide perspective. My argument is that a theory of feminist ethics provides that wider perspective, for its different sort of methodology is sensitive to both the personal and the social dimensions of issues. For that reason, I believe it is the only ethical perspective suitable for evaluating issues of this sort.

READING ENDNOTES

1. I appreciate the helpful criticism I have received from colleagues in the Dalhousie Department of Philosophy, the Canadian Society for Women in Philosophy, and the Women's Studies program of the University of Alberta where earlier versions of this paper were read. I am particularly grateful for the careful criticism it has received from Linda Williams and Christine Overall.
2. Susan Sherwin, 'A Feminist Approach to Ethics,' *Dalhousie Review* 64, 4 (Winter 1984–85) 704-13.
3. Paul Ramsey, 'Shall we Reproduce?' *Journal of the American Medical Association* 220 (June 12, 1972), 1484.
4. Leon Kass, '"Making Babies" Revisited,' *The Public Interest* 54 (Winter 1979), 32—60.
5. Joseph Card Ratzinger and Alberto Bovone, 'Instruction on Respect for Human Life in its Origin and on the Dignity of Procreation: Replies to Certain Questions of the Day' (Vatican City: Vatican Polyglot Press 1987), 23–4.
6. *Ibid.*, 28.
7. Michael Bayles, *Reproductive Ethics* (Englewood Cliffs, NJ: Prentice-Hall 1984) 15.
8. Ratzinger and Bovone, 28.

9. Samuel Gorovitz, *Doctors' Dilemmas: Moral Conflict and Medical Care* (New York: Oxford University Press 1982), 168.

10. *Ibid.*, 173.

11. Bayles, 66.

12. I owe this observation to Linda Williams.

13. H. Tristram Englehardt, *The Foundations of Bioethics* (Oxford: Oxford University Press 1986), 237.

14. *Ibid.*, 241.

15. Anita Direcks, 'Has the Lesson Been Learned?' *DES Action Voice* 28 (Spring 1986), 1–4; and Nikita A. Crook, 'Clomid,' DES Action/Toronto Factsheet #442 (available from 60 Grosvenor St., Toronto, M5S 1B6).

16. Bayles, 32. Though Bayles is not a deontologist, he does concisely express a deontological concern here.

17. Gorovitz, 177.

18. Michael Soules, 'The In Vitro Fertilization Pregnancy Rate: Let's Be Honest with One Another,' *Fertility and Sterility* 43, 4 (1985) 511–13.

19. Christine Overall, *Ethics and Human Reproduction: A Feminist Analysis* (Allen and Unwin, forthcoming), 104 ms.

20. Englehardt, 239.

21. Bayles, 31.

22. Robert G. Edwards and David J. Sharpe, 'Social Values and Research in Human Embryology,' *Nature* 231 (May 14, 1971), 87.

23. Ratzinger and Bovone, 33.

24. *Ibid.*, 34.

25. Many authors are now working on an understanding of what feminist ethics entail. Among the Canadian papers I am familiar with, are Kathryn Morgan's 'Women and Moral Madness,' Sheila Mullett's 'Only Connect: The Place of Self-Knowledge in Ethics,' both in this volume, and Leslie Wilson's 'Is a Feminine Ethics Enough?' *Atlantis* (forthcoming).

26. Sherwin, 'A Feminist Approach to Ethics.'

27. Kathryn Payne Addelson, 'Moral Revolution,' in Marilyn Pearsall, ed., *Women and Values* (Belmont, CA: Wadsworth 1986), 291—309.

28. Carol Gilligan, *In a Different Voice* (Cambridge, MA: Harvard University Press 1982).

29. Nell Noddings, *Caring* (Berkeley: University of California Press 1984).

30. Annette Baier, 'What Do Women Want in a Moral Theory?' *Nous* 19 (March 1985) 53–64, and 'Trust and Antitrust,' *Ethics* 96 (January 1986) 231–60.

31. Linda Williams presents this position particularly clearly in her invaluable work 'But What Will They Mean for Women? Feminist Concerns About the New Reproductive Technologies,' No. 6 in the *Feminist Perspective* Series, CRIAW.

32. Marilyn Frye vividly describes the phenomenon of inter-relatedness which supports sexist oppression by appeal to the metaphor of a bird cage composed of thin wires, each relatively harmless in itself, but, collectively, the wires constitute an overwhelming barrier to the inhabitant of the cage. Marilyn Frye, *The Politics of Reality: Essays in Feminist Theory* (Trumansburg, NY: The Crossing Press 1983), 4–7.

QUESTIONS

1. Why do some people think IVF risks undermining the sense of identity and familial connectedness to one's parents? Is this plausible? If there were such risks to children born from IVF, would they be sufficient to support a ban? What else would we have to ban if we accepted this line?

2. What moral problems arise from the creation of surplus fertilized eggs?

3. Many people raised concerns about where IVF would lead in terms of further reproductive technologies and research possibilities. Have many of these "slippery slope" concerns turned out to be justified?

4. Given the benefits and risks and actual harms of IVF, would a utilitarian likely support its use or not?

5. Sherwin thinks deontologists would support the use of this technology. Why? Are there reasons to think that the decision might actually be harder for deontologists to make than Sherwin suggests?

6. In a system like ours, with socialized universal medical care, do the costs of IVF take on a special moral significance? Do they raise questions about the proper use of scarce medical resources?

7. IVF increases reproductive freedom of choice for women, which is usually regarded as a good thing by feminists. But Sherwin suggests that it may not similarly increase autonomy for women. What are its autonomy-limiting features? What does this tell us about the relationship between options (choice) and autonomy?

8. Many of the concerns Sherwin raises about the actual practice of IVF have been superseded by time. For example, marriage is no longer a requirement and single and lesbian women now have access to IVF. Does this suggest that new technologies that provide a benefit only to some at first tend to become more fairly available to all over time? Is such a conjecture supported by other examples you can think of?

9. What are the social influences that Sherwin thinks explain the desire to have biological children in our society? How are they all influenced by patriarchy?

10. How does feminist ethics differ from the traditional moral theories we have studied? Why does it result in an expanded set of concerns and questions?

11. Why is all feminist analysis at least in part practical? Why is all feminist analysis at least in part political?

12. What concerns are raised by the medicalization of pregnancy and birth?

✦ ✦ ✦

Debra Satz, Markets in Women's Sexual Labor

Debora Satz examines various theories to see which most easily captures our intuition that women should not sell their sexual capacities. Satz first examines an economic analysis, which defines legitimate social arrangements as those that efficiently allocate resources (via a cost/benefit analysis). She suggests that while the public's outrage over prostitution leads to an indirect argument against prostitution, it nevertheless fails to capture our intuitions adequately. In the first place, it takes for granted the current distribution of goods, and so it ignores the possibility of an unjust allocation of resources (which is likely under patriarchy). Second, it seems that there is something special about the repugnance that some feel regarding prostitution that makes it illegitimate to consider it as simply another cost. Lastly, the economic analysis cannot take into account that there seems to be something special about some goods that make it inappropriate to put them on the market (like citizenship or friendship). She next examines essentialism. Essentialists hold that there is something about sexual intimacy that itself accounts for the inappropriateness of markets in women's sexual labour. But whether it is couched in terms of bodily integrity or human dignity, Satz finds essentialism unacceptable as well. It seems unlikely that renting out the body is selling one's essential self, or that one can consistently maintain this line and not be opposed to factory work. Alternately, human dignity seems perfectly securable if we regulate prostitution to ensure better working conditions.

Satz instead endorses the egalitarian method. Women and men are provably unequal in material circumstances and social status. This is wrong. Prostitution is wrong because it reinforces the unequal social status of women in societies like our own. Prostitution presents us with a class of women who are sexually subservient to men. There is no reciprocal class of men who satisfy women. This lends credibility to the myth that men have strong sexual needs that must be satisfied by women.

Satz concludes by examining whether this requires that prostitution be banned by law. Here she presents us with an interesting thesis: that even though prostitution is morally objectionable, it might be better to regulate it rather than ban it outright. The law does not necessarily protect women best by banning this (presumed) morally objectionable practice. This flies in the face of a common presumption—if a practice is found morally illegitimate, the law ought to ban it. The relationship between the law and morality is an interesting one, and one that too little time is spent examining.

✦ ✦ ✦

Debra Satz, "Markets in Women's Sexual Labor," *Ethics* 106 (Oct. 1995): 63–85. © 1995 The University of Chicago. Reprinted with permission of University of Chicago Press and the author.

Markets in Women's Sexual Labor

DEBRA SATZ

There is a widely shared intuition that markets are inappropriate for some kinds of human endeavor: that some things simply should not be bought and sold. For example, virtually everyone believes that love and friendship should have no price. The sale of other human capacities is disputed, but many people believe that there is something about sexual and reproductive activities that makes their sale inappropriate. I have called the thesis supported by this intuition the asymmetry thesis.[1] Those who hold the asymmetry thesis believe that markets in reproduction and sex are asymmetric to other labor markets. They think that treating sexual and reproductive capacities as commoditites, as goods to be developed and exchanged for a price, is worse than treating our other capacities as commodities. They think that there is something wrong with commercial surrogacy and prostitution that is not wrong with teaching and professional sports.

The intuition that there is a distinction between markets in different human capacities is a deep one, even among people who ultimately think that the distinction does not justify legally forbidding sales of reproductive capacity and sex. I accept this intuition, which I continue to probe in this article. In particular, I ask: What justifies taking an asymmetric attitude toward markets in our sexual capacities? What, if anything, is problematic about a woman selling her sexual as opposed to her secretarial labor? And, if the apparent asymmetry can be explained and justified, what implications follow for public policy?

In this article, I sketch and criticize two popular approaches to these questions. The first, which I call the economic approach, attributes the wrongness of prostitution to its consequences for efficiency or welfare. The important feature of this approach is its treatment of sex as a morally indifferent matter: sexual labor is not to be treated as a commodity if and only if such treatment fails to be efficient or welfare maximizing. The second, the "essentialist" approach, by contrast, stresses that sales of sexual labor are wrong because they are inherently alienating or damaging to human happiness. In contrast to these two ways of thinking about the immorality of prostitution, I will argue that the most plausible support for the asymmetry thesis stems from the role of commercialized sex and reproduction in sustaining a social world in which women form a subordinated group. Prostitution is wrong insofar as the sale of women's sexual labor reinforces broad patterns of sex discrimination. My argument thus stresses neither efficiency nor sexuality's intrinsic value but, rather, equality. In particular, I argue that contemporary prostitution contributes to, and also instantiates, the perception of women as socially inferior to men.

On the basis of my analysis of prostitution's wrongness, there is no simple conclusion as to what its legal status ought to be. Both criminalization and decriminalization may have the effect of exacerbating the inequalities in virtue of which I claim that prostitution is wrong. Nonetheless, my argument does have implications for the form of prostitution's regulation, if legal, and its prohibition and penalties, if illegal. Overall, my argument tends to support decriminalization.

The argument I will put forward here is qualified and tentative in its practical conclusions, but its theoretical point is not. I will argue that the most plausible account of prostitution's wrongness turns on its relationship to the pervasive social inequality between men and women. If, in fact, no causal relationship obtains between prostitution and gender inequality, then I do not think that prostitution is morally troubling.[2] This is a controversial claim. In my evaluation of prostitution, consideration of the actual social conditions which many, if not most, women face plays a crucial role. It will follow from my analysis that male prostitution raises distinct issues and is not connected to injustice in the same way as female prostitution.

On my view, prostitution is not wrong irrespective of its cultural and economic context. Moreover, prostitution is a complex phenomenon. I begin, accordingly, with the question, Who is a prostitute?

WHO IS A PROSTITUTE?

While much has been written on the history of prostitution, and some empirical studies of prostitutes themselves have been undertaken, the few philosophers writing on this subject have tended to treat prostitution as if the term referred to something as obvious as "table."[3] But it does not. Not only is it hard to draw a sharp line between prostitution and practices which look like prostitution, but as historians of the subject have emphasized, prostitution today is also a very different phenomenon from earlier forms of commercial sex.[4] In particular, the idea of prostitution as a specialized occupation of an outcast and stigmatized group is of relatively recent origin.[5]

While all contemporary prostitutes are stigmatized as outsiders, prostitution itself has an internal hierarchy based on class, race, and gender. The majority of prostitutes—and all those who walk the streets—are poor. The majority of streetwalkers in the United States are poor black women. These women are a world apart from prostitution's upper tier. Consider three cases: a streetwalker in Boston, a call girl on Park Avenue, and a male prostitute in San Fransisco's tenderloin district. In what way do these three lives resemble one another? Consider the three cases:

1. A fourteen-year-old girl prostitutes herself to support her boyfriend's heroin addiction. Later, she works the streets to support her own habit. She begins, like most teenage streetwalkers, to rely on a pimp for protection. She is uneducated and is frequently subjected to violence in her relationships and with her customers. She also receives no social security, no sick leave or maternity leave, and—most important—no control as to whether or not she has sex with a man. The latter is decided by her pimp.

2. Now imagine the life of a Park Avenue call girl. Many call girls drift into prostitution after "run of the mill promiscuity," led neither by material want nor lack of alternatives.[6] Some are young college graduates, who upon graduation earn money by prostitution while searching for other jobs. Call girls can earn between $30,000 and $100,000 annually. These women have control over the entire amount they earn as well as an unusual degree of independence, far greater than in most other forms of work. They can also decide who they wish to have sex with and when they wish to do so.[7] There is little resemblance between their lives and that of the Boston streetwalker.

3. Finally, consider the increasing number of male prostitutes. Most male prostitutes (but not all) sell sex to other men.[8] Often the men who buy such sex are themselves married. Unfortunately, there is little information on male prostitutes; it has not been well studied as either a historical or a contemporary phenomenon.[9] What we do know suggests that like their female counterparts, male prostitutes cover the economic spectrum. Two important differences between male and female prostitutes are that men are more likely to work only part time and that they are not generally subject to the violence of male pimps; they tend to work on their own.

Are these three cases distinct? Many critics of prostitution have assumed that all prostitutes were women who entered the practice under circumstances which included abuse and economic desperation. But that is a false assumption: the critics have mistaken a part of the practice for the whole.[10] For example, although women who walk the streets are the most visible, they constitute only about 20 percent of the prostitute population in the United States.[11]

The varying circumstances of prostitution are important because they force us to consider carefully what we think may be wrong with prostitution. For example, in the first case, the factors which seem crucial to our response of condemnation are the miserable background conditions, the prostitute's vulnerability to violence at the hands of her pimp or client, her age, and her lack of control over whether she has sex with a client. These conditions could be redressed through regulation without forbidding commercial sexual exchanges between consenting adults.[12] The second class of prostitution stands in sharp contrast. These women engage in what seems to be a voluntary activity, chosen among a range of decent alternatives. Many of these women sell their sexual capacities without coercion or regret. The third case rebuts arguments that prostitution has no other purpose than to subordinate women.

In the next section, I explore three alternative explanations of prostitution's wrongness, which I refer to respectively as economic, essentialist, and egalitarian.

WHAT IS WRONG WITH PROSTITUTION?

The Economic Approach

Economists generally frame their questions about the best way to distribute a good without reference to its intrinsic qualities. They tend to focus on the quantitative features of a good and not its qualities.[13] Economists tend to endorse interference with a market in some good only when the results of that market are inefficient or have adverse effects on welfare.

An economic approach to prostitution does not specify a priori that certain sales are wrong: no act of commodification is ruled out in advance.[14] Rather, this approach focuses on the costs and benefits that accompany such sales. An economic approach to contracts will justify inalienability rules—rules which forbid individuals from entering into certain transactions—in cases where there are costly externalities to those transactions and in general where such transactions are inefficient. The economic approach thus supports the asymmetry thesis when the net social costs of prostitution are greater than the net social costs incurred by the sale of other human capacities.

What are the costs of prostitution? In the first place, the parties to a commercial sex transaction share possible costs of disease and guilt.[15] Prostitution also has costs to third parties: a man who frequents a prostitute dissipates financial resources which might otherwise be directed to his family; in a society which values intimate marriage, infidelity costs a man's wife or companion in terms of mistrust and suffering (and therefore prostitution may sometimes lead to marital instability); and prostitutes often have diseases which can be spread to others. Perhaps the largest third-party costs to prostitution are "moralisms":[16] many people find the practice morally offensive and are pained by its existence. (Note that 'moralisms' refers to people's preferences about moral issues and not to morality as such.)

The economic approach generates a contingent case for the asymmetry thesis, focusing on prostitution's "moral" costs in terms of public opinion or the welfare costs to prostitutes or the population as a whole (e.g., through the spread of diseases). Consideration of the limitations on sexual freedom which can be justified from a welfare standpoint can be illuminating and forces us to think about the actual effects of sexual regulations.[17] Nevertheless, I want to register three objections to this approach to justifying the asymmetry thesis.

First, and most obvious, both markets and contractual exchanges function within a regime of property rights and legal entitlements. The economic approach ignores the background system of distribution within which prostitution occurs. Some background systems, however, are unjust. How do we know whether prostitution itself is part of a morally acceptable system of property rights and entitlements?

Second, this type of approach seems disabled from making sense of distinctions between goods in cases where these distinctions do not seem to reflect mere differences in the net sum of costs and benefits. The sale of certain goods seems to many people simply unthinkable—human life, for example. While it may be possible to justify prohibitions on slavery by appeal to costs and benefits (and even count moralisms in the sum), the problem is that such justification makes contingent an outcome which reasonable people do not hold contingently. It also makes little sense, phenomenologically, to describe the moral repugnance people feel toward slavery as "just a cost."[18]

Let me elaborate this point. There seems to be a fundamental difference between the "goods" of my person and my external goods, a difference whose nature is not completely explained by appeal to information failures and externalities. "Human capital" is not just another form of capital. For example, my relationship with my body and my capacities is more intimate than my relationship with most external things. The economic approach fails to capture this distinction.

Richard Posner—one of the foremost practitioners of the economic approach to law—illustrates the limits of the economic approach when he views a rapist as a "sex thief."[19] He thus overlooks the fact that rape is a crime of violence and assault.[20] He also ignores the qualitative differences between my relationship with my body and my car. But that there are such differences is obvious. The circumstances in which I sell my capacities have a much more profound effect on who I am and who I become—through effects on my desires, capacities, and values—than the circumstances in which I sell my Honda Civic. Moreover, the idea of sovereignty over body and mind is closely related to the idea of personal integrity, which is a crucial element of any reasonable scheme of liberty. The liberty to exercise sovereignty over my car has a lesser place in any reasonable scheme of liberties than the liberty to be sovereign over my body and mind.[21]

Third, some goods seem to have a special status which requires that they be shielded from the market if their social meaning or role is to be preserved. The sale of citizenship rights or friendship does not simply produce costs and benefits: it transforms the nature of the goods sold. In this sense, the market is not a neutral mechanism of exchange: there are some goods whose sale transforms or destroys their initial meaning.

These objections resonate with objections to prostitution for which its wrongness is not adequately captured by summing up contingent welfare costs and benefits. These objections resonate with moralist and egalitarian concerns. Below I survey two other types of arguments which can be used to support the asymmetry thesis: (1) essentialist arguments that the sale of sexual labor is intrinsically wrong because it is alienating or contrary to human flourishing and happiness; and (2) my own egalitarian argument that the sale of sex is wrong because, given the background conditions within which it occurs, it tends to reinforce gender inequality. I thus claim that contemporary prostitution is wrong because it promotes injustice, and not because it makes people less happy.

The Essentialist Approach

Economists abstract from the qualities of the goods that they consider. By contrast essentialists hold that there is something intrinsic to the sphere of sex and intimacy that accounts for the distinction we mark between it and other types of labor. Prostitution is not wrong simply because it causes harm; prostitution constitutes a harm. Essentialists hold that there is some intrinsic property of sex which makes its commodification wrong. Specific arguments differ, however, in what they take this property to be. I will consider two popular versions of essentialism: the first stresses the close connection between sex and the self; the second stresses the close connection between sex and human flourishing.[22]

Some feminist critics of prostitution have argued that sexual and reproductive capacities are more crucially tied to the nature of our selves than our other capacities.[23] The sale of sex is taken to cut deeper into the self, to involve a more total alienation from the self. As Carole Pateman puts it, "Whan a prostitute contracts out use of her body she is thus selling *herself* in a very real sense. Women's selves are involved in prostitution in a different manner from the involvement of the self in other occupations."[24] The realization of women's selfhood requires, on this view, that some of the capacities embodied in their persons, including their sexuality, remain "market-inalienable."[25]

Consider an analogous strategy for accounting for the value of bodily integrity in terms of its relationship to our personhood. It seems right to say that a world in which the boundaries of our bodies were not (more or less) secure would be a world in which our sense of self would be fundamentally shaken. Damage to, and violation of, our bodies affects us in a "deeper" way, a more significant way, than damage to our external property. Robbing my body of a kidney is a violation different in kind than robbing my house of a stereo, however expensive. Distributing kidneys from healthy people to sick people through a lottery is a far different act than using a lottery to distribute door prizes.[26]

But this analogy can only be the first step in an argument in favor of treating either our organs or sexual capacities as market-inalienable. Most liberals think that individual sovereignty over mind and body is crucial for the exercise of fundamental liberties. Thus, in the absence of clear harms, most liberals would reject legal bans on voluntary sales of body parts or sexual capacities. Indeed, the usual justification of such bans is harm to self: such sales are presumed to be "desperate exchanges" that the individual herself would reasonably want to foreclose. American law blocks voluntary sales of individual organs and body parts but not sales of blood on the assumption that only the former sales are likely to be so harmful to the individual that given any reasonable alternative, she herself would refrain from such sales.

Whatever the plausibility of such a claim with respect to body parts, it is considerably weaker when applied to sex (or blood). There is no strong evidence that prostitution is, at least in the United States, a desperate exchange. In part this reflects the fact that the relationship people have with their sexual capacities is far more diverse than the relationship they have with their body parts. For some people, sexuality is a realm of ecstatic communion with another, for others it is little more than a sport or distraction. Some people will find consenting to be sexually used by another person enjoyable or adequately compensated by a wage. Even for the same person, sex can be the source of a range of experiences.

Of course, the point cannot simply be that, as an empirical matter, people have differing conceptions of sexuality. The critics of prostitution grant that. The point is whether, and within what range, this diversity is desirable.[27]

Let us assume, then, in the absence of compelling counterargument, that an individual can exercise sovereignty through the sale of her sexual capacities. Margaret Radin raises a distinct worry about the effects of widespread prostitution on human flourishing. Radin's argument stresses that widespread sex markets would promote inferior forms of personhood. She says that we can see this is the case if we "reflect on what we know now about human life and choose the best from among the conceptions available to us."[28] If prostitution were to become common, Radin argues, it would have adverse effects on a form of personhood which itself is intrinsically valuable. For example, if the signs of affection and intimacy were frequently detached from their usual meaning, such signs might well become more ambiguous and easy to manipulate. The marks of an intimate relationship (physical intimacy, terms of endearment, etc.) would no longer signal the existence of intimacy. In that case, by obscuring the nature of sexual relationships, prostitution might undermine our ability to apply the criteria for coercion and informational failure.[29] Individuals might more easily enter into damaging relationships and lead less fulfilling lives as a result.

Radin is committed to a form of perfectionism which rules out the social practice of prostitution as incompatible with the highest forms of human development and flourishing. But why should perfectionists condemn prostitution while tolerating practices such as monotonous assembly line work where human beings are often mere appendages to machines? Monotonous wage labor, moreover, is far more widespread than prostitution.[30] Can a consistent perfectionist give reasons for differentiating sexual markets from other labor markets?

It is difficult to draw a line between our various capacities such that only sexual and reproductive capacities are essential to the flourishing self. In a money economy like our own, we each sell the use of many human capacities. Writers sell the use of their ability to write, advertisers sell the use of their ability to write jingles, and musicians sell the use of their ability to write and perform symphonies. Aren't these capacities also closely tied to our personhood and its higher capacities?[31] Yet the mere alienation of the use of these capacities, even when widespread, does not seem to threaten personal flourishing.

An alternative version of the essentialist thesis views the commodification of sex as an assault on personal dignity.[32] Prostitution degrades the prostitute. Elizabeth Anderson, for example, discusses the effect of commodification on the nature of sex as a shared good, based on the recognition of mutual attraction. In commercial sex, each party now values the other only instrumentally, not intrinsically. And, while both parties are thus prevented from enjoying a shared good, it is worse for the prostitute.

The customer merely surrenders a certain amount of cash; the prostitute cedes her body: the prostitute is thus degraded to the status of a thing. Call this the degradation objection.

I share the intuition that the failure to treat others as persons is morally significant; it is wrong to treat people as mere things. But I am skeptical as to whether this intuition supports the conclusion that prostitution is wrong. Consider the contrast between slavery and prostitution. Slavery was, in Orlando Patterson's memorable phrase, a form of "social death": it denied to enslaved individuals the ability to press claims, to be—in their own right—sources of value and interest. But the mere sale of the use of someone's capacities does not necessarily involve a failure of this kind, on the part of either the buyer or the seller.[33] Many forms of labor, perhaps most, cede some control of a person's body to others. Such control can range from requirements to be in a certain place at a certain time (e.g., reporting to the office), to requirements that a person (e.g., a professional athlete) eat certain foods and get certain amounts of sleep, or maintain good humor in the face of the offensive behavior of others (e.g., airline stewardesses). Some control of our capacities by others does not seem to be ipso facto destructive of our dignity.[34] Whether the purchase of a form of human labor power will have this negative consequence will depend on background social macrolevel and microlevel institutions. Minimum wages, worker participation and control, health and safety regulations, maternity and paternity leave, restrictions on specific performance, and the right to "exit" one's job are all features which attenuate the objectionable aspects of treating people's labor as a mere economic input. The advocates of prostitution's wrongness in virtue of its connection to self-hood, flourishing and degradation have not shown that a system of regulated prostitution would be unable to respond to their worries. In particular, they have not established that there is something wrong with prostitution irrespective of its cultural and historical context.

There is, however, another way of interpreting the degradation objection which draws a connection between the current practice of prostitution and the lesser social status of women.[35] This connection is not a matter of the logic of prostitution per se but of the fact that contemporary prostitution degrades women by treating them as the sexual servants of men. In current prostitution, prostitutes are overwhelmingly women and their clients are almost exclusively men. Prostitution, in conceiving of a class of women as needed to satisfy male sexual desire, represents women as sexual servants to men. The degradation objection, so understood, can be seen as a way of expressing an egalitarian concern since there is no reciprocal ideology which represents men as servicing women's sexual needs. It is to this egalitarian understanding of prostitution's wrongness that I turn in the next section.

The Egalitarian Approach

While the essentialists rightly call our attention to the different relation we have with our capacities and external things, they overstate the nature of the difference between our sexual capacities and our other capacities with respect to our personhood, flourishing, and dignity.[36] They are also insufficiently attentive to the background conditions in which commercial sex exchanges take place. A third account of prostitution's wrongness stresses its causal relationship to gender inequality. I have defended this line of argument with respect to markets in women's reproductive labor.[37] Can this argument be extended to cover prostitution as well?

The answer hinges in part on how we conceive of gender inequality. On my view, there are two important dimensions of gender inequality, often conflated. The first dimension concerns inequalities in the distribution of income, wealth, and opportunity. In most nations, including the United States, women form an economically and socially disadvantaged group. The statistics regarding these disadvantages, even in the United States, are grim.

1. *Income inequality.*—In 1992, given equal hours of work, women in the United States earned on average sixty-six cents for every dollar earned by a man.[38] Seventy-five percent of full-time working women (as opposed to 37 percent of full-time working men) earn less than twenty thousand dollars.[39]

2. *Job segregation.*—Women are less likely than men to fill socially rewarding, high-paying jobs. Despite the increasing entrance of women into previously gender-segregated occupations, 46 percent of all working women are employed in service and administrative support jobs such as secretaries, waitresses, and health aides. In the United States and Canada, the extent of job segregation in the lowest-paying occupations is increasing.[40]

3. *Poverty.*—In 1989, one out of five families were headed by women. One-third of such women-headed families live below the poverty line, which was $13,359 for a family of four in 1990.[41] In the United States, fathers currently owe mothers 24 billion dollars in unpaid child support.[42]

4. *Unequal division of labor in the family.*—Within the family, women spend disproportionate amounts of time on housework and rearing children. According to one recent study, wives employed full time outside the home do 70 percent of the housework; full-time housewives do 83 percent.[43] The unequal family division of labor is itself caused by and causes labor market inequality: given the lower wages of working women, it is more costly for men to participate in household labor.

Inequalities in income and opportunity form an important part of the backdrop against which prostitution must be viewed. While there are many possible routes into prostitution, the largest number of women who participate in it are poor, young, and uneducated. Labor market inequalities will be part of any plausible explanation of why many women "choose" to enter into prostitution.

The second dimension of gender inequality does not concern income and opportunity but status.[44] In many contemporary contexts, women are viewed and treated as inferior to men. This inferior treatment proceeds via several distinct mechanisms.

1. *Negative stereotyping.*—Stereotypes persist as to the types of jobs and responsibilities a woman can assume. Extensive studies have shown that people typically believe that men are more dominant, assertive, and instrumentally rational than women. Gender shapes beliefs about a person's capacities: women are thought to be less intelligent than their male equals.[45]

2. *Unequal power.*—Men are able to asymmetrically sanction women. The paradigm case of this is violence. Women are subjected to greater amounts of violence by men than is the reverse: every fifteen seconds a woman is battered in the United States. Battering causes more injury (excluding deaths) to women than car accidents, rape, and muggings combined.[46] Four million women a year are physically assaulted by their male partners.[47]

3. *Marginalization.*—People who are marginalized are excluded from, or absent from, core productive social roles in society—roles which convey self-respect and meaningful contribution.[48] At the extremes, marginalized women lack the means for their basic survival: they are dependent on state welfare or male partners to secure the basic necessities of life. Less severely marginalized women lack access to central and important social roles. Their activities are confined to peripheral spheres of social organization. For example, the total number of women who have served in Congress since its inception through 1992 is 134. The total number of men is 11,096. In one-third of governments worldwide, there are no women in the decision-making bodies of the country.[49]

4. *Stigma.*—A woman's gender is associated, in some contexts, with stigma, a badge of dishonor. Consider rape. In crimes of rape, the complainant's past behavior and character are central in determining whether a crime has actually occurred. This is not true of other crimes: "mail fraud" (pun intended) is not dismissed because of the bad judgment or naïveté of the victims. Society views rape differently, I suggest, because many people think that women really want to be forced into sex. Women's lower status thus influences the way that rape is seen.

Both forms of inequality—income inequality and status inequality—potentially bear on the question of prostitution's wrongness. Women's decisions to enter into prostitution must be viewed against the background of their unequal life chances and their unequal opportunities for income and rewarding work. The extent to which women face a highly constrained range of options will surely be relevant to whether, and to what degree, we view their choices as autonomous. Some women may actually loathe or judge as inferior the lives of prostitution they "choose." Economic inequality may thus shape prostitution.

We can also ask, Does prostitution itself shape employment inequalities between men and women? In general, whenever there are significant inequalities between groups, those on the disadvantageous side will be disproportionately allocated to subordinate positions. What they do, the positions they occupy, will serve to reinforce negative and disempowering images of themselves. In this sense, prostitution can have an effect on labor-market inequality, associating women with certain stereotypes. For example, images reinforced by prostitution may make it less likely for women to be hired in certain jobs. Admittedly the effect of prostitution on labor-market inequality, if it exists at all, will be small. Other roles which women disproportionately occupy—secretaries, housecleaners, babysitters, waitresses, and saleswomen—will be far more significant in reinforcing (as well as constituting) a gender-segregated division of labor.

I do not think it is plausible to attribute to prostitution a direct causal role in income inequality between men and women. But I believe that it is plausible to maintain that prostitution makes an important and direct contribution to women's inferior social status. Prostitution shapes and its itself shaped by custom and culture, by cultural meanings about the importance of sex, about the nature of women's sexuality and male desire.[50]

If prostitution is wrong it is because of its effects on how men perceive women and on how women perceive themselves. In our society, prostitution represents women as the sexual servants of men. It supports and embodies the widely held belief that men have strong sex drives which must be satisfied—largely through gaining access to some woman's body. This belief underlies the mistaken idea that prostitution is the "oldest" profession, since it is seen as a necessary consequence of human (i.e., male) nature. It also underlies the traditional conception of marriage, in which a man owned not only his wife's property but her body as well. It should not fail to startle us that until recently, most states did not recognize the possibility of "real rape" in marriage.[51] (Marital rape remains legal in two states: North Carolina and Oklahoma.)

Why is the idea that women must service men's sexual needs an image of inequality and not mere difference? My argument suggests that there are two primary, contextual reasons:

First, in our culture, there is no reciprocal social practice which represents men as serving women's sexual needs. Men are gigolos and paid escorts—but their sexuality is not seen as an independent capacity whose use women can buy. It is not part of the identity of a class of men that they will service women's sexual desires. Indeed, male prostitutes overwhelmingly service other men and not women. Men are not depicted as fully capable of commercially alienating their sexuality to women; but prostitution depicts women as sexual servants of men.

Second, the idea that prostitution embodies an idea of women as inferior is strongly suggested by the high incidence of rape and violence against prostitutes, as well as the fact that few men seek out or even contemplate prostitutes as potential marriage partners. While all women in our society are potential targets of rape and violence, the mortality rates for women engaged in streetwalking prostitution are roughly forty times higher than that of nonprostitute women.[52]

My suggestion is that prostitution depicts an image of gender inequality, by constituting one class of women as inferior. Prostitution is a "theater" of inequality—it displays for us a practice in which women are subordinate to men. This is especially the case where women are forcibly controlled by their (male) pimps. It follows from my conception of prostitution that it need not have such a negative effect when the prostitute is male. More research needs to be done on popular images and conceptions of gay male prostitutes, as well as on the extremely small number of male prostitutes who have women clients.

The negative image of women who participate in prostitution, the image of their inferior status, is objectionable in itself. It constitutes an important form of inequality—unequal status—based on attitudes of superiority and disrespect. Unfortunately, this form of inequality has largely been ignored by political philosophers and economists who have focused instead on inequalities in income and opportunity. Moreover, this form of inequality is not confined to prostitutes. I believe that the negative image of women prostitutes has third party effects: it shapes and influences the way women as a whole are seen. This hypothesis is, of course, an empirical one. It has not been tested largely because of the lack of studies of men who go to prostitutes. Most extant studies of prostitution examine the behavior and motivations of the women who enter into the practice, a fact which itself raises the suspicion that prostitution is viewed as "a problem about the women who are prostitutes ... [rather than] a problem about the men who demand to buy them."[53] In these studies, male gender identity is taken as a given.

To investigate prostitution's negative image effects on female prostitutes and on women generally we need research on the following questions: (1) What are the attitudes of men who visit women prostitutes toward prostitutes? How do their attitudes compare with the attitudes of men who do not visit prostitutes toward women prostitutes? (2) What are the attitudes of men who visit women prostitutes toward women generally? What are the attitudes of men who do not visit women prostitutes toward women generally? (3) What are the attitudes of women toward women prostitutes? (4) What are the attitudes of the men and women involved in prostitution toward themselves? (5) Given the large proportion of African-American women who participate in prostitution, in what ways does prostitution contribute to male attitudes toward these women? (6) Does prostitution contribute to or diminish the likelihood of crimes of sexual violence? (7) What can we learn about these questions through cross-national studies? How do attitudes in the United States about women prostitutes compare with those in countries with more egalitarian wage policies or less status inequality between men and women?

The answers to these questions will reflect social facts about our culture. Whatever plausibility there is to the hypothesis that prostitution causally contributes to gender status inequality, it gains this plausibility from its surrounding cultural context.

I can imagine hypothetical circumstances in which prostitution would not have a negative image effect, where it could mark a reclaiming of women's sexuality. Margo St. James and other members of Call Off Your Old Tired Ethics (COYOTE) have argued that prostitutes can function as sex therapists, fulfilling a legitimate social need as well as providing a source of experiment and alternative conceptions of sexuality and gender.[54] I agree that in a different culture, with different assumptions about men's and women's gender identities, prostitution might not have unequalizing effects. But I think that St. James and others have minimized the cultural stereotypes that surround contemporary prostitution and their power over the shape of the practice. Prostitution, as we know it, is not separable from the larger surrounding culture which marginalizes, stereotypes, and stigmatizes women. Rather than providing an alternative conception of sexuality, I think that we need to look carefully at what men and women actually learn in prostitution. I do not believe that ethnographic studies of prostitution would support COYOTE's claim that prostitution contributes to images of women's dignity and equal standing.

If, through its negative image of women as sexual servants of men, prostitution reinforces women's inferior status in society, then it is wrong. Even though men can be and are prostitutes, I think that it is unlikely that we will find such negative image effects on men as a group. Individual men may be degraded in individual acts of prostitution: men as a group are not.

Granting all of the above, one objection to the equality approach of prostitution's wrongness remains. Is prostitution's negative image effect greater than that produced by other professions in which women largely service men, for example, secretarial labor? What is special about prostitution?

The negative image effect undoubtedly operates outside the domain of prostitution. But there are two significant differences between prostitution and other gender-segregated professions.

First, most people believe that prostitution, unlike secretarial work, is especially objectionable. Holding such moral views of prostitution constant, if prostitution continues to be primarily a female occupation, then the existence of prostitution will disproportionately fuel negative images of women.[55] Second, and relatedly, the particular image of women in prostitution is more of an image of inferiority than that of a secretary. The image embodies a great amount of objectification, of representing the prostitute as an object without a will of her own. Prostitutes are far more likely to be victims of violence than are secretaries: as I mentioned, the mortality rate of women in prostitution is forty times that of other women. Prostitutes are also far more likely to be raped: a prostitute's "no" does not, to the male she services, mean no.

My claim is that, unless such arguments about prostitution's causal role in sustaining a form of gender inequality can be supported, I am not persuaded that something is morally wrong with markets in sex. In particular, I do not find arguments about the necessary relationship between commercial sex and diminished flourishing and degradation convincing. If prostitution is wrong, it is not because of its effects on happiness or personhood (effects which are shared with other forms of wage-labor); rather, it is because the sale of women's sexual labor may have adverse consequences for achieving a significant form of equality between men and women. My argument for the asymmetry thesis, if correct, connects prostitution to injustice. I now turn to the question of whether, even if we assume that prostitution is wrong under current conditions, it should remain illegal.

Should Prostitution be Legalized?

It is important to distinguish between prostitution's wrongness and the legal response that we are entitled to make to that wrongness. Even if prostitution is wrong, we may not be justified in prohibiting it if that prohibition makes the facts in virtue of which it is wrong worse, or if its costs are too great for other important values, such as autonomy and privacy. For example, even if someone accepts that the contemporary division of labor in the family is wrong, they may still reasonably object to government surveillance of the family's division of household chores. To determine whether such surveillance is justified, we need know more about the fundamental interests at stake, the costs of surveillance and the availability of alternative mechanisms for promoting equality in families. While I think that there is no acceptable view which would advocate governmental surveillance of family chores, there remain a range of plausible views about the appropriate scope of state intervention and, indeed, the appropriate scope of equality considerations.[56]

It is also important to keep in mind that in the case of prostitution, as with pornography and hate speech, narrowing the discussion of solutions to the single question of whether to ban or not to ban shows a poverty of imagination. There are many ways of challenging existing cultural values about the appropriate division of labor in the family and the nature of women's sexual and reproductive capacities—for example, education, consciousness-raising groups, changes in employee leave policies, comparable worth programs, etc. The law is not the only way to provide women with incentives to refrain from participating in prostitution. Nonetheless, we do need to decide what the best legal policy toward prostitution should be.

I begin with an assessment of the policy which we now have. The United States is one of the few developed Western countries which criminalizes prostitution.[57] Denmark, the Netherlands, West Germany, Sweden, Switzerland, and Austria all have legalized prostitution, although in some of these countries it is restricted by local ordinances.[58] Where prostitution is permitted, it is closely regulated.

Suppose that we accept that gender equality is a legitimate goal of social policy. The question is whether the current legal prohibition on prostitution in the United States promotes gender equality. The answer I think is that it clearly does not. The current legal policies in the United States arguably exacerbate the factors in virtue of which prostitution is wrong.

The current prohibition on prostitution renders the women who engage in the practice vulnerable. First, the participants in the practice seek assistance from pimps in lieu of the contractual and legal remedies which are denied them. Male pimps may protect women prostitutes from their customers and from the police, but the system of pimp-run prostitution has enormous negative effects on the women at the lowest rungs of prostitution. Second, prohibition of prostitution raises the dilemma of the "double bind": if we prevent prostitution without greater redistribution of income, wealth, and opportunities, we deprive poor women of one way—in some circumstances the only way—of improving their condition.[59] Analogously, we do not solve the problem of homelessness by criminalizing it.

Furthermore, women are disproportionately punished for engaging in commercial sex acts. Many state laws make it a worse crime to sell sex than to buy it. Consequently, pimps and clients ("johns") are rarely prosecuted. In some jurisdictions, patronizing a prostitute is not illegal. The record of arrests and convictions is also highly asymmetric. Ninety percent of all convicted prostitutes are women. Studies have shown that male prostitutes are arrested with less frequency than female prostitutes and receive shorter sentences. One study of the judicial processing of 2,859 male and female prostitutes found that judges were more likely to find defendants guilty if they were female.[60]

Nor does the current legal prohibition on prostitution unambiguously benefit women as a class because the cultural meaning of current governmental prohibition of prostitution is unclear. While an unrestricted regime of prostitution—a pricing system in women's sexual attributes—could have negative external consequences on women's self-perceptions and perceptions by men, state prohibition can also reflect a view of women which contributes to their inequality. For example, some people support state regulation because they believe that women's sexuality is for purposes of reproduction, a claim tied to traditional ideas about women's proper role.

There is an additional reason why banning prostitution seems an inadequate response to the problem of gender inequality and which suggests a lack of parallel with the case of commercial surrogacy. Banning prostitution would not by itself—does not—eliminate it. While there is reason to think that making commercial surrogacy arrangements illegal or unenforceable would diminish their occurrence, no such evidence exists about prostitution. No city has eliminated prostitution merely through criminalization. Instead, criminalized prostitution thrives as a black market activity in which pimps substitute for law as the mechanism for enforcing contracts. It thereby makes the lives of prostitutes worse than they might otherwise be and without clearly counteracting prostitution's largely negative image of women.

If we decide to ban prostitution, these problems must be addressed. If we decide not to ban prostitution (either by legalizing it or decriminalizing it), then we must be careful to regulate the practice to address its negative effects. Certain restrictions on advertising and recruitment will be needed in order to address the negative image effects that an unrestricted regime of prostitution would perpetuate. But the current regime of prostitution has negative effects on the prostitutes themselves. It places their sexual capacities largely under the control of men. In order to promote women's autonomy, the law needs to ensure that certain restrictions—in effect, a Bill of Rights for Women—are in place.[61]

1. No woman should be forced, either by law or by private persons, to have sex against her will. (Recall that it is only quite recently that the courts have recognized the existence of marital rape.) A woman who sells sex must be able to refuse to give it; she must not be coerced by law or private persons to perform.

2. No woman should be denied access, either by law or by private persons, to contraception or to treatment for sexually transmitted diseases, particularly AIDS, or to abortion (at least in the first trimester).

3. The law should ensure that a woman has adequate information before she agrees to sexual intercourse. The risks of venereal and other sexually transmitted diseases, the risks of pregnancy, and the laws protecting a woman's right to refuse sex should all be generally available.

4. Minimum age of consent laws for sexual intercourse should be enforced. These laws should ensure that women (and men) are protected from coercion and do not enter into sexual relationships until they are in a position to understand what they are consenting to.

5. The law should promote women's control over their own sexuality by pro-hibiting brokerage. If what is wrong with prostitution is its relation to gender inequality, then it is crucial that the law be brought to bear primarily on the men who profit from the use of women's sexual capacities.

Each of these principles is meant to establish and protect a woman's right to con-trol her sexual and reproductive capacities and not to give control of these capacities to others. Each of these principles is meant to protect the conditions for women's con-sent to sex, whether commercial or not. Each of these principles also seeks to counter the degradation of women in prostitution by mitigating its nature as a form of female servitude. In addition, given that a woman's choices are shaped both by the range of available opportunities and by the distribution of entitlements in society, it is crucial to attend to the inferior economic position of women in American society and those social and economic factors which produce the unequal life chances of men and women.

Conclusion

If the arguments I have offered here are correct, then prostitution is wrong in virtue of its contributions to perpetuating a pervasive form of inequality. In different cir-cumstances, with different assumptions about women and their role in society, I do not think that prostitution would be especially troubling—no more troubling than many other labor markets currently allowed. It follows, then, that in other circum-stances, the asymmetry thesis would be denied or less strongly felt. While the idea that prostitution is intrinsically degrading is a powerful intuition (and like many such intuitions, it persists even after its proponents undergo what Richard Brandt has termed "cognitive therapy," in which errors of fact and inference are corrected), I believe that this intuition is itself bound up with well-entrenched views of male gender identity and women's sexual role in the context of that identity.[62] If we are troubled by prostitution, as I think we should be, then we should direct much of our energy to putting forward alternative models of egalitarian relations between men and women.

READING ENDNOTES

I am grateful to the support of a Rockefeller Fellowship at Princeton University's Center for Human Values. Earlier versions of this article were presented at Swarthmore College, Princeton University, and Oxford University. I am grateful to the audiences at these institutions and in particular to Elizabeth Anderson, Michael Blake, C. A. J. Coady, Amy Gutmann, George Kateb, Andrew Koppelman, Arthur Kuflik, Peter de Marneffe, Thomas Pogge, Adam Swift, Stuart White, and Elisabeth Wood. I also thank two anonymous reviewers at *Ethics*, as well as the editors of the journal.
1. Debra Satz, "Markets in Women's Reproductive Labor," *Philosophy and Public Affairs* 21 (1992): 107–31.

2. What would remain troubling would be the miserable and unjust background circumstances in which much prostitution occurs. That is, if there were gender equality between the sexes but a substantial group of very poor men and women were selling sex, this would indeed be troubling. We should be suspicious of any labor contract entered into under circumstances of desperation.

3. Laurie Shrage, "Should Feminists Oppose Prostitution?" *Ethics* 99 (1989): 347–61, is an important exception. See also her new book, *Moral Dilemmas of Feminism: Prostitution, Adultery and Abortion* (New York: Routledge, 1994).

4. The fact that monetary exchange plays a role in maintaining many intimate relationships is a point underscored by George Bernard Shaw in *Mrs. Warren's Profession* (New York: Garland, 1981).

5. Compare Judith Walkowitz, *Prostitution and Victorian Society* (Cambridge: Cambridge University Press, 1980); Ruth Rosen, *Prostitution in America: 1900–1918* (Baltimore: Johns Hopkins University Press, 1982); B. Hobson, *Uneasy Virtue: The Politics of Prostitution and the American Reform Tradition* (Chicago: University of Chicago Press, 1990).

6. John Decker, *Prostitution: Regulation and Control* (Littleton, Colo.: Rothman, 1979), p. 191.

7. Compare Harold Greenwald, *The Elegant Prostitute: A Social and Psychoanalytic Study* (New York: Walker, 1970), p. 10.

8. For discussion of male prostitutes who sell sex to women, see H. Smith and B. Van der Horst, "For Women Only—How It Feels to Be a Male Hooker," *Village Voice* (March 7, 1977). Dictionary and common usage tends to identify prostitutes with women. Men who sell sex to women are generally referred to as "gigolos," not "prostitutes." The former term encompasses the sale of companionship as well as sex.

9. Male prostitutes merit only a dozen pages in John Decker's monumental study of prostitution. See also D. Drew and J. Drake, *Boys for Sale: A Sociological Study of Boy Prostitution* (Deer Park, N.Y.: Brown Book Co., 1969); D. Deisher, "Young Male Prostitutes," *Journal of American Medical Association* 212 (1970): 1661–66; Gita Sereny, *The Invisible Children: Child Prostitution in America, West Germany and Great Britain* (London: Deutsch, 1984). I am grateful to Vincent DiGirolamo for bringing these works to my attention.

10. Compare Kathleen Barry, *Female Sexual Slavery* (New York: Avon, 1979). If we consider prostitution as an international phenomenon, then a majority of prostitutes are desperately poor and abused women. Nevertheless, there is a significant minority who are not. Furthermore, if prostitution were legalized, it is possible that the minimum condition of prostitutes in at least some countries would be raised.

11. Priscilla Alexander, "Prostitution: A Difficult Issue for Feminists," in *Sex Work: Writings by Women in the Sex Industry*, ed. P. Alexander and F. Delacoste (Pittsburgh: Cleis, 1987).

12. Moreover, to the extent that desperate background conditions are the problem it is not apparent that outlawing prostitution is the solution. Banning prostitution may only remove a poor woman's best option: it in no way eradicates the circumstances which led her to such a choice. See M. Radin, "Market-Inalienability," *Harvard Law Review* 100 (1987): 1849–1937, on the problem of the "double bind."

13. Sometimes the qualitative aspects of a good have quantitative effects and so for that reason need to be taken into account. It is difficult, e.g., to establish a market for used cars given the uncertainties of ascertaining their qualitative condition. Compare George Akerlof, "The Market for Lemons: Qualitative Uncertainty and the Market Mechanism," *Quarterly Journal of Economics* 84 (1970): 488–500.

14. For an attempt to understand human sexuality as a whole through the economic approach, see Richard Posner, *Sex and Reason* (Cambridge, Mass.: Harvard University Press, 1992).

15. Although two-thirds of prostitutes surveyed say that they have no regrets about choice of work. Compare Decker, pp. 165–66. This figure is hard to interpret, given the high costs of thinking that one has made a bad choice of occupation and the lack of decent employment alternatives for many prostitutes.

16. See Guido Calabresi and A. Douglas Melamed, "Property Rules, Liability Rules and Inalienability: One View of the Cathedral," *Harvard Law Review* 85 (1972): 1089–1128.

17. Economic analysis fails to justify the laws we now have regarding prostitution. See below.

18. See Radin, pp. 1884 ff.

19. Posner, *Sex and Reason*, p. 182. See also R. Posner, "An Economic Theory of the Criminal Law," *Columbia Law Review* 85 (1985): 1193–1231. "The prohibition against rape is to the sex and marriage 'market' as the prohibition against theft is to explicit markets in goods and services" (p. 1199).

20. His approach in fact suggests that rape be seen as a "benefit" to the rapist, a suggestion that I think we should be loathe to follow.

21. I do not mean to claim however that such sovereignty over the body is absolute.

22. This section draws from and enlarges upon Satz.

23. Prostitution is, however, an issue which continues to divide feminists as well as prostitutes and former prostitutes. On the one side, some feminists see prostitution as dehumanizing and alienating and linked to male domination. This is the view taken by the prostitute organization Women Hurt in Systems of Prostitution Engaged in Revolt (WHISPER). On the other side, some feminists see sex markets as affirming a woman's right to autonomy, sexual pleasure, and economic welfare. This is the view taken by the prostitute organization COYOTE.

24. Carole Pateman, *The Sexual Contract* (Stanford, Calif.: Stanford University Press, 1988), p. 207; emphasis added.

25. The phrase is Radin's.

26. J. Harris, "The Survival Lottery," *Philosophy* 50 (1975): 81–87.

27. As an example of the ways in which the diversity of sexual experience has been culturally productive, see Lynn Hunt, ed., *The Invention of Pornography* (New York: Zone, 1993). Many of the essays in this volume illustrate the ways in which pornography has historically contributed to broader social criticism.

28. Radin, p. 1884.

29. An objection along these lines is raised by Margaret Baldwin ("Split at the Root: Feminist Discourses of Law Reform," *Yale Journal of Law and Feminism* 5 [1992]: 47–120). Baldwin worries that prostitution undermines our ability to understand a woman's capacity to consent to sex. Baldwin asks, Will a prostitute's consent to sex be seen as consent to a twenty dollar payment? Will courts determine sentences in rape trials involving prostitutes as the equivalent of parking fine violations (e.g., as another twenty dollar payment)? Aren't prostitutes liable to have their fundamental interests in bodily integrity discounted? I think Baldwin's worry is a real one, especially in the context of the current stigmatization of prostitutes. It could be resolved, in part, by withholding information about a woman's profession from rape trials.

30. Radin is herself fairly consistent in her hostility to many forms of wage labor. She has a complicated view about decommodification in nonideal circumstances which I cannot discuss here.

31. Also notice that many forms of labor we make inalienable—e.g., bans on mercenaries—cannot be justified by that labor's relationship to our personhood.

32. Elizabeth Anderson, *Value in Ethics and Economics* (Cambridge, Mass.: Harvard University Press, 1993), p. 45.

33. Actually, the prostitute's humanity is a part of the sex transaction itself. Whereas Posner's economic approach places sex with another person on the same scale as sex with a sheep, for many people the latter is not a form of sex at all (*Sex and Reason*). Moreover, in its worst forms, the prostitute's humanity (and gender) may be crucial to the john's experience of himself as superior to her. See Catharine MacKinnon, *Toward a Feminist Theory of the State* (Cambridge, Mass.: Harvard University Press, 1989).

34. Although this statement might have to be qualified in the light of empirical research. Arlie Hochschild, e.g., has found that the sale of "emotional labor" by airline stewardesses and insurance salesmen distorts their responses to pain and frustration (*The Managed Heart: The Commercialization of Human Feeling* [New York: Basic, 1983]).

35. I owe this point to Elizabeth Anderson, who stressed the need to distinguish between different versions of the degradation objection and suggested some lines of interpretation (conversation with author, Oxford University, July 1994).

36. More generally, they raise questions about the desirability of a world in which people use and exploit each other as they use and exploit other natural objects, insofar as this is compatible with Pareto improvements.

37. See Satz.

38. U.S. Department of Labor, Women's Bureau (Washington, D.C.: Government Printing Office, 1992).

39. D. Taylor, "Women: An Analysis," in *Women: A World Report* (London: Methuen, 1985). Taylor reports that while on a world scale women "perform nearly two-thirds of all working hours [they] receive only one tenth of the world income and own less than one percent of world resources."

40. J. David-McNeil, "The Changing Economic Status of the Female Labor Force in Canada," in *Towards Equity: Proceedings of a Colloquium of the Economic Status of Women in the Labor Market*," ed. Economic Council of Canada (Ottawa: Canadian Government Publication Centre, 1985).

41. S. Rix, ed., *The American Woman, 1990–91* (New York: Norton, 1990), cited in Woman's Action Coalition, ed., *WAC Stats: The Facts about Women* (New York: New Press, 1993), p. 41.

42. Report of the Federal Office of Child Support Enforcement, 1990.

43. Rix, ed. Note also that the time women spend doing housework has not declined since the 1920s despite the invention of labor saving technologies (e.g., laundry machines and dishwashers).

44. My views about this aspect of gender inequality have been greatly clarified in discussions and correspondence with Elizabeth Anderson and Elisabeth Wood during 1994.

45. See Paul Rosenkrantz, Susan Vogel, Helen Bees, Inge Broverman, and David Broverman, "Sex-Role Stereotypes and Self-Concepts in College Students," *Journal of Consulting and Clinical Psychology* 32 (1968): 286–95.

46. L. Heise, "Gender Violence as a Health Issue" (Violence, Health and Development Project, Center for Women's Global Leadership, Rutgers University, New Brunswick, N.J., 1992).

47. L. Heise, "Violence against Women: The Missing Agenda," in *Women's Health: A Global Perspective* (New York: Westview, 1992), cited in Woman's Action Coalition, ed., p. 55. More than one-third of female homicide victims are killed by their husbands or boyfriends.

48. I am indebted here to the discussion of Iris Young in *Justice and the Politics of Difference* (Princeton, N.J.: Princeton University Press, 1990).

49. Ruth Leger Sivard, *Women … a World Survey* (Washington, D.C.: World Priorities, 1985).

50. Shrage ("Should Feminists Oppose Prostitution?) argues that prostitution perpetuates the following beliefs which oppress women: (1) the universal possession of a potent sex drive; (2) the "natural" dominance of men; (3) the pollution of women by sexual contact; and (4) the reification of sexual practice.

51. Susan Estrich, *Real Rape* (Cambridge, Mass.: Harvard University Press, 1987).

52. Baldwin, p. 75. Compare the Canadian Report on Prostitution and Pornography; also M. Silbert, "Sexual Assault on Prostitutes," research report to the *National Center for the Prevention and Control of Rape*, November 1980, for a study of street prostitutes in which 70 percent of those surveyed reported that they had been raped while walking the streets.

53. Carole Pateman, "Defending Prostitution: Charges against Ericsson," *Ethics* 93 (1983): 561–65, p. 563.

54. See also, S. Schwartzenbach, "Contractarians and Feminists Debate Prostitution," *New York University Review of Law and Social Change* 18 (1990–91): 103–30.

55. I owe this point to Arthur Kuflik.

56. For example, does the fact that racist joke telling reinforces negative stereotypes and perpetuates racial prejudice and inequality justify legal bans on such joke telling? What are the limits on what we can justifiably use the state to do in the name of equality? This is a difficult question. I only note here that arguments which justify state banning of prostitution can be consistent with the endorsement of stringent protections for speech. This is because speech and expression are arguably connected with basic fundamental human interests—with forming and articulating conceptions of value, with gathering information, with testifying on matters of conscience—in a

way that prostitution (and some speech, e.g., commercial speech) is not. Even if we assume, as I think we should, that people have fundamental interests in having control over certain aspects of their bodies and lives, it does not follow that they have a fundamental interest in being free to sell themselves, their body parts, or any of their particular capacities.

57. Prostitution is legalized only in several jurisdictions in Nevada.

58. These countries have more pay equity between men and women than does the United States. This might be taken to undermine an argument about prostitution's role in contributing to income inequality. Moreover, women's status is lower in some societies which repress prostitution (such as those of the Islamic nations) than in those which do not (such as those of the Scandinavian nations). But given the variety of cultural, economic, and political factors and mechanisms which need to be taken into account, we need to be very careful in drawing hasty conclusions. Legalizing prostitution might have negative effects on gender equality in the United States, even if legal prostitution does not correlate with gender inequality in other countries. There are many differences between the United States and European societies which make it implausible to think that one factor can alone be explanatory with respect to gender inequality.

59. Radin, pp. 1915 ff.

60. J. Lindquist et al., "Judicial Processing of Males and Females Charged with Prostitution," *Journal of Criminal Justice* 17 (1989): 277–91. Several state laws banning prostitution have been challenged on equal protection grounds. These statistics support the idea that prostitution's negative image effect has disproportionate bearing on male and female prostitutes.

61. In this section, I have benefited from reading Cass Sunstein, "Gender Difference, Reproduction and the Law" (University of Chicago Law School, 1992, unpublished manuscript). Sunstein believes that someone committed to gender equality will, most likely, advocate a legal ban on prostitution.

62. Richard B. Brandt, *A Theory of the Good and the Right* (Oxford: Clarendon, 1979).

DEFINITIONS AND EXPLANATIONS

Perfectionism: Perfectionism is a moral and political theory that is typically contrasted with libertarianism and liberalism. It begins with a conception of human flourishing (an ideal of human excellence and the best human life) and builds its moral and political theory upon that basis. Perfectionists begin with a substantive theory of what a good life is like and then they develop a conception of which moral norms and social institutions would enable individuals to realize that ideal (so far as is possible given human limitations). As a result, perfectionists reject the liberal view that the state should be neutral between competing conceptions of the good life and the liberal commitment to tolerating all ways of life. Rather, the state should operate so as to help people realize their highest human capacities and to live a life that is objectively valuable. This objective value (the specific conception of a good life and human flourishing that any individual perfectionist develops) is typically expressed in terms of what is good for people given human nature. If they take human nature as a given, and as dictating certain things as good or bad for people, or certain ways of life as being suited to our natures, they are developing an **essentialist** theory. It has this name because it takes some characteristics of human beings to be fixed, essential points of our nature, such that we cannot understand what it means to be human or develop a conception of human flourishing without taking into account those essential facts about human nature.

QUESTIONS

1. What is the "asymmetry thesis"?

2. What analysis of prostitution is given by proponents of the economic approach?

3. If an economic approach denies that any sales can be ruled out *a priori*, as inherently wrong, what kind of theory of value and morality must they be relying on? Have any previous theorists we have read been relying upon this kind of approach?

4. Satz raises three objections to the economic approach to prostitution. What are they?

5. How much importance should we give to the widely-held conviction that some things are simply not commodities that can be sold? What does the feeling of "moral repugnance" add to the condemnation of slavery or prostitution?

6. What is the moral significance we attach to our relationship with our own bodies and minds, compared to external goods?

7. How can the sale of some things destroy their social meaning or value? Can you think of other examples of this phenomenon not found in the reading?

8. What is the essentialist approach to prostitution?

9. Satz considers the argument that selling sex is inherently alienating and destructive of the self and personal integrity. The argument proceeds by analogy with the sale of organs. Why does Satz reject this argument against prostitution?

10. Why does Satz reject the argument that prostitution is destructive of human flourishing?

11. What is the degradation argument against prostitution? Why does Satz reject it?

12. What are the two dimensions of gender inequality that Satz thinks are most significant for assessing prostitution?

13. Why does gender inequality throw into doubt the autonomy of any decision to enter into prostitution? Do these reasons apply equally to the street walker and the call girl that Satz described earlier?

14. How does prostitution contribute to women's inferior social status?

15. Why is prostitution uniquely likely to contribute to the inferior social status of women, compared with other gender-segregated professions?

16. Given the three bases of analysis that Satz provides, where do Clark and Sherwin fit? Are they proponents of the economic approach, the essentialist/perfectionist approach, or the inequality approach?

17. Even though prostitution is morally wrong in our society, Satz does not support its criminalization and advocates instead for its regulation. Why?

✦ ✦ ✦

Christine Overall, Surrogate Motherhood

Christine Overall concerns herself with uncovering the inadequacy of two commonly used models of surrogate motherhood: the free market model and the prostitution model. The free market model argues that surrogacy contracts are just like any other, and the surrogate is simply filling a market demand. Overall suggests that this model is simple-minded. It ignores the morally problematic aspects of surrogacy: among them that the selling of babies is morally questionable, that the bulk of the payment for the transaction is not passed along to the mother, and that the practice may be exploitive. She contrasts it with the prostitution model of surrogate motherhood. In the prostitution model, feminists recognize that the practice is likely only appealing as a job for some women because they have been socialized to realize their self-worth mainly through reproduction. On the one hand, women should be free to choose to bear children, but on the other, society should not endorse this choice of employment, because it reaffirms patriarchy. Further similarities to prostitution are brought to light when it is seen that the father is primarily involved in the surrogate relationship. Instead of a couple contracting for this service, it can be argued that the employer is really the man. Finally, as with prostitution, surrogacy is usually entertained as a course of action due to poverty. A questionable motive and a lack of viable life choices both serve to give strength to the supposition that this choice is non-autonomous.

Ultimately, Overall rejects both models. The vast power differential between the surrogate and the wealthy man, and the number of doctors and lawyers who are involved, suggest that the surrogate will lack agency during the pregnancy. The surrogate could not be said to be employed. And so the free market model fails. Alternately the prostitution model is not radical enough to capture the fundamental problematic feature of surrogacy. Allowing surrogacy legitimizes a conceptual framework where being an instrument of another's desire is a legitimate choice for women but one which society looks upon with disfavour.

We need to clarify what, exactly, is appealing about this critique. Is it the case that choosing to be of instrumental value is itself something that women ought not to be allowed to do? Is the changing of the conceptual framework more important than respecting women's choices? Are these choices unworthy of respect because they are unfree? Much hinges upon the answers to these questions. Failing to object to instrumental use suggests that we might allow surrogacy contracts, but change society's reaction to surrogates. Objecting to instrumental use, on the other hand, requires us to further restrict our employment opportunities perhaps even so far as to suggest that no manual labour positions at all are acceptable.

✦ ✦ ✦

Christine Overall, "Surrogate Motherhood," *Canadian Journal of Philosophy* Supplementary Volume 13 (1987): 285–305. © 1987 *Canadian Journal of Philosophy*. Reprinted with permission of the *Canadian Journal of Philosophy*, University of Calgary Press.

Surrogate Motherhood

CHRISTINE OVERALL

I INTRODUCTION

This paper will explore some moral and conceptual aspects of the practice of surrogate motherhood. Although I put forward a number of criticisms of existing ideas about this subject, I do not claim to offer a fully developed position. Instead what I have tried to do is to call into question what seem to be some generally accepted assumptions about surrogate motherhood, and to lend plausibility to my view that surrogate motherhood may be morally troubling for reasons not always fully recognized by other writers on this issue. These reasons go beyond the fairly obvious consequentialist concerns (already well discussed in the press) about its effects on the persons—particularly the child—involved.[1] A concern for the well being of a child produced by a surrogate is, I believe, entirely justified, but my focus in this paper will be upon the surrogate mother herself.

Surrogate motherhood is typically resorted to when the female member of a married couple is unable—for one of a variety of possible reasons—to bear a child. The 'commissioning couple'[2] pays a fee to a surrogate, who is artificially inseminated with the husband's sperm, gestates the child, and surrenders it to the couple, on payment of a fee. (I emphasize that I am interested here in the commercial forms of surrogate motherhood, not in those far rarer cases in which a woman bears a child for a friend or relative.) Usually the husband's name will be listed on the infant's birth certificate;[3] the infertile wife, however, will have to formally adopt the child in order to become its legal mother.[4]

What does surrogate motherhood suggest about the social use of human reproductive faculties, about women's relationship to their bodies, and about the interrelationships of males and females? Part of the reason for the failure to fully recognize these questions lies in the frameworks used to discuss the practice. Hence, my general aim has been to reexamine those frameworks, and to subject them to critical analysis.

I want to discover what surrogate motherhood really is. And in so doing, I am not seeking some hidden essence of the practice, but rather I am wondering how we ought most reasonably to look at it.

I shall present two different points of view about surrogate motherhood, which I call the free market model and the prostitution model.[5] Of the two, the prostitution model is better. But it shares with the free market model certain assumptions about reproductive labour and reproductive choice, assumptions which, I shall show, turn out to be highly implausible, and only obscure our understanding of what surrogate motherhood really is.

II THE FREE MARKET MODEL

According to the free market model, surrogate motherhood is, at its best, a desirable, useful, and indeed necessary service which uncoerced women may offer for purchase by childless but fertile men and their infertile wives.

This approach is defended by lawyer John A. Robertson, who regards surrogate motherhood as one type of what he calls 'collaborative reproduction,' that is, reproduction in which '[a] third person provides a genetic or gestational factor not present in ordinary paired reproduction.'[6] Other types include adoption and the use of artificial insemination by donor [AID]. For Robertson, there are few, if any, important social or moral differences among the various forms of collaborative reproduction.[7] Indeed, in some respects resort to surrogate motherhood may be preferable to agency adoption, because it is

> an alternative to the nonmarket, agency system of allocating children for adoption, which has contributed to long queues for distributing healthy white babies. This form of independent adoption is controlled by the parties, planned before conception, involves a genetic link with one parent, and enables both the father and the mother of the adopted child to be selected in advance.[8]

Robertson lists other benefits of surrogate motherhood, such as the alleviation of suffering and satisfaction of desires of the infertile.[9] But it is clear that for Robertson, the major benefit of the use of a surrogate is that it involves the uncoerced exercise of economic choice. The commissioning couple obtains the type of child they want[10] and at the time they choose. The couple freely decides to invest their money in their preferred form of consumer good: a child. As one adopted mother of a baby born to a surrogate said, 'My God, people spend more on a Mercedes than we spent on Alexander. It's an alternative for people who want infants.'[11]

Of course, since the cost of hiring a surrogate mother is now $22,000 to $25,000,[12] and growing, this service is not, in fact, available to all. Robertson calls it 'a consumption item for the middle classes.' Its limited accessibility is not, he claims, unjust to poor couples, because it does not leave them worse off than they were before.[13] Philosopher Michael D. Bayles also uses this defence and mentions some others. He says that the price will drop if many women decide, because of the attractive fees, to become surrogates, and more children will become available for adoption. 'In general,' says Bayles, 'one should not accept limitations on otherwise permissible activities because poor people cannot afford them, but should try to raise the income of the poor or subsidize the activities so that poor people can afford them.'[14]

Furthermore, the surrogate, like the commissioning couple, also exercises free choice, according to Robertson. Equality of opportunity has been extended: like the sperm donor, a woman is now free to sell her reproductive capacities.[15] She chooses, in effect, a particular type of temporary (though by no means part-time!) job. Robertson states that surrogates 'choose the surrogate role primarily because the fee provides a better economic opportunity than alternative occupations ... '[16] Thus, Jane Doe chooses to be a surrogate mother rather than a waitress, let's say, because the pay for the former is (or appears to be) better. High school guidance counselors take note: female students should be alerted to the existence of this new employment opportunity.

It should be remarked at this point that there might be some question as to how rewarding the payment for the surrogate mothering really is. Much of the money paid by the couple goes toward lawyers' fees, medical and travel expenses, and insurance; surrogate mothers usually receive about $10,000.[17] This means that a women who becomes pregnant at the very first attempt at artificial insemination would earn around $1.50 per hour for her full-time 24-hour-per-day 'job' as a pregnant women.

Nevertheless, says Robertson, the payment of a fee (such as it is) is crucial to the surrogate mothering contract, for 'few surrogates will volunteer for altruistic reasons alone.' A ban on fees is not necessary to protect the surrogate from coercion or exploitation, since the surrogate has made 'a considered, knowing choice, often with the assistance of counsel, before becoming pregnant.'[18] Bayles elaborates this suggestion. Poor women, he says, are not exploited in being offered attractive payments to be surrogates. After all, 'other people are attracted by large fees to become lawyers or physicians.' It is true that poor, uneducated women might not have many alternative forms of employment, but this fact is not a good reason to ban even this form of opportunity. In fact, it would be unjust to deprive them of the opportunity, providing their decision to become a surrogate is an informed one.[19] Philosopher Alan Rassaby expresses this idea more bluntly. 'Given a choice between poverty and exploitation,' he says, 'many people may prefer the latter.'[20]

Robertson does not fail to recognize some potential problems in surrogate motherhood. These problems mainly concern the possibility of psychological suffering of the parties to the contract between the surrogate and the commissioning couple, harms to the child, the artificial manipulation of the natural process of reproduction, and difficulties resulting from noncompliance with the contract. Robertson apparently regards such problems as just a manifestation of the pains of the human condition: they are not unique to surrogate motherhood. Furthermore, they can be significantly diminished by providing good medical and legal services.

Robertson summarizes his discussion of possible problems in surrogate mother-hood in a most significant statement. 'The morality of surrogate mothering,' he says, 'depends on how the duties and responsibilities of the role are carried out, rather than on the mere fact that a couple produces a child with the aid of a collaborator.'[21] For Robertson what is important is 'not what we do—but how we do it.'[22] No further analysis of 'what we do' in surrogate mothering is needed. All that is required is rea-sonable 'public scrutiny, through regulation of the process of drawing up the contract rather than its specific terms,'[23] of how surrogate mothering is carried out.

III THE PROSTITUTION MODEL

At the very least, the free market model for surrogate motherhood seems naive. Among its problems are the assumptions that the commodification of babies is morally acceptable; that the high cost to the commissioning couple, along with the low fee to the mother, is not unjust; that surrogate mothers choose freely to sell their services at a fair price and are therefore not the victims of exploitation; that the prac-tice of surrogate motherhood requires only legal regulation in order to prevent prob-lems; and that *what* surrogate motherhood is is in no need of further analysis.

The second point of view on surrogate motherhood, which I have called the pros-titution model, is, at first sight, quite different from the first, for it calls into question at least some of the assumptions made by the free market model. It is usually advanced by feminist writers, but it is nowhere as fully expressed and developed as the free market model. Instead, it is necessary to piece it together from a variety of rather brief commentaries.

According to this second point of view, surrogate motherhood is a type of delib-erate exploitation of women's reproductive capacities, and is in that way akin to pros-titution.

An outline of this sort of analysis is provided by Mary Kay Blakely, in a short paper whose very title, 'Surrogate Mothers: For Whom Are They Working?' invites us to examine our underlying assumptions about surrogate motherhood. She suggests that the practice is governed by racist and sexist beliefs.[24] Surrogate motherhood, she says, raises issues concerning ownership of children, 'the conceit of patriarchal genetics,'[25] infertility as a failing in women, and finally 'guilt and money, and how women earn both.'[26] But these comments just hint at a feminist analysis, and Blakely herself never answers the provocative question in the title of her paper.

In response to Blakely's paper, another writer[27] states that recognition of a woman's right to control her own body and to make decisions about childbearing do not imply a license to exploit one's body. Surrogate mothers may feel a sense of ful-fillment at least partly because childbearing has been, historically, almost the only realm for which women gain recognition.[28] Thus, while women should have a 'right to choose' in regard to surrogate motherhood, 'society's endorsement of this choice as a valid female occupation' would be a mistake, because it would serve as an affirmation of the tradition of fulfillment through childbearing.

A possible answer to the question, for whom are surrogates working, is provided by feminist Susan Ince. In her investigation of the operation of a surrogate motherhood broker, she found that the infertile wife, who is the raison d'être of the surrogate industry, is 'notably absent' from the surrogate motherhood relationship. The company investigated by Ince urged each 'girl' to find ways to include the biological father (the husband of the infertile woman) in her pregnancy and birth, for example, by sending a 'nice note' to the father after conception, and later, a tape of the baby's heartbeat.[29] Furthermore, the contract used by the company makes it clear that it is the father who is the purchaser; it is he to whom the child product belongs, and to whom it must be delivered.[30] The preeminence of the father over his infertile wife is emphasized by the fact that her consent is not usually required for his participation in the surrogate motherhood arrangement. (This contrasts with the regular procedures governing the use of AID: consent of the husband is usually required before a woman is artificially inseminated.) Thus, Susan Ince's analysis suggests that the true employer of the surrogate is not the so-called commissioning couple, but only the male who provides the sperm.

That suggestion renders more plausible the claim that surrogate motherhood is like prostitution. The comparison is used briefly by philosopher Mary B. Mahowald, who also challenges the assumption of the free market model that women freely choose the job of surrogate mother. Expressing concern about women's rights to self-determination regarding their own bodies, she writes,

> Most prostitutes are driven to their "trade" by economic and emotional pressures largely beyond their control; and surrogacy? What either practice says about society is more telling than what it says about the individual. Accordingly, we might more appropriately critique the social conditions that make these options genuine and unavoidable for individual women, than worry about the legal complaints arising from their practice.[31]

Finally, feminist Andrea Dworkin has also written about surrogate motherhood in the course of a longer discussion of prostitution. She argues that the scientific separation of sex from reproduction, and of reproduction from sex, now 'enable women to sell their wombs within the terms of the brothel model.'[32] Thus, reproduction can become the sort of commodity that sex is now. All reproductive technologies 'make the womb extractable from the woman as a whole person in the same way the vagina (or sex) is now.'[33] A surrogate mother is, Dworkin says, a 'reproductive prostitute.'[34]

IV THE TWO MODELS: SIMILARITIES AND CRITIQUE

The free market model and the prostitution model of surrogate motherhood appear to be rather different. The former states that surrogate motherhood is a freely chosen arrangement between two or more human beings operating to the potential benefit of all concerned. The latter sees surrogate motherhood as akin to prostitution, a type of exploitive employment by men into which the women involved enter, not freely, but out of economic necessity or social coercion. The two viewpoints are, consequently, sharply divided as to the moral justification of the practice: the free market model regards it as acceptable, the prostitution model as morally questionable; and also as to social policy, with the free market model seeing surrogacy as in need only of legal regulation, while the prostitution model sees it as necessitating a dramatic restructuring of society so that women will not be forced into being surrogate mothers.

Nevertheless, despite these apparent differences, closer examination of the two viewpoints on surrogate mothers reveals that they share several assumptions in common. I shall discuss two items of agreement between them: the first concerns the idea of reproductive labour, which is expressed in this context by treating surrogate motherhood as a job; the second concerns the concept of reproductive choice.

a) Reproductive Labour: Surrogate Motherhood as a Job

In a very literal sense, the surrogate mother is engaging in reproductive labour: her body is doing the work necessary to produce a human being. Moreover, she is being paid for this work. Hence, surrogate motherhood appears to be, or to be like, a job. This is an assumption shared by both the free market model and the prostitution model, and even by the women themselves.[35] Just as, for example, a music teacher might sell her pedagogical services privately to individual students, or a lawyer might sell her legal services to clients, or a prostitute might sell her sexual services to customers, the surrogate mother sells her reproductive services to the commissioning couple, or, more accurately, to a man, or possibly a series of individual men.

To treat surrogate motherhood as a job appears only too consistent with other traditional uses of women's reproductive labour. For, as feminist writers have pointed out, under usual circumstances, such labour is either a species of volunteer work, which women supposedly undertake for sheer love of it, or, in less congenial circumstances, it is a type of slavery.[36] Thus, the fee paid to the surrogate mother at least appears to put reproductive labour on a more equal footing with other forms of paid labour than it ordinarily possesses.

But *if* surrogate motherhood is to be regarded as a job, then we are forced to accept the peculiar implications which follow from it. For example, consider this: The free market model assumes that the surrogate is employed by the commissioning couple; the prostitution model suggests that she is employed by the man who provides the sperm. But closer investigation makes it at least as plausible to say that the surrogate is self-employed.

Surrogate motherhood is similar in several respects to a small-scale, owner-operated business. The woman, after all, operates out of her own home; she provides the equipment for carrying out the labour; and her earnings are controlled (or limited) by the amount of work she is willing to do (that is, by the number of babies she is willing to produce). I would even venture that if the government found out about her income, it would require her to pay taxes directly to the state.[37] The surrogate motherhood brokers who bring buyers and sellers together are not the employers of the women; they explicitly disavow any responsibility for adverse outcomes,[38] and they do not pay the woman for her services. But then, neither are the couple, or the biological father, the employer of the woman, any more than a lawyer's clients or a music teacher's pupils are their employers.

Thus, *if* surrogate motherhood is a job involving the selling of reproductive labour on a private basis, then an answer, at least as plausible as any other, to Blakely's question, for whom is the surrogate working, is: herself.

Now of course, I do not really want to claim that surrogate mothers are self-employed. I simply want to explore the implications that follow from treating surrogate motherhood as a job. They reveal, I think, that there is an error in seeing surrogate motherhood as being, or being like, a job involving the selling of one's reproductive services. For if the surrogate mother is self-employed, then we are led to see her as an individual whose activities must be regulated in order to protect both those who specifically hire her services, and the general public, from any potential dangers or failure of responsibility in her exercise of her vocation.[39] Indeed, legislation to govern surrogate motherhood has already been proposed which is designed to safeguard lawyers, doctors, the commissioning couple, and the potential baby, by providing legal and financial penalties to be exacted if the mother should abort, engage in negligent behaviour, or fail to surrender the child, in violation of the terms of her contract.[40] The idea that the surrogate mother is self-employed thus leads us to a concern for the licensing of surrogates; for setting appropriate fees;[41] for requisite training, qualifications, screening, advertising, insurance, and contracts. Moreover, if surrogate motherhood is a job, then it appears that our only worry, if there is one at all, for the women involved must be whether it is a good job: Our concern will be directed toward improving their working conditions, raising their income, providing insurance, perhaps even offering a pension plan, and so on.

But all of these concerns entirely lose sight of part of what seems to be implicit in, and correct about, the feminist critique of surrogate motherhood: namely, that the surrogate mother is *herself* in need of protection from the lawyers, doctors, and infertile couples who wish to make use of her services. The assumption that surrogate motherhood is, or is like, a job essentially misrepresents the power relations which are defined by the practice. The immediate locus of power in the surrogate arrangement is in a necessarily rather wealthy man who pays the fee and provides the sperm, and in the person, usually a male lawyer, who represents him, and receives a commission for his services. But the wider network of control is constituted by the authority relations defined in patriarchy, in the context of which reproduction is usually labour done by women for men. It seems highly unlikely that in becoming a surrogate mother, a woman is invested with power and independence which she would otherwise not possess in the exercise of her reproductive capacities. As in the case of prostitution, the mere payment of a small fee in no way changes the possibility that she is a victim of exploitation, and the nature of the exploitation is not such that an increase in fees or improved working conditions will change it.

b) Reproductive Choice

But in order to give more substance to this contention, I shall now introduce some analysis of the second item on which the two models of surrogate motherhood agree. Both of them assume that individuals ought, perhaps within certain limits, to have the freedom to choose what sort of job to take up (whether, let's say, to become a secretary or a waitress, or whether to choose self-employment as a doctor or as a surrogate mother). And becoming a surrogate mother is assumed to be, at least potentially, one possible result of the exercise of that free choice, in particular, free choice concerning the use of one's reproductive capacities.

Of course, the two models disagree as to whether this freedom really exists in the case of surrogate motherhood: the free market model says it does; the prostitution model says it does not. And in this respect, the prostitution model is, I would argue, correct. A question raised by the Canadian Advisory Council on the Status of Women about prostitution applies almost verbatim to surrogate motherhood: 'Can a person of minimal education and financial well-being be said truly to choose a way of life that is stigmatized by much of society, that is physically dangerous at times, that leaves her with little control over her earning power, and that can cause her considerable legal complications?'[42]

In one of the psychological studies so far undertaken on the characteristics of women who apply to be surrogate mothers, it was discovered that 40% of the sample were unemployed or receiving some form of financial aid, or both. Moreover, 72% of the women had an education level of high school graduation or less.[43] The researcher, Philip J. Parker, also found that a large majority of the group had been pregnant previously; when pregnant these women 'felt more content, complete, special, and adequate and often felt an inner glow; some felt more feminine and attractive and enjoyed the extra attention afforded them.'[44] In this sample, 35% of the women either had had a voluntary abortion or had relinquished a child for adoption, a fact which led Parker to surmise that these women 'felt (often unconsciously) that surrogate motherhood would help them master unresolved feelings they had regarding a previous voluntary loss of fetus or baby.'[45] Considering all of these factors, the candidates for surrogate motherhood seem not only to be motivated by very real financial need, but also to be influenced by quite traditional role expectations about the importance of pregnancy and motherhood in women's lives.[46]

It is most ironic that after uncovering this information about applicants for surrogate motherhood, Parker emphasizes the importance of ensuring that every applicant for surrogate motherhood is 'competent' and is 'voluntarily and freely making an informed choice, free of coercion and undue influence.'[47] In my view, there is a fundamental contradiction between the fact that social conditions such as those delineated in Parker's study create the demand for surrogate motherhood, and permit reproductive services to become a commodity, and the fact that the women involved are perceived as able to make a free choice.[48] Yet the free market proponents of surrogate motherhood are likely to use that alleged free choice to defend the practice, by asking, rhetorically, what right the state has to deny women the exercise of her free will in selling her reproductive capacities.[49]

Perhaps the cause of the disagreement between the two models as to whether surrogate motherhood is the result of free choice is a failure to examine what reproductive choice means. Both models appear to assume that the main moral question about reproductive choice is whether or not it exists—in this context, whether the women who become surrogate mothers freely choose this use of their reproductive capacities. But I contend that the idea of reproductive choice is in need of further analysis: It is more complex than proponents of the two models appear to realize.

Sociologist Barbara Katz Rothman has sounded some warnings about the meanings of reproductive choice. Examining the varieties of choices offered by reproductive technology—options for fetal monitoring, contraceptive use, abortion, prenatal diagnosis, and infertility treatments—Rothman argues that apparent expansions of choice often result in the loss of other choices because they become socially less acceptable, or in the existence of choices which we are, paradoxically, forced to make.[50] Thus reproductive choice sometimes turns out to be more apparent than real.

This sort of insight can be applied to surrogate motherhood. We should be asking what options may be foreclosed for some women by the existence of the apparent choice of selling one's reproductive services. To this question I can offer only a tentative response. For individual women, the existence of surrogate motherhood as an apparent choice may tend to obscure or override other possible interpretations of their lives. Just as the overwhelming presence of the role of housewife presented itself, until recently, as the only 'choice' for women, so also surrogacy may appear to be the only possible escape route for some women with few resources and opportunities. A woman may reason, in effect, that if all else fails, she can still become a surrogate mother. If surrogate motherhood becomes a socially approved 'choice,' it will affect how women see the use of their reproductive capacities, and their relationships to their children, as well as the social construction of women's reproductive roles.

So far, what I have said about reproductive choice does not go much beyond what feminists have said about it in other contexts. However, I want to suggest a second reason to reconsider the notion of reproductive choice in the context of surrogate motherhood: it can lead to an uncritical acceptance of the many ways in which women's reproductive capacities may be used. In endorsing an uncritical freedom of reproductive choice, we may also be implicitly endorsing all conceivable alternatives that an individual might adopt; we thereby abandon the responsibility for evaluating substantive actions in favour of advocating merely formal freedom of choice.[51] We must think very carefully about whether surrogate motherhood is a 'choice' which we want to recognize in this way.

This brings me to a more fundamental reservation about the idea of reproductive choice in the context of surrogate motherhood: Is becoming a surrogate mother really the sort of thing one can freely choose? What I am trying to get at here could perhaps be more clearly expressed by asking whether surrogate motherhood is genuinely a part of what we ought to *mean* by the exercise of reproductive choice.

The problem is not merely that surrogate motherhood may not be freely chosen by those women who take it up. The problem is that there is a real moral danger in the sort of conceptual framework which presents surrogate motherhood as even a *possible* freely chosen alternative for women.

This becomes apparent when we consider whether the practice of surrogacy would raise fewer moral questions if only middle-class, economically advantaged women became surrogate mothers. (And in fact, some commentators have suggested that such women may be a substantial component of the applicants for surrogate motherhood.[52] A study by Darrell D. Franks of a very small sample of such applicants found that nine out of ten of the women 'were of modest to moderate means'— although in many cases this turned out to mean that they were supported by a husband or boyfriend.[53]) No woman is forced into becoming a surrogate mother at the point of a gun, and middle class women are not, apparently, forced into it by economic expediency. But the absence of these or comparable compelling conditions does not mean that it makes sense to say that a woman is therefore making a choice to be a surrogate, and is thereby exercising a type of reproductive freedom.

Surrogate motherhood is not and cannot be merely one career choice among others. It is not a real alternative. It is implausible to suppose that fond parents would want it for their daughters. We are unlikely to set up training courses for surrogate mothers. Schools holding 'career days' for their future graduates will surely not invite surrogate mothers to address the class on the advantages of their 'vocation.' And surrogate motherhood does not seem to be the sort of thing one would put on one's curriculum vitae.[54]

Surrogate motherhood is no more a real job option than selling one's blood or one's gametes or one's bodily organs can be real job options. All of these commercial transactions involve an extreme form of personal and bodily alienation. Surrogate mothering is 'at the extreme end of the spectrum of alienated labour,' for the surrogate mother must contract out all of the 'so-called "normal" love, pride, satisfaction, and attachment in, for, and to the product of her labour.'[55] In surrogate motherhood, the woman gives up the use of her body, the product of her reproductive labour, and that reproductive labour itself, to persons who pay to make them their own.[56] In so doing, she surrenders her individuality, for becoming a surrogate mother involves receiving a fee, not for labour which is the unique expression of one's personal capacities and talents, but only for the exercise of one's reproductive capacities. As one applicant for surrogate motherhood aptly expressed it: 'I'm only an incubator.'[57]

Now, some have claimed that reproductive labour is not impersonal: that some form of personal expression enters into it by means of, for example, choices as to what is consumed during pregnancy, the type of activities one engages in, and the moods and feelings one experiences. But while these factors can indeed affect the nature of the pregnancy and its outcome (that is, not only the health of the baby, but one's own wellbeing), for the most part the course of the pregnancy and even of childbirth is outside the control of the woman involved. This is emphasized by Mary O'Brien, in a discussion of Marx's comparison of the architect and the bee.

> [M]other and architect are quite different. The woman cannot realize her visions, cannot make them come true, by virtue of the reproductive labour in which she involuntarily engages, if at all. Unlike the architect, her will does not influence the shape of her product. Unlike the bee, she knows that her product, like herself, will have a history. Like the architect, she knows what she is doing; like the bee, she cannot help what she is doing.[58]

For this reason, the woman who engages in paid reproductive labour is permitted no moral significance as an individual. In fact, as Andrea Dworkin points out, when women are defined and used as a sex class, as they are when they are paid for their reproductive or sexual services, the individual woman becomes a fiction.[59] It is clear that, within certain broadly defined limits—for example, being fertile, being white, being healthy, even being pretty—the women who work as surrogate mothers are interchangeable. Despite some superficial attention to finding the 'right' woman—and indeed, sometimes the hiring father is encouraged to choose his woman on the basis of data supplied by the lawyer or agency[60]—the women involved are defined solely as gestators, without reference to their individual characteristics or potential.[61]

Thus, surrogate motherhood is not and cannot be a freely chosen job because the practice is such that it recognizes no individual who can make the choice. The institution defines the individual woman out of existence. All that is left is what the press has referred to as a 'womb for rent.' In surrogate motherhood, there can be no doubt, a commercial transaction takes place, but it is not a transaction between equals, or even between potential equals. Although the woman involved may rightly be described as being freely chosen by a man, who pays her fee and who thus exercises a special type of reproductive choice, she does not freely choose him. The man who pays the fee and provides the sperm has merely leased for nine months a part of her body, together with its reproductive capacities, and has purchased outright the egg from which the baby grows. A woman can no more choose to be a surrogate mother than a room can choose to be leased, or a pet can choose to be bought. Surrogate motherhood is no more a job than being occupied, for a fee, is a job.

V CONCLUSION

Thus, a close examination of the practice of surrogate motherhood leads to the rejection of two assumptions made both by those who praise and by those who condemn it, that is, by the free market model and by the prostitution model. Surrogate motherhood is not a job. And to become a surrogate mother is not the sort of thing that we should mean by the exercise of reproductive choice.

While in no way wanting to glorify some hypothetical form of 'natural' motherhood, I nevertheless believe that this examination of what surrogate motherhood is, that is, within what framework or set of assumptions it should be understood, shows both that the commercial form of surrogate motherhood as it now exists is not the sort of social practice which should be fostered or benignly tolerated, and that it is part of a broader context of morally and conceptually dubious assumptions about women's role in reproduction.

READING ENDNOTES

1. The usual approach to moral questions about the practice of surrogate motherhood is simply to list the possible problems that might arise within a surrogate motherhood arrangement. For examples of this sort of approach, see Robert T. Francoeur, *Utopian Motherhood: New Trends in Human Reproduction* (Garden City, NY: Doubleday 1970), 102–6, and Council for Science and Society, *Human Procreation: Ethical Aspects of the New Techniques* (Oxford: Oxford University Press 1984), 66–70.
2. This is the term used by Mary Warnock in *A Question of Life: The Warnock Report on Human Fertilisation and Embryology* (Oxford: Basil Blackwell 1985), 42.
3. Michael D. Bayles, *Reproductive Ethics* (Englewood Cliffs, NJ: Prentice-Hall 1984), 22.
4. See also John A. Robertson, 'Surrogate Mothers: Not So Novel After All,' *The Hastings Center Report* 13 (October 1983), 29, and Council for Science and Society, 67. There are also other forms of surrogate motherhood, for example, those in which the surrogate gestates an embryo which is not the product of her own egg, but which was produced through in vitro fertilization of another women's ovum, or was obtained through the process of uterine lavage. These raise issues comparable to those in standard surrogate motherhood cases, but may be complicated further by the fact that the child which is produced is not genetically related to the gestating mother.
5. There are others—such as Herbert T. Krimmel's view that surrogate motherhood is immoral primarily because of the motivations of the persons involved and the effects on the children produced—which I shall not discuss here. See 'The Case Against Surrogate Parenting,' *The Hastings Center Report* 13 (October 1983), 35–9. Cf. *A Matter of Life*, 45.
6. Robertson, 28.
7. Bayles also compares the issues surrounding surrogate motherhood to those in AID (23). Cf. Alan B. Rassaby, 'Surrogate Motherhood: The Position and Problems of Substitutes,' in William Walters and Peter Singer, eds., *Test-Tube Babies* (Melbourne: Oxford University Press 1982), 103, and Suzanne M. Patterson, 'Parenthood by Proxy: Legal Implications of Surrogate Birth,' *Iowa Law Review* 385 (1982), 390–1.
8. Robertson, 28.
9. Cf. Rassaby, 104.
10. For example, white, not black: '[A]lmost every adopting white couple wants a healthy white baby, and the great majority of young, pregnant, white American women do not give up their babies for adoption' (Cynthia Gorney, 'For Love and Money,' *California Magazine* [October 1983], 91).
11. *Ibid.*, 155.
12. Margaret Munro, '"Rent-a-Womb" Trade Thriving Across Canada-U.S. Border,' *The Montreal Gazette* (21 January 1985) D-11.
13. Robertson, 29.
14. Bayles, 26; cf. Rassaby, 103.
15. *A Matter of Life* also cites this claim as a possible justification for surrogacy: '[C]arrying mothers … have a perfect right to enter into such agreements if they so wish, just as they have a right to use their own bodies in other ways, according to their own decision' (45). Cf. Council for Science and Society, 66.
16. Robertson, 29.
17. Munro, D-11.
18. Robertson, 32-3.
19. Bayles, 25.
20. Rassaby, 103. Cf. William A.W. Walters and Peter Singer, 'Conclusions—And Costs,' in *Test-Tube Babies*, 138.
21. Robertson, 32.

22. *Ibid.*, 33.

23. *Ibid.*, 34.

24. Advertisements for prospective surrogates usually make it clear that applicants should be white. And the commissioning couple may 'try again' for a boy if the pregnancy produces a female infant (Mary Kay Blakely, 'Surrogate Mothers: For Whom Are They Working?' *Ms.* 11 [March 1983], 18 and 20). She could also have added class considerations. Cf. Rosalind Pollack Petchesky, 'Reproductive Freedom: Beyond "A Woman's Right to Choose,"' in Catharine R. Stimpson and Ethel Spector Person, eds., *Women: Sex and Sexuality* (Chicago: University of Chicago Press 1980), 92–116, for a discussion of class distinctions in the availability of other reproductive services, such as abortion and contraception.

25. Susan Ince states: 'The need to continue patriarchal lineage, to make certain the child has the sperm and name of the buyer, is primary' ('Inside the Surrogate Industry,' in Rita Arditti, Renate Duelli Klein, and Shelley Minden, eds., *Test-Tube Women: What Future for Motherhood?* [London: Pandora Press 1984], 112).

26. Blakely, 20.

27. Susan E. Nash, letter, *Ms.* 11 (June, 1983), 5.

28. Some confirmation for this appears in a recent brief discussion of the motives of surrogate mothers. One woman wrote, 'When I first heard of surrogate motherhood, my immediate thoughts were, "Goodness, I could do that! I can't cook, I can't play tennis or do tapestries, but I am good at being pregnant and giving birth."' Quoted in Carl Wood and Ann Westmore, *Test-Tube Conception* (Englewood Cliffs, NJ: Prentice-Hall 1984), 113.

29. Ince, 102.

30. *Ibid.*, 112.

31. Letter, *The Hastings Center Report* 14 (June, 1984), 43.

32. Andrea Dworkin, *Right-Wing Women* (New York: Perigee Books 1983), 181.

33. *Ibid.*, 187.

34. *Ibid.*, 188.

35. Munro, D-11.

36. Elizabeth W. Moen, 'What Does "Control Over Our Bodies" Really Mean?', *International Journal of Women's Studies* 2 (March/April 1979), 133.

37. I owe these ideas to Ted Worth.

38. Ince, 107.

39. This point of view is taken most noticeably by Bernard D. Hirsch, in 'Parenthood by Proxy,' *Journal of the American Medical Association* 249 (April 22/29 1983), 2251–2.

40. This seems to be reflected in surrogate motherhood contracts: the contract signed by the mother is often longer, and specifies more limitations, than that signed by the commissioning couple. ('Nothing Left to Chance in "Rent-A-Womb" Agreements,' *The Toronto Star* [January 13, 1985].) See also Theresa M. Mady, 'Surrogate Mothers: The Legal Issues,' *American Journal of Law and Medicine* 7 (Fall 1981), 351.

41. 'One wonders … whether fair compensation for being a surrogate mother should be determined simply by market forces,' William J. Winslade, 'Surrogate Mothers: Private Right or Public Wrong?', *Journal of Medical Ethics* 7 (1981), 154.

42. Canadian Advisory Council on the Status of Women, *Prostitution in Canada* (March 1984), 84.

43. Philip J. Parker, 'Motivation of Surrogate Mothers: Initial Findings,' *American Journal of Psychiatry* 140 (January 1983), 117.

44. *Ibid.*, 118.

45. *Ibid.*

46. Cf. the findings of Darrell D. Franks, 'Psychiatric Evaluation of Women in Surrogate Mother Program,' *American Journal of Psychiatry* 138 (October 1981) 1378–9.

47. Philip J. Parker, 'Surrogate Motherhood: The Interaction of Litigation, Legislation and Psychiatry,' *International Journal of Law and Psychiatry* 5 (1982), 352.

48. Dworkin, 182.

49. *Ibid.*, 180; cf. *Prostitution in Canada*, 69 and Ince, 99.

50. Barbara Katz Rothman, 'The Meanings of Choice in Reproductive Technology,' in *Test-Tube Women*, 23–33. Cf. Kathleen McDonnell, *Not An Easy Choice: A Feminist Re-Examines Abortion* (Toronto: The Women's Press 1984), 71–2, and Petchesky, 101, on abortion as a 'free' choice.

51. An unlimited advocacy of the further development of reproductive choice would seem to imply, for example, an unlimited 'right' to choose the sex of one's children, through selective abortion, a 'right' which appears to be potentially gynecidal. See McDonnell, 79, and Petchesky, 100.

52. John Robertson, 'John Robertson Replies,' *The Hastings Center Report* 14 (June 1984), 43.

53. Franks, 1379.

54. Lorraine Code, 'Commentary on "Surrogate Motherhood" by Christine Overall,' unpublished paper (February 1985), 3.

55. *Ibid.*, 4. The effects on the woman of giving up her child—effects which are at least hinted at by women who change their minds about surrendering the baby once it is born—must be counted as part of the exploitation and psychological costs to the mother of the practice of surrogate motherhood.

56. Cf. Mary O'Brien, *The Politics of Reproduction* (Boston: Routledge & Kegan Paul 1981), 58–9, on alienation and appropriation.

57. Parker, 'Motivation of Surrogate Mothers: Initial Findings,' 118.

58. *Ibid.*, 38.

59. Dworkin, 182.

60. Munro, D-11.

61. It is worth noting that this loss of individuality will be exacerbated in the near future when embryo transfers become routine, and the surrogate mother contributes only her reproductive services to the production of the baby.

QUESTIONS

1. What is the "free market model" of surrogate motherhood? Why is this an apt name for it? What does it imply about the permissibility of the practice?

2. What is the "prostitution model" of surrogate motherhood? Why is this an apt name for it? What does it imply about the permissibility of the practice?

3. Overall thinks that both the free market and prostitution models presuppose a false conception of surrogate motherhood as a job. Why is it false?

4. Do the facts that many surrogates are "motivated by very real financial need" and are "influenced by quite traditional role expectations about the importance of pregnancy and motherhood in women's lives" support the conclusion that the choice to be a surrogate cannot be free or autonomous? Would not the same facts often influence women to marry and have children? Should this choice be denied to them?

5. Does the analogy with prostitution that Overall considers in questioning whether the choice to be a surrogate (or prostitute) can be a free one, break down given that the two are so differently valued in society?

6. How reasonable is Overall's analysis of reproductive choice? Is it likely that making surrogacy an option will actually reduce the options available to those who would otherwise choose it (given that they are poor, undereducated, etc. by Overall's own lights)?

7. Does Overall's analysis suggest that she is willing to restrict the choices of some women to advance the causes of feminism, such as transforming the social construction of women's reproductive roles?

8. Why might allowing freedom of reproductive choice of one kind (surrogacy) lead us to be uncritically accepting of all possible uses of reproductive capacities?

9. Does Overall provide any argument for thinking that we should not view the decision to become a surrogate mother as a free choice? Is she inviting readers to share her value judgement about such a choice? Is her judgement that such a choice lacks value consistent with her claim that, under patriarchy, child bearing and mothering are the only valuable roles for women?

10. Must surrogacy involve an alienation of one's self, one's labour, and one's individuality? Why is it a uniquely alienating form of labour?

11. Would Overall's reasons for wanting to ban commercial surrogacy apply equally to altruistic surrogate arrangements?

12. Is the label "surrogate *motherhood*" misleading?

✦ ✦ ✦

George W. Harris, Fathers and Fetuses

George W. Harris argues that there are occasions where it would be morally impermissible for a woman to have an abortion due to it being a violation of the father's autonomy. He examines five thought experiments involving pregnant women who decide to abort in different circumstances in order to make his case. In the first, a woman is raped and the man wants her to bring the fetus to term. In the second, the woman and man have a casual sexual relationship and the man wants her to bring the fetus to term. In the third, the woman and man are married, the woman has been secretly ambivalent about having kids, while letting her husband believe that she eventually wants kids, and the man wants her to bring the fetus to term. In the fourth, the woman and man are married, the woman does not want kids but does not tell her husband, who wants her to bring the fetus to term. In the fifth, the woman and man are married, the woman wants to intentionally hurt the man, so she gets pregnant and then aborts the fetus.

Harris suggests that in the third, fourth, and fifth cases, a wrong is done to the father, and in the fourth and fifth case it is impermissible to have an abortion. Assuming that the fetus is both the woman's and the man's, in some sense, Harris reasons as follows: In the third case, the father's autonomy was interfered with by the negligence of the mother in failing to clarify her desires. Although this is a wrong done to the father, the woman's fault of negligence is, however, not sufficient to require that she not abort. In the fourth case, the husband's autonomy was interfered with by deceit. The fault of deceit is sufficient to require that the mother not abort. The conclusions regarding the fifth case are the same as the fourth.

Harris' second case is also of interest. The woman and the man had been engaging in the permissible plan of having a sexual relationship, and so the woman has no reason not to abort. It was never a part of the plan that she be pregnant. The man's further interest in being a father has no legitimate claim on her on this analysis. Similarly, he notes, the woman would then have no claim on the man for support. Those committed to the moral ideal of equal concern for autonomous choices seem to be further committed to rejecting the idea that men have a duty to aid women in these circumstances. This leaves any duty to aid based in the rights of the future child unexamined, but this in turn requires a thoughtful examination of the rights of future persons, which may in turn require a denial of abortion on demand, as we have seen in Sterba's paper.

✦ ✦ ✦

George W. Harris, "Fathers and Fetuses," *Ethics* 96:3 (April 1986): 594–603. © The University of Chicago Press. Reprinted with permission of the University of Chicago Press and the author.

Fathers and Fetuses

George W. Harris

Conspicuously absent from most discussions of the abortion issue are considerations of third-party interests, especially those of the father. A survey of the literature reveals an implicit assumption by most writers that the issue is to be viewed as a two-party conflict—the rights of the fetus versus the rights of the mother—and that an adequate analysis of the balance of these rights is sufficient to determine the conditions under which abortion is morally impermissible. I shall argue, however, that in some cases it would be morally impermissible for a woman to have an abortion because it would be a wrongful harm to the father and a violation of his autonomy. Moreover, I shall argue for this on principles that I believe require a strong stand on women's rights.

I

The issue I wish to discuss then is whether or not it would ever be morally wrong for a woman to have an abortion on the grounds that it would be a wrong done to the father. I leave aside the issue of the rights of the fetus since I do not consider here whether abortion under the circumstances raised might be wrong on other grounds.

Consider then the following cases which are arranged to elucidate the moral considerations involved in the analysis. The extreme cases 1 and 5 are included not so much for their intrinsic importance but because of the light they shed on the analysis of cases 2, 3, and 4. Now, to the cases.

1. Karen, a healthy twenty-five-year-old woman, becomes pregnant as the result of being raped by a man with severe psychological problems. After therapy and significant improvement in his mental health, the man recognizes what he has done and is willing to accept liability for the harms he has caused and even punishment should the victim deem it necessary. His only plea is that Karen carry the fetus to term and then give it to him if she does not care to raise the child herself. Unable, however, to disassociate the fetus from the trauma of the rape, Karen decides to abort.

2. Jane and Jack, two attractive, healthy individuals, meet at a party given by mutual friends. During the weeks and months that follow, a casual but pleasant sexual relationship develops between them. As a result, Jane becomes pregnant. But after learning of the pregnancy, Jack reveals that he is a moderately serious Catholic and from a combined sense of guilt, responsibility, and parental instinct proposes that they be married. Jane, on the other hand, being neither Catholic nor desirous of a husband, decides to abort. Respecting her religious differences and her right to marry whomever she pleases, Jack offers to pay all of Jane's medical expenses, to take complete responsibility for the child after it is born, and to pay her a large sum of money to carry the fetus to term. Jane nonetheless decides to proceed with the abortion.

3. Susan and Charles, both in perfect health, are in the fifth year of their marriage. Aside from his love for Susan, the prospect of raising a family is the most important thing in Charles's life—more important than career, possessions, sports, or any of the other things thought to be of the utmost importance to men. Susan, on the other hand, is secretly ambivalent about having children due to her indecisiveness between having a career and having a family. But because of her love for Charles and the fear of causing him what she believes might be unnecessary anxiety, she allows him to believe that her reluctance is only with when rather than with whether to have children. And despite reasonable efforts at birth control, Susan becomes pregnant just at a point at which her career takes a significant turn for the better. In the situation, it is a career rather than children that she wants, and she decides to have an abortion. Distraught, Charles tries to dissuade her by offering to forgo his own career and to take on the role traditionally reserved for mothers. But to no avail.

4. Michelle and Steve, like Susan and Charles, are also in the fifth year of their marriage. And Steve, like Charles, is equally and similarly desirous of a family. Michelle, however, knows all along that she does not want children but avoids discussing the issue with Steve, allowing him to think that the beginning of their family is just a matter of time. She believes that eventually she can disabuse him of the values of family life in favor of a simple life together. But due to the unpleasantness of broaching the subject, Michelle procrastinates and accidentally becomes pregnant. And despite Steve's expectations, his pleas, and his offer to take on the major responsibilities of raising the child, Michelle decides to abort.

5. Anne is a man hater. Resentment brought on in part by traditional male chauvinistic attitudes toward women has led her to stereotype all men as little more than barbarians. Mark is a reasonably decent man, who, like Charles and Steve, desires very much to be a parent. After meeting Mark, Anne devises a plan to vicariously vent her rage through Mark on the entire male sex. Carefully playing the role of a conventionally attractive woman with traditional life plans, she sets out to seduce Mark. Soon he falls in love with her and, thinking that he has met the ideal mate, proposes marriage. She accepts and after the wedding convinces Mark that if they are to have a happy married life and a healthy environment in which to raise children he must give up his

lucrative realty business and the house he inherited from his parents. Valuing his life with Anne and the prospects of a family more than his career, he sells the business at a considerable loss and takes a less lucrative job. He also sells his home and buys another, again at a considerable financial loss. Finally, Anne becomes pregnant. Initially, she plays the adorable expectant mother, intentionally heightening Mark's expectations. But later she has an abortion. Relishing Mark's horror, she further reveals her scheme and explains that his pain and loss are merely the just deserts of any man for the things that men have done to women.

In all these cases, the issue is this: if we assume that all the men could be acceptable parents and that the pregnancies are physically normal, would any of the abortions by the women in these cases constitute a moral wrong done to any of the men? In the following sections, I shall argue that only in the third, fourth, and fifth cases is a wrongful harm done to the father and that only in the fourth and fifth cases would it be morally impermissible for the woman to proceed with the abortion. By a "wrongful harm," I shall mean a harm that could reasonably have been avoided. I shall argue that in the cases where abortion is claimed to be morally impermissible it is so on the grounds that it violates the father's autonomy; that is, it invades the man's morally legitimate interest in self-determination. The Kantian notion of treating persons as ends—as autonomous agents in pursuit of morally legitimate interests— underlies my argument. Its role will become clearer as the argument proceeds.

II

Much of the analysis presented here turns on the issue of when it is morally significant to say that the fetus is the father's as well as the mother's. One of the things that a woman can do without violating her interest in the autonomous control of her own body is to have a baby. I do not mean that she can do this alone but that, with the cooperation of a man, she can become pregnant as a matter of unencumbered choice. And though things are a bit more difficult for a man, one of the things he can do with his body, in cooperation with a woman, is to bring new life into the world. The interest in autonomy and the interest in procreation are therefore quite compatible and are common to both women and men. The significance of this, I believe, is that when a man and a woman autonomously decide to become parents together, a harm done to the fetus by a third party without the consent of both parents is a prima facie wrong done both to the man and to the woman because it is an interference with his autonomy as well as with hers. Moreover, a harm done to the fetus is a harm done to the man as well as to the woman because the fetus is both the object and the result of his pursuing a morally legitimate interest, that is, the interest in procreation. To harm the fetus, then, is to invade the morally legitimate interest in procreation of both the father and the mother and thereby to interfere with the man's as well as the woman's autonomy. Further exploration of these observations, I believe, is crucial to the analysis of the cases already presented.

In the first case, Karen's abortion, whatever its moral standing relative to the fetus, is not a wrong done to the man who raped her. This is true despite the fact that the man was not in control of his behavior and therefore was not responsible for his actions. The biological connection between the fetus and the father in this case is not sufficient to establish that the fetus is a morally legitimate object of interest for the man. The reason is obvious. Although procreation is a morally legitimate interest that men can have, the pursuit of this interest is restricted by the requirement that men respect the autonomy of women in this regard. And since the fetus was forced upon Karen by the man, she is not required to view the fetus as a legitimate object of interest for him. The fetus then is his only in a biological sense. Any harm done to the fetus is therefore neither a violation of his autonomy nor a harm done to him by Karen. It is important to note, however, that she could decide to keep it without violating her own or anyone else's autonomy. And this makes the fetus hers in a way that it is not the man's.

Similarly, in the second case, the fetus is Jane's in a way that it is not Jack's. The reasons, however, are slightly different than in the first case. Although Jane and Jack here each autonomously decide to pursue their interests in sex, neither has decided to pursue an interest in procreation. The fact that Jack has neglected to reveal his beliefs about abortion vitiates any claim he has that a harm done to the fetus is a violation of his autonomous pursuit of procreation. Rather, he has left it to Jane to assume that his only interest is in the pleasure of sex with her, and it is only this interest that she has a moral obligation to honor in terms of his autonomy. Had she promised him love and a family in order to have sex with him, she would have violated his autonomy both in regard to his interest in sex with love and his interest in procreation. Neither of these has occurred here. But though Jane is free from considerations of Jack's autonomy in deciding whether to abort or to keep the fetus, she could decide to keep it without violating her own sense of autonomy. It is this fact that makes the fetus hers in a way that it is not Jack's.

Yet by parity of reasoning, Jack is equally free from any responsibility to Jane in terms of the fetus should she decide to keep it. For, like Jane, he has not given his consent to the use of his body for the pursuit of her interest in procreation. He could, however autonomously decide to take on the responsibility for the fetus. But she could not lay claim to a violation of her autonomy if he did not so choose. Had he promised her love and a family in order to have sex with her, he would have violated her autonomy in regard to her interest in sex with love and her interest in procreation. But since he has done neither of these, she has no valid claim that the fetus is a moral liability for him.[1] Thus the pursuit of casual sex can be quite compatible with the principle of autonomy; it is nonetheless morally perilous for both men and women.

In the third case, Charles is the victim of a wrongful harm and his autonomy has been violated. Due to the fact that both men and women have a morally legitimate interest in procreation, couples have an obligation to each other to be forthright and informative about their desires and reservations about family planning. Such forthrightness is necessary if each is to pursue morally legitimate interests without violating the autonomy of the other. Susan, in this case, has clearly been negligent in this responsibility to Charles. She has allowed him to believe that his sex life with her is more than casual and includes more than an expression of his love for her; it is, in part, a legitimate pursuit of his interest in procreation.

Moreover, he has not violated her autonomy as the rapist did with Karen in the first case. Consequently, the fetus is a morally legitimate object of interest for him, and to harm it is to harm Charles—a harm that could reasonably have been avoided by Susan had she told him about her reservations and informed him that should a pregnancy occur she might very well decide in favor of abortion. And it is no excuse that she had not led Charles to believe that she would carry through with any pregnancy, for she has led him to believe that she would carry through with some pregnancy and has now made a decision that thwarts any such expectation. As a result of Susan's negligence, then, the abortion causes a wrongful harm to Charles and is a violation of his autonomy because the fetus is his as well as hers.

But does it follow from this that the abortion is morally impermissible for Susan? The abortion would be morally impermissible if and only if she has a moral obligation to carry the fetus to term. And the issue we are considering here is whether she has such an obligation to Charles. By withholding important information relevant to her own interest in procreation, she has violated his autonomy in regard to two of his legitimate interests—his interest in procreation and his interest in respecting her autonomy in regard to procreation. Therefore, since the fetus is the legitimate result of his pursuing a morally legitimate interest in a morally legitimate way with due respect for her autonomy, the fetus is his as well as hers, and she has a prima facie obligation to him not to harm it. What considerations then could possibly absolve her of her obligation to Charles?

The answer cannot be found in ranking the interest in a career over an interest in procreation; I cannot see that a career is a more legitimate means of self-determination than procreation or vice versa. Rather, I believe that the answer can be found in Susan's general interest in the control of her own body when compared with the nature of her negligence. To undertake a pregnancy is a serious investment of a woman's bodily and psychological resources—an undertaking that is not similarly possible for a man. The fetus then is a threat to the mother's autonomy in a way that it is not to the father's. And though Susan is responsible for being forthright about such matters, it is certainly understandable for a woman, as it is for a man, to be undecided about how to rank an interest in a career versus an interest in a possible family. Moreover, it is understandable, though far from mature or laudable, for a person to find it difficult to talk with his or her spouse about such matters when the spouse has strong desires for a family. To say that Susan has an obligation to carry his fetus to term in this case and to sacrifice the control of her own body is, it seems to me, to overestimate the fault of her negligence by not allowing for understandable weaknesses in regard to the responsibilities of autonomy. But we must be careful not to underestimate it. She has caused Charles a serious harm, and she has violated his autonomy. For that, she is guilty.

The fourth case is much like the third except the violation of Steve's autonomy and the consequent wrongful harm are done with deceit rather than negligence. The burden to overcome the prima facie obligation not to harm the fetus is therefore stronger for Michelle than it was for Susan because Michelle could have been expected more reasonably to have avoided the harm. Again it is understandable, though neither mature nor laudable, for a person who is deeply in love with someone with significantly different life plans, perhaps as a result of self-deception, to think that the other person can be brought around to seeing things the other way. But it is not excusable. Surely, given the importance the interest in procreation plays in the lives of some people, a normal adult can be expected on the grounds of the other person's autonomy to be honest in such situations. If so, then in the absence of countervening moral considerations it would be a wrong to Steve for Michelle to have the abortion.

The fifth case involves malicious deceit with the intent to cause harm. Only a crazed ideologue could think that the harm caused Mark is not wrongful. And only someone who things that men have no legitimate moral interest in procreation could think that Anne's plan does not involve a violation of his autonomy. The fetus is clearly a morally legitimate object of interest for him and therefore his as well as hers. To harm the fetus then is a prima facie harm done to Mark. And given the extent of his sacrifices, the intensity of his expectations, and the depravity of Anne's intentions, it is difficult to see how the general interest in the autonomous control of one's own body could ever be morally significant enough to allow a woman like Anne to culminate the harm she has planned by having the abortion unless the fetus seriously threatened her most fundamental welfare. To think that the general interest in the autonomous control of one's body allows a woman this kind of freedom is to sanctify female autonomy and to trivialize male autonomy—the mirror image of the chauvinism Anne claims to despise. Assuming then that Anne is physically healthy and the pregnancy is not a threat to her fundamental welfare, for her to abort is morally wrong. She has an obligation to Mark to carry through with the pregnancy.

III

Someone might argue, however, that the wrongs in these cases can be accounted for on moral grounds that are independent of special considerations of the father or the fetus. The negligence of Susan, the deceit of Michelle, the malice of Anne, all—it might be argued—are wrongs independent of abortion, and there is nothing special about abortion and these wrongs.

Certainly negligence, deceit, and malice are wrongs independent of abortion, but it does not follow from this that there is nothing special about the wrongs here. Susan, Michelle, and Anne would, respectively be guilty of negligence, deceit, and malice even had Charles, Steve, and Mark turned out unknowingly to be sterile. But the fact that the men were not sterile and the fact that the women did become pregnant make possible an additional wrong that is special to the abortion issue and that involves fathers and fetuses. The nonmalicious deceit of Michelle illustrates this well. Had Steve been unknowingly sterile, Michelle would have wronged him by lying to him, but she would not have wrongfully harmed him. In fact, the particular harm Anne planned to inflict upon Mark would have been impossible had he been sterile. And had he been knowingly sterile, Anne could not have violated his autonomy by invading an interest that was impossible for him to pursue. Nonetheless, she would have wronged him in other ways. The fact that these other wrongs can affect a man's legitimate interest in procreation gives them special significance here.

It might also be objected that one disquieting implication of the argument is that abortion would be said to constitute a "wrongful harm" to anyone and anything that has a "morally legitimate interest" in it. So, for example, in an underpopulated country like Norway or Australia, society might have a morally legitimate interest in childbearing, and every woman opting for an abortion might be said to do a "wrongful harm to society." Or grandparents might have a "morally legitimate" interest in grandchildren being born; and a woman aborting would be said to have done a "wrongful harm" to the would-be grandparents.[2]

Certainly these results are unacceptable, but I do not believe that they are consistent with the concept of autonomy I have in mind here. We might distinguish between interests that are prima facie morally legitimate and those that are morally legitimate *simpliciter* or legitimate after all moral considerations are in. An interest that is prima facie morally legitimate is one that in itself is a morally permissible interest to have. The interest in sex and the interest in procreation are two such interests, as are the interests in grandparents having grandchildren and the interest of a country in having a larger population. But one way in which prima facie morally legitimate interests can fail to be morally legitimate *simpliciter* is for a person who has these interests to pursue them in ways that are morally illegitimate.

Assume that the rapist has an interest in sex (which is doubtful, at least that it is his primary interest.) This interest fails to be morally legitimate *simpliciter* when the pursuit of it invades the morally legitimate interest his victim has in her choice of sexual partners. And it is the primacy of the importance of individual choice and its moral legitimacy that is at the heart of the concept of autonomy employed here. Thus a prima facie morally legitimate interest can fail to be morally legitimate *simpliciter* if it is pursued in a way that does not respect the autonomy of others to pursue their morally legitimate interests. So like the rapist who has an interest in sex, there is nothing wrong with what the country wants in wanting a larger population or in what potential grandparents want in wanting grandchildren. These interests become morally illegitimate, however, when the autonomy of the women involved is violated by the rapist, the country, or the grandparents in the pursuit of their interests. And it is the importance of autonomy to my argument that prevents the disquieting implication.

A final objection might be that too much of the argument turns on the extremity and implausibility of case 5. There is an ambiguity, however, in the charge of "implausibility." On the one hand, it might mean that the case is far-fetched in that cases like it are not at all likely to occur. Or on the other hand, it might mean that the analysis of the case is either unconvincing or that it sheds no light on the other cases.

The first construal of the charge renders it irrelevant. We hope that there are and will be no such cases. But this is beside the point. If the analysis of the case can be defended against the charge of implausibility of the second kind, the case serves to shed light on moral issues in other contexts. This is what Judith Jarvis Thomson's violinist example and Jane English's mad scientist example are designed to do.[3] And no one thinks that these examples are implausible on the grounds that they are unlikely to occur. Those who think of these examples as implausible think so on grounds that they are misleading or otherwise uninformative in terms of analysis.[4] The objection then turns on the second construal of the charge.

That the analysis is unconvincing might be argued either by claiming that Anne has not wronged Mark or that the wrong is independent of the abortion issue. Since I do not believe that anyone would upon reflection seriously claim the former and since I have already addressed the latter claim, the second charge must turn on the claim that the case fails to illuminate the issues in other contexts. But I believe that it does illuminate the issues of other cases. Most important, it establishes that a serious wrong that a woman can do to a man is to harm him by killing his fetus, and it shows how this might involve other wrongs that are done with intentional malice. Once these two points are established, the issue naturally arises as to whether the wrong of harming a man by killing his fetus might be done in other ways involving other wrongs that are not accompanied by malicious intent. I have argued that abortion constitutes a wrongful harm in cases involving neglect and nonmalicious deceit. Viewed from this perspective, cases 3 and 4 are illuminated by case 5. And viewed from this perspective, we can see that there are other ways—ways that are more likely to occur—in which we can wrong others by failing to take their autonomy and their interests seriously than just in cases where we intentionally and maliciously set out to do so. The latter cases are easy to recognize; the former are not always. Being alive to this is important and that is why cases 3 and 4 and perhaps other more subtle ones are most important in the analysis.

IV

I have spoken about the rights of autonomy. It is time now to say something about its responsibilities. On any plausible view of the importance of autonomy, anyone who claims to have a right that others respect his or her autonomy must recognize the obligation to take seriously the autonomy of others. Men and women in their relations with each other as members of the opposite sex have not always done this. Let me briefly mention two ways in which men and women have failed in this responsibility.

The first has to do with equality. If the interest in procreation and the interest in, say, a career are equally legitimate, then a man cannot consistently require a woman with whom he is involved to take seriously his interest in a family if he does not take seriously her interest in a career. It is notoriously true that many men are chauvinistic in this regard. But by the same token, a woman cannot consistently require a man with whom she is involved to take seriously her interest in a career if she does not take seriously his interest in a family. This does not mean that she must have children with him, but it does mean that in working out her relationship with him she must grant that men have as legitimate an interest in being parents as do women. I am not sure that many women— nor for that matter that many men—are emotionally prepared to admit this. Although we are making some progress in thinking that women have an equal right to a career as men and that men have equal obligations in child rearing as women, we are still hesitant to think that a man could be an equal to a women in parenthood.

The second way in which men and women have failed to take each other's autonomy seriously involves forthrightness. Men, it is said with some justification, are unwilling to talk about their feelings. This often puts an unfair burden on the woman with whom a man is involved to understand what his interests are, and without adequate information regarding his interests, the woman is poorly positioned to respect his autonomy in regard to those interests. Thus one aspect of the responsibility to be forthright involves letting the other person know what your interests are so that your autonomy can be respected. This was Jack's failure in case 2.

Another aspect of the responsibility to be forthright has to do with allowing the other person to make an informed choice. Certainly, it is an interference with another person's autonomy to purposefully provide them with or knowingly allow them to believe erroneous information relevant to their choices. This is what Susan, Michelle, and Anne have done in the cases considered. Such motivation to be less than forthright is not always selfish, but it is almost always a failure to take autonomy seriously.

V

To summarize. In order for a man to lay claim to the fetus being his in a sense that the mother is obligated to respect, the fetus must be the result of his pursuing the legitimate interest in procreation in a morally legitimate way. In cases 1 and 2, the men— in different ways—have not satisfied the requirement of acting in a way that is consistent with the responsibilities of autonomy. It would therefore not be a wrong done to these men for Karen and Jane to have their abortions. However, when a man has satisfied the requirements of autonomy in regard to the interest in procreation both in regard to himself and to his sexual partner, the woman has a prima facie obligation to him not to harm the fetus. And unless there is some countervening moral consideration to override this prima facie obligation, the abortion of the fetus is morally impermissible. I have argued that the latter is true in cases 4 and 5.

READING ENDNOTES

1. These observations do not contradict the practice of the courts in holding liable for support men who have simply become uninterested in their wives and children. What is being maintained is that the fact that a man is the biological father of a child is not sufficient either to give him rights to the child or to put him under an obligation to it or to the mother.
2. I owe this objection to Robert Goodin. The grandparents case was also mentioned to me by James F. Hill.
3. See Judith Jarvis Thompson, "A Defense of Abortion, "*Philosophy and Public Affairs* 1 (1971): 47–66; and Jane English, "Abortion and the Concept of a Person," *Canadian Journal of Philosophy* 5 (1975): 233–43.
4. I find these examples quite helpful, especially English's.

QUESTIONS

1. Is Harris' understanding of a "wrongful harm" acceptable as a moral notion? Is it sufficient for a harm to be wrongful just that it could reasonably have been avoided?

2. Imagine that an intentionally pregnant married woman is attacked by a stranger and the fetus dies as a result. Does this thought experiment lend support to Harris' contention that if a third party harms a fetus that person may thereby harm the autonomy and interests of both the mother and father of the fetus?

3. When is a fetus (procreation) a "morally legitimate object of interest" for a man? For a woman?

4. Why does Harris think that only a father who has a legitimate interest in a fetus can have responsibilities to it (or its mother)?

5. In those cases in which Harris thinks men have a legitimate interest in a fetus, is the fact that the men are all married to the women who are pregnant playing a role in his thinking? Does it reinforce the worry raised by many previous authors that our society thinks of women and children as the property of men?

6. What constraint does the requirement that we must respect women's autonomy place on the legitimate interests others can have in her decisions regarding whether to bear children?

7. Does Harris' analysis ignore the unique position that women occupy relative to any fetus they carry?

Chapter Endnotes

Chapter 1

1. Though our method obviously draws very heavily on Rawls' method of reflective equilibrium, we do not use that term in order to avoid confusion where our method differs from his.

Chapter 2

1. Jeremy Bentham, *An Introduction to the Principles of Morals and Legislation* (1789) I, III.
2. *Ibid.*, IV, II.
3. *Ibid.*, IV, III.
4. *Ibid.*, IV, IV.
5. *Ibid.*, IV, V.
6. John Stuart Mill, *Utilitarianism* (1861), Chapter 2.
7. *Ibid.*
8. Bentham, *Principles of Morals and Legislation*, I, II.
9. *Ibid.*, I, X.
10. *Ibid.*, footnote added in 1822 to I, XIII.
11. *Ibid.*, XVII, II.
12. Though Bentham is often represented as an act utilitarian, it is unclear, to us at least, that he intended his doctrine to be understood in this narrow way, given that his primary interest was in the actions of governments: general laws and institutional arrangements. Sidgwick was an act utilitarian, however, while Mill was just as clearly a rule utilitarian.
13. See J.J.C. Smart's contribution to *Utilitarianism: For and Against*, edited by J.J.C. Smart and Bernard Williams (New York: Cambridge University Press, 1973). This remains highly recommended reading for anyone interested in utilitarian theory.

Chapter 3

1. Immanuel Kant, *Grounding for the Metaphysics of Morals* (1785), Preface 389.
2. *Ibid.*, First Section 393.
3. *Ibid.*, First Section 394.
4. *Ibid.*, First Section 402.
5. *Ibid.*, Second Section 421.
6. See *ibid.*, Second Section 424.
7. *Ibid.*, Second Section 429. "Respect for persons" is one common name for this principle, as is "the end in itself" principle.
8. *Ibid.*, Second Section 431.
9. *Ibid.*, Second Section 417.
10. *Ibid.*, Second Section 420.
11. For the actual discussion by Kant see *ibid.*, Second Section 421–425.
12. For the actual discussion by Kant see *ibid.*, Second Section 429–430.

Chapter 4

1. John Stuart Mill, *On Liberty* (London: 1859), Chapter 1.
2. *Ibid.*
3. *Ibid.*
4. For Mill's discussion of the issue, see Chapter 4 of *On Liberty*.
5. *Ibid.*, Chapter 4.
6. John Locke, *Second Treatise of Government* (1690).

7. This discussion is loosely influenced by years of discussion with our good friend Jan Narveson. Narveson's position is even stronger than the one advanced here, however, for he insists that all rights (including the right to life and liberty) just are property rights. See his book, *The Libertarian Idea* (Temple University Press, 1988); reprinted recently by Broadview Press. See also his application of libertarian principles to a number of practical moral, social, and political issues in his collections of essays, *Moral Matters* (Broadview Press, 1998) and *Respecting Persons in Theory and in Practice* (Rowan and Littlefield, 2002).

8. Robert Nozick identified original acquisition and transfer as the basic grounds of property rights in *Anarchy, State and Utopia* (New York: Basic Books, 1974).

Chapter 5

1. Some libertarians are also willing to expand the range of rights to include not just negative liberty but positive welfare rights as well, but they insist that if such an extension is to be justified it must be shown that the individuals who are so governed by such a system do (or would) agree to it.

2. It must always be kept in mind any time one hears that "the state" or "the government" ought to pay for anything that governments do not have money. They are not productive agencies and they have no goods to distribute, including money. Whenever a claim is made that the government should pay compensation or for some service (like education and healthcare), what is really being said is that taxpayers should pay compensation or for the service. Governments provide services only by taking the money from some of its citizens to pay for them. Thus all claims upon the government are actually claims upon (some) fellow citizens, namely those who pay taxes.

3. This example is further complicated if we think that those who have a right to an education are children, since they are not yet autonomous agents. To whom, then, is the duty to provide educational opportunities owed? To parents, as the owners of children? To the children themselves, as potential autonomous persons?

4. John Rawls, *A Theory of Justice* (Cambridge, MA: The Belknap Press of Harvard University Press, 1971), §15, p. 92.

5. *Ibid.*, §60, p. 396.

6. The whole of *A Theory of Justice* is devoted to establishing this particular theory of justice.

7. The most important of which, for our purposes, is Will Kymlicka, *Liberalism, Community and Culture* (Oxford: Clarendon Press of Oxford University Press, 1989).

8. To use the apt phrase of another very prominent liberal, Ronald Dworkin.

Chapter 6

1. Catharine MacKinnon, *Toward a Feminist Theory of the State* (Cambridge, MA: Harvard University Press, 1989).

2. Carol Gilligan, *In a Different Voice* (Cambridge, MA: Harvard University Press, 1982).

3. Patricia Smith, "Introduction" to *Feminist Jurisprudence*, Patricia Smith, ed. (New York: Oxford University Press, 1993), p. 3.

Key Terms Index

The following key terms are defined throughout the text.